ACCA

S T U D Y   T E X T

PAPER F1

ACCOUNTANT IN BUSINESS

D1494730

In this new syllabus first edition approved by ACCA

- We **discuss** the **best strategies** for studying for ACCA exams
- We **highlight** the **most important elements** in the syllabus and the **key skills** you will need
- We **signpost** how each chapter links to the syllabus and the study guide
- We **provide** lots of **exam focus points** demonstrating what the examiner will want you to do
- We **emphasise key points** in regular **fast forward summaries**
- We **test your knowledge** of what you've studied in **quick quizzes**
- We **examine your understanding** in our **exam question bank**
- We **reference** all the important topics in our **full index**

BPP's **i-Learn** and **i-Pass** products also support this paper.

FOR EXAMS IN DECEMBER 2007 AND JUNE 2008

BPP
LEARNING MEDIA

First edition February 2007

ISBN 9780 7517 3286 3

British Library Cataloguing-in-Publication Data
A catalogue record for this book is available from the
British Library

Published by

BPP Learning Media Ltd
BPP House, Aldine Place
London W12 8AA

www.bpp.com/learningmedia

Printed in Great Britain

We are grateful to the Association of Chartered Certified
Accountants for permission to reproduce the pilot paper
questions. The suggested solutions to the pilot paper
have been prepared by BPP Learning Media Ltd.

Your learning materials, published by BPP Learning
Media Ltd, are printed on paper sourced from
sustainable, managed forests.

Contents

The BPP Learning Media Effective Study Package

Distance Learning from BPP Professional Education

You can access our exam-focussed interactive e-learning materials over the **Internet**, via BPP Learn Online, hosted by BPP Professional Education.

BPP Learn Online offers **comprehensive tutor support**, **revision guidance** and **exam tips**.

Visit www.bpp.com/acca/learnonline for further details.

Learning to Learn Accountancy

BPP's ground-breaking **Learning to Learn Accountancy** book is designed to be used both at the outset of your ACCA studies and throughout the process of learning accountancy. It challenges you to consider how you study and gives you helpful hints about how to approach the various types of paper which you will encounter. It can help you **focus your studies on the subject and exam**, enabling you to **acquire knowledge**, **practise and revise efficiently and effectively**.

How the BPP ACCA-approved Study Text can help you pass

How the BPP ACCA-approved Study Text can help you pass

Tackling studying

We know that studying for a number of exams can seem daunting, particularly when you have other commitments as well.

- We therefore provide guidance on **what you need to study efficiently and effectively** – to use the limited time you have in the best way possible

- We explain the **purposes** of the **different features** in the BPP Study Text, demonstrating how they help you and improve your chances of passing

Developing exam awareness

We never forget that you're aiming to pass your exams, and our Texts are completely focused on helping you do this.

- In the section **Studying F1** we introduce the key themes of the syllabus, describe the skills you need and summarise how to succeed

- The **Introduction** to each chapter of this Study Text sets the chapter in the context of the syllabus and exam

- We provide specific tips, **Exam focus points**, on what you can expect in the exam and what to do (and not to do!) when answering questions

And our Study Text is **comprehensive**. It covers the syllabus content. No more, no less.

Using the Syllabus and Study Guide

We set out the Syllabus and Study Guide in full.

- Reading the **introduction to the Syllabus** will show you what **capabilities** (skills) you'll have to demonstrate, and how this exam links with other papers.

- The topics listed in the **Syllabus** are the **key topics** in this exam. By quickly looking through the Syllabus, you can see the breadth of the paper. Reading the Syllabus will also highlight topics to look out for when you're reading newspapers or *student accountant* magazine.

- The **Study Guide** provides the **detail**, showing you precisely what you'll be studying. Don't worry if it seems a lot when you look through it; BPP's Study Text will carefully guide you through it all.

- Remember the Study Text shows, at the start of every chapter, which areas of the Syllabus and Study Guide are covered in the chapter.

Testing what you can do

Testing yourself helps you develop the skills you need to pass the exam and also confirms that you can recall what you have learnt.

- We include **Questions** within chapters and the **Exam Question Bank** provides lots more practice.

- Our **Quick Quizzes** test whether you have enough knowledge of the contents of each chapter.

- Question practice is particularly important if English is not your first written language. ACCA offers an **International Certificate in Financial English** promoting language skills within the international business community.

BPP
LEARNING MEDIA

Example chapter

Topic list

The Topic list gives an overview of the chapter.

Introduction

The Introduction sets the chapter in the context of the whole syllabus.

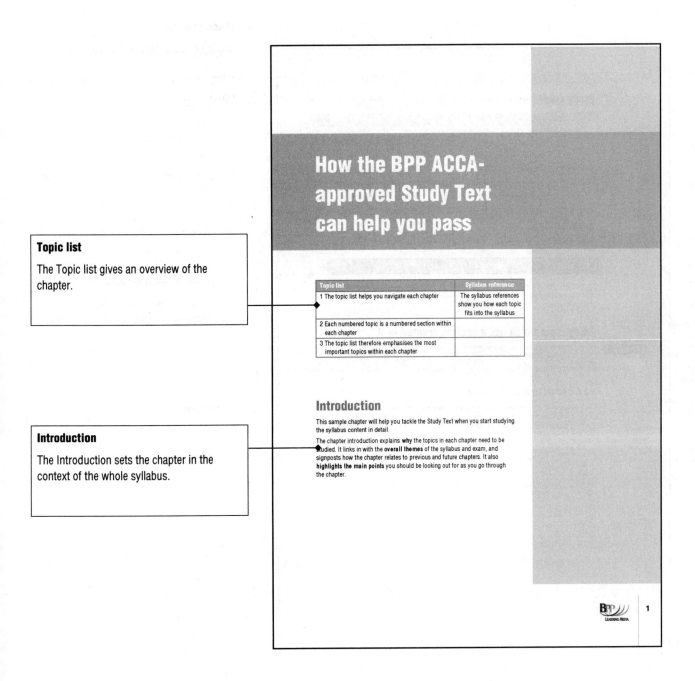

How the BPP ACCA-approved Study Text can help you pass

Topic list	Syllabus reference
1 The topic list helps you navigate each chapter	The syllabus references show you how each topic fits into the syllabus
2 Each numbered topic is a numbered section within each chapter	
3 The topic list therefore emphasises the most important topics within each chapter	

Introduction

This sample chapter will help you tackle the Study Text when you start studying the syllabus content in detail.

The chapter introduction explains **why** the topics in each chapter need to be studied. It links in with the **overall themes** of the syllabus and exam, and signposts how the chapter relates to previous and future chapters. It also **highlights the main points** you should be looking out for as you go through the chapter.

BPP
LEARNING MEDIA

1

Study guide

The Study guide links with ACCA's own guidance.

Exam guide

The Exam guide describes the examinability of the chapter.

Knowledge brought forward

Knowledge brought forward shows you what you need to remember from previous exams.

Fast forward

Fast forwards allow you to preview and review each section easily.

Study guide

	Intellectual level
We list the topics in ACCA's Study guide that are covered in each chapter	The intellectual level indicates the depth in which the topics will be covered

Exam guide

The Exam guide highlights ways in which the main topics covered in each chapter may be examined.

Knowledge brought forward from earlier studies

Knowledge brought forward boxes summarise information and techniques that you are **assumed to know** from your earlier studies. As the exam may test your knowledge of these areas, you should **revise** your previous study material if you are unsure about them.

1 Key topic which has a section devoted to it

FAST FORWARD — Fast forwards give you a **summary** of the content of each of the main chapter sections. They are listed together in the roundup at the end of each chapter to allow you to review each chapter quickly.

1.1 Important topic within section

The headings within chapters give you a good idea of the **importance** of the topics covered. The larger the header, the more important the topic is. The headers will help you navigate through the chapter and locate the areas that have been highlighted as important in the front pages or in the chapter introduction.

Example

Examples show you how theory is put into practice.

Key term

Key terms are the core vocabulary.

Exam focus point

Exam focus points provide specific links to the exam.

Formula to learn

You must remember these formulae in the exam.

Question

Questions provide vital practice of what you've learnt.

Case Study

Case Studies link what you've learnt with the business environment.

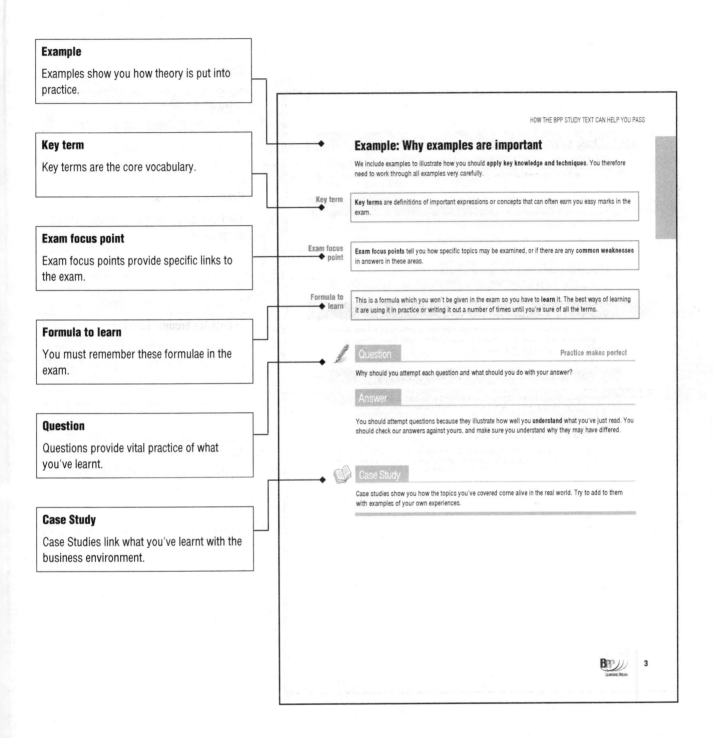

HOW THE BPP STUDY TEXT CAN HELP YOU PASS

Example: Why examples are important

We include examples to illustrate how you should **apply key knowledge and techniques**. You therefore need to work through all examples very carefully.

Key term

Key terms are definitions of important expressions or concepts that can often earn you easy marks in the exam.

Exam focus point

Exam focus points tell you how specific topics may be examined, or if there are any **common weaknesses** in answers in these areas.

Formula to learn

This is a formula which you won't be given in the exam so you have to **learn** it. The best ways of learning it are using it in practice or writing it out a number of times until you're sure of all the terms.

Question · Practice makes perfect

Why should you attempt each question and what should you do with your answer?

Answer

You should attempt questions because they illustrate how well you **understand** what you've just read. You should check our answers against yours, and make sure you understand why they may have differed.

Case Study

Case studies show you how the topics you've covered come alive in the real world. Try to add to them with examples of your own experiences.

BPP LEARNING MEDIA 3

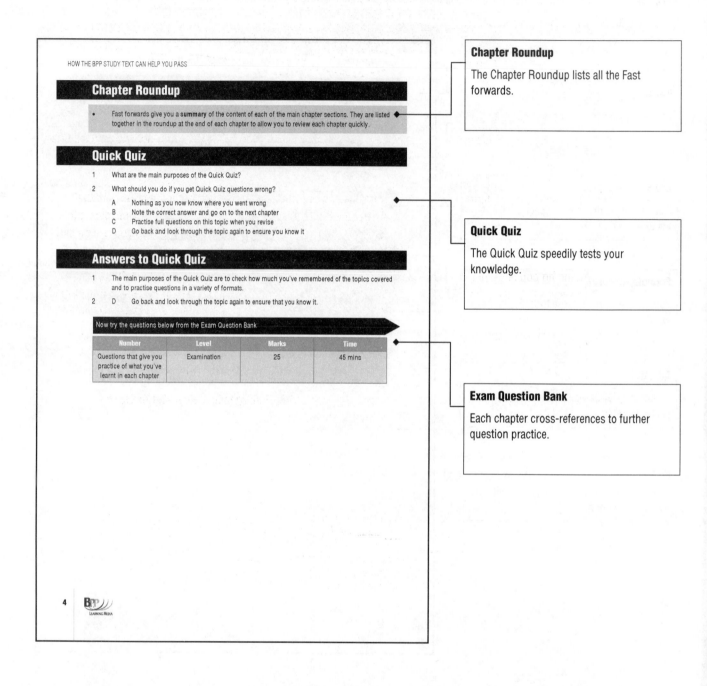

Learning styles

BPP's guide to studying, *Learning to Learn Accountancy*, provides guidance on identifying how you learn and the variety of intelligencies that you have. We shall summarise some of the material in *Learning to Learn Accountancy*, as it will help you understand how to you are likely to approach the Study Text:

If you like	Then you might focus on	How the Study Text helps you
Word games, crosswords, poetry	Going through the detail in the Text	Chapter introductions, Fast forwards and Key terms help you determine the detail that's most significant
Number puzzles, Sudoku, Cluedo	Understanding the Text as a logical sequence of knowledge and ideas	Chapter introductions and headers help you follow the flow of material
Drawing, cartoons, films	Seeing how the ways material is presented show what it means and how important it is	The different features and the emphasis given by headers and emboldening help you see quickly what you have to know
Attending concerts, playing a musical instrument, dancing	Identifying patterns in the Text	The sequence of features within each chapter helps you understand what material is really crucial
Sport, craftwork, hands on experience	Learning practical skills such as preparing a set of accounts	Examples and question practice help you develop the practical skills you need

If you want to learn more about developing some or all of your intelligencies, *Learning to Learn Accountancy* shows you plenty of ways in which you can do so.

Studying efficiently and effectively

BPP
LEARNING MEDIA

What you need to study efficiently and effectively

Positive attitude

Yes there is a lot to learn. But look at the most recent ACCA pass list. See how many people have passed. They've made it; you can too. Focus on all the **benefits** that passing the exam will bring you.

Exam focus

Keep the exam firmly in your sights throughout your studies.

- Remember there's lots of **helpful guidance** about F1 in this first part of the Study Text.
- Look out for the **exam references** in the Study Text, particularly the types of question you'll be asked.

Organisation

Before you start studying you must organise yourself properly.

- We show you how to **timetable** your study so that you can ensure you have enough time to cover all of the syllabus – and revise it.
- Think carefully about the way you take **notes**. You needn't copy out too much, but if you can summarise key areas, that shows you understand them.
- Choose the notes **format** that's most helpful to you; lists, diagrams, mindmaps.
- Consider the **order** in which you tackle each chapter. If you prefer to get to grips with a theory before seeing how it's applied, you should read the explanations first. If you prefer to see how things work in practice, read the examples and questions first.

Active brain

There are various ways in which you can keep your brain active when studying and hence improve your **understanding** and **recall** of material.

- Keep asking yourself how the topic you're studying fits into the **whole picture** of this exam. If you're not sure, look back at the chapter introductions and Study Text front pages.
- Go carefully through every **example** and try every **question** in the Study Text and in the Exam Question Bank. You will be thinking deeply about the syllabus and increasing your understanding.

Review, review, review

Regularly reviewing the topics you've studied will help fix them in your memory. Your BPP Texts help you review in many ways.

- Important points are emphasised **in bold**.
- **Chapter Roundups** summarise the **Fast forward** key points in each chapter.
- **Quick Quizzes** test your grasp of the essentials.

BPP Passcards present summaries of topics in different visual formats to enhance your chances of remembering them.

Timetabling your studies

As your time is limited, it's vital that you calculate how much time you can allocate to each chapter. Following the approach below will help you do this.

Step 1   Calculate how much time you have

Work out the time you have available per week, given the following.

- The standard you have set yourself

- The time you need to set aside for work on the Practice & Revision Kit, Passcards, i-Learn and i-Pass

- The other exam(s) you are sitting

- Practical matters such as work, travel, exercise, sleep and social life

Hours

Note your time available in box A.   A [   ]

Step 2   Allocate your time

- Take the time you have available per week for this Study Text shown in box A, multiply it by the number of weeks available and insert the result in box B.   B [   ]

- Divide the figure in box B by the number of chapters in this Study Text and insert the result in box C.   C [   ]

Remember that this is only a rough guide. Some of the chapters in this Study Text are longer and more complicated than others, and you will find some subjects easier to understand than others.

Step 3   Implement your plan

Set about studying each chapter in the time shown in box C. You'll find that once you've established a timetable, you're much more likely to study systematically.

Short of time: Skim study technique

You may find you simply do not have the time available to follow all the key study steps for each chapter, however you adapt them for your particular learning style. If this is the case, follow the **Skim study** technique below.

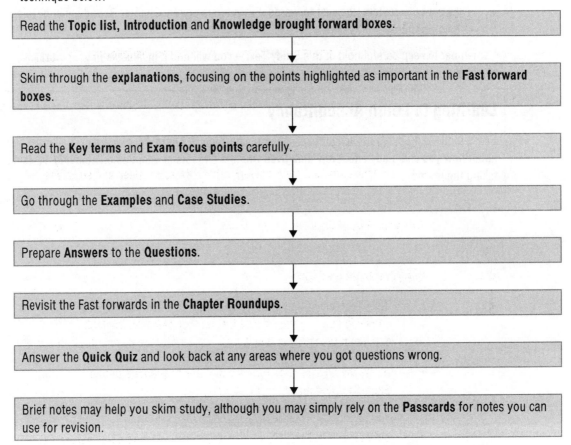

Read the **Topic list, Introduction** and **Knowledge brought forward boxes**.

Skim through the **explanations**, focusing on the points highlighted as important in the **Fast forward boxes**.

Read the **Key terms** and **Exam focus points** carefully.

Go through the **Examples** and **Case Studies**.

Prepare **Answers** to the **Questions**.

Revisit the Fast forwards in the **Chapter Roundups**.

Answer the **Quick Quiz** and look back at any areas where you got questions wrong.

Brief notes may help you skim study, although you may simply rely on the **Passcards** for notes you can use for revision.

Revision

When you are ready to start revising, you should still refer back to this Study Text.

- As a source of **reference** (you should find the index particularly helpful for this)

- As a way to **review** (the Fast forwards, Exam focus points, Chapter Roundups and Quick Quizzes help you here)

Remember to keep careful hold of this Study Text – you will find it invaluable in your work.

Learning to Learn Accountancy

BPP's guide to studying for accountancy exams, **Learning to Learn Accountancy**, challenges you to think about how you can study effectively and gives you lots and lots of vital tips on studying, revising and taking the exams.

Studying F1

Approaching F1

1 What the paper is about

The overall aim of the *Accountant in Business* syllabus is to introduce accountancy firmly in its context as a central business function. This encompasses:

- Business structure and management
- Environmental analysis and influences
- Accounting and its relationship with other business functions
- Regulation and the accounting profession
- Audit and internal control
- People management issues

The six broad areas of the syllabus are not given specific weightings, indicating that questions on the examination paper could be drawn **from any source**. The syllabus areas are as follows.

- **Business organisation structure, governance and management**

  How the organisation is structured and governed. You will study organisational concepts, the influence of organisational culture and the role of IT and the importance of effective information systems. Ethics, governance and social responsibility are also important here.

- **Key environmental influences**

  It is important to understand the macro-economic environment within which a business operates. The PEST framework provides a useful way to analyse direct environmental influences.

- **History and role of accounting**

  The purpose of the accounting function merits specific consideration in this syllabus and this section provides a theoretical basis for the detailed analysis of the accounting function which follows.

- **Specific functions of accounting and internal financial control**

  This section of the syllabus examines the detailed aspects of accounting systems in a typical organisation, internal financial control and audit. This function plans and monitors business performance, and also has a key role to play in detecting and preventing fraud.

- **Leading and managing individuals and teams**

  It is important to understand how the management and motivation of staff aligns with wider organisational objectives. This section of the syllabus explores both theoretical and practical aspects of what is generally termed 'people management'.

- **Recruiting and developing effective employees**

  The recruitment and development of employees is another important organisational activity. Ensuring that employees develop constructive relationships and work effectively is a way of making sure that they contribute towards organisational objectives.

2 What's required

This exam tests two intellectual levels in its questions: knowledge and comprehension, and application and analysis. You will need to be familiar with the basic models and theories associated with organisations, business functions and people management, and be able to apply these basic ideas to questions where ideas are explored.

There are several broad question types on the Pilot Paper:

- 'True or false' for one mark
- Multiple choice questions with one correct response for two marks
- Sentence completion ('fill in the gap') for one mark

So, despite the fact that the questions are all short ones carrying only one or two marks, it is still possible for higher skills of explanation to be tested.

3 How to pass

Cover the whole syllabus

The exam consists of 40 two mark questions and 10 one mark questions. With 50 questions at his disposal, the examiner has plenty of scope to test all major areas of the syllabus. For this reason it is not advisable to study the syllabus selectively, as the format of the exam enables all topics to be tested in some way.

Practise

The text gives you ample opportunity to practise by providing questions within chapters, quick quiz questions and the Pilot Paper.

Syllabus

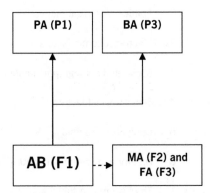

AIM

To introduce knowledge and understanding of the business and its environment and the influence this has on how organisations are structured and on the role of the accounting and other key business functions in contributing to the efficient, effective and ethical management and development of an organisation and its people and systems.

MAIN CAPABILITIES

On successful completion of this paper, candidates should be able to:

A Explain how the organisation is structured, governed and managed by – and on behalf of – its external, connected and internal stakeholders

B Identify and describe the key environmental influences and constraints on how the business operates in general and how these affect the accounting function in particular

C Describe the history, purpose, and position of accounting in the organisation and the roles of other functional areas

D Identify and explain the functions of accounting systems and internal controls in planning, monitoring and reviewing performance and in preventing fraud and business failure

E Recognise the principles of authority and leadership and how teams and individuals behave and are managed, disciplined and motivated in pursuit of wider departmental and organisational aims and objectives

F Recruit and develop effective employees, using appropriate methods and procedures, while developing constructive relationships through effective communication and interpersonal skills

RELATIONAL DIAGRAM OF MAIN CAPABILITIES

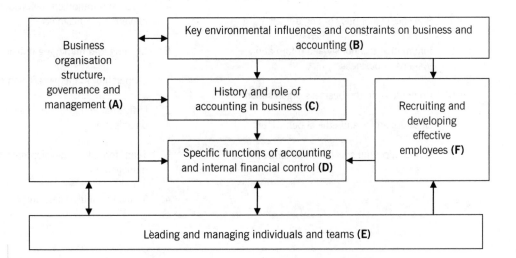

RATIONALE

The *Accountant in Business* syllabus acts as an introduction to business structure and purpose, and to accountancy as a central business function. The syllabus commences with an examination of the structure and governance of businesses, briefly introducing ethics. It then looks at business in the context of its environment, including economic, legal, and regulatory influences on such aspects as governance, employment, health and safety, data protection and security. From there, it focuses on accounting, how it originated, how it is organised, its critical importance in business planning and control, and how it affects other business functions.

The syllabus then introduces students to the accounting profession and to certain aspects of the regulatory framework as they affect accounting, auditing and governance. The syllabus also covers accounting, auditing, and internal control as specific business functions and how these should be supported by effective management information systems. Finally, the syllabus introduces key management and people issues such as individual and team behaviour, leadership, motivation and personal effectiveness.

DETAILED SYLLABUS

A   Business organisation structure, governance and management

1.   The business organisation and its structure

2.   The formal and informal business organisation

3.   Organisational culture in business

4.   Stakeholders of business organisations

5.   Information technology and information systems in business

6.   Committees in the business organisation

7.   Business ethics and ethical behaviour

8.   Governance and social responsibility in business

B   Key environmental influences and constraints on business and accounting

1.   Political and legal factors

2.   Macro-economic factors

3.   Social and demographic factors

4.   Technological factors

5.   Competitive factors

C   History and role of accounting in business

1.   The history and function of accounting in business

2.   Law and regulation governing accounting

3.   Financial systems, procedures and IT applications

4.   The relationship between accounting and other business functions

D   Specific functions of accounting and internal financial control

1.   Accounting and finance functions within business

2.   Internal and external auditing and their functions

3.   Internal financial control and security within business organisations

4.   Fraud and fraudulent behaviour and their prevention in business.

E   Leading and managing individuals and teams

1.   Leadership, management and supervision

2.   Individual and group behaviour in business organisations

3.   Team formation, development and management

4.   Motivating individuals and groups

F **Recruiting and developing effective employees**

1. Recruitment and selection, managing diversity, and equal opportunity.

2. Techniques for improving personal effectiveness at work and their benefits

3. Features of effective communication

4. Training, development, and learning in the maintenance and improvement of business performance

5. Review and appraisal of individual performance

APPROACH TO EXAMINING THE SYLLABUS

The syllabus is assessed by a two hour paper-based or computer-based examination. Questions will assess all parts of the syllabus and will test knowledge and some comprehension or application of this knowledge. The examination will consist of 40 two mark questions, and 10 one mark questions.

Study Guide

A BUSINESS ORGANISATIONAL STRUCTURE, GOVERNANCE AND MANAGEMENT

1. The business organisation and its structure

a) Identify the different types of organisation:[1]
   i) Commercial
   ii) Not-for-profit
   iii) Public sector
   iv) Non-governmental organisations
   v) Cooperatives

b) Describe the different ways in which organisations may be structured: entrepreneurial, functional, matrix, divisional, departmental, by geographical area and by product.[1]

c) Describe the roles and functions of the main departments in a business organisation: [1]
   i) research and development
   ii) purchasing
   iii) production
   iv) direct service provision
   v) marketing
   vi) administration
   vii) finance.

d) Explain the characteristics of the strategic, tactical and operational levels in the organisation in the context of the Anthony hierarchy.[1]

e) Explain the role of marketing in an organisation: [1]
   i) the definition of marketing
   ii) the marketing mix
   iii) the relationship of the marketing plan to the strategic plan

f) Explain basic organisational structure concepts: [2]
   i) separation of direction and management
   ii) span of control and scalar chain
   iii) tall and flat organisations

g) Explain centralisation and decentralisation and list their advantages and disadvantages.[1]

2. The formal and informal business organisation

a) Explain the informal organisation and its relationship with the formal organisation.[1]

b) Describe the impact of the informal organisation on the business.[2]

3. Organisational culture in business

a) Define organisational culture.[1]

b) Describe the factors that shape the culture of the organisation.[1]

c) Explain the contribution made by writers on culture:[1]
   i) Schein – determinants of organisational culture
   ii) Handy – four cultural stereotypes
   iii) Hofstede – international perspectives on culture

4. Stakeholders of business organisations

a) Define the internal stakeholder and list the different categories of internal stakeholder.[1]

b) Define connected and external stakeholders and explain their impact on the organisation.[1]

c) Identify the main stakeholder groups and the objectives of each group.[1]

d) Explain how the different stakeholder groups interact and how their objectives may conflict with one another.[1]

5. Information technology and information systems in business

a) Discuss the types of information technology and information systems used by the business organisation.[1]

b) List the attributes of good quality information.[1]

c) Explain how the type of information differs and the purposes for which it is applied at different levels of the organisation: strategic, tactical and operational.[1]

d) Identify the different sources of internal and external information.[1]

e) Describe the main features of information systems used within the organisation.[1]

6. Committees in the business organisation

a) Explain the purposes of committees.[1]

b) Describe the types of committee used by business organisations.[1]

c) List the advantages and disadvantages of committees.[1]

d) Explain the roles of the Chair and Secretary of a committee.[1]

7. Business ethics and ethical behaviour

a) Define business ethics and explain the importance of ethics to the organisation and to the individual.[1]

b) Identify influences that determine whether behaviour and decisions are ethical or unethical.[1]

c) Identify the factors that distinguish a profession from other types of occupation.[1]

d) Explain the role of the accountant in promoting ethical behaviour.[1]

e) Recognise the purpose of international and organisational codes of ethics and codes of conduct, IFAC, ACCA etc.[1]

8. Governance and social responsibility in business

a) Recognise the concept of separation between ownership and control.[1]

b) Define corporate governance and social responsibility and explain their importance in contemporary organisations.[1]

c) Explain the responsibility of organisations to maintain appropriate standards of corporate governance and corporate social responsibility.[1]

d) Briefly explain the main recommendations of best practice in effective corporate governance:[1]
   i) Non-executive directors
   ii) Remuneration committees
   iii) Audit committees
   iv) Public oversight

e) Explain how organisations take account of their social responsibility objectives through analysis of the needs of internal, connected and external stakeholders.[1]

f) Identify the social and environmental responsibilities of business organisations to internal, connected and external stakeholders. [1]

B KEY ENVIRONMENTAL INFLUENCES AND CONSTRAINTS ON BUSINESS AND ACCOUNTING

1. Political and legal factors

a) Define environmental forces in terms of political, legal, economic, social and technological factors.[1]

b) Explain how the political system and government policy affect the organisation.[1]

c) Describe the sources of legal authority, including supra-national bodies, national and regional governments.[1]

d) Explain how the law protects the employee and the implications of employment legislation for the manager and the organisation.[1]

e) Identify the principles of data protection and security.[1]

f) Explain how the law promotes and protects health and safety in the workplace.[1]

g) Recognise the responsibility of the individual and organisation for compliance with laws on data protection, security and health and safety.[1]

2. Macro-economic factors

a) Define macro-economic policy.[1]

b) Explain the main determinants of the level of business activity in the economy and how variations in the level of business activity affect individuals, households and businesses.[1]

c) Explain the impact of economic issues on the individual, the household and the business: [1]
   i) inflation
   ii) unemployment
   iii) stagnation
   iv) international payments disequilibrium.

d) Describe the main types of economic policy that may be implemented by government and supra-national bodies to maximise economic welfare.[1]

e) Recognise the impact of fiscal and monetary policy measures on the individual, the household and businesses.[1]

3. Social and demographic factors

a) Explain the medium and long-term effects of social and demographic trends on business outcomes and the economy.[1]

b) Describe the impact of changes in social structure, values, attitudes and tastes on the organisation.[2]

c) Identify and explain the measures that governments may take in response to the medium and long-term impact of demographic change.[2]

4. Technological factors

a) Explain the effects of technological change on the organisation structure and strategy:[1]
   i) Downsizing
   ii) Delayering
   iii) Outsourcing

b) Describe the impact of information technology and information systems development on business processes.[1]

5. Competitive factors

a) Explain the factors that influence the level of competitiveness in an industry or sector.[1]

b) Describe the activities of an organisation that affect its competitiveness:[1]
   i) purchasing
   ii) production
   iii) marketing
   iv) service

C HISTORY AND ROLE OF ACCOUNTING IN BUSINESS

1. The history and function of accounting in business

a) Briefly explain the history and development of the accounting and finance role in business.[1]

b) Explain the overall role and separate functions of the accounting department.[1]

2. Law and regulation governing accounting

a) Explain basic legal requirements in relation to keeping and submitting proper records and preparing financial accounts.[1]

b) Explain the broad consequences of failing to comply with the legal requirements for maintaining accounting records.[1]

c) Explain how the international accountancy profession regulates itself through the establishment of reporting standards and their monitoring.[1]

3. Financial systems, procedures and IT applications

a) Explain how business and financial systems and procedures are formulated and implemented to reflect the objectives and policies of the organisation.[1]

b) Describe the main financial systems used within an organisation:[1]
   i) purchases and sales invoicing
   ii) payroll
   iii) credit control
   iv) cash and working capital management.

c) Explain why appropriate controls are necessary in relation to business and IT systems and procedures.[2]

d) Understand business uses of computers and IT software applications:[1]
   i) Spreadsheet applications
   ii) Database systems

e) Describe and compare the relative benefits and limitations of manual and automated financial systems that may be used in an organisation.[2]

4. The relationship between accounting and other business functions

a) Explain the relationship between accounting and purchasing/procurement.[1]

b) Explain financial considerations in production and production planning.[1]

c) Identify the financial issues associated with marketing.[1]

d) Identify the financial costs and benefits of effective service provision.[1]

D SPECIFIC FUNCTIONS OF ACCOUNTING AND INTERNAL FINANCIAL CONTROL

1. Accounting and finance functions within business

a) Explain the contribution of the accounting function to the formulation, implementation, and control of the organisation's policies, procedures, and performance.[2]

b) Identify and describe the main accounting and reporting functions in business:[1]
   i) recording financial information
   ii) codifying and processing financial information
   iii) preparing financial statements

c) Identify and describe the main management accounting and performance management functions in business:[1]
   i) recording and analysing costs and revenues
   ii) providing management accounting information for decision-making

   iii) planning and preparing budgets and exercising budgetary control.

d) Identify and describe the main finance and treasury functions:[1]
   i) calculating and mitigating business tax liabilities
   ii) evaluating and obtaining finance
   iii) managing working capital
   iv) treasury and risk management.

2. Internal and external auditing and their functions

a) Define internal and external audit.[1]

b) Explain the main functions of the internal auditor and the external auditor.[1]

3. Internal financial control and security within business organisations

a) Explain internal control and internal check.[1]

b) Explain the importance of internal financial controls in an organisation.[2]

c) Describe the responsibilities of management for internal financial control.[1]

d) Describe the features of effective internal financial control procedures in an organisation.[2]

e) Identify and describe features for protecting the security of IT systems and software within business.[1]

f) Describe general and application systems controls in business.[1]

4. Fraud and fraudulent behaviour and their prevention in business.

a) Explain the circumstances under which fraud is likely to arise.[1]

b) Identify different types of fraud in the organisation.[1]

c) Explain the implications of fraud for the organisation.[2]

d) Explain the role and duties of individual managers in the fraud detection and prevention process.[1]

E LEADING AND MANAGING INDIVIDUALS AND TEAMS

1. Leadership, management and supervision

a) Define leadership, management and supervision and the distinction between these terms.[1]

b) Explain the nature of management:[1]
   i) scientific/classical theories of management Fayol, Taylor
   ii) the human relations school – Mayo
   iii) the functions of a manager – Mintzberg, Drucker

c) Explain the areas of managerial authority and responsibility.[2]

d) Explain the qualities, situational, functional and contingency approaches to leadership with reference to the theories of Adair, Fiedler, Bennis, Kotter and Heifetz.[2]

e) Explain leadership styles and contexts: using the models of Ashridge, and Blake and Mouton.[2]

2. Individual and group behaviour in business organisations

a) Describe the main characteristics of individual and group behaviour.[1]

b) Outline the contributions of individuals and teams to organisational success.[1]

c) Identify individual and team approaches to work.[1]

3. Team formation, development and management

a) Explain the differences between a group and a team.[1]

b) Define the purposes of a team.[1]

c) Explain the role of the manager in building the team and developing individuals within the team.[1]
   i) Belbin's team roles theory
   ii) Tuckman's theory of team development

d) List the characteristics of effective and ineffective teams.[1]

e) Describe tools and techniques that can be used to build the team and improve team effectiveness.[1]

4. Motivating individuals and groups

a) Define motivation and explain its importance to the organisation, teams and individuals.[1]

b) Explain content and process theories of motivation: Maslow, Herzberg, McGregor, and Vroom.[2]

c) Explain and identify types of intrinsic and extrinsic reward.[1]

d) Explain how reward systems can be designed and implemented to motivate teams and individuals.[1]

F. RECRUITING AND DEVELOPING EFFECTIVE EMPLOYEES

1. Recruitment and selection, managing diversity and equal opportunity

a) Explain the importance of effective recruitment and selection to the organisation.[1]

b) Describe the recruitment and selection processes and explain the stages in these processes.[1]

c) Describe the roles of those involved in the recruitment and selection processes.[1]

d) Describe the methods through which organisations seek to meet their recruitment needs.[1]

e) Explain the advantages and disadvantages of different recruitment and selection methods.[1]

f)   Explain the purposes of a diversity policy within the human resources plan.[2]

g)   Explain the purpose and benefits of an equal opportunities policy within human resource planning.[2]

h)   Explain the practical steps that an organisation may take to ensure the effectiveness of its diversity and equal opportunities policy.[1]

2.   **Techniques for improving personal effectiveness at work and their benefits**

a)   Explain the purposes of personal development plans.[1]

b)   Describe how a personal development plan should be formulated, implemented, monitored and reviewed by the individual.[1]

c)   Explain the importance of effective time management.[1]

d)   Describe the barriers to effective time management and how they may be overcome.[1]

e)   Describe the role of information technology in improving personal effectiveness.[1]

f)   Explain the purposes and processes of coaching, mentoring and counselling and their benefits.[1]

3.   **Features of effective communication**

a)   Define communications.[1]

b)   Explain a simple communication model: sender, message, receiver, feedback, noise.[1]

c)   Explain formal and informal communication and their importance in the workplace.[1]

d)   Identify the consequences of ineffective communication.[1]

e)   Describe the attributes of effective communication.[1]

f)   Describe the barriers to effective communication and identify practical steps that may be taken to overcome them.[1]

g)   Describe the main methods and patterns of communication.[1]

4.   **Training, development and learning in the maintenance and improvement of business performance**

a)   Explain the importance of learning in the workplace.[2]

b)   Describe the learning process: Honey and Mumford, Kolb.[1]

c)   Describe the role of the human resources department and individual managers in the learning process.[1]

d)   Describe the training and development process: identifying needs, setting objectives, programme design, delivery and validation.[1]

e)   Explain the terms 'training', 'development' and 'education' and the characteristics of each.[1]

f)   List the benefits of effective training and development in the workplace.[1]

5.   **Review and appraisal of individual performance**

a)   Explain the importance of performance assessment.[1]

b)   Explain how organisations assess the performance of human resources.[1]

c)   Define performance appraisal and describe its purposes.[1]

d)   Describe the performance appraisal process.[1]

e)   Explain the benefits of effective appraisal.[2]

f)   Identify the barriers to effective appraisal and how these may be overcome.[1]

g)   Explain how the effectiveness of performance appraisal may be evaluated.[2]

The exam paper

The syllabus is assessed by a two-hour paper-based or computer-based examination. Questions will assess all parts of the syllabus and will test knowledge and some comprehension or application of this knowledge. The examinations will consist of 40 two mark questions and 10 one mark questions.

The Pilot Paper for the syllabus is reproduced on pages 35–43.

Pilot paper

Paper F1

Accountant in Business

Time allowed: 2 hours

Do NOT open this paper until instructed by the supervisor.

During reading and planning time only the question paper may be annotated. You must NOT write in your answer booklet until instructed by the supervisor.

This question paper must not be removed from the examination hall.

Warning

The pilot paper cannot cover all of the syllabus nor can it include examples of every type of question that will be included in the actual exam. You may see questions in the exam that you think are more difficult than any you see in the pilot paper.

ALL FIFTY questions are compulsory and MUST be attempted

1   Span of control is concerned with the number of levels of management in an organisation.

    A   True

    B   False   **(1 mark)**

---

2   Which of the following is the main function of marketing?

    A   To maximise sales volume

    B   To identify and anticipate customer needs

    C   To persuade potential consumers to convert latent demand into expenditure

    D   To identify suitable outlets for goods and services supplied   **(2 marks)**

---

3   Which one of the following has become an established best practice in corporate governance in recent years?

    A   An increasingly prominent role for non-executive directors

    B   An increase in the powers of external auditors

    C   Greater accountability for directors who are in breach of their fiduciary duties

    D   A requirement for all companies to establish an internal audit function   **(2 marks)**

---

4   According to Charles Handy's four cultural stereotypes, which of the following organisations would adopt a task culture?

    A   The cost accounting department of a large steel producing company

    B   The consulting division of a 'big four' accountancy firm

    C   A civil service department

    D   A small clothes and design fashion house   **(2 marks)**

---

5   At what stage of the planning process should a company carry out a situation analysis?

    A   When converting strategic objectives into tactical plans

    B   When formulating a mission statement

    C   When validating the effectiveness of plans against outcomes

    D   When formulating strategic objectives   **(2 marks)**

---

6   Which one of the following is a potential advantage of decentralisation?

    A   Greater control by senior management

    B   Risk reduction in relation to operational decision-making

    C   More accountability at lower levels

    D   Consistency of decision-making across the organisation   **(2 marks)**

---

7   Which one of the following is an example of an internal stakeholder?

    A   A shareholder

    B   An non-executive director

    C   A manager

    D   A supplier   **(2 marks)**

8 According to Mendelow, companies must pay most attention to the needs of which group of stakeholders?

    A   Those with little power and little interest in the company

    B   Those with a high level of power but little interest in the company

    C   Those with little power but a high level of interest in the company

    D   Those with a high level of power and a high level of interest in the company   **(2 marks)**

9 What is the responsibility of a Public Oversight Board?

    A   The establishment of detailed rules on internal audit procedures

    B   The commissioning of financial reporting standards

    C   The creation of legislation relating to accounting standards

    D   The monitoring and enforcement of legal and compliance standards   **(2 marks)**

10 The ageing population trend in many European countries is caused by a increasing birth rate and an increasing mortality rate.

    A   True

    B   False   **(1 mark)**

11 Which one of the following is consistent with a government's policy objective to expand the level of economic activity?

    A   An increase in taxation

    B   An increase in interest rates

    C   An increase in personal savings

    D   An increase in public expenditure   **(2 marks)**

12 Which of the following is the name given to unemployment arising from labour in the market place being of the wrong type or available in the wrong place?

    A   Structural unemployment

    B   Cyclical unemployment

    C   Frictional unemployment

    D   Marginal unemployment   **(2 marks)**

13 When an organisation carries out an environmental scan, it analyses which of the following?

    A   Strengths, weaknesses, opportunities and threats

    B   Political, economic, social and technological factors

    C   Strategic options and choice

    D   Inbound and outbound logistics   **(2 marks)**

14 Which of the following is data protection legislation primarily designed to protect?

    A   All private individuals and corporate entities on whom only regulated data is held

    B   All private individuals on whom only regulated data is held

    C   All private individuals on whom any data is held

    D   All private individuals and corporate entities on whom any data is held   **(2 marks)**

15   Which of the following types of new legislation would provide greater employment opportunities in large companies?

    A   New laws on health and safety
    B   New laws to prevent discrimination in the workplace
    C   New laws making it more difficult to dismiss employees unfairly
    D   New laws on higher compensation for employer breaches of employment contracts

(2 marks)

16   The total level of demand in the economy is made up of consumption, ... , government expenditure and net gains from international trade.

Which of the following correctly completes the sentence above.

    A   Savings
    B   Taxation
    C   Investment

(1 mark)

17   Which set of environmental factors does a lobby group intend to directly influence?

    A   Political
    B   Technological
    C   Demographic
    D   Economic

(2 marks)

18   The use of advanced technology solutions in order to maximise the productivity and effectiveness of call centre operations is an application of the principles established by which school of management thought?

    A   Human relations
    B   Empirical
    C   Scientific
    D   Administrative

(2 marks)

19   The original role of the accounting function was which one of the following?

    A   Providing management information
    B   Recording financial information
    C   Maintaining financial control
    D   Managing funds efficiently

(2 marks)

20   Tax avoidance is a legal activity whilst tax evasion is an illegal activity.

Is this statement true or false?

    A   True
    B   False

(1 mark)

21   The system used by a company to record sales and purchases is an example of which of the following?

    A   A transaction processing system
    B   A management information system
    C   An office automation system
    D   A decision support system

(2 marks)

22   The implementation of a budgetary control system in a large organisation would be the responsibility of the internal auditor.

Is this statement true or false?

A   True
B   False   **(1 mark)**

23   Which type of organisation would have the retail prices it charges to personal consumers subject to close scrutiny by a regulator?

A   A multinational corporation
B   A multi-divisional conglomerate
C   A national utilities company
D   A financial services provider   **(2 marks)**

24   The central bank has announced a 2% increase in interest rates.

This decision has the most impact on which department of a large company?

A   Marketing
B   Treasury
C   Financial accounting
D   Production   **(2 marks)**

25   The major purpose of the International Accounting Standards Board (IASB) is to ensure consistency in ....

Which two words complete this sentence?

A   Financial control
B   Corporate reporting
C   External auditing   **(1 mark)**

26   X Co has a financial accountant and a management accountant.

Which group of activities would fall within the responsibility of the financial accountant?

A   Payroll, purchase ledger, sales invoicing
B   Inventory valuation, budgetary control and variance analysis
C   Fraud avoidance, segregation of duties, internal review and control
D   Funds management, risk assessment, project and investment appraisal   **(2 marks)**

27   In an economic environment of high price inflation, those who owe money will gain and those who are owed money will lose.

Is this statement true or false?

A   True
B   False   **(1 mark)**

28   To whom is the internal auditor primarily accountable?

A   The directors of the company
B   The company as a separate entity
C   The shareholders of the company
D   The employees of the company   **(2 marks)**

29 Which one of the following is a DISADVANTAGE of a computerised accounting system over a manual accounting system?

    A   A computerised system is more time consuming to operate
    B   The operating costs of a computerised system are higher
    C   The computerised system is more costly to implement
    D   A computerised system is more error prone   **(2 marks)**

30 The identification, evaluation, testing and reporting on internal controls is a feature of which of the following?

    A   Operational audit
    B   Transactions audit
    C   Social responsibility audit
    D   Systems audit   **(2 marks)**

31 What is the primary responsibility of the external auditor?

    A   To verify all the financial transactions and supporting documentation of the client

    B   To ensure that the client's financial statements are reasonably accurate and free from bias

    C   To report all financial irregularities to the shareholders of the client

    D   To ensure that all the client's financial statements are prepared and submitted to the relevant authorities on time   **(2 marks)**

32 Which of the following are substantive tests used for in the context of external audit of financial accounts?

    A   To establish whether a figure is correct
    B   To investigate why a figure is incorrect
    C   To investigate whether a figure should be included
    D   To establish why a figure is excluded   **(2 marks)**

33 In the context of fraud, 'teeming and lading' is most likely to occur in which area of operation?

    A   Sales
    B   Quality control
    C   Advertising and promotion
    D   Despatch   **(2 marks)**

34 In order to establish an effective internal control system that will minimise the prospect of fraud, which one of the following should be considered first?

    A   Recruitment policy and checks on new personnel
    B   Identification of areas of potential risk
    C   Devising of appropriate sanctions for inappropriate behaviour
    D   Segregation of duties in critical areas   **(2 marks)**

35 The leadership style that least acknowledges the contribution that subordinates have to make is

....

Which word correctly completes this sentence?

    A   Authoritarian
    B   Autocratic
    C   Assertive   **(1 mark)**

36 The Blake and Mouton managerial grid examines the relationship between 'concern for production' and which of the following?

A   Concern for people
B   Concern for sales
C   Concern for quality
D   Concern for service

(2 marks)

37 Jackie leads an established team of six workers. In the last month, two have left to pursue alternative jobs and one has commenced maternity leave. Three new staff members have joined Jackie's team.

Which one of Tuckman's group stages will now occur?

A   Norming
B   Forming
C   Performing
D   Storming

(2 marks)

38 Richard is a valuable member of his team. He is enthusiastic and curious, highly communicative and has a capacity for contacting people and exploring anything new.

Which of Belbin's team roles does Richard fulfil?

A   Monitor-evaluator
B   Plant
C   Resource-investigator
D   Company worker

(2 marks)

39 Which one of the following statements is correct in relation to monetary rewards in accordance with Herzberg's Two-Factor theory?

A   Pay increases are a powerful long-term motivator
B   Inadequate monetary rewards are a powerful dissatisfier
C   Monetary rewards are more important than non-monetary rewards
D   Pay can never be used as a motivator

(2 marks)

40 Which one of the following is a characteristic of a team as opposed to a group?

A   Members agree with other members
B   Members negotiate personal roles and positions
C   Members arrive at decisions by consensus
D   Members work in cooperation

(2 marks)

41 According to Victor Vroom:

Force (or motivation) = ... × expectancy

Which of the following words completes Vroom's equation.

A   Needs
B   Valence
C   Opportunity

(1 mark)

42 According to Handy's 'shamrock' organisation model, which one of the following is becoming progressively less important in contemporary organisations?

A The permanent, full-time work force
B The part-time temporary work force
C The role of independent sub-contractors
D The role of technical support functions (2 marks)

43 Which pattern of communication is the quickest way to send a message?

A The circle
B The chain
C The Y
D The wheel (2 marks)

44 Poor quality lateral communication will result in which of the following?

A Lack of direction
B Lack of coordination
C Lack of delegation
D Lack of control (2 marks)

45 Role playing exercises using video recording and playback would be most effective for which type of training?

A Development of selling skills
B Regulation and compliance
C Dissemination of technical knowledge
D Introduction of new processes or procedures (2 marks)

46 In the context of marketing, the 'four P's' are price, place, promotion and ....

Which word correctly completes this sentence?

A Processes
B Production
C Product (1 mark)

47 In relation to employee selection, which type of testing is most appropriate for assessing the depth of knowledge of a candidate and the candidate's ability to apply that knowledge?

A Intelligence testing
B Personality testing
C Competence testing
D Psychometric testing (2 marks)

48 A company has advertised for staff who must be at least 1.88 metres tall and have been in continuous full-time employment for at least five years.

Which of the following is the legal term for this unlawful practice?

A Direct discrimination
B Indirect discrimination
C Victimisation
D Implied discrimination (2 marks)

49   Which one of the following is most appropriate for the purpose of supporting the individual through the learning process with a view to promoting career development?

A   Buddy
B   Counsellor
C   Mentor
D   Instructor   (2 marks)

50   Gils is conducting an appraisal interview with his assistant Jill. He initially invites Jill to talk about the job, her aspirations, expectations and problems. He adopts a non-judgmental approach and offers suggestions and guidance.

This is an example of which approach to performance appraisal?

A   Tell and sell approach
B   Tell and listen approach
C   Problem solving approach
D   360 degree approach   (2 marks)

Part A
Business organisational structure, governance and management

Business organisation and structure

Topic list	Syllabus reference
1 Types of organisation	A1 (a)
2 Organisational structure	A1 (b)(f)
3 Levels of strategy in the organisation	A1 (d)
4 Organisational departments and functions	A1 (c)(e); C4 (a)–(d); D1(a)-(d)
5 Centralisation and decentralisation	A1(g)
6 Committees	A6 (a)–(d)

Introduction

Organisations develop out of the need to **co-ordinate** work, but this can be achieved in different ways. In this chapter we identify the different types of organisation **(Section 1)**.

There are various influences upon organisational structure **(Section 2)**. Most firms have some sort of **organisation hierarchy** reflecting the levels of strategy-making **(Section 3)**. We can see the **strategic apex** (eg Board of Directors) at the top, through ranks of **middle managers** to the **operating core** where the work is done. Of course, firms which employ many people need to group people into departments on some basis: this involves choices as to **departmentation (Section 4)**, and the level of centralisation that is operated **(Section 5)**. The chapter concludes with a discussion of the work of committees **(Section 6)**. Committees are one of the main mechanisms for organisational consultation and communication.

Study guide

		Intellectual level
A1	**The business organisation and its structure**	
(a)	Identify the different types of organisation:	1
(i)	Commercial	
(ii)	Not-for-profit	
(iii)	Public sector	
(iv)	Non-governmental organisations	
(v)	Cooperatives	
(b)	Describe the different ways in which organisations may be structured: entrepreneurial, functional, matrix, divisional, departmental, by geographical area and by product.	1
(c)	Describe the roles and functions of the main departments in a business organisation:	1
(i)	Research and development	
(ii)	Purchasing	
(iii)	Production	
(iv)	Direct service provision	
(v)	Marketing	
(vi)	Administration	
(vii)	Finance	
(d)	Explain the characteristics of the strategic, tactical and operational levels in the organisation in the context of the Anthony hierarchy.	1
(e)	Explain the role of marketing in an organisation:	1
(i)	The definition of marketing	
(ii)	The marketing mix	
(iii)	The relationship of the marketing plan to the strategic plan	
(f)	Explain basic organisational structure concepts:	1
(i)	Separation of direction and management	
(ii)	Span of control and scalar chain	
(iii)	Tall and flat organisations	
(g)	Explain centralisation and decentralisation and list their advantages and disadvantages	1
A6	**Committees in the business organisation**	
(a)	Explain the purpose of committees	1
(b)	Describe the types of committee used by business organisations	1
(c)	List the advantages and disadvantages of committees	1
(d)	Explain the roles of the Chair and Secretary of a committee	1

Study guide cont'd

		Intellectual level
C4	**The relationship between accounting and other business functions**	
(a)	Explain the relationship between accounting and purchasing/procurement	1
(b)	Explain financial considerations in production and production planning	1
(c)	Identify the financial issues associated with marketing	1
(d)	Identify the financial costs and benefits of effective service provision	1
D1	**Accounting and finance functions within business**	
(a)	Explain the contribution of the accounting function to the formulation, implementation, and control of the organisation's policies, procedures, and performance	2
(b)	Identify and describe the main accounting and reporting functions in business:	1
(i)	Recording financial information	
(ii)	Codifying and processing financial information	
(iii)	Preparing financial statements	
(c)	Identify and describe the main management accounting and performance management functions in business:	1
(i)	Recording and analysing costs and revenues	
(ii)	Providing management accounting information for decision-making	
(iii)	Planning and preparing budgets and exercising budgetary control	
(d)	Identify and describe the main finance and treasury functions:	1
(i)	Calculating and mitigating business tax liabilities	
(ii)	Evaluating and obtaining evidence	
(iii)	Managing working capital	
(iv)	Treasury and risk management	

Exam guide

This chapter lays the foundation for an understanding of what organisations are, what they do and how they do it. Organisational structure concepts **(Section 2)** represent a higher level of knowledge. According to the Study Guide you must be able to apply knowledge to exam questions.

1 Types of organisation

1.1 What all organisations have in common

> An **organisation** is: 'a *social arrangement* which pursues collective *goals*, which *controls* its own performance and which has a *boundary* separating it from its environment'.

Here are some examples of organisations.

- A multinational car manufacturer (eg Ford)
- An accountancy firm (eg Ernst and Young)
- A charity (eg Oxfam)

- A local authority
- A trade union (eg Unison)
- An army

Here is how the definition applies to two of the organisations listed above.

Characteristic	Car manufacturer	Army
Social arrangement	People work in different divisions, making different cars	Soldiers are in different regiments
Collective goals	Sell cars, make money	Defend the country
Controls performance	Costs and quality are reviewed and controlled	Strict disciplinary procedures, training
Boundary	Physical: factory gates Social: employment status	Physical: barracks Social: different rules than for civilians

(a) Organisations are preoccupied with **performance**, and meeting or improving their standards.

(b) Organisations contain formal, documented **systems and procedures** which enable them to control what they do.

(c) Different people do different things, or **specialise** in one activity.

(d) They pursue a **variety of objectives** and goals.

(e) Most organisations obtain **inputs** (eg materials), and **process** them into **outputs** (eg for others to buy).

1.2 Why do organisations exist?

Organisations can achieve results which individuals cannot achieve by themselves.

(a) Organisations **overcome people's individual limitations**, whether physical or intellectual.

(b) Organisations **enable people to specialise** in what they do best.

(c) Organisations **save time**, because people can work together or do two aspects of a different task at the same time.

(d) Organisations **accumulate** and share **knowledge**.

(e) Organisations enable **synergy**: by bringing *together* two individuals their combined output will exceed their output if they continued working separately.

In brief, organisations enable people to be **more productive**.

1.3 How organisations differ

The common elements of organisations were described in paragraph 1.1, but organisations also differ in many ways. Here are some possible differences.

Factor	Example
Ownership (public vs private)	Private sector: owned by private owners/shareholders. Public sector: owned by the government
Control	By the owners themselves, by people working on their behalf, or indirectly by government-sponsored regulators
Activity (ie what they do)	Manufacturing, healthcare
Profit or non-profit **orientation**	Business exists to make a profit. The army, on the other hand, is not profit orientated
Legal status	Limited company or partnership
Size	Family business, multinational corporation.
Sources of **finance**	Borrowing, government funding, share issues
Technology	High use of technology (eg computer firms) vs low use (eg corner shop)

1.4 What the organisation does

Organisations do many different types of work. Here are some examples.

Industry	Activity
Agriculture	Producing and processing food
Manufacturing	Acquiring raw materials and, by the application of labour and technology, turning them into a product (eg a car)
Extractive/raw materials	Extracting and refining raw materials (eg mining)
Energy	Converting one resource (eg coal) into another (eg electricity)
Retailing/distribution	Delivering goods to the end consumer
Intellectual production	Producing **intellectual property** eg software, publishing, films, music etc
Service industries	These include retailing, distribution, transport, banking, various business services (eg accountancy, advertising) and public services such as education, medicine

1.5 Profit vs non-profit orientation

An important difference in the list above is between profit orientated ('commercial') and non profit orientated organisations. The basic difference in outlook is expressed in the diagram below. Note the distinction between **primary** and **secondary** goals. A primary goal is the most important: the other goals support it.

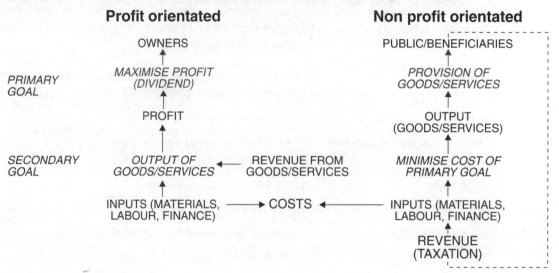

1.6 Private vs public sector

> **Private sector**: organisations not owned or run by central or local government, or government agencies
>
> **Public sector**: organisation owned or run by central or local government or government agencies

1.7 Private sector businesses

A business organisation exists to make a profit. In other words, the costs of its activities should be less than the revenues it earns from providing goods or services. Profits are not incidental to its activities but the driving factor.

Business organisations come in all different shapes and sizes, and there is a choice of legal structure.

1.7.1 Legal status

Someone setting up a business can choose to go into business **alone**, take on one or more **partners** who also share the profits of the business, or set up a **limited company**.

1.7.2 Limited companies

> A **limited company** has a separate legal personality from its owners (shareholders). The shareholders cannot normally be sued for the debts of the business unless they have given some personal guarantee. Their risk is generally restricted to the amount that they have invested in the company when buying the shares. This is called **limited liability.**

Whereas sole traderships and partnerships are normally small business, limited company status is used for businesses of any size.

The **ownership** and **control** of a limited company are **legally separate** even though they may be vested in the same individual or individuals.

(a) **Shareholders are the owners** but have limited rights, as shareholders, over the day to day running of the company. They provide capital and receive a return. Shareholders could be large institutional investors (such as insurance companies and pension funds), private individuals, or employees.

(b) **Directors are appointed by shareholders to run the company**. In the UK, the board of directors controls management and staff, and is accountable to the shareholders, but it has responsibilities towards both groups – owners and employees alike.

    (i) **Executive directors** participate in the daily operations of the organisation.

    (ii) **Non-executive directors** are invited to join in an advisory capacity, usually to bring their particular skills or experience to the discussions of the board to exercise some overall guidance.

(c) **Operational management** usually consists of career managers who are recruited to operate the business, and are accountable to the board.

1.7.3 Types of limited company

In the UK, limited companies come in two types: **private limited companies** (eg X Limited) and **public limited companies** (eg X plc). They differ as follows.

(a) **Number of shareholders.** Most private companies are owned by only a small number of shareholders. Public companies generally are owned by a wider proportion of the investing public.

(b) **Transferability of shares.** Shares in public companies can be offered to the general public. In practice this means that they can be traded on a stock exchange. Shares in private companies, on the other hand, are rarely transferable without the consent of the shareholders.

(c) **Directors as shareholders.** The directors of a private limited company are more likely to hold a substantial portion of the company's shares than the directors of a public company.

(d) **Source of capital**

    (i) A private company's share capital will normally be provided from three sources.

        – The founder or promoter
        – Business associates of the founder or employer
        – Venture capitalists

    (ii) A public company's share capital, in addition, can be raised from the public directly, or through institutional investors, using recognised markets.

Many companies start in a small way, often as family businesses which operate as private companies, then grow to the point where they become public companies and can invite investors to subscribe for shares. The new capital thus made available enables the firm to expand its activities and achieve the advantages of large scale operation. In the UK firms can get a **listing** on the Alternative Investment Market (AIM) or a full listing on the Stock Exchange.

1.7.4 Advantages and disadvantages of limited companies

Advantages

- **More money** available for investment.
- **Reduces risk** for investors thanks to limited liability.
- **Separate legal personality.** A company can own property, make contracts etc.
- **Ownership** is legally **separate** from **control**. Investors need not get involved in operations.
- **No restrictions on size**. Some companies have millions of shareholders.
- **Flexibility**. Capital and enterprise can be brought together.

Disadvantages

- Legal **compliance costs**. Because of limited liability, the financial statements of most limited companies have to be **audited**, and then published for shareholders.

- **Shareholders** have **little** practical **power**, other than to sell their shares to a new group of managers, although they can vote to sack the directors.

1.7.5 Co-operative societies and mutual associations

Co-operatives are businesses owned by their workers or customers, who share the profits. Here are some of the features they have in common.

- Open membership
- Democratic control (one member, one vote)
- Distribution of the surplus in proportion to purchases
- Promotion of education.

 Case Study

A major example of a co-operative in the UK is the *Co-operative Retail Store* network. In addition there is the *Co-operative Wholesale Society* and the *Co-operative Bank*. Another example is the *John Lewis Partnership*.

Mutual associations are similar to co-operatives in that they are 'owned' by their members rather than outside investors.

(a)   Some financial companies used to be mutual associations. However, building societies in the UK such as the Abbey National and the Halifax converted from being mutual associations to being banks. The Nationwide Building Society has held out against this, so far citing the lower interest rates it can offer to borrowers.

(b)   Some **insurance companies** are mutual associations, such as Equitable Life. Again there are no external shareholders to satisfy.

 Question   **Types of organisation**

Florence Nightingale runs a successful and growing small business as a sole trader. She wishes to expand the business and has her eyes on Scutari Ltd, a small private limited company in the same line. After the acquisition, she runs the two businesses as if they were one operation making no distinction between them. What is the legal form of the business she is running?

Answer

This is quite a tricky question. For example, if suppliers have contracts with Scutari Ltd, the contract is with the company, and Florence is not legally liable for the company's debts. If their contracts are with Florence, then they are dealing with her personally. Florence has to make a choice.

(a)   She can run the entire business as a sole trader, in which case Scutari Ltd's assets must be transferred to her

(b)   She can run her entire business as a limited company, in which case she would contribute the assets of her business as capital to the company

(c)   She can ensure that the two business are legally distinct in their assets, liabilities, income and expenditure.

1.8 The public sector

The **public sector** comprises all organisations owned and run by the government and local government. Here are some examples.

- NHS hospitals
- The armed forces
- Publicly funded agencies such as English Heritage
- Most schools and universities
- Government departments

Public sector organisations have a variety of objectives.

- The Benefits Agency administers part of the social security system.

- The Post Office makes a **profit** from mail services, although it does have a **social function** too.

1.8.1 Key characteristics of the public sector

(a)   **Accountability**, ultimately, to Parliament

(b)   **Funding.** The public sector can obtain funds in three main ways.

    (i)   Raising taxes
    (ii)   Making charges (eg for prescriptions)
    (iii)   Borrowing

(c)   **Demand for services.** There is a relationship between the price charged for something and the 'demand'. In the public sector demand for many services is practically limitless.

(d)   **Limited resources.** Despite the potentially huge demand for public services, constraints on government expenditure mean that resources are limited and that demand cannot always be met.

1.8.2 Advantages

(a)   **Fairness**. The public sector can ensure that everyone has access to health services.

(b)   **Filling the gaps left by the private sector**, by providing **public goods** such as streetlighting.

(c)   **Public interest**. Governments once believed the public interest was best served if the state ran certain services.

(d)   **Economies of scale**. Costs can be spread if everything is centralised.

(e)   **Cheaper finance**. Taxes or borrowing backed by government guarantees might be cheaper than borrowing at commercial rates.

(f)   **Efficiency**. The public sector is sometimes more efficient than the private sector. The UK's NHS, despite its well publicised problems, has lower administration costs and serves more of the population than the private sector does in the US.

1.8.3 Disadvantages

(a)   **Accountability.** Inefficiency may be ignored as taxpayers bear losses.

(b)   **Interference.** Politicians may not be familiar with the operation of a business and yet political pressures and indecision may influence adversely the decision making process. Pressures to get elected may lead to the deferral of necessary but unpopular decisions.

(c)   **Cost.** There can be conflict between economy of operation and adequacy of service. The public will demand as perfect a service as possible but will not wish to bear the cost involved.

1.9 Non-governmental organisations

FAST FORWARD

A non-governmental organisation (NGO) is an independent voluntary association of people acting together for some common purpose (other than achieving government office or making money).

Non-governmental organisations (NGOs) are bodies which are not directly linked with national government. The description 'NGO' generally applies to groups whose primary aim is not a commercial one, but within this the term is applied to a diverse range of activities, aimed at promoting social, political or environmental change.

Case Study

The UK has a significant number of NGOs providing information on conservation matters. The Farming and Wildlife Advisory Service, for example, is a non-government organisation which provides farmers with practical advice on managing farm operations in order to support wildlife, landscape, archaeology and other conservation issues.

NGOs need to engage in fund raising and mobilisation of resources (donations, volunteer labour, materials). This process may require quite complex levels of organisation. The following are some organisational features of NGOs.

- Staffing by volunteers as well as full time employees
- Finance from grants or contracts
- Skills in advertising and media relations
- Some kind of national 'headquarters'
- Planning and budgeting expertise

It can be seen, therefore, that NGOs may need to possess an efficient level of organisation structure, much in the same way as a traditional commercial undertaking.

2 Organisational structure

2.1 Components of the organisation

Mintzberg believes that *all* organisations can be analysed into five components, according to how they relate to the work of the organisation, and how they prefer to co-ordinate.

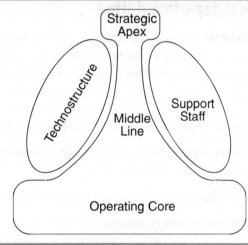

Component	Job	Preferred means of co-ordination
Strategic apex	Ensures the organisation follows its mission. Manages the organisation's relationship with the environment.	Direct supervision (especially in small businesses)
Operating core	People **directly** involved in the process of obtaining inputs, and converting them into outputs	Mutual adjustment; standardisation of skills
Middle line	Converts the desires of the strategic apex into the work done by the operating core	Standardisation of outputs (results)
Technostructure	• Analysers determine the best way of doing a job • Planners determine outputs (eg goods must achieve a specified level of quality) • Personnel analysts standardise skills (eg training programmes)	Standardisation of work processes or outputs
Support staff	Ancillary services such as public relations, legal counsel, the cafeteria. Support staff do not plan or standardise production. They function independently of the operating core.	Mutual adjustment

In most organisations, tasks and people are grouped together in some rational way: on the basis of specialisation, say, or shared technology or customer base. This is known as **departmentation**. Different patterns of departmentation are possible, and the pattern selected will depend on the individual circumstances of the organisation.

FAST FORWARD

Organisations can be **departmentalised** on a **functional** basis (with separate departments for production, marketing, finance etc), a **geographical** basis (by region, or country), a **product** basis (eg worldwide divisions for product X, Y etc), a **brand** basis, or a **matrix** basis (eg someone selling product X in country A would report to both a product X manager and a country A manager). Organisation structures often feature a variety of these types, as **hybrid** structures.

2.2 Functional departmentation

Functional organisation involves grouping together people who do similar tasks. Primary functions in a manufacturing company might be production, sales, finance, and general administration. Sub-departments of marketing might be market research, advertising, PR and so on.

Advantages include:

(a)   **Expertise is pooled** thanks to the division of work into specialist areas.

(b)   It **avoids duplication** (eg one management accounts department rather than several) and enables economies of scale.

(c)   It **facilitates** the recruitment, management and development of functional specialists.

(d)   It suits **centralised** businesses.

Disadvantages include:

(a)   It focuses on internal **processes** and **inputs**, rather than the **customer** and **outputs**, which are what ultimately drive a business. Inward-looking businesses are less able to adapt to changing demands.

(b)   **Communication problems** may arise between different functions, which each have their own jargon.

(c)   **Poor co-ordination**, especially if rooted in a tall organisation structure. Decisions by one function/department involving another might have to be referred upwards, and dealt with at a higher level, thereby increasing the burdens on senior management.

(d)   Functional structures create **vertical barriers** to information and work flow. Management writer *Peters* suggests that customer service requires 'horizontal' flow between functions – rather than passing the customer from one functional department to another.

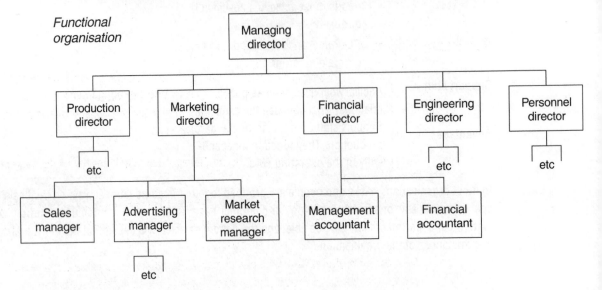

Functional organisation

2.3 Geographic departmentation

Where the organisation is structured according to geographic area, some authority is retained at Head Office but day-to-day operations are handled on a **territorial** basis (eg Southern region, Western region). Many sales departments are organised territorially.

There are **advantages** to geographic departmentation.

(a) There is **local decision-making** at the point of contact between the organisation (eg a salesperson) and its customers, suppliers or other stakeholders.

(b) It may be **cheaper** to establish area factories/offices than to service markets from one location (eg costs of transportation and travelling may be reduced).

But there are **disadvantages** too.

(a) **Duplication** and possible loss of economies of scale might arise. For example, a national organisation divided into ten regions might have a customer liaison department in each regional office. If the organisation did all customer liaison work from head office (centralised) it might need fewer managerial staff.

(b) **Inconsistency** in methods or standards may develop across different areas.

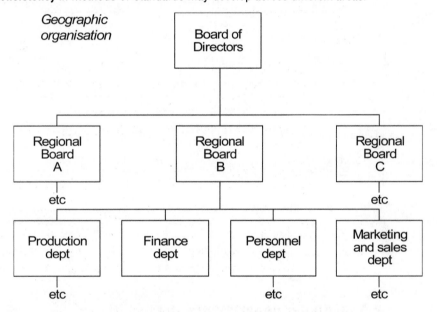

Geographic organisation

2.4 Product/brand departmentation

Some organisations group activities on the basis of **products** or product lines. Some functional departmentation remains (eg manufacturing, distribution, marketing and sales) but a divisional manager is given responsibility for the product or product line, with authority over personnel of different functions.

Advantages include:

(a) **Accountability**. Individual managers can be held accountable for the profitability of individual products.

(b) **Specialisation**. For example, some salespeople will be trained to sell a specific product in which they may develop technical expertise and thereby offer a better sales service to customers.

(c) **Co-ordination**. The different functional activities and efforts required to make and sell each product can be co-ordinated and integrated by the divisional/product manager.

Disadvantages include:

(a) It **increases the overhead costs** and managerial complexity of the organisation.

(b) Different product divisions may **fail to share resources** and customers.

A **brand** is the name (eg 'Persil') or design which identifies the products or services of a manufacturer or provider and distinguishes them from those of competitors. (Large organisations may produce a number of different brands of the same basic product, such as washing powder or toothpaste.) Branding brings the product to the attention of buyers and creates brand **recognition**, **differentiation** and **loyalty**: often customers do not realise that two 'rival' brands are in fact produced by the same manufacturer.

(a) Because each brand is packaged, promoted and sold in a distinctive way, the need for specialisation may make brand departmentation effective. As with product departmentation, some functional departmentation remains but brand managers have responsibility for the brand's marketing and this can affect every function.

(b) Brand departmentation has similar advantages/disadvantages to product departmentation.

Product/brand organisation

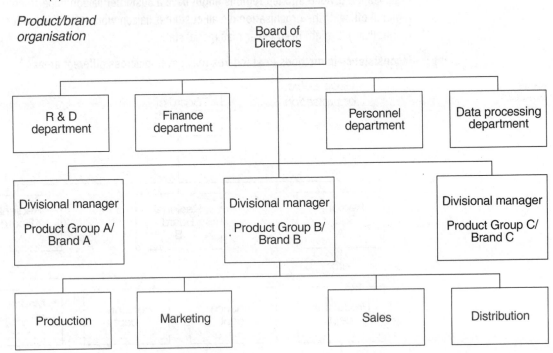

2.5 Customer departmentation

An organisation may organise its activities on the basis of types of customer, or market segment.

(a) Departmentation by customer is commonly associated with **sales departments** and selling effort, but it might also be used by a jobbing or contracting firm where a team of managers may be given the responsibility of liaising with major customers (eg discussing specifications and completion dates, quality of work, progress chasing etc).

(b) Many businesses distinguish between **business customers** and **consumers**.

Question   Types of organisation

Looking at the 'Product/Brand Organisation' chart following Section 2.4 above, what types of organisation can you identify, and why are these appropriate for their purposes? What *added* type of organisation might this firm use, and in what circumstances?

Answer

- At the head office level, there is *functional* organisation. This enables standardisation of policy and activity in key 'staff' or support functions shared by the various divisions.

- At divisional level, there is *product/brand* organisation. This allows the distinctive culture and attributes of each product/brand to be addressed in production processes and marketing approach.

- For each product/brand, there is *functional* organisation, enabling specialist expertise to be directed at the different activities required to produce, market and distribute a product.

- This firm may further organise its marketing department by *customer*, if its customer base includes key (high-value, long-term) customer accounts with diverse service needs, for example.

- It may further organise its sales and distribution departments by *geographical area*, if the customer base is internationally or regionally dispersed: local market conditions and values, and logistical requirements of distribution, can then be taken more specifically into account.

2.6 Divisionalisation

FAST FORWARD

In a **divisional structure** some activities are **decentralised** to business units or regions.

Key term

Divisionalisation is the division of a business into autonomous regions or product businesses, each with its own revenues, expenditures and capital asset purchase programmes, and therefore each with its own profit and loss responsibility.

Each division of the organisation might be:

- A subsidiary company under the holding company
- A profit centre or investment centre within a single company
- A strategic business unit (SBU) within the larger company, with its own objectives

Successful divisionalisation requires certain key conditions.

(a) Each division must have **properly delegated authority**, and must be held properly accountable to head office (eg for profits earned).

(b) Each unit must be **large enough** to support the quantity and quality of management it needs.

(c) The unit must not rely on head office for excessive **management support**.

(d) Each unit must have a **potential for growth** in its own area of operations.

(e) There should be **scope and challenge** in the job for the management of each unit.

(f) If units deal with each other, it should be as an **'arm's length' transaction**.

The advantages and disadvantages of divisionalisation may be summarised as follows.

Advantages	Disadvantages
Focuses the attention of management below 'top level' on business performance.	In some businesses, it is impossible to identify completely independent products or markets for which separate divisions can be set up.
Reduces the likelihood of unprofitable products and activities being continued.	Divisionalisation is only possible at a fairly senior management level, because there is a limit to how much discretion can be used in the division of work. For example, every product needs a manufacturing function and a selling function.
Encourages a greater attention to efficiency, lower costs and higher profits.	There may be more resource problems. Many divisions get their resources from head office in competition with other divisions.
Gives more authority to junior managers, and so grooms them for more senior positions in the future (planned managerial succession).	
Reduces the number of levels of management. The top executives in each division should be able to report directly to the chief executive of the holding company.	

2.7 Hybrid structures

Organisation structures are rarely composed of only one type of organisation. 'Hybrid' structures may involve a mix of functional departmentation, ensuring specialised attention to key functions, with elements of (for example):

(a)   Product organisation, to suit the requirements of brand marketing or production technologies.

(b)   Customer organisation, particularly in marketing departments, to service key accounts.

(c)   Territorial organisation, particularly of sales and distribution departments, to service local requirements for marketing or distribution in dispersed regions or countries.

2.8 The simple structure (or entrepreneurial structure)

FAST FORWARD

> The strategic apex exerts a pull to centralise, leading to the **simple structure**.

The **strategic apex** wishes to retain control over decision-making, and so exercises what *Mintzberg* describes as a **pull to centralise**. Mintzberg believes that this leads to a **simple structure**.

Simple structure

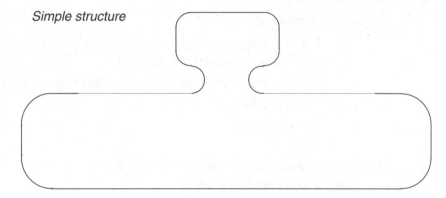

(a) **The simple structure is characteristic of small, young organisations**. The strategic apex is a small group, or possibly one person, which exercises direct control over the people making up the operating core. There is little, if any, role for technical or support staff.

(b) In small firms, a single entrepreneur or management team will dominate (as in the power culture). If it grows, the organisation might need more managerial skills than the apex can provide. Strategies might be made on the basis of the manager's hunches.

(c) Centralisation is advantageous as it reflects management's full knowledge of the operating core and its processes. However, senior managers might intervene too much.

(d) It is risky as it depends on the expertise of one person. Such an organisation might be prone to **succession crises**. This problem is often encountered in family businesses.

(e) This structure can handle an environment that is relatively simple but fast moving, where standardisation cannot be used to co-ordinate activities.

(f) **Co-ordination is achieved by direct supervision**, with few formal devices. It is thus flexible.

(g) This structure has its own particular characteristics: wide span of control; no middle line and hence minimal hierarchy; and no technostructure, implying little formalisation or standardisation of behaviour.

2.9 Matrix and project organisation

Where hybrid organisation 'mixes' organisation types, **matrix** organisation actually *crosses* functional and product/customer/project organisation.

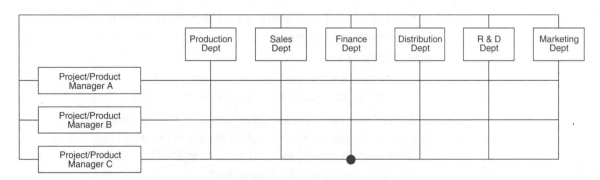

The employees represented by the dot in the above diagram, for example, are responsible to:

- The finance manager for their work in accounting and finance for their functional department; and
- To the project manager C for their work on the project team: budgeting, management reporting and payroll relevant to the project, say.

Advantages of matrix organisation include:

(a)   Greater **flexibility** of:

(i)   **People**. Employees develop an attitude geared to accepting change, and departmental monopolies are broken down.

(ii)   **Workflow and decision-making**. Direct contact between staff encourages problem solving and big picture thinking.

(iii)   **Tasks and structure**. The matrix structure may be readily amended, once projects are completed.

(b)   **Inter-disciplinary co-operation** and a mixing of skills and expertise, along with **improved communication** and **co-ordination**.

(c)   **Motivation and employee development**: providing employees with greater participation in planning and control decisions.

(d)   **Market awareness**: the organisation tends to become more customer/quality focused.

(e)   **Horizontal workflow**: bureaucratic obstacles are removed, and department specialisms become less powerful.

There are **disadvantages**, however.

(a)   **Dual authority** threatens a **conflict** between functional managers and product/ project/area managers.

(b)   An individual with two or more bosses may suffer stress from **conflicting demands** or **ambiguous roles**.

(c)   **Cost**: product management posts are added, meetings have to be held, and so on.

(d)   **Slower decision making** due to the added complexity.

2.10 The new organisation

Some recent trends have emerged from the focus on **flexibility** as a key organisational value.

(a)   **Flat structures.** The flattening of hierarchies does away with levels of organisation which lengthened lines of communication and decision making. Flat structures are more responsive, because there is a more direct relationship between the organisation's strategic centre and the operational units serving the customer.

(b)   **'Horizontal structures'.** There is increased recognition that functional versatility (through multi-functional project teams and multi-skilling, for example) is the key to flexibility.

(c)   **'Chunked' and 'unglued' structures**. So far, this has meant teamworking and decentralisation, or empowerment, creating smaller and more flexible units within the overall structure.

(d)   **Output-focused structures**. The key to all the above trends is the focus on results, and on the customer, instead of internal processes and functions for their own sake.

(e)   **'Jobless' structures.** The employee becomes not a job-holder but a seller of skills. This is a concrete expression of the concept of **employability**, which says that a person needs to have a portfolio of skills which are valuable on the open labour market: employees need to be mobile, moving between organisations.

2.11 The shamrock organisation

Largely driven by pressure to reduce personnel costs, there has been an increase in the use of part-time and temporary contracts of employment. These allow rapid down-sizing in times of recession or slow growth and can save on the costs of benefits such as pensions, holiday pay and health insurance. The growth in the proportion of the workforce employed on such less-favourable contracts has attracted political attention but continues. It has produced the phenomenon of the **flexible firm** or, as *Handy* calls it, the **shamrock organisation**.

Key term

> *Handy* defines the **shamrock organisation** as a 'core of essential executives and workers supported by outside contractors and part-time help'. This structure permits the buying-in of services as needed, with consequent reductions in overhead costs. It is also known as the **flexible firm**.

Professional core

The first leaf of the shamrock is the **professional core**. It consists of professionals, technicians and managers whose skills define the organisation's core competence. This core group defines what the company does and what business it is in. They are essential to the continuity and growth of the organisation. Their pay is tied to organisational performance and their relations will be more like those among the partners in a professional firm than those among superiors and subordinates in today's large corporation.

Self-employed professionals

The next leaf is made up of **self-employed professionals or technicians** or smaller specialised organisations who are hired on contract, on a project-by-project basis. They are paid in fees for results rather than in salary for time. They frequently **telecommute**. No benefits are paid by the core organisation, and the worker carries the risk of insecurity.

Contingent work force

The third leaf comprises the **contingent work force**, whose employment derives from the external demand for the organisation's products. There is no career track for these people and they perform routine jobs. They are usually temporary and part-time workers who will experience short periods of employment and long periods of unemployment. They are paid by the hour or day or week for the time they work.

Consumers

A fourth leaf of the shamrock may exist, consisting of **consumers** who do the work of the organisation. Examples are shoppers who bag their own groceries and purchasers of assemble-it-yourself furniture.

This type of organisation provides three kinds of flexibility.

(a) **Personnel costs** can respond to market conditions of supply and demand for different types of labour and to the employer's financial position.

(b) Overall **personnel numbers** can be changed as required.

(c) The **skills** available can be modified fairly rapidly and multi-skilling can be encouraged.

Exam focus point

> This 'shamrock' model appears on the Pilot Paper.

2.12 Span of control

FAST FORWARD

> **Span of control** or **'span of management'** refers to the number of subordinates responsible to a superior.

Key term

> The **span of control** refers to the number of subordinates immediately reporting to a superior official.

In other words, if a manager has five subordinates, the span of control is five.

Classical theorists suggest the following.

(a) There are physical and mental **limitations** to any given manager's ability to control people, relationships and activities.

(b) There needs to be **tight managerial control** from the top of an organisation downward.

(c) The span of control should therefore be **restricted**, to allow maximum control consistent with the manager's capabilities: usually between three and six. If the span of control is too wide, too much of the manager's time will be taken up with routine problems and supervision, leaving less time for planning. Even so, subordinates may not get the supervision, control and communication that they require.

(d) On the other hand, if the span is too **narrow**, the manager may fail to delegate, keeping too much routine work to himself and depriving subordinates of decision-making authority and responsibility. There may be a tendency to interfere in or over-supervise the work that is delegated to subordinates – and the relative costs of supervision will thus be unnecessarily high. Subordinates tend to be dissatisfied in such situations, having too little challenge and responsibility and perhaps feeling that the superior does not trust them.

A number of factors influence the span of control.

(a) A manager's **capabilities** limit the span of control: there are physical and mental limitations to any single manager's ability to control people and activities.

(b) The **nature of the manager's workload**

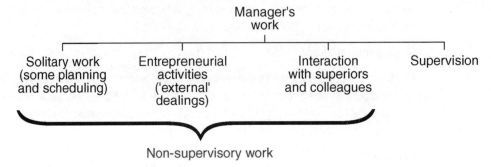

The more non-supervisory work in a manager's workload:

(i) The narrower the span of control
(ii) The greater the delegation of authority to subordinates

(c) The **geographical dispersion** of subordinates: dispersed teams require more effort to supervise.

(d) **Subordinates' work:** if all subordinates do similar tasks, a wide span is possible. If **close group cohesion** is desirable, a narrow span of control might be needed.

(e) The **nature of problems** that a supervisor might have to help subordinates with. Time consuming problems suggest a narrow span of control.

(f) The degree of **interaction between subordinates**. If subordinates can help each other, a wide span is possible.

(g) The amount of **support** that supervisors receive from other parts of the organisation or from *technology* (eg computerised work monitoring, or 'virtual meetings' with dispersed team members).

2.13 Tall and flat organisations

FAST FORWARD

Recent trends have been towards **delayering** organisations of levels of management. In other words, **tall organisations** (with many management levels, and narrow spans of control) are turning into **flat organisations** (with fewer management levels, wider spans of control) as a result of technological changes and the granting of more decision-making power to front line employees.

The span of control concept has implications for the length of the **scalar chain**

Key terms

Scalar chain: the chain of command from the most senior to the most junior.

A **tall organisation** is one which, in relation to its size, has a large number of levels of management hierarchy. This implies a *narrow* span of control.

A **flat organisation** is one which, in relation to its size, has a small number of hierarchical levels. This implies a *wide* span of control.

Exam focus point

All of the highlighted key terms above are specified in the Study Guide.

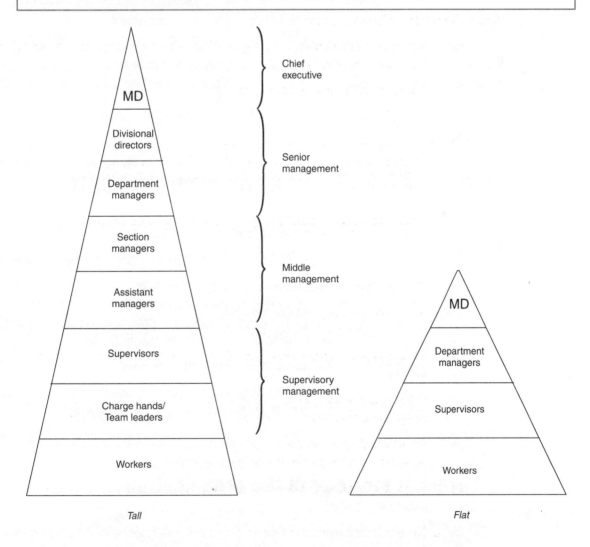

Tall

Flat

The advantages and disadvantages of these organisational forms can be summarised as follows.

Tall organisation

For	Against
Narrow control spans	Inhibits delegation
Small groups enable team members to participate in decisions	Rigid supervision can be imposed, blocking initiative
A large number of steps on the promotional ladders – assists management training and career planning	The same work passes through too many hands
	Increases administration and overhead costs
	Slow decision making and responses, as the strategic apex is further away

Flat organisation

For	Against
More opportunity for delegation	Requires that jobs *can* be delegated. Managers may only get a superficial idea of what goes on. If they are overworked they are more likely to be involved in crisis management
Relatively cheap	Sacrifices control
In theory, speeds up communication between strategic apex and operating core	Middle managers are often necessary to convert the grand vision of the strategic apex into operational terms

2.14 Delayering

Key term

> **Delayering** is the reduction of the number of management levels from bottom to top.

Many organisations are delayering. Middle line jobs are vanishing. Organisations are increasing the average span of control, reducing management levels and becoming flatter.

(a) **Information technology** reduces the need for middle managers to process information.

(b) **Empowerment**. Many organisations, especially service businesses, are keen to delegate authority down the line to the lowest possible level. Front-line workers in the operating core are allowed to take decisions, in order to increase responsiveness to customer demands. This perhaps removes the need for some middle management jobs.

(c) **Economy**. Delayering reduces managerial/supervisory costs.

(d) **Fashion**. Delayering is fashionable: if senior managers believe that tall structures are inherently inflexible, they might cut the numbers of management levels.

This topic is also covered in Chapter 7, when discussing the impact of technology on the organisation.

3 Levels of strategy in the organisation

FAST FORWARD

There are many levels of strategy in an organisation.

- **Corporate**: the general direction of the whole organisation
- **Business**: how the organisation or its SBUs tackle particular markets
- **Operational/functional**: specific strategies for different departments of the business

Any level of the organisation can have objectives and devise strategies to achieve them. The strategic management process is multi-layered.

It is generally agreed that there are **three levels of strategy**: **corporate**, **business** and **functional/operational**. The distinction between corporate and business strategy arises because of the development of the **divisionalised** business organisation, which typically has a corporate centre and a number of strategic business units (SBUs).

 Case Study

Chandler described how four large US corporations found that the best way to divide strategic responsibility was to have the corporate HQ allocate resources and exercise overall financial control while the SBUs were each responsible for their own product-market strategies. Functional operational strategies can then be developed for component parts of SBUs.

3.1 Corporate strategies

Key term

> **Corporate strategy** is concerned with what types of business the organisation is in. It 'denotes the most general level of strategy in an organisation' (*Johnson and Scholes*).

Levels of strategy

CORPORATE STRATEGY

What businesses are we (or want to be) in?

How do we enter or exit?

| BUSINESS STRATEGY | BUSINESS STRATEGY | BUSINESS STRATEGY |

Strategies relevant to a particular area

Strategic Business Unit (SBU)   SBU   SBU

FUNCTIONAL STRATEGIES

R&D	OPERATIONS	MARKETING	HRM	IT/IS	FINANCE
• Products	• Capacity	• Orientation	• Recruitment	• Systems	• Sources
• Processes	• Process technology	• Marketing mix	• Selection	• Technology	• Uses
• Design	• Work flows	• Product planning	• HRD	• Management	
• Development	• Quality	• Marketing information	• Appraisal		
• Testing	• Outsourcing	• Segmentation	• Reward		
		• Services			

STRATEGIES INVOLVING MANY FUNCTIONS (EG CHANGE MANAGEMENT, TOTAL QUALITY, RE-ENGINEERING)

Defining aspects of corporate strategy

Characteristic	Comment
Scope of activities	Strategy and strategic management impact upon the whole organisation: all parts of the business operation should support and further the strategic plan.
Environment	The organisation counters threats and exploits opportunities in the environment (customers, clients, competitors).
Resources	Strategy involves choices about allocating or obtaining corporate resources now and in future.
Values	The value systems of people with power in the organisation influence its strategy.
Timescale	Corporate strategy has a long-term impact.
Complexity	Corporate strategy involves uncertainty about the future, integrating the operations of the organisation and change.

3.2 Business strategy

Key term

> **Business strategy**: how an organisation approaches a particular product market area.

Business strategy can involve decisions such as whether to segment the market and specialise in particularly profitable areas, or to compete by offering a wider range of products.

 Case Study

Mercedes-Benz wished to expand its product range to include four wheel drive vehicles and smaller cars; eventually the company merged with Chrysler.

As we noted earlier, some large, diversified firms have separate **strategic business units** (SBUs) dealing with particular areas. Business strategy for such large organisations is strategy at the SBU level.

3.3 Functional/operational strategies

Functional/operational strategies deal with specialised areas of activity.

Functional area	Comment
Marketing	Devising products and services, pricing, promoting and distributing them, in order to satisfy customer needs at a profit. Marketing and corporate strategies are interrelated.
Production	Factory location, manufacturing techniques, outsourcing and so on.
Finance	Ensuring that the firm has enough financial resources to fund its other strategies by identifying sources of finance and using them effectively.
Human resources management	Secure personnel of the right skills in the right quantity at the right time, and to ensure that they have the right skills and values to promote the firm's overall goals.

Functional area	Comment
Information systems	A firm's information systems are becoming increasingly important, as an item of expenditure, as administrative support and as a tool for competitive strength. Not all information technology applications are strategic, and the strategic value of IT will vary from case to case.
R&D	New products and techniques.

3.4 The Anthony hierarchy

Robert Anthony classified managerial activity as follows:

(a) **Strategic management** (carried out by senior management) is concerned with direction-setting, policy making and crisis handling.

(b) **Tactical management** (carried out by middle management) is concerned with establishing means to the corporate ends, mobilising resources and innovating (finding new ways to achieve business goals).

(c) **Operational management** (carried out by supervisors and operatives) is concerned with routine activities to carry out tactical plans.

Exam focus point

It can be seen from this analysis that one of the basic organisational structure concepts is that of the separation between direction-setting for the business, and day-to-day management processes. This distinction is specifically itemised in the Study Guide.

4 Organisational departments and functions

4.1 Research and development

FAST FORWARD

Research may be **pure**, **applied** or **development**. It may be intended to improve **products** or **processes**. R&D should support the organisation's strategy and be closely co-ordinated with marketing.

Key terms

Pure research is original research to obtain new scientific or technical knowledge or understanding. There is no obvious commercial or practical end in view.

Applied research is also original research work like pure research, but it has a specific practical aim or application (eg research on improvements in the effectiveness of medicines etc).

Development is the use of existing scientific and technical knowledge to produce new (or substantially improved) products or systems, prior to starting commercial production operations.

Many organisations employ **specialist staff** to conduct research and development (R&D). They may be organised in a separate functional department of their own. In an organisation run on a product division basis, R&D staff may be employed by each division.

4.1.1 Product and process research

There are two categories of R&D.

> **Product research** is based on creating new products and developing existing ones, in other words the organisation's 'offer' to the market.
>
> **Process research** is based on improving the way in which those products or services are made or delivered, or the efficiency with which they are made or delivered.

Product research – new product development

The new product development process must be carefully controlled; new products are a major source of competitive advantage but can cost a great deal of money to bring to market. A screening process is necessary to ensure that resources are concentrated on projects with a high probability of success.

Process research

Process research involves attention to how the goods/services are produced. Process research has these aspects.

(a)   **Processes** are crucial in service industries (eg fast food), as part of the services sold.

(b)   **Productivity**. Efficient processes save money and time.

(c)   **Planning**. If you know how long certain stages in a project are likely to take, you can plan the most efficient sequence.

(d)   **Quality management** for enhanced quality.

R&D should be closely co-ordinated with marketing

(a)   Customer needs, as identified by marketers, should be a vital input to new product developments.

(b)   The R&D department might identify possible changes to product specifications so that a variety of marketing mixes can be tried out and screened.

 Case Study

An example of the relationship of R&D to marketing was described in an article in the *Financial Times* about the firm *Nestlé*, which invested £46m a year in research and approximately £190m on development. *Nestlé* had a central R&D function, but also regional development centres. The central R&D function was involved in basic research. 'Much of the lab's work was only tenuously connected with the company's business... When scientists joined the lab, they were told "Just work in this or that area. If you work hard enough, we're sure you'll find something"'. The results of this approach were:

(a)   The research laboratory was largely cut off from development centres.
(b)   Much research never found commercial application.

As part of *Nestlé's* wider reorganisation, which restructured the business into strategic business units (SBU's), formal links were established between R&D and the SBUs. This meant that research procedures have been changed so that a commercial time horizon is established for projects.

4.2 Purchasing

Purchasing makes a major contribution to cost and quality management in any business and in retail is a vital element of strategy. The purchasing mix is:

- Quantity
- Price
- Quality
- Delivery

Purchasing is 'the acquisition of material resources and business services for use by the organisation'.

4.2.1 Importance of purchasing

Cost. Raw materials and subcomponents purchases are a major cost for many firms.

Quality. The quality of input resources affects the quality of outputs and the efficiency of the production function.

Strategy. In retailing, buying goods for resale is one of the most important activities of the business.

Position of purchasing within the organisation

Where purchasing is of strategic importance, the most senior purchasing executive may be on the **board of directors** or, at least, report to the managing director.

Where raw materials are an important cost, the purchasing officer may work in the **production function**.

In any event, the purchasing officer must **liaise with the finance department**, especially with regard to payment of creditors.

The purchasing manager's responsibilities

(a) **Inputs for production.** Acquiring raw materials, components, sub-assemblies, consumable stores and capital equipment for the production function.

(b) **Inputs for administration.** Purchasing supplies and equipment for all areas of the business (eg microcomputers, motor cars, telephone systems, office furniture, paper and other stationery items).

(c) **Cost control.** Ensuring that the organisation obtains value for money over the long term consistent with quality.

(d) **Liaison with the R&D** department to find suppliers for materials which are to the specifications required by the designers.

(e) **Supplier management**. Locating suppliers and dealing with them (eg discussing prices, discounts, delivery lead times, specifications; chasing late deliveries; sanctioning payments).

(f) Obtaining **information** on availability, quality, prices, distribution and suppliers for the evaluation of purchasing alternatives.

(g) Maintenance of **inventory levels.**

4.2.2 The purchasing mix

The purchasing manager has to obtain the best purchasing mix.

- Quantity
- Quality
- Price
- Delivery

(a) **Quantity**. The size and timing of purchase orders will be dictated by the balance between two things.

    (i) Delays in production caused by insufficient inventory

    (ii) Costs of holding inventory: tied up capital, storage space, deterioration, insurance, risk of pilferage.

A system of inventory control will set **optimum reorder levels** (the inventory level at which supplies must be replenished so as to arrive in time to meet demand) to ensure **economic order quantities** (EOQ) are obtained for individual inventory items.

(b) **Quality**. The production department will need to be consulted about the quality of goods required for the manufacturing process, and the marketing department about the quality of goods acceptable to customers. Purchased components might be an important constituent of product quality.

(c) **Price**. Favourable short-term trends in prices may influence the buying decision, but purchasing should have an eye to the best **value** over a period of time – considering quality, delivery, urgency of order, inventory-holding requirements and so on.

(d) **Delivery**. The **lead time** between placing and delivery of an order can be crucial to efficient inventory control and production planning. The reliability of suppliers' delivery arrangements must also be assessed.

4.2.3 Purchasing and profits

The professionalism of the purchasing function affects profit in three ways. Effective purchasing does three things.

- It obtains the **best value for money**, giving the company more flexibility in its pricing strategy.

- It assists in meeting **quality targets**, with an impact on a firm's long-term marketing strategy if quality is an issue.

- It minimises the amount of purchased material held as inventory, so minimising inventory-holding costs.

4.3 Production

The production function plans, organises, directs and controls the necessary activities to provide products and services, creating outputs which have added value over the value of inputs.

Activity	Example
Obtain **inputs** to the production 'system', such as plant facilities, materials and labour.	Inputs: timber, screws, nails, adhesives, varnish, stain, templates, cutting tools, carpenters
Adding of value The activities below occupy most of the production manager's attention. • Scheduling jobs on machines • Assigning labour to jobs • Controlling the quality of production and/or service delivery • Improving methods of work • Managing materials and equipment, to avoid waste	Operations: sawing, sanding, assembly, finishing
Create **outputs,** ie finished products and services	Outputs: tables, chairs, cabinets, and so on

4.3.1 Production management decisions

Longer-term decisions

These are related to setting up the production organisation.

- Selection of equipment and processes
- Job design and methods
- Factory location and layout
- Ensuring the right number and skills of employees

Short-term decisions

These are concerned with the running and control of the organisation.

- Production and control
- Quality management
- Maintenance
- Labour control and supervision
- Inventory control

4.3.2 Relationships with other functions

Longer term decisions, particularly relating to design and the innovation of improved products, cannot be taken by the production department alone; its activities must be **integrated with other functions** in the firm.

- **Product design** is co-ordinated with **R&D**. Production should advise R&D as to the consequences of particular designs for the manufacturing process.

- **Job design** will involve consultation with **human resources** specialists.

- The quantities needed to be produced will be notified by the **sales department**.

- The **human resources department** will be involved in managing the work force.

- The **finance department** might indicate the resources available for new equipment.

4.4 Service operations

> **Services** are intangible, cannot be stored, are inherently variable in quality and nature and their purchase results in no transfer of property. The people and processes involved in providing them are therefore of paramount importance.

Many products have a service element. Service businesses include health care, restaurants, tourism, financial services, education and all the professions.

Key term

> **Service** '... any activity of benefit that one party can offer to another that is essentially intangible and does not result in the ownership of anything. Its production may or may not be tied to a physical product.'
>
> (P Kotler, *Social Marketing*)

4.4.1 The nature of services

Intangibility. Unlike goods there are no substantial material or physical aspects to a service. A service cannot be packaged in a bag and carried home, such as a live musical performance.

Inseparability. Many services are **created** at the same time as they are **consumed**, for example, dental treatment. Associated with this is **perishability**. Services cannot be stored. The services of a dentist are purchased for a **period of time**. The service they offer cannot be used later.

Variability. It may be hard to attain precise standardisation of the service offered. The quality of the service may depend heavily on **who** (or what) delivers the service, and exactly **when** it takes place.

Ownership. Services differ from consumer goods: they do **not normally result in the transfer of property**. The purchase of a service only confers on the customer access to or a right to use a facility, not ownership.

4.4.2 Implications of service provision

Poor service quality on one occasion (eg lack of punctuality of trains, staff rudeness, a bank's incompetence) is likely to lead to **widespread distrust** of everything the organisation does.

Complexity. If the service is intangible offering a complicated future benefit then attracting customers means promoting an attractive image and ensuring that the service lives up to its reputation, consistently.

Pricing of services is often complicated, especially if large numbers of people are involved in providing the service.

Human resources management is a key ingredient in the services marketing mix, as so many services are produced and consumed in a specific social context.

Dimensions of service operations

Determinants	Comments
Tangibles	The physical evidence, such as the quality of fixtures and fittings of the company's service area, must be consistent with the desired image.
Reliability	Getting it right first time is very important, not only to ensure repeat business, but, in financial services, as a matter of ethics, if the customer is buying a future benefit.
Responsiveness	The staff's willingness to deal with the customer's queries must be apparent.
Communication	Staff should talk to customers in non-technical language which they can understand.
Credibility	The organisation should be perceived as honest, trustworthy and as acting in the best interests of customers.

Determinants	Comments
Security	This is specially relevant to medical and financial services organisations. The customer needs to feel that the conversations with bank service staff are private and confidential. This factor should influence the design of the service area.
Competence	All the service staff need to appear competent in understanding the product range and interpreting the needs of the customers. In part this can be achieved through training programmes.
Courtesy	Customers (even rude ones) should perceive service staff as polite, respectful and friendly. This basic requirement is often difficult to achieve in practice, although training programmes can help.
Understanding customers' needs	The use of computer-based customer databases can be very impressive in this context. The service personnel can then call up the customer's records and use these data in the service process, thus personalising the process. Service staff need to meet customer needs rather than try to sell products. This is a subtle but important difference.
Access	Minimising queues, having a fair queuing system and speedy but accurate service are all factors which can avoid customers' irritation building up. A pleasant relaxing environment is a useful design factor in this context.

4.5 Marketing

FAST FORWARD

The **marketing function** manages an organisation's relationships with its customers.

Key term

Marketing is 'the management process which identifies, anticipates and satisfies customer needs profitably'.
(Chartered Institute of Marketing)

4.5.1 Models of marketing

Marketing activities in organisations can be grouped broadly into four roles.

(a) **Sales support**: the emphasis in this role is essentially reactive: marketing supports the direct sales force. It may include activities such as telesales or telemarketing, responding to inquiries, co-ordinating diaries, customer database management, organising exhibitions or other sales promotions, and administering agents. These activities usually come under a sales and marketing director or manager.

(b) **Marketing communications**: the emphasis in this role is more proactive: marketing promotes the organisation and its product or service at a tactical level. It typically includes activities such as providing brochures and catalogues to support the sales force.

(c) **Operational marketing**: the emphasis in this role is for marketing to support the organisation with a co-ordinated range of marketing activities including marketing research; brand management; product development and management; corporate and marketing communications; and customer relationship management. Given this breadth of activities, planning is also a function usually performed in this role but at an operational or functional level.

(d) **Strategic marketing**: the emphasis in this role is for marketing to contribute to the creation of competitive strategy. As such, it is practised in customer-focused and larger organisations. In a large or diversified organisation, it may also be responsible for the coordination of marketing departments or activities in separate business units.

Operational marketing activities

- Research and analysis
- Contributing to strategy and marketing planning
- Managing brands
- Implementing marketing programmes
- Measuring effectiveness
- Managing marketing teams

The operational marketing role, where it exists, will be performed by a marketing function in a business.

4.5.2 Marketing strategy and corporate strategy

So, what is the relationship between marketing and strategic management? The two are closely linked since there can be no corporate plan which does not involve products/services and customers.

Corporate strategic plans aim to guide the overall development of an organisation. Marketing planning is subordinate to corporate planning but makes a significant contribution to it and is concerned with many of the same issues. The marketing department is probably the most important source of information for the development of corporate strategy. The corporate audit of product/market strengths and weaknesses, and much of its external environmental analysis is directly informed by the **marketing audit**.

Specific marketing strategies will be determined within the overall corporate strategy. To be effective, these plans will be interdependent with those for other functions of the organisation.

(a)   The **strategic** component of marketing planning focuses on the direction which an organisation will take in relation to a specific market, or set of markets, in order to achieve a specified set of objectives.

(b)   Marketing planning also requires an **operational** component that defines tasks and activities to be undertaken in order to achieve the desired strategy. The **marketing plan** is concerned uniquely with **products** and **markets**.

Marketing management aims to ensure the company is pursuing effective policies to promote its products, markets and distribution channels. This involves exercising strategic control of marketing, and the means to apply strategic control is known as the **marketing audit**. Not only is the marketing audit an important aspect of **marketing control**, it can be used to provide much information and analysis for the **corporate planning process**.

Exam focus point

> The relationship between marketing and the overall strategic plan is specified in the Study Guide. The marketing function has been highlighted by the examiner as one of particular importance for organisational success, so it is vital that you take this topic area seriously.

4.5.3 Marketing orientation

Different organisations have different orientations towards the customer.

Orientation	Description
Production orientation	'Customers will buy whatever we produce – our job is to make as many as we can'. (Demand exceeds available supply.)
Product orientation, a variant of production orientation	'Add more features to the product – demand will pick up'. Such firms do not research what customers actually want.

Orientation	Description
Sales orientation	Customers are naturally sales resistant so the product must be sold actively and aggressively and customers must be persuaded to buy them.
Marketing orientation	The key task of the organisation is to determine the needs, wants and values of a target market and to adapt the organisation to delivering the desired satisfactions more effectively and efficiently than its competitors.

Market orientation   *Sales/production orientation*

```
Determine customer needs          Determine whether product
                                        can be made
         │                                  │
         ▼                                  ▼
   Invest resources                   Invest resources
         │                                  │
         ▼                                  ▼
  Make product/service                 Make product
         │                                  │
         ▼                                  ▼
Market the product/service (Profit   Sell the product (profit via
   via customer satisfaction)           increased turnover)
         │
         ▼
    Market feedback
```

4.5.4 Satisfying customer needs: the marketing mix

Before you continue, recall the Chartered Institute of Marketing's definition at the beginning of this section. The last word is **profitably**. After all, customers would be absolutely delighted if you were to satisfy **all** their needs for exotic holidays, caviar, champagne, private jets and so forth, for nothing. The marketing orientation is a way of doing business that seeks to provide satisfaction of customer wants at a **profit**.

Key term

> The **marketing mix** is the set of controllable variables and their levels that an organisation uses to influence the target market. These variables are product, price, place and promotion and are known as the 4Ps.

There is thus a balance to be achieved between organisational capacity and customer requirements. This balance is expressed in the **marketing mix,** which is the framework in which the customer and the business deal with each other.

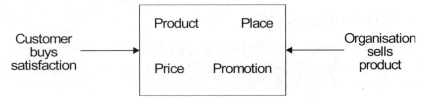

Customer buys satisfaction → | Product   Place |
| Price   Promotion | ← Organisation sells product

Product

The **product** element of the marketing mix is what is being sold, whether this be widgets, power stations, haircuts, holidays or financial advice. (A product could be a **service**.) Product issues include:

- Design (size, shape)
- Features
- Quality and reliability
- Packaging

- Safety
- Ecological friendliness
- What it does
- Image

The **implication of the marketing orientation** is that the **product or service** is not a 'thing' with 'features' but, from the customer's point of view is a **package of benefits, which meets a need or provides a solution** to a problem.

Core and augmented product

(a)   The **core product** is a product's essential features. The core product of a credit card is the ability to borrow up to a certain limit and pay off in varied instalments.

(b)   **Augmentations** are additional benefits. Most credit cards offer travel insurance, for instance.

Marketing managers make the following distinction.

(a)   Product **class**. This is a broad category of product, such as cars, washing machines and so forth. This corresponds to the core or generic product identified above.

(b)   Product **form**. This category refers to the different types of product within a product class. The product class 'cars' may have several forms, including five-door hatchbacks, four-wheel drive vehicles, hearses and so forth.

(c)   **Brand or make**. This refers to the particular brand or make of the product form. For example, the Nissan Micra, Vauxhall Corsa and Rover 100 are, broadly speaking, examples of the same product form.

We have already identified the **product life cycle**. A product may be expected to go through the stages of introduction, growth, maturity, decline and senility. A **different marketing approach is appropriate to each stage**, and different levels of sales and profit can be expected. Note that the product life cycle is a **model** of what **might** happen, **not a law** prescribing what **will** happen. In other words, not all products go through these stages or even have a life cycle.

Marketing personnel do not decide how the product appears. Production and design staff must also be consulted.

Place: distribution

Place covers two main issues.

(a)   **Outlets.** Where products are sold, for example in supermarkets, shops.

(i)   For most consumer goods, this involves one or more **intermediaries**, such as wholesalers, and then retailers.

(ii)   **Direct distribution** occurs when a firm runs its own shops or, via **mail order,** uses the postal service to bypass intermediaries.

(b)   **Logistics**

Even where intermediaries are used, a manufacturer still has to distribute products to wholesalers and retailers. Logistics is the management of to warehouses, storage and transportation.

Promotion: marketing communications

Promotion in the marketing mix includes all marketing communications, by which the public knows about the product or service.

Promotion is traditionally the main responsibility of marketing personnel, and is their most visible role. Promotion is intended to stimulate the potential customer through four behavioural stages.

- **Awareness** of the product
- **Interest** in the product
- **Desire** to buy
- **Action:** an actual purchase

(AIDA)

Some types of promotion

- **Advertising**: newspapers, TV, cinema, internet web-sites
- **Sales promotion**: money-off coupons, 'two for the price of one' offers
- **Direct selling** by sales personnel.
- **Public relations:** crisis management, obtaining favourable press coverage

Price

Products have to be sold at a price which meets the organisation's profit objectives. Pricing is a very practical matter and important part of marketing work.

(a) The **price element of the mix** itself covers the basic price, discounts, credit terms and interest free credit.

(b) **Price is influenced by demand** and the product's stage in its life cycle.

    (i) **Penetration** pricing: a low price is charged to persuade as many people as possible to buy the product in its early stages.

    (ii) **Skimming**: prices are set to cream off the highest level of profits even though this restricts the number of people able to afford the product.

(c) **Price is also part of the image** of the product: rightly or wrongly, a high-priced product is often assumed to be of better quality than a cheaply priced product. A high price also conveys an image of exclusivity.

(d) Price is a weapon against **competitors**.

Service marketing

In addition, for **services** (eg hospital care, air travel) there are three more Ps.

3 Ps

(a) The **people** who deliver the service (eg smiling or surly staff).
(b) The **processes** by which the service is delivered (eg queuing systems at Disneyworld).
(c) The **physical evidence** of the service (such as a glossy brochure).

Question	Marketing concept

'An accounts department is not making goods and selling them and so does not need the marketing concept.' Is this a fair comment?

Answer

No.

(a) The accounts department supplies information to various other parts of the organisation. Providing information is its service, and the other parts of the organisation are, effectively, its customers.

(b) An accounts department deals with customers all the time, especially credit customers: after all it sends out the bills and collects the money. As its activities are directly involved with customers, it must take the marketing philosophy on board, too.

4.5.5 The ideal marketing mix

The ideal marketing mix is one which holds a **proper balance** between each of these elements.

(a) One marketing activity in the mix will not be fully effective unless proper attention is given to all the other activities. For example, if a company launches a costly promotion campaign which emphasises the superior quality of a product, the outlay on advertising, packaging and personal selling will be wasted if the quality does not live up to customer expectations.

(b) A company might also place too much emphasis on one aspect of the marketing mix, and much of the effort and expenditure might not be justified for the additional returns it obtains. It might for example, place too much importance on price reductions to earn higher profits, when in fact a smaller price reduction and greater spending on sales promotion or product design might have a more profitable effect.

4.6 Administration

In many organisations administrative functions are carried out at head office as much as is possible. When this is the case, the administration function is said to be **centralised**. A **centralised** administration department involves as many administrative tasks as possible being carried out at a single central location.

4.6.1 Advantages of a centralised administration office

(a) **Consistency** – for example the same account codes are likely to be used no matter which part of the organisation submits an invoice. Everyone uses the same data and information.

(b) It gives better **security/control** over operations and it is easier to enforce standards.

(c) **Head office** is in a better position to know what is going on.

(d) There may be **economies of scale** available, for example in purchasing computer equipment and supplies.

(e) Administration staff are in a **single location** and more expert staff are likely to be employed. Career paths may be more clearly defined.

4.6.2 Disadvantages of a centralised administration office

(a) Local offices might **have to wait** for tasks to be carried out.

(b) **Reliance on head office**. Local offices are less self-sufficient.

(c) A system fault or hold-up at head office will **impact across the organisation**.

4.7 The finance function

In many companies, the finance function is one of the most important expert roles in the organisation.

Note that Chapter 8 also looks at the role of the finance function in the context of the **specific role** of accounting in the organisation.

Role

- **Raising money**, ensuring it is available for those who need it
- **Recording and controlling** what happens to money, eg payroll and credit control.
- Providing **information to managers** to help them make decisions
- **Reporting** to stakeholders such as shareholders and tax authorities

Central / non Central

4.7.1 The importance of finance and finance management

A distinction can be made between 'financial management' and 'management of finance'.

(a) **Financial management**

    (i) Investment decisions

    (ii) Financing decisions (how to pay for investments)

    (iii) Dividend decisions (how much to give to shareholders)

    (iv) Operating decisions that affect profits (such as decisions on cost reductions or price increases).

(b) **Management of finance** is the responsibility for the handling of cash, invoices and other financial documents and for recording the affairs of the business in the books of account.

4.7.2 Raising money: sources of finance

A company might raise new funds from the following sources, using the expertise in its treasury department if it has one.

(a) **The capital markets**, such as the Stock Exchange or the Alternative Investment Market. **Capital markets** are markets for trading **long-term** financial instruments such as equities and debentures. Companies will go to them for three services.

    (i) New share issues, for example by companies acquiring a stock market listing for the first time

    (ii) Rights issues (ie when existing companies issue shares to investors for money)

    (iii) Issues of loan capital

(b) **Money markets**, on the other hand, are markets for trading **short term** financial instruments, bills of exchange and certificates of deposits.

(c) **Retained earnings**: profits earned in a year may be kept in the company as opposed to being distributed to shareholders.

(d) **Bank borrowings** (on a short or long term basis). Interest payments cannot be reduced to reflect changed circumstances.

(e) **Government sources** (grants, tax reliefs)

(f) **Venture capital**

(g) The **international money and capital markets** (eurocommercial paper, eurobonds and eurocurrency borrowing)

Question   **Finance function**

What sources of finance are available to a public sector organisation?

Answer

- Taxation of incomes and company profits, excise, sales tax (VAT) receipts (central government)
- Sale of gilts (government securities) to investors
- Borrowing from external sources (eg issuing eurobonds)
- Council tax
- User fees (eg charge for using a leisure facility)

- Retail prices (eg train fares)
- Other special charges (eg the 'nuclear levy' on electricity bills)
- Charging overseas users (eg universities for overseas students)
- Funds from central government
- Issuing of municipal bonds (on the money markets)
- Long-term loan finance (eg for local authorities)

Management at this level involves

(a) Decisions as to the **right mix of share and loan capital.**

(b) Decisions as to **when that capital should be raised** (eg to fund a major acquisition).

(c) **Keeping these important shareholders and lenders informed** about the company and its prospects.

Much of the **internal** financial management of a company is conducted with the shareholders' return in mind. For example, a company embarking on an investment project will assess its worth by the return or value expected.

4.7.3 Financial accounting

(a) **Recording financial transactions.** Financial accounting covers the classification and recording of transactions in monetary terms in accordance with established concepts, principles, accounting standards and legal requirements. It presents as accurate a view as possible of the effect of those transactions over a period of time and at the end of the time. The Companies Act **requires** directors of companies to maintain adequate records to show transactions, assets and liabilities and from which accounts can be prepared to show profit or loss for the accounting reference period and a balance sheet, detailing assets and liabilities and capital at the end of that reference period.

(b) **Reporting to shareholders.** In addition, the information must be reported to the **shareholders** in accordance with the detailed disclosure requirements of the Companies Act. All this information will be subject to statutory **audit**. Other organisations, such as building societies and charities are subject to similar legislation.

4.7.4 Treasury management

Treasury management **plans and controls** the **sources and uses of funds** by the organisation. This is achieved by a range of techniques.

(a) **Cash budgeting**, daily, weekly, monthly, quarterly and annually

(b) Arranging **a bank overdraft facility**; borrowing funds in the money markets and capital markets

(c) **Repaying** sums borrowed when the loans mature

(d) Comparing actual **cash flows** against budget

(e) Possibly, the **cashier's duties** of making payments to suppliers, paying wages and banking receipts

(f) Managing **foreign currency dealings**, to limit the firm's exposure to the risk of losses arising from changes in exchange rates.

4.7.5 Working capital and other matters

A company's management of its working capital is vital for business success. Working capital consists of cash, accounts receivable, accounts payable and inventory.

Receivables can be managed by effective **credit control**. Poor credit control has its own penalties.

(a) **Irrecoverable debts**. Sales revenue is not received for goods sold. In effect this is the same as giving away the goods.

(b) A company which cannot collect its debts in time might have to use bank **overdraft finance** to pay its bills. If the bank is concerned about the security of its loan, this might mean the company is vulnerable to increases in interest rates, and the bank's credit decisions.

Payables. Many companies delay paying suppliers as long as possible. In effect they are using suppliers as a sort of credit finance. Payments to suppliers are an outflow of funds. However, in the long term it may be more important to establish reliable commercial relationships with them than squeeze every pound out of them in the short term. Large companies are now required to disclose their policies on paying suppliers in their annual financial statements.

Inventory. Inventory levels are a focus of some of the production systems discussed earlier. Inventory holding costs must always be managed.

The finance department is often responsible for **payroll**. HR and production provide details of wage rates, time sheets and so forth.

4.7.6 Management accounting information

The finance function plays a critical role in providing information to management to assist in **planning, decision making and control.** This is called management accounting.

(a) **Planning**

    (i) The finance function draws up **budgets** which direct and allocate resources.

    (ii) The finance function also produces **forecasts** of anticipated future results.

(b) **Decision making**. The finance function is often involved in assessing and modelling the expenditure and cash flow implications of proposed decisions.

(c) **Control**

    (i) **Budgets are also used to monitor performance**. The finance function regularly provides information comparing budgeted revenues and costs for a period, with **actual results** and with comparisons from previous months.

    (ii) **Management accountants** are involved in assessing the contribution which products, services, processes and other operations make to overall profitability.

    (iii) **Costing based on predetermined standards** provides the information which enables managers to identify weaknesses and look for remedies all in a timely manner.

The success of management accountants in meeting their job objectives will depend upon two things.

- The **quality of the information** they provide
- Whether the information they provide to other managers is used properly

4.7.7 Co-ordination with other departments

Instead of being seen as helpers and advisers to other managers, management accountants are sometimes regarded as an adversary who tries to **find fault**. However, close co-ordination with other departments is essential.

(a) The **purchase ledger section** relies on the purchasing department to send copies of purchase orders and confirm the validity of invoices received from suppliers, and also to inform the purchase ledger staff about any despatches concerning goods received, or purchases returns. The section also relies on the cashier to inform it of all payments of invoices.

(b) The **sales ledger section** relies on **sales staff** to send copies of sales order or confirmations of goods delivered to customers, and on the cashier to pass on information about payments received.

(c) The sales ledger section must also co-operate with **debt collection staff**, by helping to prepare monthly statements and lists of aged debtors. **Credit control** work and the work of the debt collection staff are also closely interdependent, relying on the free exchange of information between them.

(d) The **financial accounting** staff responsible for the preparation of the annual accounts might rely on the management accounting staff for data about inventory records, so as to place a value on closing inventory in the accounts.

As **information providers** to other managers in other departments in the organisation, accountants cannot be fully effective unless they work in co-operation with these other managers.

4.7.8 The finance department and strategic planning

The role of finance is three-fold.

(a) Finance is a **resource**, which can be deployed so that objectives are met.

(b) A firm's objectives are often **expressed in financial or semi-financial terms**.

(c) **Financial controls** are often used to plan and control the implementation of strategies. Financial indicators are often used for detailed performance assessment.

As a planning medium and tool for monitoring, financial management makes a variety of strategic contributions.

(a) **Ensuring that resources of finance are available**. Issues of raising equity or loan capital are important here. The amount of resources that the strategy will consume needs to be assessed, and the likely cost of those resources established. Cash flow forecasting will also be necessary.

(b) **Integrating the strategy into budgets** for revenues, operating costs and capital expenditure over a period. The budgeting process serves as a planning tool and a means of financial control and monitoring.

(c) **Establishing the necessary performance measures**, in line with other departments for monitoring strategic objectives.

(d) **Establishing priorities**, if, for example, altered conditions make some aspects of the strategy hard to fulfil.

(e) **Assisting in the modelling process**. Financial models are simplified representations of the business. It is easier to experiment with models, to see the effect of changes in variables, than with the business itself.

4.8 Human resources

Key term

> **Human resource management** (HRM) is the process of evaluating an organisation's human resource needs, finding people to fill those needs, and getting the best work from each employee by providing the right incentives and job environment – with the overall aim of helping achieve organisational goals.

4.8.1 Scope of human resource management

FAST FORWARD

> **Human resource management** (HRM) is concerned with the most effective use of human resources. It deals with organisation, staffing levels, motivation, employee relations and employee services.

Human resource management (HRM) is concerned with a strategic approach to people at work and their relationships as they arise in the working environment.

The objectives of HRM

It is possible to identify **four main objectives of HRM**.

(a) To develop an effective human component for the organisation which will respond effectively to change.

(b) To obtain and develop the human resources required by the organisation and to use and motivate them effectively.

(c) To create and maintain a co-operative climate of relationships within the organisation.

(d) To meet the organisation's social and legal responsibilities relating to the human resource.

4.8.2 Why is HRM important?

Effective human resource management and employee development are strategically necessary for the following reasons.

(a) To **increase productivity**. Developing employee skills might make employees more productive, hence the recent emphasis on public debate on the value of training.

(b) To **enhance group learning**. Employees work more and more in multi-skilled teams. Each employee has to be competent at several tasks. Some employees have to be trained to work together (ie in teamworking skills).

(c) To **reduce staff turnover**. Reducing staff turnover, apart from cutting recruitment costs, can also increase the effectiveness of operations. In service businesses, such as hotels, or retail outlets, reductions in staff turnover can be linked with repeat visits by customers. As it is cheaper to keep existing customers than to find new ones, this can have a significant effect on profitability.

(d) To **encourage initiative.** Organisations can gain significant advantage from encouraging and exploiting the present and potential abilities of the people within them.

4.8.3 The human resource cycle

A relatively simple model that provides a framework for explaining the nature and significance of HRM is the human resource cycle (*Devanna* 1984).

Human resource cycle

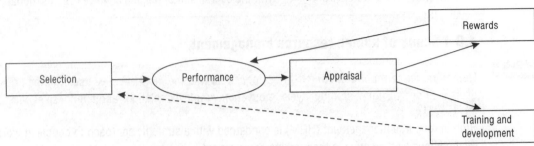

Selection is important to ensure the organisation obtains people with the qualities and skills required.

Appraisal enables targets to be set that contribute to the achievement of the overall strategic objectives of the organisation. It also identifies skills and performance gaps, and provides information relevant to reward levels.

Training and development ensure skills remain up-to-date, relevant, and comparable with (or better than) the best in the industry.

The **reward system** should motivate and ensure valued staff are retained.

Performance depends upon each of the four components and how they are co-ordinated.

These topics are all covered in Part F of the Study Text.

4.8.4 The HR plan

FAST FORWARD

HRM planning should be based on the **organisation's strategic planning processes**, with relation to analysis of the labour market, forecasting of the external supply and internal demand for labour, job analysis and plan implementation.

Human resource planning concerns the acquisition, utilisation, improvement and return of an enterprise's human resources. Human resource planning deals with:

* Recruitment
* Retention (company loyalty, to retain skills and reduce staff turnover)
* Downsizing (reducing staff numbers)
* Training and retraining to enhance the skills base

The process of human resources planning

1. STRATEGIC ANALYSIS

* of the environment
* of the organisation's manpower strengths and weaknesses, opportunities and threats
* of the organisation's use of employees
* of the organisation's objectives

2. FORECASTING

* of internal demand and supply
* of external supply

4.8.5 Control over the HR plan

Once the HR plan has been established, regular **control reports** should be produced.

(a) **Actual** numbers recruited, leaving and promoted should be compared with **planned** numbers. Action may be required to correct any imbalance – depending upon the cause.

(b) Actual pay, conditions of employment and training should be compared with assumptions in the HR plan. Do divergences explain any excessive staff turnover?

(c) Periodically, the HR plan itself should be reviewed and brought up to date.

5 Centralisation and decentralisation

5.1 What is centralisation?

> **FAST FORWARD**
>
> A **centralised** organisation is one in which authority is concentrated in one place.

We can look at centralisation in two ways.

(a) **Geography**. some functions may be centralised rather than 'scattered' in different offices, departments or locations.

So, for example, secretarial support, IT support and information storage (filing) may be centralised in specialist departments (whose services are shared by other functions) rather than carried out by staff/equipment duplicated in each departmental office.

(b) **Authority**. Centralisation also refers to the extent to which people have to refer decisions upwards to their superiors. Decentralisation therefore implies increased delegation, empowerment and autonomy at lower levels of the organisation.

5.2 Advantages and disadvantages of centralisation

> **FAST FORWARD**
>
> **Centralisation** offers greater control and co-ordination; **decentralisation** offers greater flexibility.

The table below summarises some of the arguments in favour of centralisation and decentralisation.

Pro centralisation	Pro decentralisation/delegation
Decisions are made at one point and so are easier to co-ordinate.	Avoids overburdening top managers, in terms of workload and stress.
Senior managers can take a wider view of problems and consequences.	Improves motivation of more junior managers who are given responsibility.
Senior management can balance the interests of different functions – eg by deciding on the resources to allocate to each.	Greater awareness of local problems by decision makers. (Geographically dispersed organisations are often decentralised on a regional/area basis for this reason.)
Quality of decisions is (theoretically) higher due to senior managers' skills and experience.	Greater speed of decision making, and response to changing events, since no need to refer decisions upwards. This is particularly important in rapidly changing markets.
Possibly cheaper, by reducing number of managers needed and so lower costs of overheads.	Helps develop the skills of junior managers: supports managerial succession.

Pro centralisation	Pro decentralisation/delegation
Crisis decisions are taken more quickly at the centre, without need to refer back.	Separate spheres of responsibility can be identified: controls, performance measurement and accountability are better.
Policies, procedures and documentation can be standardised organisation-wide.	Communication technology allows decisions to be made locally, with information and input from head office if required.

6 Committees

Within an organisation, committees can consist entirely of executives or may be instruments for joint consultation between employers and employees. They are a key part of organisational communication processes, which are covered in Chapter 14.

6.1 Purposes of committees

(a) **Creating new ideas**. Group creativity may be achieved by a brainstorming committee or think tank.

(b) They can be an excellent means of **communication**. For example, they can be used to exchange ideas and get feedback before a decision is taken or to inform managers about policies, plans, actual results and so on.

(c) They are democratic, because they allow for greater **participation** in the decision-making process. **Problem solving** can be facilitated by consultations between interested parties.

(d) **Combining abilities**. Committees enable the differing skills of its various members to be brought together to deal with a problem. In theory, the quality of committee decisions should be of a high standard.

(e) **Co-ordination**. Committees should enable the maximum co-ordination of all parties involved in a decision to be achieved, for example in co-ordinating the budgets of each department and compiling a master budget.

(f) **Representation**. Committees enable all relevant interests to be involved in the decision-making process and they bring together the specialised knowledge of working people into a working combination.

(g) Making **recommendations** for others to follow is a key output from committee processes.

6.1.1 The committee Chair

There are a number of recognised qualities of a good Chair (though common sense may dictate many others, varying with circumstances)

(a) The Chair will have to give **immediate rulings** on points of dispute or doubt, so he or she should have:

    (i) A sound knowledge of the relevant issues

    (ii) An ability to make up his/her mind

    (iii) Skill in communicating clearly, but tactfully and in a courteous manner

(b) The Chair should be and be seen to be **impartial**. There will be times when criticism is expressed which he/she personally may find unfair, or there is a strong clash of opinion between other committee members. In either situation, whatever his/her personal views, the Chair should treat opponents with equal fairness.

(c) The Chair should have the **discretion** to know when to insist on **strict observance** of correct procedure, and when a certain amount of **relaxation** will ease the tension.

(d) The Chair should be **punctual** and regular in attendance at meetings. If he/she cannot give the duties the appropriate amount of time and attention, he/she should consider resigning.

6.1.2 The committee secretary

(a) Duties **before** committee meeting:

(i) Fixing the date and time of the meeting
(ii) Choosing and preparing the location of the meeting
(iii) Preparing and issuing various documents

(b) Duties **at** the meeting: assisting the Chair, making notes

(c) Duties **after** the meeting: preparing minutes, acting on and communicating decisions

6.2 Types of committee

Committees can be classified according to the **power** they exercise.

(a) **Executive committees** have the power to govern or administer. The board of directors of a limited company is itself a 'committee' appointed by the shareholders, to the extent that it governs or administers.

(b) **Standing committees** are formed for a particular purpose on a **permanent basis**. Their role is to deal with routine business delegated to them at weekly or monthly meetings.

(c) **Ad hoc committees** are formed to complete a particular task (eg fact-finding and reporting on a particular problem before being wound up).

(d) **Sub-committees** may be appointed by committees to relieve the parent committee of some of its routine work.

(e) **Joint committees** may be formed to co-ordinate the activities of two or more committees, for example, representatives from employers and employees may meet in a Joint Consultative Committee. This kind of committee can either be permanent or appointed for a special purpose.

(f) **Management committees** in many businesses contain executives at a number of levels not all the decisions in a firm need to be taken by the Board.

6.3 Advantages of committees

(a) **Consolidation of power and authority**. The pooled authority of a committee may enable a decision to be made for which an individual's authority would not be sufficient. Examples of a **plural executive** include a Board of Directors or the Cabinet of the government.

(b) **Delegation** of power and authority (eg to subcommittee)

(c) **Blurring responsibility.** When a committee makes a decision, no individual will be held responsible for the consequences of the decision.

(d)   **Delay**. A committee is used to gain time (eg a manager may set up a committee to investigate a problem when he or she wants to delay his decision, or a company may refer a labour relations problem to a committee to defer a crisis with a trade union).

6.4 Disadvantages of committees

(a)   They are **apt to be too large for constructive action**, since the time taken by a committee to resolve a problem tends to be in direct proportion to its size.

(b)   Committees are **time-consuming and expensive**. In addition to the cost of highly paid executives' time, secretarial costs will be incurred.

(c)   **Delays may occur if matters of a routine nature are entrusted to committees**; committees must not be given responsibilities which they would carry out inefficiently.

(d)   **Operations may be jeopardised by the frequent attendance of executives at meetings**, and by distracting them from their real duties.

(e)   **Incorrect or ineffective decisions** may be made, if members are unfamiliar with the issues. Occasionally, there may be a **total failure to reach any decision at all.**

(f)   The fact that there is no individual responsibility for decisions might invite **compromise** instead of clear-cut decisions. Moreover, members may avoid responsibility for poor results arising from decisions taken in committee. Weak management can hide behind committee decisions.

6.5 Using committees successfully

(a)   Well-defined areas of authority, timescales of operations and purpose should be specified in writing.

(b)   The **Chair** should have the qualities of leadership to co-ordinate and motivate the other committee members.

(c)   The committee should not be so large as to be unmanageable.

(d)   The members of the committee should have the necessary skills and experience to do the committee's work; where the committee is expected to liaise with functional departments, the members must also have sufficient status and influence with those departments.

(e)   Minutes of the meetings should be taken and circulated by the **Secretary**, with any action points arising out of the meetings notified to the members responsible for doing the work.

(f)   Above all, an efficient committee must provide benefits that justify its cost.

(g)   Finally, if at all possible, the committee should be allowed plenty of time to reach decisions, enabling members to form sub-groups.

Chapter Roundup

- A non-governmental organisation (NGO) is an independent voluntary association of people acting together for some common purpose (other than achieving government office or making money).

- Mintzberg believes that *all* organisations can be analysed into five components, according to how they relate to the work of the organisation, and how they prefer to co-ordinate.

- Organisations can be **departmentalised** on a **functional** basis (with separate departments for production, marketing, finance etc), a **geographical** basis (by region, or country), a **product** basis (eg worldwide divisions for product X, Y etc), a **brand** basis, or a **matrix** basis (eg someone selling product X in country A would report to both a product X manager and a country A manager). Organisation structures often feature a variety of these types, as **hybrid** structures.

- In a **divisional structure** some activities are **decentralised** to business units or regions.

- The strategic apex exerts a pull to centralise, leading to the **simple structure**.

- **Span of control** or **'span of management'** refers to the number of subordinates responsible to a superior.

- Recent trends have been towards **delayering** organisations of levels of management. In other words, **tall organisations** (with many management levels, and narrow spans of control) are turning into **flat organisations** (with fewer management levels, wider spans of control) as a result of technological changes and the granting of more decision-making power to front line employees.

- There are many levels of strategy in an organisation.

    - **Corporate**: the general direction of the whole organisation
    - **Business**: how the organisation or its SBUs tackle particular markets
    - **Operational/functional**: specific strategies for different departments of the business

- Research may be **pure**, **applied** or **development**. It may be intended to improve **products** or **processes**. R&D should support the organisation's strategy and be closely co-ordinated with marketing.

- **Purchasing** makes a major contribution to cost and quality management in any business and in retail is a vital element of strategy. The purchasing mix is:

    - Quantity   – Price
    - Quality   – Delivery

- The **production function** plans, organises, directs and controls the necessary activities to provide products and services, creating outputs which have added value over the value of inputs.

- **Services** are intangible, cannot be stored, are inherently variable in quality and nature and their purchase results in no transfer of property. The people and processes involved in providing them are therefore of paramount importance.

- The **marketing function** manages an organisation's relationships with its customers.

- **Human resource management** (HRM) is concerned with the most effective use of human resources. It deals with organisation, staffing levels, motivation, employee relations and employee services.

- **HRM planning** should be based on the **organisation's strategic planning processes**, with relation to analysis of the labour market, forecasting of the external supply and internal demand for labour, job analysis and plan implementation.

- A **centralised** organisation is one in which authority is concentrated in one place.

- **Centralisation** offers greater control and co-ordination; **decentralisation** offers greater flexibility.

- Within an organisation, committees can consist entirely of executives or may be instruments for joint consultation between employers and employees. They are a key part of organisational communication processes, which are covered in Chapter 14.

Quick Quiz

1   Define organisation.

2   Differentiate between private and public sector.

3   What are co-operative societies?

4   What, in Mintzberg's view, are the five component parts of an organisation?

5   What is functional organisation?

6   What is divisionalisation?

7   What is matrix organisation?

8   What is span of control?

9   What is meant by scalar chain?

10   Distinguish between tall and flat organisations.

11   What is delayering?

12   What is the main intention behind R & D?

13   What are the elements of the purchasing mix?

14   What is the role of the production function?

15   Define marketing.

16   What is the role of the finance function?

17   How does the finance function relate to strategic planning?

18   What are the four main objectives of HRM?

19   Why is selection important?

20   Identify some types of committee.

BPP
LEARNING MEDIA

Answers to Quick Quiz

1   An organisation is: 'a *social arrangement* which pursues collective *goals*, which *controls* its own performance and which has a *boundary* separating it from its environment'.

2   **Private sector**: organisations not owned or run by central or local government, or government agencies.

   Public sector: organisations owned or run by central or local government or government agencies.

3   Businesses owned by their workers or customers who share the profit.

4   Strategic apex; technostructure; support staff; middle line; operating core.

5   Grouping people together who do similar tasks.

6   Division of a business into autonomous regions or product businesses, each with its own profit and loss responsibility.

7   A hybrid of organisation types, crossing functional and product/customer/project boundaries.

8   The number of subordinates responsible to a superior.

9   The chain of command from the most senior to the most junior.

10   A tall organisation has a long chain of command. A flat organisation has a short chain of command.

11   The reduction of the number of management levels from the bottom to the top.

12   To improve products or processes and so support the organisation's strategy.

13   Quality; Quality; Price; Delivery

14   To control the necessary activities to provide products (or services) creating outputs which have added value over the value of inputs.

15   'The management process which identifies, anticipates and satisfies customer needs profitably'.

   Chartered Institute of Marketing

16   • To raise money, ensuring it is available for those who need it.
   • To record and control what happens to money
   • To provide information to managers for decision-making
   • Reporting to stakeholders

17   • Ensuring that resources of finance are available
   • Integrating the strategy into budgets
   • Establishing the necessary performance measures
   • Establishing priorities
   • Assisting in the modelling process

18   • To develop an effective human component for the company
   • To obtain, develop and motivate staff
   • To create positive relationships
   • To ensure compliance with social and legal responsibilities

19   It ensures that the organisation obtains people with the qualities and skills required.

20   Executive committees; standing committees; Ad hoc committees; sub-committees; joint committees; management committees.

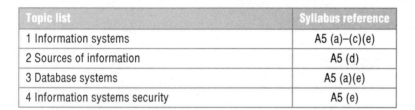

Information technology and systems

Topic list	Syllabus reference
1 Information systems	A5 (a)–(c)(e)
2 Sources of information	A5 (d)
3 Database systems	A5 (a)(e)
4 Information systems security	A5 (e)

Introduction

The role of information has changed from that of simply recording transactions and providing accounting information to a central and strategic role, fulfilling a range of purposes (**Section 1**). Designing information systems so that they capture all of the relevant information from the various sources is a key challenge.

(**Section 2**) A range of ICT systems has been created to support strategic tactical and operational decision making (**Section 3**), and because of the central of importance of information its security has become a key issue (**Section 4**).

Study guide

		Intellectual level
A5	**Information technology and information systems in business**	
(a)	Discuss the types of information technology and information systems used by the business organisation.	1
(b)	List the attributes of good quality information.	1
(c)	Explain how the type of information differs and the purposes for which it is applied at different levels of the organisation: strategic, tactical and operational.	1
(d)	Identify the different sources of internal and external information.	1
(e)	Describe the main features of information systems used within the organisation.	1

Exam guide

The choice of suitable systems to meet a specific business information requirements could be the topic of a question.

1 Information systems

FAST FORWARD

Information takes many forms and has many uses within the organisation. Organisations require **different types of information system** to provide **different levels of information** in a **range of functional areas**, supporting the distinction between strategic, tactical and operational decision making.

1.1 Why do organisations need information?

Key terms

Data is the raw material for data processing. Data consists of numbers, letters and symbols and relates to facts, events and transactions.

Information is data that has been processed in such a way as to be meaningful to the person who receives it.

FAST FORWARD

Organisations require **information** for a range of **purposes**.

- Planning
- Controlling
- Recording transactions
- Performance measurement
- Decision making

1.1.1 Planning

Once any decision has been made, it is necessary to plan **how to implement** the steps necessary to make it effective. Planning requires a knowledge of, among other things, available **resources**, possible **time-scales** for implementation and the likely **outcome under alternative scenarios**.

1.1.2 Controlling

Once a plan is implemented, its actual performance must be controlled. Information is required to assess **whether it is proceeding as planned** or whether there is some unexpected deviation from plan. It may consequently be necessary to take some form of corrective action.

1.1.3 Recording transactions

Information about **each transaction or event** is required for a number of reasons. Documentation of transactions can be used as **evidence** in a case of dispute. There may be a **legal requirement** to record transactions, for example for accounting and audit purposes. Detailed information on production costs can be built up, allowing a better **assessment of profitability**. Similarly, labour utilised in providing a particular service can be measured. Structured systems can be installed to capture transactions data.

1.1.4 Performance measurement

Just as individual operations need to be controlled, so overall performance must be measured in order to enable **comparisons against budget or plan** to be carried out. This may involve the collection of information on, for example, costs, revenues, volumes, time-scale and profitability.

1.1.5 Decision making

Information is also required to make informed decisions. This completes the full circle of organisational activity.

1.2 The qualities of good information

Good information has a number of specific qualities: the mnemonic **ACCURATE** is a useful way of remembering them.

The **qualities of good information** are outlined below – in mnemonic form. If you think you have seen this before, note that the second A here stands for **'Authoritative'**, an increasingly important concern given the huge **proliferation of information sources** available today.

Quality	Example
Accurate	Figures should **add up**, the degree of **rounding** should be appropriate, there should be **no typos**, items should be allocated to the **correct category**, **assumptions should be stated** for uncertain information (no spurious accuracy).
Complete	Information should includes everything that it **needs** to include, for example external data if relevant, or comparative information.
Cost-beneficial	It should not **cost more** to obtain the information than the **benefit** derived from having it. Providers of information should be given efficient means of collecting and analysing it. Presentation should be such that users do not waste time working out what it means.
User-targeted	The **needs of the user** should be borne in mind, for instance senior managers may require summaries, junior ones may require detail.
Relevant	Information that is **not needed** for a decision should be omitted, no matter how 'interesting' it may be.
Authoritative	The **source** of the information should be a reliable one (**not**, for instance, 'Joe Bloggs Predictions Page' on the Internet unless Joe Bloggs is known to be a reliable source for that type of information.

Quality	Example
Timely	The information should be available **when it is needed**.
Easy to use	Information should be **clearly presented**, **not excessively long**, and sent using the **right medium** and **communication channel** (e-mail, telephone, hard-copy report etc).

Exam focus point

> The qualities of information are specifically mentioned in the Study Guide.

1.3 Information in the organisation

A modern organisation requires a **wide range of systems** to hold, process and analyse information. We will now examine the various information systems used to serve organisational information requirements.

Organisations require different types of information system to provide different **levels of information** in a range of functional areas. One way of portraying this concept is shown on the following diagram (taken from *Laudon* and *Laudon*, *Management Information Systems*).

Types of information systems

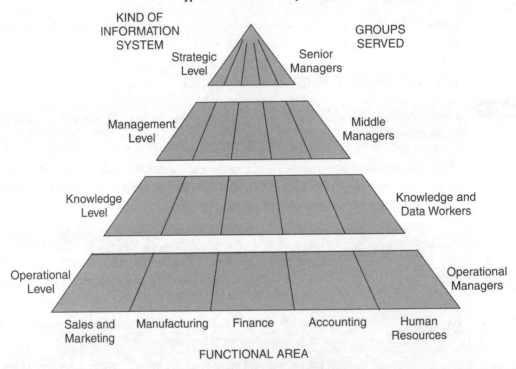

System level	System purpose
Strategic	To help senior managers with long-term planning. Their main function is to ensure changes in the external environment are matched by the organisation's capabilities.
Management/ tactical	To help middle managers monitor and control. These systems check if things are working well or not. Some management– level systems support non-routine decision making such as 'what if?' analyses.
Knowledge	To help knowledge and data workers design products, distribute information and perform administrative tasks. These systems help the organisation integrate new and existing knowledge into the business and to reduce the reliance on paper documents.

System level	System purpose
Operational	To help operational managers track the organisation's day-to-day operational activities. These systems enable routine queries to be answered, and transactions to be processed and tracked.

1.3.1 Example

Finance subsystem

- The **operational level** would deal with cash receipts and payments, bank reconciliations and so forth.

- The **tactical level** would deal with cash flow forecasts and working capital management.

- **Strategic level** financial issues are likely to be integrated with the organisation's commercial strategy, but may relate to the most appropriate source of finance (eg long-term debt, or equity).

The type of information at each level can be seen in the table below.

	Inputs	Process	Outputs
Strategic	Plans, competitor information, overall market information	Summarise Investigate Compare Forecast	Key ratios, ad hoc market analysis, strategic plans
Management/tactical	Historical and budget data	Compare Classify Summarise	Variance analyses Exception reports
Operational	Customer orders, programmed inventory control levels, cash receipts/payments	Update files Output reports	Updated file listings, invoices

Although opinions differ and not all categories are agreed, we can identify seven **types of information system**.

- Executive Support Systems (ESS)
- Management Information Systems (MIS)
- Decision-Support Systems (DSS)
- Expert systems
- Knowledge Work Systems (KWS)
- Office Automation Systems (OAS)
- Transaction Processing Systems (TPS)

1.4 Executive Support Systems (ESS)

An **Executive Support System (ESS)** pools data from internal and external sources and makes information available to senior managers in an easy-to-use form. ESS help senior managers make strategic, unstructured decisions.

An ESS should provide senior managers with easy access to key **internal and external** information. The system summarises and tracks strategically critical information, possibly drawn from internal MIS and DSS, but also including data from external sources eg competitors, legislation, external databases such as Reuters.

An ESS is likely to have the following features.

- Flexibility
- Quick response time
- Sophisticated data analysis and modelling tools

1.5 Management Information Systems (MIS)

> **Management Information Systems (MIS)** convert data from mainly internal sources into information (eg summary reports, exception reports). This information enables managers to make timely and effective decisions for planning, directing and controlling the activities for which they are responsible.

An MIS provides regular reports and (usually) on-line access to the organisation's current and historical performance.

MIS usually transform data from underlying transaction processing systems into summarised files that are used as the basis for management reports.

MIS have the following characteristics:

- Support **structured** decisions at operational and management control levels
- Designed to report on existing operations
- Have little analytical capability
- Relatively **inflexible**
- Have an internal focus

1.6 Decision Support Systems (DSS)

> **Decision Support Systems (DSS)** combine data and analytical models or data analysis tools to support semi-structured and unstructured decision making.

DSS are used by management to assist in making decisions on issues which are subject to high levels of uncertainty about the problem, the various **responses** which management could undertake or the likely **impact** of those actions.

Decision support systems are intended to provide a wide range of alternative information gathering and analytical tools with a major emphasis upon **flexibility** and **user-friendliness**.

DSS have more analytical power than other systems enabling them to analyse and condense large volumes of data into a form that aids managers make decisions. The objective is to allow the manager to consider a number of **alternatives** and evaluate them under a variety of potential conditions.

1.7 Expert systems

> An **expert system** is a computer program that captures human expertise in a limited domain of knowledge.

Expert system software uses a **knowledge base** that consists of **facts, concepts** and the **relationships** between them on a particular domain of knowledge and uses pattern-matching techniques to 'solve' problems.

For example, many financial institutions now use expert systems to process straightforward **loan applications**. The user enters certain key facts into the system such as the loan applicant's name and most recent addresses, their income and monthly outgoings, and details of other loans. The system will then:

(a)   **Check the facts** given against its database to see whether the applicant has a good previous credit record.

(b)   **Perform calculations** to see whether the applicant can afford to repay the loan.

(c)   **Make a judgement** as to what extent the loan applicant fits the lender's profile of a good risk (based on the lender's previous experience).

(d)   Suggest a decision.

An organisation can **use an expert system** when a number of **conditions** are met.

(a)   The problem is **well defined**.
(b)   The expert can define **rules** by which the problem can be solved.
(c)   The **investment** in an expert system is cost-justified.

1.8 Knowledge Work Systems (KWS)

Key terms

> **Knowledge Work Systems (KWS)** are information systems that facilitate the creation and integration of new knowledge into an organisation.
>
> **Knowledge Workers** are people whose jobs consist of primarily creating new information and knowledge. They are often members of a profession such as doctors, engineers, lawyers and scientists.

KWS help knowledge workers create new knowledge and expertise. Examples include:

- Computer Aided Design (CAD)
- Computer Aided Manufacturing (CAM)
- Specialised financial software that analyses trading situations

1.9 Office Automation Systems (OAS)

Key term

> **Office Automation Systems (OAS)** are computer systems designed to increase the productivity of data and information workers.

OAS support the major activities performed in a typical office such as document management, facilitating communication and managing data. Examples include:

- Word processing, desktop publishing, and digital filing systems
- E-mail, voice mail, videoconferencing, groupware, intranets, schedulers
- Spreadsheets, desktop databases

1.10 Transaction Processing Systems (TPS)

Key term

> A **Transaction Processing System (TPS)** performs and records routine transactions.

TPS are used for routine tasks in which data items or transactions must be processed so that operations can continue. TPS support most business functions in most types of organisations. The following table shows a range of TPS applications.

Transaction processing systems					
	Sales/ marketing systems	**Manufacturing/ production systems**	**Finance/ accounting systems**	**Human resources systems**	**Other types (eg university)**
Major functions of system	• Sales management • Market research • Promotion Pricing • New products	• Scheduling • Purchasing Shipping/ receiving • Engineering • Operations	• Budgeting • General ledger • Billing • Management accounting	• Personnel records • Benefits • Salaries • Labour relations • Training	• Admissions • Student academic records • Course records • Graduates
Major application systems	• Sales order information system • Market research system • Pricing system	• Materials resource planning • Purchase order control • Engineering • Quality control	• Nominal ledger • Accounts receivable /payable • Budgeting • Funds management	• Payroll • Employee records • Employee benefits • Career path systems	• Registration • Student record • Curriculum/ class control systems • Benefactor information system

1.10.1 Batch processing and on-line processing

A TPS will process transactions using either **batch** processing or on-line processing.

Batch processing involves transactions being **grouped** and **stored** before being processed at regular intervals, such as daily, weekly or monthly. Because data is not input as soon as it is received the system will not always be up-to-date.

The lack of up-to-date information means batch processing is usually not suitable for systems involving customer contact. Batch processing is suitable for internal, regular tasks such as payroll.

On-line processing involves transactions being input and **processed immediately**. An airline ticket sales and reservation system is an example.

1.11 System dependencies and integration

FAST FORWARD

The ease of which data flows from one system to another depends on the **extent of integration** between systems.

The types of system we have identified exchange data with each other. The ease with which data flows from one system to another depends on the extent of **integration** between systems. The level of integration will depend on the nature of the organisation and the systems involved.

Interrelationships between systems are shown in the following diagram from *Loudon and Loudon*.

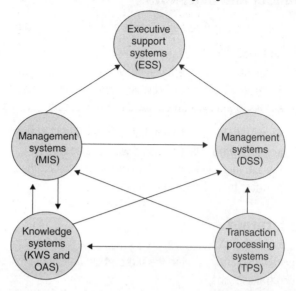

1.12 Information systems: levels, types and functions

Examples of the levels and types of information system we have discussed in this section are shown in the following diagram.

TYPES OF SYSTEMS	Strategic-Level Systems				
Executive Support Systems (ESS)	5-year sales trend forecasting	5-year operating plan	5-year budget forecasting	Profit planning	Human resource planning

	Management-Level Systems				
Management Information Systems (MIS)	Sales management	Inventory control	Annual budgeting	Capital investment analysis	Relocation analysis
Decision Support Systems (DSS)	Sales region analysis	Production scheduling	Cost analysis	Pricing/ profitability analysis	Contract cost analysis

	Knowledge-Level System		
Knowledge Work Systems (KWS)	Engineering workstations	Graphics workstations	Managerial workstations
Office Automation Systems (OAS)	Word processing	Document imaging	Electronic calendars

	Operational-Level Systems				
Transaction Processing Systems (TPS)		Machine control	Securities trading	Payroll	Compensation
	Order tracking	Plant scheduling		Accounts payable	Training & development
	Order processing	Material movement control	Cash management	Accounts receivable	Employee record keeping
	Sales and Marketing	Manufacturing	Finance	Accounting	Human Resources

BPP
LEARNING MEDIA

1.13 Intranets and extranets

Organisations are increasingly using **intranets** and **extranets** to **disseminate information**.

(a) An **intranet** is like a mini version of the Internet (covered in the following section). Organisation members use networked computers to access information held on a server. The user interface is a browser – similar to those used on the Internet. The intranet offers access to information on a wide variety of topics, and often includes access to the Internet.

(b) An **extranet** is an intranet that is accessible to **authorised outsiders**, using a valid username and password. The username will have access rights attached – determining which parts of the extranet can be viewed. Extranets are becoming a very popular means for business partners to exchange information.

1.14 The Internet

FAST FORWARD

Many organisations are now utilising **the Internet** as a means of gathering and disseminating information, and conducting transactions.

Key term

The **Internet** is a global network connecting millions of computers.

The Internet is the name given to the technology that allows any computer with a telecommunications link to **send and receive information** from any other suitably equipped computer.

The **World Wide Web** is the multimedia element which provides facilities such as full-colour, graphics, sound and video. Web-sites are points within the network created by members who wish to provide an information point for searchers to visit and benefit by the provision of information and/or by entering into a transaction.

Almost all companies have a **Website** on the Internet. A site is a collection of screens providing **information in text and graphic form**, any of which can be viewed simply by clicking the appropriate button, word or image on the screen.

1.14.1 Current uses of the Internet

The scope and potential of the Internet are still developing. Its uses already embrace the following:

(a) **Dissemination** of information.

(b) **Product/service development** – through almost instantaneous test marketing.

(c) **Transaction processing** (electronic commerce or e-commerce) – both business-to-business and business-to-consumer.

(d) **Relationship enhancement** – between various groups of stakeholders.

(e) **Recruitment** and job search – involving organisations worldwide.

(f) **Entertainment** – including music, humour, art, games and some less wholesome pursuits!

It is estimated that approximately 60% of the adult population of the UK use the Internet on a regular basis.

The Internet provides opportunities to organise for and to automate tasks which would previously have required more costly interaction with the organisation. These have often been called low-touch or zero-touch approaches.

Question

Which of the following statements is **incorrect**?

A   Expert systems exist that can help decide credit worthiness.

B   A management information system is normally capable or producing exception reports.

C   Batch processing systems are not appropriate if information is required to be up-to-date at all times

D   An expert system always provides the correct solution to a problem

Answer

D. An expert system can produce an incorrect answer. The answer produced by the system depends on the quality of the data and rules held by the system. The other statements are all correct.

2 Sources of information

Data and **information** come from **sources** both **inside** and **outside** an organisation. An organisation's information systems should be designed so as to obtain – or **capture** – all the relevant data and information required.

2.1 Internal information

Capturing data and information from inside the organisation involves designing a system for collecting or measuring data and information which sets out procedures for:

- What data and information is collected
- How frequently
- By whom
- By what methods
- How data and information is processed, filed and communicated

2.1.1 The accounting records

The accounting ledgers provide an excellent source of information regarding what has happened in the past. This information may be used as a basis for predicting future events eg budgeting.

Accounting records can provide more than purely financial information. For example an inventory control system includes purchase orders, goods received notes and goods returned notes that can be analysed to provide information regarding the speed of delivery or the quality of supplies. Sales ledgers can provide sales information for the marketing function.

2.1.2 Other internal sources

Much information that is not strictly part of the accounting records nevertheless is closely tied in to the accounting system.

(a)   Information about **personnel** will be linked to the **payroll** system. Additional information may be obtained from this source if, say, a project is being costed and it is necessary to ascertain the availability and rate of pay of different levels of staff, or the need for and cost of recruiting staff from outside the organisation.

(b)   Much information will be produced by a **production** department about machine capacity, fuel consumption, movement of people, materials, and work in progress, set up times, maintenance requirements and so on. A large part of the traditional work of cost accounting involves ascribing costs to the **physical information** produced by this source.

(c)   Many **service** businesses, notably accountants and solicitors, need to keep detailed records of the **time spent** on various activities, both to justify fees to clients and to assess the efficiency and profitability of operations.

Staff themselves are one of the primary sources of internal information. Information may be obtained either informally in the course of day-to-day business or through meetings, interviews or questionnaires.

2.1.3 External information

Formal collection of data from outside sources includes the following.

(a)   A company's **tax specialists** will be expected to gather information about changes in tax law and how this will affect the company.

(b)   Obtaining information about any new legislation on health and safety at work, or employment regulations, must be the responsibility of a particular person – for example the company's **legal expert** or **company secretary** – who must then pass on the information to other managers affected by it.

(c)   Research and development (R & D) work often relies on information about other R & D work being done by another company or by government institutions. An **R & D official** might be made responsible for finding out about R & D work in the company.

(d)   **Marketing managers** need to know about the opinions and buying attitudes of potential customers. To obtain this information, they might carry out market research exercises.

Informal gathering of information from the environment occurs naturally, consciously or unconsciously, as people learn what is going on in the world around them – perhaps from newspapers, television reports, meetings with business associates or the trade press.

Organisations hold external information such as invoices, letters, advertisements and so on **received from customers and suppliers**. But there are many occasions when an active search outside the organisation is necessary.

Key term

> The phrase **environmental scanning** is often used to describe the process of gathering external information, which is available from a wide range of sources.

(a)   The government.

(b)   Advice or information bureaux eg Reuters.

(c)   Consultants.

(d)   Newspaper and magazine publishers.

(e)   There may be specific reference works which are used in a particular line of work.

(f)   Libraries and information services.

(g)   Increasingly businesses can use each other's systems as sources of information, for instance via extranets or electronic data interchange (EDI).

(h)   **Electronic sources** of information are becoming increasingly important.

(i)   For some time there have been 'viewdata' services such as **Prestel** offering a very large bank of information gathered from organisations such as the Office for National Statistics, newspapers and the British Library. **Topic** offers information on the stock market. Companies like **Reuters** operate primarily in the field of provision of information – often in electronic form.

(ii)   The **Internet** is a vast source of information.

2.2 Efficient data collection

To produce meaningful information it is first necessary to capture the underlying data. The method of **data collection** chosen will depend on the nature of the **organisation**, **cost** and **efficiency**. Some common data collection methods are listed below.

- Document reading methods
- Magnetic ink character recognition (MICR)
- Optical mark reading (OMR)
- Scanners and optical character recognition (OCR)
- Bar coding and Electronic Point of Sale (EPOS)
- Electronic Funds Transfer at the Point of Sale (EFTPOS)
- Magnetic stripe cards
- Smart cards
- Touch screens
- Voice recognition

3 Database systems

FAST FORWARD

The term '**database system**' is used to describe a wide range of systems that utilise a central pool of data.

As shown in the following illustration, a 'database system' can, (and for our purposes usually does), involve much more than a single database package such as Microsoft Access.

Key terms

A **database** is a collection of structured data which may be manipulated to select or sort some or all of the data held. The database provides convenient access to data for a wide variety of users and user needs.

A **database management system (DBMS)** is the software that builds, manages and provides access to a database. It allows a systematic approach to the storage and retrieval of data.

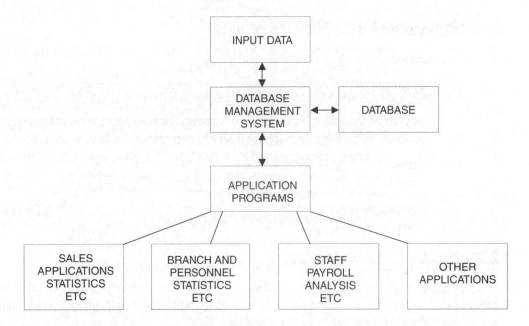

3.1 Characteristics of a database

A database has three major **characteristics**.

- It should be **shared**
- It should provide for the **needs of different users** with different requirements
- It should be **capable of evolving** to meet **future** needs

3.2 Using a database

There are four main operations in using a database.

(a)   Creating the database **structure**, ie the structure of files and records.

(b)   **Entering data** on to the database files, and **amending/updating** it.

(c)   **Retrieving and manipulating** the data.

(d)   Producing **reports**.

3.3 Entering and maintaining data

When entering data into a new database the following issues may have to be addressed.

(a)   The **compatibility** between systems is not just a matter of whether one system's files are computer-sensible to another system. It may extend to matters such as **different systems of coding**, different formats for personal data (with/without a contact name, with/without phone or fax number, and so on), different field sizes.

(b)   **Access to data should not suffer**. Users will be attempting to extract information from a much larger pool. The system must be designed in such a way that they do not have to wade through large amounts of data that is irrelevant.

(c)   As well as offering the potential for new kinds of report the system must continue to **support existing reporting**. **Extensive consultation** with users is essential.

(d)   Once the data has been amalgamated the business faces the task of ensuring that it is **secure**. A systems failure will now mean that no part of the business can operate, rather than at most just one part.

3.4 Retrieval and manipulation of data

Data can be retrieved and manipulated in a variety of ways.

(a) By **specifying the required parameters** – for example from a database of employee records, records of all employees in the sales department who have been employed for over 10 years and are paid less than $20,000 pa could be extracted. Search and retrieve parameters (queries) can be stored for future use.

(b) Retrieved data can be **sorted** on any specified field (for example for employees, sorting might be according to grade, department, age, experience, salary level etc).

(c) Some **calculations** on retrieved data can be carried out – such as calculating **totals** and **average** values.

3.5 Advantages and disadvantages of a database system

The **advantages** of a database system are as follows.

(a) Avoidance of **unnecessary duplication** of data.

(b) Data is looked upon as serving the **organisation as a whole**, not just for individual departments. The database concept encourages management to regard data as a resource that must be **properly managed.**

(c) The installation of a database system encourages management to **analyse data**, relationships between data items, and how data is used in different applications.

(d) **Consistency** – because data is only held once, the possibility of departments holding conflicting data on the same subject is reduced.

(e) Data on file is independent of the user programs that access the data. This allows **greater flexibility** in the ways that data can be used. New programs can be easily introduced to make use of existing data in a different way.

(f) Developing **new application programs** with a database system is easier because the programmer is not responsible for the file organisation.

The **disadvantages** of database systems relate mainly to security and control.

(a) There are problems of **data security** and **data privacy**. There is potential for unauthorised access to data. Administrative procedures for data security must supplement software controls.

(b) Since there is only one set of data, it is essential that the data should be **accurate** and free from corruption.

(c) Since data is held once, but its use is widespread, the impact of **system failure** would be greater.

(d) If an organisation develops its own database system from scratch, **initial development costs** will be high.

4 Information systems security

Information is a **valuable resource** and a key tool in the quest for a competitive advantage. **Security** controls, integrity controls and contingency controls are used to protect data and information.

As such, measures need to be taken to ensure data and information entering an organisation's information systems is **reliable** and **accurate**. Once captured by the system, the information must be kept secure and any processing must preserve accuracy.

Key term

Security means the protection of data from unauthorised modification, disclosure or destruction, and the protection of the information system from the degradation or non-availability of services.

The measures an organisation can take to protect information and information systems can be classified into:

- Security controls
- Integrity controls
- Contingency controls

These are examined in more detail in Chapter 9 in the context of control and systems security.

Chapter Roundup

- Information takes many forms and has many uses within the organisation. Organisations require **different types of information system** to provide **different levels of information** in a **range of functional areas**, supporting the distinction between strategic, tactical and operational decision making.

- Organisations require **information** for a range of **purposes**.

  - Planning
  - Controlling
  - Recording transactions
  - Performance measurement
  - Decision making

- **Good information** has a number of specific qualities: the mnemonic **ACCURATE** is a useful way of remembering them.

- The ease of which data flows from one system to another depends on the **extent of integration** between systems.

- Many organisations are now utilising **the Internet** as a means of gathering and disseminating information, and conducting transactions.

- Data and **information** come from **sources** both **inside** and **outside** an organisation. An organisation's information systems should be designed so as to obtain – or **capture** – all the relevant data and information required.

- The term '**database system**' is used to describe a wide range of systems that utilise a central pool of data.

- **Information** is a **valuable resource** and a key tool in the quest for a competitive advantage. Security controls, integrity controls and contingency controls are used to protect data and information.

Quick Quiz

1   List five uses of information.

2   List five characteristics of strategic information.

3   List five characteristics of tactical information.

4   List five characteristics of operational information.

5   Match the following abbreviations with the appropriate description.

TPS, OAS, KWS, MIS, DSS, ESS.

(a)   Information systems that facilitate the creation and integration of new knowledge into an organisation

(b)   A system that pools data from internal and external sources and makes information available to senior managers in an easy-to-use form.

(c)   Computer systems designed to increase the productivity of data and information workers.

(d)   A system that converts data, mainly from internal sources into information (eg summary reports, exception reports).

(e)   A system that combines data and analytical models or data analysis tools to support semi-structured and unstructured decision making.

(f)   A system to perform and record routine transactions.

6   'Full integration across all organisational information systems is vital.' Do you agree with this statement? Justify your answer (very briefly).

Answers to Quick Quiz

1   Planning, controlling, recording transactions, measuring performance and making decisions.

2   [Five of]

Derived from both internal and external sources

Summarised at a high level

Relevant to the long term

Concerned with the whole organisation

Often prepared on an 'ad hoc' basis

Both quantitative and qualitative

Uncertain, as the future cannot be predicted accurately

3   [Five of]

Primarily generated internally (but may have a limited external component)

Summarised at a lower level

Relevant to the short and medium term

Concerned with activities or departments

Prepared routinely and regularly

Based on quantitative measures

4   [Five of]

Derived from internal sources

Detailed, being the processing of raw data

Relevant to the immediate term

Task-specific

Prepared very frequently

Largely quantitative

5   (a)   Knowledge Work Systems (KWS).
     (b)   Executive Support Systems (ESS).
     (c)   Office Automation Systems (OAS).
     (d)   Management Information Systems (MIS).
     (e)   Decision Support Systems (DSS).
     (f)   Transaction Processing Systems (TPS).

6   Disagree. A high degree of integration is usually desirable, but in all cases the costs of integration should be considered against the value of the expected benefits integration would bring.

Influences on organisational culture

Topic list	Syllabus reference
1 What is culture?	A3 (a)
2 Organisation culture	A3 (b)
3 Culture and structure	A3 (c)
4 The informal organisation	A2 (a)(b)
5 Stakeholder goals and objectives	A4 (a)–(d)

Introduction

Organisation culture is, broadly, the distinctive way an organisation does things: its particular 'style'. We explore how this reveals itself in **Sections 1 and 2** of this chapter.

Like **structure**, the concept of **culture** gives us a way of talking about how organisations 'work'. The contributions of Schein, Handy and Hofstede are specifically mentioned in the Study Guide. Particular structures suit particular cultures – as we see in **Section 3**: Handy's is a useful model, which should be learned in detail. The impact of national culture on organisational culture outlined by Hofstede is useful when discussing management in multi-national and cross-cultural contexts. With increasing globalisation and workforce diversity, this is useful awareness.

Section 4 examines the importance of informal networks in shaping organisational culture.

The objectives, policies, procedures and management/leadership style of an organisation will all be influenced (in part) by its culture. Another influence is exerted by stakeholders. Different stakeholder groups have different degrees of power and interest, and management must respond to each in a different way. These are examined in **Section 5**.

Study guide

		Intellectual level
A2	**The formal and informal business organisation**	
(a)	Explain the informal organisation and its relationship with the formal organisation.	1
(b)	Describe the impact of the informal organisation on the business.	2
A3	**Organisational culture in business**	
(a)	Define organisational culture.	1
(b)	Describe the factors that shape the culture of the organisation.	1
(c)	Explain the contribution made by writers on culture:	1
(i)	Schein – determinants of organisational culture	
(ii)	Handy – four cultural stereotypes	
(iii)	Hofstede – international perspectives on culture	
A4	**Stakeholders of business organisations**	
(a)	Define the internal stakeholder and list the different categories of internal stakeholder.	1
(b)	Define connected and external stakeholders and explain their impact on the organisation.	1
(c)	Identify the main stakeholder groups and the objectives of each group.	1
(d)	Explain how the different stakeholder groups interact and how their objectives may conflict with one another.	1

Exam guide

Cultural influences provide a good source of potential exam questions. There is such a question on the pilot paper. Stakeholders too are very important – worth four marks on the pilot paper.

1 What is culture?

1.1 Spheres of culture

FAST FORWARD

Culture is 'the collective programming of the mind which distinguishes the members of one category of people from another' *(Hofstede)*. It may be identified as ways of behaving, and ways of understanding, that are shared by a group of people.

Edgar Schein (1985) defines organisational culture as 'the set of shared, taken-for-granted implicit assumptions that a group holds and that determines how it perceives, thinks about and reacts to its environment'. He also suggests that the culture of an organisation is grounded in the founder's basic beliefs, values and assumptions, and embedded in the organisation over time – what Schein calls 'the residue of success'.

Culture may therefore be identified as ways of behaving, and ways of understanding, that are shared by a group of people. Referring to it as: 'The way we do things round here', Schein says that organisational culture matters because cultural elements determine strategy, goals and modes of operating.

Culture can be discussed on many different levels. The 'category' or 'group' of people whose shared behaviours and meanings may constitute a culture include:

- A nation, region or ethnic group
- Women versus men ('gender culture')
- A social class (eg 'working class culture')
- A profession or occupation
- A type of business (eg 'advertising culture')
- An organisation ('**organisational culture**')

If you are a male (or female) accountant in an organisation operating in a given business sector in a particular region of your country of residence (which may not be your country of origin), you may be influenced by all these different spheres of culture!

1.2 Elements of culture

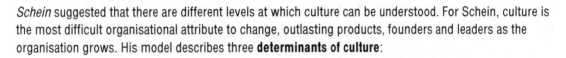

FAST FORWARD

Elements of culture include:

- Observable behaviour
- Underlying values and beliefs which give meaning to the observable elements
- Hidden assumptions, which unconsciously shape values and beliefs

Schein suggested that there are different levels at which culture can be understood. For Schein, culture is the most difficult organisational attribute to change, outlasting products, founders and leaders as the organisation grows. His model describes three **determinants of culture**:

(a) **The first level:** The **observable**, expressed or 'explicit' elements of culture.

    (i) **Behaviour**: norms of personal and interpersonal behaviour; customs and rules about behaviours that are 'acceptable' or unacceptable.

    (ii) **Artefacts**: concrete expressions such as architecture and interior design (eg of office premises), dress codes and symbols.

    (iii) **Attitudes**: patterns of collective behaviour such as greeting styles, business formalities, social courtesies and ceremonies.

(b) **The second level:** Beneath these observable phenomena lie **values and beliefs** and the professed culture, which give the behaviours and attitudes their special meaning and significance. For example, the design of office space may imply status and honour, or reflect the importance of privacy within a culture: it 'means' more than the observable features. Values and beliefs may be overtly expressed in slogans or the mission statement.

(c) **The third level:** Beneath values and beliefs lie **assumptions**: foundational ideas ('unspoken rules') that are no longer consciously recognised or questioned by the culture, but which 'programme' its ways of thinking and behaving.

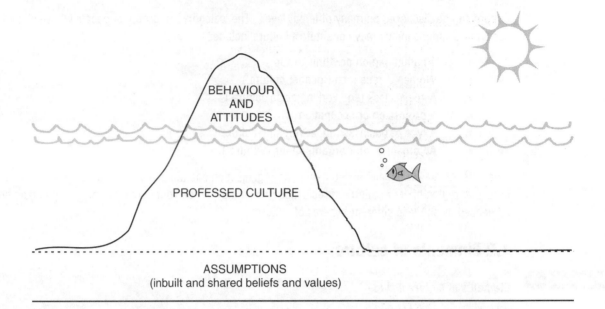

2 Organisation culture

Organisation culture may be defined as:

*   'The collection of traditions, values, policies, beliefs and attitudes that constitute a pervasive context for everything we do and think in an organisation' *(Mullins)*

*   'A pattern of beliefs and expectations shared by the organisation's members, and which produce norms which powerfully shape the behaviour of individuals and groups in the organisation' *(Schwartz & Davies)*

*   'The way we do things around here'

(These are definitions cited by the ACCA.)

2.1 Manifestations of culture in organisations

Organisation culture is **'the way we do things round here'**.

Examples of organisation culture include the following.

Item	Example
Beliefs and values, which are often unquestioned	'The customer is always right'.
Behaviour	In the City of London, standard business dress is still generally taken for granted and even 'dress down Fridays' have their rules.
Artefacts	Microsoft encourages communication between employees by setting aside spaces for the purpose.
Rituals	In some firms, sales people compete with each other, and there is a reward, given at a ceremony, for the salesperson who does best in any period.
Symbols	Corporate logos are an example of symbols, but they are directed outwards. Within the organisation, symbols can represent power: dress, make and model of car, office size and equipment and access to facilities can all be important symbols.

Manifestations of culture in an organisation may thus include:

- How formal the organisation structure is
- Communication: are senior managers approachable?
- Office layout
- The type of people employed
- Symbols, legends, corporate myths
- Management style
- Freedom for subordinates to show initiative
- Attitudes to quality
- Attitudes to risk
- Attitudes to the customer
- Attitudes to technology

Question	Manifestations of culture

What do you think would differentiate the culture of:

- A regiment in the Army
- An advertising agency?

Answer

Here are some hints. The Army is very disciplined. Decisions are made by officers; behaviour between ranks is sometimes very formal. The organisation values loyalty, courage and discipline and team work. Symbols and artefacts include uniforms, medals, regimental badges and so on. Rituals include corporate expressions such as parades and ceremonies.

An advertising agency, with a different mission, is more fluid. Individual flair and creativity, within the commercial needs of the firm, is expected. Artefacts may include the style of creative offices, awards or prizes, and the agency logo. Rituals may include various award ceremonies, team meetings and social gatherings.

2.2 What shapes organisation culture?

Influences on organisational culture include:

(a) The organisation's **founder**. A strong set of values and assumptions is set up by the organisation's founder, and even after he or she has retired, these values have their own momentum. Or, to put it another way, an organisation might find it hard to shake off its original culture.

(b) The organisation's **history**.

    (i) Culture reflects the era when the organisation was founded.

    (ii) The effect of history can be determined by stories, rituals and symbolic behaviour. They legitimise behaviour and promote priorities.

(c) **Leadership and management style**. An organisation with a strong culture recruits and develops managers who naturally conform to it, who perpetuate the culture.

(d) The **organisation's environment**. As we have seen, nations, regions, occupations and business types have their own distinctive cultures, and these will affect the organisation's style.

FAST FORWARD

Cultural values can be used to guide organisational processes without the need for tight control. They can also be used to motivate employees, by emphasising the heroic dimension of the task. Culture can also be used to drive change, although – since values are difficult to change – it can also be a powerful force for preserving the *status quo*.

3 Culture and structure

FAST FORWARD

Harrison classified four types of culture, to which **Handy** gave the names of Greek deities.

- **Power** culture (Zeus) is shaped by one individual
- **Role** culture (Apollo) is a bureaucratic culture shaped by rationality, rules and procedures
- **Task** culture (Athena) is shaped by a focus on outputs and results
- **Existential** or person culture (Dionysus) is shaped by the interests of individuals.

Writing in 1972, Harrison suggested that organisations could be classified into four types. His work was later popularised by Charles Handy in his book *'Gods of Management'*. The four types are differentiated by their structures, processes and management methods. The differences are so significant as to create **distinctive cultures**, to each of which Handy gives the name of a Greek God.

Zeus Power culture	**Apollo** Role culture
The organisation is controlled by a key central figure, owner or founder. Power is direct, personal, informal. Suits small organisations where people get on well.	Classical, rational organisation: bureaucracy. Stable, slow-changing, formalised, impersonal. Authority based on position and function.
Athena Task culture	**Dionysus** Person culture
Management is directed at outputs: problems solved, projects completed. Team-based, horizontally-structured, flexible, valuing expertise – to get the job done.	The purpose of the organisation is to serve the interests of the individuals who make it up: management is directed at facilitating, administering.

3.1 Power culture

Zeus is the god representing the **power culture** or **club culture**. Zeus is a dynamic entrepreneur who rules with snap decisions. Power and influence stem from a central source, perhaps the owner-directors or the founder of the business. The degree of formalisation is limited, and there are few rules and procedures. Such a firm is likely to be organised on a functional basis.

(a) The organisation is capable of adapting quickly to meet change.

(b) Personal influence decreases as the size of an organisation gets bigger. The power culture is therefore best suited to smaller entrepreneurial organisations, where the leaders have direct communication with all employees.

(c) Personnel have to get on well with each other for this culture to work. These organisations are clubs of 'like-minded people introduced by the like-minded people, working on empathetic initiative with personal contact rather than formal liaison.'

3.2 Role culture

Apollo is the god of the **role culture** or **bureaucracy**. There is a presumption of logic and rationality.

(a) These organisations have a formal structure, and operate by well-established rules and procedures.

(b) Individuals are required to perform their job to the full, but not to overstep the boundaries of their authority. Individuals who work for such organisations tend to learn an expertise without experiencing risk; many do their job adequately, but are not over-ambitious.

(c) The bureaucratic style, as we have seen, can be very efficient in a stable environment, when the organisation is large and when the work is predictable.

3.3 Task culture

Athena is the goddess of the **task culture**. Management is seen as completing a succession of projects or solving problems.

(a) The task culture is reflected in project teams and task forces. In such organisations, there is no dominant or clear leader. The principal concern in a task culture is to get the job done. Therefore the individuals who are important are the experts with the ability to accomplish a particular aspect of the task.

(b) Performance is judged by results.

(c) Task cultures are expensive, as experts demand a market price.

(d) Task cultures also depend on variety, and to tap creativity requires a tolerance of perhaps costly mistakes.

3.4 Person culture

Dionysus is the god of the **existential** or **person culture**. In the three other cultures, the individual is subordinate to the organisation or task. An existential culture is found in an organisation whose purpose is to serve the interests of the individuals within it. These organisations are rare, although an example might be a partnership of a few individuals who do all the work of the organisation themselves (with perhaps a little secretarial or clerical assistance): for example, barristers (in the UK) work through chambers.

Management positions in these organisations are often lower in status than the professionals and are labelled secretaries, administrators, bursars, registrars or clerks.

The organisation depends on the talent of the individuals; management is derived from the consent of the managed, rather than the delegated authority of the owners.

Exam focus point

> Do not neglect the key link between *culture* and *structure*! It is the subject of a question on the pilot paper.

3.5 A contingency approach

When thinking about these four types of culture, remember that they do not necessarily equate to specific organisation types, though some styles of organisation culture may accompany particular organisation structures. Also, it is quite possible for different cultures to prevail in different parts of the same organisation, especially large ones with many departments and sites. In other words, as the contingency approach says: 'it all depends'.

Case Study

Handy cites a pharmaceutical company which at one time had all its manufacturing subcontracted, until the turnover and cost considerations justified a factory of its own. The company hired nine talented individuals to design and run the factory. Result:

(a)   The *design team* ran on a task culture, with a democratic/consultative leadership style, using project teams for certain problems. This was successful while the factory was being built.

(b)   After its opening, the *factory*, staffed by 400, was run on similar lines. There were numerous problems. Every problem was treated as a project, and the workforce resented being asked to help sort out 'management' problems. In the end, the factory was run in a slightly more autocratic way. Handy states that this is a classic case of a task culture (to set something up) being superseded by a role culture (to run it). Different cultures suit different businesses.

Handy also matched appropriate cultural models to Robert **Anthony's** classification of managerial activity, which we discussed in Chapter 1.

(a)   **Strategic management** (carried out by senior management) is concerned with direction-setting, policy making and crisis handling. It therefore suits a **power culture**.

(b)   **Tactical management** (carried out by middle management) is concerned with establishing means to the corporate ends, mobilising resources and innovating (finding new ways of achieving goals). It therefore suits a **task culture**.

(c)   **Operational management** (carried out by supervisors and operatives) is concerned with routine activities to carry out tactical plans. It therefore suits a **role culture**.

 Question   **Classifications of culture**

Review the following statements. Ascribe each of them to one of Handy's four corporate cultures.

People are controlled and influenced by:

(a)   The personal exercise of rewards, punishments or charisma

(b)   Impersonal exercise of economic and political power to enforce procedures and standards of performance

(c)   Communication and discussion of task requirements leading to appropriate action motivated by personal commitment to goal achievement

(d)   Intrinsic interest and enjoyment in the activities to be done, and/or concern and caring for the needs of the other people involved

Answer

(a)   Zeus/power culture
(b)   Apollo/role culture
(c)   Athena/task culture
(d)   Dionysus/person culture

3.6 The impact of national culture

National culture influences organisation culture in various ways. One model of these effects is the 'Hofstede model' which describes four dimensions on which cultures differ:

- Power distance
- Uncertainty avoidance
- Individuality/collectivity
- Masculinity/femininity

Different countries have different ways of doing business, and different cultural values and assumptions which influence business and management styles.

Case Study

'French managers see their work as an intellectual challenge, requiring the remorseless application of individual brainpower. They do not share the Anglo-Saxon view of management as an interpersonally demanding exercise, where plans have to be constantly "sold" upward and downward using personal skills. 'Selection interviewers need to allow for cultural influences on interviewees' behaviour. For instance, Chinese applicants in Singapore tend to defer to the interviewer, whom they treat as 'superior', and to focus on the group or family, besides avoiding self-assertion… Hence, applicants from a Chinese background may be disadvantaged when being interviewed for jobs with multi-national companies that are heavily influenced by Anglo-American culture.' *(Guirdham)*

(Harvard Business Review)

3.7 The Hofstede model

Hofstede (1984) carried out cross-cultural research at 66 national offices of IBM and formulated one of the most influential models of work-related cultural differences.

The Hofstede model describes four main dimensions of difference between national cultures, which impact on all aspects of management and organisational behaviour: motivation, team working, leadership style, conflict management and HR policies.

(a) **Power distance**: the extent to which unequal distribution of power is accepted.

    (i) *High* PD cultures (as in Latin, near Eastern and less developed Asian countries) accept greater centralisation, a top-down chain of command and closer supervision. Subordinates have little expectation of influencing decisions.

    (ii) *Low* PD cultures (as in Germanic, Anglo and Nordic countries) expect less centralisation and flatter organisational structures. Subordinates expect involvement and participation in decision-making. (Japan is a medium PD culture.)

(b) **Uncertainty avoidance**: the extent to which security, order and control are preferred to ambiguity, uncertainty and change.

    (i) *High* UA cultures (as in Latin, near Eastern and Germanic countries and Japan) respect control, certainty and ritual. They value task structure, written rules and regulations, specialists and experts, and standardisation. There is a strong need for consensus: deviance and dissent are not tolerated. The work ethic is strong.

    (ii) *Low* UA cultures (as in Anglo and Nordic countries) respect flexibility and creativity. They have less task structure and written rules; more generalists and greater variability. There is more tolerance of risk, dissent, conflict and deviation from norms.

(c)   **Individualism**: the extent to which people prefer to live and work in individualist (focusing on the 'I' identity) or collectivist (focusing on the 'we' identity) ways.

    (i)   *High* Individualism cultures (as in Anglo, more developed Latin and Nordic countries) emphasise autonomy and individual choice and responsibility. They prize individual initiative. The organisation is impersonal and tends to defend business interests: task achievement is more important than relationships. Management is seen in an individual context.

    (ii)   *Low* Individualism (or Collectivist) cultures (as in less developed Latin, near Eastern and less developed Asian countries) emphasise interdependence, reciprocal obligation and social acceptability. The organisation is seen as a 'family' and tends to defend employees' interests: relationships are more important than task achievement. Management is seen in a team context. (Japan and Germany are 'medium' cultures on this dimension.)

(d)   **Masculinity**: the extent to which social gender roles are distinct. (Note that this is different from the usual sense in which the terms 'masculine' and 'feminine' are used.)

    (i)   *High* Masculinity cultures (as in Japan and Germanic and Anglo countries) clearly differentiate gender roles. Masculine values of assertiveness, competition, decisiveness and material success are dominant. Feminine values of modesty, tenderness, consensus, focus on relationships and quality of working life are less highly regarded, and confined to women.

    (ii)   *Low* Masculinity (or Feminine) cultures (as in Nordic countries) minimise gender roles. Feminine values are dominant – and both men and women are allowed to behave accordingly.

Question   National culture and management style

According to the Hofstede model, what issues might arise in the following cases?

(a)   The newly-appointed Spanish (more developed Latin) R & D manager of a UK (Anglo) firm asks to see the Rules and Procedures Manual for the department.

(b)   A US-trained (Anglo) manager attempts to implement a system of Management by Objectives in Thailand (less developed Asian).

(c)   A Dutch (Nordic) HR manager of a US (Anglo) subsidiary in the Netherlands is instructed to implement downsizing measures.

Answer

(a)   A high-UA manager, expecting to find detailed and generally adhered-to rules for everything, may be horrified by the ad-hocracy of a low-UA organisation: if (s)he attempts to impose a high-UA culture, there may be resistance from employees and management.

(b)   A high-individuality manager may implement MbO on the basis of individual performance targets, results and rewards: this may fail to motivate collectivist workers, for whom group processes and performance is more important.

(c)   A low-masculinity manager may try to shelter the workforce from the effects of downsizing, taking time for consultation, retraining, voluntary measures and so on: this may seem unacceptably 'soft' to a high-masculinity parent firm.

4 The informal organisation

4.1 What is the 'informal organisation?

An **informal organisation** always exists alongside the formal one. This consists of social relationships, informal communication networks, behavioural norms and power/influence structures, all of which may 'by-pass' formal organisational arrangements. This may be detrimental or beneficial to the organisation, depending how it is managed.

An **informal organisation** exists side by side with the formal one, whose key structural characteristics and features were examined in detail in Chapter 1. When people work together, they establish social relationships and customary ways of doing things. Unlike the formal organisation, the **informal organisation** is loosely structured, flexible and spontaneous. It embraces such mechanisms as:

(a) Social relationships and groupings (eg cliques) within – or across – formal structures

(b) The 'grapevine', 'bush telegraph', or informal communication which by-passes the formal reporting channels and routes

(c) Behavioural norms and ways of doing things, both social and work-related, which may circumvent formal procedures and systems (for good or ill). New members must 'learn the ropes' and get used to 'the way we do things here'

(d) Power/influence structures, irrespective of organisational authority: informal leaders are those who are trusted and looked to for advice

4.2 Benefits of the informal organisation

Benefits of the informal organisation for managers include the following.

(a) **Employee commitment**. The meeting of employees' social needs may contribute to morale and job satisfaction, with benefits in reduced absenteeism and labour turnover.

(b) **Knowledge sharing.** The availability of information through informal networks can give employees a wider perspective on their role in the task and the organisation, potentially stimulating 'big picture' problem-solving, cross-boundary co-operation and innovation.

(c) **Speed.** Informal networks and methods may sometimes be more efficient in achieving organisational goals, where the formal organisation has rigid procedures or lengthy communication channels, enabling decisions to be taken and implemented more rapidly.

(d) **Responsiveness**. The directness, information-richness and flexibility of the informal organisation may be particularly helpful in conditions of rapid environmental change, facilitating both the mechanisms and culture of anti-bureaucratic responsiveness.

(e) **Co-operation**. The formation and strengthening of interpersonal networks can facilitate teamworking and co-ordination across organisational boundaries. It may reduce organisational politics – or utilise it positively by mobilising effective decision-making coalitions and by-passing communication blocks.

4.3 Managerial problems of informal organisation

Each of the positive attributes of informal organisation could as easily be detrimental if the power of the informal organisation is directed towards goals unrelated to, or at odds with, those of the formal organisation.

(a)   Social groupings may act collectively against organisational interests, strengthened by collective power and information networks. Even if they are aligned with organisational goals, group/network maintenance may take a lot of time and energy away from tasks.

(b)   The grapevine is notoriously inaccurate and can carry morale-damaging rumours.

(c)   The informal organisation can become too important in fulfilling employees' needs: individuals can suffer acutely when excluded from cliques and networks.

(d)   Informal work practices may 'cut corners', violating safety or quality assurance measures.

Managers can **minimise problems** by:

(a)   Meeting employees' **needs** as far as possible via the *formal* organisation: providing information, encouragement, social interaction and so on

(b)   Harnessing the **dynamics** of the informal organisation – for example by using informal leaders to secure employee commitment to goals or changes

(c)   Involving **managers** themselves in the informal structure, so that they support information sharing, the breaking down of unhelpful rules and so on

Exam focus point

> Culture impacts on other topics, such as motivation, leadership and teams. It is also an important and fashionable topic in its own right – including the influence of national cultures, with increasingly globalised management.

 Case Study

The *Harvard Business Review* reported the significance of informal relationships.

- They are often reasons for high staff turnover.
- They indicate where people *actually* look for advice.
- They indicate who people trust.

A senior manager in a Californian-based computer company was having difficulty in getting staff to work together on a strategic plan. The co-ordinator on the task force could not get the others to work together because of his weak position on the 'trust network'. A replacement co-ordinator was then appointed who was more trusted by a wider group of people and who was able to get people to work together. Thus the senior manager exploited the informal organisation.

4.4 Group norms

A work group establishes **norms** or acceptable levels and methods of behaviour, to which all members of the group are expected to conform. This group attitude will have a negative effect on an organisation if it sets unreasonably low production norms. Groups often apply unfair treatment or discrimination against others who break their rules.

Norms are partly the product of role and role expectations of how people in certain positions behave, as conceived by people in related positions.

 Case Study

In a classic experiment by Sherif, participants were asked to look at a fixed point of light in a black box in a darkroom. Although the point of light is fixed, it so happens that in the darkness, it *appears* to move. Each participant was asked to say how far the light moved, and their individual estimates were recorded.

They were next put into a small group where each member of the group gave their own estimates to the others. From this interchange of opinions, individuals began to change their minds about how far the light had moved, and a group 'norm' estimate emerged.

When the groups were broken up, each individual was again asked to re-state his estimate; significantly, they retained the group norm estimate and rejected their previous individual estimate.

The experiment showed the effect of group psychology on establishing norms for the individual himself; even when, as in the case of the experiment, there is no factual basis for the group norm.

The general nature of group pressure is to require the individual to share in the group's own identity, and individuals may react to group norms and customs in a variety of ways.

- **Compliance** – toeing the line without real commitment
- **Internalisation** – full acceptance and identification
- **Counter-conformity** – rejecting the group and/or its norms

There are some circumstances which put strong pressure on the individual.

- The issue is not clear-cut.
- The individual lacks support for his own attitude or behaviour.
- The individual is exposed to other members of the group for a length of time.

Norms may be reinforced in various ways by the group.

(a) **Identification**: the use of badges, symbols, perhaps special modes of speech, in-jokes and so on – the marks of belonging, prestige and acceptance. There may even be initiation rites which mark the boundaries of membership.

(b) **Sanctions** of various kinds. Deviant behaviour may be dealt with by ostracising or ignoring the member concerned, by ridicule or reprimand, even by physical hostility. The threat of expulsion is the final sanction.

The group's power to induce conformity depends on the degree to which the individual values his membership of the group and the rewards it may offer, or wishes to avoid the negative sanctions at its disposal.

4.4.1 The Hawthorne Studies

The work of the **human relations school** of management theory sheds light on the importance of groups within an organisation. Interesting findings emerged from studies conducted at the Hawthorne plant of the *Western Electric Company*.

 Case Study

The experiments arose from an attempt by Western Electric to find out the effects of lighting standards on worker *productivity*. As a test, it moved a group of workers into a special room with variable lighting, and moved another group of workers into a room where the lighting was kept at normal standards. To the astonishment of the company management, productivity shot up in both rooms. When the lighting was then reduced in the first room, as a continuation of the test, not only did productivity continue to rise in the first room, but it also rose still further in the second room.

The conclusions of the studies were that individual members must be seen as part of a group, and that *informal* groups exercise a powerful influence in the workplace: supervisors and managers need to take account of social needs if they wish to secure commitment to organisational goals.

The Hawthorne studies were the first major attempt to undertake genuine social research, and to redirect attention to human factors at work. They are enduringly popular with managers, not least because they have an apparent simplicity and a straightforward, enthusiastically 'sold' message that 'happy workers are more productive', without over-attention to academic rigour, cautious qualification etc.

By modern standards of research, however, the methodology was 'less than rigorous in many respects' (G A Cole, *Personnel Management*). Human relations ideas were applied throughout the Western Electric Company – but didn't work. The programme was time-costly, as well as expensive; enthusiasm waned as the founders left. The conditions which made the initial experiments a success (the sense of status enjoyed by the workers in the Relay Assembly Test Room, because of their participation in the research) were no longer present when the experimental situation (the counselling service) was made available organisation-wide.

5 Stakeholder goals and objectives

Managers are not completely free to set objectives: they have different groups of stakeholders to consider. The influence of stakeholders varies from organisation to organisation.

FAST FORWARD

Stakeholders are those individuals or groups that, potentially, have an interest in what the organisation does.

 Case Study

Shiseido

(From the *Financial Times*).

Shiseido, one of the world's largest cosmetics companies, follows an un-Japanese, investor friendly strategy: setting rising targets for return on equity and stressing high standards of disclosure. The company maintains investor relations offices in the US, UK and Switzerland.

The company is pushing for globalisation, aiming to be the world's number one cosmetics company and to generate a quarter of its sales outside Japan.

International shareholders are becoming more intent on getting information in line with global standards – return on assets and equity, efficiency of management of assets, and so on. They are also more persistent about questioning investments that do not seem to be paying their way.

There are three broad types of stakeholder in an organisation, as follows.

- **Internal** stakeholders (employees, management)
- **Connected** stakeholders (shareholders, customers, suppliers, financiers)
- **External** stakeholders (the community, government, pressure groups)

5.1 Internal stakeholders: employees and management

Because **employees and management** are so intimately connected with the company, their objectives are likely to have a strong influence on how it is run. They are interested in the following issues.

(a)   The **organisation's continuation and growth**. Management and employees have a special interest in the organisation's continued existence.

(b)   Managers and employees have **individual interests** and goals which can be harnessed to the goals of the organisation.

Internal stakeholder	Interests to defend	Response risk
Managers and employees	• Jobs/careers • Money • Promotion • Benefits • Satisfaction	• Pursuit of 'systems goals' rather than shareholder interests • Industrial action • Negative power to impede implementation • Refusal to relocate • Resignation

5.2 Connected stakeholders

If management performance is measured and rewarded by reference to changes in **shareholder value** then shareholders will be happy, because managers are likely to encourage long-term share price growth.

Connected stakeholder	Interests to defend	Response risk
Shareholders (corporate strategy)	• Increase in shareholder wealth, measured by profitability, P/E ratios, market capitalisation, dividends and yield • Risk	• Sell shares (eg to predator) or boot out management
Bankers (cash flows)	• Security of loan • Adherence to loan agreements	• Denial of credit • Higher interest charges • Receivership
Suppliers (purchase strategy)	• Profitable sales • Payment for goods • Long-term relationship	• Refusal of credit • Court action • Wind down relationships
Customers (product market strategy)	• Goods as promised	• Buy elsewhere

 Case Study

A survey of FTSE 100 companies conducted by the *Financial Times* asked what part leading shareholders play in the running of companies and what top directors think of their investors.

Almost half of those surveyed felt that their main shareholders 'rarely or never' offered any useful comments about their business. 69% of respondents however felt that their major investors understood their business well or very well. 89% did not feel hampered by shareholders in taking the correct long term strategy.

Almost all directors felt their biggest shareholders were in it for the long term. This latter point probably reflects the fact that the top ten fund managers own 36 per cent of the FTSE 100 – few fund managers can afford to move out of a FTSE 100 company altogether and therefore remain long term shareholders whether the investment is liked or not.

There is a perceived trend towards greater involvement and communication. To quote one director: 'Investors are much more sensitive to their responsibilities than in the past because they are looked on as the guardians of the corporate conscience.'

5.3 External stakeholders

External stakeholder groups – the government, local authorities, pressure groups, the community at large, professional bodies – are likely to have quite diverse objectives.

External stakeholder	Interests to defend	Response risk
Government	• Jobs, training, tax	• Tax increases • Regulation • Legal action
Interest/pressure groups	• Pollution • Rights • Other	• Publicity • Direct action • Sabotage • Pressure on government
Professional bodies	• Members' ethics	• Imposition of ethical standards

5.4 Another approach

Stakeholders may also be analysed by reference to whether they have a **contractual relationship** with the organisation. Stakeholders who have such a relationship are called **primary stakeholders**, while those who do not are known as **secondary stakeholders**. The primary stakeholder category thus includes **internal** and **connected** stakeholders, while the secondary stakeholders category equates to **external** stakeholder status.

5.5 Stakeholder conflict

Since their interests may be widely different, **conflict between stakeholders** can be quite common. Managers must take the potential for such conflict into account when setting policy and be prepared to deal with it if it arises in a form that affects the organisation.

A relationship in which **conflict** between stakeholders is vividly characterised is that between **managers and shareholders**. The relationship can run into trouble when the managers' decisions focus on maintaining the corporation as a **vehicle for their managerial skills** while the shareholders wish to see radical changes so as to enhance their **dividend stream and increase the value of their shares**. The shareholders may feel that the business is a **managerial corporation** run for the benefit of managers and employees without regard for the objectives of the owners. The conflict in this case can be seriously detrimental to the company's stability.

(a)   Shareholders may **force resignations and divestments of businesses**, while managers may seek to preserve their empire and provide growth at the same time by undertaking risky policies.

(b)   In most cases, however, managers cannot but acknowledge that the shareholders have the **major stake** as owners of the company and its assets. Most companies therefore focus on making profits and increasing the market value of the company's shares, sometimes at the expense of the long term benefit of the company. Hence long term strategic plans may be 'hijacked' by the need to make a sizeable profit in one particular year; planning horizons are reduced and investment in long term business prospects may be shelved.

Clearly, each stakeholder group considers itself in some way **a client of the organisation**, thus broadening the debate about organisation effectiveness.

5.6 Dependency

A firm might depend on a stakeholder group at any particular time.

(a)   A firm with persistent cash flow problems might depend on its bankers to provide it with money to stay in business at all.

(b)   In the long term, any firm depends on its customers.

The degree of dependence or reliance can be analysed according to these criteria.

(a)   **Disruption**. Can the stakeholder disrupt the organisation's plans (eg a bank withdrawing overdraft facilities)?

(b)   **Replacement**. Can the firm replace the relationship?

(c)   **Uncertainty**. Does the stakeholder cause uncertainty in the firm's plans? A firm with healthy positive cash flows and large cash balances need not worry about its bank's attitude to a proposed investment.

The way in which the relationship between company and stakeholders is conducted is a function of the parties' **relative bargaining strength** and the philosophy underlying **each party's objectives**. This can be shown by means of a spectrum.

	Weak	Stakeholders' bargaining strength			Strong
Company's conduct of relation-ship	Command/ dictated by company	Consultation and consideration of stakeholders' views	Negotiation	Participation and acceptance of stakeholders' views	Democratic voting by stakeholders	Command/ dictated by stakeholders

5.7 Stakeholder mapping: power and interest

Mendelow suggests that stakeholders may be positioned on a matrix whose axes are power held and likelihood of showing an interest in the organisation's activities. These factors will help define the type of relationship the organisation should seek with its stakeholders.

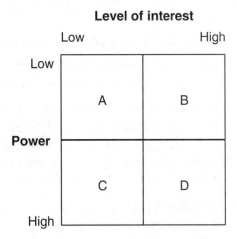

Level of interest

(a)   **Key players** are found in segment D: strategy must be *acceptable* to them, at least. An example would be a major customer. These stakeholders may even participate in decision-making.

(b)   Stakeholders in segment C must be treated with care. While often passive, they are capable of moving to segment D. They should, therefore be **kept satisfied.** Large institutional shareholders might fall into segment C.

(c)   Stakeholders in segment B do not have great ability to influence strategy, but their views can be important in influencing more powerful stakeholders, perhaps by lobbying. They should therefore be **kept informed.** Community representatives and charities might fall into segment B.

(d)   Minimal effort is expended on segment A.

A single stakeholder map is unlikely to be appropriate for all circumstances. In particular, stakeholders may move from quadrant to quadrant when different potential future strategies are considered.

Stakeholder mapping is used to assess the **significance** of stakeholder groups. This in turn has implications for the organisation.

(a)   The framework of **corporate governance** should recognise stakeholders' levels of interest and power.

(b)   It may be appropriate to seek to **reposition** certain stakeholders and discourage others from repositioning themselves, depending on their attitudes.

(c)   Key **blockers** and **facilitators** of change must be identified.

Each of these groups has three basic choices.

- **Loyalty**. They can do as they are told.

- **Exit**. For example by selling their shares, or getting a new job.

- **Voice**. They can stay and try to change the system. Those who choose **voice** are those who can, to varying degrees, influence the organisation. Influence implies a degree of power and willingness to exercise it.

Existing structures and systems can channel stakeholder influence.

(a)   They are the **location of power**, giving groups of people varying degrees of influence over strategic choices.

(b)   They are **conduits of information**, which shape strategic decisions.

(c)   They **limit choices** or give some options priority over others. These may be physical or ethical constraints over what is possible.

(d)   They **embody culture**.

(e)   They **determine the successful implementation** of strategy.

(f)   The **firm has different degrees of dependency** on various stakeholder groups. A company with a cash flow crisis will be more beholden to its bankers than one with regular cash surpluses.

So, different stakeholders will have their own views as to strategy. As some stakeholders have **negative power**, in other words power to impede or disrupt the decision, their likely response might be considered.

Exam focus point

Every exam is likely to have at least one question on stakeholders. In an exam question, you might have to:

- Identify the stakeholders in the situation, or
- Identify what their particular interests are

5.8 The strategic value of stakeholders

The firm can make strategic gains from managing stakeholder relationships. This was highlighted by a recent report by the Royal Society of Arts on *Tomorrow's Company*. Studies have revealed the following correlations.

(a) A correlation between **employee** and **customer loyalty** (eg reduced staff turnover in service firms generally results in more repeat business).

(b) **Continuity** and **stability** in relationships with employees, customers and suppliers is important in enabling organisations to respond to certain types of change, necessary for business as a sustained activity.

Responsibilities towards customers are mainly those of providing a product or service of a quality that customers expect, and of dealing honestly and fairly with customers.

Responsibilities towards suppliers are expressed mainly in terms of trading relationships.

(a) The organisation's size could give it considerable power as a buyer. One ethical guideline might be that the organisation should not use its power unscrupulously.

(b) Suppliers might rely on getting prompt payment in accordance with the terms of trade negotiated with its customers.

(c) All information obtained from suppliers and potential suppliers should be kept confidential.

5.9 Measuring stakeholder satisfaction

We have already considered ways in which stakeholders may be classified and given some instances of their probable interests. Measuring the success the organisation achieves in satisfying of stakeholder interests is likely to be difficult, since many of their expectations relate to **qualitative** rather than **quantitative** matters. It is, for example, difficult to measure good corporate citizenship. On the other hand, some of the more important stakeholder groups do have fairly specific interests, the satisfaction of which should be fairly amenable to measurement. Here are some examples of possible measures.

Stakeholder group	Measure
Employees	Staff turnover; pay and benefits relative to market rate; job vacancies
Government	Pollution measures; promptness of filing annual returns; accident rate; energy efficiency
Distributors	Share of joint promotions paid for; rate of running out of inventory

Chapter Roundup

- **Culture** is 'the collective programming of the mind which distinguishes the members of one category of people from another' (*Hofstede*). It may be identified as ways of behaving, and ways of understanding, that are shared by a group of people.

- **Elements of culture** include:
    - Observable behaviour
    - Underlying values and beliefs which give meaning to the observable elements
    - Hidden assumptions, which unconsciously shape values and beliefs

- Organisation culture is **'the way we do things round here'**.

- **Cultural values** can be used to guide organisational processes without the need for tight control. They can also be used to motivate employees, by emphasising the heroic dimension of the task. Culture can also be used to drive change, although – since values are difficult to change, it can also be a powerful force for preserving the status quo.

- **Harrison** classified four types of culture, to which **Handy** gave the names of Greek deities.

    - **Power** culture (Zeus) is shaped by one individual
    - **Role** culture (Apollo) is a bureaucratic culture shaped by rationality, rules and procedures
    - **Task** culture (Athena) is shaped by a focus on outputs and results
    - **Existential** or person culture (Dionysus) is shaped by the interests of individuals

- **National culture** influences organisation culture in various ways. One model of these effects is the 'Hofstede model' which describes four dimensions on which cultures differ:

    - Power distance
    - Uncertainty avoidance
    - Individuality/collectivity
    - Masculinity/femininity

- An **informal organisation** always exists alongside the formal one. This consists of social relationships, informal communication networks, behavioural norms and power/influence structures, all of which may 'by-pass' formal organisational arrangements. This may be detrimental or beneficial to the organisation, depending how it is managed.

- **Stakeholders** are those individuals or groups that, potentially, have an interest in what the organisation does.

Quick Quiz

1   What are the elements of culture?

2   'Bureaucracy' is another name for a:

    A   Power culture
    B   Role culture
    C   Task culture
    D   Existential culture

3   A project team is most likely to be a role culture. *True or false?*

4   List the four dimensions of cultural difference according to the Hofstede model.

5   List the potential benefits of the informal organisation.

6   What is a stakeholder?

7   Who are the most important stakeholders in Mendelow's matrix?

Answers to Quick Quiz

1   Observable phenomena (behaviour, artefacts, rituals), values and beliefs, assumptions

2   B   Role culture

3   False: it is most likely to be a task culture

4   Power distance, uncertainty avoidance, individuality, masculinity

5   Meeting of employee needs offering morale and job satisfaction; knowledge sharing; speed of operation; responsiveness to change; support for teamworking and co-ordination

6   Those individuals and groups that potentially have an interest in what the organisation does.

7   Those stakeholders in segment D, ie those with a high level of interest in the organisation and high power

Ethical considerations

Topic list	Syllabus reference
1 A framework of rules	A7 (b)
2 Management accountability	A7 (a)
3 The ethical environment	A7 (b)
4 Ethics in organisations	A7 (a)
5 Accountants and ethics	A7 (c)(d)
6 A code of ethics for accountants	A7 (c)–(e)

Introduction

Ethical conduct is a matter of continuing debate. This chapter begins by considering why society developed a framework of rules in **Section 1**. There have been many examples of misbehaviour at all levels of large organisations in recent years, including but not limited to the frauds associated with Enron. All professional bodies are alarmed by these events and what they say about ethical standards in everyday life. They are determined to do everything they can to promote and ensure high standards of behaviour among their members. Ethics has an increased focus in this syllabus.

In **Section 2**, we look at the idea of managers' **accountability** and **fiduciary responsibility**. The vital theme here is that even at the highest level, managers are not autonomous: they are always responsible to someone for their actions.

Section 3 looks at the wider background to ethical behaviour. Organisations are embedded in society and must respond not only to established ideas about ethical conduct, but also to current public concerns, including some current notions about social responsibility.

Section 4 is about the way organisations manage ethical problems and, in particular, about the desirability of building and maintaining an ethical culture.

Sections 5 and 6 consider in particular why ethics are relevant to accountants, and the qualities that accountants should demonstrate. In particular, you are encouraged to make yourself familiar with **ACCA's own ethical code**.

Study guide

		Intellectual level
A7	**Business ethics and ethical behaviour**	
(a)	Define business ethics and explain the importance of ethics to the organisation and to the individual.	1
(b)	Identify influences that determine whether behaviour and decisions are ethical or unethical.	1
(c)	Identify the factors that distinguish a profession from other types of occupation.	1
(d)	Explain the role of the accountant in promoting ethical behaviour.	1
(e)	Recognise the purpose of international and organisational codes of ethics and codes of conduct, IFAC, ACCA etc.	1

Exam guide

Ethics does not appear on the pilot paper, but it is something that is relevant to all professional and organisational behaviour, so it could be included in a question on any topic on future papers.

1 A framework of rules

The society we live in could not exist without **rules and standards**. Think about it, what would life be like if everyone went about doing exactly what they felt like?

People may decide not to turn up for work. This would mean shops not opening, and that you could not buy food. What we consider **crime would spiral out of control** as members of the public decide to take what they want and the police would only tackle criminals if they felt like it. **Businesses would not function** and the financial markets could not operate.

As society developed from prehistoric tribes to the complex interrelationships we have today, rules regulating behaviour had also to evolve. This is because humans recognised the need for everyone to work together for the good of the group.

1.1 Development of society

Imagine a prehistoric tribe. They would have started as individuals, roaming for food and shelter to keep themselves alive. By working as a group, some could **find shelter**, while others **hunted** for things to eat. It would be no good if the hunters ate all the food they found, and those who found shelter refused to let the hunters into the shelter. The shelter finders would **starve** to death while the hunters would **freeze**.

Humans have evolved from these tribes and have built a strong society that has revolutionised our planet. This has only been possible because **individuals have worked together**, guided by rules.

1.2 A need for rules

Back in prehistoric times, there were no laws, no courts and no police. Rules would have **developed through need**. The tribe would have a collective idea of what was **right** and **wrong** for the good of the group and would have **punished** a group member who stepped out of line, for example by taking food from others.

Further rules developed as society grew and eventually the first **laws** were laid down to control the larger populations. **Religion** played a major role in developing the rules for the individual, and many of these rules are still in place today.

Business law is relatively new, and has only developed over the last couple of hundred years with **industrialisation** and the needs that grew from it.

1.3 How do the rules fit together?

FAST FORWARD

There are three main sources of rules that regulate behaviour of individuals and businesses. These are:

- The law
- Non-legal rules and regulations
- Ethics

The diagram below shows how the three sources of regulation fit together.

Point A shows a company's current behaviour. It indicates that it is currently breaking the law. It could be treating its employees in an illegal way such as breaking health and safety laws.

The company wants to move to point B. This means taking the maximum care of employees that is expected by society. To get to this point, the company needs to meet its legal and non-legal obligations first.

The law is the minimum level of behaviour required. Any standard of behaviour below it is considered illegal and warrants punishment by society.

By meeting non-legal regulations (such as the rules of your workplace), you meet a higher level of behaviour than just the legal requirements.

Ethical behaviour is seen as the highest level of behaviour that society expects. Your behaviour goes further than just meeting your legal and non-legal obligations.

2 Management accountability

FAST FORWARD

Organisations are not autonomous; they exist to serve some external purpose, usually manifested in a group such as shareholders in a company or trustees of a charity. In particular, the **strategic apex must not lose sight of this accountability**. All managers have a **duty of faithful service** to the external purpose of the organisation and this lies most heavily on the shoulders of those at the strategic apex.

An organisation's managers are collectively responsible for the conduct of its affairs. This is true whatever the nature of the organisation, whether it is a charity or a commercial enterprise, a government or a trade union. As we discussed earlier, there is a **scalar chain of authority and accountability** that runs hierarchically up and down the organisation. Junior managers are accountable to more senior ones and so on up the chain until the strategic apex is reached. The question then arises: to whom are the managers at the strategic apex accountable for the activities of the organisation as a whole? As a matter of principle, we can say that there should be some external entity on behalf of which the strategic apex manages the organisation and to which it is accountable.

Question
Accountability

Who are the strategic apex managers of the following organisations and to whom are they accountable?

(a)   A charity
(b)   The government of a democracy
(c)   A trade union

Answer

(a)   The strategic apex of a charity is likely to be similar in nature to the board of a company, consisting of heads of departments, such as fundraising and operations, together with some non-executive directors. Their collective responsibility is likely to be to subscription-paying members of the institution assembled in a general meeting, where these exist, or possibly to a supervisory board, or even to a court of law. In any event, the actions of the managers in dealing with the interests of those the charity is intended to benefit will be the main concern.

(b)   The strategic apex of a democratic government is called the Cabinet and, again, consists of senior politicians with functional and advisory roles. The external body to which it is responsible is the electorate, which has the power collectively to expel it from office and install a completely different government.

(c)   The strategic apex of a trade union will consist of senior executives and, depending on its constitution, is likely to be responsible to the membership of the union. The extent of this responsibility will depend on local law and tradition and may be discharged for example, through postal ballots or, less satisfactorily, through mass meetings.

2.1 Fiduciary responsibility

Organisations are not autonomous: that is to say, they do not exist to serve their own purposes or those of their senior managers. They exist to serve some external purpose and their managers have a duty to run them in a way that serves that purpose, whether it be to relieve distress (a charity), to keep the peace and manage the economy (a government), to promote the interests of its members (a trade union) or to make a profit (a business). Managers have a **fiduciary responsibility** (or duty of faithful service) in this respect and their behaviour must always reflect it.

2.2 The objectives of commercial organisations

The general objective of a commercial organisation is to make a profit. It is possible to argue that wider objectives should be acknowledged and that the interests of people other than the owners should be served. This is the 'stakeholder view'. Nevertheless, whatever an organisation's objectives may be, it is the duty of its managers to seek to attain them.

2.3 Example

Managers need not be actually corrupt in order to fail in their fiduciary duty. The CEO who sets in motion a takeover bid that will enhance his prestige; the head of department who 'empire builds'; and the IT manager who buys an unnecessarily sophisticated enterprise resource management system are all failing in their fiduciary duty even though they receive no material benefit themselves.

2.4 Business objectives and management discretion

There are differing views about the extent to which external pressures modify business objectives and form boundaries to the exercise of management discretion.

(a) **The stakeholder view of company objectives** is that many groups of people have a stake or legitimate interest in what the company does. Shareholders own the business, but there are also suppliers, managers, workers and customers. A business depends on appropriate relationships with these groups, otherwise it will find it hard to function. Each of these groups has its own objectives, so that a compromise or balance is required.

(b) **The consensus theory of company objectives** was developed by *Cyert and March*. They argued that managers run a business, but do not own it, and they do not necessarily set objectives for the company, but rather they look for objectives which suit their own inclinations. Objectives emerge as a consensus of the differing views of shareholders, managers, employees, suppliers, customers and society at large, but (in contrast to the stakeholder view) **they are not all selected or controlled by management**.

3 The ethical environment

FAST FORWARD

Ethics and morality are about right and wrong behaviour. Western thinking about ethics tends to be based on ideas about **duty** and **consequences**. Unfortunately, such thinking often fails to indicate a single clear course of action. Ethical thinking is also influenced by the concepts of **virtue** and **rights**.

Key term

Ethics: a set of moral principles to guide behaviour

Whereas the political environment in which an organisation operates consists of laws, regulations and government agencies, the social environment consists of the customs, attitudes, beliefs and education of society as a whole, or of different groups in society; and the ethical environment consists of a set (or sets) of well-established rules of personal and organisational behaviour.

3.1 Ethical principles

Much of the practical difficulty with ethics lies in the absence of an **agreed basis** for decision-making. Effective **legal systems** are certain in their effects upon the individual. While the complexity of such matters as tax law can make it difficult to determine just what the law says in any given case, it is still possible to determine the issue in court. Once the law is decided it is definite and there is little scope for argument.

The **certainty of legal rules** does not exist in ethical theory. Different ideas apply in different cultures. The two main important ideas in the Western ethical tradition are **duty** and **consequences**.

3.2 Ethics based on consequences

This approach judges actions by reference to their outcomes or consequences. **Utilitarianism**, propounded by *Jeremy Bentham*, is the best known version of this approach and can be summed up as choosing the action that is likely to result in the **greatest good for the greatest number of people**.

3.3 Ethics based on duty

We use **duty** as a label for the ethical approach technically called **deontology** (which means much the same thing as 'duty' in Greek). This set of ideas is associated with the German thinker *Immanuel Kant* and is based upon the idea that behaviour should be governed by **absolute moral rules** that apply in all circumstances.

3.4 Rights and virtues

The idea that individuals have natural **inherent rights** that should not be abused is a further, long-established influence on Western ethical thinking and one that has led to the development of law to protect certain 'human rights'.

Virtue ethics continues to exert a subtle influence. The idea is that if people cultivate **virtue**, their behaviour is likely to be inherently ethical. Today it is suggested that managers should attempt to incorporate such virtues as firmness, fairness, objectivity, charity, forethought, loyalty and so on into their daily behaviour and decision-making.

Question	Categorical imperative

Is the statement below correct or incorrect?

'In Kant's approach to ethics, it is important to consider the consequences of an action in order to determine whether it is right or wrong.'

Answer

This statement is incorrect. Kant believes that certain rules must be obeyed no matter what the consequences may be.

3.5 Social attitudes

Social attitudes, such as a belief in the merits of education, progress through science and technology, and fair competition, are significant for the management of a business organisation. Other beliefs have either gained strength or been eroded in recent years:

(a) There is a growing belief in preserving and improving the quality of life by reducing working hours, reversing the spread of pollution, developing leisure activities and so on. Pressures on organisations to consider the environment are particularly strong because most environmental damage is irreversible and some is fatal to humans and wildlife.

(b) Many pressure groups have been organised in recent years to protect social minorities and under-privileged groups. Legislation has been passed in an attempt to prevent racial discrimination and discrimination against women and disabled people.

(c) Issues relating to the environmental consequences of corporate activities are currently debated, and respect for the environment has come to be regarded as an unquestionable good.

The ethical environment refers to justice, respect for the law and a moral code. The conduct of an organisation, its management and employees will be measured against ethical standards by the customers, suppliers and other members of the public with whom they deal.

3.6 Ethical problems facing managers

Managers have a duty (in most enterprises) to aim for profit. At the same time, modern ethical standards impose a duty to guard, preserve and enhance the value of the enterprise for the good of all touched by it, including the general public. Large organisations tend to be more often held to account over this than small ones.

In the area of **products and production**, managers have responsibility to ensure that the public and their own employees are protected from danger. Attempts to increase profitability by cutting costs may lead to dangerous working conditions or to inadequate safety standards in products. In the United States, **product liability litigation** is so common that this legal threat may be a more effective deterrent than general ethical standards. The *Consumer Protection Act 1987* and EU legislation generally is beginning to ensure that ethical standards are similarly enforced in the UK.

Another ethical problem concerns **payments by companies to government or municipal officials** who have power to help or hinder the payers' operations. In *The Ethics of Corporate Conduct, Clarence Walton* refers to the fine distinctions which exist in this area.

(a) **Extortion**. Foreign officials have been known to threaten companies with the complete closure of their local operations unless suitable payments are made.

(b) **Bribery**. This refers to payments for services to which a company is not legally entitled. There are some fine distinctions to be drawn; for example, some managers regard political contributions as bribery.

(c) **Grease money**. Multinational companies are sometimes unable to obtain services to which they are legally entitled because of deliberate stalling by local officials. Cash payments to the right people may then be enough to oil the machinery of bureaucracy.

(d) **Gifts**. In some cultures (such as Japan) gifts are regarded as an essential part of civilised negotiation, even in circumstances where to Western eyes they might appear ethically dubious. Managers operating in such a culture may feel at liberty to adopt the local customs.

Business ethics are also relevant to competitive behaviour. This is because a market can only be free if competition is, in some basic respects, fair. There is a distinction between competing aggressively and competing unethically. The dispute between *British Airways* and *Virgin* centred around issues of business ethics.

3.7 Social responsibility and businesses

Arguably, institutions like hospitals, schools and so forth exist because health care and education are seen to be desirable social objectives by government at large, if they can be afforded.

However, where does this leave businesses? How far is it reasonable, or even appropriate, for businesses to exercise 'social responsibility' by giving to charities, voluntarily imposing strict environmental objectives on themselves and so forth?

Social responsibility action is likely to have an adverse effect on shareholders' interests.

(a) **Additional costs** such as those of environmental monitoring
(b) **Reduced revenues** as a result of refusing to supply certain customers
(c) **Diversion of employee effort** away from profitable activities
(d) **Diversion of funds** into social projects

However, it is possible to argue that being socially responsible is in shareholders' interests, possibly over the longer term.

Corporate social responsibility is examined in more detail in Chapter 5.

3.8 Specific environmental responsibilities

Businesses are widely regarded as having a duty to safeguard the **natural environment**. There are six areas for action.

(a) **Environmental auditing** to monitor such things as legal compliance, waste treatment, and emissions.

(b) **Economic action**: charges for environmental damage should be made internally to give managers an incentive to avoid it.

(c) **Accounting action**: a separate set of accounts incorporating **shadow prices** to represent environmental costs is prepared.

(d) **Ecological approach**: aspects of the business such as a product or a location are selected for examination to ascertain their environmental impact.

(e) **Production** is managed to minimise inputs of materials and energy.

(f) **Quality** management is applied using the principle of continuous improvement in environmental performance.

3.9 Examples of social and ethical objectives

Companies are not passive in the social and ethical environment. Many organisations pursue a variety of social and ethical objectives.

(a) **Employees**

    (i) A minimum wage, perhaps with adequate differentials for skilled labour
    (ii) Job security (over and above the protection afforded by legislation)
    (iii) Good conditions of work (above the legal minima)
    (iv) Job satisfaction
    (v) Promotion of diversity and equal opportunities
    (vi) A healthy and safe workplace

(b) **Customers** may be regarded as entitled to receive a safe product of good quality at a reasonable price.

(c) **Suppliers** may be offered regular orders and timely payment in return for reliable delivery and good service.

(d) **Society as a whole**

    (i) Control of pollution and use of sustainable resources
    (ii) Provision of financial assistance to charities, sports and community activities
    (iii) Not producing undesirable goods

4 Ethics in organisations

> Ethical conduct by all members should be a major concern for management. Inside the organisation, a **compliance based** approach highlights **conformity with the law**. An **integrity based** approach suggests a **wider remit**, incorporating ethics in the organisation's **values and culture**. Organisations sometimes issue codes of conduct to employees. Many employees are bound by professional codes of conduct.

Companies have to follow legal standards, or else they will be subject to fines and their officers might face similar charges. Ethics in organisations relates to **social responsibility** and **business practice.**

People that work for organisations bring their own values into work with them. Organisations contain a variety of ethical systems.

(a) **Personal ethics** deriving from a person's upbringing, religious or non-religious beliefs, political opinions, personality and so on.

(b) **Professional ethics** (eg ACCA's code of ethics, medical ethics).

(c) **Organisation cultures** (eg 'customer first'). We discussed culture in an earlier chapter; culture, in denoting what is normal behaviour, also denotes what is the right behaviour in many cases.

(d) **Organisation systems**. Ethics might be contained in a formal code, reinforced by the overall statement of values. A problem might be that ethics does not always save money, and there is a real cost to ethical decisions. Besides, the organisation has different ethical duties to different stakeholders. Who sets priorities?

Ethical problems can be approached from several directions, as we have attempted to show. Unfortunately, this means that difficult problems rarely have clear solutions and it is usually possible for the opportunist manager to find authority to support any decision. The Chartered Certified Accountant must make an effort to do the right thing bearing in mind the variety of ethical assumptions that other people may make; the varying expectations of legitimate stakeholders; and the attitudes of legislators and pressure groups.

 Case Study

Organisation systems and targets do have ethical implications. The *Harvard Business Review* reported that the US retailer, Sears Roebuck was deluged with complaints that customers of its car service centre were being charged for unnecessary work: apparently this was because mechanics had been given targets of the number of car spare parts they should sell.

4.1 Leadership practices and ethics

The role of culture in determining the ethical climate of an organisation can be further explored by a brief reflection on the role of leaders in setting the ethical standard. A culture is partly a collection of symbols and attitudes, embodying certain truths about the organisation. Senior managers are also symbolic managers; inevitably they decide priorities; they set an example, whether they like it or not.

4.2 Two approaches to managing ethics

Lynne Paine (*Harvard Business Review*, March-April 1994) suggests that ethical decisions are becoming more important as penalties, in the US at least, for companies which break the law become tougher. Paine suggests that there are two approaches to the management of ethics in organisations.

- **Compliance**-based
- **Integrity**-based

4.2.1 Compliance-based approach

A compliance-based approach is primarily designed to ensure that the company **acts within the letter of the law**, and that violations are prevented, detected and punished. Some organisations, faced with the legal consequences of unethical behaviour take legal precautions such as those below.

- Compliance procedures to detect misconduct
- Audits of contracts
- Systems for employees to report criminal misconduct without fear of retribution
- Disciplinary procedures to deal with transgressions

4.2.2 Integrity-based programmes

An integrity-based approach combines a concern for the law with an **emphasis on managerial responsibility** for ethical behaviour. Integrity strategies strive to define companies' guiding values, aspirations and patterns of thought and conduct. When integrated into the day-to-day operations of an organisation, such strategies can help prevent damaging ethical lapses, while tapping into powerful human impulses for moral thought and action.

Whistleblowing is the disclosure by an employee of illegal, immoral or illegitimate practices on the part of the organisation. This may appear to be in the public interest, but confidentiality is very important in the accountants' code of ethics. Whistle-blowing frequently involves **financial loss** for the whistleblower.

(a)   Whistle-blowers may lose their jobs.

(b)   A whistle-blower who is a member of a professional body cannot, sadly, rely on that body to take a significant interest, or even offer a sympathetic ear. Some professional bodies have narrow interpretations of what is meant by ethical conduct. For many the duties of **commercial confidentiality** are felt to be more important.

In the UK, the Public Interest Disclosure Act 1998 offers some protection to whistle-blowers, but both the subject of the disclosure and the way in which it is made must satisfy the requirements of the Act.

Exam focus point

> The ethics codes described above can be related to mission, culture and control strategies. A compliance-based approach suggests that bureaucratic control is necessary; an integrity based approach relies on cultural control.

5 Accountants and ethics

FAST FORWARD

> As an accountant, your values and attitudes **flow through** everything you do professionally. They contribute to the **trust** the wider community puts in the profession and the **perception** it has of it.

Key reasons for accountants to behave ethically:

(a)   Ethical issues may be a matter of law and regulation and accountants are expected to apply them

(b)   The profession requires members to conduct themselves and provide services to the public according to certain standards. By upholding these standards, the profession's reputation and standing is protected

(c)   An accountant's ethical behaviour serves to protect the public interest

5.1 Approaches to accountancy ethics

Professionals will have their own idea of what behaviour is ethical and what is not. Although there will be differences, collectively there are common views and values that shine through.

To help individuals judge whether or not they are acting ethically in particular circumstances, guidance should be given (usually by a governing body) that clarifies the matter. Such guidance is usually known as a '**Code of ethics**' or '**Code of conduct**'.

6 A code of ethics for accountants

FAST FORWARD

The **International Federation of Accountants** (IFAC) is an international body representing all the major accountancy bodies across the world. Its mission is to develop the **high standards** of professional accountants and enhance the quality of services they provide.

6.1 IFAC and the ACCA

To enable the development of high standards, IFAC's ethics committee established a **code of ethics**. The code indicates a minimum level of conduct that all accountants must adhere. As a member of IFAC, ACCA released its own code of ethics, designed to align to the IFAC code.

For further information visit www.ifac.org.

6.1.1 Fundamental principles of the ACCA Code of Ethics and Conduct

Members are required to comply with the following fundamental principles.

- Integrity
- Objectivity
- Professional competence and due care
- Confidentiality
- Professional behaviour

(For more on the ACCA's code of ethics, visit its website at www.acca.org.uk.)

6.2 Personal qualities expected of an accountant

In meeting the fundamental principles, certain qualities are expected you. As a student of ACCA (and a future member) you need to develop the following qualities to ensure you meet the fundamental principles.

- Personal qualities
- Professional qualities

FAST FORWARD

The personal qualities that an accountant should demonstrate are:

- Reliability
- Responsibility
- Timeliness
- Courtesy
- Respect

6.2.1 Reliability

Your clients and colleagues trust that your work meets **professional standards**. Failure to meet the standards will reduce their **confidence** in your ability to do the job. If this happens consistently, the reliability of your future work will be called into question.

When taking on work, you must ensure it gets done. You should resolve any problems in good time and not leave them to the last minute.

6.2.2 Responsibility

In the work place, you should take '**ownership**' of your work. This means ensuring it is **complete** and meets the requirements of **professional standards**. You should not expect others to do your work for you.

Your work may put you in a position of responsibility, and you should conduct yourself in a manner that respects this. For example, you may be asked to review confidential payroll information. It is important that you recognise the need to safeguard the information, and not take any undue risks that could result in the information becoming public.

6.2.3 Timeliness

Clients and work colleagues rely on you to produce work within a specified time frame. They also rely on you to be on time for work and your appointments, **failure** do so as can be **costly** as it wastes both your time and that of others.

6.2.4 Courtesy

You should conduct yourself with **courtesy** and **consideration** towards your clients, colleagues, and all others that you come into contact with during the performance your work. The way you behave reflects both **on you** and the **accountancy profession**, so it is important to leave those you meet with a good impression.

6.2.5 Respect

As an accountant, you should respect others by developing **constructive relationships** and recognising the **values** and **rights** of others. It is perfectly reasonable to disagree with their point of view, but you should not bring the disagreement down to a personal level.

6.3 Professional qualities expected of an accountant

FAST FORWARD

The professional qualities an accountant should demonstrate are:

- Independence
- Scepticism
- Accountability
- Social responsibility

6.3.1 Independence

The principle of objectivity requires an '**independent mind**'. This means putting all considerations not relevant to the task in hand to one side – enabling you to complete your work free from bias or prejudice.

You must also be seen to be independent. This is known as '**independence in appearance**', and means you should demonstrate your independence by avoiding situations that could cause a reasonable observer to question your objectivity. For example, by not accepting a valuable gift from an audit client that you are about to report on, even if the client's motive is entirely innocent.

6.3.2 Scepticism

The principle of integrity means that you should develop a healthy sense of scepticism. **You should question information given to you**. Ask yourself, does the information make sense, is there other evidence that supports it, where did it come from, and why was it given to me?

By questioning, you will form your own opinion regarding its quality and reliability, reducing the risk of misinformation.

6.3.3 Accountability

You should recognise that you are accountable for your own judgements and decisions. Where these are called into question you should not pass undue responsibility onto others.

6.3.4 Social responsibility

As we saw earlier, accountants have a public duty as well as a duty to their employer or clients. This public duty can also be referred to as social responsibility – the provision of specific benefits to society as a whole.

You should be aware that your work may affect the public in some way. For example:

(a)   **Audit work**. Your work may affect an entity's financial result which members of the public use when making investment decisions. The public rely on audits to ensure the accounts are correct and free from error.

(b)   **Accountancy work**. Your work in preparing sole trader or limited company accounts will affect their profit and therefore the amount of tax collected.

(c)   **Investment decisions**. You may be asked to work on a major investment decision that your company will be making. The wrong decision could cost your company significant sums of money, and public shareholders their dividends.

Remember – although the effect one accountant has on society may be small, collectively, accountants have a significant influence.

Chapter Roundup

- There are three main sources of rules that regulate behaviour of individuals and businesses. These are:
  - The law
  - Non-legal rules and regulations
  - Ethics

- Organisations are not autonomous; they exist to serve some external purpose, usually manifested in a group such as shareholders in a company or trustees of a charity. In particular, the **strategic apex must not lose sight of this accountability**. All managers have a **duty of faithful service** to the external purpose of the organisation and this lies most heavily on the shoulders of those at the strategic apex.

- Ethics and morality are about right and wrong behaviour. Western thinking about ethics tends to be based on ideas about **duty** and **consequences**. Unfortunately, such thinking often fails to indicate a single clear course of action. Ethical thinking is also influenced by the concepts of **virtue** and **rights**.

- Ethical conduct by all members should be a major concern for management. Inside the organisation, a **compliance based** approach highlights **conformity with the law**. An **integrity based** approach suggests a **wider remit**, incorporating ethics in the organisation's **values and culture**. Organisations sometimes issue codes of conduct to employees. Many employees are bound by professional codes of conduct.

- As an accountant, your values and attitudes **flow through** everything you do professionally. They contribute to the **trust** the wider community puts in the profession and the **perception** it has of it.

- The **International Federation of Accountants** (IFAC) is an international body representing all the major accountancy bodies across the world. Its mission is to develop the **high standards** of professional accountants and enhance the quality of services they provide.

- The personal qualities that an accountant should demonstrate are:
  - Reliability
  - Responsibility
  - Timeliness
  - Courtesy
  - Respect

- The professional qualities an accountant should demonstrate are:
  - Independence
  - Scepticism
  - Accountability
  - Social responsibility

Quick Quiz

1   Ethics are a set of .... that ....
....

2   What is the name given to guidance issued (usually by a governing body) to individuals to judge whether they are acting ethically in particular circumstances?

3   List five personal qualities expected of an accountant.

(a)   R..

(b)   R..

(c)   T..

(d)   C..

(e)   R..

4   What is fiduciary responsibility?

5   Why might social responsibility have an adverse effect on shareholders' interests?

6   What is a compliance-based approach to ethics designed to ensure?

7   Why should accountants behave ethically?

8   What is IFAC's mission?

Answers to Quick Quiz

1   Moral principles, guide behaviour

2   Code of Ethics or Code of Conduct

3   (a)   Reliability
     (b)   Responsibility
     (c)   Timeliness
     (d)   Courtesy
     (e)   Respect

4   A duty of faithful service

5   Social responsibility action may

- Incur additional costs (for example, environmental monitoring)
- Decrease revenues (if, say, a company refused to supply to certain customers)
- Divert employee effort away from profitable activities
- Divert funds away from the business into social projects

6   That the company acts within the letter of the law and that violations are prevented, detected and punished

7
- Ethics may be a matter of law; accountants are expected to apply them
- Public expectations of professional conduct; safeguarding the profession's reputation
- To protect the public interest

8   To develop high standards of professional accountants and enhance the quality of the service they provide.

Corporate governance and social responsibility

Topic list	Syllabus reference
1 Principles of corporate governance	A8 (a) (c)
2 Developments in corporate governance	A8 (b)
3 Role of the board	A8 (c) (d)
4 Reporting on corporate governance	A8 (d)
5 Corporate social responsibility	A8 (b) (c)
6 Ethics, law, governance and social responsibility	A8 (e) (f)

Introduction

There have been a number of reports worldwide on corporate governance, but understanding the underlying principles of corporate governance are more important than getting to grips with the detailed provisions laid down in each report. **Sections 1 and 2** of this chapter cover the main areas of corporate governance.

Section 3 and 4 go on to discuss the role of the board and how it communicates with shareholders.

Corporate social responsibility is covered in **Sections 5 and 6** of the chapter. While some argue that business has a social responsibility for the cost of its activities, this is controversial. However, there does now seem to be widespread acceptance that commercial organisations should devote some of their resources to the promotion of wider social aims that are not necessarily mandated by either law or the rules of ethics.

Study guide

		Intellectual level
A8	**Governance and social responsibility in business**	
(a)	Recognise the concept of separation between ownership and control.	1
(b)	Define corporate governance and social responsibility and explain their importance in contemporary organisations.	1
(c)	Explain the responsibility of organisations to maintain appropriate standards of corporate governance and corporate social responsibility.	1
(d)	Briefly explain the main recommendations of best practice in effective corporate governance:	1
(i)	Non-executive directors	
(ii)	Remuneration committees	
(iii)	Audit committees	
(iv)	Public oversight	
(e)	Explain how organisations take account of their social responsibility objectives through analysis of the needs of internal, connected and external stakeholders.	1
(f)	Identify the social and environmental responsibilities of business organisations to internal, connected and external stakeholders.	1

Exam guide

Corporate governance and social responsibility is an issue for all corporate bodies, both commercial and not-for-profit. 'Best practice' in corporate governance features in a question on the Pilot Paper.

1 Principles of corporate governance

FAST FORWARD

> Most corporate governance reports are based around the principles of **integrity**, **accountability**, **independence** and **good management** but there is disagreement on how much these principles need to be supplemented by detailed rules.

1.1 Perspectives on governance

Debates about the place of governance are founded on three differing views associated with the **ownership** and **management** of organisations.

1.1.1 Stewardship theory

Some approaches to good governance view the management of an organisation as the **stewards** of its assets, charged with their employment and deployment in ways consistent with the overall strategy of the organisation. With this approach, power is seen to be vested in the stewards, that is the executive managers.

Other interest groups take little or no part in the running of the company and receive relevant information via established reporting mechanisms; audited accounts, annual reports etc. Technically, shareholders or member/owners have the right to dismiss their stewards if they are dissatisfied by their stewardship, via a vote at an annual general meeting.

1.1.2 Agency theory

Another approach to governance is enshrined in **agency theory**. This takes the stance that, rather than acting as stewards, management will act in an **agency capacity**, seeking to service their own self-interest and looking after the performance of the company only where its goals are co-incident with their own.

1.1.3 Stakeholder theory

The stakeholder approach takes a much more **'organic' view** of the organisation, imbuing it with a 'life' of its own, in keeping with the notion of a separate legal personage. Effectively stakeholder theory is a development of the notion of stewardship, stating that management has a **duty of care, not just to the owners** of the company in terms of maximising shareholder value, but also to the **wider community** of interest, or stakeholders.

1.2 Governance principles

Most corporate governance codes are based on a set of principles founded upon ideas of what corporate governance is meant to achieve. This list is based on a number of reports.

(a) To **minimise risk**, especially financial, legal and reputational risks, by requiring compliance with accepted good practice in the jurisdiction in question and ensuring appropriate systems of financial control are in place, in particular systems for monitoring risk, financial control and compliance with the law.

(b) To **ensure adherence** to and **satisfaction** of the **strategic objectives** of the organisation, thus aiding effective management.

(c) To **fulfil responsibilities to all stakeholders** and to **minimise potential conflicts of interest** between the owners, managers and wider stakeholder community, however defined and to treat each category **fairly**.

(d) To **establish clear accountability** at senior levels within an organisation.

(e) To **maintain the independence** of those who scrutinise the behaviour of the organisation and its senior executive managers. Independence is particularly important for **non-executive directors**, and **internal and external auditors.**

(f) To **provide accurate and timely reporting of trustworthy/independent financial and operational data** to both the management and owners/members of the organisation to give them a true and balanced picture of what is happening in the organisation.

(g) To **encourage more proactive involvement** of owners/members in the effective management of the organisation through recognising their responsibilities of oversight and input to decision making processes via voting or other mechanisms.

(h) To **promote integrity**, that is **straightforward dealing** and **completeness**.

1.3 Principles vs rules

A continuing debate on corporate governance is whether the guidance should predominantly be in the form of principles, or whether there is a need for detailed laws or regulations.

The Hampel report in the UK came out very firmly in favour of a principles-based approach. The committee preferred relaxing the regulatory burden on companies and was against treating the corporate governance codes as sets of prescriptive rules. The report stated that there may be **guidelines** which will normally be appropriate but the differing circumstances of companies meant that sometimes there are valid reasons for exceptions.

However a number of commentators criticised the Hampel report for this approach. Some critics have commented that the principles set out in the Hampel report are so broad that they are of very little use as a guide to best corporate governance practice. For example the suggestion that non-executive directors from a wide variety of backgrounds can make a contribution is seen as not strong enough to encourage companies away from recruiting directors by means of the 'old boy network'.

2 Developments in corporate governance

Good corporate governance involves **risk management** and **internal control, accountability** to stakeholders and other shareholders and conducting business in an **ethical and effective way.**

2.1 What is corporate governance?

Key term

> **Corporate governance** is the system by which organisations are directed and controlled by senior officers.

Although mostly discussed in relation to large quoted companies, governance is an issue for all bodies corporate; commercial and not for profit.

There are a number of elements in corporate governance:

(a) The management and **reduction of risk** is fundamental in all definitions of good governance.

(b) **Overall performance enhanced** by **good supervision** and **management** within **set best practice guidelines** underpins most definitions.

(c) Good governance provides a **framework** for an organisation to pursue its strategy in an **ethical and effective** way from the perspective of all stakeholder groups affected, and offers safeguards against misuse of resources, physical or intellectual.

(d) Good governance is not just about externally established codes, it also requires a willingness to **apply the spirit** as well as the letter of the law.

(e) **Accountability** is generally a major theme in all governance frameworks. There is a free flow of information in the form of accounts and other reports. However, issues of commercial confidentiality can get in the way of too much 'openness'.

Extensive abuses have led to a variety of measures intended to improve the quality of corporate governance.

(a) The development of **accounting standards** has been driven in part by the need to prevent abuses in financial reporting.

(b) The various professional bodies all have their own **codes of professional conduct**.

(c) A series of major financial scandals has led to government intervention in the UK in the form of **commissions on standards of behaviour**, each producing its code of conduct.

2.2 The driving forces of governance development

Corporate governance issues came to prominence in the USA during the 1970s and in the UK and Europe from late 1980s. The main, but not the only, drivers associated with the increasing demand for the development of governance were:

(a) **Increasing internationalisation and globalisation** meant that investors, and institutional investors in particular, began to invest outside their home countries. The King report in South Africa highlights the role of the free movement of capital, commenting that investors are promoting governance in their own self-interest.

(b)   The **differential treatment of domestic and foreign investors**, both in terms of reporting and associated rights/dividends caused many investors to call for parity of treatment.

(c)   Issues concerning **financial reporting** were raised by many investors and were the focus of much debate and litigation. Shareholder confidence in many instances was eroded and, while focus solely on accounting and reporting issues is inadequate, the regulation of practices such as off-balance sheet financing has led to greater transparency and a reduction in risks faced by investors.

(d)   The characteristics of individual countries may have a **significant influence** in the way corporate governance has developed. The King report emphasises the importance of qualities that are fundamental to the South African culture such as collectiveness, consensus, helpfulness, fairness, consultation and religious faith in the development of best practice.

(e)   An increasing number of **high profile corporate scandals** and collapses including Polly Peck International, BCCI, and Maxwell Communications Corporation prompted the development of governance codes in the early 1990s. However the scandals since then have raised questions about further measures that may be necessary.

 Case Study

In the UK the Cadbury committee was set up in May 1991 because of the lack of confidence which was perceived in financial reporting and in the ability of external auditors to provide the assurances required by the users of financial statements. The main difficulties were considered to be in the relationship between external auditors and boards of directors. In particular, the commercial pressures on both directors and auditors caused pressure to be brought to bear on auditors by the board and the auditors often capitulated.

Problems were also perceived in the ability of the board of directors to control their organisations. The lack of board accountability in many of these company collapses demonstrated the need for action.

2.2.1 The development of UK corporate governance

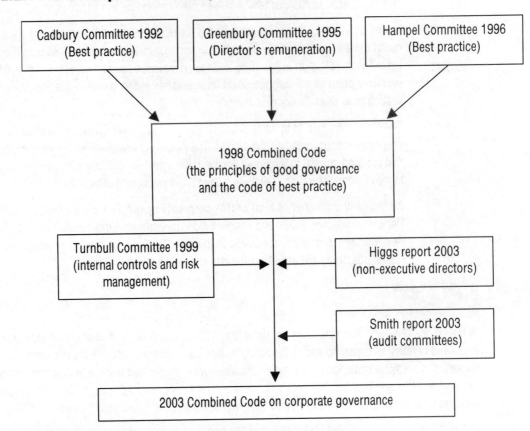

2.3 Features of poor corporate governance

The scandals over the last 25 years have highlighted the need for guidance to tackle the various risks and problems that can arise in organisations' systems of governance.

2.3.1 Domination by a single individual

A feature of many corporate governance scandals has been boards dominated by a single senior executive with other board members merely acting as a rubber stamp. Sometimes the single individual may bypass the board to action his own interests.

Even if an organisation is not dominated by a single individual, there may be other weaknesses. The organisation may be run by a small group centred round the chief executive and chief financial officer, and appointments may be made by personal recommendation rather than a formal, objective process.

2.3.2 Lack of involvement of board

Boards that meet irregularly or fail to consider systematically the organisation's activities and risks are clearly weak. Sometimes the failure to carry out proper oversight is due to a **lack of information** being provided.

2.3.3 Lack of adequate control function

An obvious weakness is a **lack of internal audit.**

Another important control is **lack of adequate technical knowledge** in key roles, for example in the audit committee or in senior compliance positions. A rapid turnover of staff involved in accounting or control may suggest inadequate resourcing, and will make control more difficult because of lack of continuity.

2.3.4 Lack of supervision

Employees who are not properly supervised can create large losses for the organisation through their own incompetence, negligence or fraudulent activity. The behaviour of Nick Leeson, the employee who caused the collapse of Barings bank was not challenged because he appeared to be successful, whereas he was using unauthorised accounts to cover up his large trading losses. Leeson was able to do this because he was in charge of dealing and settlement, a systems weakness or **lack of segregation of key roles** that was featured in other financial frauds.

2.3.5 Lack of independent scrutiny

External auditors may not carry out the necessary questioning of senior management because of fears of losing the audit, and internal audit do not ask awkward questions because the chief financial officer determines their employment prospects. Often corporate collapses are followed by criticisms of external auditors, such as the Barlow Clowes affair where poorly planned and focused audit work failed to identify illegal use of client monies.

2.3.6 Lack of contact with shareholders

Often board members may have grown up with the company but lose touch with the interests and views of shareholders. One possible symptom of this is the payment of remuneration packages that do not appear to be warranted by results.

2.3.7 Emphasis on short-term profitability

Emphasis on success or getting results can lead to the **concealment of problems or errors,** or **manipulation of accounts** to **achieve desired results**.

2.3.8 Misleading accounts and information

Often misleading figures are symptomatic of other problems (or are designed to conceal other problems) but clearly poor quality accounting information is a major problem if markets are trying to make a fair assessment of the company's value. Giving out misleading information was a major issue in the UK's Equitable Life scandal where the company gave contradictory information to savers, independent advisers, media and regulators.

Question	Governance

Techpoint plc is a medium-sized public company that produces a range of components used in the manufacture of computers.

The board of directors consists of chairman Max Mallory, chief executive Richard Mallory, finance director Linda Mallory all of whom are siblings. There are five other unrelated executive directors. All directors receive bonuses based on sales. The company's sales are made by individual salesmen and women each of whom have the authority to enter the company into contracts unlimited in value without the need to refer to a superior or consult with other departments. It is this flexibility that has enabled the company to be very profitable in past years. However, a number of bad contracts in the current year have meant that the finance director has re-classed them as 'costs' to maintain healthy sales and to protect the directors' bonuses.

What are the corporate governance issues at Techpoint plc?

Answer

The main corporate governance issues are:

(a) **Domination by a small group**

All the key directors are related which gives them power over the other executives.

(b) **Short-term view**

Directors' bonuses are based on short-term sales and have resulted in the manipulation of accounts to achieve them.

(c) **Lack of supervision**

The sales force can tie the company into large loss-making contracts without any checks. There is no authorisation or communication with other departments which means the company may take on contracts that it cannot fulfil. The company has been hit hard with bad contracts in the current year.

2.4 Risks of poor corporate governance

Clearly the ultimate risk is of the organisation **making such large losses** that **bankruptcy** becomes inevitable. The organisation may also be closed down as a result of **serious regulatory breaches,** for example misapplying investors' monies.

2.5 Reports on corporate governance

A number of reports have been produced in various countries aiming to address the risk and problems posed by poor corporate governance.

2.5.1 United Kingdom

There were three significant corporate governance reports in the United Kingdom during the 1990s. The **Cadbury and Hampel reports** covered general corporate governance issues, whilst the **Greenbury report** concentrated on remuneration of directors.

The recommendations of these three reports were merged into a **Combined Code** in 1998, with which companies listed on the London Stock Exchange are required to comply.

Since the publication of the Combined Code a number of reports in the UK have been published about specific aspects of corporate governance.

- The **Turnbull report** focused on risk management and internal control
- The **Smith report** discussed the role of audit committees
- The **Higgs report** focused on the role of the non-executive director

2.5.2 USA

Corporate scandals, particularly the Enron scandal, in the United States over the last few years have led to the Sarbanes-Oxley Act 2002 and consequent changes to the listing rules that companies quoted on Wall Street have to fulfil. The primary aim of this Act is to protect investors through improving the accuracy and reliability of corporate disclosures, and placing accountability for this upon the senior management of the organisation.

The Act implemented tight controls in corporate financial and accounting processes. The Act also established the Public Company Accounting oversight Board (PCAOB). Its aim is to protect investors and other stakeholders by ensuring that the auditor of a company's financial statements has adhered to strict guidelines. While this applies chiefly to US auditing firms, the principle of **public oversight** is applicable to other countries in that regulation of the auditing profession (whether through registration and inspection, or self-regulation) is seen as very important both in improving audit quality and emphasising the importance of compliance with standards in a company's control environment.

Exam focus point

The responsibilities of a Public Oversight Board appear on the Pilot Paper.

2.5.3 South Africa

South Africa's major contribution to the corporate governance debate has been the **King report**, first published in 1994 and updated in 2002 to take account of developments in South Africa and elsewhere in the world.

The King report differs in emphasis from other guidance by advocating an integrated approach to corporate governance in the interest of a wide range of stakeholders – embracing the social, environmental and economic activities of a company's activities. The report encourages activism by shareholders, business and the financial press and relies heavily on disclosure as a regulatory measure.

3 Role of the board

FAST FORWARD

The board should be responsible for taking major **policy** and **strategic** decisions.

Directors should have a **mix of skills** and their **performance** should be assessed regularly.

Appointments should be conducted by formal procedures administered by a **nomination committee**.

3.1 Scope of role

The King report provides a good summary of the role of the board.

> 'To define the purpose of the company and the values by which the company will perform its daily existence and to identify the stakeholders relevant to the business of the company. The board must then develop a strategy combining all three factors and ensure management implements that strategy.'

If the board is to act effectively, its role must be defined carefully. The Cadbury report suggests that the board should have a **formal schedule of matters** specifically reserved to it for decision. Some would be decisions such as **mergers and takeovers** that are **fundamental** to the business and hence should not be taken just by executive managers. Other decisions would include **acquisitions and disposals of assets of the company** or its subsidiaries that are material to the company and **investments, capital projects, bank borrowing** facilities, **loans** and their repayment, foreign currency transactions, all above a certain size (to be determined by the board).

Other tasks the board should perform include:

- Monitoring the chief executive officer
- Overseeing strategy
- Monitoring risks and control systems
- Monitoring the human capital aspects of the company in regard to succession, morale, training, remuneration etc.
- Ensuring that there is effective communication of its strategic plans, both internally and externally

3.2 Attributes of directors

In order to carry out effective scrutiny, directors need to have **relevant expertise** in industry, company, functional area and governance. The board as a whole needs to contain a **mix of expertise** and show a **balance** between **executive management** and **independent non-executive directors**. The King report stresses the importance also of having a good **demographic balance.**

New and existing directors should also have **appropriate training** to develop the knowledge and skills required.

3.2.1 Nomination committee

In order to ensure that balance of the board is maintained, the board should set up a **nomination committee,** to oversee the process for board appointments and make recommendations to the board. The nomination committee needs to consider the balance between executives and independent non-executives, the skills possessed by the board, the need for continuity and the desirable **size** of the board. Recent corporate governance guidance has laid more stress on the need to attract board members from a **diversity** of backgrounds.

3.3 Possession of necessary information

As we have seen above, in many corporate scandals, the board were not given full information. The UK's Higgs report stresses that it is the responsibility both of the Chair to decide what information should be made available, and directors to satisfy themselves that they have **appropriate information** of **sufficient quality** to make sound judgements. The King report highlights the importance of the board receiving **relevant non-financial information**, going beyond assessing the financial and qualitative performance of the company, looking at **qualitative measures** that involve **broader stakeholder interests**.

3.4 Performance of board

Appraisal of the board's performance is an important control over it. The Higgs report recommends that **performance of the board** should be **assessed** once a year. **Separate appraisal** of the chairman and chief executive should also be carried out, with links to the remuneration process.

3.5 Increased accountability and responsibility

Corporate governance rules have created standards of *'best practice'* that all companies, not just listed ones, are encouraged to follow.

These standards have raised public expectations of directors' conduct, and widened the range of stakeholders taking an interest in a company's governance.

Directors now **face increased risk** of:

- **Legal action**, as they are now more accountable for their actions and responsible to a wider range of stakeholders.

- **Dismissal**, as service contracts are shorter in length and directors must stand for re-election by the shareholders regularly.

Directors have had to alter their behaviour to counter these increased risks. They are devoting more time to meeting the requirements of *'best practice'*, and to investor/stakeholder relations.

However, this would result in director's attention being diverted away from making the company profitable, potentially damaging the long-term success of the business.

3.6 Division of responsibilities

All reports acknowledge the importance of having a division of responsibilities at the head of an organisation. The simplest way to do this is to require the roles of **Chair** and **chief executive** to be held by two different people.

This division has not been made mandatory in the UK. The Cadbury report recommended that if the posts were held by the same individual, there should be a **strong independent element** on the board with a recognised senior member. The UK's Higgs report suggested that a senior independent non-executive director should be appointed who would be available to shareholders who have concerns that were not resolved through the normal channels.

FAST FORWARD

> **Division of responsibilities** at the head of an organisation is most simply achieved by separating the roles of Chair and chief executive.
>
> **Independent non-executive directors** have a key role in governance. Their number and status should mean that their views carry significant weight.

3.7 Non-executive directors

Key term

> **Non-executive directors** have no executive (managerial) responsibilities.

Non-executive directors should provide a **balancing influence**, and play a key role in **reducing conflicts of interest** between management (including executive directors) and shareholders. They should provide reassurance to shareholders, particularly institutional shareholders, that management is acting in the interests of the organisation.

3.7.1 Role of non-executive directors

The UK's Higgs report provides a useful summary of the role of non-executive directors:

(a) **Strategy**: non-executive directors should contribute to, and challenge the direction of, strategy.

(b) **Performance**: non-executive directors should scrutinise the performance of management in meeting goals and objectives, and monitor the reporting of performance.

(c) **Risk**: non-executive directors should satisfy themselves that financial information is accurate and that financial controls and systems of risk management are robust.

(d) **Directors and managers**: non-executive directors are responsible for determining appropriate levels of remuneration for executives, and are key figures in the appointment and removal of senior managers and in succession planning.

3.7.2 Advantages of non-executive directors

Non-executive directors can bring a number of advantages to a board of directors.

(a) They may have **external experience and knowledge which executive directors do not possess.** The experience they bring can be in many different fields. They may be executive directors of other companies, and thus have experience of different ways of approaching corporate governance, internal controls or performance assessment. They can also bring knowledge of markets within which the company operates.

(b) Non-executive directors can provide a **wider perspective** than executive directors who may be more involved in detailed operations.

(c)   Good non-executive directors are often a **comfort factor** for third parties such as investors or suppliers.

(d)   The English businessman Sir John Harvey-Jones has pointed out that there are **certain roles** non-executive directors are well-suited to play. These include 'father-confessor' (being a confidant for the Chair and other directors), 'oil-can' (intervening to make the board run more effectively) and acting as 'high sheriff' (if necessary taking steps to remove the Chair or chief executive).

(e)   The most important advantage perhaps lies in the dual nature of the non-executive director's role. Non-executive directors are **full board members** who are expected to have the level of knowledge that full board membership implies. At the same time they are meant to provide the so-called **strong, independent element** on the board. This should imply that they have the knowledge and detachment to be able to assess fairly the remuneration of executive directors when serving on the remuneration committee, and to be able to discuss knowledgeably with auditors the affairs of the company on the audit committee.

3.7.3 Problems with non-executive directors

Nevertheless there are a number of difficulties connected with the role of non-executive director.

(a)   In many organisations, non-executive directors may **lack independence**. There are in practice a number of ways in which non-executive directors can be linked to a company, as suppliers or customers for example. Even if there is no direct connection, potential non-executive directors are more likely to agree to serve if they admire the company's Chair or its way of operating.

(b)   There may be a **prejudice in certain companies** against widening the recruitment of non-executive directors to include people proposed other than by the board or to include stakeholder representatives.

(c)   High-calibre non-executive directors may gravitate towards the **best-run companies**, rather than companies which are more in need of input from good non-executives.

(d)   Non-executive directors may have **difficulty imposing** their views upon the board. It may be easy to dismiss the views of non-executive directors as irrelevant to the company's needs. This may imply that non-executive directors need good persuasive skills to influence other directors. Moreover, if executive directors are determined to push through a controversial policy, it may prove difficult for the more disparate group of non-executive directors to oppose them effectively.

(e)   Sir John Harvey-Jones has suggested that not enough emphasis is given to the role of non-executive directors in **preventing trouble**, in warning early on of potential problems. Contrawise, when trouble does arise, non-executive directors may be expected to play a major role in rescuing the situation, which they may not be able to do.

(f)   Perhaps the biggest problem which non-executive directors face is the **limited time** they can devote to the role. If they are to contribute valuably, they are likely to have time-consuming other commitments. In the time they have available to act as non-executive directors, they must contribute as knowledgeable members of the full board and fulfil their legal responsibilities as directors. They must also serve on board committees. Their responsibilities mean that their time must be managed effectively, and they must be able to focus on areas where the value they add is greatest.

3.7.4 Number of non–executive directors

Most corporate governance reports acknowledge the importance of having a significant presence of non-executive directors on the board. The question has been whether organisations should follow the broad principles expressed in the Cadbury report:

> 'The board should include non-executive directors of sufficient character and number for their views to carry significant weight.'

or whether they should follow prescriptive guidelines. New York Stock Exchange rules now require listed companies to have a majority of non-executive directors.

3.7.5 Independence of non-executive directors

Various safeguards can be put in place to ensure that non-executive directors remain independent. Those suggested by the corporate governance reports include:

(a)   Non-executive directors should have **no business**, **financial** or other **connection** with the company, apart from fees and shareholdings. Recent reports such as the UK's Higgs report have widened the scope of business connections to include anyone who has been an employee or had a material business relationship over the last few years, or served on the board for more than ten years.

(b)   They should **not take part in share option schemes** and their service should not be pensionable, to maintain their independent status.

(c)   **Appointments** should be for a **specified term** and reappointment should not be automatic. The board as a whole should decide on their nomination and selection.

(d)   Procedures should exist whereby non-executive directors may take **independent advice**, at the company's expense if necessary.

Exam focus point

> In the context of non-executive directors, watch out for threats to, or questions over, their independence. The increased role for non-executive directors is the subject of a question on the Pilot Paper.

3.8 Remuneration

FAST FORWARD

> Directors' remuneration should be set by a **remuneration committee** consisting of independent non-executive directors.
>
> Remuneration should be dependent upon **organisation** and **individual performance**.
>
> Accounts should disclose **remuneration policy** and (in detail) the **packages of individual directors.**

3.8.1 Need for guidance

Directors being paid excessive salaries and bonuses has been seen as one of the major corporate abuses for a large number of years. It is thus inevitable that the corporate governance provisions have targeted it.

The **Greenbury committee** in the UK set out principles which are a good summary of what remuneration policy should involve.

- Directors' remuneration should be set by **independent members** of the board

- Any form of bonus should be related to **measurable performance** or enhanced shareholder value

- There should be **full transparency of directors' remuneration** including pension rights in the annual accounts

3.8.2 Remuneration committee

The remuneration committee plays the key role in establishing remuneration arrangements. In order to be effective, the committee needs both to **determine** the organisation's **general policy** on the **remuneration of executive directors** and **specific remuneration packages** for each director.

Measures to ensure that the committee is **independent** include not just requiring that the committee is staffed by non-executive directors, but also placing limits on the members' connection with the organisation. Measures to ensure independence include stating that the committee should have no personal interests other than as shareholders, no conflicts of interest and no day-to-day involvement in running the business.

3.8.3 Establishing remuneration arrangements

However the committee must also take into account the wider picture. Packages will need to **attract, retain and motivate directors** of sufficient quality, whilst at the same time taking into account shareholders' interests as well. However assessing executive remuneration in an imperfect market for executive skills may prove problematic.

The committee needs to be mindful of the **implications** of **all aspects** of the package. Particularly sensitive areas include terms of **share option schemes**, the phasing of rewards, and the pension consequences of various elements of the remuneration package.

Share options can be used to **align management and shareholder interests**, particularly options held for a long time when value is dependent on long-term performance.

Length of service contracts can be a particular problem. If service contracts are too long, and then have to be terminated prematurely, the perception often arises that the amounts paying off directors for the remainder of the contract are essentially rewards of failure. Corporate governance guidance has indicated that service contracts greater than 12 months need to be carefully considered.

Other issues the remuneration committee have to consider include:

(a) The **differentials at management/director level** (difficult with many layers of management)

(b) The **ability of managers to leave**, taking clients and knowledge to a competitor or their own new business

(c) **Individual performance** and additional work/effort

(d) The company's **overall performance**

3.9 Internal control and audit committees

3.9.1 Internal control

FAST FORWARD

> Boards should regularly review **risk management** and **internal control**, and carry out a wider review annually, the results of which should be disclosed in the accounts.

Note that we will be discussing internal control in detail in Chapter 9 of the text, in the context of specific accounting functions., In this section we shall focus on the role of the board in maintaining internal control.

The USA's Sarbanes-Oxley regulations have forced American boards to look carefully at internal controls and in particular:

(a) **Disclose to the auditors** and **audit committee** deficiencies in the operation of internal controls

(b)   In the accounts, **acknowledge their responsibility** for **internal control**, and assess its effectiveness based on an evaluation within 30 days prior to the report

3.9.2 Review of internal controls

The UK's **Turnbull committee** suggested that review of internal controls should be an **integral part** of the **company's operations**; the board, or board committees, should actively consider reports on control issues from others operating internal controls. We shall look in detail at this review in Chapter 9.

3.9.3 Audit committee

> Audit committees of **independent non-executive directors** should liaise with **external audit, supervise internal audit**, and **review** the **annual accounts** and **internal controls**.

Exam focus point

> Audit committees are very significant because of their responsibilities for supervision and overall review. In particular they should have a close interest in the work of internal audit; the Cadbury report emphasised the importance of internal audit having unrestricted access to the audit committee.

The Cadbury committee summed up the benefits that an audit committee can bring to an organisation.

> 'If they operate effectively, audit committees can bring significant benefits. In particular, they have the potential to:
>
> (a)   improve the quality of financial reporting, by reviewing the financial statements on behalf of the Board;
>
> (b)   create a climate of discipline and control which will reduce the opportunity for fraud;
>
> (c)   enable the non-executive directors to contribute an independent judgement and play a positive role;
>
> (d)   help the finance director, by providing a forum in which he can raise issues of concern, and which he can use to get things done which might otherwise be difficult;
>
> (e)   strengthen the position of the external auditor, by providing a channel of communication and forum for issues of concern;
>
> (f)   provide a framework within which the external auditor can assert his independence in the event of a dispute with management;
>
> (g)   strengthen the position of the internal audit function, by providing a greater degree of independence from management;
>
> (h)   increase public confidence in the credibility and objectivity of financial statements.'

The Cadbury committee warned, however, that the effectiveness of the audit committee may be compromised if it acts as a **'barrier'** between the external auditors and the main (executive) board, or if it allows the main board to **'abdicate its responsibilities** in the audit area' as this will weaken the board's responsibility for reviewing and approving the financial statements. The audit committee must also avoid falling under the influence of a **dominant board member** or getting in the way of exercise of the 'entrepreneurial skills' of the management.

Audit committees are now compulsory for companies trading on the New York Stock Exchange.

In order to be effective, the audit committee has to be well-staffed. The UK's Smith committee recommended that the **audit committee** should consist entirely of **independent non-executive directors** (excluding the Chair), and should include at least one member with **significant and recent financial experience**.

3.10 The main duties of the audit committee

3.10.1 Review of financial statements and systems

The committee should review both the **quarterly** (if published) and **annual accounts**. This should involve assessment of the judgements made about the overall appearance and presentation of the accounts, key accounting policies and major areas of judgement. The Cadbury report lists the other main features the review should cover.

As well as reviewing the accounts, the committee's review should cover the financial reporting and budgetary systems. This involves considering **performance indicators** and **information systems** that allow **monitoring** of the **most significant business and financial risks**, and the progress towards financial objectives. The systems should also highlight developments that may require action (for example large variances), and communicate these to the right people.

3.10.2 Liaison with external auditors

The audit committee's tasks here will include:

(a) Being responsible for the **appointment or removal of the external auditors** as well as fixing their remuneration.

(b) Considering whether there are **any other threats to external auditor independence.** In particular the committee should consider **non-audit services** provided by the external auditors, paying particular attention to whether there may be a **conflict of interest.**

(c) **Discussing the scope of the external audit** prior to the start of the audit. This should include consideration of whether external audit's coverage of all areas and locations of the business is fair, and how much external audit will rely on the work of internal audit.

(d) Acting as a **forum for liaison** between the external auditors, the internal auditors and the finance director.

(e) **Helping the external auditors to obtain the information** they require and in resolving any problems they may encounter.

(f) **Making themselves available** to the external auditors for consultation, with or without the presence of the company's management.

(g) Dealing with any **serious reservations** which the external auditors may express either about the accounts, the records or the quality of the company's management.

3.10.3 Review of internal audit

The review should cover the following aspects of internal audit.

- **Standards** including **objectivity**, **technical knowledge** and **professional standards**
- **Scope** including how much emphasis is given to different types of review
- **Resources**
- **Reporting arrangements**
- **Work plan**, especially review of controls and coverage of high risk areas
- **Liaison** with external auditors
- **Results**

The head of internal audit should have direct access to the audit committee.

3.10.4 Review of internal control

The audit committee should play a significant role in reviewing internal control.

(a)   Committee members can use their own experience to **monitor** continually the **adequacy** of **internal control systems**, focusing particularly on the control environment, management's attitude towards controls and overall management controls.

(b)   The audit committee's review should cover **legal compliance** and **ethics**, for example listing rules or environmental legislation. Committee members should check that there are systems in place to promote compliance. They should review reports on the operation of **codes of conduct** and review violations.

(c)   The committee should also address the risk of **fraud**, ensuring employees are aware of risks and that there are mechanisms in place for staff to report fraud, and fraud to be investigated.

(d)   Each year the committee should be responsible for **reviewing the company's statement on internal controls** prior to its approval by the board.

(e)   The committee should consider the **recommendations of the auditors** in the management letter and management's response. Because the committee's role is ongoing, it can also ensure that recommendations are publicised and see that actions are taken as appropriate.

(f)   The committee may play a **more active supervisory role**, for example reviewing major transactions for reasonableness.

3.10.5 Review of risk management

The audit committee can play an important part in the review of risk recommended by the Turnbull report This includes confirming that there is a **formal policy** in place for **risk management** and that the policy is backed and regularly monitored by the board. They should also **review** the **arrangements**, including training, for ensuring that managers and staff are aware of their responsibilities. They should use their own knowledge of the business to confirm that risk management is updated to **reflect current positions and strategy**.

3.10.6 Investigations

The committee will also be involved in implementing and reviewing the results of **one-off investigations**. The Cadbury report recommends that audit committees should be given specific authority to investigate matters of concern, and in doing so have access to sufficient resources, appropriate information and outside professional help.

4 Reporting on corporate governance

Annual reports must **convey** a **fair and balanced view** of the organisation. They should state whether the organisation has complied with governance regulations and codes, and give specific disclosures about the board, internal control reviews, going concern status and relations with stakeholders.

4.1 Reporting requirements

The London Stock Exchange requires the following general disclosures:

(a)   A **narrative statement** of how companies have **applied the principles** set out in the Combined Code, providing explanations which enable their shareholders to assess how the principles have been applied

(b)   A **statement** as to whether or not they **complied** throughout the accounting period with the **provisions** set out in the Combined Code. Listed companies that did not comply throughout the accounting period with all the provisions must specify the provisions with which they did not comply, and give reasons for non-compliance

The corporate governance reports also suggest that the directors should **explain** their **responsibility for preparing accounts**. They should **report that the business is a going concern**, with supporting assumptions and qualifications as necessary.

In addition further statements may be required depending on the jurisdiction such as:

(a)   Information about the **board of directors**: the composition of the board in the year, information about the independence of the non-executives, frequency of and attendance at board meetings, how the board's performance has been evaluated. The King report suggests a charter of responsibilities should be disclosed

(b)   Brief report on the **remuneration, audit and nomination committees** covering terms of reference, composition and frequency of meetings

(c)   Information about **relations with auditors** including reasons for change and steps taken to ensure auditor objectivity and independence when non-audit services have been provided

(d)   A statement that the directors have reviewed the **effectiveness** of **internal controls**, including risk management

(e)   A statement on relations and **dialogue with shareholders**

(f)   A statement that the company is a **going concern**

(g)   **Sustainability reporting,** defined by the King report as including the nature and extent of social, transformation, ethical, safety, health and environmental management policies and practices

(h)   An **operating and financial review.** The UK's Accounting Standards Board summarised the purpose of such a review:

> 'The Operating and Financial Review (OFR) should set out the directors' analysis of the business, in order to provide to investors a historical and prospective analysis of the reporting entity 'through the eyes of management'. It should include discussion and interpretation of the performance of the business and the structure of its financing, in the context of known or reasonably expected changes in the environment in which it operates.'

Furthermore the information organisations provide cannot just be backward-looking. The King report points out investors want a forward-looking approach and to be able to assess companies against a **balanced scorecard.** Companies will need to weigh the need to keep commercially sensitive information private with the expectations that investors will receive full and frank disclosures.

5 Corporate social responsibility

FAST FORWARD

There is a fundamental split of views about the nature of corporate responsibility.

- The **strong stakeholder view** that a range of goals should be pursued
- The view that the business organisation is a purely **economic force**, subject to law

Expectations about the exercise of **social responsibility** by organisations are subject to the same split of views as corporate ethical responsibility. One definition of corporate social responsibility is that set of actions which the organisation is not obliged to take, taken for the well-being of stakeholders and the public.

BPP
LEARNING MEDIA

5.1 Corporate social responsibility

Businesses, particularly large ones, are subject to increasing expectations that they will exercise **social responsibility**. This is an ill-defined concept, but appears to focus on the provision of specific benefits to society in general, such as charitable donations, the creation or preservation of employment, and spending on environmental improvement or maintenance. A great deal of the pressure is created by the activity of minority action groups and is aimed at businesses because they are perceived to possess extensive resources. The momentum of such arguments is now so great that the notion of social responsibility has become almost inextricably confused with the matter of ethics. It is important to remember the distinction. Social responsibility and ethical behaviour are not the same thing.

In this context, you should remember that a business managed with the sole objective of maximising shareholder wealth can be run in just as ethical a fashion as one in which far wider stakeholder responsibility is assumed. On the other hand, there is no doubt that many large businesses have behaved irresponsibly in the past and some continue to do so.

5.1.1 Strategies for social responsibility

Proactive strategy	A strategy which a business follows where it is prepared to take full responsibility for its actions. A company which discovers a fault in a product and recalls the product without being forced to, before any injury or damage is caused, acts in a proactive way.
Reactive strategy	This involves allowing a situation to continue unresolved until the public, government or consumer groups find out about it.
Defence strategy	This involves minimising or attempting to avoid additional obligations arising from a particular problem.
Accommodation strategy	This approach involves taking responsibility for actions, probably when one of the following happens. • Encouragement from special interest groups • Perception that a failure to act will result in government intervention

5.2 Against corporate social responsibility

Milton Friedman argued against corporate social responsibility along the following lines.

(a)   Businesses do not have responsibilities, only people have responsibilities. Managers in charge of corporations are responsible to the owners of the business, by whom they are employed.

(b)   These employers may have charity as their aim, but 'generally [their aim] will be to make as much money as possible while conforming to the basic rules of the society, both those embodied in law and those embodied in ethical custom.'

(c)   If the statement that a manager has social responsibilities is to have any meaning, 'it must mean that he is to act in some way that is not in the interest of his employers.'

(d)   If managers do this they are, generally speaking, spending the owners' money for purposes other than those they have authorised.

5.3 The stakeholder view

FAST FORWARD

How much organisations consider the interests of other stakeholders will depend on their **legal responsibilities** and their view of stakeholders as partners.

The **stakeholder view** is that many groups have a stake in what the organisation does. This is particularly important in the business context, where shareholders own the business but employees, customers and government also have particularly strong claims to having their interests considered. This is fundamentally an argument derived from **natural law theory** and is based on the notion of individual and collective **rights**.

 Case Study

Some business leaders have made a case for becoming ecologically and socially sustainable:

- 'Institutions that operate so as to capitalise all gain in the interests of the few, while socialising all loss to the detriment of the many, are ethically, socially and operationally unsound ... This must change.' – Dee Hock, Founder, President and CEO Emeritus of Visa International, the credit card organisation.

- 'Far from being a soft issue grounded in emotion and ethics, sustainable development involves cold, rational business logic'. – Robert B. Shapiro, Chairman of Monsanto, the US multinational.

- 'The gap between rhetoric and reality is increasing. I would tell multinationals they have to watch out ... they are much more vulnerable because they have to be accountable to the public everyday.' – Thilo Bode, Executive Director of Greenpeace.

- Explaining his company's forays into renewable energy and enhanced support for the communities where it does business: 'These efforts have nothing to do with charity, and everything to do with our long-term self interests ... our shareholders want performance today, and tomorrow, and the day after.' – Sir John Browne, CEO of British Petroleum/Amoco.

6 Ethics, law, governance and social responsibility

6.1 A brief recap

This chapter has developed the concept of corporate governance and business social responsibility. Since the management and owners of companies are not necessarily the same people, it is important for management to be encouraged to act in the best interests of the owners and other stakeholders.

6.2 Interaction of ethics, law, governance and social responsibility

By pulling together all we have already studied, we find

- Ethics are values and principles that society **expects** companies and individuals to follow
- Laws are rules that a company and individuals **must** follow

Corporate governance requirements and social responsibility may be viewed as additional rules and guidance for companies and individuals. They bridge the gap between what the law requires and what society expects. This is because the law does not always encourage them to behave in an ethical or socially responsible manner.

6.2.1 Levels of regulation

One way of examining how the subjects are related is to look at how regulated they are.

The relationship between law, governance, social responsibility and ethics			
Law	**Corporate governance**	**Social responsibility**	**Ethics**
Rules individuals and companies **must follow.** The **minimum level of behaviour** society allows.	**Publicly listed companies only** are regulated. Others are **encouraged** to follow 'best practice'.	**No regulation.** Individuals and companies have a free choice. **Some social pressure** to act in a socially responsible manner.	**Values and principles.** Individuals and companies are **expected to follow.** Adopting an ethical position is down to free choice.
More regulation, less freedom of choice.		Less regulation more freedom of choice.	

From the table above we can see that the law is highly regulated, corporate governance is less regulated and, social responsibility and ethics have no regulation as adoption is down to free choice.

6.2.2 Effect on corporate behaviour

Perhaps more importantly, we should examine the effect each has on corporate behaviour.

An important point to remember is that companies do not make decisions by themselves. Human individuals (usually the directors) make the significant policy choices.

The following diagram demonstrates the interaction of law, ethics and social responsibility on the company.

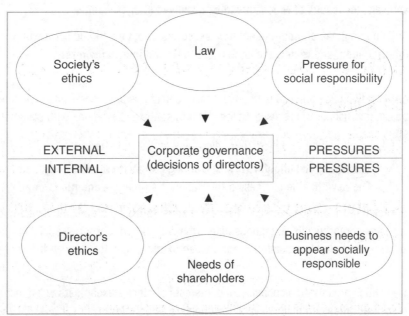

We can see that many factors will influence the behaviour of a company. The main external influence is the law as it sets the minimum level of behaviour expected. Society's ethical views and needs for social responsibility will have an influence as companies will respect them as far as necessary to remain profitable.

Directors are greatly influenced by the need to deliver the results that shareholders require, for example increasing the company's share price or dividend. To achieve this may require breaking their own personal ethical beliefs.

Remember, businesses do not necessarily have to act ethically. In most cases they are run for the benefit of the owners (the shareholders) rather than for the benefit of society as a whole.

Chapter Roundup

- Most corporate governance reports are based around the principles of **integrity, accountability, independence** and **good management** but there is disagreement on how much these principles need to be supplemented by detailed rules.

- Good corporate governance involves **risk management** and **internal control, accountability** to stakeholders and other shareholders and conducting business in an **ethical and effective way.**

- The board should be responsible for taking major **policy** and **strategic** decisions.

    Directors should have a **mix of skills** and their **performance** should be assessed regularly.

    Appointments should be conducted by formal procedures administered by a **nomination committee.**

- **Division of responsibilities** at the head of an organisation is most simply achieved by separating the roles of chairman and chief executive.

    Independent non-executive directors have a key role in governance. Their number and status should mean that their views carry significant weight.

- Directors' remuneration should be set by a **remuneration committee** consisting of independent non-executive directors.

    Remuneration should be dependent upon **organisation** and **individual performance.**

    Accounts should disclose **remuneration policy** and (in detail) the **packages of individual directors.**

- Boards should regularly review **risk management** and **internal control**, and carry out a wider review annually, the results of which should be disclosed in the accounts.

- Audit committees of **independent non-executive directors** should liaise with **external audit, supervise internal audit**, and **review** the **annual accounts** and **internal controls.**

- Annual reports must **convey** a **fair and balanced view** of the organisation. They should state whether the organisation has complied with governance regulations and codes, and give specific disclosures about the board, internal control reviews, going concern status and relations with stakeholders.

- There is a fundamental split of views about the nature of corporate responsibility.

    - The **strong stakeholder view** that a range of goals should be pursued
    - The view that the business organisation is a purely **economic force**, subject to law

    Expectations about the exercise of **social responsibility** by organisations are subject to the same split of views as corporate ethical responsibility. One definition of corporate social responsibility is that set of actions which the organisation is not obliged to take, taken for the well-being of stakeholders and the public.

- How much organisations consider the interests of other stakeholders will depend on their **legal responsibilities** and their view of stakeholders as partners.

Quick Quiz

1   Define corporate governance.

2   Give four examples of symptoms of poor corporate governance.

3   How can an organisation ensure that there is a division of responsibilities at its highest level?

4   Audit committees are generally staffed by executive directors.

   True   ☐

   False   ☐

5   List the main responsibilities of audit committees.

6   Which two of the following are symptoms of poor corporate governance

   A   Lack of board involvement
   B   Bonuses for directors
   C   The finance director also performing the role of company secretary
   D   Inadequate supervision

7   What is 'the stakeholder view'?

8   What are the four strategies for social responsibility?

Answers to quick quiz

1 The system by which organisations are directed and controlled.

2 • Domination by a single individual
   • Lack of board involvement
   • Inadequate control function
   • Inadequate supervision
   • Lack of independent scrutiny
   • Lack of contact with shareholders
   • Excessive emphasis on short-term profitability
   • Misleading accounts

3 • Splitting the roles of chair and chief executive
   • Appointing a senior independent non-executive director
   • Having a strong independent element on the board with a recognised leader

4 False. They should be staffed by non-executive directors (excluding the chair).

5 • Review of financial statements and systems
   • Liaison with external auditors
   • Review of internal audit
   • Review of internal control
   • Review of risk management
   • Investigations

6 A. Lack of board involvement. D. Inadequate supervision.

7 This view is that many groups have a stake in what the organisation does.

8 • Proactive strategy
   • Reactive strategy
   • Defence strategy
   • Accommodation strategy

Part B
Key environmental influences

The macro-economic environment

Topic list	Syllabus reference
1 Government policies and objectives	B2 (a) (d)
2 Fiscal policy	B2 (e)
3 Monetary policy	B2 (e)
4 The determination of national income	B2 (b)
5 The business cycle	B2 (b)
6 Inflation and its consequences	B2 (c)(i)
7 Unemployment	B2 (c)(ii)
8 The objective of economic growth	B2 (c)(iii)
9 The balance of payments	B2 (c)(iv)

Introduction

In this chapter we present an overview of the goals of macroeconomic policy concentrating on fiscal policy and monetary policy.

We consider the role of fiscal policy (**Section 2**) in affecting demand and examine the types of taxation and the role of taxation in creating incentives, followed by a discussion of the conduct of monetary policy (**Section 3**).

In macroeconomics we are concerned with spending, investment, price levels, employment and output in the economy as a whole (**Section 4**).

Broadly speaking, macroeconomists divide into the two camps of the Keynesians and the monetarists. These two camps have had differing ideas about how national income can be made to grow, how full employment can be achieved and how booms and slumps of trade cycles can be smoothed out (**Section 5**).

The Keynesians and monetarists also differ in their views about the causes of inflation, and the effectiveness of government measures to stimulate the economy (**Sections 6-8**).

The balance of payments (**Section 9**) is a statistical 'accounting' record of a country's international trade transactions (the purchase and sale of goods and services) and capital transactions (the acquisition and disposal of assets and liabilities) with other countries during a period of time.

Study guide

		Intellectual level
B2	**Macro-economic factors**	
(a)	Define macro-economic policy.	1
(b)	Explain the main determinants of the level of business activity in the economy and how variations in the level of business activity affect individuals, households and businesses.	1
(c)	Explain the impact of economic issues on the individual, the household and the business:	1
(i)	Inflation	
(ii)	Unemployment	
(iii)	Stagnation	
(iv)	International payments disequilibrium.	
(d)	Describe the main types of economic policy that may be implemented by government and supra-national bodies to maximise economic welfare.	1
(e)	Recognise the impact of fiscal and monetary policy measures on the individual, the household and businesses.	1

Exam guide

You might consider macro-economic factors to be a peripheral area of this syllabus, but the detail in this chapter does lend itself to the type of questions which are set under this examination. On the Pilot Paper there were nine marks available for questions covering macro-economics topics.

1 Government policies and objectives

Macro-economics is the study of the aggregated effects of the decisions of individual economic units (such as households or businesses). It looks at a complete national economy, or the international economic system as a whole.

FAST FORWARD

Macroeconomic policy objectives relate to economic growth, inflation, unemployment and the balance of payments.

1.1 Economic policy objectives

All modern governments are expected to manage their national economies to some extent. Electorates generally suppose that government action can support or hinder the growth of prosperity and look to them for serviceable macroeconomic policies. There are four main objectives of economic policy, though debate continues about their relative priority.

(a) **To achieve economic growth**, and growth in national income per head of the population. Growth implies an increase in national income in real terms. Increases caused by price inflation are not real increases at all.

(b) **To control price inflation** (to achieve stable prices). This has become a central objective of UK economic policy in recent years.

(c) **To achieve full employment**. Full employment does not mean that everyone who wants a job has one all the time, but it does mean that unemployment levels are low, and involuntary unemployment is short-term.

(d) **To achieve a balance between exports and imports** (on the country's balance of payments accounts) over a period of years. The wealth of a country relative to others, a country's creditworthiness as a borrower, and the goodwill between countries in international relations might all depend on the achievement of an external balance over time.

1.2 Government spending

Governments spend money. Expenditure must be allocated between departments and functions such as health, social services, education, transport, defence, grants to industry, and so on.

- Wages and salaries to employees
- Materials, supplies and services
- Capital equipment
- Interest on borrowings and repayments of capital
- Benefits and pensions to those entitled to such

1.3 Significance of government tax and spending decisions to companies

(a) Expenditure decisions by government affect **suppliers to the government** such as producers of defence equipment, medicines and medical equipment, school text books.

(b) There is a **'knock-on' effect** throughout the economy of government spending; that is, companies might supply companies which in turn supply the government.

(c) Taxation affects **consumers' purchasing power**.

(d) **Taxes** on company profits and tax allowances affect the after-tax return on investment that companies achieve.

(e) **Investment** by the public sector will tend to be directed towards activities in which the public sector is involved or on fulfilling social needs. Hence industries in these fields will benefit.

(f) Public sector investment might have a longer **time scale** (eg health) or have less quantifiable economic benefits (eg education) than the private sector is able to cope with.

1.4 Economic planning

At one time, many people believed the government should plan economic activity in detail. This is now out of favour, and has been discredited as a result of the failure of communism in the eastern bloc and China and its unhappy history in Western Europe. In this model, government is a **director** of economic activity.

Economic planning on a lesser scale, with the government as an **enabler** of private sector activity and as corrector of market imperfections, still has a role, however.

(a) Government's most important economic role is the legal system relating to business. Law relating to property, contracts in corporation, competition, employment and so on provides a framework which enables businesses to be done with confidence.

(b) Government also has a responsibility for macro-economic management. Such management, like to legal framework, should provide stable conditions in which business can operate with confidence.

(c)   Governments can raise **trade barriers** to protect domestic industry, although the trend has been to lower such barriers.

(d)   Governments can **subsidise exports, or promote them** in other ways (eg by trade missions, export credit insurance and so forth).

(e)   Governments can also encourage **inward investment** by foreign countries. This has been UK government policy since the early 1980s, and has had particular success in attracting investment by Japanese companies.

(f)   **Regional policy** is an example of small scale economic planning.

   (i)   Tax incentives or grants for investing in certain areas

   (ii)   Relaxing or enforcing town and county planning restrictions

   (iii)   Developing **new towns** to reduce population pressure in major conurbations, although this policy is perhaps a thing of the past

   (iv)   Promotion of infrastructure developments (eg roads, rail, airports)

The government also attempts to influence businesses by persuasion and exhortation.

1.5 State influences over organisations

Government influences are outlined in the diagram below.

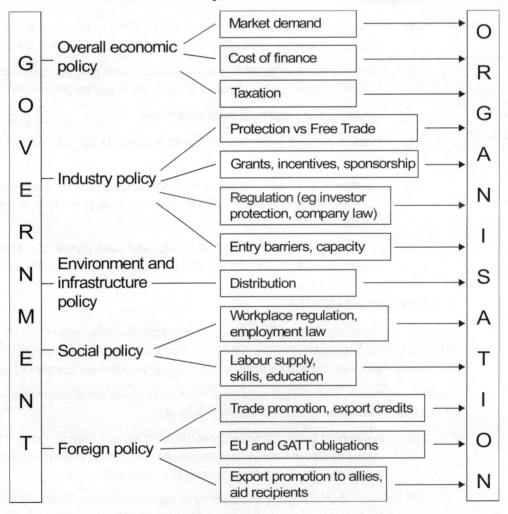

1.6 Government influence over commercial decisions

Decision	Comment
Output capacity	Grants or tax incentives to invest
Competition	• Forbid or allow takeovers/mergers • Outlaw anti-competitive practices • Opening markets to new entrants (eg gas)
Monopolies	Break them up; regulate them
Sales demand	Government policy affects demand

1.7 Government influence over operational decisions

Decision	Comment
Health and safety	Legislation, regulations
Employment	Equal opportunities legislation
Consumers	Product safety standards
Tax	Sales tax procedures, income tax, accounting control

2 Fiscal policy

FAST FORWARD

Fiscal policy provides a method of managing **aggregate demand** in the economy.

2.1 Fiscal policy and the Budget

A feature of fiscal policy is that a government must **plan** what it wants to spend, and so how much it needs to raise in income or by borrowing. It needs to make a plan in order to establish how much taxation there should be, what form the taxes should take and so which sectors of the economy (firms or households, high income earners or low income earners) the money should come from. This formal planning of fiscal policy is usually done once a year and is set out in **the Budget**.

The two components of the budget which the government determines and through which it exercises its fiscal policy are:

(a) **Expenditure**. The government, at a national and local level, spends money to provide goods and services, such as a health service, public education, a police force, roads, public buildings and so on, and to pay its administrative work force. It may also, perhaps, provide finance to encourage investment by private industry, for example by means of grants.

(b) **Revenues**. Expenditure must be financed, and the government must have income. Most government income comes from **taxation**, albeit some income is obtained from **direct charges** to users of government services such as National Health Service charges.

A third element of the fiscal policy is:

(c) **Borrowing**. To the extent that a government's expenditure exceeds its income it must borrow to make up the difference. The amount that the government must borrow each year is now known as the **Public Sector Net Cash Requirement (PSNCR)** in the UK Its former name was **Public Sector Borrowing Requirement (PSBR).** Where the government borrows from has an impact on the effectiveness of fiscal policy.

2.2 Budget surplus and budget deficit

> If a government decides to use fiscal policy to influence demand in the economy, it can choose either expenditure changes or tax changes as its policy instrument.

Suppose, for example, that the government wants to stimulate demand in the economy.

If the government kept its own spending at the same level, but **reduced levels of taxation**, it would **stimulate demand** in the economy because firms and households would have more of their own money after tax for consumption or saving/investing.

(a) **It can increase demand directly by spending more itself** – eg on the health service or education, and by employing more people itself.

    (i) This extra spending could be financed by higher taxes, but this would reduce spending by the private sector of the economy because the private sector's after-tax income would be lower.

    (ii) The extra government spending could also be financed by extra government borrowing. Just as individuals can borrow money for spending, so too can a government.

(b) **It can increase demand indirectly by reducing taxation** and so allowing firms and individuals more after-tax income to spend (or save).

    (i) Cuts in taxation can be matched by cuts in government spending, in which case total demand in the economy will not be stimulated significantly, if at all.

    (ii) Alternatively, tax cuts can be financed by more government borrowing.

Just as aggregate demand in the economy can be boosted by either more government spending or by tax cuts, financed in either case by a higher PSNCR, so too can demand in the economy be reduced by cutting government spending or by raising taxes, and using the savings or higher income to cut government borrowing.

Expenditure changes and tax changes are not mutually exclusive options, of course. A government has several options.

(a) Increase expenditure and reduce taxes, with these changes financed by a higher PSNCR
(b) Reduce expenditure and increase taxes, with these changes reducing the size of the PSNCR
(c) Increase expenditure and partly or wholly finance this extra spending with higher taxes
(d) Reduce expenditure and use these savings to reduce taxes

When a government's income exceeds its expenditure, and there is a negative PSNCR or **Public Sector Debt Repayment (PSDR),** we say that the government is running a **budget surplus**. When a government's expenditure exceeds its income, so that it must borrow to make up the difference, there is a PSNCR and we say that the government is running a **budget deficit**.

2.3 Functions of taxation

Taxation has several functions.

(a) **To raise revenues for the government** as well as for local authorities and similar public bodies (eg the European Union).

(b) **To discourage certain activities regarded as undesirable**. The imposition of Development Land Tax in the United Kingdom in the mid-70s (since abolished) was partially in response to growth in property speculation.

(c) **To cause certain products to be priced to take into account their social costs**. For example, smoking entails certain social costs, including especially the cost of hospital care for those suffering from smoking-related diseases, and the government sees fit to make the price of tobacco reflect these social costs.

(d) **To redistribute income and wealth**. Higher rates of tax on higher incomes will serve to redistribute income. UK inheritance tax goes some way towards redistributing wealth.

(e) **To protect industries from foreign competition.** If the government levies a duty on all imported goods much of the duty will be passed on to the consumer in the form of higher prices, making imported goods more expensive. This has the effect of transferring a certain amount of demand from imported goods to domestically produced goods.

(f) **To provide a stabilising effect on national income**. Taxation reduces the effect of the multiplier, and so can be used to dampen upswings in a trade cycle – ie higher taxation when the economy shows signs of a boom will slow down the growth of money GNP and so take some inflationary pressures out of the economy.

2.4 Qualities of a good tax

Features of a good tax can be identified.

- **Flexibility**. It should be adjustable so that rates may be altered up or down.
- **Efficiency**. It should not harm initiative, but evasion should be difficult.
- It should attain its purpose **without distorting economic behaviour**.

Note the following distinctions.

(a) A **regressive tax** takes a higher **proportion** of a poor person's salary than of a rich person's. Television licences and road tax are examples of regressive taxes since they are the same for all people.

(b) A **proportional tax** takes the **same proportion** of income in tax from all levels of income. Schedule E income tax with a basic of tax at 23% is proportional tax, but only within a limited range of income.

(c) A **progressive tax** takes a **higher proportion** of income in tax as income rises. Income tax as a whole is progressive, since the first part of an individual's income is tax-free due to personal allowances and the rate of tax increases in steps in the UK from 20p in £1 to 40p in £1 as taxable income rises.

FAST FORWARD

Direct taxes have the quality of being **progressive** or **proportional**. Income tax is usually progressive, with high rates of tax charged on higher bands of taxable income. **Indirect taxes** can be **regressive**, when the taxes are placed on essential commodities or commodities consumed by poorer people in greater quantities.

2.5 Direct and indirect taxes

FAST FORWARD

A government must decide how it intends to raise tax revenues, from **direct or indirect taxes**, and in what proportions tax revenues will be raised from each source.

A **direct tax** is paid direct by a person to the Revenue authority. Examples of direct taxes in the UK are income tax, corporation tax, capital gains tax and inheritance tax. A direct tax can be levied on income and profits, or on wealth. Direct taxes tend to be progressive or proportional taxes. They are also usually unavoidable, which means that they must be paid by everyone.

An **indirect tax** is collected by the Revenue authority from an intermediary (a supplier) who then attempts to pass on the tax to consumers in the price of goods they sell. Indirect taxes are of two types.

Key terms

> A **specific tax** is charged as a *fixed sum* per unit sold.
>
> An **ad valorem tax** is charged as a *fixed percentage* of the price of the good.

3 Monetary policy

FAST FORWARD

> **Monetary policy** uses money supply, interest rates or credit controls to influence aggregate demand.

Key terms

> **Monetary policy**: government policy on the money supply, the monetary system, interest rates, exchange rates and the availability of credit.
>
> **Fiscal policy**: government policy on taxation, public borrowing and public spending.
>
> Monetary and fiscal policies attempt to attain the macroeconomic policy objectives by influencing aggregate demand.

Question

Effects of policy

How are businesses affected by fiscal and monetary policy?

Answer

Businesses are affected by a government's tax policy (eg corporation tax rates) and monetary policy (high interest rates increase the cost of investment, and depress consumer demand).

3.1 Objectives of monetary policy

Exam focus point

> Questions on monetary policy will often focus on its impact on the business sector.

Monetary policy can be used as a means towards achieving ultimate economic objectives for inflation, the balance of trade, full employment and real economic growth. To achieve these **ultimate objectives**, the authorities will set **intermediate objectives** for monetary policy.

In the UK, the ultimate objective of monetary policy in recent years has been principally to reduce the rate of inflation to a sustainable low level. The intermediate objectives of monetary policy have related to the level of interest rates, growth in the money supply, the exchange rate for sterling, the expansion of credit and the growth of national income.

3.2 The money supply as a target of monetary policy

To monetarist economists, the **money supply** is an obvious intermediate target of economic policy. This is because they claim that an increase in the money supply will raise prices and incomes and this in turn will raise the demand for money to spend.

When such a policy is first introduced, the short-term effect would be unpredictable for three reasons.

    (a)   The effect on interest rates might be erratic.

(b)   There might be a time lag before anything can be done. For example, it takes time to cut government spending and hence to use reduction in government borrowing as an instrument of monetary policy.

(c)   There might be a time lag before control of the money supply alters expectations about inflation and wage demands.

Growth in the money supply, if it is a monetary policy target, should therefore be a **medium-term target**.

3.3 Interest rates as a target for monetary policy

The authorities might decide that **interest rates** – the price of money – should be a target of monetary policy. This would be appropriate if it is considered that there is a direct relationship between interest rates and the level of expenditure in the economy, or between interest rates and the rate of inflation.

A rise in interest rates will raise the price of borrowing in the internal economy for both companies and individuals. If companies see the rise as relatively permanent, rates of return on investments will become less attractive and **investment plans may be curtailed**. Corporate profits will fall as a result of higher interest payments. Companies will reduce inventory levels as the cost of having money tied up in inventory rises. Individuals should be expected to reduce or postpone consumption in order to reduce borrowings, and should become less willing to borrow for house purchase.

Although it is generally accepted that there is likely to be a connection between interest rates and investment (by companies) and consumer expenditure, **the connection is not a stable and predictable one**, and interest rate changes are only likely to affect the level of expenditure after a **considerable time lag**.

Other effects of raising interest rates

(a)   High interest rates will keep the value of sterling higher than it would otherwise be. This will keep the cost of exports high, and so discourage the purchase of exports. This may be necessary to protect the balance of payments and to prevent 'import-cost-push' inflation. UK manufacturers have complained bitterly about this effect and BMW cited it as one of the reasons for disposing of Rover.

(b)   High interest rates will attract foreign investors into sterling investments, and so provide capital inflows which help to finance the large UK balance of payments deficit.

An important reason for pursuing an interest rate policy is that the authorities are able to influence interest rates much more effectively and rapidly than they can influence other policy targets, such as the money supply or the volume of credit. As we have already seen, in 1997 the new Labour Government of the UK placed responsibility for interest rate decisions with the Bank of England, which sets rates with the objective of meeting the government's inflation target.

3.4 The exchange rate as a target of monetary policy

Why the exchange rate is a target

(a)   If the exchange rate falls, exports become cheaper to overseas buyers and so more competitive in export markets. Imports will become more expensive and so less competitive against goods produced by manufacturers at home. A fall in the exchange rate might therefore be good for a domestic economy, by giving a **stimulus to exports** and **reducing demand for imports**.

(b)   An increase in the exchange rate will have the opposite effect, with dearer exports and cheaper imports. If the exchange rate rises and imports become cheaper, there should be a reduction in the rate of domestic inflation. A fall in the exchange rate, on the other hand, tends to increase the cost of imports and adds to the rate of domestic inflation.

When a country's economy is heavily dependent on overseas trade, as the UK economy is, it might be appropriate for government policy to establish a target exchange value for the domestic currency. However, the exchange rate is dependent on both the domestic rate of inflation and the level of interest rates. Targets for the exchange rate cannot be achieved unless the rate of inflation at home is first brought under control.

3.5 Targets and indicators

An economic indicator provides information about economic conditions and might be used as a way of judging the performance of government.

(a) A **leading indicator** is one which gives an advance indication of what will happen to the economy in the future. It can therefore be used to predict future conditions. For example, a fall in the value of sterling by, say, 2% might be used to predict what will happen to the balance of payments and to the rate of inflation.

(b) A **coincident indicator** is one which gives an indication of changes in economic conditions **at the same time** that these changes are occurring. For example, if the narrow money supply rises by 5%, this might 'confirm' that the rate of increase in GDP over the same period of time has been about the same, 5% in 'money' terms.

(c) A **lagging indicator**, you will have guessed, is one which 'lags behind' the economic cycle. Unemployment, to take an example, often continues to rise until after a recession has ended and only starts to fall again after recovery has begun.

There are a number of monetary indicators.

(a) The size of the money stock

(b) Interest rates such as the banks' base rate of interest, the Treasury bill rate and the yield on long-dated government securities

(c) The exchange rate against the US dollar, or the trade-weighted exchange rate index

(d) The size of the government's borrowing

(e) Government borrowing as a percentage of Gross Domestic Product

3.6 Monetary policy and fiscal policy

Monetary policy can be made to act as a subsidiary support to fiscal policy and demand management. Since budgets are once-a-year events, a government must use non-fiscal measures in between budgets to make adjustments to its control of the economy.

(a) A policy of **low interest rates** or the absence of any form of credit control might stimulate bank lending, which in turn would increase expenditure (demand) in the economy.

(b) **High interest rates might** act as a deterrent to borrowing and so reduce spending in the economy.

(c) Strict **credit controls** (for example restrictions on bank lending) might be introduced to reduce lending and so reduce demand in the economy.

Alternatively, monetary policy might be given prominence over fiscal policy as the most effective approach by a government to achieving its main economic policy objectives. This might not however be possible: from 1990 to 1992, for example, monetary policy in the UK was heavily constrained by the need to set interest rates at levels which maintained sterling's position in the European exchange rate mechanism (ERM). From 1997, the Government has given the Bank of England the role of setting interest rates, although it is still the government which sets an inflation target. If the UK joined a single European currency, interest rates would largely be determined at the European level.

3.7 Monetary policy, inflation control and economic growth

Monetarists argue that monetary control will put the brake on inflation, but how does this help the economy? We might argue like this.

(a) High inflation increases **economic uncertainty**. Bringing inflation under control will restore business confidence and help international trade by stabilising the exchange rate.

(b) A resurgence of business confidence through lower interest rates (due to less uncertainty and lower inflation) will **stimulate investment** and real output.

(c) A **controlled growth in the money supply** will provide higher incomes for individuals to purchase the higher output.

4 The determination of national income

FAST FORWARD

Equilibrium national income is determined using aggregate supply and aggregate demand analysis.

4.1 Aggregate demand and supply equilibrium

Aggregate demand (AD) is total planned or desired consumption demand in the economy for consumer goods and services and also for capital goods, no matter whether the buyers are households, firms or government.

4.2 Full-employment national income

If one aim of a country's economic policy is full employment, then the ideal equilibrium level of national income will be where AD and AS are in balance at the full employment level of national income, without any inflationary gap – in other words, where aggregate demand at current price levels is exactly sufficient to encourage firms to produce at an output capacity where the country's resources are fully employed.

4.3 Inflationary gaps

In a situation where resources are already fully employed, there may be an **inflationary gap** since increases in demand will cause price changes, but no variations in real output.

A shift in demand or supply will not only change the national income, it will also change price levels.

Example

If you are not sure about this point, a simple numerical example might help to explain it better. Suppose that in Ruritania there is full employment and all other economic resources are fully employed. The country produces 1,000 units of output with these resources. Total expenditure (that is, aggregate demand) in the economy is 100,000 Ruritanian dollars, or 100 dollars per unit. The country does not have any external trade, and so it cannot obtain extra goods by importing them. Because of pay rises and easier credit terms for consumers, total expenditure now rises to 120,000 Ruritanian dollars. The economy is fully employed, and cannot produce more than 1,000 units. If expenditure rises by 20%, to buy the same number of units, it follows that prices must rise by 20% too. In other words, when an economy is at full employment, any increase in aggregate demand will result in price inflation.

4.4 Deflationary gap

In a situation **where there is unemployment of resources** there is said to be a **deflationary gap**. Prices are fairly constant and real output changes as aggregate demand varies. A deflationary gap can be described as the extent to which the aggregate demand function will have to shift upward to produce the full employment level of national income.

4.5 Stagflation

In the 1970s there was a problem with **stagflation**: a combination of unacceptably high unemployment and unacceptably high inflation. One of the causes was diagnosed as the major rises in the price of crude oil that took place. The cost of energy rose and this had the effect of rendering some production unprofitable

National income fell, and both prices and unemployment rose. Any long term major increase in costs (a **price shock**) is likely to have this effect.

4.6 Summary

An equilibrium national income will be reached where aggregate demand equals aggregate supply. There are two possible equilibria.

(a)   One is at a level of demand which exceeds the productive capabilities of the economy at full employment, and there is insufficient output capacity in the economy to meet demand at current prices. There is then an **inflationary gap**.

(b)   The other is at a level of employment which is below the full employment level of national income. The difference between actual national income and full employment national income is called a **deflationary gap**. To create full employment, the total national income (expenditure) must be increased by the amount of the deflationary gap.

5 The business cycle

FAST FORWARD

> **Business cycles** or **trade cycles** are the continual sequence of rapid growth in national income, followed by a slow-down in growth and then a fall in national income. After this recession comes growth again, and when this has reached a peak, the cycle turns into recession once more.

5.1 Phases in the business cycle

Four main phases of the business cycle can be distinguished.

- Recession
- Depression
- Recovery
- Boom

Recession tends to occur quickly, while recovery is typically a slower process.

5.2 Diagrammatic explanation

At point A in the diagram below, the economy is entering a recession. In the recession phase, consumer demand falls and many investment projects already undertaken begin to look unprofitable. Orders will be cut, inventory levels will be reduced and business failures will occur as firms find themselves unable to sell their goods. Production and employment will fall. The general price level will begin to fall. Business and consumer confidence are diminished and investment remains low, while the economic outlook appears to be poor. Eventually, in the absence of any stimulus to aggregate demand, a period of full **depression** sets in and the economy will reach point B.

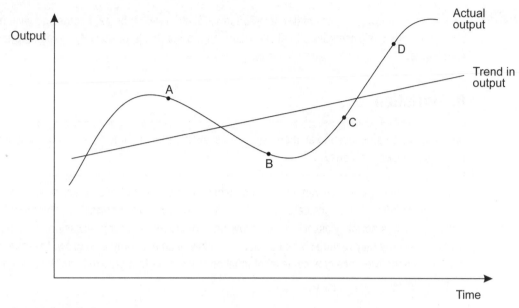

The business cycle

5.3 Analysis of the phases

Recession can begin relatively quickly because of the speed with which the effects of declining demand will be felt by businesses suffering a loss in sales revenue. The knock-on effects of destocking and cutting back on investment exacerbate the situation and add momentum to the recession. Recovery can be slow to begin because of the effect of recession on levels of confidence.

At point C the economy has reached the **recovery** phase of the cycle. Once begun, the phase of recovery is likely to quicken as confidence returns. Output, employment and income will all begin to rise. Rising production, sales and profit levels will lead to optimistic business expectations, and new investment will be more readily undertaken. The rising level of demand can be met through increased production by bringing existing capacity into use and by hiring unemployed labour. The average price level will remain constant or begin to rise slowly.

In the recovery phase, decisions to purchase new materials and machinery may lead to benefits in efficiency from new technology. This can enhance the relative rate of economic growth in the recovery phase once it is under way.

As recovery proceeds, the output level climbs above its trend path, reaching point D, in the **boom** phase of the cycle. During the boom, capacity and labour will become fully utilised. This may cause bottlenecks in some industries which are unable to meet increases in demand, for example because they have no spare capacity or they lack certain categories of skilled labour, or they face shortages of key material inputs. Further rises in demand will, therefore, tend to be met by increases in prices rather than by increases in production. In general, business will be profitable, with few firms facing losses. Expectations of the future may be very optimistic and the level of investment expenditure high.

It can be argued that wide fluctuations in levels of economic activity are damaging to the overall economic well-being of society. The inflation and speculation which accompanies boom periods may be inequitable in their impact on different sections of the population, while the bottom of the trade cycle may bring high unemployment. Governments generally seek to stabilise the economic system, trying to avoid the distortions of a widely fluctuating trade cycle.

6 Inflation and its consequences

FAST FORWARD

High rates of **inflation** are harmful to an economy. Inflation redistributes income and wealth. Uncertainty about the value of money makes business planning more difficult. Constantly changing prices impose extra costs.

6.1 Inflation

Key term

> **Inflation** is the name given to an increase in price levels generally. It is also manifest in the decline in the purchasing power of money.

Historically, there have been very few periods when inflation has not been present. We discuss below why high rates of inflation are considered to be harmful. However, it is important to remember that **deflation** (falling prices) is normally associated with low rates of growth and even recession. It would seem that a healthy economy may require some inflation. Certainly, if an economy is to grow, the money supply must expand, and the presence of a low level of inflation will ensure that growth is not hampered by a shortage of liquid funds.

6.2 Why is inflation a problem?

An economic policy objective which now has a central place in the policy approaches of the governments of many developed countries is that of stable prices. Why is a *high* rate of price inflation harmful and undesirable?

6.2.1 Redistribution of income and wealth

Inflation leads to a redistribution of income and wealth in ways which may be undesirable. Redistribution of wealth might take place from accounts payable to accounts receivable. This is because debts lose 'real' value with inflation. For example, if you owed $1,000, and prices then doubled, you would still owe $1,000, but the **real value** of your debt would have been halved. In general, in times of inflation those with economic power tend to gain at the expense of the weak, particularly those on fixed incomes.

6.2.2 Balance of payments effects

If a country has a higher rate of inflation than its major trading partners, its exports will become relatively expensive and imports relatively cheap. As a result, the balance of trade will suffer, affecting employment in exporting industries and in industries producing import-substitutes. Eventually, the exchange rate will be affected.

6.2.3 Uncertainty of the value of money and prices

If the rate of inflation is imperfectly anticipated, no one has certain knowledge of the true rate of inflation. As a result, no one has certain knowledge of the value of money or of the real meaning of prices. If the rate of inflation becomes excessive, and there is 'hyperinflation', this problem becomes so exaggerated that money becomes worthless, so that people are unwilling to use it and are forced to resort to barter. In less extreme circumstances, the results are less dramatic, but the same problem exists. As prices convey less information, the process of resource allocation is less efficient and rational decision-making is almost impossible.

6.2.4 Resource costs of changing prices

A fourth reason to aim for stable prices is the resource cost of frequently changing prices. In times of high inflation substantial labour time is spent on planning and implementing price changes. Customers may also have to spend more time making price comparisons if they seek to buy from the lowest cost source.

6.2.5 Economic growth and investment

It is sometimes claimed that inflation is harmful to a country's economic growth and level of investment. A study by *Robert Barro* (*Bank of England Quarterly Bulletin*, May 1995) examined whether the evidence available supports this view. Barro found from data covering over 100 countries from 1960 to 1990 that, on average, an increase in inflation of ten percentage points per year reduced the growth rate of real GDP per capita by 0.2 to 0.3 percentage points per year, and lowered the ratio of investment to GDP by 0.4 to 0.6 percentage points. Although the adverse influence of inflation on economic growth and investment appears small, this could affect a country's standard of living fairly significantly over the long term.

6.3 Consumer price indices

We have already referred to the way in which inflation erodes the real value of money. In order to measure changes in the real value of money as a single figure, we need to group all goods and services into a single price index.

A consumer price index is based on a chosen 'basket' of items which consumers purchase. A weighting is decided for each item according to the average spending on the item by consumers.

Consumer price indices may be used for several purposes, for example as an indicator of inflationary pressures in the economy, as a benchmark for wage negotiations and to determine annual increases in government benefits payments. Countries commonly have more than one consumer price index because one composite index may be considered too wide a grouping for different purposes.

6.3.1 The RPI and the CPI

RPI

One important measure of the general rate of inflation in the UK used over many years has been the **Retail Prices Index (RPI)**. The RPI measures the percentage changes month by month in the average level of prices of the commodities and services, including housing costs, purchased by the great majority of households in the UK. The items of expenditure within the RPI are intended to be a representative list of items, current prices for which are collected at regular intervals.

In December 2003, it was confirmed that the standardised European measure, sometimes called the Harmonised Index of Consumer Prices (HICP) was now to be used as the basis for the UK's inflation target. The UK HICP is called the **Consumer Prices Index (CPI)**. The CPI excludes most housing costs.

CPI

6.3.2 The underlying rate of inflation

The term **underlying rate of inflation** is usually used to refer to the RPI adjusted to exclude mortgage costs and sometimes other elements as well (such as the local council tax). The effects of interest rate changes on mortgage costs help to make the RPI fluctuate more widely than the underlying rate of inflation.

RPIX is the underlying rate of inflation measured as the increase in the RPI excluding mortgage interest payments. Another measure, called **RPIY**, goes further and excludes the effects of sales tax (VAT) changes as well.

6.4 Causes of inflation

The following can cause inflation:

- Demand pull factors
- Cost push factors
- Import cost factors
- Expectations
- Excessive growth in the money supply

6.4.1 Demand pull inflation

Demand pull inflation arises from an excess of aggregate demand over the productive capacity of the economy.

Demand pull inflation occurs when the economy is buoyant and there is a high aggregate demand, in excess of the economy's ability to supply.

(a) Because aggregate demand exceeds supply, prices rise.

(b) Since supply needs to be raised to meet the higher demand, there will be an increase in demand for factors of production, and so factor rewards (wages, interest rates, and so on) will also rise.

(c) Since aggregate demand exceeds the output capability of the economy, it should follow that demand pull inflation can only exist when unemployment is low. A feature of inflation in the UK in the 1970s and early 1980s, however, was high inflation coupled with high unemployment.

Key term

Demand pull inflation: inflation resulting from a persistent excess of aggregate demand over aggregate supply. Supply reaches a limit on capacity at the full employment level.

6.4.2 Cost push inflation

Cost push inflation arises from increases in the costs of production.

Cost push inflation occurs where the costs of factors of production rise regardless of whether or not they are in short supply. This appears to be particularly the case with wages.

Key term

Cost push inflation: inflation resulting from an increase in the costs of production of goods and services, eg through escalating prices of imported raw materials or from wage increases.

6.4.3 Import cost factors

Import cost push inflation occurs when the cost of essential imports rise regardless of whether or not they are in short supply. This has occurred in the past with the oil price rises of the 1970s. Additionally, a fall in the value of a country's currency will have import Cost push effects since a weakening currency increases the price of imports.

6.4.4 Expectations and inflation

A further problem is that once the rate of inflation has begun to increase, a serious danger of **expectational inflation** will occur. This means, regardless of whether the factors that have caused inflation are still persistent or not, there will arise a generally held view of what inflation is likely to be, and so to protect future income, wages and prices will be raised now by the expected amount of future inflation. This can lead to the vicious circle known as the **wage-price spiral**, in which inflation becomes a relatively permanent feature because of people's expectations that it will occur.

6.4.5 Money supply growth

Monetarists have argued that inflation is caused by **increases in the supply of money**. There is a considerable debate as to whether increases in the money supply are a **cause** of inflation or whether increases in the money supply are a **symptom** of inflation. Monetarists have argued that since inflation is caused by an increase in the money supply, inflation can be brought under control by reducing the rate of growth of the money supply.

7 Unemployment

7.1 The rate of unemployment

Key term

The **rate of unemployment** in an economy can be calculated as:

$$\frac{\text{Number of unemployed}}{\text{Total workforce}} \times 100\%$$

The number of unemployed at any time is measured by government statistics. If the flow of workers through unemployment is constant then the size of the unemployed labour force will also be constant.

Flows into unemployment are:

(a) Members of the working labour force **becoming** unemployed

- Redundancies
- Lay-offs
- Voluntary quitting from a job

(b) People **out** of the labour force **joining** the unemployed

- School leavers without a job
- Others (for example, carers) rejoining the workforce but having no job yet

Flows out of unemployment are:

- Unemployed people finding jobs
- Laid-off workers being re-employed
- Unemployed people stopping the search for work

In the UK, the monthly unemployment statistics published by the Office for National Statistics (ONS) count only the jobless who receive benefits.

The ONS also produce figures based on a quarterly survey of the labour force known as the International Labour organisation measure (ILO measure) that provides seasonally adjusted monthly data. This figure is considered to be more useful because it is also an internationally comparable measure.

7.2 Consequences of unemployment

Unemployment results in the following problems.

(a) **Loss of output**. If labour is unemployed, the economy is not producing as much output as it could. Thus, total national income is less than it could be.

(b) **Loss of human capital**. If there is unemployment, the unemployed labour will gradually lose its skills, because skills can only be maintained by working.

(c) **Increasing inequalities in the distribution of income**. Unemployed people earn less than employed people, and so when unemployment is increasing, the poor get poorer.

(d) **Social costs**. Unemployment brings social problems of personal suffering and distress, and possibly also increases in crime such as theft and vandalism.

(e) **Increased burden of welfare payments**. This can have a major impact on government fiscal policy.

7.3 Causes of unemployment

Unemployment may be classified into several categories depending on the underlying causes.

Category	Comments
Real wage unemployment	This type of unemployment is caused when the supply of labour exceeds the demand for labour, but real wages do not fall for the labour market to clear. This type of unemployment is normally caused by strong trade unions which resist a fall in their wages. Another cause of this type of unemployment is the minimum wage rate, when it is set above the market clearing level.
Frictional	It is inevitable that some unemployment is caused not so much because there are not enough jobs to go round, but because of the *friction* in the labour market (difficulty in matching quickly workers with jobs), caused perhaps by a lack of knowledge about job opportunities. In general, it takes time to match prospective employees with employers, and individuals will be unemployed during the search period for a new job. Frictional unemployment is temporary, lasting for the period of transition from one job to the next.
Seasonal	This occurs in certain industries, for example building, tourism and farming, where the demand for labour fluctuates in seasonal patterns throughout the year.
Structural	This occurs where long-term changes occur in the conditions of an industry. A feature of structural unemployment is high regional unemployment in the location of the industry affected.
Technological	This is a form of structural unemployment, which occurs when new technologies are introduced. (a) Old skills are no longer required. (b) There is likely to be a labour saving aspect, with machines doing the job that people used to do. With automation, employment levels in an industry can fall sharply, even when the industry's total output is increasing.

Category	Comments
Cyclical or demand-deficient	It has been the experience of the past that domestic and foreign trade go through cycles of boom, decline, recession, recovery, then boom again, and so on.
	(a) During recovery and boom years, the demand for output and jobs is high, and unemployment is low.
	(b) During decline and recession years, the demand for output and jobs falls, and unemployment rises to a high level.
	Cyclical unemployment can be long-term, and a government might try to reduce it by doing what it can to minimise a recession or to encourage faster economic growth.

Seasonal employment and frictional unemployment will be short-term. Structural unemployment, technological unemployment, and cyclical unemployment are all longer term, and more serious.

Exam focus point

Frictional unemployment is the subject of a question on the Pilot Paper.

7.4 Government employment policies

Job creation and reducing unemployment should often mean the same thing, but it is possible to create more jobs without reducing unemployment.

(a) This can happen when there is a greater number of people entering the jobs market than there are new jobs being created. For example, if 500,000 new jobs are created during the course of one year, but 750,000 extra school leavers are looking for jobs, there will be an increase in unemployment of 250,000.

(b) It is also possible to reduce the official unemployment figures without creating jobs. For example, individuals who enrol for a government financed training scheme are taken off the unemployment register, even though they do not have full-time jobs.

A government can try several options to create jobs or reduce unemployment.

(a) **Spending more money directly on job**s (for example hiring more civil servants)

(b) **Encouraging growth** in the private sector of the economy. When aggregate demand is growing, firms will probably want to increase output to meet demand, and so will hire more labour.

(c) **Encouraging training in job skills**. There might be a high level of unemployment amongst unskilled workers, and at the same time a shortage of skilled workers. A government can help to finance training schemes, in order to provide a 'pool' of workers who have the skills that firms need and will pay for.

(d) **Offering grant assistance to employers** in key regional areas

(e) **Encouraging labour mobility** by offering individuals financial assistance with relocation expenses, and improving the flow of information on vacancies

Other policies may be directed at **reducing real wages to market clearing levels**.

(a) Abolishing **closed shop** agreements, which restrict certain jobs to trade union members
(b) Abolishing **minimum wage regulations**, where such regulations exist

Question

Match the terms (a), (b) and (c) below with definitions A, B and C.

(a)   Structural unemployment
(b)   Cyclical unemployment
(c)   Frictional unemployment

A   Unemployment arising from a difficulty in matching unemployed workers with available jobs
B   Unemployment occurring in the downswing of an economy in between two booms
C   Unemployment arising from a long-term decline in a particular industry

Answer

The pairings are (a) C, (b) B and (c) A.

8 The objective of economic growth

8.1 Economic growth

This may be measured by increases in the **real** gross national product (GNP) per head of the population.

It is not unusual to find economic growth measured simply as increases in total GNP, regardless of inflation and changes in population size. Over periods in which the population changes relatively little, this approach will be satisfactory.

Economic growth may be **balanced** when all sectors of the economy expand together or **unbalanced**. Less developed countries in particular find it difficult to achieve economic growth, because many of the factors necessary for growth are absent in these countries.

Actual economic growth is the annual percentage increase in national output, which typically fluctuates in accordance with the trade cycle. **Potential economic growth** is the rate at which the economy would grow if all resources (eg people and machinery) were utilised.

8.2 Actual growth

Actual growth in the long run is determined by two factors.

- The growth in **potential output**
- The growth in **aggregate demand (AD)**.

These factors should move in step with one another.

8.3 Potential growth

The causes of growth in **potential** output are the determinants of the capacity of the economy (the supply side) rather than actual spending (the demand side), and are as follows.

(a)   There may be increases in the **amount of resources** available.

   (i)   **Land and raw materials**. Land is virtually in fixed supply, but new natural resources are continually being discovered.

   (ii)   **Labour** (the size of the working population). The output per head will be affected by the proportion of the population which is non-working.

(iii) **Capital** (eg machinery).

(b) Increases in the **productivity of resources** may result from technological progress or changed labour practices, for example.

8.4 Factors needed for sustained economic growth

Sustained economic growth depends heavily on an adequate level of new investment, which will be undertaken if there are **expectations** of future growth in demand. After investment has taken place on the basis of expectations, the level of income will increase, by the operation of the multiplier. But there is no reason why the actual level of income should end up increasing as much as the investing business people thought it would. It follows that investment, a factor in growth, is dependent on **business confidence** in the future, which is reflected in expectations of growth in consumption.

8.5 Natural resources

The rate of extraction of natural resources will impose a limit on the rate of growth. Production which uses up a country's natural resources, such as oil, coal and other minerals, depletes the stock of available resources; it is therefore, in a sense, **disinvestment**.

8.6 Technological progress

Technological progress is a very important source of faster economic growth.

- The same amounts of the factors of production can produce a higher output.
- New products will be developed, thus adding to output growth.

There can be technical progress in the labour force. If workers are better educated and better trained they will be able to produce more. For example, if there is a fault in the production process, a skilled worker will be able to deal with it quickly, whereas an unskilled worker one might have to call for a superior instead.

Technological progress can be divided into three types.

(a) **Capital saving**: technical advances that use less capital and the same amount of labour per unit of output.

(b) **Neutral**: technical advances that require labour and capital in the same proportions as before, using less of each per unit of output.

(c) **Labour-saving**: technical advance that uses less labour and the same amount of capital per unit of output.

If technological progress is of type (c) and the new technology seems to be labour-saving, then unemployment will rise unless there is either a simultaneous **expansion of demand** or a **reduction in hours** worked by each person. In the latter case there is no productivity increase associated with the technological progress.

Technological progress may therefore stimulate growth but at the same time conflict with the goal of full employment. A further consequence of this could be that those people in work would benefit from economic growth in the form of higher wages, but those people put out of work by the new technology would be left with a lower income. There is thus a danger that the rich will get richer and the poor will get poorer in spite of economic growth, and this would be regarded by many people as an undesirable development.

8.7 External trade influences on economic growth

An improvement in the **terms of trade** (the quantity of imports that can be bought in exchange for a given quantity of exports) means that more imports can be bought or alternatively a given volume of exports will earn higher profits. This will boost investment and hence growth. The rate of growth of the rest of the world is important for an economy that has a large foreign trade sector. If trading partners have slow growth, the amount of exports a country can sell to them will grow only slowly, and this limits the country's own opportunities for investment and growth.

8.8 Advantages and disadvantages of economic growth

Economic growth should lead to a higher income per head which can in turn lead to higher levels of consumption and a better standard of living.

A country with economic growth is more easily able to provide welfare services without creating intolerable tax burdens on the community.

There are possible disadvantages to growth, however.

(a)   Growth implies faster use of **natural resources**. Without growth, these resources would last longer.

(b)   Much economic activity tends to create **pollution**, such as acid rain and nuclear waste. It leads to emissions which threaten to produce disruptive climatic changes through an increase in the 'greenhouse effect'. It results in more roads, new and larger towns, and less unspoilt countryside.

(c)   There is a danger that some sections of the population, unable to adapt to the demands for new skills and more training, will not find jobs in the developing economy. This **structural unemployment** might create a large section of the community which gains no benefit from the increase in national income.

(d)   In order to achieve growth, firms need to **invest more** and this requires financing. This finance can only come from **higher savings** which in turn require the population to consume less. In the short-run, therefore, higher growth requires a cut in consumption.

9 The balance of payments

FAST FORWARD

The **balance of payments accounts** consist of a current account with visibles and invisibles sections and transactions in capital (external assets and liabilities including official financing).

9.1 The nature of the balance of payments

Exam focus point

Confusion of the balance of payments with the government budget is common. Make sure that the distinction is clear in *your* mind.

Under the current method of presentation of the UK balance of payments statistics, **current account** transactions are sub-divided into four parts.

- Trade in goods
- Trade in services
- Income
- Transfers

Before 1996, the term **visibles** was used in official statistics for trade in goods and the term **invisibles** was used for the rest. These terms have now been dropped in order to give more emphasis to the balances for trade in goods and services, although you may still find them mentioned.

Income is divided into two parts.

(a) Income from employment of UK residents by overseas firms

(b) Income from capital investment overseas

Transfers are also divided into two parts:

(a) Public sector payments to and receipts from overseas bodies such as the EU. Typically these are interest payments

(b) Non-government sector payments to and receipts from bodies such as the EU

The **capital account** balance is made up of public sector flows of **capital** into and out of the country, such as government loans to other countries.

The balance on the **financial account** is made up of flows of capital to and from the non-government sector, such as direct investment in overseas facilities; portfolio investment (in shares, bonds and so on); and speculative flows of currency. Movements on government foreign currency reserves are also included under this heading.

When journalists or economists speak of the balance of payments they are usually referring to the deficit or surplus on the **current account**, or possibly to the surplus or deficit on trade in goods only (this is also known as the **balance of trade**).

Exam focus point

Do not equate a trade surplus or deficit with a 'profit' or 'loss' for the country. A country is not like a company and the trade balance has nothing to do with profits and losses.

9.2 Equilibrium in the balance of payments

A balance of payments is in equilibrium if, over a period of years, the exchange rate remains stable and autonomous credits and debits are equal in value (the annual trade in goods and services is in overall balance). However, equilibrium will not exist if these things require the government to introduce measures which create unemployment or higher prices, sacrifice economic growth or impose trade barriers (eg import tariffs and import quotas).

9.3 Surplus or deficit in the current account

FAST FORWARD

A surplus or deficit on the balance of payments usually means a **surplus or deficit on the current account**.

A problem arises for a country's balance of payments when the country has a deficit on current account year after year, although there can be problems too for a country which enjoys a continual current account **surplus**.

The problems of a **deficit** on the current account are probably the more obvious. When a country is continually in deficit, it is importing more goods and services that it is exporting. This leads to two possible consequences.

(a) It may borrow more and more from abroad, to build up external liabilities which match the deficit on current account, for example encouraging foreign investors to lend more by purchasing the government's gilt-edged securities.

(b)   It may sell more and more of its assets. This has been happening recently in the USA, for example, where a large deficit on the US current account has resulted in large purchases of shares in US companies by foreign firms.

Even so, the demand to buy the country's currency in the foreign exchange markets will be weaker than the supply of the country's currency for sale. As a consequence, there will be pressure on the exchange rate to depreciate in value.

If a country has a **surplus** on current account year after year, it might invest the surplus abroad or add it to official reserves. The balance of payments position would be strong. There is the problem, however, that if one country which is a major trading nation (such as Japan) has a continuous surplus on its balance of payments current account, other countries must be in continual deficit. These other countries can run down their official reserves, perhaps to nothing, and borrow as much as they can to meet the payments overseas, but eventually, they will run out of money entirely and be unable even to pay their debts. Political pressure might therefore build up within the importing countries to impose tariffs or import quotas.

9.4 How can a government rectify a current account deficit?

The government of a country with a balance of payments deficit will usually be expected to take measures to reduce or eliminate the deficit. A deficit on current account may be rectified by one or more of the following measures.

(a)   A depreciation of the currency (called **devaluation** when deliberately instigated by the government, for example by changing the value of the currency within a controlled exchange rate system).

(b)   Direct measures to restrict imports, such as tariffs or import quotas or exchange control regulations.

(c)   Domestic deflation to reduce aggregate demand in the domestic economy.

The first two are **expenditure switching** policies, which transfer resources and expenditure away from imports and towards domestic products while the last is an **expenditure reducing** policy.

Chapter Roundup

- **Macroeconomic policy objectives** relate to economic growth, inflation, unemployment and the balance of payments.

- **Fiscal policy** provides a method of managing **aggregate demand** in the economy.

- If a government decides to use fiscal policy to influence demand in the economy, it can choose either expenditure changes or tax changes as its policy instrument.

- **Direct taxes** have the quality of being **progressive** or **proportional**. Income tax is usually progressive, with high rates of tax charged on higher bands of taxable income. **Indirect taxes** can be **regressive**, when the taxes are placed on essential commodities or commodities consumed by poorer people in greater quantities.

- A government must decide how it intends to raise tax revenues, from **direct or indirect taxes**, and in what proportions tax revenues will be raised from each source.

- **Monetary policy** uses money supply, interest rates or credit controls to influence aggregate demand.

- **Equilibrium national income** is determined using aggregate supply and aggregate demand analysis.

- **Business cycles** or **trade cycles** are the continual sequence of rapid growth in national income, followed by a slow-down in growth and then a fall in national income. After this recession comes growth again, and when this has reached a peak, the cycle turns into recession once more.

- High rates of **inflation** are harmful to an economy. Inflation redistributes income and wealth. Uncertainty about the value of money makes business planning more difficult. Constantly changing prices impose extra costs.

- **Demand pull inflation** arises from an excess of aggregate demand over the productive capacity of the economy.

- **Cost push inflation** arises from increases in the costs of production.

- The **balance of payments accounts** consist of a current account with visibles and invisibles sections and transactions in capital (external assets and liabilities including official financing).

- A surplus or deficit on the balance of payments usually means a **surplus or deficit on the current account**.

Quick Quiz

1 What is the difference between fiscal policy and monetary policy?

2 What are the components of the UK National Debt?

3 Outline how the government may use fiscal policy to influence aggregate demand.

4 What is:

(a) A regressive tax?
(b) A proportional tax?
(c) A progressive tax?

5 Distinguish between direct taxation and indirect taxation.

6 The government of a certain country decides to introduce a poll tax, which will involve a flat rate levy of £200 on every adult member of the population. This new tax could be described as:

A Regressive
B Proportional
C Progressive
D Ad valorem

7 High rates of personal income tax are thought to have a disincentive effect. This refers to the likelihood that the high rates of tax will:

A Encourage illegal tax evasion by individuals
B Lead to a reduction in the supply of labour
C Lead to a reduction in savings by individuals
D Discourage consumer spending and company investments

8 Which of the following will *not* be the immediate purpose of a tax measure by the government?

A To discourage an activity regarded as socially undesirable.
B To influence interest rates.
C To protect a domestic industry from foreign competition.
D To price certain products so as to take into account their social cost.

9 Which of the following government aims might be achieved by means of fiscal policy? 1. A redistribution of income between firms and households. 2. A reduction in aggregate monetary demand. 3. A change in the pattern of consumer demand.

A Objectives 1 and 2 only
B Objectives 1 and 3 only
C Objectives 2 and 3 only
D Objectives 1, 2 and 3

10 What are the two main types of inflation?

11 What effect does an increase in interest rates have on the exchange rate?

12 Other things remaining the same, an increase in the money supply will tend to reduce:

A Interest rates
B Liquidity preference
C The volume of bank overdrafts
D Prices and incomes

13   According to monetarist economists, which of the following consequences will result from an increase in the money supply? 1. Households will have excess money. 2. Households will use this money to buy more bonds, equities and physical goods. 3. Interest rates will rise. 4. The demand for money will respond to the change in interest rates. 5. Expenditure in the economy will increase.

A   1, 2 and 5 only will happen
B   3 and 5 only will happen
C   1, 2, 4 and 5 only will happen
D   3, 4 and 5 will all happen

14   How might a government try to influence the volume of investment by firms?

15   Injections into the economy are:

A   Consumption and Investment
B   Investment and Government Expenditure
C   Investment, Government Expenditure and Export Demand
D   Consumption, Investment, Government Expenditure and Export Demand

16   A deflationary gap occurs when:

A   Aggregate demand is insufficient to buy up all the goods and services the company is capable of producing.

B   Aggregate demand is more than sufficient to buy up all the goods and services produced by an economy.

C   A government attempts to spend its way out of recession.

D   A government is cutting its level of expenditure.

Answers to quick quiz

1   A government's fiscal policy is concerned with taxation, borrowing and spending; and their effects upon the economy. Monetary policy is concerned with money, the money supply, interest rates, inflation and the exchange rate.

2   The UK National Debt has two main parts: marketable instruments (Treasury bills and gilt-edged securities) and non marketable debt, which chiefly comprises National Savings & Investments.

3   A government can increase demand by spending more itself or by reducing taxation so that firms and households have more after-tax income to spend.

4   A regressive tax takes a higher proportion of a poor person's income than a rich person's. A progressive tax takes a higher proportion of a rich person's income and a lower proportion of a poor person's. A proportional tax takes the same proportion of all incomes.

5   Direct taxes are levied on income while indirect taxes are levied on expenditure. Indirect taxes are regressive. Direct taxes can be progressive.

6   A   A flat-rate poll tax, with no concession for the lower-paid, would take a higher proportion of the income of lower-income earners than of higher income earners. This is a regressive tax system.

7   B   The disincentive effect refers specifically to the disincentive of individuals to work.

8   B   The main purpose of taxation will be to raise revenue for the government. Other aims might be to redistribute wealth or affect demand in the economy. Changes in rate of tax do not have a direct influence on interest rates, which can be influenced by a government's *monetary* policies.

9   D   Objective 1 could be achieved by raising (or lowering) taxes on firms and lowering (or raising) taxes on households. Objective 2 could be achieved by raising taxation in order to reduce consumers' disposable income and so to reduce aggregate expenditure in the economy: these consequences should lead to a fall in the demand for money. Objective 3 can be achieved either by taxing income or by means of selective indirect taxes on certain goods.

10   Demand pull and Cost push

11   It attracts foreign investment, thus increasing the demand for the currency. The currency typically strengthens as a result.

12   A   Lower interest rates should be a consequence of an increase in the money supply, with a movement along the liquidity preference curve rather than a shift in the liquidity preference curve.

13   A   The question describes the transmission mechanism, which is the link between an excess of money supply over demand (or money demand over supply) and changes in expenditure in the economy. According to monetarists, an increase in the money supply creates excess supply over demand. Households use the excess money to buy bonds (and so interest rates *fall*), equities and physical goods (and so expenditure in the economy rises). The demand for money is interest-rate inelastic, according to monetarists (but not according to Keynesians) and so this does not increase in response to any interest rate fall.

14   Lower interest rates, investment grants and tax incentives may encourage investment. Governments can also stimulate demand by tax cuts or lower interest rates and improve business confidence by business friendly and growth enhancing policies like deregulation and controlling inflation. Policies to encourage technological development may also lead to increased investment.

15   C

16   A

7

The business environment

Topic list	Syllabus reference
1 Analysing the environment	B1 (a)
2 The political and legal environment	B1 (b)(c)
3 Employment protection	B1 (d)
4 Health and safety	B1 (f)(g)
5 Data protection and security	B1 (e)
6 Social and demographic trends	B3 (a)(c)
7 Cultural trends	B3 (b)
8 The impact of technology on organisations	B4 (a)(b)
9 Competitive forces	B5 (a)
10 Converting resources: the value chain	B5 (b)

Introduction

The aim of environmental analysis (**Section 1**) is to review the environment for **opportunities** and **threats**, and to secure environmental fit. An organisation has many interchanges with its environment. It draws inputs from it and outputs goods and services to it. The environment is a major source of uncertainty.

An organisation is affected by **general environmental trends**, usefully summarised in the **PEST** model (**Section 2**). The PEST model is drawn out into its component elements in **Sections 3 to 8**, which cover legal aspects (employment legislation, health and safety and data protection), social and cultural trends and the impact of technology on organisations. External competitive forces, as identified by Michael Porter, are covered in **Section 9**.

The internal capabilities of the organisation are analysed in the value chain framework (**Section 10**), and we conclude the chapter with this. Whilst the value chain has an internal rather than an external focus, it is included in this chapter as a method of improving a company's competitive position in the wider market.

Study guide

		Intellectual level
B1	**Political and legal factors**	
(a)	Define environmental forces in terms of political, legal, economic, social and technological factors.	1
(b)	Explain how the political system and government policy affect the organisation.	1
(c)	Describe the sources of legal authority, including supra-national bodies, national and regional governments.	1
(d)	Explain how the law protects the employee and the implications of employment legislation for the manager and the organisation.	1
(e)	Identify the principles of data protection and security.	1
(f)	Explain how the law promotes and protects health and safety in the workplace.	1
(g)	Recognise the responsibility of the individual and organisation for compliance with laws on data protection, security and health and safety.	1
B3	**Social and demographic factors**	
(a)	Explain the medium and long-term effects of social and demographic trends on business outcomes and the economy.	1
(b)	Describe the impact of changes in social structure, values, attitudes and tastes on the organisation.	2
(c)	Identify and explain the measures that governments may take in response to the medium and long-term impact of demographic change.	2
B4	**Technological factors**	
(a)	Explain the effects of technological change on the organisation structure and strategy:	1
(i)	Downsizing	
(ii)	Delayering	
(iii)	Outsourcing	
(b)	Describe the impact of information technology and information systems development on business processes	1
B5	**Competitive factors**	
(a)	Explain the factors that influence the level of competitiveness in an industry or sector.	1
(b)	Describe the activities of an organisation that affect its competitiveness:	1
(i)	Purchasing	
(ii)	Production	
(iii)	Marketing	
(iv)	Service	

Exam guide

The topics covered in this large chapter are heavily tested on the Pilot Paper, so it is a very important one. Questions on the Pilot Paper cover population trends, environmental factors and scanning, data protection legislation and employment legislation.

1 Analysing the environment

FAST FORWARD

> Whatever the overall strategic management method used, no organisation is likely to achieve its aims if it fails to take into account the **characteristics of the environment** in which it operates.

The environment is everything that surrounds an organisation, physically and socially.

Environmental analysis is one of the inputs to the strategy-making process. *Johnson and Scholes* suggest the following procedure:

Step 1   Assess the nature of the environment (eg is it changing?).

Step 2   Identify those influences which have affected the organisation in the past or which are likely to do so in future.

Step 3   Prepare a structural analysis identifying the 'key forces at work in the immediate or competitive environment'

↓

These steps should identify important developments. Then the following questions should be asked.

↓

Step 4   What is the organisation's position in relation to other organisations?

Step 5   What threats and/or opportunities are posed by the environment?

An organisation's environment may be examined in a number of ways.

(a)   **Global/local**. Some organisations operate worldwide. However, they still have to be sensitive to the local requirements of the countries or markets they operate in or export to. Some companies are much more exposed to global competition than others.

(b)   **General/task**: this is the method we will use.

    (i)   The **general (or macro) environment** covers all those factors influencing all organisations indirectly, such as general economic trends, population growth new technology. These are abbreviated as PEST (political-legal, economic, social-cultural, technological) factors. *PEST*

    (ii)   The **task or (micro) environment** includes those areas which have a direct impact on the organisation, such as its ability to acquire raw materials, its competitors and its customers. *Porter* analyses the task environment into **five competitive forces**, which are discussed in Section 9.

The distinction is not hard and fast, and is drawn for convenience only.

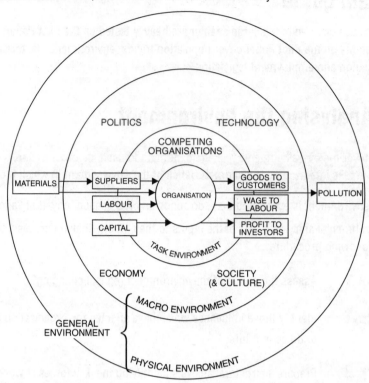

The environment is a source of **uncertainty**. In other words, decision-makers do not have sufficient information about environmental factors, and many things are out of their control. The overall degree of uncertainty may be assessed along two axes: simplicity/complexity and stability/dynamism.

(a) **Simplicity/complexity**

    (i) The **variety of influences** faced by an organisation. The more open an organisation is, the greater the variety of influences. The greater the number of markets the organisation operates in, the greater the number of influences to which it is subject.

    (ii) The amount of **knowledge necessary**. Some environments, to be handled successfully, require knowledge. All businesses need to have knowledge of the tax system, for example, but only pharmaceuticals businesses need to know about mandatory testing procedures for new drugs.

    (iii) The **interconnectedness** of environmental influences causes complexity. Importing and exporting companies are sensitive to exchange rates, which themselves are sensitive to interest rates. Interest rates then influence a company's borrowing costs. Scenario-building and modelling are ways of dealing with complexities to develop an understanding of environmental conditions.

(b) **Stability/dynamism**

    (i) An area of the environment is stable if it remains the same. (For example, investors get nervous about a change in government.) Firms which can predict demand face a stable environment.

    (ii) An unstable environment changes often. The environment of many fashion goods is unstable.

As a rule of thumb, use the following checklist for uncertainty.

- **Simple** (few environmental influences to worry about) and stable: low uncertainty
- **Complex and stable**: low to moderate uncertainty
- **Simple and unstable**: moderate to high uncertainty
- **Complex and unstable**: high uncertainty

1.1 The changing environment

Changes in the business environment have been driven by a number of developments. Here are some of the changes that have happened.

- (a) **Globalisation** of business – increased competition and global customers as domestic markets become saturated. Companies are able to compete easily anywhere in the world

- (b) **Science and technology** developments, especially in communications (the Internet) and transport (particularly air travel)

- (c) Mergers, acquisitions and strategic **alliances**

- (d) Changing **customer values** and behaviour

- (e) Increased **scrutiny of business decisions** by government and the public

- (f) Increased **liberalisation** of trade, and **deregulation** and co-operation between business and government have eased access to foreign markets

- (g) Changes in **business practices** - downsizing, outsourcing and re-engineering

- (h) Changes in the **social and business relationships** between companies and their employees, customers and other stakeholders

As companies have become exposed to more international competition, at the same time as having greater access to international markets, their preferred choice of **organisational structure** has been affected. This has been evident, as discussed earlier, in the shift away from mechanistic and bureaucratic organisations towards flatter structures with more flexible operating arrangements. Network forms of organisation and 'virtual' organisations are another manifestation of this trend. The need for strategic **international alliances** has increased with the need to understand and access foreign markets. The development of **communications technology** (email, the Internet) is the key factor that has made such relationships possible.

Some firms have been changing the structure of their workforces for the sake of greater flexibility in responding to competitor activity or customer needs. This so-called '**flexible firm**' comprises a **core** of full-time permanent staff with the key scarce skills, and **peripheral** part-timers and temporary or contract workers. This workforce can be flexed in a number of ways to meet changes in the market.

2 The political and legal environment

FAST FORWARD

Government policy influences the economic environment, the framework of laws, industry structure and certain operational issues. Political instability is a cause of risk. Different approaches to the **political environment** apply in different countries. **International trade** is subject to a further layer of international law and regulation.

The **political environment** affects the firm in a number of ways.

- A basic legal framework generally exists

- The government can take a particular stance on an issue of direct relevance to a business or industry

- The government's overall conduct of its economic policy is relevant to business

Exam focus point

PEST analysis is a useful tool to employ as an initial survey of conditions and options.

2.1 The political and legal environment

Laws come from common law, parliamentary legislation and government regulations derived from it, and obligations under treaties such as those establishing the European Union.

Legal factors affecting all companies

Factor	Example
General legal framework: contract, tort, agency	Basic ways of doing business, negligence proceedings
Criminal law	Theft (eg of documents in Lanica's failed bid for the Co-op), insider dealing, bribery, deception
Company law	Directors and their duties, reporting requirements, takeover proceedings, shareholders' rights, insolvency
Employment law	Trade Union recognition, Social Chapter provisions, minimum wage, unfair dismissal, redundancy, maternity, Equal Opportunities
Health and Safety	Fire precautions, safety procedures
Data protection	Use of information about employees and customers
Marketing and sales	Laws to protect consumers (eg refunds and replacement, 'cooling off' period after credit agreements), what is or isn't allowed in advertising
Environment	Pollution control, waste disposal
Tax law	Corporation tax payment, Collection of income tax (PAYE) and National Insurance contributions, sales tax (VAT)

Some legal and regulatory factors affect **particular industries**, if the public interest is served. For example, electricity, gas, telecommunications, water and rail transport are subject to **regulators** (Offer, Ofgas, Oftel, Ofwat, Ofrail) who have influence over market access, competition and pricing policy (can restrict price increase)

This is because either:

- The industries are, effectively, monopolies
- Large sums of public money are involved (eg in subsidies to rail companies)

2.2 The impact of government

Porter notes several ways whereby the **government** can directly affect the **economic structure** of an industry. They are explained below.

Capacity expansion	Government policy can encourage firms to increase or cut their capacity.
	(a) The UK tax system offers 'capital allowances' to encourage investment in equipment
	(b) A variety of incentives, funded by the EU and national governments, exist for locating capacity in a particular area
	(c) **Incentives** are used to encourage investment by overseas firms. Different countries in the EU have 'competed' for investment from Japan, for example
Demand	• The government is a major customer
	• Government can also influence demand by legislation, tax reliefs or subsidies
Divestment and rationalisation	In some European countries, the state takes many decisions regarding the selling off or closure of businesses, especially in sensitive areas such as defence.

Emerging industries	Can be promoted by the government or damaged by it.
Entry barriers	Government policy can discourage firms from entering an industry, by restricting investment or competition or by making it harder, by use of quotas and tariffs, for overseas firms to compete in the domestic market.
Competition	(a) The government's **purchasing decisions** will have a strong influence on the strength of one firm relative to another in the market (eg armaments).
	(b) **Regulations and controls** in an industry will affect the growth and profits of the industry – eg minimum product quality standards.
	(c) As a supplier of **infrastructure** (eg roads), the government is also in a position to influence competition in an industry.
	(d) Governments and supra-national institutions such as the EU might impose policies which keep an industry **fragmented**, and prevent the concentration of too much market share in the hands of one or two producers.

In some industries, governments regulate the adoption of **new products**. This is well illustrated by the pharmaceuticals industry, where new drugs or medicines must in many countries undergo stringent testing and obtain government approval before they can be marketed.

National and EU institutions also affect the operating activities of some organisations, for example:

- Anti-discrimination legislation
- Health and safety legislation
- Product safety and standardisation (especially EU standards)
- Workers' rights (eg unfair dismissal, maternity leave)
- Training and education policies can determine the 'standard' of recruits

Question

Government impact

How do you think government policy affects the pharmaceutical industry in your country?

Answer

Using the example of the UK.

(a) The government must authorise most new drugs (eg for safety before they can be sold).

(b) The UK government is a major purchaser of pharmaceuticals, for the national health service, and so has significant buying power.

(c) Health education policies affect consumer demand.

(d) Funding of universities affects the science base for recruitment.

(e) Employment practices, such as working hours, are influenced by EU employment directives.

2.3 Influencing government

Businesses are able to influence government policies in a number of ways.

(a)   They can employ **lobbyists** to put their case to individual ministers or civil servants.

(b)   They can give MPs **non-executive directorships**, in the hope that the MP will take an interest in all legislation that affects them.

(c)   They can try to **influence public opinion**, and hence the legislative agenda, by advertising.

Of particular importance is the need to influence the decision making processes of the European Commission. EU regulations, for practical purposes, take priority over national law. They are arrived at after a great deal of negotiation, and for this reason alone, are difficult to change. It is therefore much better to influence the **drafting process** of new regulations than to try and get them changed once they have been implemented.

The EU will have an increasing role in the conduct of **European businesses** in:

- Product standards
- Environmental protection
- Monetary policy (a European Central Bank might set interest rates)
- Research and development
- Regional policy
- Labour costs (wages, pensions)

2.4 Political risk and political change

Changes in UK law are often predictable. A government will publish a **green paper** discussing a proposed change in the law, before issuing a **white paper** and passing a bill through Parliament. Plans should be formulated about what to do if the change takes place.

However, it is **political change** which complicates the planning activities of many firms. Many economic forecasts ignore the implications of a change in government policy.

(a)   At **national level**, political influence is significant and includes legislation on trading, pricing, dividends, tax, employment as well as health and safety (to list but a few).

(b)   Politics at **international level** also has a direct bearing on organisations. EU directives affect all countries in the EU.

The **political risk** in a decision is the risk that political factors will invalidate the strategy and perhaps severely damage the firm. Examples are wars, political chaos, corruption and nationalisation.

2.5 International trade

The political environment is of particular importance in **international trade**. Such trade is governed by an extra layer of legislation contained in treaties and agreements and is potentially subject to a **higher level of political risk**. This may be manifested in a variety of ways, such as taxation law, labour regulation and economic policy on such matters as ownership. At worst, there is a threat of expropriation or nationalisation. Failure to repress lawlessness and corruption are further complicating factors, as is open or covert refusal to consider international bidders for government contracts.

2.6 Regional trading organisations

The **EU** is the most integrated of the regional trading organisations, aspiring to a single market in goods, services and factors of production.

Countries in various regions have entered into closer economic arrangements such as NAFTA (USA, Canada, Mexico), the EU, Mercosur (Brazil, Argentina, Uruguay, Paraguay and now Chile). The **EU** is the world's largest single market, but is unusual in that it features a common political decision-making process (Council of Ministers, Commission, Parliament) and a single currency.

The EU single market programme has involved areas as diverse as harmonising technical standards, opening up areas such as telecommunications to competition, consumer protection, mutual recognition of professional qualifications and so on.

2.6.1 The European Union

The European Union operates a single European market, allowing for the free movement of labour, goods and services, and free competition.

- **Physical barriers** (eg customs inspection) on goods and service have been removed for most products.

- **Technical standards** (eg for quality and safety) should be harmonised.

- Governments should not discriminate between EU companies in awarding public works contracts.

- Telecommunications are now subject to **greater competition.**

- It should be possible to provide **financial services** in any country.

- Measures are being taken to rationalise **transport services.**

- There should be **free movement of capital** within the community.

- **Professional qualifications** awarded in one member state should be recognised in the others.

- The EU is taking a co-ordinated stand on matters related to **consumer protection.**

- A common currency, the Euro, has been widely adopted within the EU.

2.7 International trade liberalisation: the World Trade Organisation (WTO)

The **World Trade Organisation** was set up to promote free trade and resolve disputes between trading partners.

The theory of **comparative advantage** suggests that **free trade** is the best way to promote global economic growth and, by implication, domestic prosperity. In other words, people should be free to buy and sell goods and services anywhere in the world.

Many countries have limited or controlled their trading activities, with varying success. **Protectionist measures to restrict competition** from overseas include:

- **Quotas** on the number of items that can be imported (eg Japanese cars)
- **Import bans** (eg Brazil prohibited the import of cheap US-made computers)
- **Restrictions** on foreign ownership of certain industries (eg defence)
- **Tariffs**

3 Employment protection

Much legislation (and not enough economic knowledge) has been aimed at the idea of 'employment protection'. As a result, all forms of **termination of employment** must be treated with great care.

3.1 Retirement

In the UK, many employees are taking **early retirement** perhaps as a result of corporate downsizing, but many people still search for work at an older age and there are pressure groups seeking to ban **ageism** in recruitment. Retirement ages for men and women are being **equalised**.

Organisations **encourage retirement** for a variety of reasons.

- Promotion opportunities for younger workers
- Early retirement is an alternative to redundancy
- The age structure of an organisation may become unbalanced
- The cost of providing pensions rises with age

3.2 Resignation

People resign for many reasons, personal and occupational. Employees who are particularly valuable should be encouraged to stay. Particular problems the employee has been experiencing (eg salary) may be solvable, though not always in the short term.

In any case, an **exit interview**, when the leaver explains the decision to go, is a valuable source of information.

The **period of notice** required for the employee to leave should be set out in the contract of employment, but some leeway may be negotiated on this.

3.3 Dismissal

There are three forms of termination that constitute dismissal under UK law.

(a) The termination of an employee's contract **by the employer**

(b) The ending of a fixed-term contract **without renewal** on the same terms: in effect, there is no such thing as a fixed-term contract of employment.

(c) Resignation by the **employee** where the **employer's conduct** breaches the contract of employment. This is **constructive dismissal**

The **statutory minimum** period of notice to be given is determined by the employee's length of continuous service in the employer's service. Longer periods may be written into the contract, at the employer's discretion, and by agreement. Either party may waive his right to notice, or accept payment in lieu of notice. An employee is entitled to a written statement of the **reasons** for dismissal.

3.4 Wrongful dismissal

Wrongful dismissal is dismissal that breaches the **contract of employment**. An example would be failure to give the contractual period of notice (assuming the circumstances did not justify summary dismissal).

3.5 Unfair dismissal

The legal concept of unfair dismissal gives protection to the employee against **arbitrary** dismissal; that is dismissal without good reason. A dismissal need not be wrongful to be unfair. The basic principle is that any dismissal is potentially unfair. Under employment protection legislation, the employee has to **prove** that he has been dismissed. The onus is then on the **employer to prove** that the dismissal was **fair**.

Potentially fair grounds for dismissal

(a) **Redundancy,** provided that the selection for redundancy was fair.

(b) **Legal impediment:** the employee could not continue to work in his present position without breaking a legal duty or restriction.

(c) **Non-capability,** provided adequate training and warnings had been given.

(d) **Misconduct,** provided warnings suitable to the offence have been given.

(e) **Other substantial reason:** for example, the employee is married to a competitor.

Automatically unfair dismissal

- Unfair selection for redundancy
- Membership and involvement in a trade union
- Pregnancy
- Insisting on documented payslips and employment particulars
- Carrying out certain activities in connection with health and safety at work

The Conciliation Officer or Industrial Tribunal to whom a complaint of unfair dismissal is made may order various **remedies**, subject to the circumstances of the case.

- **Re-instatement**: giving the employee the old job back.
- **Re-engagement**: giving the employee a job comparable to the old one.
- **Compensation**: which may include redundancy pay, breach of contract and punitive award.

Incompetence or misconduct

(a) **Incompetence** means that the employee's best efforts have not reached the standard required.

(b) If the employee has **deliberately not** done his best, however, this is **misconduct**.

The solution to these difficulties lies partly in the hands of the HRM function, which has a number of responsibilities.

(a) Ensuring that **standards of performance and conduct** are set, clearly defined and communicated to all employees

(b) **Warning** employees where a gap is perceived between standard and performance

(c) Giving a clearly defined and reasonable **period for improvement** - with help and advice where necessary, and clear improvement targets

(d) Ensuring that **disciplinary procedures** and the ultimate consequences of continued failure are made clear

If such procedures are formulated, the employer will not only feel that the employee has been given every chance to redeem the situation, but will also be in a strong position at a tribunal in rebutting a complaint of unfair dismissal.

3.6 Disciplinary procedures

The use of a disciplinary system can be evidence in certain situations that an employee has not been dismissed unfairly.

3.7 Redundancy

Redundancy is dismissal under two circumstances.

(a) The employer has ceased to carry on the business at all or in the place where the employee was employed.

(b) The requirements of the business for employees to carry out work of a particular kind have ceased or diminished or are expected to.

Compensation is a legal entitlement, and encourages employees to accept redundancy without damage to industrial relations.

The employee is **not entitled** to compensation in three circumstances.

(a) The employer has made an offer of suitable alternative employment and the employee has **unreasonably** rejected it.

(b) The employee is of pensionable age or over, or has less than two years' continuous employment.

(c) The employee's conduct merits **dismissal without notice**.

There are certain legal minima for compensation offered, based on age and length of service.

3.7.1 Procedure for handling redundancies

From a purely humane point of view, it is obviously desirable to consult with employees or their representatives. Notice of impending redundancies is a legal duty for redundancies over a certain number.

The impact of a redundancy programme can be reduced in several ways.

- Retirement of staff over the normal retirement age
- Early retirement to staff approaching normal retirement age
- Restrictions on recruitment to reduce the workforce over time by natural wastage
- Dismissal of part-time or short-term contract staff
- Offering retraining and/or redeployment within the organisation
- Seeking voluntary redundancies

Where management have to choose between individuals doing the same work, they may dismiss the less competent or require people to re-apply for the job. The LIFO principle may be applied, so that newcomers are dismissed before long-serving employees.

Many large organisations provide benefits in excess of the statutory minimum, with regard to consultation periods, terms, notice periods, counselling and aid with job search, training in job-search skills and so on.

Many firms provide advice and **outplacement** counselling, to help redundant employees find work elsewhere.

3.8 Equal opportunities

Some groups are discriminated against with little or no justification. This applies particularly in employment matters. The law and an extensive bureaucracy exist to redress the balance. Equal opportunities is covered more fully in Chapter 17.

4 Health and safety

People should be able to be confident that they will not be exposed to excessive risk when they are at work. This means that risk and danger must be actively managed.

4.1 Importance of maintaining health and safety at work

- An employer has **legal obligations** under UK and EU law.
- Accidents and illness **cost the employer money**.
- The company's **image** in the marketplace and society may suffer.

The **major legislation in the UK** covers a number of Acts of Parliament. EU law will become more important in the future. The most important piece of legislation in this area in the UK is the Health and Safety at Work Act 1975.

4.2 Employers' duties

A senior manager must be specified as responsible for ensuring that problems are solved and rules observed.

(a)   All **work practices** must be safe.

(b)   The work **environment** must be safe and healthy.

(c)   All plant and equipment must be maintained to the necessary standard.

(d)   Information, instruction, training and supervision should **encourage safe working practices**. Employers must provide training and information to all staff.

(e)   The safety policy should be clearly **communicated** to all staff.

(f)   Employers must carry out **risk assessments**, generally in writing, of all work hazards. Assessment should be continuous. They must **assess the risks to anyone else affected by their work activities.**

(g)   They must **share hazard and risk information** with other employers, including those on adjoining premises, other site occupiers and all subcontractors coming onto the premises.

(h)   They must **introduce controls** to reduce risks.

(i)   They should **revise safety policies** in the light of the above, or initiate safety policies if none were in place previously.

(j)   They must **identify employees** who are especially at risk.

(k)   They must employ competent safety and health **advisers**.

The Safety Representative Regulations provide that a **safety representative** may be appointed by a recognised trade union, and for **safety committees** to be set up at the request of employee representatives. Safety representatives are entitled to paid time off work to carry out their duties.

4.3 Employees' duties

(a)   Take reasonable care of themselves and others

(b)   Allow the employer to carry out his or her duties (including enforcing safety rules)

(c)   Not interfere intentionally or recklessly with any machinery or equipment

(d)   Inform the employer of any situation which may be a danger (this does not reduce the employer's responsibilities in any way)

(e)   Use all equipment properly

Question

What aspects of your own work environment (if any) do you think are:

- A hindrance to your work?
- A source of dissatisfaction?
- A hazard to your health or safety?

4.4 Accident and safety policies

Accidents are **expensive**

(a)   Time is lost by the injured employee and other staff.

(b)   Direct costs are incurred by disruption to operations at work; damage and repairs and modification to the equipment; compensation payments or fines resulting from legal action; increased insurance premiums.

(c)   Output from the injured employee on return to work is often reduced.

(d)   Recruiting and training a replacement for the injured worker will have its own cost.

An employee who is injured as a result of either the **employer's failure to take reasonable care** or a breach of **statutory duty** can **sue**.

(a)   An employee is not deemed to consent to the risk of injury because he or she is aware of the risk. It is the employer's duty to provide a safe working system.

(b)   Employees can become inattentive or careless in doing work which is monotonous or imposes stress. This factor too must be allowed for in the employer's safety precautions.

(c)   The employer should encourage and insist on proper use of safety equipment.

(d)   Many dangers can be caused by carelessness or other fault of an otherwise competent employee, possibly by his mere thoughtlessness.

Reducing the frequency and severity of accidents

(a)   Develop safety consciousness among staff.

(b)   Develop effective consultative **participation**.

(c)   Give adequate **instruction** in safety rules and measures.

(d)   **Materials handling should be minimised**.

(e)   **Good maintenance** pays dividends.

(f)   Implement in full the **code of practice** for the industry.

(g)   **Safety inspections** should be carried out regularly.

Accident reporting systems

(a)   Accidents should be reported on an **accident report form** and records kept . Accidents resulting in death, major injury (such as the loss of an eye or a finger) or more than three days off work for the victim must be notified to the Health and Safety Executive.

(b)   **Statistical trends** should be monitored to reveal areas where recurring accidents suggest the need for special investigation, but only more serious incidents will have to be followed-up in depth.

(c)   **Follow-up** should be clearly aimed at preventing recurrence - not placing blame.

(d)   Risk audit or sampling should be carried out regularly to prevent accidents.

(e) There should be a procedure for reporting 'near-misses', anonymously if necessary to encourage openness.

4.5 Health and safety policy

In order to enhance safety awareness, promote good practice and comply with legal obligations, many employers have a **health and safety policy** for their staff. Such a policy will have a number of features.

(a) Statement of **principles**
(b) Detail of **safety procedures**
(c) **Compliance with the law**
(d) **Detailed instructions** on how to use equipment
(e) **Training requirements**

Senior managers **must set a good example**.

(a) **Visibly reacting to breaches** of the policy (eg if the fire doors are blocked open, remove the blockage).

(b) **Ensuring that the policy is communicated** to staff (eg memoranda, newsletters).

(c) **Setting priorities for operations**.

(d) Involving staff in the health and safety process.

5 Data protection and security

FAST FORWARD

Privacy is the right of the individual not to suffer unauthorised disclosure of information.

Key term

Privacy is the right of the individual to control the use of information about him or her, including information on financial status, health and lifestyle (ie prevent unauthorised disclosure).

5.1 Why is privacy an important issue?

In recent years, there has been a growing fear that the ever-increasing amount of **information** about individuals held by organisations could be misused.

In particular, it was felt that an individual could easily be harmed by the existence of computerised data about him or her which was inaccurate or misleading and which could be **transferred to unauthorised third parties** at high speed and little cost.

In the UK the current legislation covering this area is the **Data Protection Act 1998**.

5.2 The Data Protection Act 1998

FAST FORWARD

The (UK) **Data Protection Act 1998** protects individuals about whom data is held. Both manual and computerised information must comply with the Act.

The Data Protection Act 1998 is an attempt to protect the **individual**. The terms of the Act cover data about individuals – **not data about corporate bodies**.

5.3 Definitions of terms used in the Act

In order to understand the Act it is necessary to know some of the technical terms used in it.

Key terms

> **Personal data** is information about a living individual, including expressions of opinion about him or her. Data about organisations is not personal data.
>
> **Data users** are organisations or individuals who control personal data and the use of personal data.
>
> A **data subject** is an individual who is the subject of personal data.

5.4 The data protection principles

The UK Data Protection Act includes eight Data Protection Principles with which data users must comply.

> DATA PROTECTION PRINCIPLES
>
> Schedule 1 of the Act contains the data protection principles.
>
> 1   Personal data shall be processed fairly and lawfully and, in particular, shall not be processed unless:
>
>   (a)   At least one of the conditions in Schedule 2 is met (see paragraph 5.5.3 (c) later in this chapter).
>
>   (b)   In the case of sensitive personal data, at least one of the conditions in Schedule 3 is also met (see 4.5.3 (d)).
>
> 2   Personal data shall be obtained only for one or more specified and lawful purposes, and shall not be further processed in any manner incompatible with that purpose or those purposes.
>
> 3   Personal data shall be adequate, relevant and not excessive in relation to the purpose or purposes for which they are processed.
>
> 4   Personal data shall be accurate and, where necessary, kept up to date.
>
> 5   Personal data processed for any purpose or purposes shall not be kept for longer than is necessary for that purpose or those purposes.
>
> 6   Personal data shall be processed in accordance with the rights of data subjects under this Act.
>
> 7   Appropriate technical and organisational measures shall be taken against unauthorised or unlawful processing of personal data and against accidental loss or destruction of, or damage to, personal data.
>
> 8   Personal data shall not be transferred to a country or territory outside the European Economic Area unless that country or territory ensures an adequate level of protection for the rights and freedoms of data subjects in relation to the processing of personal data.

The Act has two main aims:

   (a)   To protect **individual privacy**. Previous UK law only applied to **computer-based** information. The 1998 Act applies to **all personal data, in any form.**

   (b)   To **harmonise data protection legislation** so that, in the interests of improving the operation of the single European market, there can be a **free flow of personal data** between the member states of the EU.

5.4.1 The rights of data subjects

The Act establishes the following rights for data subjects.

(a) A data subject may seek **compensation** through the courts for damage and any associated distress caused by the **loss**, **destruction** or **unauthorised disclosure** of data about himself or herself or by **inaccurate data** about himself or herself.

(b) A data subject may apply to the courts for **inaccurate data** to be **put right** or even **wiped off** the data user's files altogether. Such applications may also be made to the Registrar.

(c) A data subject may obtain **access** to personal data of which he or she is the subject. (This is known as the 'subject access' provision.) In other words, a data subject can ask to see his or her personal data that the data user is holding.

(d) A data subject can **sue** a data user for any **damage or distress** caused to him by personal data about him which is **incorrect** or **misleading** as to matter of **fact** (rather than opinion).

Question

Data protection

Your managing director has asked you to recommend measures that your company, which is based in the UK, could take to ensure compliance with data protection legislation. Suggest what measures should be taken.

Pay close attention to the newspapers and the *ACCA student accountant* for details of developments in legislation.

Answer

Measures could include the following.

- Obtain consent from individuals to hold any sensitive personal data you need.
- Supply individuals with a copy of any personal data you hold about them if so requested.
- Consider if you may need to obtain consent to process personal data.
- Ensure you do not pass on personal data to unauthorised parties.

6 Social and demographic trends

6.1 Population and the labour market

Population affects an organisation's supply of labour and hence its policies towards recruiting and managing human resources. This section uses the example of the UK.

Growing populations offer a larger labour market.

- Increasing birth rates mean more young people.
- Falling death rates mean more elderly people – some of these will continue working.

The changing age structure of the labour force. Fewer young people might mean that young people will become more expensive. The number of 16 year olds entering the labour force peaked in the late 1970s, but has been falling ever since.

Women are increasing their participation in the labour force.

The increasing participation of women occurs for four reasons.

- More part time jobs
- Rising male unemployment as many industries which employed men have declined
- The growth of the service sector

- An increase in the average age at which women have children

6.2 Implications for employers

How organisations can cope with these demographic and educational trends

Step 1   Establish the **labour market** the organisation is in (eg young people, part time workers). In other words, 'Who do we want to recruit?'

Step 2   Discover the organisation's **catchment areas** (ie location of potential recruits).

Step 3   Discern the **supply side trends** in the catchment area labour force (eg how many school leavers are expected? what is the rate of growth/decline of local population?).

Step 4   Examine **education trends** in the area.

Step 5   Assess the **demand from other employers** for the **skills** you need (eg if there is a large concentration of, say, electronics companies in the region, then they will be interested in hiring people with similar skills).

Step 6   Assess whether some of your demand can be satisfied by a supply from **other sources.**

Organisations will need proper resourcing strategies to make sure their demand for labour is properly met.

Professionalism in recruitment

- Research the labour market
- Segment the labour market
- Conduct a proper job analysis to be certain of the skills needed
- Target potential employees, and sell the company to them
- Get recruitment right

Tapping unused labour resources

(a)   **Older workers**. Some companies in the retail sector have targeted older workers (over-40s and over-45s) because of their qualities.

   (i)   Skills and experience.
   (ii)   High regard for customer service.
   (iii)   Stabilising influence on younger staff.
   (iv)   Contribution to better staff retention rates.

(b)   **Encouraging women returners**. Female participation in the workforce is increasing, and more women are entering higher education. In practice, women spend far more on household and childcare tasks than men Employers can take positive steps to encourage female returners.

   (i)   **Child care facilities**. Private child care is expensive.

   (ii)   **Career break schemes**. Women may be allowed to take time off for a few years to have children and return to the same job, subject to a satisfactory performance record.

   (iii)   **Corporate** culture and **policies** such as equal opportunities policies, training schemes, assertiveness courses and so on.

6.3 Family life cycle

An example of a use of demography by marketing people is **family life cycle** (FLC). This is a summary of demographic variables.

- It combines the effects of age, marital status, career status (income) and the presence or absence of children.

- It is able to identify the various stages through which households progress. It is clear that particular products and services can be marketed to people at specific stages of the life cycle.

6.4 Social structures and class

> **Social class:** 'The basic idea of class is that a society can be divided into broad strata which comprise individuals, whose members share common features, such as type of *occupation, income level, education background* and other variables.' (*Palmer and Worthington*)

In sociological terms, a class is more than a group of people with various things in common, however. Classes fit into a social structure, in which some classes have advantage over others.

- Access to power
- Educational attainment
- Income
- Inherited wealth
- Status or esteem

Membership of a class categorises people according to two things.

- What they have in common
- Their relationship with other classes

At one time, class was easy to determine by inheritance and by the relationship each group had to the means of production. Now matters are much more complex.

It is possible to infer shared values, attitudes and behaviour within a social class, as distinct from those of a higher or lower class: some research has been able to relate consumption behaviour to class standing. (This makes social class an attractive proposition for market segmentation.)

In Britain, a complex social class system is usually encapsulated in the popular terms: 'working class', 'middle class' and 'upper class'. People have stereotypes about the attributes of a particular class, and the topic tends to be very emotive on the basis of these stereotyped perceptions.

(a) **Subjective definitions** of class relate to the way in which people consider themselves. (A white-collar job, an owned home or particular leisure pursuits may cause a person to identify himself as 'middle class'.)

(b) **Reputational definitions** ask people to describe **other people's class**, not their own.

(c) **Objective** measures of social class consist of selected demographic (mainly socio-economic) variables: income, education and **occupation** are the most common.

6.5 Socio-economic position, income and wealth

Whilst there are some real differences between the groups, 'social class' for marketing or planning purposes should be used with caution.

(a) **Definition.** It is not exactly or consistently defined. (Is it economic interest? status? wealth? background? access to power? educational achievement?)

(b) **Social mobility** (moving from class to class) may make it difficult to use the concept in a meaningful way.

(c) **Aspiration.** People commonly perceive themselves to be in a different class to that in which they are objectively classified, and/or may aspire to membership of a higher class: their consumption behaviour will be affected accordingly.

(d) **Dual income families.** Conventional gradings take into consideration the occupation of the head of the household, but with dual-income families, fluctuating family/household patterns, the mobility of labour and changes in employment circumstances (eg redundancy or insolvency), this may give a rather misleading picture.

(e) **Cause or effect?** 'It is certainly the case that people in the same social class have many things in common - the same monopoly or lack of access to scarce resources, for example; the same good or bad standards of housing; the same access to, or restrictions on, educational opportunity; the same shared experiences of comfort, travel, hardship or enjoyment. But all of these cultural characteristics are the **consequences** of social class rather than the causes of it. People's **lifestyles are a reflection of their economic condition** in society, **not the reason** for their position.'

6.6 Socio-economic position, income and wealth

Question	Socio-economic status

'Comparing people's income is a simple matter. All you need to do is compare income after direct tax and social security contributions to see how well off people are.'

Do you agree with this statement?

Answer

Unfortunately the issue is not that simple. Firstly, there is indirect taxation (VAT). Households on different incomes are more or less exposed to this. Secondly, there is the issue of mortgage interest relief, which is not available to people renting their accommodation. Thirdly, there are additional social benefits such as education. It is hard to combine all these factors together.

6.7 Buying patterns

Buying behaviour is an important aspect of marketing. Many factors influence the buying decisions of individuals and households. Demography and the class structure are relevant in that they can be both **behavioural determinants** and **inhibitors**.

(a) **Behavioural determinants encourage** people to buy a product or service. They include the individual's personality, culture, social class, and the importance of the purchase decision (eg a necessity such as food or water, or a luxury).

(b) **Inhibitors** are factors that make the person **less likely** to purchase something (eg low income).

Socio-economic status can be related to buying patterns in a number of ways, both in the amount people have to spend and what they spend it on. It affects both the quantity of goods and services supplied, and the proportion of their income that households spend on goods and services.

7 Cultural trends

Organisations are part of the wider social environment. Examples of how cultural trends can change organisations are given in this section.

7.1 Health and diet issues

There have been significant changes in the UK in attitudes to diet and health.

(a) **Smoking**. Most obvious has been a decrease in cigarette smoking, but it remains 'the greatest cause of preventable death' in Britain, accounting for 1 in 6 deaths. It is more common in manual than non-manual occupations.

(b) **Asthma** now affects over 2 million people in England. The number of hospital admissions has increased strikingly: some have linked this to increased pollution from motor vehicle exhaust.

British people are slowly moving to a healthier diet: In addition, there has been an increase in vegetarianism, and 'green consumerism'. This includes a concern with 'organic food' now found in many supermarkets.

7.2 Impact of health and diet on businesses

Growing market for sports-related goods (even though, as is the case with running shoes, sporting goods might be purchased as fashion accessories).

Employee health. Employers are concerned with the effect of ill-health on productivity. Some employers provide gyms and physical recreation facilities. Others offer counselling programmes to employees who are alcohol abusers.

New foods. Some foods have added vitamins.

A market for **new sorts of convenience food**.

Organic foods (grown without artificial pesticides, hormones etc) are more popular. Issues of food heath (eg BSE) will surface more often.

7.3 Women in work

Over the past few decades, many more women have entered the labour force. *Social Trends* estimates that the proportion of women **economically active** in the UK labour force has increased. (Economically active includes full and part time employment and self employment). More than five times as many women as men are part-timers.

7.3.1 Discrimination

There was once widespread discrimination against women.

- There were legal restrictions on female employment (eg mining work).

- Employers were concerned that women would leave work to have children.

- Women had little influence in trade unions.

- Segregation was reinforced at school. Subjects such as home economics were often compulsory for girls, while subjects such as woodwork and metalwork were offered only to boys.

The Sex Discrimination Act 1975 ensures that **non-discrimination**, in most cases, applies to all aspects of employment.

Key terms

> **Overt discrimination** is where one group is treated less favourably than another.
> **Indirect discrimination** makes it harder for somebody of a particular group to fulfil requirements.

Furthermore, the principle of **equal pay for equal work** and for **equal value** is enshrined in legislation. This is covered in more detail in Chapter 16.

7.3.2 Promotion and seniority

Women still occupy fewer senior positions than men.

(a) In some professions or jobs (eg accountancy) female participation is relatively recent, so that the **age profile** of the female participants means that women are predominantly young.

(b) Part time work, in which female employment is concentrated, rarely offers opportunities for promotion.

(c) There might still be subtle discrimination (a 'glass ceiling') at higher levels and more obvious discrimination at lower levels.

(d) Women still take most responsibility for child rearing.

Some employers have begun to address the underlying problems of equal opportunities with active policies.

(a) Instituting an **Equal Opportunities Policy**

(b) Appointing **Equal Opportunities Managers** reporting directly to the Human Resources Director

(c) **Flexible hours** or part-time work and term-time contracts to help women to combine a career with family responsibilities

(d) **Career-break** or **return-to-work** schemes for women

(e) **Posting managerial vacancies** internally, gives more opportunities for movement up the ladder to women currently at lower levels of the organisation

(f) **Assertiveness training**

(g) **Awareness training** for managers, to encourage them to think about equal opportunity policy

(h) The provision of **workplace nurseries** for working mothers would be a boon to many female workers. Employers appear reluctant to bear the cost.

(i) **Positive action to encourage** job and training applications from women. Note that positive discrimination as such (employing somebody less well qualified) is unlawful.

7.4 Environmentalism

Issues relating to the effect of an organisation's activities on the physical environment have come to the fore in recent years. Why?

(a) **Prosperity** has encouraged people to pay attention to the quality of life.

(b) **Expansion of media coverage** of famines and long term environmental trends (eg **global warming**) has fuelled public concern.

(c) **Disasters** (eg Chernobyl, BSE) have aroused public attention.

(d) **Greater scientific knowledge.** It only recently became possible to measure the hole in the ozone layer and assess its causes.

(e) **Tangible deterioration** in the environment (eg traffic congestion).

7.5 The business response

(a) **'Green products'.** Companies like The Body Shop have cleverly exploited ecological friendliness as a marketing tool. Supermarkets now stock cleaning products which are supposed to be kind to nature.

(b) **Changed practices.** Bad publicity has led to improvements. A consumer campaign to boycott tuna from companies whose methods of fishing endangered the lives of dolphins has led to changed fishing techniques.

(c) **Limits.** There may be a limit to how much consumers are prepared to alter their lifestyles, or pay, for the sake of ecological correctness.

(d) **Education and confusion.** Consumers may be imperfectly educated about environmental issues. For example, much recycled paper has simply replaced paper produced from trees from properly managed (ie sustainably developed) forests. There is widespread confusion as to green labelling.

(e) **Environmental impact assessments**: companies review not just the finished product but their production processes too.

As far as **pollution** goes, there has been a longish history on environmental legislation. This is still mainly a problem of the industrialised west. It is likely that government will take an increased interest in this area. Companies might have to face a variety of measures designed to deal with the pollution. Some examples are given below.

(a) **Government fees**. UK firms must pay a **Landfill Tax** on hazardous waste.

(b) **Government regulations**. Fines might be imposed for persistent breach of pollution guidelines, and pollution might be monitored by government inspectors. The government is currently focusing on how to discourage car usage and on the desirability of environmentally friendly transport.

(c) **Government targets.** The UK government has outlined targets for recycling and carbon dioxide emissions.

(d) **Tradeable permits**. A means of regulating pollution is to charge for it, raising the price over a period.

(e) **Commercial opportunities**. Companies **might** benefit from the commercial opportunities proposed by environmentalism, but this is no certainty.

(f) **Relocation.** Firms might **relocate** the business to a country where environmental standards are less strict, or have a lower priority in relation to other economic and social objectives, such as economic growth.

8 The impact of technology on organisations

8.1 Organisation structure

> Information systems and information technology have played a significant role in the development of the modern business environment including encouraging the **flattening** of **organisation hierarchies** and widening **spans of control**.

Information systems and information technology have played a significant role in the development of the modern business environment. For example, modern communications technology makes decentralised organisations possible, allowing decision making to be passed down to 'empowered' workers or outsourced to external companies.

There is a trend towards smaller, more **agile companies**. **Flexibility** and speed are increasingly seen as the key to competitive advantage. Advances in IT have allowed complex operating processes to be accelerated and made feedback information available almost immediately.

8.1.1 Span of control

As we saw in Chapter 1, span of control, or 'span of management', refers to the number of subordinates responsible to a superior. If a manager has five subordinates, the span of control is five.

Business automation and rationalisation, and improved management information systems, have often resulted in reduced staffing levels. In particular, layers of middle management have been removed in many organisations. This has been termed **'delayering'**. Managers or staff 'lower down' the hierarchy have been empowered to make decisions previously made by middle managers. Information technology has therefore had the effect of flattening organisation hierarchies and **widening spans of control**.

There is no universally 'correct' size for the span of control. The appropriate span of control will depend on:

(a) **Ability of the manager**. A good organiser and communicator will be able to control a larger number. The manager's work-load is also relevant.

(b) **Ability of the subordinates**. The more experienced, able, trustworthy and well-trained subordinates are, the easier it is to control larger numbers.

(c) **Nature of the task**. It is easier for a supervisor to control a large number of people if they are all doing routine, repetitive or similar tasks.

(d) The **geographical dispersal** of the subordinates, and the **communication system** of the organisation.

(e) The availability of **good quality information** to assist in decision making.

8.1.2 Tall and flat organisations

An **information system**, such as an intranet, can help provide organisation unity and coherency in flat, decentralised organisations.

The trend towards flatter structures is evidenced by talk of an 'e-lance economy', characterised by shifting **coalitions** of small firms collaborating on particular **projects**.

8.1.3 Organisation structure and information systems

The structure of an organisation and the way in which the organisation's information system is arranged are **related** issues.

Centralised systems means holding and processing data in a central place, such as a computer centre at head office. Data will be collected at 'remote' (ie geographically separate) offices and other locations and sent in to the central location.

Decentralised systems have the data/information processing carried out at several different locations, away from the 'centre' or 'head office'.

8.2 Other effects of IT on organisations

FAST FORWARD

Other **effects of IT on organisations** include:

- Routine processing (bigger volumes, greater speed, greater accuracy)
- Digital information and record keeping
- New skills required and new ways of working
- Reliance on IT
- New methods of communication and of providing customer service
- Interoperability (encourages collaboration across organisation boundaries) and open systems
- The view of information as a valuable resource
- The view of information as a commodity which can be bought, sold or exchanged ('information market')

8.2.1 Routine processing

Information technology enables the processing of data to be performed in bigger volumes, at greater speed and with greater accuracy.

8.2.2 Digital information and record keeping

Information storage and transmission is now largely digital rather than paper-based. However, many people like 'hard copies' and print out information as required. Far from reducing the use of paper, computer systems seem to have encouraged greater use of paper.

The nature and quality of management information has also changed.

(a) Managers have access to more information – for example from an ESS. Information is also likely to be more timely, accurate, reliable and up-to-date.

(b) More detailed planning is possible through the use of models (eg spreadsheets).

(c) Information for control should be more readily available.

(d) Decision making should improve as a consequence of better quality information.

8.2.3 Employment issues

The infiltration of IT into almost every area of business means that the vast majority of employees are now expected to utilise information technology. IT skills are required and new ways of working have emerged.

8.2.4 Technological change

A reliance on information technology commits an organisation to **continual change**. Systems are likely to be superseded after a few years.

8.2.5 Customer service

Information technology has enabled organisations to provide better customer service. Customer databases, EDI, extranets, websites and datamining can all be applied to improving service levels.

8.2.6 Information markets

The term **'information market'** reflects the growing view that information is a **commodity** which can be bought, sold or exchanged.

There has been a growing realisation that information is a resource and that it has many of the characteristics of any other resource. A key theme of this syllabus is the benefits which information, properly managed and used, can bring to an organisation.

8.2.7 Developments in communications

Communications technology is probably having a greater impact on organisational life than computers are at present. **E-mail** provides a quick and **efficient** means of communicating worldwide.

Voice mail systems allow **flexibility** in communication time and location. Computer Telephony Integration (CTI) systems can **route** incoming calls (they can be frustrating, particularly for callers with non-standard enquiries). CTI also enables information about callers to be gathered and stored allowing **personalised** communication.

Computer conferencing systems and organisation-wide **bulletin boards** encourage **communication** – both formal and **informal**.

Video-conferencing allows face-to-face contact between people who are spread widely across the world. If a video-conference is deemed sufficient, **travel costs** can be reduced.

8.3 IT and the employee/employer relationship

The widespread use of information technology in the workplace has affected the relationship between **employers and employees**:

- Reduced need to follow the chain-of-command
- Information overload
- Nature of work
- Close business relationships regardless of geographical location
- More flexible working arrangements
- Greater monitoring and control

Delayering has gone hand in hand with a trend towards **downsizing** whereby large numbers of managers and staff have been made redundant.

 Case Study

Downsizing is not that recent, but it is part of a relentless quest by companies to keep efficient.

(a) *Air New Zealand.* In late 2005 and early 2006 Air New Zealand outsourced 120 cleaning positions as well as axing 110 jobs from its aircraft engine sector. In an increasingly competitive and volatile market it also shed 470 head office jobs.

(b) *Rolls Royce.* Between 2001 to 2005, much of Rolls Royce's aircraft engine manufacturing operations was transferred from Hillingdon to Inchinnan. The workforce was reduced by over a third and the company increased its efficiency.

(c) *Harley Davidson*, in the US, cut the number of production controllers at one of its plants from 27 to 1.

Reasons for this trend are as follows.

(a) Information technology makes the information processing work of middle managers redundant.

(b) The trend towards team-working, whereby responsibility is devolved to groups of workers, renders redundant the directing and controlling role of middle managers.

8.4 Homeworking and supervision

Advances in communications technology have, for some tasks, reduced the need for the **actual presence of an individual in the office**. This is particularly true of tasks involving computers.

(a) The employee can, for example, do tasks involving data entry at home.

(b) The keyed-in data can be sent over a telecommunications link to head office.

(c) Some firms see benefits in employing the services of a pool of freelance workers, when there is a demand. This approach is being adopted in publishing and journalism.

This is sometimes known as homeworking (or, occasionally, telecommuting if it involves IT). The practice is not new in itself, but it is relatively new to the management of the office.

8.5 Outsourcing

Outsourcing is the contracting out of specified operations or services to an external vendor. There are various outsourcing options available, with different levels of control maintained 'in-house'. Outsourcing has **advantages** (eg use of highly skilled people) and **disadvantages** (eg lack of control).

Key term

Outsourcing is the contracting out of specified operations or services to an external vendor.

8.5.1 Types of outsourcing

There are four **broad classifications** of outsourcing, as described in the following table.

Classification	Comment
Ad-hoc	The organisation has a short-term requirement for increased IS/IT skills. An example would be employing programmers on a short-term contract to help with the programming of bespoke software.
Project management	The development and installation of a particular IS/IT project is outsourced. For example, a new accounting system.
Partial	Some IT/IS services are outsourced. Examples include hardware maintenance, network management or ongoing website management.
Total	An external supplier provides the vast majority of an organisation's IS/IT services; eg third party owns or is responsible for IT equipment, software and staff.

8.5.2 The advantages and disadvantages of outsourcing

Advantages of outsourcing

The **advantages** of outsourcing are as follows.

(a)   Outsourcing can remove uncertainty about **cost**, as there is often a long-term contract where services are specified in advance for a **fixed price**. If computing services are inefficient, the costs will be borne by the FM company. This is also an incentive to the third party to provide a high quality service.

(b)   Long-term contracts (maybe up to ten years) encourage **planning** for the future.

(c)   Outsourcing can bring the benefits of **economies of scale**. For example, a FM company may conduct research into new technologies that benefits a number of their clients.

(d)   A specialist organisation is able to retain **skills and knowledge**. Many organisations would not have a sufficiently well-developed IT department to offer IT staff opportunities for career development. Talented staff would leave to pursue their careers elsewhere.

(e)   New skills and knowledge become available. A specialist company can **share** staff with **specific expertise** between several clients. This allows the outsourcing company to take advantage of new developments without the need to recruit new people or re-train existing staff, and without the cost.

(f)   **Flexibility** (contract permitting). Resources may be able to be scaled up or down depending upon demand. For instance, during a major changeover from one system to another the number of IT staff needed may be twice as large as it will be once the new system is working satisfactorily.

An outsourcing organisation is more able to arrange its work on a **project** basis, whereby some staff will expect to be moved periodically from one project to the next.

Disadvantages of outsourcing

Some possible **drawbacks** are outlined below.

(a)   It is arguable that information and its provision is an **inherent part of the business** and of management. Unlike office cleaning, or catering, an organisation's IT services may be too important to be contracted out. Information is at the heart of management.

(b)   A company may have highly **confidential information** and to let outsiders handle it could be seen as **risky** in commercial and/or legal terms.

(c)   If a third party is handling IS/IT services there is no onus upon internal management to keep up with new developments or to suggest new ideas. Consequently, opportunities to gain **competitive advantage** may be missed. Any new technology or application devised by the third party is likely to be available to competitors.

(d)   An organisation may find itself **locked in** to an unsatisfactory contract. The decision may be very difficult to reverse. If the service provider supplies unsatisfactory levels of service, the effort and expense the organisation would incur to rebuild its own computing function or to move to another provider could be substantial.

(e)   The use of an outside organisation does not encourage awareness of the potential **costs** and benefits of IS/IT within the organisation. If managers cannot manage in-house IS/IT resources effectively, then it could be argued that they will not be able to manage an arrangement to outsource effectively either.

9 Competitive forces

FAST FORWARD

The **competitive environment** is structured by five forces: **barriers to entry; substitute products**; the bargaining power of **customers**; the bargaining power of **suppliers; competitive rivalry**.

In discussing competition, *Porter* (*Competitive Strategy*) distinguishes between factors which characterise the nature of competition.

(a) **In one industry compared with another** (eg in the chemicals industry compared with the clothing retail industry, some factors make one industry as a whole potentially more profitable than another (ie yielding a bigger return on investment).

(b) Factors **within a particular industry** lead to the competitive strategies that individual firms might select.

Five **competitive forces** influence the state of competition in an industry, which collectively determine the profit (ie long-run return on capital) potential of the industry as a whole. **Learn them.**

- The threat of **new entrants** to the industry
- The threat of **substitute** products or services
- The bargaining power of **customers**
- The bargaining power of **suppliers**
- The **rivalry** amongst current competitors in the industry

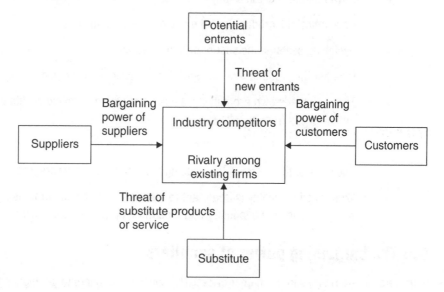

9.1 The threat of new entrants (and barriers to entry to keep them out)

A new entrant into an industry will bring extra capacity and more competition. The strength of this threat is likely to vary from industry to industry and depends on two things.

- The strength of the **barriers to entry**. Barriers to entry discourage new entrants.
- The likely **response of existing competitors** to the new entrant.

9.2 The threat from substitute products

A **substitute product** is a good or service produced by **another industry** which satisfies the same customer needs.

 Case Study

The Channel Tunnel

Passengers have several ways of getting to London to Paris, and the pricing policies of the various industries transporting them there reflects this.

(a)   'Le Shuttle' carries cars in the Channel Tunnel. Its main competitors come from the *ferry* companies, offering a substitute service. Therefore, you will find that Le Shuttle sets its prices with reference to ferry company prices, and vice versa.

(b)   Eurostar is the rail service from London to Paris/Brussels. Its main competitors are not the ferry companies but the *airlines.* Prices on the London-Paris air routes fell with the commencement of Eurostar services, and some airlines have curtailed the number of flights they offer.

9.3 The bargaining power of customers

Customers want better quality products and services at a lower price. Satisfying this want might force down the profitability of suppliers in the industry. Just how strong the position of customers will be depends on a number of factors.

* How much the customer buys

* How critical the product is to the customer's own business

* Switching costs (ie the cost of switching supplier)

* Whether the products are standard items (hence easily copied) or specialised

* The customer's own profitability: a customer who makes low profits will be forced to insist on low prices from suppliers

* Customer's ability to bypass the supplier (or take over the supplier)

* The skills of the customer purchasing staff, or the price-awareness of consumers

* When product quality is important to the customer, the customer is less likely to be price-sensitive, and so the industry might be more profitable as a consequence

9.4 The bargaining power of suppliers

Suppliers can exert pressure for higher prices. The ability of suppliers to get higher prices depends on several factors.

* Whether there are just **one or two dominant suppliers** to the industry, able to charge monopoly or oligopoly prices

* The threat of **new entrants** or substitute products to the **supplier's industry**

* Whether the suppliers have **other customers** outside the industry, and do not rely on the industry for the majority of their sales

* The **importance of the supplier's product** to the customer's business

* Whether the supplier has a **differentiated product** which buyers need to obtain

* Whether **switching costs** for customers would be high

 LEARNING MEDIA

9.5 The rivalry amongst current competitors in the industry

The **intensity of competitive rivalry** within an industry will affect the profitability of the industry as a whole. Competitive actions might take the form of price competition, advertising battles, sales promotion campaigns, introducing new products for the market, improving after sales service or providing guarantees or warranties. Competition can stimulate demand, expanding the market, or it can leave demand unchanged, in which case individual competitors will make less money, unless they are able to cut costs.

10 Converting resources: the value chain

FAST FORWARD

The **value chain** describes those activities of the organisation that add value to purchased inputs. Primary activities are involved in the production of goods and services. Support activities provide necessary assistance. **Linkages** are the relationships between activities. Managing the value chain, which includes relationships with outside suppliers, can be a source of strategic advantage.

The **value chain** model of corporate activities offers a bird's eye view of the firm and what it does. Competitive advantage arises out of the way in which firms organise and perform **activities** to add value.

10.1 Value activities

Key term

Value activities are the means by which a firm creates value in its products.

Activities incur costs, and, in combination with other activities, provide a product or service which earns revenue.

10.2 Example

Let us explain this point by using the example of a **restaurant**. A restaurant's activities can be divided into buying food, cooking it, and serving it (to customers). There is no reason, in theory, why the customers should not do all these things themselves, at home. The customer however, is not only prepared to **pay for someone else** to do all this but also **pays more than the cost of** the resources (food, wages and soon). The ultimate value a firm creates is measured by the amount customers are willing to pay for its products or services above the cost of carrying out value activities. A firm is profitable if the realised value to customers exceeds the collective cost of performing the activities.

(a) Customers **purchase value**, which they measure by comparing a firm's products and services with similar offerings by competitors.

(b) The business **creates value** by carrying out its activities either more efficiently than other businesses, or by combining them in such a way as to provide a unique product or service.

Question — **Value activities**

Outline different ways in which the restaurant can create value.

Answer

Here are some ideas. Each of these options is a way of organising the activities of buying, cooking and serving food in a way that customers will value.

(a) It can become more efficient, by automating the production of food, as in a fast food chain.

(b)   The chef can develop commercial relationships with growers, so he or she can obtain the best quality fresh produce.

(c)   The chef can specialise in a particular type of cuisine (eg Nepalese, Korean).

(d)   The restaurant can be sumptuously decorated for those customers who value atmosphere and a sense of occasion, in addition to a restaurant's purely gastronomic pleasures.

(e)   The restaurant can serve a particular type of customer (eg celebrities).

10.3 The value chain

Porter (in *Competitive Advantage*) grouped the various activities of an organisation into a **value chain**. Here is a diagram.

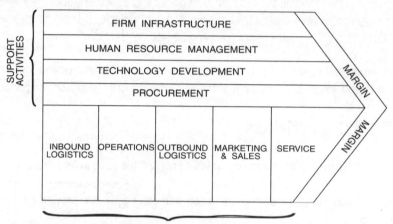

The **margin** is the excess the customer is prepared to **pay** over the **cost** to the firm of obtaining resource inputs and providing value activities. It represents the **value created** by the **value activities** themselves and by the **management of the linkages** between them.

Exam focus point

This diagram is worth committing to memory as the terms may be referred to in an exam question.

Primary activities are directly related to production, sales, marketing, delivery and service.

Activity	Comment
Inbound logistics	Receiving, handling and storing inputs to the production system: warehousing, transport, inventory control and so on.
Operations	Convert resource inputs into a final product. Resource inputs are not only materials. People are a resource especially in service industries.
Outbound logistics	Storing the product and its distribution to customers: packaging, testing, delivery and so on.
Marketing and sales	Informing customers about the product, persuading them to buy it, and enabling them to do so: advertising, promotion and so on.
After sales service	Installing products, repairing them, upgrading them, providing spare parts and so forth.

Support activities provide purchased inputs, human resources, technology and infrastructural functions to support the primary activities.

Quick Quiz

1 Why is environmental analysis important?

2 Give four types of legal factor affecting a company.

3 How can businesses influence government policy?

4 It is a basic principle of employment legislation that any dismissal is potentially unfair. True or false?

5 What is a 'data subject'?

6 How can senior managers promote health and safety awareness?

7 Why is the routine processing of data, that has been made possible by advances in IT, of benefit to an organisation?

8 What are the effects of downsizing?

9 What are the five competitive forces?

10 What are the primary activities in the value chain?

11 The purpose of value chain analysis is to understand customer price and quality preferences. True or false?

Answers to quick quiz

1   The environment is everything that surrounds an organisation and so understanding it is one of the key inputs to the strategy-making process.

2   **Four from:**

   General legal framework (eg contract)
   Criminal
   Company
   Employment
   Health and safety
   Data protection
   Marketing and sales
   Environment
   Taxation

3   Employ lobbyists; hand out non-executive directorships, try to influence public opinion.

4   True. The employee then needs to prove that he or she has been dismissed, and the employer needs to prove that it was fair.

5   An individual who is the subject of personal data.

6   • Visibly reacting to policy breaches
     • Ensuring that the policy is communicated
     • Setting priorities
     • Involving staff in the health and safety process

7   Greater volumes of data can be processed more quickly and with greater accuracy.

8   It can make organisations leaner and more flexible, but also can reduce capacity.

9   • Threat of new entrants
     • Threat of substitute products
     • Bargaining power of customers
     • Bargaining power of suppliers
     • Rivalry amongst current competition

10   Inbound logistics; operations; outbound logistics; marketing and sales; after sales service

11   False. The main purpose is to understand how the company creates value from its various activities.

Part C
History and role of accounting

The role of
accounting

Topic list	Syllabus reference
1 The purpose of accounting information	C1 (a)(b)
2 Nature, principles and scope of accounting	C1 (b)
3 The regulatory system	C2 (a)(c)
4 Control over business transactions	C3 (a)
5 The main business financial systems	C3 (b)(c)
6 Manual and computerised accounting systems	C3 (e)
7 Databases and spreadsheets	C3 (d)

Introduction

It is important to understand why accounts are prepared. **Sections 1 and 2** of
this chapter introduce some basic ideas about accounts and give an indication
of their purpose. You also need to consider what makes accounting information
useful, and the qualities which such information should have.

We outline the standard setting process in **Section 3**.

Sections 4 and 5 examine the main transactions and financial systems
undertaken by a business, before going on to consider manual and
computerised financial systems in **Section 6**.

Questions may ask you to discuss the advantages and disadvantages of
databases and spreadsheets (**Section 7**).

Study guide

		Intellectual level
C1	**The history and function of accounting in business**	
(a)	Briefly explain the history and development of the accounting and finance role in business.	1
(b)	Explain the overall role and separate functions of the accounting department.	1
C2	**Law and regulation governing accounting**	
(a)	Explain basic legal requirements in relation to keeping and submitting proper records and preparing financial accounts.	1
(b)	Explain the broad consequences of failing to comply with the legal requirements for maintaining accounting records.	1
(c)	Explain how the international accountancy profession regulates itself through the establishment of reporting standards and their monitoring.	1
C3	**Financial systems, procedures and IT applications**	
(a)	Explain how business and financial systems and procedures are formulated and implemented to reflect the objectives and policies of the organisation.	1
(b)	Describe the main financial systems used within an organisation:	1
(i)	Purchases and sales invoicing	
(ii)	Payroll	
(iii)	Credit control	
(iv)	Cash and working capital management.	
(c)	Explain why appropriate controls are necessary in relation to business and IT systems and procedures.	2
(d)	Understand business uses of computers and IT software applications:	1
(i)	Spreadsheet applications	
(ii)	Database systems	
(e)	Describe and compare the relative benefits and limitations of manual and automated financial systems that may be used in an organisation.	2
D1	**Accounting and finance functions within business**	
(a)	Explain the contribution of the accounting function to the formulation, implementation, and control of the organisation's policies, procedures, and performance.	2
(b)	Identify and describe the main accounting and reporting functions in business:	1
(i)	Recording financial information	
(ii)	Codifying and processing financial information	
(iii)	Preparing financial statements	

		Intellectual level
(c)	Identify and describe the main management accounting and performance management functions in business:	1
(i)	Recording and analysing costs and revenues	
(ii)	Providing management accounting information for decision-making	
(iii)	Planning and preparing budgets and exercising budgetary control.	
(d)	Identify and describe the main finance and treasury functions:	1
(i)	Calculating and mitigating business tax liabilities	
(ii)	Evaluating and obtaining finance	
(iii)	Managing working capital	
(iv)	Treasury and risk management.	

Exam guide

The specifics of accounting systems are highly likely to be examined. The business needs of the users of accounting information are also a 'hot topic'.

1 The purpose of accounting information

1.1 What is accounting?

FAST FORWARD

Accounting is a way of recording, analysing and summarising transactions of a business.

- The transactions are recorded in 'books of prime entry'.
- The transactions are then analysed and posted to the ledgers.
- Finally the transactions are summarised in the financial statements.

The accounting function is part of the broader business system, and does not operate in isolation. It handles the financial operations of the organisation, but also provides information and advice to other departments.

Accounts are produced to aid management in planning, control and decision-making and to comply with statutory regulations. **The accounting system must be adequate to fulfil these functions**. An organisation's accounting systems are affected by the nature of its business transactions and the sort of business it is.

Factor	Example
Size	A small business like a greengrocer will have a simple, accounting system, where the main accounting record will probably be the till roll. A large retail business, such as a chain of supermarkets, will have elaborate accounting systems covering a large number of product ranges and sites.
Type of organisation	A service business might need to record the time employees take on particular jobs. Accounting on a job or client basis might also be a feature of service businesses. A public sector organisation, such as a government department, may be more concerned with the monitoring of expenditure against performance targets than recording revenue. A manufacturing company will account both for unit sales and revenue, but needs to keep track of costs for decision-making purposes and so forth.
Organisation structure	In a business managed by area, accounts will be prepared on an area basis. In a functional organisation, the accounts staff are in a separate department.

Be aware that accounting work has to comply with a wide range of regulations to avoid penalties, including law such as the Companies Act. As a result, it tends to be rather formalised and procedural in order to make sure that nothing is overlooked. Organisations often lay down their accounting rules and procedures in writing, and this may form part of an organisation manual or procedures manual.

1.2 The need for accounts

Renaissance scholar *Luca Pacioli* wrote the first printed explantion of double-entry bookkeeping in 1494. Double-entry bookkeeping involves entering every transaction as a **debit** in one account and a corresponding **credit** in another account, and ensuring that they 'balance'. Pacioli's description of the method was widely influential.

The first English book on the subject was written in 1543. The practice of double entry bookkeeping has barely changed since then and is standard across the world, based upon the concept that every transaction has a dual effect that balances to zero.

The original role of the accounting function was to record financial information and this is still its main focus.

Why do businesses need to produce accounts? If a business is being run efficiently, why should it have to go through all the bother of accounting procedures in order to produce financial information?

A business should produce information about its activities because there are various groups of people who want or need to know that information. This sounds rather vague: to make it clearer, we should look more closely at the classes of people who might need information about a business. We need also to think about what information in particular is of interest to the members of each class.

Large businesses are usually of interest to a greater variety of people than small businesses, so we will consider the case of a large public company whose shares can be purchased and sold on the Stock Exchange.

1.3 Users of financial statements and accounting information

The people who might be interested in financial information about a large public company may be classified as follows.

(a) **Managers of the company**. These are people appointed by the company's owners to supervise the day-to-day activities of the company. They need information about the company's financial situation as it is currently and as it is expected to be in the future. This is to enable them to manage the business efficiently and to take effective control and planning decisions.

(b) **Shareholders of the company**, ie the company's owners. These will want to assess how effectively management is performing its stewardship function. They will want to know how profitably management is running the company's operations and how much profit they can afford to withdraw from the business for their own use.

(c) **Trade contacts**, including suppliers who provide goods to the company on credit and customers who purchase the goods or services provided by the company. **Suppliers** will want to know about the company's ability to pay its debts; **customers** need to know that the company is a secure source of supply and is in no danger of having to close down.

(d) **Providers of finance to the company**. These might include a bank which permits the company to operate an overdraft, or provides longer-term finance by granting a loan. The bank will want to ensure that the company is able to keep up with interest payments, and eventually to repay the amounts advanced.

(e) **Her Majesty's Revenue and Customs**, who will want to know about business profits in order to assess the tax payable by the company.

(f) **Employees of the company**. These should have a right to information about the company's financial situation, because their future careers and the size of their wages and salaries depend on it.

(g) **Financial analysts and advisers**, who need information for their clients or audience. For example, stockbrokers will need information to advise investors in stocks and shares; credit agencies will want information to advise potential suppliers of goods to the company; and journalists need information for their reading public.

(h) **Government and their agencies.** Governments and their agencies are interested in the allocation of resources and therefore in the activities of enterprises. They also require information in order to provide a basis for national statistics.

(i) **The public**. Enterprises affect members of the public in a variety of ways. For example, enterprises may make a substantial contribution to a local economy by providing employment and using local suppliers. Another important factor is the effect of an enterprise on the environment, for example as regards pollution.

Accounting information is organised into financial statements to satisfy the **information needs** of these different groups. Not all will be equally satisfied.

Managers of a business need the most information, to help them take their planning and control decisions; and they obviously have 'special' access to information about the business, because they can get people to give them the types of statements they want. When managers want a large amount of information about the costs and profitability of individual products, or different parts of their business, they can arrange to obtain it through a system of cost and management accounting.

Question

Information

It is easy to see how 'internal' people get hold of accounting information. A manager, for example, can just go along to the accounts department and ask the staff there to prepare whatever accounting statements he needs. But external users of accounts cannot do this. How, in practice, can a business contact or a financial analyst access accounting information about a company?

Answer

The answer is that limited companies (though not other forms of business such as partnerships) are required to make certain accounting information public. They do so by sending copies of the required information to the Registrar of Companies at Companies House. The information filed at Companies House is available, at a fee, to any member of the public who asks for it. Other sources include financial comment in the press and company brochures.

In addition to management information, financial statements are prepared and perhaps published for the benefit of other user groups.

(a) The **law** provides for the provision of some information. The Companies Acts require every company to publish accounting information for its shareholders; and companies must also file a copy of their accounts with the Registrar of Companies, so that any member of the public who so wishes can go and look at them.

(b) The **HM Revenue and Customs** authorities will receive the information they need to make tax assessments.

(c)   A **bank** might demand a forecast of a company's expected future cash flows as a pre-condition of granting an overdraft.

(d)   The **professional accountancy bodies** have been jointly responsible for issuing **accounting standards** and some standards require companies to publish certain additional information. Accountants, as members of these professional bodies, are placed under a strong obligation to ensure that company accounts conform to the requirements of the standards.

(e)   Some companies provide, voluntarily, specially prepared financial information for issue to their employees. These statements are known as **employee reports**.

Exam focus point	You may be asked about what information would be needed by managers, employees or shareholders.

1.3.1 Non-commercial undertakings

It is not only businesses that need to prepare accounts. **Charities and clubs**, for example, prepare financial statements every year. Accounts also need to be prepared for **government** (public sector organisations).

1.4 Qualities of good accounting information

FAST FORWARD	You should be able to identify the qualities of good accounting information.

Below are some features that accounting information should have if it is to be useful.

(a)   **Relevance**. The information provided should satisfy the needs of information users. In the case of company accounts, clearly a wide range of information will be needed to satisfy a wide range of users.

(b)   **Comprehensibility**. Information may be difficult to understand because it is skimpy or incomplete; but too much detail is also a defect which can cause difficulties of understanding.

(c)   **Reliability**. Information will be more reliable if it is independently verified. The law requires that the accounts published by limited companies should be verified by auditors, who must be independent of the company and must hold an approved qualification.

(d)   **Completeness**. A company's accounts should present a rounded picture of its economic activities.

(e)   **Objectivity**. Information should be as objective as possible. This is particularly the case where conflicting interests operate and an unbiased presentation of information is needed. In the context of preparing accounts, where many decisions must be based on judgement rather than objective facts, this problem often arises. Management are often inclined to paint a rosy picture of a company's profitability to make their own performance look impressive. By contrast, auditors responsible for verifying the accounts are inclined to take a more prudent view so that they cannot be held liable by, say, a supplier misled into granting credit to a shaky company.

(f)   **Timeliness**. The usefulness of information is reduced if it does not appear until long after the period to which it relates, or if it is produced at unreasonably long intervals. What constitutes a long interval depends on the circumstances: management of a company may need very frequent (perhaps daily) information on cash flows to run the business efficiently; but shareholders are normally content to see accounts produced annually.

(g)   **Comparability**. Information should be produced on a consistent basis so that valid comparisons can be made with information from previous periods and with information produced by other sources (for example the accounts of similar companies operating in the same line of business).

1.5 The structure of accounting functions

We have already spent some time looking at the accounting function in Chapter 1, so what follows is something of a re-cap to put it into the context of its specific role, as covered by this chapter. In UK companies, the head of the accounting management structure is usually the **finance director**. The finance director has a seat on the **board of directors** and is responsible for routine accounting matters and also for broad financial policy.

In many larger companies the finance director has one or more deputies below him.

(a)   Some responsibilities of the **Financial Controller**

- Routine accounting
- Providing accounting reports for other departments
- Cashiers' duties and cash control

(b)   Management accounting is such an important function that a **Management Accountant** is often appointed with status equal to the financial controller and separate responsibilities.

- Cost accounting
- Budgets and budgetary control
- Financial management of projects

(c)   A very large organisation might have a **Treasurer** in charge of treasury work.

- Raising funds by borrowing
- Investing surplus funds on the money market or other investment markets
- Cash flow control

Sections in the accounts department

(a)   The **financial accounts** section is divided up into sections, with a supervisor responsible for each section (eg for credit control, payroll, purchase ledger, sales ledger etc).

(b)   Similarly, **management accounting** work is divided up, with a number of cost accountants as supervisors of sections responsible for keeping cost records of different items (eg materials, labour, overheads; or production, research and development, marketing).

(c)   Some companies that spend large amounts on **capital projects** might have a section assigned exclusively to capital project appraisal (payback appraisal, DCF appraisal, sensitivity analysis, the capital budget).

An accounts function is depicted in the diagram on the next page. People are grouped together by the type of work they do. In an area structure, accounts staff might be dispersed throughout the different regions of an organisation. Management accounting work is often decentralised to departments because it provides vital information for management control purposes.

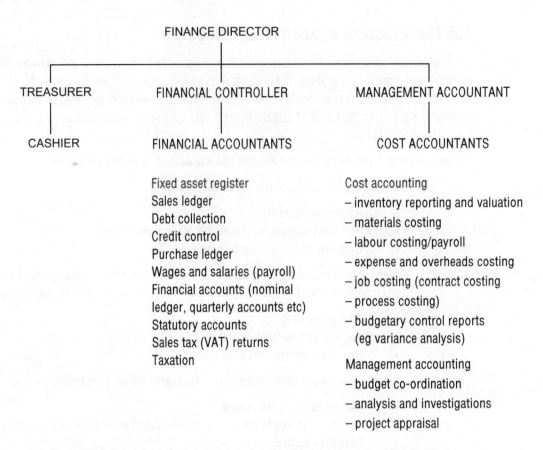

FINANCE DIRECTOR

TREASURER   FINANCIAL CONTROLLER   MANAGEMENT ACCOUNTANT

CASHIER   FINANCIAL ACCOUNTANTS   COST ACCOUNTANTS

Fixed asset register
Sales ledger
Debt collection
Credit control
Purchase ledger
Wages and salaries (payroll)
Financial accounts (nominal
ledger, quarterly accounts etc)
Statutory accounts
Sales tax (VAT) returns
Taxation

Cost accounting
– inventory reporting and valuation
– materials costing
– labour costing/payroll
– expense and overheads costing
– job costing (contract costing
– process costing)
– budgetary control reports
  (eg variance analysis)

Management accounting
– budget co-ordination
– analysis and investigations
– project appraisal

Many organisations have an **internal audit department**. This functions as an internal financial control. One of its responsibilities is to control the risks of fraud and error. For this reason it should be separate from the finance department and the chief internal auditor should report to the audit committee of the board of directors, bypassing the Financial Director. Internal audit is covered in Chapter 9.

2 Nature, principles and scope of accounting

FAST FORWARD

You may have a wide understanding of what accounting is about. Your job may be in one area or type of accounting, but you must understand the breadth of work which an accountant undertakes.

2.1 Financial accounting and management accounting

Key term

> **Financial accounting** is mainly a method of reporting the results and financial position of a business.

It is not primarily concerned with providing information towards the more efficient conduct of the business. Although financial accounts are of interest to management, their principal function is to satisfy the information needs of persons not involved in the day-to-day running of the business.

This is particularly clear in the context of the published accounts of limited companies. **Accounting Standards** (and company law) prescribe that a company should **produce accounts to be presented to the shareholders**. There are usually detailed regulations on what the accounts must contain and this enables shareholders to assess how well the directors (or management board) have run the company. Also there are certain outsiders who need information about a company: suppliers, customers, employees, tax authorities, the general public. Their information needs are satisfied, wholly or in part, by the company's published financial statements.

> **Management (or cost) accounting** is a management information system which analyses data to provide information as a basis for managerial action. The concern of a management accountant is to present accounting information in the form most helpful to management.

2.2 The application of information

Financial reporting is not an optional extra. The published accounts are an important source of communication with outsiders. Reported levels of profit determine the return that investors can receive. They also indirectly affect the company's cost of capital by affecting the share price.

The **management accountant** is even nearer the policy making and management process. This is because the management accountant is not primarily interested in reporting to interested parties external to the organisation. After all, the requirements of external users of accounts may be different to those involved in managing and running the business in several respects.

- Aggregation of information
- Classification of data
- Level of detail
- The period covered

Internally, accountants therefore provide information for **planning and controlling** the business.

- Competitors performance
- Cost/profit centre performance
- Desirability of investments
- Past cost information
- Product profitability
- Sensitivity analysis
- Alternative options

The accountant provides information essential for the current management and decision-making of the business. If line decisions are assessed in accounting terms, even in part, then the accountant will be involved in them. Accountants assess the future financial consequences of certain decisions.

2.2.1 Control and stewardship

The accountant's staff authority is generally expressed in procedures and rules. For example, capital investment is analysed in financial terms. People have formal expenditure limits. In many respects, money and funds are a business's lifeblood, and monitoring their flow is a necessary precaution. If the flow of funds dries up a business can fail very easily. **Proper financial control ensures that the business is adequately financed to meet its obligations.**

> It is important that you understand this distinction between management accounting and financial accounting. The accounting statements drawn up by a management accountant are often prepared and presented very differently from those of the financial accountant; for example, they do not need to comply with company law or accounting standards. You should bear in mind the different reasons for preparing management and financial accounts, and the different people to whom they are addressed.

2.3 Financial management

Financial management is a separate discipline from both management accounting and financial accounting, although in a small organisation the three roles may be carried out by the same person.

The financial manager is responsible for raising finance and controlling financial resources, including the following decisions.

- Should the firm borrow from a bank or raise funds by issuing shares?
- How much should be paid as a dividend?
- Should the firm spend money on new machinery?
- How much credit should be given to customers?
- How much discount should be given to customers who pay early?

The subject of financial management will be considered in your more advanced studies.

2.4 Auditing

The annual accounts of a limited company must generally be **audited** by a person independent of the company. In practice, this often means that the members of the company appoint a firm of registered auditors to investigate the financial statements and report as to whether or not they show a true and fair view of the company's results for the year and its financial position at the end of the year.

When the auditors have completed their work they must prepare a **report** explaining the work that they have done and the **opinion** they have formed.

In simple cases they will be able to report that they have carried out their work in accordance with the Auditing Standards and that, in their opinion, the accounts show a true and fair view and are properly prepared in accordance with company legislation. This is described as an **unqualified** (or 'clean') audit report.

Sometimes the auditors may disagree with management on a point in the accounts. If they are unable to persuade the management to change the accounts, and if the item at issue is large or otherwise important, it is the auditors' duty to prepare a **qualified report**, setting out the matter(s) on which they disagree with the management.

The financial statements to which the auditors refer in their report comprise the following.

- The income statement
- The balance sheet
- The cash flow statement
- Supporting notes

The auditors' report is included as a part of the company's published accounts. It is addressed to the members of the company (not to the management).

2.4.1 Internal audit

Internal auditors are employees of the company whose duties are fixed by management and who report on the effectiveness of internal control systems.

2.5 Other departments and sections

Accounting management provides a good example of the **need for close co-ordination** between managers and sections, and this need is particularly acute in financial accounts work because of the **internal controls dividing up responsibilities**.

Department	Accounts section	Relationship
Purchases dept (PD)	Purchase ledger (PL)	PD advises PL of purchase orders
		PD indicates valid invoices
	Cashier (C)	C informs PD and PL of payment
Human resources dept	Payroll	Personnel gives details of wage rates, starters and leavers, to payroll
Sales dept (SD) **Credit control (CC)**	Sales ledger (SL)	SD advises SL of sales order
		SL might give CC information about overdue debts
		SL might give details about debtors ageing and other reports
Operations, inventory controllers	Cost accounting staff	Operations might give details of movements of inventory, so that the accounts staff can value inventory and provide costing reports
Senior management	Financial accounting and cost accounting staff	The accounts department as a whole produces management information for decision making and control

Importance of the relationship

The accounts department is crucial to the organisation.

- If it provides the wrong information, managers will make bad decisions
- If it confuses the data, important transactions might slip through the net, and fraud may result
- There is a legal duty to ensure that accounting records are in good order

3 The regulatory system

FAST FORWARD

You should be able to outline the factors which have shaped the development of financial accounting.

3.1 Introduction

You may be aware that there have been considerable upheavals in financial reporting, mainly in response to criticism. The purpose of this section is to give a **general picture** of some of the factors which have shaped financial accounting. We will concentrate on the accounts of limited companies because this is the type of organisation whose accounts are most closely regulated by statute or otherwise.

The following factors can be identified.

- Company law
- Accounting concepts and individual judgement
- Accounting standards
- The European Union
- Other international influences
- Generally accepted accounting practice (GAAP)

3.2 Company law

Limited companies are required by law (the UK Companies Act 1985 or CA 1985 for example) to prepare and publish accounts annually. The form and content of the UK accounts are regulated primarily by CA 1985, but must also comply with accounting standards.

3.3 Accounting concepts and individual judgement

Financial statements are prepared on the basis of a number of fundamental accounting concepts (or accounting principles as they are called in the UK Companies Act 1985). Many figures in financial statements are derived from the application of judgement in putting those concepts into practice.

It is clear that different people exercising their judgement on the same facts can arrive at very different conclusions. Other examples of areas where the judgement of different people may differ are as follows.

- Valuation of buildings in times of rising property prices.

- Research and development. Is it right to treat this only as an expense? In a sense it is an investment to generate future revenue.

- Accounting for inflation.

- Brands such as 'Jaffa Cakes' or 'Walkman'. Are they assets in the same way that a forklift truck is an asset?

Working from the same data, different groups of people would produce very different financial statements. If the exercise of judgement is completely unfettered any comparability between the accounts of different organisations will disappear. This will be all the more significant in cases where deliberate manipulation occurs in order to present accounts in the most favourable light.

3.4 UK Accounting standards

In an attempt to deal with some of the subjectivity, and to achieve comparability between different organisations, **accounting standards** were developed.

3.4.1 The old UK regime

Between 1970 and 1990 the standards (Statements of Standard Accounting Practice or SSAPs) were devised by the **Accounting Standards Committee**. However, it was felt that these standards were too much concerned with detailed rules in which companies found it all too easy to find loopholes.

3.4.2 The current UK regime

The Accounting Standards Committee was replaced in 1990 by the **Financial Reporting Council**. Its subsidiary the **Accounting Standards Board** (ASB), issues standards 'concerned with principles rather than fine details'. Its standards are called Financial Reporting Standards (FRSs). However it adopted all existing SSAPs and some of these are still relevant although most have been replaced by FRSs. It is supported in its aim by the Urgent Issues Task Force and the Review Panel.

The **Urgent Issues Task Force (UITF)** is an offshoot of the ASB. Its function is to tackle urgent matters not covered by existing standards and for which, given the urgency, the normal standard setting process would not be practicable.

The **Financial Reporting Review Panel** (FRRP) is concerned with the examination and questioning of departures from accounting standards by large companies.

3.4.3 Accounting Standards and the law

The Companies Act 1985 requires companies to include a note to the accounts stating that the accounts have been prepared in accordance with **applicable accounting standards** or, alternatively, giving details of material departures from those standards, with reasons. The Review Panel and the Secretary of State for Trade and Industry have the power to apply to the court for revision of the accounts where non-compliance is not justified.

These provisions mean that accounting standards now have the force of law, whereas previously they had no legal standing in statute.

Question

Recap

Without looking:

(a)   Why do we need accounting standards?
(b)   Who produces them?
(c)   Who looks into departures from accounting standards?
(d)   Do they have the force of law?

Answer

(a)   See Section 3.4
(b)   The ASB
(c)   The FRRP
(d)   Yes

3.5 The European Union

Since the United Kingdom became a member of the European Union (EU) it has been obliged to comply with legal requirements decided on by the EU. It does this by enacting UK laws to implement EU directives. For example, the Companies Act 1989 was enacted in part to implement the provisions of the seventh and eighth directives, which deal with consolidated accounts and auditors.

Exam focus point

> Although your syllabus does not require you to be an expert on EU procedure, you should be aware that the form and content of company accounts can be influenced by international developments.

3.6 International Accounting Standards Board

One important influence on financial accounting is the **International Accounting Standards Board** (IASB). The forerunner of the IASB was set up in 1973 to work for the improvement and harmonisation of financial reporting. Its members are the professional accounting bodies. The structure of the IASB was reorganised in May 2000.

The objectives of the IASB are:

(a)   To **develop**, in the public interest, a single set of high quality, understandable and enforceable **global accounting standards** that require high quality, transparent and comparable information in financial statements and other financial reporting to help participants in the world's capital markets and other users make economic decisions.

(b)   To promote the use and **rigorous application** of those standards.

(c) To bring about **convergence of national accounting standards** and International Accounting Standards to high quality solutions.

3.6.1 The use and application of International Accounting Standards (IASs)

IASs have helped both to improve and to harmonise financial reporting around the world. The standards are used:

- As national requirements, often after a national process
- As the basis for all or some national requirements
- As an international benchmark for those countries which develop their own requirements
- By regulatory authorities for domestic and foreign companies
- By companies themselves

3.7 Generally Accepted Accounting Practice (GAAP)

This term signifies all the rules, from whatever source, which govern accounting.

Key term

> **GAAP** is a set of rules governing accounting. The rules may derive from:
> - Company law (mainly CA 1985)
> - Accounting standards
> - International accounting standards and statutory requirements in other countries (particularly the US)
> - Stock Exchange requirements

3.8 True and fair view

Key term

> **True and fair view** is not defined in company law or accounting standards. For practical purposes, it can be taken to mean accurate and not misleading.

Company law requires that:

- The balance sheet must give a **true and fair view of the state of affairs** of the company as at the end of the financial year.

- The profit and loss account must give a **true and fair view of the profit or loss** of the company for the financial year.

3.8.1 True and fair 'override'

The Companies Act 1985 states that the directors may depart from any of its provisions if these are inconsistent with the requirement to give a true and fair view. This is commonly referred to as the 'true and fair override'. It has been treated as an important loophole in the law and has been the cause of much argument, and dissatisfaction within the accounting profession.

Question   Forces

List the forces that have shaped financial accounting, stating the effect of each.

Answer

(a) **Company law** requires companies to prepare accounts and regulates their form and content.
(b) **Accounting concepts** are applied by individuals using their **subjective judgement**.
(c) **Accounting standards** help to eliminate subjectivity.
(d) The **European Union** issues directives on accounting matters which we must apply.

(e) **International Accounting Standards** aim to harmonise accounting round the world.

(f) **GAAP** is a collection of rules from various sources, governing accounting.

4 Control over business transactions

4.1 Office organisation

There are a number of areas or functions to be administered and managed within a business. For example, the 'head office' of a business may cover the following areas:

- Purchasing
- Human resources
- Finance
- Sales and marketing
- General administration

4.1.1 Purchasing

Whether a business manufactures products or sells bought in products, there will be a large purchasing function, either purchasing raw materials for manufacture or purchasing finished goods for resale. The function of the purchasing department will be to ensure that the business purchases from suppliers providing the best overall deal in terms of price, service, delivery time and quality. The purchasing department will also be responsible for ensuring that only necessary purchases are made by the business.

4.1.2 Human resources

Any business that employs a significant number of people is likely to have a human resources function. This area of the office will be responsible for the hiring and firing of staff, for training of staff and for the general welfare of the employees.

4.1.3 Finance

The finance function is also very wide-ranging. On a day to day level the accounts department will deal with the sending invoices to customers, receiving invoices from suppliers, payment of suppliers, receiving money from customers and making other payments such as purchases of non-current assets and payment of employees. The higher levels of management in the accounting function may also be responsible for management of the cash balances and for the overall financing of the organisation.

4.1.4 Sales and marketing

The selling and marketing function will deal with all aspects of taking sales orders, advertising, and any sales personnel.

4.1.5 General administration

General administration functions are very wide-ranging but might include secretarial support, dealing with telephone queries and arranging matters such as rent of properties.

Question

Which of the following is not a function of the purchasing department?

A   Ensuring that only required goods are purchased
B   Ensuring that suppliers used give the best price
C   Paying suppliers' invoices
D   Negotiating discounts with suppliers

Answer

The answer is C. Paying suppliers' invoices.

4.2 Policies

As you will be starting to realise in any reasonable sized business there will be a lot of different transactions and roles being carried out by many different people in the organisation. As with any entity, in order for the management to keep control of the activities there will have to be some form of rules and procedures.

For example there must be **authorisation policies** for the purchase of non-current assets, procedures for choosing new suppliers, procedures for accepting new customers etc.

In smaller organisations where only a handful of individuals are involved in the transactions of the business such procedures and best practices can be **communicated orally by management**. However in larger organisations where there are very many people carrying out functions possibly at a number of different geographical locations then a more formal procedure is needed to ensure that the correct procedures and practices are followed.

This often takes the form of a **policy manual** which will set out the required procedures for all of the various functions of the business. Every employee will be expected to have read the areas relevant to their functions and the policy manual should always be readily available for easy reference.

Although a policy manual is to be recommended as a form of control over the activities of employees care must be taken that strict adherence to the rules does not create inflexibility and in cases of doubt a more senior member of the staff should be consulted.

4.3 Business transactions

It was mentioned earlier that businesses come in all shapes and forms. However there will be a number of types of transactions which will be common to most businesses:

- Making sales
- Making purchases
- Paying expenses
- Paying employees
- Purchasing non-current assets

This diagram shows, in a simplified form, the flow of funds, documentation and information.

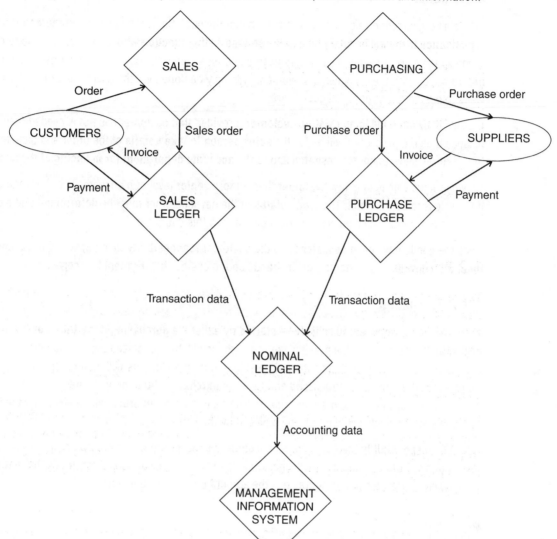

Effective systems and procedures should ensure that:

- Relationships with customers are effectively managed
- Relationships with suppliers are effectively managed
- Office functions interrelate properly and are not duplicated

Within the overall system, which we can consider to be how each department relates to the other departments and to outside bodies, there will be sub-systems. For instance, the purchase ledger function will have its own system, which will be designed to ensure that only authorised payments are made, that no invoice ever gets paid twice and that expenses are coded to the correct accounts.

Weaknesses in office procedures may be signalled by:

- Arguments over job functions
- Missing paperwork
- Disputes with customers/suppliers
- Goods not delivered

4.3.1 Sales

In a retail organisation sales are of course made on the shop floor. However in a **manufacturing organisation** there will normally be a **sales and marketing function** whose responsibility is to **market** the organisation's **products** and take orders from customers. Often the day to day responsibility for taking orders will be with the salesmen and women. This may be done over the telephone or may be via personal visits to customers or potential customers.

If a sale is being made to an **existing customer**, provided that customer has not exceeded their credit balance then the procedure will be for the **sales person** to **take details** of the order and pass those details to the stores department **for despatch** and to the **accounts department for invoicing** of the customer.

However if the sale is to a **new customer** then a more **senior** level of management will have to be involved if the sale is to be on credit. The **credit status** of the new customer must be **determined** and a decision made as to whether sales on credit should be made to this customer.

Once the **goods** have been **despatched** to the customer **responsibility** then **passes** to the **accounting function** to invoice the customer for the goods and to ensure that payment is received.

4.3.2 Purchases

The making of **purchases** will initially be **started** by either the **purchasing department or** the **stores department**. The need for the purchase of more goods will be recognised by, for example, the stores manager when he realises that an item of inventory is running low. He will then **complete** a **purchase requisition** which must be **authorised** and then the **purchasing function** will determine the most **appropriate supplier** on the basis of price, delivery and quality. An order will be placed by the purchasing function and the goods will normally be received by the stores department.

After this **responsibility** then goes to the **accounting department** which will await the arrival of the invoice for the goods from the suppliers, will check that the invoice is accurate and for goods that have in fact been received and then in due course pay the amount due to the supplier.

4.3.3 Overheads

Organisations will incur a variety of expenses such as rent and rates, insurance, telephone bills, energy bills, advertising expenses etc. In some cases these will be incurred by a specific department of the business such as the marketing department entering investing in an advertising campaign or alternatively the receipt of the telephone bill will be part of the **general administration of the business**.

When bills for **expenses** are received they will be passed to the **accounting function** which will check that the expense has been incurred or is reasonable and then will process the expense for payment.

4.3.4 Payroll

Every week and/or every month the employees of the business must be paid. For this process to take place there are a lot of calculations to be made and a lot of paperwork to be filled out. In **larger organisations** there will be **payroll department** which will deal with this otherwise it will be the **responsibility** of the payroll clerk in the **accounting function**.

The payroll function will determine the gross pay for each employee, based upon a variety of different remuneration schemes, and then will calculate the statutory and other deductions that must be made and will then calculate the net pay due to the employee. Finally the payroll function must then organise the method of payment to the employees.

4.3.5 Capital expenditure

From time to time an organisation will need to purchase non-current assets. These are **assets** that are to be **used** in the business for the **medium to long term** rather than being purchased for resale. This will include items such as machinery, cars, computer equipment, office furniture etc.

In order for the purchase of non-current assets to be put in motion the manager of the department which requires the asset must firstly fill out a **purchase requisition**. As most non-current assets are relatively expensive this will probably have to be **authorised** by more **senior management**. Once the requisition has been authorised the purchasing function will then find the most appropriate supplier for the assets.

Once a purchase order has been placed the details will then be passed to the **accounting function** which will then process and pay the invoice when it is received.

Question   Purchasing function

Which of the following personnel in an organisation would not be involved in the purchase of materials?

A   Credit controller
B   Stores manager
C   Accountant
D   Purchasing manager

Answer

A. The credit controller chases unpaid debts.

4.4 Control over transactions

As you may have noticed in the last section any transaction that a business is involved in will tend to involve a number of different people within the organisation. You will have also noticed the requirement for transactions to be authorised.

The management of a reasonably large business cannot have the time to personally be involved in every transaction of the business. However in order to keep control of the sources of income of the business and the expenditure that the business incurs it is important that transactions are authorised by a responsible member of the management team.

In particular this means that management must have control over the following areas:

(a)   **Sales on credit made to new customers**. If a sale is made on credit the goods are sent out with a promise from the customer to pay in the future therefore the management of the business must be as certain as they can be that this new customer can, and will, pay for the goods which means that the credit controller must be happy that the new customer has a good credit rating and is fairly certain to pay for the goods.

(b)   **Purchases of goods or non-current assets and payments for expenses**. This is money going out of the business therefore it is essential that these are necessary and valid expenditures so a responsible official must authorise them.

(c)   **Payroll**. One of the largest payments made by most organisations is that of the wages bill for their employees. It is essential that only bona fide employees are paid for the actual hours that they have worked therefore authorisation of the payroll is a very important part of any business.

4.5 Financial control procedures

Financial control procedures exist specifically to ensure that:

- Financial transactions are properly carried out
- The assets of the business are safeguarded
- Accurate and timely management information is produced

These are some examples of financial control procedures:

- Cheques over a certain amount to need two signatories
- Authorisation limits for purchase orders
- Authorisation for petty cash and expenses claims
- Effective credit control procedures
- Computer security procedures and access levels

Weaknesses in financial control procedures may be signalled by:

- Cash or cheques going missing
- Excessive bad or doubtful debts
- Debtors not paying within credit terms
- Suppliers not being paid on time
- Unauthorised purchases being made
- Failure to produce accounts or other reports at the specified time

5 The main business financial systems

5.1 Controlling the payroll system

Key controls over payroll cover:

- Documentation and authorisation of staff changes
- Calculation of wages and salaries
- Payment of wages and salaries
- Authorisation of deductions

The purpose of a payroll system is to compute the gross wages and salaries of employees and produce payslips, cheques and/or listings sent to banks instructing them to make payments. A computerised payroll system will be expected to carry out these tasks in accordance with how much employees should receive, how they should receive it and when it should be paid. The system should also be able to calculate tax deductions, national insurance deductions, savings, loan repayments etc, as well as printing various other outputs connected with employees' pay.

5.1.1 Data held on a payroll file

Payroll files will consist of an individual record for each employee.

    (a)   **Standing** data on each employee will include:

        (i)   Personal details (eg name, employee number, job grade, address etc)
        (ii)   Rate of pay
        (iii)   Details of deductions (including tax code)
        (iv)   Holidays

(b)   **Variable** (transaction) data will include:

   (i)   Gross pay to date
   (ii)   Tax to date
   (iii) Pension contributions etc

5.1.2 Inputs to a payroll system

The main inputs into a **wages system** (ie into a weekly-paid payroll) are as follows.

(a)   Clock cards or time sheets (sometimes both are used). Details of overtime worked will normally be shown on these documents. Sometimes payroll might be directly linked to an electronic time recording system.

(b)   Amount of bonus, or appropriate details if the bonus is calculated by the computer.

Salary systems (ie a monthly-paid payroll) are similar to those for wages but it is usual for the monthly salary to be generated by the computer from details held on the master file and therefore (with the exception of overtime, bonuses etc) there is no need for any transaction input. So the inputs for a salary system are just overtime, bonuses etc (because the basic salary is already on the master file).

5.1.3 Processing in a payroll system

The primary action involved in processing a payroll is calculating an employee's gross pay, calculating and implementing the various deductions in order to find net pay, and then making payment by the appropriate method.

In the case of wages, this means taking the input data on hours worked and pay details, and calculating the weekly wage due to the employee. The same calculation is carried out every week.

In the case of salaries, payroll processing might just mean picking an option to pay all the monthly-paid employees the same amount as they received the previous month. This could happen in theory, but in practice there are usually some amendments to make to the monthly pay details, and these are implemented during payroll processing.

5.1.4 Outputs from a payroll system

Typical outputs in a payroll system are:

(a)   Payslips

(b)   Payroll (this is often a copy of the payslips)

(c)   Payroll analysis, including analysis of deductions (tax, national insurance etc) and details for costing purposes

(d)   Various forms required for income tax purposes

(e)   Coin analysis, cheques, credit transfer forms

(f)   In some cases, a floppy disk with payment details for despatch to the bank and payment through the BACS system

Segregation of duties within the payroll department is particularly important. Well-planned fraud, such as the payment of 'ghost' employees, then requires collusion involving two or more people, and is consequently less likely to take place.

The most important aims of the control system relating to wages and salaries are:

Feature	Aims
Setting of wages and salaries	• **Employees** are **only paid** for **work** that they have **done** • **Gross pay** has been **calculated correctly** and **authorised**
Recording of wages and salaries	• **Gross** and **net pay** and **deductions** are **accurately recorded** on the payroll • **Wages** and **salaries paid** are **recorded correctly** in the **bank** and **cash records** • Wages and salaries are **correctly recorded** in the **general ledger**
Payment of wages and salaries	• The **correct employees** are **paid**
Deductions	• Statutory and non-statutory **deductions** have been **calculated correctly** and are **authorised** • The **correct amounts** are **paid** to the **taxation authorities**

5.1.5 Controls

While in practice separate arrangements are generally made for dealing with wages and salaries, the considerations involved are broadly similar and for convenience the two aspects are here treated together.

Responsibility for the preparation of pay sheets should be delegated to a suitable person, and adequate staff appointed to assist him. The extent to which the staff responsible for preparing wages and salaries may perform other duties should be clearly defined. In this connection full advantage should be taken where possible of the **division of duties**, and checks available where automatic wage-accounting systems are in use.

Setting of wages and salaries

- **Staffing** and **segregation of duties**

- **Maintenance of personnel records** and regular checking of wages and salaries to details in personnel records

- **Authorisation** required for:
    - Engagement and discharge of employees
    - Changes in pay rates
    - Overtime
    - Non-statutory deductions (for example pension contributions)
    - Advances of pay

- **Recording** of **changes** in **personnel** and **pay rates**

- **Recording** of hours worked by **timesheets, clocking in and out** arrangements

- **Review of hours worked**

- **Recording** of **advances** of **pay**

- **Holiday pay** arrangements

- **Answering queries**

- **Review** of **wages against budget**

Recording of wages and salaries

- **Bases** for **compilation** of payroll
- **Preparation, checking** and **approval** of payroll
- Dealing with **non-routine matters**

Payment of cash wages

- **Segregation of duties**
    - Cash sheet preparation
    - Filling of pay packets
    - Distribution of wages

- **Authorisation** of **wage cheque**

- **Custody** of cash
    - Encashment of cheque
    - Security of pay packets
    - Security of transit arrangements
    - Security and prompt banking of unclaimed wages

- **Verification of identity**

- **Recording** of distribution

Payment of salaries

- **Preparation** and **signing** of cheques and bank transfer lists
- **Comparison** of **cheques** and **bank transfer list** with payroll
- **Maintenance** and **reconciliation** of wages and salaries bank account

Deductions from pay

- **Maintenance** of **separate employees' records**, with which pay lists may be compared as necessary

- **Reconciliation** of **total pay** and **deductions** between one pay day and the next

- **Surprise cash counts**

- **Comparison** of actual pay totals with **budget estimates** or standard costs and the investigation of variances

- **Agreement** of **gross earnings** and **total tax deducted** with income tax returns to the Inland Revenue

Appropriate arrangements should be made for dealing with statutory and other authorised deductions from pay, such as national insurance, income tax, pension fund contributions, and savings held in trust. A primary consideration is the establishment of adequate controls over the **records,** and **authorisation** of deductions.

5.2 The purchases and sales cycles

FAST FORWARD

The purchases and sales systems will be the most important components of most company accounting systems.

5.2.1 Purchase and sales systems

Purchasing is an important area to control, especially where items of high value are concerned. There are likely to be specific authorisation procedures for the purchase of non-current assets.

5.2.2 Inputs to a purchase ledger system

Bearing in mind what we expect to see held on a purchase ledger, typical data input into a purchase ledger system is:

- Details of purchases recorded on invoices
- Details of returns to suppliers for which credit notes are received
- Details of payments to suppliers
- Adjustments

5.2.3 Processing in a purchase ledger system

The primary action involved in updating the purchase ledger is adjusting the amounts outstanding on the supplier accounts. These amounts will represent money owed to the suppliers. This processing is identical to updating the accounts in the sales ledger, except that the sales ledger balances are debits (receivables) and the purchase ledger balances are credits (payables).

5.2.4 Outputs from a purchase ledger system

Typical outputs in a computerised purchase ledger are as follows.

(a)   Lists of transactions posted - produced every time the system is run.

(b)   An analysis of expenditure for nominal ledger purposes. This may be produced every time the system is run or at the end of each month.

(c)   List of payables balances together with a reconciliation between the total balance brought forward, the transactions for the month and the total balance carried forward.

(d)   Copies of suppliers' accounts. This may show merely the balance b/f, current transactions and the balance c/f. If complete details of all unsettled items are given, the ledger is known as an **open-ended ledger**.

(e)   Any purchase ledger system can be used to produce details of payments to be made. For example:

   (i)   Remittance advices (usually a copy of the ledger account)
   (ii)   Cheques
   (iii)   Credit transfer listings

(f)   Other special reports may be produced for:

   (i)   Costing purposes
   (ii)   Updating records about fixed assets
   (iii)   Comparisons with budget
   (iv)   Aged creditors list

Businesses have to ensure that only **properly authorised purchases** which are necessary for the business are made. All stages of the purchase process – ordering, receiving goods and being charged for them – should be documented and matched. In this way it can be ensured that the business gets what it ordered and only pays for what it orders and receives. The purchase ledger makes it possible for the business to keep track of what it owes each supplier.

The most important aims of the control system relating to payables and purchases are:

Feature	Aims
Ordering	• All **orders for**, and expenditure on, **goods and services** are properly **authorised**, and are for **goods and services** that are actually **received** and are **for the company** • **Orders** are only **made** to **authorised suppliers** • **Orders** are **made** at **competitive prices**
Receipt and invoices	• **Goods and services** received are **used** for the **organisation's purposes** and not private purposes • **Goods and services** are **only accepted** if they have been **ordered**, and the **order** has been authorised • All **goods and services received** are accurately **recorded** • **Liabilities** are **recognised** for all **goods and services** that have been **received** • All **credits** to which business is due are **claimed** • **Receipt** of goods and services is **necessary** to **establish** a **liability**
Accounting	• All **expenditure** is **authorised** and is for goods that are **actually received** • All **expenditure** that is made is **recorded** correctly in the nominal and purchase ledger • All **credit notes** that are received are **recorded** in the nominal and purchase ledger • All **entries** in the **purchase ledger** are **made** to the **correct purchase ledger accounts** • **Cut-off** is **applied correctly** to the purchase ledger

5.2.5 Controls

FAST FORWARD

The purchasing system tests will be based around:

- Buying (authorisation)
- Goods inwards (custody)
- Accounting (recording)

The following controls should be in place over **ordering**.

- **Central policy** for choice of suppliers
- Evidence needed of **requirements** for purchase before purchase authorised (re-order quantities and re-order levels)
- **Order forms** prepared only when a purchase requisition has been received
- **Authorisation** of order forms
- **Prenumbered order forms**
- **Safeguarding** of blank order forms
- **Review** of orders not received
- **Monitoring** of **supplier terms** and taking advantage of favourable conditions (bulk order, discount)

The client should carry out the following checks on **goods received** and **invoices** from **suppliers.**

(a) **Examination** of goods inwards

(i) Quality
(ii) Quantity
(iii) Condition

(b)   **Recording arrival** and **acceptance** of goods (prenumbered goods received notes)

(c)   **Comparison** of **goods received notes** with **purchase orders**

(d)   **Referencing** of supplier invoices; numerical sequence and supplier reference

(e)   **Checking** of **suppliers' invoices**

  (i)   Prices, quantities, accuracy of calculation
  (ii)   Comparison with order and goods received note

(f)   **Recording return of goods** (prenumbered good returned notes)

(g)   Procedures for **obtaining credit notes** from suppliers

The following controls should be in place over **accounting procedures**.

(a)   **Segregation** of **duties:** accounting and checking functions

(b)   Prompt **recording** of **purchases** and **purchase returns** in day books and ledgers

(c)   **Regular maintenance** of **purchase ledger**

(d)   **Comparison** of **supplier statements** with **purchase ledger balances**

(e)   **Authorisation** of **payments**

  (i)   Authority limits

  (ii)   Confirmation that goods have been received, accord with purchase order, and are properly priced and invoiced

(f)   **Review** of **allocation** of expenditure

(g)   **Reconciliation** of **purchase ledger** control account to total of purchase ledger balances

(h)   **Cut-off** accrual of unmatched goods received notes at year-end

5.3 Controlling the sales cycle

FAST FORWARD

Like the purchase cycle, the sales system tests will be based around:

- Selling (authorisation)
- Goods outwards (custody)
- Accounting (recording)

For sales, businesses want to give credit only to customers who will pay their debts. The processes of handling sales, matched orders, despatching goods and invoicing all need to be **documented** and **matched**, so that customers receive what they ordered and are correctly billed. The **sales ledger** makes it possible to keep track of what is owed by each customer.

5.3.1 Input to a sales ledger system

Bearing in mind what we expect to find in a sales ledger, we can say that typical data input into sales ledger system is as follows.

(a)   **Amendments**

  (i)   Amendments to customer details, eg change of address or credit limit
  (ii)   Insertion of new customers
  (iii) Deletion of 'non-active' customers

(b)   **Transaction data relating to**:

    (i)   Sales transactions, for invoicing

    (ii)   Customer payments

    (iii) Credit notes

    (iv) Adjustments (debit or credit items)

Some computerised sales ledgers produce invoices, so that basic sales data is input into the system. But other businesses might have a specialised invoicing module, so that the sales ledger package is not expected to produce invoices. The invoice details are already available (as output from the specialised module) and are input into the sales ledger system rather than basic sales data.

5.3.2 Processing in a sales ledger system

The primary action involved in updating the sales ledger is modifying the amount outstanding on the customer's account. How the amount is modified depends on what data is being input (ie whether it is an invoice, credit note, remittance etc).

5.3.3 Outputs from a sales ledger system

Typical outputs in a computerised sales ledger are as follows.

(a)   **Day book listing**. A list of all transactions posted each day. This provides an audit trail - information which the auditors of the business can use when carrying out their work. Batch and control totals will be included in the listing.

(b)   **Invoices** (if the package is one which is expected to produce invoices.)

(c)   **Statements**. End of month statements for customers.

(d)   **Aged receivables list**. Probably produced monthly.

(e)   **Sales analysis reports**. These will analyse sales according to the sales analysis codes on the sales ledger file.

(f)   **Customers reminder letters**. Letters can be produced automatically to chase late payers when the due date for payment goes by without payment having been received.

(g)   **Customer lists** (or perhaps a selective list). The list might be printed on to adhesive labels, for sending out customer letters or marketing material.

(h)   **Responses to enquiries**, perhaps output on to a VDU screen rather than as printed copy, for fast response to customer enquiries.

(i)   **Output onto disk file for other modules,** eg to the inventory control module and the nominal ledger module, if these are also used by the organisation, and the package is not an integrated one.

There are a number of controls which need to be in place over sales and receivables. Bear in mind that, quite apart from safeguarding actual transactions, there must be no possibility of turnover figures being falsified. A number of people may have bonuses and commissions based on them!

The most important aims of the control system relating to receivables and sales are these:

Feature	Aims
Ordering and granting of credit	• **Goods** and **services** are **only supplied** to **customers** with **good credit ratings** • **Customers** are encouraged to **pay promptly** • **Orders** are **recorded correctly** • **Orders** are **fulfilled**
Despatch and invoicing	• All **despatches** of goods are **recorded** • All **goods and services** sold are **correctly invoiced** • All **invoices** raised **relate to goods and services** that have been **supplied** by the business • **Credit notes** are only given for **valid reasons**
Recording, accounting and credit control	• All sales that have been **invoiced** are **recorded** in the nominal and sales ledgers • All **credit notes** that have been **issued** are **recorded** in the nominal and sales ledgers • All **entries** in the sales ledger are **made** to the **correct** sales ledger **accounts** • **Cut-off** is applied correctly to the sales ledger • Potentially **doubtful debts** are **identified**

5.3.4 Controls

FAST FORWARD

The tests of controls of the **sales system** will be based around:

- Selling (authorisation)
- Goods outwards (custody)
- Accounting (recording)

The following controls relate to the **ordering** and **credit control** process; note the importance of controls over credit terms, ensuring that goods are only sent to customers who are likely to pay promptly.

(a)　**Segregation** of duties; credit control, invoicing and inventory despatch

(b)　**Authorisation** of **credit terms** to customers

　　(i)　References/credit checks obtained
　　(ii)　Authorisation by senior staff
　　(iii)　Regular review

(c)　**Authorisation** for changes in **other customer data**

　　(i)　Change of address supported by letterhead

　　(ii)　Requests for deletion supported by evidence balances cleared/customer in liquidation

(d)　**Orders** only **accepted** from **customers** who have no credit problems

(e)　**Sequential numbering** of blank **order documents**

(f)　**Matching** of **customer orders** with production orders and despatch notes

The following checks relate to **despatches** and **invoice preparation**.

(a) **Authorisation** of **despatch** of **goods**

    (i)   Despatch only on sales order

    (ii)   Despatch only to authorised customers

    (iii)   Special authorisation of despatches of goods free of charge or on special terms

(b) **Examination** of **goods outwards** as to quantity, quality and condition

(c) **Recording** of **goods outwards**

(d) **Agreement** of **goods outwards records** to **customer orders**, **despatch notes** and **invoices**

(e) **Prenumbering** of despatch notes and delivery notes and regular checks on sequence

(f) **Condition** of **returns checked**

(g) Recording of goods returned on **goods returned notes**

(h) **Signature** of **delivery notes** by customers

(i) Preparation of invoices and credit notes

    (i)   **Authorisation** of **selling prices**/use of **price lists**

    (ii)   **Authorisation** of **credit notes**

    (iii)   **Checks on prices**, **quantities**, **extensions** and totals on invoices and credit notes

    (iv)   **Sequential numbering of** blank invoices and credit notes, and regular tests on sequence

(j) **Inventory records updated**

(k) **Matching** of **sales invoices** with despatch and delivering notes and sales orders

(l) Regular **review** for **orders** which have not yet been delivered

The following controls relate to **accounting** and **recording**.

(a) **Segregation of duties:** recording sales, maintaining customer accounts and preparing statements

(b) **Recording** of **sales invoices** sequence and **control** over **spoilt invoices**

(c) **Matching** of **cash receipts** with **invoices**

(d) **Retention** of **customer remittance advices**

(e) **Separate recording** of **sales returns, price adjustments** etc

(f) **Cut-off procedures** to ensure goods despatched and not invoiced (or vice versa) are properly dealt within the correct period

(g) Regular **preparation** of **receivables statements**

(h) **Checking** of **receivables' statements**

(i) **Safeguarding** of **receivables statements** so that they cannot be altered before despatch

(j) **Review** and **follow-up** of **overdue accounts**

(k) **Authorisation** of **writing off** of **bad debts**

(l) **Reconciliation** of **sales ledger control account**

(m) **Analytical review** of **sales ledger** and **profit margins**

5.4 Controlling cash

Cash and petty cash must be regularly reconciled.

Although we still talk in terms of cash, very few business transactions involve its use. Even at the retail level, many purchases are now being made by debit and credit card.

When we consider sales and purchases made on credit between businesses, transfer of funds will probably be by:

- Company cheque
- Bank transfer
- Internet transfer, or in some cases
- Standing order/direct debit

The only use of cash in non-retail businesses will probably be for petty cash. So what controls need to be in place?

5.4.1 Control over receipts

In any business controls over cash **receipts** are fundamental if the company is to keep a healthy cash position. **Control over cash receipts** will concentrate on three main areas.

- Receipts must be **banked promptly**.
- The **record of receipts must be complete.**
- The loss of receipts through **theft or accident** must be prevented.

The difference between these three controls can be demonstrated with an example.

5.4.2 Example: control over cash receipts

Suppose that your company sells goods for $10,000 during the month of April to XYZ & Co. You receive a payment of $10,000 by cheque along with a remittance advice which shows exactly which invoices the cheque covers.

(a)   You examine the cheque to ensure it is valid and completed correctly and you pay it in to the company account within 24 hours as company policy dictates (**banked promptly**).

(b)   A colleague records the cheque details and compares the amount of the cheque to the remittance advice (**checking for completeness**). Usually the payment would also be checked against the total amount owed by the customer as part of the completeness check.

(c)   The **segregation of duties** between the person who banks the money and the person who records it is considered to be a very good control to prevent **theft and accidental loss**. This prevents the fraud known as 'teeming and lading' where receipts for customers are misappropriated and this is then covered up by misposting future receipts.

(d)   Now that cheques can only be paid into the account in whose name they are made out, the opportunities for misappropriation of cheque receipts are much less.

5.4.3 Controls over payments

Controls over payments by a business must be **strict**. This should apply to all payments, from the smallest to the largest. The need for controls should be fairly obvious: if any business allowed some of its employees to pay out its money without needing to obtain permission, the scope for cheating and dishonesty would be very wide.

There are three main steps in applying controls over payments.

Step 1 Obtaining **documentary evidence** of the reason why the payment is being made and the amount of the payment. In the case of payments to suppliers, the documentary evidence will be a supplier's invoice (or statement).

Step 2 **Authorisation** of the payment, which means giving formal 'official' approval to make the payment.

Step 3 **Restricting the authority to actually make the payment** to certain specified individuals.

The difference between Steps 1, 2 and 3 can be illustrated with an example.

5.4.4 Example: controlling a payment

Suppose that a company buys goods costing $5,000.

Step 1 It will receive an invoice from the supplier. This is the **documentary evidence** of the reason for and amount of the payment.

Step 2 The invoice will be approved by the purchasing director. This approval is the **authorisation of the payment**.

Step 3 At some time later, the payment will be made to the supplier, probably by cheque. For a payment of $5,000, perhaps only the finance director or managing director will be permitted to sign the cheque, and so the **authority to make the payment** would be limited to these two people.

5.4.5 Authorisation

Every payment must be approved by an **authorised person**. This person will often be a manager or supervisor in the department that initiated the expense, but every organisation has its own system. The following control limits must be set.

- **Which individuals** can authorise particular expenses
- The **maximum amount** of expenditure that an individual can authorise

The controls described above are designed to **prevent** fraud and error in the cash cycle. The most important controls designed to **detect** fraud and error which may already have taken place are **reconciliations**.

Petty cash should be reconciled whenever there is a need to replenish the float. The vouchers plus the remaining cash should equal the original float. If this balances, the only other check needed is to make sure that the vouchers are all valid and authorised.

A **bank reconciliation** should be done at least once a month. Many businesses, even those with sophisticated computer systems, still keep a manual cash book. If not, a printout of the bank record from the computer can be used. This is reconciled to the bank statement. There will always be differences, but they should come into the following categories.

- Timing differences due to unpresented cheques
- Timing differences due to uncredited lodgements
- Standing orders and direct debits not entered in the cash book
- Bank charges not entered in the cash book
- Funds received by transfer and not recorded in the cash book

6 Manual and computerised accounting systems

Most accounting systems are computerised and anyone training to be an accountant should be able to work with them. The most important point to remember is that the **principles** of computerised accounting are the same as those of **manual accounting**.

Most reference to computerised accounting talks about accounting **packages**. This is a rather general term, but most of us can probably name the accounting package that we use at work. An accounting package consists of several accounting **modules**, eg sales ledger, nominal ledger.

We are going to look specifically at 'applications software', that is packages of computer programs that carry out specific tasks.

(a)   Some applications are devoted specifically to an accounting task, for example a payroll package, a non-current asset register or a inventory control package.

(b)   Other applications have many uses in business, including their use for accounting purposes. Examples of this are databases and spreadsheets, which are covered in Section 7.

6.1 Accounting packages

Accounting functions retain the same names in computerised systems as in more traditional written records. Computerised accounting still uses the familiar ideas of day books, ledger accounts, double entry, trial balance and financial statements. The principles of working with computerised sales, purchase and nominal ledgers are exactly what would be expected in the manual methods they replace.

The only difference is that these various books of account have become invisible. Ledgers are now computer files which are held in a computer-sensible form, ready to be called upon.

6.2 Manual systems v computerised systems

FAST FORWARD

> In **many situations manual systems are inferior to computerised systems** in terms of productivity, speed, accessibility, quality of output, incidence of errors, 'bulk' and when making corrections.

Disadvantages of **manual systems** include the following.

Disadvantage	Comment
Productivity	**Productivity** is usually lower, particularly in routine or operational situations such as transaction processing.
Slower	Processing is **slower** where large volumes of data need to be dealt with.
Risk of errors	The **risk of errors** is greater, especially in repetitive work like payroll calculations.
Less accessible	Information on manual systems is generally **less accessible**. Access to information is often restricted to one user at a time.
Alterations	It is difficult to make **corrections**. If a manual document contains errors or needs updating it is often necessary to recreate the **whole** document from scratch.
Quality of output	**Quality of output** is less consistent and often not well-designed. At worst, hand-written records may be illegible and so completely useless.
Bulk	Paper based systems are generally very **bulky** both to handle and to store.

However, don't assume that computerised systems are best in every situation. For example, a post-it note stuck on a colleague's desk with a brief message may in some cases be quicker than typing up an e-mail message.

6.3 Coding

Computers require vital information to be expressed in the form of codes. For example, nominal ledger accounts might be coded individually by means of a two-digit code:

00	Ordinary share capital
01	Share premium
05	Income statement
15	Purchases
22	Receivables control account
41	Payables control account
42	Interest
43	Dividends

In the same way, individual accounts must be given a unique code number in the sales ledger and purchase ledger.

6.3.1 Example: coding

When an invoice is received from a supplier (example code 1234) for $3,000 for the purchase of raw materials, the transaction might be coded for input to the computer as:

	Nominal ledger			Inventory	
Supplier Code	Debit	Credit	Value	Code	Quantity
1234	15	41	$3,000	56742	150

Code 15 in our example represents purchases, and code 41 the payables control account from the list in Paragraph 4.8. This single input could be used to update the purchase ledger, the nominal ledger, and the inventory ledger. The inventory code may enable further analysis to be carried out, perhaps allocating the cost to a particular department or product. Thus the needs of both financial accounting and cost accounting can be fulfilled at once.

6.4 Modules

> A **module** is a program which deals with one particular part of a business accounting system.

An accounting package will consist of several modules. A simple accounting package might consist of only one module (in which case it is called a stand-alone module), but more often it will consist of several modules. The name given to a set of several modules is a **suite**. An accounting package, therefore, might have separate modules for:

- Invoicing
- Inventory
- Sales ledger
- Purchase ledger
- Nominal ledger
- Payroll
- Cash book
- Job costing
- Non-current asset register
- Report generator

6.5 Integrated software

Control is enhanced by an **integrated accounting system**.

Each module may be integrated with the others, so that data entered in one module will be passed automatically or by simple operator request through into any other module where the data is of some relevance. For example, if there is an input into the invoicing module authorising the despatch of an invoice to a customer, there might be **automatic links**:

(a) To the sales ledger, to update the file by posting the invoice to the customer's account

(b) To the inventory module, to update the inventory file by:

(i) Reducing the quantity and value of inventory in hand
(ii) Recording the inventory movement

(c) To the nominal ledger, to update the file by posting the sale to the sales account

(d) To the job costing module, to record the sales value of the job on the job cost file

(e) To the report generator, to update the sales analysis and sales totals which are on file and awaiting inclusion in management reports.

A diagram of an **integrated accounting system** is given below.

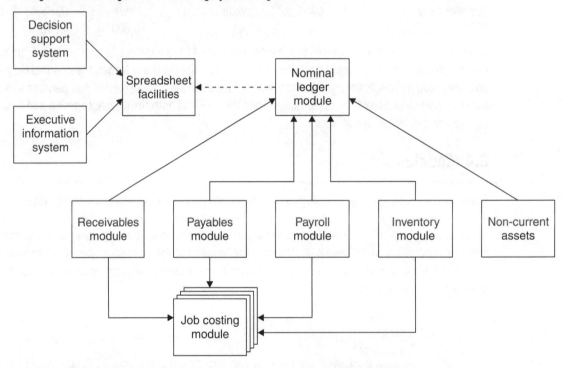

6.5.1 Advantages

(a) It becomes possible to make just one entry in one of the ledgers which automatically updates the others.

(b) Users can specify reports, and the software will automatically extract the required data from all the relevant files.

(c) Both of the above simplify the workload of the user, and the irritating need to constantly load and unload disks is eliminated.

6.5.2 Disadvantages

(a) Usually, it requires more computer memory than separate (stand-alone) systems - which means there is less space in which to store actual data.

(b) Because one program is expected to do everything, the user may find that an integrated package has fewer facilities than a set of specialised modules.

7 Databases and spreadsheets

A **database** may be described as a 'pool' of data, which can be used by any number of applications. Its use is not restricted to the accounts department.

The database approach can also be summarised diagrammatically.

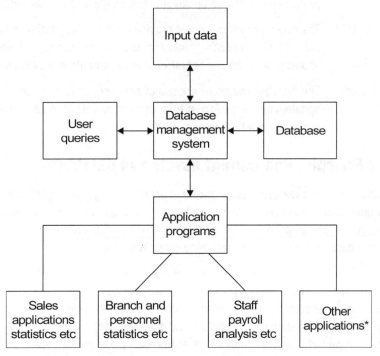

* The range of applications which make use of a database will vary widely, depending on what data is held in the database files.

Note the following from the diagram.

(a) Data is input, and the DBMS software organises it into the database. If you like, you can think of the database as a vast library of fields and records, waiting to be used.

(b) Various application programs (sales, payroll etc) are 'plugged into' the DBMS software so that they can use the database, or the same application used by different departments can all use the database.

(c) As there is only one pool of data, there is no need for different departments to keep many different files with duplicated information.

7.1 Objectives of a database

The main virtues of a database are as follow.

(a)	There is **common data** for all users to share.
(b)	The extra effort of keeping **duplicate files** in different departments is avoided.
(c)	Conflicts between departments who use **inconsistent data are avoided**.

A database should have four major objectives.

(a)	It should be **shared**. Different users should be able to access the *same data* in the database for their own processing applications (and at the *same time* in some systems) thus removing the need for duplicating data on different files.
(b)	The **integrity** of the database must be preserved. This means that one user should not be allowed to alter the data on file so as to spoil the database records for other users. However, users must be able to update the data on file, and so make valid alterations to the data.
(c)	The database system should provide for the needs of different users, who each have their own processing requirements and data access methods. In other words, the database should provide for the **operational requirements of all its users**.
(d)	The database should be capable of **evolving**, both in the short term (it must be kept updated) and in the longer term (it must be able to meet the future data processing needs of users, not just their current needs).

7.2 Example: Non-current assets and databases

An organisation, especially a large one, may possess a large quantity of non-current assets. Before computerisation these would have been kept in a manual non-current asset register. A database enables this non-current asset register to be stored in an electronic form. A database file for non-current assets might contain most or all of the following categories of information.

(a)	Code number to give the asset a unique identification in the database
(b)	Type of asset (for example motor car, leasehold premises), for published accounts purposes
(c)	More detailed description of the asset (for example serial number, car registration number, make)
(d)	Physical location of the asset (for example address)
(e)	Organisational location of the asset (for example accounts department)
(f)	Person responsible for the asset (for example in the case of a company-owned car, the person who uses it)
(g)	Original cost of the asset
(h)	Date of purchase
(i)	Depreciation rate and method applied to the asset
(j)	Accumulated depreciation to date
(k)	Net book value of the asset
(l)	Estimated residual value
(m)	Date when the physical existence of the asset was last verified
(n)	Supplier

Obviously, the details kept about the asset would depend on the type of asset it is.

Any kind of computerised non-current asset record will improve efficiency in accounting for non-current assets because of the ease and speed with which any necessary calculations can be made. Most obvious is the calculation of the depreciation provision which can be an extremely onerous task if it is done monthly and there are frequent acquisitions and disposals and many different depreciation rates in use.

The particular advantage of using a database for the non-current asset function is its flexibility in generating reports for different purposes. Aside from basic cost and net book value information a database with fields such as those listed above in the record of each asset could compile reports analysing assets according to location say, or by manufacturer. This information could be used to help compare the performance of different divisions, perhaps, or to assess the useful life of assets supplied by different manufacturers. There may be as many more possibilities as there are permutations of the individual pieces of data.

7.3 Spreadsheets

FAST FORWARD

Spreadsheets, too, are often used both in financial accounting and cost accounting.

Key term

A **spreadsheet** is essentially an electronic piece of paper divided into rows and columns with a built in pencil, eraser and calculator. It provides an easy way of performing numerical calculations.

The intersection of each column and row of a spreadsheet is referred to as a cell. A cell can contain text, numbers or formulae. Use of a formula means that the cell which contains the formula will display the results of a calculation based on data in other cells. If the numbers in those other cells change, the result displayed in the formula cell will also change accordingly. With this facility, a spreadsheet is used to create financial models.

Below is a spreadsheet processing budgeted sales figures for three geographical areas for the first quarter of the year.

	A	B	C	D	E
1	**BUDGETED SALES FIGURES**				
2		Jan	Feb	Mar	Total
3		£'000	£'000	£'000	£'000
4	North	2,431	3,001	2,189	7,621
5	South	6,532	5,826	6,124	18,482
6	West	895	432	596	1,923
7	Total	9,858	9,259	8,909	28,026

7.4 The use of spreadsheets

Spreadsheets have many uses, both for accounting and for other purposes. It is perfectly possible, for example, to create proforma balance sheets and income statements on a spreadsheet, or set up the notes for financial accounts, like the non-current assets note.

Chapter Roundup

- Accounting is a way of recording, analysing and summarising transactions of a business.

- You should be able to identify the qualities of good accounting information.

- You may have a wide understanding of what accounting is about. Your job may be in one area or type of accounting, but you must understand the breadth of work which an accountant undertakes.

- You should be able to outline the factors which have shaped the development of financial accounting.

- Key controls over payroll cover:

    - Documentation and authorisation of staff charges
    - Calculation of wages and salaries
    - Payment of wages and salaries
    - Authorisation of deductions

- The purchases and sales systems will be the most important components of most company accounting systems.

- The purchasing system tests will be based around:

    - Buying (authorisation)
    - Goods inwards (custody)
    - Accounting (recording)

- The tests of controls of the **sales system** will be based around:

    - Selling (authorisation)
    - Goods outwards (custody)
    - Accounting (recording)

- Cash and petty cash must be regularly reconciled.

- In **many situations manual systems are inferior to computerised systems** in terms of productivity, speed, accessibility, quality of output, incidence of errors, 'bulk' and when making corrections.

- Control is enhanced by an **integrated accounting system**.

- A **database** may be described as a 'pool' of data, which can be used by any number of applications. Its use is not restricted to the accounts department.

- **Spreadsheets**, too, are often used both in financial accounting and cost accounting.

Quick Quiz

1   What is the fundamental objective of company annual reports?

2   Identify eight user groups who need accounting information.

3   What are the two main financial statements drawn up by accountants?

4   What are the qualities of useful accounting information?

5   Which of the following factors have not influenced financial accounting?

    A   National legislation
    B   Economic factors
    C   Accounting standards
    D   GAAP

6   What are the objectives of the International Accounting Standards Committee?

7   What does GAAP stand for?

8   What is meant by a 'true and fair' view?

9   What are the key elements in authorisation of credit terms to customers?

10 What should auditors check when reviewing sales invoices?

11 How can a company ensure that quantities of goods ordered do not exceed those that are required?

12 What are the important checks that should be made on invoices received from suppliers?

13 What do the key controls over payroll cover?

14 What are the three main steps in controlling payments?

15 What are the advantages of computerised accounting?

16 What sort of data is input into a sales ledger system?

17 What is the open item method of processing?

18 What should be the four major objectives of a database?

19 What are the advantages of using a database to maintain non-current asset records?

20 What is a spreadsheet?

Answers to Quick Quiz

1   To provide information about the financial position, performance and changes in financial position of an enterprise that is useful to a wide range of users in making economic decisions.

2   Managers; shareholders; trade contacts; lenders; Her Majesty's Revenue and Customs; analysts and advisors; Government and their agencies; the public.

3   The income statement and the balance sheet.

4   Relevance; comprehensibility; reliability; completeness; objectivity; timelines; comparability

5   B   Economic factors do not influence the development of financial accounting; all the others do (see Section 5.1).

6   To develop a single set of high quality, understandable and enforceable global accounting standards; to promote their use; to bring about convergence of national accounting standards and International Accounting Standards

7   Generally accepted accounting principles.

8   The financial statements must be 'accurate and not misleading'.

9   Authorisation of credit terms to customers

   (i)   References/credit checks obtained
   (ii)   Authorisation by senior staff
   (iii)   Regular review

10 When reviewing sales invoices auditors should check

   (i)   Authorisation of selling prices/use of price lists
   (ii)   Authorisation of credit notes
   (iii)   Checks on prices, quantities, extensions and totals on invoices and credit notes
   (iv)   Sequential numbering of blank invoices and credit notes, and regular tests on sequence

11 Evidence is needed of requirements for purchases before the purchases are authorised (re-order quantities and re-order levels).

12 Invoices should be checked for prices, quantities, accuracy of calculations and comparison with the order and goods received note.

13 Controls cover documentation and authorisation of staff changes, calculation and payment of wages and salaries, and authorisation of deductions.

14 The three steps are: obtaining documentary evidence of the amount and reason for payment, obtaining authorisation and restricting the authority to actually make the payment to certain specified individuals.

15 Computerised accounting systems

   –   Increased productivity
   –   Allow faster processing of data
   –   Reduce risk of error
   –   Are more secure (access to records restricted)
   –   Standardises presentation
   –   More convenient than paper-based records

16 Amendments to customer details (changed address, new customers, deletion of 'non-active' customers) and transaction data (sales, payments, adjustments).

17 Payments are credited to specific invoices, so that late payment of invoices can be identified.

18   A database should

      –   be shared
      –   have the integrity of its data preserved
      –   provide for the operational requirements of all users
      –   be capable of evolving

19   The amount of detail that can be kept about each individual asset and the ease in analysing this information into different reports and calculations (eg depreciation, profit on sale).

20   A series of cells arranged in columns and rows which can contain calculations, numbers or text. Calculations can be performed upon the contents of other cells.

Part D

Specific functions of accounting and internal financial control

Control, security and audit

Topic list	Syllabus reference
1 Internal control systems	D3 (a)(b)
2 Internal control environment and procedures	D3 (c)(d)
3 Internal audit and internal control	D2 (a)(b)
4 External audit	D2 (a)(b)
5 IT systems security and safety	D3 (e)
6 Building controls into an information system	D3 (f)

Introduction

In this chapter we move to the main elements of internal control systems that organisations operate (**Section 1**). Controls must be linked to organisational objectives and the main risks that organisations face (**Section 2**). In addition internal control systems do not just consist of the controls themselves but also the control environment within which controls operate.

Internal audit is a key part of the control system of larger companies (**Section 3**) and the external audit function exists to review controls and report upon the financial statements (**Section 4**).

Organisations are becoming increasingly **reliant on computerised information systems**. It is vital therefore to ensure these systems are secure – to protect the information held on them, to ensure operations run smoothly, to prevent theft and to ensure compliance with legislation (**Sections 5 and 6**).

Security and legal issues are likely to crop up regularly in the examination.

Study guide

		Intellectual level
D2	**Internal and external auditing and their functions**	
(a)	Define internal and external audit.	1
(b)	Explain the main functions of the internal auditor and the external auditor.	1
D3	**Internal financial control and security within business organisations**	
(a)	Explain internal control and internal check.	1
(b)	Explain the importance of internal financial controls in an organisation.	2
(c)	Describe the responsibilities of management for internal financial control.	1
(d)	Describe the features of effective internal financial control procedures in an organisation.	2
(e)	Identify and describe features for protecting the security of IT systems and software within business.	1
(f)	Describe general and application systems controls in business.	1

Exam guide

The syllabus regards internal control as a specific and very important business function, supported by effective and secure management information.

1 Internal control systems

FAST FORWARD

Internal controls should help organisations counter risks, maintain the quality of reporting and comply with laws and regulations. They provide reasonable assurance that the organisations will fulfil their objectives.

Key term

An **internal control** is any action taken by management to enhance the likelihood that established objectives and goals will be achieved. Management plans, organises and directs the performance of sufficient actions to provide reasonable assurance that objectives and goals will be achieved. Thus, control is the result of proper planning, organising and directing by management.   (*Institute of Internal Auditors*)

1.1 Direction of control systems

In order for internal controls to function properly, they have to be well-directed. Managers and staff will be more able (and willing) to implement controls successfully if it can be demonstrated to them what the objectives of the control systems are, whilst objectives provide a yardstick for the board when they come to monitor and assess how controls have been operating.

1.2 Turnbull guidelines

The UK's Turnbull report provides a helpful summary of the main purposes of an internal control system.

Turnbull comments that internal control consists of 'the **policies**, **processes**, **tasks**, **behaviours** and other aspects of a company that taken together:

(a)   Facilitate its **effective** and **efficient operation** by enabling it to respond appropriately to significant **business**, **operational, financial, compliance** and other risks to achieving the company's objectives. This includes the **safeguarding of assets** from inappropriate use or from loss and fraud and ensuring that **liabilities** are **identified** and **managed**.

(b)   Help ensure the **quality** of **internal** and **external reporting**. This requires the **maintenance** of **proper records and processes** that generate a flow of **timely, relevant and reliable information** from within and without the organisation.

(c)   Help ensure **compliance with applicable laws and regulations,** and also with internal policies with respect to the conduct of business'

The Turnbull report goes on to say that a sound system of internal control reduces but does not eliminate the possibilities of **poorly-judged decisions**, **human error, deliberate circumvention of controls**, **management override of controls** and **unforeseeable circumstances.** Systems will provide reasonable (not absolute) assurance that the company will not be hindered in achieving its business objectives and in the orderly and legitimate conduct of its business, but won't provide certain protection against all possible problems.

1.3 Need for control framework

FAST FORWARD

> Internal control frameworks include the **control environment** within which **internal controls** operate. Other important elements are the **risk assessment and response processes,** the **sharing of information** and **monitoring** the environment and operation of the control system.

Organisations need to consider the overall framework of controls since controls are unlikely to be very effective if they are developed sporadically around the organisation, and their effectiveness will be very difficult to measure by internal audit and ultimately by senior management.

1.4 Control environment and control procedures

Key term

> The **internal control system** comprises the **control environment** and **control procedures**. It includes all the policies and procedures (internal controls) adopted by the directors and management of an entity to assist in achieving their objective of ensuring, as far as practicable, the orderly and efficient conduct of its business, including adherence to internal policies, the safeguarding of assets, the prevention and detection of fraud and error, the accuracy and completeness of the accounting records, and the timely preparation of reliable financial information. Internal controls may be incorporated within computerised accounting systems. However, the internal control system extends beyond those matters which relate directly to the accounting system.

Perhaps the simplest framework for internal control draws a distinction between

- **Control environment** – the overall context of control, in particular the attitude of directors and managers towards control

- **Control procedures** – the detailed controls in place

We shall examine both these elements in detail in the next two sections.

The Turnbull report on Internal Control also highlights the importance of

- **Information** and **communication processes**
- **Processes** for **monitoring** the **continuing effectiveness** of the system of internal control

1.5 Limitations of internal controls

However, any internal control system can only provide the directors with **reasonable assurance** that their objectives are reached, because of **inherent limitations** which is why auditors cannot obtain all their evidence from tests of the systems of internal control. The limitations include

- The **costs** of control **not outweighing** their **benefits**
- The **potential** for **human error** or **fraud**
- **Collusion** between employees
- The possibility of controls being **by-passed** or **overridden by management**
- Controls being designed to cope with routine and **not non-routine transactions**
- Controls depending on the method of data processing – they should be **independent** of the method of data processing

2 Internal control environment and procedures

FAST FORWARD

> The **control environment** is influenced by **management's attitude** towards control, the **organisational structure** and the **values** and **abilities** of employees.

2.1 Nature of control environment

Key term

> The **control environment** is the overall attitude, awareness and actions of directors and management regarding internal controls and their importance in the entity. The control environment encompasses the management style, and corporate culture and values shared by all employees. It provides the background against which the various other controls are operated.

The following factors are reflected in the control environment.

- The **philosophy** and **operating style** of the directors and management
- The entity's **organisational structure** and methods of assigning authority and responsibility (including segregation of duties and supervisory controls)
- The directors' **methods of imposing control**, including the internal audit function, the functions of the board of directors and personnel policies and procedures
- The **integrity, ethical values** and **competence** of directors and staff

The Turnbull report highlighted a number of elements of a strong control environment.

- **Clear strategies** for dealing with the significant risks that have been identified
- The company's **culture, code of conduct, human resource policies** and **performance reward systems** supporting the business objectives and risk management and internal control systems
- Senior management demonstrating through its actions and policies commitment to **competence, integrity** and **fostering a climate of trust** within the company
- **Clear definition** of **authority, responsibility** and **accountability** so that decisions are made and actions are taken by the appropriate people
- **Communication** to employees what is expected of them and scope of their freedom to act
- People in the company having the **knowledge, skills** and **tools** to support the achievements of the organisation's objectives and to manage effectively its risks

However, a strong control environment does not, by itself, ensure the effectiveness of the overall internal control system although it will have a major influence upon it.

The control environment will have a major impact on the establishment of business objectives, the structuring of business activities, and dealing with risks.

Controls can be classified in various ways including **administrative** and **accounting; prevent, detect** and **correct; discretionary** and **non-discretionary; voluntary** and **mandated; manual** and **automated**.

The mnemonic **SPAMSOAP** can be used to remember the main types of control.

Key term

Control procedures are those policies and procedures in addition to the control environment which are established to achieve the entity's specific objectives.   (Auditing Practices Board)

2.2 Classification of control procedures

You may find internal controls classified in different ways, and these are considered below. Classification of controls can be important because different classifications of control are tested in different ways.

2.2.1 Administrative controls and accounting controls

Administrative controls are concerned with achieving the objectives of the organisation and with implementing policies. The controls relate to the following aspects of control systems.

- Establishing a suitable organisation structure
- The division of managerial authority
- Reporting responsibilities
- Channels of communication

Accounting controls aim to provide accurate accounting records and to achieve accountability. They apply to the following.

- The recording of transactions
- Establishing responsibilities for records, transactions and assets

2.2.2 Prevent, detect and correct controls

Prevent controls are controls that are designed to prevent errors from happening in the first place. Examples of **prevent controls** are as follows.

- Checking invoices from suppliers against goods received notes before paying the invoices

- Regular checking of delivery notes against invoices, to ensure that all deliveries have been invoiced

- Signing of goods received notes, credit notes, overtime records and so forth, to confirm that goods have actually been received, credit notes properly issued, overtime actually authorised and worked and so on

 Question   **Prevent controls**

How can prevent controls be used to measure performance and efficiency?

Answer

In the above examples the system outputs could include information, say, about the time lag between delivery of goods and invoicing:

(a) As a measure of the **efficiency of the invoicing section**

(b) As an **indicator of the speed and effectiveness** of **communications** between the despatch department and the invoicing department

(c) As **relevant background information** in assessing the effectiveness of cash management

You should be able to think of plenty of other examples. Credit notes reflect customer dissatisfaction, for example: how quickly are they issued?

Detect controls are controls that are designed to detect errors once they have happened. Examples of **detect controls** in an accounting system are bank reconciliations and regular checks of physical inventory against book records of inventory.

Correct controls are controls that are designed to minimise or negate the effect of errors. An example of a **correct control** would be back-up of computer input at the end of each day, or the storing of additional copies of software at a remote location.

2.2.3 Discretionary and non-discretionary controls

Discretionary controls are controls that, as their name suggests, are subject to human discretion.

Non-discretionary controls are provided automatically by the system and cannot be bypassed, ignored or overridden. For example, checking the signature on a purchase order is discretionary, whereas inputting a PIN number when using a cash dispensing machine is a non-discretionary control.

2.2.4 Voluntary and mandated controls

Voluntary controls are chosen by the organisation to support the management of the business.

Mandated controls are required by law and imposed by external authorities.

2.2.5 Manual and automated controls

Manual controls demonstrate a one-to-one relationship between the processing functions and controls, and the human functions.

Automated controls are programmed procedures designed to prevent, detect and correct errors all the way through processing.

Manual controls are often used in conjunction with automated controls, for example when an exception report is reviewed.

2.2.6 General and application controls

These controls are used to reduce the risks associated with the computer environment. **General controls** are controls that relate to the environment in which the application system is operated. **Application controls** are controls that prevent, detect and correct errors and irregularities as transactions flow through the business system. These are covered in more detail in Section 6.

2.2.7 Financial and non-financial controls

Financial controls focus on the key transaction areas, with the emphasis being on the **safeguarding of assets** and the **maintenance of proper accounting records** and **reliable financial information**.

Non-financial controls tend to concentrate on wider performance issues. **Quantitative non-financial controls** include numeric techniques such as **performance indicators**, the **balanced scorecard** and **activity-based management**. **Qualitative non-financial controls** include many topics we have already discussed, such as organisational structures, rules and guidelines, strategic plans and human resource policies.

2.3 Types of financial control procedure

The UK Auditing Practices Board's SAS 300 *Accounting and internal control systems and risk assessments* lists some specific control procedures.

- **Approval** and **control** of **documents**
- Controls over **computerised applications** and the information technology environment
- **Checking** the **arithmetical accuracy** of the records
- Maintaining and reviewing **control accounts** and trial balances
- **Reconciliations**
- **Comparing** the results of cash, security and inventory **counts** with **accounting records**
- **Comparing internal data** with **external sources** of information
- **Limiting** direct physical **access** to assets and records

The old UK Auditing Practices Committee's guideline *Internal controls* gave a useful summary that is often remembered as a mnemonic, 'SPAMSOAP'.

(a) **Segregation of duties**. For example, the chairman/Chief Executive roles should be split.

(b) **Physical**. These are measures to secure the custody of assets, eg only authorised personnel are allowed to move funds on to the money market.

(c) **Authorisation and approval**. All transactions should require authorisation or approval by an appropriate responsible person; limits for the authorisations should be specified, eg a remuneration committee is staffed by non-executive directors (NEDs) to decide directors' pay.

(d) **Management** should provide control through analysis and review of accounts, eg variance analysis, provision of internal audit services.

(e) **Supervision** of the recording and operations of day-to-day transactions. This ensures that all individuals are aware that their work will be checked, reducing the risk of falsification or errors, eg budgets, managers' review, exception or variance reports.

(f) **Organisation**: identify reporting lines, levels of authority and responsibility. This ensures everyone is aware of their control (and other) responsibilities, especially in ensuring adherence to management policies, eg avoid staff reporting to more than one manager. Procedures manuals will be helpful here.

(g) **Arithmetical and accounting**: to check the correct and accurate recording and processing of transactions, eg reconciliations, trial balances.

(h) **Personnel**. Attention should be given to selection, training and qualifications of personnel, as well as personal qualities; the quality of any system is dependent upon the competence and integrity of those who carry out control operations, eg use only qualified staff as internal auditors.

2.4 Internal checks

Internal controls should not be confused with **internal checks**, which have a more restricted definition.

Key term

> **Internal checks** are defined as the checks on the day-to-day transactions whereby the work of one person is proved independently or is complementary to the work of another, the object being the prevention or early detection of errors and fraud. It includes matters such as the delegation and allocation of authority and the division of work, the method of recording transactions and the use of independently ascertained totals, against which a large number of individual items can be proved.

Internal checks are an important feature of the day-to-day control of financial transactions and the accounting system. **Arithmetical** internal checks include pre-lists, post-lists and control totals.

Key terms

> A **pre-list** is a list that is drawn up before any processing takes place.
>
> A **post-list** is a list that is drawn up during or after processing.
>
> A **control total** is a total of any sort used for control purposes by comparing it with another total that ought to be the same.

A pre-list total is a control total, so that for example, when cash is received by post and a pre-list prepared and the receipts are recorded individually in the cash book, and a total of amounts entered in the cash book is obtained by adding up the individual entries, the control total obtained from the cash book can be compared with, and should agree with, the pre-list control total. Control totals, as you should already be aware, are frequently used within computer processing.

2.5 Aims of internal checks

Segregate tasks, so that the responsibility for particular actions, or for defaults or omissions, can be traced to an individual person.

Create and preserve the records that act as confirmation of physical facts and accounting entries.

Break down routine procedures into separate steps or stages, so as to facilitate an even flow of work and avoid bottlenecks.

Reduce the possibility of fraud and error. The aim should be to **prevent** fraud and error rather than to be able to **detect** it after it has happened. Efficient internal checks make extensive fraud virtually impossible, except by means of collusion between two or more people.

Internal checks, importantly, imply a **division of work**, so that the work of one person is either **proved independently** or else is complementary to the work of another person.

Question	Internal checks

The Geton Company specialises in providing cleaning services. It is currently undertaking an expansion programme, much of which is achieved by supplying services previously carried out by employees of client organisations. In many cases these same employees are then recruited by Geton to work on the contracts using the improved procedures developed through its specialisation in this type of work.

For each large contract, or a number of small contracts in the same location, a supervisor is appointed to oversee the activities of the employees and to provide basic control data for hours worked, materials issued, use of equipment and so on. Invoices are prepared centrally as are wages. These are paid weekly in arrears via BACS. Each supervisor has a van in which the materials are kept and replenished from a central store. Equipment is normally kept at the purchasing organisation.

As a senior accounts assistant with Geton you have been asked to oversee the clerical activities associated with the work of the supervisors.

(a)   Outline and explain the basic data you would expect to be completed by the supervisor.
(b)   Explain what checks you would apply to confirm the correctness of the data provided.

Answer

(a)   *Basic data to be completed by the supervisor*

   (i)   **Materials usage**. This will be determined by records of the use of van materials by job, materials drawn from central store to replenish the van and so forth. To assess usage the quantity and type of materials held as inventory at the beginning and the end of the week may need to be recorded, unless a running total is kept. Although the supervisor keeps the van topped up, it is not certain whether there is a minimum level kept in the van.

   (ii)   **Van expenses**. It is a relatively simple matter to record the miles run on company business. Supervisors will need to keep receipts for amounts paid for petrol and oil, to enable reimbursement. Alternatively, a company charge card might be used.

   (iii)   **Hours worked**. For each employee, the employee's name, grade if appropriate, hours at basic rate, and hours at overtime rates, type or category of work (if the company analyses its time in this way) should be recorded.

(b)   *Checks to ensure data accuracy*

Geton can take a variety of approaches. They could require a great deal of documentation to ensure that errors do not arise. They could have a roaming inspection department to check on compliance with recording procedures. Other controls include the following.

   (i)   **Materials usage**

   - Comparison between different jobs for reasonableness
   - Van inventory counts
   - Reconciliation of van inventory counts with recorded usage
   - Materials usage could be part of the budget

   (ii)   **Van expenses**

   (1)   The company will not pay for private mileage so the mileage recorded must be reasonable. Van mileages can be checked. Supervisors might be required to log journeys and to produce all garage receipts, including those for cleaning the van.

   (2)   A mileage budget could be established to check for the reasonableness of any claims. Again, mileage on a job can be compared with other similar jobs.

   (iii)   **Work done**

   (1)   A budget can be set for each job. Actual hours worked can be compared to it: the difference may be perfectly reasonable but the supervisor will have to explain any significant variance. On occasions, a member of the inspection team can carry out further checks.

   (2)   The job to be done should be specified and the job specification might arise out of the contract itself. One of the supervisor's jobs will be to ensure that the work is done as required. In addition, an inspection team may visit the site now and then to ensure that standards are adhered to. Clients can also be sent questionnaires asking them about their satisfaction with the service.

2.6 Characteristics of a good internal control system

(a) **A clearly defined organisation structure**

    (i) **Different operations must be separated** into appropriate divisions and sub-divisions.

    (ii) Officers must **be appointed to assume responsibility** for each division.

    (iii) **Clear lines of responsibility** must exist between each division and sub-division and the board.

    (iv) There must be overall **co-ordination of the company's activities** (through corporate planning).

(b) **Adequate internal checks**

    (i) **Separation of duties** for **authorising** a transaction, **custody** of the assets obtained by means of the transaction and **recording** the transaction.

    (ii) **'Proof measures'** such as control totals, pre-lists and bank reconciliations should be used.

(c) **Acknowledgement** of work done: persons who carry out a particular job should acknowledge their work by means of signatures, initials, rubber stamps and so on.

(d) Protective devices for **physical security**.

(e) **Formal documents should acknowledge the transfer of responsibility for goods**. When goods are received, a goods received note should be used to acknowledge receipt by the storekeeper.

(f) **Pre-review:** the authorisation of a transaction (for example a cash payment, or the purchase of an asset) should not be given by the person responsible without first checking that all the proper procedures have been carried out.

(g) A clearly defined **system for authorising transactions** within specified spending limits.

(h) **Post-review:** completed transactions should be reviewed after they have happened; for example, monthly statements of account from suppliers should be checked against the purchase ledger accounts of those suppliers.

(i) There should be **authorisation, custody** and **re-ordering** procedures.

    (i) Funds and property of the company should be kept under **proper custody**. Access to assets (either direct or by documentation) should be **limited to authorised personnel**.

    (ii) Expenditure should only be incurred after authorisation and all expenditures are properly accounted for.

    (iii) All revenue must be properly accounted for and received in due course.

(j) **Personnel** should have the capabilities and qualifications necessary to carry out their responsibilities properly.

(k) An **internal audit** department should be able to verify that the control system is working and to review the system to ensure that it is still appropriate for current circumstances.

2.7 Limitations on the effectiveness of internal controls

Not only must a control system include sufficient controls, but also these **controls must be applied properly and honestly**.

(a) Internal controls depending on **segregation of duties can be avoided by the collusion** of two or more people responsible for those duties.

(b) **Authorisation controls can be abused** by the person empowered to authorise the activities.

(c) **Management can often override the controls they have set up themselves.**

3 Internal audit and internal control

3.1 Internal audit

Key term

Internal audit has been defined as:

An independent appraisal activity established within an organisation as a service to it. It is a control which functions by examining and evaluating the adequacy and effectiveness of other controls. The investigative techniques developed are applied to the analysis of the effectiveness of all parts of an entity's operations and management.

The work of internal audit is distinct from the external audit which is carried out for the benefit of shareholders only and examines published accounts. **Internal audit is part of the internal control system**.

3.2 The need for internal audit

FAST FORWARD

The role of internal audit will **vary** according to the **organisation's objectives** but is likely to include review **of internal control systems, risk management, legal compliance** and **value for money**.

The Turnbull report in the UK stated that listed companies without an internal audit function should **annually review** the need to have one, and listed companies with an internal audit function should review annually its **scope, authority** and **resources**.

Turnbull states that the need for internal audit will depend on:

- The **scale, diversity** and **complexity** of the company's activities
- The number of employees
- Cost-benefit considerations
- **Changes** in the organisational structures, reporting processes or underlying information systems
- **Changes** in **key risks**
- **Problems** with **internal control systems**
- An **increased number** of **unexplained** or **unacceptable** events

Although there may be alternative means of carrying out the routine work of internal audit, those carrying out the work may be involved in operations and hence lack **objectivity**.

3.3 Objectives of internal audit

The role of the internal auditor has expanded in recent years as internal auditors seek to monitor all aspects (not just accounting) of the business, and add value to their organisation. The work of the internal auditor is still prescribed by management, but it may cover the following broad areas.

(a) **Review of the accounting and internal control systems**. The establishment of adequate accounting and internal control systems is a responsibility of management and the directors. Internal audit is often assigned specific responsibility for the following tasks.

- Reviewing the design of the systems
- Monitoring the operation of the systems by risk assessment and detailed testing
- Recommending cost effective improvements

Review will cover both financial and non-financial controls.

(b)   **Examination of financial and operating information**. This may include review of the means used to identify, measure, classify and report such information and specific enquiry into individual items including detailed testing of transactions, balances and procedures.

(c)   **Review of the economy, efficiency and effectiveness** of operations.

(d)   **Review of compliance** with laws, regulations and other external requirements and with internal policies and directives and other requirements including appropriate authorisation of transactions.

(e)   **Review of the safeguarding of assets**.

(f)   **Review of the implementation of corporate objectives**. This includes review of the effectiveness of planning, the relevance of standards and policies, the company's corporate governance procedures and the operation of specific procedures such as communication of information.

(g)   **Identification of significant business** and financial **risks, monitoring** the **organisation's overall risk management policy** to ensure it operates effectively, and **monitoring** the **risk management strategies** to ensure they continue to operate effectively.

(h)   **Special investigations** into particular areas, for example suspected fraud.

3.4 Internal audit and risk management

Internal audit will play a significant part in the organisation's risk management processes, being required to assess and advise on how risks are countered. Internal audit's work will be influenced by the organisation's **appetite** for bearing risks, but internal audit will assess:

- The **adequacy of the risk management and response processes** for identifying, assessing, managing and reporting on risk

- The risk management and control **culture**

- The **internal controls** in operation to **limit risks**

- The **operation and effectiveness** of the **risk management processes**

The areas auditors will concentrate on will depend on the **scope** and **priority** of the assignment and the **risks identified**. Where the risk management framework is insufficient, auditors will have to rely on their own **risk assessment** and will focus on **recommending an appropriate framework**. Where a framework for risk management and control is embedded in operations, auditors will aim to use **management assessment of risks** and concentrate on **auditing the risk management processes**.

3.5 The features of internal audit

From these definitions the two main features of internal audit emerge.

(a)   **Independence:** although an internal audit department is part of an organisation, it should be independent of the line management whose sphere of authority it may audit.

(b)   **Appraisal:** internal audit is concerned with the appraisal of work done by other people in the organisation, and internal auditors should not carry out any of that work themselves. The appraisal of operations provides a service to management.

3.6 Types of audit

Internal audit is a management control, as it is a tool used to ensure that other internal controls are working satisfactorily. An internal audit department may be asked by management to look into any aspect of the organisation.

Five different types of audit can be distinguished. (The first three types are considered further in the following paragraphs.)

- Operational audit
- Systems audit
- Transactions audit
- Social audit
- Management investigations

Operational audits can be concerned with **any sphere** of a company's activities. Their prime objective is the monitoring of management's performance at every level, to ensure optimal functioning according to pre-determined criteria. They concentrate on the outputs of the system, and the efficiency of the organisation. They are also known as **'management'**, **'efficiency'** or **'value for money'** audits.

A **systems audit** is based on a testing and evaluation of the **internal controls** within an organisation so that those controls may be relied on to ensure that resources are being managed effectively and information provided accurately. Two types of tests are used.

(a)   **Compliance tests** seek evidence that the internal controls are being applied as prescribed.

(b)   **Substantive tests** substantiate the entries in the figures in accounts. They are used to discover **errors and omissions**.

The auditor will be interested in a variety of processing errors when performing compliance tests.

- At the wrong time
- Incompleteness
- Omission
- Error
- Fraud

The key importance of the two types of test is that **if the compliance tests reveal that internal controls are working satisfactorily, then the amount of substantive testing can be reduced**, and the internal auditor can concentrate the audit effort on those areas where controls do not exist or are not working satisfactorily.

3.7 Example

Suppose a department within a company processes travel claims which are eventually paid and recorded on the general ledger.

(a)   When conducting **compliance tests**, the internal auditor is **looking at the controls** in the travel claim section to see if they are working properly. This is not the same as looking at the travel claims themselves. For example, one of the internal controls might be that a clerk checks the addition on the travel claim and initials a box to say that he has done so. If he fails to perform this arithmetic check, then there has been a control failure - regardless of whether the travel claim had, in fact, been added up correctly or incorrectly.

(b)   When conducting **substantive tests**, the internal auditor is examining figures which he has extracted directly from the company's financial records. For this sort of test, the auditor is concerned only with establishing whether or not the figure in the ledger is correct. He or she is not concerned as to how it got there.

A transactions or probity audit aims to detect fraud and uses only substantive tests.

3.8 Accountability

The internal auditor is accountable to the highest executive level in the organisation, preferably to the audit committee of the Board of Directors. There are three main reasons for this requirement.

- The auditor needs access to all parts of the organisation.

- The auditor should be free to comment on the performance of management.

- The auditor's report may need to be actioned at the highest level to ensure its effective implementation.

<table>
<tr><td>**Exam focus point**</td><td>The accountability of the internal auditor is tested on the Pilot Paper.</td></tr>
</table>

3.9 Independence

Given an acceptable line of responsibility and clear terms of authority, it is vital that the internal auditor **is and is seen to be independent**. Independence for the internal auditor is established by three things.

- The responsibility structure
- The auditor's mandatory authority
- The auditor's own approach

Internal audit requires a highly professional approach which is objective, detached and honest. Independence is a fundamental concept of auditing and this applies just as much to the internal auditor as to the external auditor. The internal auditor should not install new procedures or systems, neither should he engage in any activity which he would normally appraise, as this might compromise his independence.

Question	Internal control systems

The Midas Mail Order Company operates a central warehouse from which all merchandise is distributed by post or carrier to the company's 10,000 customers. An outline description of the sales and cash collection system is set out below.

Sales and cash collection system

Stage	Department/ staff responsible	Documentation
1 Customer orders merchandise (Orders by phone or through the postal system)	Sales dept Sales assistants	Multiple copy order form (with date, quantities, price marked on them)
		Copies 1-3 sent to warehouse. Copy 4 sent to accounts dept. Copy 5 retained in sales dept
2 Merchandise requested from inventory rooms by despatch clerks	Storekeepers	Copies 1-3 handed to storekeepers. Forms marked as merchandise taken from inventory. (Note. If merchandise is not in inventories held, the storekeepers retain copies 1-3 until inventory room is re-filled).
		Copies 1-2 handed to despatch clerks. Copy 3 retained by store-keepers.
3 Merchandise despatched	Despatch bay Despatch clerks	Copy 2 marked when goods despatched and sent to accounts department

Stage	Department/ staff responsible	Documentation
4 Customers invoiced	Accounts dept: sales ledger clerks	2-copy invoice prepared from invoiced details on copy 2 of order form received from despatch bay
		Copy 1 of invoice sent to customer. Copy 2 retained by accounts dept and posted to sales ledger
5 Cash received (as cheques, bank giro credit, or cash)	Accounts dept: cashier	2-copy cash receipt list
		Copy 1 of cash receipt list retained by cashier
		Copy 2 passed to sales ledger clerk

(a) State four objectives of an internal control system.

(b) For the Midas Mail Order Company list four major controls which you would expect to find in the operation of the accounting system described above, and explain the objective of each of these controls.

(c) For each of the four controls identified above, describe briefly two tests which you would expect an internal auditor to carry out to determine whether the control was operating satisfactorily.

Answer

(a) **Four objectives of an internal control system**

(i) To enable management to carry on the business of the enterprise in an orderly and efficient manner

(ii) To satisfy management that their policies are being adhered to

(iii) To ensure that the assets of the company are safeguarded

(iv) To ensure, as far as possible, that the enterprise maintains complete and accurate records

(b) **Four major controls**

(i) **Control over customers' creditworthiness**. Before any order is accepted for further processing, established procedures should be followed in order to check the creditworthiness of that customer. For new customers procedures should exist for obtaining appropriate references before any credit is extended. For all existing customers there should be established credit limits and before an order is processed the sales assistants should check to see that the value of the current order will not cause the debtor's balance to rise above their agreed credit limit.

The objective of such procedures is to try to avoid the company supplying goods to debtors who are unlikely to be able to pay for them. In this way the losses suffered by the company as a result of bad debts should be minimal.

(ii) **Control over the recording of sales and debtors**. The most significant document in the system is the multiple order form. These forms should be sequentially pre-numbered and controls should exist over the supplies of unused forms and also to ensure that all order forms completed can be traced through the various stages of processing and agreed to the other documents raised and the various entries made in the accounting records.

The main objective here will be to check the completeness of the company's recording procedures in relation to the income which it has earned and the assets which it holds in the form of receivables.

(iii)   **Control over the issue of inventory and the despatch of goods**. Control procedures here should be such that goods are not issued from stores until a valid order form has been received and the fact of that issue is recorded both on the order form (copies 1-3)and in the inventory records maintained by the store-keepers.

The objectives here are to see that no goods are released from inventory without appropriate authority and that a record of inventory movements is maintained.

(iv)   **Control over the invoicing of customers**. The main control requirement here will be to use sequentially pre-numbered invoices with checks being carried out to control the completeness of the sequence. Checks should also be conducted to ensure that all invoices are matched with the appropriate order form (Copy 2) to confirm that invoices have been raised in respect of all completed orders.

The major concern here will be to ensure that no goods are despatched to customers without an invoice subsequently being raised.

(v)   (*The question merely required four controls to be considered, but for the sake of completeness, each of the five main stages in processing as indicated by the question are considered here.*)

Control over monies received. There should be controls to ensure that there is an adequate segregation of duties between those members of staff responsible for the updating of the sales records in respect of monies received and those dealing with the receipt, recording and banking of monies. There should also be a regular independent review of aged debtor balances together with an overall reconciliation of the receivables control account with the total of outstanding debts on individual customer accounts.

The objectives here are to ensure that proper controls exist with regard to the complete and accurate recording of monies received, safe custody of the asset cash and the effectiveness of credit control procedures.

(c)   Appropriate tests in relation to each of the controls identified in (b) above would be as follows.

(i)   **Controls over customers' creditworthiness**

(1)   For a sample of new accounts opened during the period check to see that suitable references were obtained before the company supplied any goods on credit terms and that the credit limit set was properly authorised and of a reasonable amount.

(2)   For a sample of customers' orders check to see that at the time they were accepted, their invoice value would not have been such as to cause the balance on that customers' account to go above their agreed credit limit.

(ii)   **Controls over the recording of sales and debtors**

(1)   On a sample basis check the completeness of the sequence of order forms and also that unused inventory of order forms are securely stored.

(2)   For a sample of order forms raised during the period ensure that they can be traced through the system such that there is either evidence that the order was cancelled or that a valid invoice was subsequently raised.

(iii)   **Control over the issue of inventory and the despatch of goods**

(1)   For a sample of entries in the inventory records check to ensure that a valid order form exists for all issues recorded as having been made.

(2)   Attend the inventory rooms to observe the procedures and check that goods are not issued unless a valid order form has been received and that the appropriate entries are made in the inventory records and on the order form at the time of issue.

(iv) **Control over the invoicing of customers**

(1) On a sample basis check the completeness of the sequence of invoices raised and also that the unused inventory of invoice forms are securely stored.

(2) For a sample of invoices raised during the period ensure that they have been properly matched with the appropriate order form (copy 2).

4 External audit

FAST FORWARD

Internal auditors are **employees** of the organisation whose work is designed to **add value** and who report to the **audit committee. External auditors** are from **accountancy firms** and their role is to **report on the financial statements to shareholders**.

Both **internal and external auditors** review controls, and **external auditors** may **place reliance** on **internal auditors' work** providing they assess its worth.

Key term

External audit is a periodic examination of the books of account and records of an entity carried out by an independent third party (the auditor), to ensure that they have been properly maintained, are accurate and comply with established concepts, principles, accounting standards, legal requirements and give a true and fair view of the financial state of the entity.

4.1 Differences between internal and external audit

The following table highlights the differences between internal and external audit.

	Internal audit	External audit
Reason	Internal audit is an activity designed to **add value** and improve an **organisation's operations**.	External audit is an exercise to enable auditors to **express an opinion on the financial statements**.
Reporting to	Internal audit reports to the **board of directors**, or others charged with governance, such as the audit committee.	The external auditors report to the **shareholders**, or members, of a company on the stewardship of the directors.
Relating to	Internal audit's work relates to the **operations of the organisation**.	External audit's work relates to the **financial statements**. They are concerned with the financial records that underlie these.
Relationship with the company	Internal auditors are very often **employees of the organisation**, although sometimes the internal audit function is outsourced.	External auditors are **independent of the company and its management**. They are appointed by the shareholders.

The table shows that although some of the procedures that internal audit undertake are very similar to those undertaken by the external auditors, the whole **basis** and **reasoning** of their work is fundamentally **different**.

The **difference** in **objectives** is particularly important. Every definition of internal audit suggests that it has a **much wider scope** than external audit, which has the objective of considering whether the accounts give a true and fair view of the organisation's financial position.

Exam focus point

> The work of internal and external audit features in questions carrying a total of nine marks on the Pilot Paper.

4.2 Relationship between external and internal audit

Co-ordination between the external and internal auditors of an organisation will minimise duplication of work and encourage a wide coverage of audit issues and areas. Co-ordination should have the following features.

- Periodic meetings to plan the overall audit to ensure adequate coverage
- Periodic meetings to discuss matters of mutual interest
- Mutual access to audit programmes and working papers
- Exchange of audit reports and management letters
- Common development of audit techniques, methods and terminology

4.3 Assessment by external auditors

Where the external auditors wish to rely on the work of the internal auditors, then the external auditors must assess the internal audit function, as with any part of the system of internal control. The following important criteria will be considered by the external auditors.

(a) **Organisational status**

Internal audit's specific status in the organisation and the effect this has on its ability to be objective. Ideally, the internal audit function should have a direct line of communication to the entity's main board or audit committee, and be free of any other operating responsibility. External auditors should consider any constraints or restrictions placed on internal audit.

(b) **Scope of function**

The nature and extent of the assignments which internal audit performs. External auditors should also consider whether management and the directors act on internal audit recommendations and how this is evidenced.

(c) **Technical competence**

Whether internal audit work is performed by persons having adequate technical training and proficiency as internal auditors. External auditors may, for example, review the policies for hiring and training the internal audit staff and their experience and professional qualifications, also how work is assigned, delegated and reviewed.

(d) **Due professional care**

Whether internal audit work is properly planned, supervised, reviewed and documented. The existence of adequate audit manuals, work programmes and working papers may be considered, also consultation procedures.

| Question | External and internal audit |

The growing recognition by management of the benefits of good internal control, and the complexities of an adequate system of internal control have led to the development of internal auditing as a form of control over all other internal controls. The emergence of internal auditors as specialists in internal control is the result of an evolutionary process similar in many ways to the evolution of independent auditing.

Required

Explain why the internal and independent auditors' review of internal control procedures differ in purpose.

Answer

The internal auditors **review and test the system of internal control** and report to management in order to **improve the information** received by managers and to help in their task of running the company. The internal auditors will recommend changes to the system to make sure that management receive objective information that is efficiently produced. The internal auditors will also have a duty to search for and discover fraud.

The external auditors **review the system of internal control** in order to **determine the extent of the substantive work** required on the year-end accounts. The external **auditors report** to the **shareholders** rather than the managers or directors. It is usual, however, for the external auditors to issue a letter of weakness to the managers, laying out any areas of weakness and recommendations for improvement in the system of internal control. The external auditors report on the **truth and fairness** of the financial statements, not directly on the system of internal control. The auditors do not have a specific duty to detect fraud, although they should plan the audit procedures so as to have reasonable assurance that they will detect any material misstatement in the accounts on which they give an opinion.

5 IT systems security and safety

FAST FORWARD

Security is the protection of data from accidental or deliberate threats and the protection of an information system from such threats.

5.1 The responsibilities of ownership

If you own **something that you value** – you **look after it**. **Information** is valuable and it deserves similar care.

Key term

> **Security**, in information management terms, means the **protection of data** from accidental or deliberate threats which might cause unauthorised modification, disclosure or destruction of data, and the **protection of the information system** from the degradation or non-availability of services.

Security refers to **technical** issues related to the computer system, psychological and **behavioural** factors in the organisation and its employees, and protection against the unpredictable occurrences of the **natural world**.

Security can be subdivided into a number of aspects.

(a) **Prevention**. It is in practice impossible to prevent all threats cost-effectively.

(b) **Detection**. Detection techniques are often combined with prevention techniques: a log can be maintained of unauthorised attempts to gain access to a computer system.

(c) **Deterrence**. As an example, computer misuse by personnel can be made grounds for disciplinary action.

(d) **Recovery procedures**. If the threat occurs, its consequences can be contained (for example checkpoint programs).

(e) **Correction procedures**. These ensure the vulnerability is dealt with (for example, by instituting stricter controls).

(f) **Threat avoidance**. This might mean changing the design of the system.

5.2 Physical threats

Physical threats to security may be natural or man made. They include fire, flooding, weather, lightning, terrorist activity and accidental damage.

The **physical environment** quite obviously has a major effect on information system security, and so planning it properly is an important precondition of an adequate security plan.

5.3 Fire

Fire is the **most serious hazard** to computer systems. Destruction of data can be even more costly than the destruction of hardware.

A fire safety plan is an essential feature of security procedures, in order to prevent fire, detect fire and put out the fire. Fire safety includes:

- **Site preparation** eg fireproof materials, fire doors
- **Detection equipment** eg smoke detector alarms
- **Extinguishing equipment** eg sprinklers and extinguishers
- **Staff awareness** of fire safety procedures

5.4 Water

Water is a serious hazard. Flooding and water damage are often encountered following firefighting activities elsewhere in a building.

This problem can be countered by the use of waterproof ceilings and floors together with the provision of adequate drainage.

In some areas flooding is a natural risk, for example in parts of central London and many other towns and cities near rivers or coasts. Basements are therefore generally not regarded as appropriate sites for large computer installations.

5.5 Weather

Wind, rain and storms can all cause substantial **damage to buildings**. In certain areas the risks are greater, for example the risk of typhoons in parts of the Far East. Many organisations make heavy use of prefabricated and portable offices, which are particularly vulnerable.

Cutbacks in maintenance expenditure may lead to leaking roofs or dripping pipes, which can invite problems of this type, and maintenance should be kept up if at all possible.

5.6 Lightning

Lightning and electrical storms can play havoc with power supplies, causing power failures coupled with power surges as services are restored. Adjustments in power supplies may be enough to affect computer processing operations (characterised by lights which dim as the country's population turns on electric kettles following a popular television program).

One way of combating this is by the use of **uninterruptible (protected) power supplies**. This will protect equipment from fluctuations in the supply. Power failure can be protected against by the use of a **separate generator** or rechargeable battery. It may be sufficient to maintain power only long enough to close down the computer system in an orderly manner.

5.7 Terrorist activity

Political terrorism is the main risk, but there are also threats from individuals with **grudges.**

In some cases there is very little that an organisation can do: its buildings may just happen to be in the wrong place and bear the brunt of an attack aimed at another organisation or intended to cause general disruption.

There are some avoidance measures that should be taken, however.

(a)   **Physical access** to buildings should be controlled (see the next section).

(b)   Organisations involved in controversial activities may consider moving into other lines of business.

(c)   The organisation should consult with police and fire authorities about potential risks, and co-operate with their efforts to avoid them.

(d)   The organisation should not advertise its presence by displaying its name and logo on the building.

5.8 Accidental damage

People are a physical threat to computer installations: there can be few of us who have not at some time spilt a cup of coffee over a desk covered with papers, or tripped and fallen doing some damage to ourselves or to an item of office equipment.

Combating accidental damage is a matter of:

(a)   Sensible **attitudes** to office behaviour.
(b)   Good office **layout**.
(c)   Eliminating hazards such as trailing cables.

Question   Fire and flooding

You are the financial controller of your organisation. The company is in the process of installing a mainframe computer, and because your department will be the primary user, you have been co-opted onto the project team with responsibility for systems installation. You have a meeting at which the office services manager will be present, and you realise that no-one has yet mentioned the risks of fire or flooding in the discussions about site selection. Make a note of the issues which you would like to raise under these headings.

Answer

(a)   **Fire**. Fire security measures can usefully be categorised as preventative, detective and corrective. Preventative measures include siting of the computer in a building constructed of suitable materials and the use of a site which is not affected by the storage of inflammable materials (eg stationery, chemicals). Detective measures involve the use of smoke detectors. Corrective measures may include installation of a sprinkler system (water-based or possibly gas-based to avoid electrical problems), training of fire officers and good sitting of exit signs and fire extinguishers.

(b)   **Flooding**. Water damage may result from flooding or from fire recovery procedures. If possible, large installations should not be situated in basements.

5.9 Physical access controls

Physical access controls are designed to prevent **intruders** getting near to computer equipment and/or storage media.

Physical access controls including the following.

(a) **Personnel**, including receptionists and, outside working hours, security guards, can help control human access.

(b) **Door locks** can be used where frequency of use is low. (This is not practicable if the door is in frequent use.)

(c) Locks can be combined with:

   (i) A **keypad system**, requiring a code to be entered.
   (ii) A **card entry system**, requiring a card to be 'swiped'.

(d) Intruder **alarms**.

The best form of access control would be one which **recognised** individuals immediately, without the need for personnel or cards. However, machines that can identify a person's fingerprints or scan the pattern of a retina are relatively more **expensive**, so their use is less widespread.

It may not be cost effective or practical to use the same access controls in all areas. The **security requirements of different departments** should be estimated, and appropriate measures taken. Some areas will be very restricted, whereas others will be relatively open.

Important aspects of physical access of control are **door locks** and **card entry systems**. Computer theft is becoming more prevalent as equipment becomes smaller and more portable.

5.9.1 Personal identification numbers (PINs)

In some organisations staff are allocated an individual **personal identification number**, or PIN, which identifies him or her to the system. Based on the security privileges allocated, the person will be **allowed** access to certain parts of a building, but prevented from accessing other areas.

5.9.2 Door locks

Conventional door locks are of value in certain circumstances, particularly where users are only required to pass through the door a **couple of times a day**. If the number of people using the door increases and the frequency of use is high, it will be difficult to persuade staff to lock a door every time they pass through it.

A 'good' lock must be accompanied by a **strong door**. Similarly, other points of entry into the room/complex must be as well protected, otherwise the intruder will simply use a **window** to gain access.

One difficulty with conventional locks is the matter of **key control**. Each person authorised to use the door will need a key. Cleaners and other contractors might also be issued with keys. Practices such as lending out keys or taking duplicate keys may be difficult to prevent.

One approach to this is the installation of **combination locks**, where a numbered keypad is located outside the door and access allowed only after the correct 'code', or sequence of digits has been entered. This will only be fully effective if users ensure the combination is kept confidential, and the combination is **changed** frequently.

5.9.3 Card entry systems

Card entry systems are a more sophisticated means of control than the use of locks, as **cards can be programmed** to allow access to certain parts of a building only, between certain times.

Cards allow a high degree of monitoring of staff movements; they can for example be used instead of clock cards to record details of time spent on site. Such cards can be incorporated into **identity cards**, which also carry the photograph and signature of the user and which must be 'displayed' at all times.

5.9.4 Computer theft

As computer equipment becomes **smaller** and **more portable**, it can be 'smuggled' out of buildings with greater ease. Indeed much equipment is specifically **designed for use off-site**.

A **log of all equipment** should be maintained. This may already exist in basic form as a part of the fixed asset register. The log should include the **make, model** and **serial number** of each item, together with some other organisation-generated code which identifies the **department** which owns the item, the **individual** responsible for the item and its **location**. Anyone taking any equipment off-site should book it out and book it back in.

Smaller items of equipment, such as laptop computers and floppy disks, should always be **locked securely away**. Larger items cannot be moved with ease and one approach adopted is the use of **bolts** to secure them to desks. This discourages 'opportunity' thieves. Larger organisations may also employ site security guards and install closed circuit camera systems.

Other possible precautions include secured containers in cars for laptops, and the locking away of CDs and other storage media.

Question	Security measures

You are the chief accountant at your company. Your department, located in an open-plan office, has five networked desktop PCs, two laser printers and a dot matrix printer.

You have just read an article suggesting that the best form of security is to lock hardware away in fireproof cabinets, but you feel that this is impracticable. Make a note of any alternative security measures which you could adopt to protect the hardware.

Answer

(a) 'Postcode' all pieces of hardware. Invisible ink postcoding is popular, but visible marking is a better deterrent. Heated soldering irons are ideal for imprinting postcodes onto objects with a plastic casing.

(b) Mark the equipment in other ways. Some organisations spray their hardware with permanent paint, perhaps in a particular colour (bright red is popular) or using stencilled shapes.

(c) Hardware can be bolted to desks. If bolts are passed through the desk and through the bottom of the hardware casing, the equipment can be rendered immobile.

(d) Ensure that the organisation's standard security procedures (magnetic passes, keypad access to offices, signing in of visitors etc) are followed.

6 Building controls into an information system

FAST FORWARD

> It is possible to **build controls into** a **computerised** information system. A **balance** must be struck between the degree of control and the requirement for a user friendly system.

Controls can be classified as:

- Security controls
- Integrity controls
- Contingency controls

6.1 Security controls

Key term

> **Security** can be defined as 'The protection of data from accidental or deliberate threats which might cause unauthorised modification, disclosure or destruction of data, and the protection of the information system from the degradation or non-availability of services'.
>
> (Lane: *Security of computer based information systems*)

Risks to data

- Human error

  - Entering incorrect transactions
  - Failing to correct errors
  - Processing the wrong files

- Technical error such as malfunctioning hardware or software

- Natural disasters such as fire, flooding, explosion, impact, lightning

- Deliberate actions such as fraud

- Commercial espionage

- Malicious damage

- Industrial action

6.2 Integrity controls

Key terms

> **Data integrity** in the context of security is preserved when data is the same as in source documents and has not been accidentally or intentionally altered, destroyed or disclosed.
>
> **Systems integrity** refers to system operation conforming to the design specification despite attempts (deliberate or accidental) to make it behave incorrectly.

Data will maintain its **integrity** if it is **complete** and **not corrupted**. This means that:

(a)   The original **input** of the data must be controlled in such a way as to ensure that the results are complete and correct.

(b)   Any **processing and storage** of data must maintain the completeness and correctness of the data captured.

(c)   That reports or other **output** should be set up so that they, too, are complete and correct.

6.2.1 Input controls

Input controls should ensure the **accuracy, completeness and validity** of input.

(a) **Data verification** involves ensuring data entered matches source documents.

(b) **Data validation** involves ensuring that data entered is not incomplete or unreasonable. Various checks can be used, depending on the data type.

    (i) **Check digits**. A digit calculated by the program and added to the code being checked to validate it eg modulus 11 method.

    (ii) **Control totals**. For example, a batch total totalling the entries in the batch.

    (iii) **Hash totals**. A system generated total used to check processing has been performed as intended.

    (iv) **Range checks**. Used to check the value entered against a sensible range, eg balance sheet account number must be between 5,000 and 9,999.

    (v) **Limit checks**. Similar to a range check, but usually based on a upper limit eg must be less than 999,999.99.

Data may be **valid** (for example in the **correct format**) but still **not match source documents**.

6.2.2 Processing controls

Processing controls should ensure the **accuracy and completeness of processing**. Programs should be subject to development controls and to rigorous testing. Periodic running of test data is also recommended.

6.2.3 Output controls

Output controls should ensure the accuracy, completeness and security of output. The following measures are possible.

- Investigation and follow-up of error reports and exception reports
- Batch controls to ensure all items processed and returned
- Controls over distribution/copying of output
- Labelling of disks/tapes

6.2.4 Back-up controls

FAST FORWARD

A **back-up** and **archive** strategy should include:

- Regular back-up of data (at least daily)
- Archive plans
- A **disaster recovery** plan including off-site storage

Back-up controls aim to maintain system and data integrity. We have classified back-up controls as an integrity control rather than a contingency control (see later this section) because back-ups should be part of the day-to-day procedures of all computerised systems.

Key term

Back-up means to make a copy in anticipation of future failure or corruption. A back-up copy of a file is a duplicate copy kept separately from the main system and only used if the original fails.

The **purpose of backing-up data** is to ensure that the most recent usable copy of the data can be recovered and restored in the event of loss or corruption on the primary storage media.

In a well-planned data back-up scheme, a copy of backed-up data is delivered (preferably daily) to a secure **off-site** storage facility.

A tape **rotation scheme** can provide a restorable history from one day to several years, depending on the needs of the business.

A well-planned **back-up and archive strategy** should include:

(a)   A plan and schedule for the **regular back-up of critical data**.

(b)   **Archive plans**.

(c)   A **disaster recovery plan** that includes off-site storage.

Regular tests should be undertaken to **verify that data backed-up can be successfully restored**.

The **intervals** at which back-ups are performed must be decided. Most organisations back up their data daily, but back-ups may need to be performed more frequently, depending on the nature of the data and of the organisation.

Even with a well planned back-up strategy some re-inputting may be required. For example, if after three hours work on a Wednesday a file becomes corrupt, the Tuesday version can be restored – but Wednesday's work will need to be re-input.

6.2.5 Archiving

A related concept is that of **archiving**. Archiving data is the process of moving data from primary storage, such as a hard disk, to tape or other portable media for long-term storage.

Archiving provides a legally acceptable **business history**, while freeing up **hard disk space**. If archived data is needed, it can be restored from the archived tape to a hard disk. Archived data can be used to recover from site-wide disasters, such as fires or floods, where data on primary storage devices is destroyed. Archiving also helps avoid the slowdown in processing which may occur if large volumes of data build up on the main operational storage.

How long data should be retained will be influenced by:

- Legal obligations
- Other business needs

Data stored for a long time should be tested periodically to ensure it is **still restorable** – it may be subject to **damage** from environmental conditions or mishandling.

6.2.6 Passwords and logical access systems

Key term

> A **password** is a set of characters which may be allocated to a person, a terminal or a facility which is required to be keyed into the system before further access is permitted.

Unauthorised persons may circumvent physical access controls. A **logical access system** can prevent access to data and program files, by measures such as the following.

- Identification of the user
- Authentication of user identity
- Checks on user authority

Virtually all computer installations use passwords. Failed access attempts may be logged. Passwords are not foolproof.

- Standard system passwords (such as 1234) given when old passwords are reset or provided to new employees, must be changed

- Passwords must never be divulged to others and must never be written down

- Passwords must be changed regularly – and changed immediately if it is suspected that the password is known by others

- Obvious passwords must not be used

Passwords are also used by administrators to control access rights for the reading, modifying and deleting functions.

6.2.7 Administrative controls

Personnel selection is important. Some employees are always in a position of trust.

- Computer security officer
- Senior systems analyst
- Database administrator

Measures to control personnel include the following.

- Careful recruitment
- Job rotation and enforced vacations
- Systems logs
- Review and supervision

For other staff, **segregation of duties** remains a core security requirement. This involves division of responsibilities into separate roles.

- Data capture and data entry
- Computer operations
- Systems analysis and programming

6.2.8 Audit trail

FAST FORWARD

> An **audit trail** shows who has accessed a system and the operations performed.

The original concept of an audit trail is to enable a manager or auditor to follow transactions stage-by-stage through a system to ensure that they have been processed correctly. The intention is to:

- **Identify errors**
- **Detect fraud**

Modern integrated computer systems have cut out much of the time-consuming stage-by-stage working of older systems, but there should still be some **means of identifying individual records** and the **input and output documents** associated with the processing of any individual transaction.

Key term

> An **audit trail** is a record showing who has accessed a computer system and what operations he or she has performed. Audit trails are useful both for maintaining security and for recovering lost transactions. Accounting systems include an audit trail component that is able to be output as a report.
>
> In addition, there are separate audit trail software products that enable network administrators to monitor use of network resources.

An audit trail should be provided so that every transaction on a file contains a **unique reference** (eg a sales system transaction record should hold a reference to the customer order, delivery note and invoice).

Typical contents of an accounting software package audit trail include the following items.

(a) A system generated **transaction number**.

(b) A meaningful reference number eg invoice number.

(c) Transaction type eg reversing journal, credit note, cashbook entry etc.

(d) Who input the transaction (user ID).

(e) Full **transaction details** eg net and gross amount, customer ID and so on.

(f) The **PC or terminal** used to enter the transaction.

(g) The **date** and **time** of the entry.

(h) Any additional reference or **narration** entered by the user.

6.2.9 Systems integrity with a PC

Possible **controls relevant to a stand-alone PC** are as follows.

(a) Installation of a **password** routine which is activated whenever the computer is booted up, and activated after periods of inactivity.

(b) The use of additional passwords on 'sensitive' files eg employee salaries spreadsheet.

(c) Any data stored on floppy disk, DVD or CD should be locked away.

(d) **Physical access controls**, for example door locks activated by swipe cards or PIN numbers, to prevent access into the room(s) where the computers are kept.

6.2.10 Systems integrity with a LAN

The main additional risk (when compared to a stand-alone PC) is the risk of a fault **spreading across the system**. This is particularly true of **viruses**. A virus introduced onto one machine could replicate itself throughout the network. All files coming in to the organisation should be scanned using **anti-virus software** and all machines should have anti-virus software running constantly.

A further risk, depending on the type of network configuration, is that an extra PC could be 'plugged in' to the network to gain access to it. The **network management software** should detect and prevent breaches of this type.

6.2.11 Systems integrity with a WAN

Additional issues, over and above those already described are related to the extensive communications links utilised by Wide Area Networks. Dedicated land lines for data transfer and encryption software may be required.

If **commercially sensitive data** is being transferred it would be necessary to specify high quality communications equipment and to use sophisticated network software to prevent and detect any security breaches.

6.3 Contingency controls

Key term

> A **contingency** is an unscheduled interruption of computing services that requires measures outside the day-to-day routine operating procedures.

The preparation of a contingency plan (also known as a disaster recovery plan) is one of the stages in the development of an organisation-wide security policy. A contingency plan is necessary in case of a major **disaster,** or if some of the **security measures** discussed elsewhere **fail**.

A **disaster** occurs where the system for some reason breaks down, leading to potential **losses** of equipment, data or funds. The system **must recover as soon as possible** so that further losses are not incurred, and current losses can be rectified.

Question

Causes of system breakdown

What actions or events might lead to a system breakdown?

Answer

System breakdowns can occur in a variety of circumstances, for example:

(a)   Fire destroying data files and equipment.

(b)   Flooding.

(c)   A computer virus completely destroying a data or program file.

(d)   A technical fault in the equipment.

(e)   Accidental destruction of telecommunications links (eg builders severing a cable).

(f)   Terrorist attack.

(g)   System failure caused by software bugs which were not discovered at the design stage.

(h)   Internal sabotage (eg logic bombs built into the software).

6.3.1 Disaster recovery plan

Any disaster recovery plan must provide for:

(a)   **Standby procedures** so that some operations can be performed while normal services are disrupted.

(b)   **Recovery procedures** once the cause of the breakdown has been discovered or corrected.

(c)   **Personnel management** policies to ensure that (a) and (b) above are implemented properly.

6.3.2 Contents of a disaster recovery plan

FAST FORWARD

A **disaster recovery plan** must cover all activities from the initial response to a 'disaster', through to damage limitation and full recovery. Responsibilities must be clearly spelt out for all tasks.

Chapter Roundup

- **Internal controls** should help organisations counter risks, maintain the quality of reporting and comply with laws and regulations. They provide reasonable assurance that the organisations will fulfil their objectives.

- Internal control frameworks include the **control environment** within which **internal controls** operate. Other important elements are the **risk assessment and response processes,** the **sharing of information** and **monitoring** the environment and operation of the control system.

- The **control environment** is influenced by **management's attitude** towards control, the **organisational structure** and the **values** and **abilities** of employees.

- Controls can be classified in various ways including **administrative** and **accounting**; **prevent**, **detect** and **correct**; **discretionary** and **non-discretionary**; **voluntary** and **mandated**; **manual** and **automated**.

  The mnemonic **SPAMSOAP** can be used to remember the main types of control.

- The role of internal audit will **vary** according to the **organisation's objectives** but is likely to include review **of internal control systems, risk management, legal compliance** and **value for money**.

- **Internal auditors** are **employees** of the organisation whose work is designed to **add value** and who report to the **audit committee**. **External auditors** are from **accountancy firms** and their role is to **report on the financial statements to shareholders**.

  Both **internal and external auditors** review controls, and **external auditors** may **place reliance** on **internal auditors' work** providing they assess its worth.

- **Security** is the protection of data from accidental or deliberate threats and the protection of an information system from such threats.

- **Physical threats** to security may be natural or man made. They include fire, flooding, weather, lightning, terrorist activity and accidental damage.

- **Physical access controls** are designed to prevent **intruders** getting near to computer equipment and/or storage media.

- Important aspects of physical access of control are **door locks** and **card entry systems**. Computer theft is becoming more prevalent as equipment becomes smaller and more portable.

- It is possible to **build controls into** a **computerised** information system. A **balance** must be struck between the degree of control and the requirement for a user friendly system.

- A **back-up** and **archive** strategy should include:

  - Regular back-up of data (at least daily)
  - Archive plans
  - A **disaster recovery** plan including off-site storage

- An **audit trail** shows who has accessed a system and the operations performed.

- A **disaster recovery plan** must cover all activities from the initial response to a 'disaster', through to damage limitation and full recovery. Responsibilities must be clearly spelt out for all tasks.

Quick Quiz

1 What according to Turnbull should a good system of internal control achieve?

2 What are the main components of the criteria of control framework?

3 What are the main factors that will be reflected in the organisation's control environment?

4 Match the control and control type

    (a) Checking of delivery notes against invoices
    (b) Back-up of computer input
    (c) Bank reconciliation

    (i) Prevent
    (ii) Detect
    (iii) Correct

5 A .... control is required by law and imposed by external authorities.

6 List the eight types of control given in SAS 300.

7 According to the Turnbull report, in which areas do internal controls particularly need to be communicated?

8 What technique can be used by managers to obtain a consistent view on the adequacy of control procedures throughout the organisation?

9 What is internal audit?

10 What are the main elements of internal audit's review of the accounting and control systems?

11 Name three key differences between internal and external audit.

12 What matters would the external auditors consider when assessing the internal audit function?

13 Internal auditors are not required to consider fraud.

    True   ☐

    False   ☐

14 What are the most important aspects of the assessment of the professional proficiency of internal audit?

15 What criteria should be used to judge the quality of internal audit reports?

16 It is possible to buy in an internal audit service from an external organisation.

    True   ☐

    False   ☐

17 List three physical access control methods.

18 List four risks to data.

19 What is the purpose of taking a back-up?

20 Why should certain duties be segregated between staff members?

Answers to Quick Quiz

1   • Facilitate effective and efficient operation by enabling it to respond to significant risks
    • Help ensure the quality of internal and external reporting
    • Help ensure compliance with applicable laws and regulations

2   • Purpose
    • Commitment
    • Capability
    • Action
    • Monitoring and learning

3   • The philosophy and operating style of the directors and management

    • The entity's organisational structure and methods of assigning authority and responsibility (including segregation of duties and supervisory controls)

    • The directors' methods of imposing control, including the internal audit function, the functions of the board of directors and personnel policies and procedures

    • The integrity, ethical values and competence of directors and staff

4   (a)   (i)
    (b)   (iii)
    (c)   (ii)

5   A **mandated** control is required by law and imposed by external authorities.

6   • Approval and control of documents
    • Controls over computerised applications and the information technology environment
    • Checking the arithmetical accuracy of the records
    • Maintaining and reviewing control accounts and trial balances
    • Reconciliations
    • Comparing the results of cash, security and stock counts with accounting records
    • Comparing internal data with external sources of information
    • Limiting direct physical access to assets and records

7   • Customer relations
    • Service levels for both internal and outsourced activities
    • Health, safety and environmental protection
    • Security of assets and business continuity
    • Expenditure
    • Accounting, financial and other reporting

8   Control self-assessment

9   Internal audit is an appraisal or monitoring activity established by management and directors, for the review of the accounting and internal control systems as a service to the entity.

10   • Reviewing the design of systems
     • Monitoring the operation of systems by risk assessment and detailed testing
     • Recommending cost effective improvements

11   External report to members, internal to directors
     External report on financial statements, internal on systems, controls and risks
     External are independent of the company, internal often employed by it

12   • Organisational status
     • Scope of function
     • Technical competence
     • Due professional care

13 False

14
- Appropriate staffing
- Knowledge, skills and disciplines
- Supervision
- Compliance with professional standards
- Human relations and communication
- Continuing education
- Due professional care

15
- Whether reports are well written
- Timeliness of reports
- Reaction from operational departments

16 True

17 Personnel (security guards), mechanical devices (eg keys), electronic devices (eg card-swipe systems, PIN keypads).

18 Human error
Hardware error
Software error
Deliberate actions
You may have come up with others.

19 To enable valid files to be restored in case of a future corruption or failure.

20 To reduce the opportunity for fraud and/or malicious damage.

Identifying and preventing fraud

10

Topic list	Syllabus reference
1 What is fraud?	D4(a)
2 Potential for fraud	D4(b)
3 Implications of fraud for the organisation	D4(c)
4 Systems for detecting and preventing fraud	D4(d)
5 Responsibility for detecting and preventing fraud	D4(d)

Introduction

This chapter considers the various types of fraud that an organisation may be prone to (**Section 1**) and which may have to be investigated by internal audit (**Chapter 9**). It is important that you are able to identify signs of fraud in different circumstances (**Section 2**).

You also need to have a good knowledge of both how fraud is prevented and detected. Although there may be significant costs involved in implementing a good system of fraud prevention, the consequences of successful fraud may be very serious, both for the reputation of the organisation and the position of its directors. **Sections 3**, **4** and **5** explore these issues

Study guide

		Intellectual level
D4	**Fraud and fraudulent behaviour and their prevention in business**	
(a)	Explain the circumstances under which fraud is likely to arise.	1
(b)	Identify different types of fraud in the organisation.	1
(c)	Explain the implications of fraud for the organisation.	2
(d)	Explain the role and duties of individual managers in the fraud detection and prevention process.	1

Exam guide

The practical aspects of fraud (where it might actually occur how it can be detected) are the most likely topics to be examined. This is certainly the case on the Pilot Paper.

1 What is fraud?

FAST FORWARD

> In a corporate context fraud can fall into one of two main categories: **removal of funds or assets** from a business or the intentional **misrepresentation of the financial position of a business**.

Key term

> **Fraud** may be generally defined as 'deprivation by deceit'. In a court case, fraud was defined as 'a false representation of fact made with the knowledge of its falsity, or without belief in its truth, or recklessly careless, whether it be true or false'.

In a corporate context, fraud can fall into one of two main categories.

Category	Comment
Removal of funds or assets from a business	The most obvious example of this is outright theft, either of cash or of other assets. However, this form of fraud also encompasses more subtle measures, such as overstatement of claims. (Paragraph 1.1)
Intentional misrepresentation of the financial position of the business	This includes the omission or misrecording of the company's accounting records. (Paragraph 1.2)

Exam focus point

> This is not an exhaustive list of examples. Every business is unique in its own way and offers different opportunities for fraud to be committed. You need to be able to think about a situation and identify for yourself areas and ways in which frauds could be occurring.

1.1 Removal of funds or assets from a business

FAST FORWARD

> **Common frauds** include payroll frauds, conspiracy with other parties and stealing assets. More subtle measures include teeming and lading and manipulation of bank reconciliations and cashbooks to conceal theft.

1.1.1 Theft of cash

Employees with access to cash may be tempted to steal it. A prime example is theft from petty cash. Small amounts taken at intervals may easily go unnoticed.

1.1.2 Theft of inventory

Similarly, employees may pilfer items of inventory. The most trivial example of this is employees taking office stationery, although larger items may be taken also. These examples are of unsophisticated types of fraud, which generally go undetected because of their immateriality. On the whole, such fraud will tend to be too insignificant to have any serious impact on results or long-term performance.

1.1.3 Payroll fraud

Employees within or outside the payroll department can perpetrate payroll fraud.

(a) Employees external to the department can falsify their timesheets, for example by claiming overtime for hours which they did not really work.

(b) Members of the payroll department may have the opportunity deliberately to miscalculate selected payslips, either by applying an inflated rate of pay or by altering the hours to which the rate is applied.

(c) Alternatively, a fictitious member of staff can be added to the payroll list. The fraudster sets up a bank account in the bogus name and collects the extra cash himself. This is most feasible in a large organisation with high numbers of personnel, where management is not personally acquainted with every employee.

1.1.4 Teeming and lading

This is one of the best known methods of fraud in the sales ledger area. Basically, **teeming and lading** is the theft of cash or cheque receipts. Setting subsequent receipts, not necessarily from the same customer, against the outstanding debt conceals the theft.

Exam focus point

> Teeming and lading is the topic of a question on the Pilot Paper.

1.1.5 Fictitious customers

This is a more elaborate method of stealing inventory. Bogus orders are set up, and goods are despatched on credit. The 'customer' then fails to pay for the goods and the cost is eventually written off as a bad debt. For this type of fraud to work, the employee must have responsibility for taking goods orders as well as the authority to approve a new customer for credit.

1.1.6 Collusion with customers

Employees may collude with customers to defraud the business by manipulating prices or the quality or quantity of goods despatched.

(a) For example, a sales manager or director could **reduce the price** charged to a customer in return for a cut of the saving. Alternatively, the employee could write off a debt or issue a credit note in return for a financial reward.

(b) Another act of collusion might be for the employee to **suppress invoices** or under-record quantities of despatched goods on delivery notes. Again, the customer would probably provide the employee with a financial incentive for doing this.

1.1.7 Bogus supply of goods or services

This typically involves senior staff who falsely invoice the firm for goods or services that were never supplied. One example would be the supply of consultancy services. To enhance authenticity, in many cases the individual involved will set up a personal company that invoices the business for its services. This type of fraud can be quite difficult to prove.

1.1.8 Paying for goods not received

Staff may collude with suppliers, who issue invoices for larger quantities of goods than were actually delivered. The additional payments made by the company are split between the two parties.

1.1.9 Meeting budgets/target performance measures

Management teams will readily agree that setting budgets and goals is an essential part of planning and an important ingredient for success. However, such targets can disguise frauds. In some cases, knowing that results are unlikely to be questioned once targets have been met, employees and/or management siphon off and pocket any profits in excess of the target.

1.1.10 Manipulation of bank reconciliations and cash books

Often the simplest techniques can hide the biggest frauds. We saw earlier how simple a technique teeming and lading is for concealing a theft. Similarly, other simple measures such as incorrect descriptions of items and use of compensating debits and credits to make a reconciliation work frequently ensure that fraudulent activities go undetected.

1.1.11 Misuse of pension funds or other assets

This type of fraud has received a high profile in the past. Ailing companies may raid the pension fund and steal assets to use as collateral in obtaining loan finance. Alternatively, company assets may be transferred to the fund at significant over-valuations.

1.1.12 Disposal of assets to employees

It may be possible for an employee to arrange to buy a company asset (eg a car) for personal use. In this situation, there may be scope to manipulate the book value of the asset so that the employee pays below market value for it. This could be achieved by over-depreciating the relevant asset.

1.2 Intentional misrepresentation of the financial position of the business

Here we consider examples in which the intention is to overstate profits. Note, however, that by reversing the logic we can also use them as examples of methods by which staff may deliberately understate profits. You should perform this exercise yourself.

1.2.1 Over-valuation of inventory

Inventory is a particularly attractive area for management wishing to inflate net assets artificially. There is a whole range of ways in which inventory may be incorrectly valued for accounts purposes.

(a)   Inventory records may be manipulated, particularly by deliberate miscounting at inventory counts.

(b)   Deliveries to customers may be omitted from the books.

(c)   Returns to suppliers may not be recorded.

(d)   Obsolete inventory may not be written off but rather held at cost on the balance sheet.

1.2.2 Irrecoverable debt policy may not be enforced

Aged receivables who are obviously not going to pay should be written off. However, by not enforcing this policy management can avoid the negative effects it would have on profits and net assets.

1.2.3 Fictitious sales

These can be channelled through the accounts in a number of ways.

Question — Sales fraud

See if you can come up with three ways of generating fictitious sales transactions or sales values.

Answer

The following are just three obvious suggestions:

(a)   Generation of false invoices
(b)   Overcharging customers for goods or services
(c)   Selling goods to friends (with a promise of buying them back at a later date)

1.2.4 Manipulation of year end events

Cut off dates provide management with opportunities for window dressing the financial statements. Sales made just before year end can be deliberately over-invoiced and credit notes issued with an apology at the start of the new year. This will enhance turnover and profit during the year just ended. Delaying the recording of pre-year-end purchases of goods not yet delivered can achieve the same objective.

1.2.5 Understating expenses

Clearly, failure to record all expenses accurately will inflate the reported profit figure.

1.2.6 Manipulation of depreciation figures

As an expense that does not have any cash flow effect, depreciation figures may be easily tampered with. Applying incorrect rates or inconsistent policies in order to understate depreciation will result in a higher profit and a higher net book value, giving a more favourable impression of financial health.

2 Potential for fraud

The UK has witnessed a number of high profile frauds, most notably the BCCI, Maxwell and Barings Bank cases. The real incidence of fraud is difficult to gauge, particularly because companies are often loath to publicise such experiences. However, all business – without exception – face the **risk of fraud**: the directors' responsibility is to manage that risk.

2.1 Prerequisites for fraud

FAST FORWARD

There are three broad pre-requisites or 'pre-conditions' that must exist in order to make fraud a possibility: dishonesty, motivation and opportunity.

These are useful to know, because if one or more of them can be eliminated, the risk of fraud is reduced!

2.1.1 Dishonesty

Honesty is a subjective quality, which is interpreted variously according to different ethical, cultural and legal norms. However, we may define dishonesty as an individual's pre-disposition or tendency to act in ways which contravene accepted ethical, social, organisational and legal norms for fair and honest dealing. This tendency may arise from:

(a)   Personality factors: a high need for achievement, status or security; a competitive desire to gain advantage over others; low respect for authority;

(b)   Cultural factors: national or familial values, which may be more 'flexible' or anti-authority than the law and practice prevailing in the organisation. (Cultural values about the ethics of business 'bribes' – or 'gifts' – for example, vary widely. 'Lying' is also a very fluid concept: some cultures value 'saving face' or agreeing over giving strictly truthful responses.)

2.1.2 Motivation

In addition to a general predisposition or willingness to act dishonestly, should the opportunity arise, the individual needs a specific motivation to do so. We will be discussing the concept of motivation in Chapter 12, but broadly, it involves a **calculation** of whether a given action is worthwhile. Individuals weigh up:

(a)   The **potential rewards** of an action: the satisfaction of some need, or the fulfilment of some goal; **in relation to**

(b)   The **potential sanctions** or negative consequences of an action, or the deprivations required to carry it through.

The individual's goal or motive for fraudulent behaviour may be:

(a)   Financial needs or wants, or envy of others (in the case of theft or fraud for monetary gain)

(b)   A desire to exercise negative power over those in authority

(c)   A desire to avoid punishment (in the case of cover ups, say)

2.1.3 Opportunity

Even if a person is willing to act dishonestly, and has a motive for doing so, (s)he must still find an opportunity or opening to do so: a 'loophole' in the law or control system that:

- Allows fraudulent activity to go undetected, or
- Makes the risk of detection acceptable, given the rewards available.

An individual will have a high incentive to commit fraud if (s)he is predisposed to **dishonesty** and the **rewards** for the particular fraud are high and there is an **opportunity** to commit fraudulent action with **little chance of detection** or with insignificant sanctions if caught.

| Question | Fraud strategies |

Just considering the three prerequisites of fraud, what immediate control strategies can you suggest for preventing fraud?

| Answer |

(a)   Don't employ people with pre-dispositions to **dishonesty**, if possible: carry out legitimate and appropriate background and CV checks when carrying out recruitment and selection. (The more opportunity for fraud there is in the job, the more carefully dishonesty should be screened.)

(b) Reduce **motivations** for fraud. This is highly subjective, but the organisation should give attention to matters such as: ensuring equity in pay and rewards; monitoring employees for signs of financial difficulty and its possible causes (eg gambling addiction) and offering counselling and support where required; providing generally good and equitable working terms and conditions; establishing clear rules and strong sanctions for fraudulent behaviour; and so on.

(c) Reduce **opportunities** for fraud. This is the function of a range of internal checks and controls, discussed in Section 4 of the chapter: separating duties so no one person has sole control over a system; requiring authorisations for expense/time sheets, cheques and so on; using data security measures such as passwords; security checks; identification on office equipment to deter theft; and so on.

2.2 Assessing the risk of fraud

FAST FORWARD

Signs of high fraud risk include indications of **lack of integrity**, **excessive pressures**, **poor control systems**, **unusual transactions** and **lack of audit evidence**.

The starting point for any management team wanting to set up internal controls to prevent and detect fraud must be an assessment of the extent to which the firm is exposed to the risk of fraud. The best approach is to consider separately the extent to which **external** and **internal** factors may present a risk of fraud.

2.2.1 External factors

Step 1 First, consider the market place as a whole. The general environment in which the business operates may exhibit factors that increase the risk of fraud. For instance, the trend to de-layer may reduce the degree of supervision exercised in many organisations, perhaps without putting anything in its place.

Step 2 Next, narrow the focus a little and consider whether the industry in which the firm operates is particularly exposed to certain types of fraud. For example, the building industry may be particularly prone to the risk of theft of raw materials, the travel industry may face risks due to the extensive use of agents and intermediaries and the retail industry must be vigilant to the abuse of credit cards.

Question

Risk factors

Think of some examples of such general external factors that might influence the degree of risk that a company is exposed to.

Answer

You might have thought of some of the following.

- Technological developments
- New legislation or regulations
- Economic or political changes
- Increased competition
- Changing customer needs

2.2.2 Internal factors

Having considered the big picture, the next step is to apply the same logic at a company level. Focus on the general and specific risks in the firm itself.

Be alert to circumstances that might increase the risk profile of a company.

- Changed operating environment
- New personnel
- New or upgraded management information systems
- New overseas operations

- Rapid growth
- New technology
- New products
- Corporate restructuring

A number of factors tend to crop up time and time again as issues that might indicate potential fraud. Attention should be drawn to them if any of these factors come to light when assessing external and internal risks.

2.2.3 Business risks

FAST FORWARD

A number of factors tend to crop up frequently as **indicators** of potential fraud situations; these can be categorised under business and personnel risks.

An alert management team will always be aware of the industry or business environment in which the organisation operates.

(a)   **Profit levels/margins deviating significantly from the industry norm**

As a rule of thumb, if things seem too good to be true, then they generally are. If any of the following happen, alarm bells should start ringing.

(i)   The company suddenly starts to exhibit profits far above those achieved by other firms in the same industry.

(ii)   Turnover rises rapidly but costs do not rise in line.

(iii)   Demand for a particular product increases significantly.

(iv)   Investors seem to find the firm unusually attractive.

Such patterns can indicate problems such as the manipulation of accounting records, collusion with existing customers or the creation of fictitious customers.

Similarly, results showing that the organisation is under-performing relative to competitors may be an indication of theft, collusion with suppliers or deliberate errors in the accounting records.

(b)   **Market opinion**

If the market has a low opinion of the firm, this might indicate something about the company's products, its people or its way of doing business.

(c)   **Complex structures**

(i)   Organisations with complex group structures, including numerous domestic and overseas subsidiaries and branches, may be more susceptible to fraud.

(ii)   The sheer size of the group can offer plenty of opportunities to 'lose' transactions or to hide things in intercompany accounts.

(iii)   Furthermore, vast staff numbers contribute to a certain degree of employee anonymity, making it easier to conceal fraudulent activities.

2.2.4 Personnel risks

Fraud is not usually an easy thing to hide. A person's behaviour often gives clues to the fact that they are engaging in fraud.

(a) **Secretive behaviour**

A High Court judge once described secrecy as 'the badge of fraud'. If an individual starts behaving in a more secretive way than is generally considered normal, then there may be cause for concern.

(b) **Expensive lifestyles**

A well-known indicator of fraud is a life-style beyond an individual's earnings. A recent case involved an Inspector of Taxes who started driving expensive sport cars, taking lavish holidays and so forth. It was later discovered that he was being paid by a wealthy businessman in return for assisting him to evade tax.

(c) **Long hours or untaken holidays**

Workaholics and staff who do not take their full holiday entitlement may be trying to prevent a temporary replacement from uncovering a fraud.

(d) **Autocratic management style**

In some organisations a sole manager or director has exclusive control over a significant part of the business. This can provide ample scope for fraud, particularly when the situation is compounded by little, if any, independent review of those activities by anyone else at a senior level.

(e) **Lack of segregation of duties**

Employees occasionally have more than one area of responsibility, particularly in small businesses where staff numbers are low. This can make it easy for the employee to conduct and conceal fraudulent actions. For example, if the employee who prepares the payslips were also the person who authorises the payments, payroll fraud would be relatively simple to put into practice.

(f) **Low staff morale**

One motive for fraud is resentment towards the firm. Staff may start defrauding the firm because they feel that they are not rewarded sufficiently for their work or because they were passed over for a promotion that they believed they deserved. Alternatively, low staff morale may lead to the breakdown of internal controls, yielding opportunities for fraud.

2.3 Potential for computer fraud

Organisations are becoming increasingly dependent on computers for operational systems as well as accounting and management information. With this dependency comes an increased **exposure** to fraud. The computer is frequently the vehicle through which fraudulent activities are carried out.

Problems particularly associated with computers.

(a) **Computer hackers**. The possibility of unknown persons trying to hack into the systems increases the potential for fraud against which the firm must protect itself.

(b) **Lack of training within the management team**. Many people have an inherent lack of understanding of how computer systems work. Senior management can often be the least computer literate. They may also be the most reluctant to receive training, preferring to delegate tasks to assistants. Without management realising it, junior staff can secure access to vast amounts of financial information and find ways to alter it.

(c)   **Identifying the risks**. Most firms do not have the resources to keep up to date with the pace of development of computer technology. This makes it ever more difficult to check that all major loopholes in controls are closed, even if management are computer literate.

(d)   **Need for ease of access and flexible systems**. In most cases, a firm uses computers in order to simplify and speed up operations. To meet these objectives, there is frequently a need for ease of access and flexible systems. However, implementing strict controls can sometimes suppress these features.

3 Implications of fraud for the organisation

Whilst it is clear that fraud is bad for business, the precise ways in which the firm is affected depends on the type of fraud being carried on.

3.1 Removal of funds or assets from a business

Immediate financial implications

Profits are lower than they should be. The business has less cash or fewer assets, and therefore the net asset position is weakened. Returns to shareholders are likely to fall as a result.

Long term effects on company performance

The reduction in working capital makes it more difficult for the company to operate effectively. In the most serious cases, fraud can ultimately result in the collapse of an otherwise successful business, such as Barings.

3.2 Intentional misrepresentation of the financial position of the business

Financial statements do not give a true and fair view of the financial situation of the business. Results may be either artificially enhanced or, less frequently, under-reported.

It is also possible that managers in charge of a particular **division** can artificially enhance their division's results, thereby deceiving senior management.

Question	Reporting results

Try to think of reasons why someone might want to:

(a)   Artificially enhance the results
(b)   Under-report the results

Answer

(a)   Reasons for overstating profits and/or net assets

   (i)   To ensure achievement on paper, may have to meet targets in order to secure a promotion, bonuses or remuneration may be linked to performance

   (ii)   Trying to conceal another form of fraud, such as theft

   (iii)   Need a healthy balance sheet to convince bank to give loan finance

   (iv)   Ailing company may be trying to entice equity investors

(b) Reasons for understating profits and/or net assets

    (i) To facilitate a private purchase of an asset from the business at less than market value

    (ii) To defraud HM Revenue & Customs by reducing taxable profits or gains

    (iii) Trying to force the share price down so that shares can be bought below market value by friends or relatives

3.2.1 If results are overstated

A company may **distribute too much** of its profits to shareholders.

Retained profits will be lower than believed, leading to potential shortfalls in working capital. This makes the day-to-day activities more difficult to perform effectively.

Incorrect decisions will be made, based on inaccurate knowledge of available resources.

The effects of fraudulent activities can also affect **stakeholders** if the financial statements upon which they rely are misrepresentations of the truth.

(a) **Investors** making decisions based on inaccurate information will find actual returns deviating from expectations.

(b) **Suppliers** will extend credit without knowing the financial position of the company.

3.2.2 If results are understated

Returns to investors may be reduced unnecessarily.

If the company is quoted on the stock exchange, the share price might fall and market strength may be eroded.

Access to loan finance may be restricted if assets are understated.

The **negative publicity** can damage the business by affecting the public's perceptions.

Legal consequences. Finally, fraudsters open themselves up to the possibility of arrest. Depending on the scale and seriousness of the offence some may even find themselves facing a prison sentence.

4 Systems for detecting and preventing fraud

4.1 Prioritising prevention

FAST FORWARD

In order to prevent fraud, managers must be aware of the **risks** and **signs** of fraud.

Prevention of fraud must be an **integral** part of **corporate strategy**. Managing the risk of fraud is a key part of managing business risks in general, and if the company's risk management procedures are poor, management of fraud risk is also likely to be unsuccessful.

Certain recent developments, notably downsizing, have however meant that certain controls that are designed to prevent fraud, for example segregation of duties, may not be possible. Hence it is equally important the control system is designed so as to **detect and investigate** fraud.

4.2 Reasons for fraud

Management must have an understanding of how and why frauds might arise. Examples include:

(a)   The risk of fraud may be increased by factors that are specific to the **industry**. Lower profit margins due to increased competition may be a temptation to manipulate results.

(b)   Factors specific to the **business** may also increase the risk of fraud.

(i)   **Personnel** factors such as extensive authority given to dominant managers.

(ii)   **Organisation** factors such as unclear structure of responsibility or lack of supervision of remote locations.

(iii)   **Strategy** factors such as a lack of a business strategy or great emphasis being placed on reward by results.

(c)   **Changes in circumstances** may also increase the risk of fraud. Often a control system may become inadequate as a result of changes in the business, particularly changes in technology or internal organisation.

(d)   Certain areas, for example cash sales are **normally high risk**.

4.3 Reasons for poor controls

Management also need to understand factors that may prevent controls from operating properly.

- Controls will not function well if there is a **lack of emphasis** on compliance or a **lack of understanding** of why the controls are required, how they should operate and who should be operating them.

- **Staff problems** such as understaffing, poor quality or poorly motivated staff can impede the operation of controls.

- **Changes in senior personnel** can lead to a lack of supervision during the transition period.

- **Emphasis on the autonomy of operational management** may lead to controls being bypassed.

4.4 General prevention policies

FAST FORWARD

Prevention policies include emphasis on **ethics** and **personnel and training procedures**. Controls within particular business areas such as **segregation of duties** and **documentation requirements** are also significant.

Management can implement certain general controls that are designed to prevent fraud.

(a)   **Emphasising ethics** can decrease the chances of fraud. Several businesses have formal codes of ethics which employees are required to sign covering areas such as gifts from customers. Management can also ensure that they set 'a good example'.

(b)   **Personnel controls** are a very important means of preventing fraud. Thorough **interviewing** and **recruitment procedures** including obtaining references can be an effective screening for dishonest employees. **Appraisal** and grievance systems can prevent staff demotivation.

(c)   **Training and raising awareness** can be important. There are many examples of frauds taking place where people who were unwittingly close were shocked that they had no idea what was happening. **Fraud awareness education** should therefore be an integral part of the training programme, particularly for managers and staff in **high risk areas** such as procurement, and staff with key roles in fraud prevention and detection, for example human resources.

4.5 Prevention of fraud in specific business areas

Controls will also be needed in specific areas of the business where a high risk of fraud has been identified.

(a) **Segregation of duties** is a key control in fraud prevention. Ultimately operational pressures may mean that segregation is incomplete. Management should nevertheless identify certain functions that must be kept separate, for example separating the cheque signing function from the authorisation of payments.

(b) **Appropriate documentation** should be required for all transactions.

(c) **Limitation controls** such as only allowing staff to choose suppliers from an approved list, or limiting access to the computer network by means of passwords can reduce the opportunities for fraud.

(d) Certain actions should be **prohibited** such as leaving a computer terminal without logging off.

(e) **Internal audit** work should **concentrate** on these areas.

4.6 Detection and prevention

A primary aim of any system of internal controls should be to **prevent fraud**. However, the very nature of fraud means that people will find ways to get around existing systems. It is equally important, therefore, to have controls in place to **detect fraud** if and when it happens.

4.7 Internal controls

FAST FORWARD

> Controls must be developed in a structured manner, taking account of the whole spectrum of risk and focusing on the key risks identified in each area of the business.

Let us think about appropriate controls that could be introduced to combat fraud.

4.8 Physical controls

Basic as it seems, physical security is an important tool in preventing fraud. Keeping tangible assets under lock and key makes it difficult for staff to access them and can go a long way towards discouraging theft.

4.9 Segregation of duties

Staff who have responsibility for a range of tasks have more scope for committing and concealing fraud. Therefore the obvious way to control the risk is to segregate duties.

If an employee's duties do not extend beyond one domain, it will be more difficult for an employee to conceal a fraud. It is more likely that it will be picked up at the next stage in the process.

So, for example, the employee responsible for recording sales orders should not be the same person responsible for maintaining inventory records. This will make it more difficult to falsify sales or inventory records, as a discrepancy between sales figures and inventory balances would show up.

Segregating responsibility for packaging goods for delivery from either of the recording tasks would also help to minimise the risk of theft and increase the likelihood of detection.

4.10 Authorisation policies

Requiring written authorisation by a senior member of staff is a good preventative tool. It increases accountability and also makes it harder to conceal a fraudulent transaction.

4.11 Customer signatures

Requiring customers to inspect and sign for receipt of goods or services ensures that they cannot claim that the delivery did not match their order.

It also provides confirmation that the delivery staff actually did their job and that what was delivered corresponded to what was recorded.

4.12 Using words rather than numbers

Insist that all quantities be written out in full. It is much more difficult to change text than to alter a figure.

4.13 Documentation

Separate documents should be used to record sales order, despatch, delivery and invoice details. A simple matching exercise will then pick up any discrepancies between them and lead to detection of any alterations.

4.14 Sequential numbering

Numbering order forms, delivery dockets or invoices makes it extremely simple to spot if something is missing.

4.15 Dates

Writing the date on forms and invoices assists in cut-off testing. For example, if a delivery docket is dated pre-year end but the sale is recorded post-year end it is possible that results are being manipulated.

4.16 Standard procedures

Standard procedures should be defined clearly for normal business operations and should be known to all staff. For example:

- Independent checks should be made on the existence of new customers.

- Credit should not be given to a new customer until his/her credit history has been investigated.

- All payments should be authorised by a senior member of staff.

- Wages/payslips must be collected in person.

Any deviations from these norms should become quite visible.

4.17 Holidays

As we have said, fraud is difficult to conceal. Enforcing holiday policy by insisting that all staff take their full holiday entitlement is therefore a crucial internal control. A two-week absence is frequently sufficient time for a fraud to come to light.

4.18 Recruitment policies

Personnel policies play a vital part in developing the corporate culture and deterring fraud. Something as obvious as checking the information and references provided by applicants may reduce the risk of appointing dishonest staff.

4.19 Computer security

This will be discussed in detail in chapter 18. However, many of the above controls (access controls, segregation of duties, authorisations and so on) will apply.

4.20 Manager and staff responsibilities

Managers and staff should be aware of their **responsibilities** to help in detecting fraud. Fraud detection is also helped by having **information readily available** and allowing **whistleblowing**.

If fraud is to be detected, it is important that everyone involved in detection should be aware of their responsibilities.

(a) **Operational managers** should be **alert for signs** of petty fraud, as well as checking the work staff have done and also being aware of what staff are doing.

(b) **Finance staff** should be alert for **unusual items** or **trends** in accounting data, also incomplete financial information.

(c) **Personnel staff** should be alert for **signs of discontent** or **low morale**, and also should (if possible) be aware of close personal relationships between staff who work together.

(d) **Internal audit staff** have responsibility for ensuring **systems** and controls are thoroughly **reviewed**. One off exercises such as surprise visits may be undertaken alongside annual audit work.

(e) **External audit staff** are required to **assess** the **risk** that fraud may have a **material impact** on a company's accounts when planning their audit work. They are required to **report** all instances of fraud found to management, unless they suspect management of being involved in the fraud. The external auditors should also report to management any material weaknesses in the accounting and internal control systems.

(f) **Non-executive directors** should **act** on **signs** of **dishonesty** by senior executive management. The **audit committee** should **review the organisation's performance** in fraud prevention and report any suspicious matters to the board.

4.20.1 Fraud officer

Many large organisations have appointed a fraud officer, who is responsible for **initiating** and **overseeing fraud investigations**, **implementing the fraud response plan**, and for **any follow-up actions**. The fraud officer should be able to **talk to staff confidentially** and be able to **provide advice** without consulting senior management.

4.21 Availability of information

It is of course important that information should be available to enable management to identify signs of actual fraud, or of an environment where fraud may occur.

(a) **Cost and management accounting systems** should **provide** promptly **information** with sufficient detail to enable management to identify parts of the business whose performance is out of line with expectations. Actual results should be compared with budgeted results and explanations sought for significant variances.

(b) **Personnel procedures** such as **staff meetings**, **appraisals** and **exit interviews** may indicate low morale or staff who are under undue pressure.

(c) **Lines of reporting** should be **clear**. Staff should know to whom they should report any suspicions of fraud.

4.22 Whistleblowing

The likelihood of fraud detection may have been increased by recent legislation in a number of countries that provides **employment protection rights** to 'whistleblowers', employees who reveal fraud or malpractice in a workplace. The legislation covers disclosure of certain 'relevant failures', including committal of a criminal offence, failure to comply with legislation, endangering health and safety or damaging the environment.

Some employers are introducing a formal concerns procedure, which sets out how potential whistleblowers should communicate their concerns.

4.23 Investigation of fraud

Organisations should establish a **fraud response plan**, setting out how the **method** and **extent** of the fraud and **possible suspects** should be investigated.

If the worst does happen there should be a **fraud response plan**, a strategy for **investigating** and **dealing with the consequences** of frauds that have occurred.

Certain actions might have to be taken as soon as the fraud comes to light. These may include **ensuring the security of the records** that will be used to investigate what has happened, and also the **securing of assets** that may be vulnerable to theft. Procedures may have to include suspending staff, changing passwords and so on.

Investigation procedures should be designed with the following aims in mind:

(a)   **Establishing** the **extent** of the loss, ascertain on whom it fell and assess how it may be recovered

(b)   **Establishing how** the fraud **occurred**

(c)   Considering **who else** may have been **implicated** in the fraud

(d)   Assessing whether the **fraud** was not detected because **existing controls** were not operating properly, or whether existing controls would have been unlikely to prevent or identify the fraud

Key decisions in fraud investigation will include who will be **carrying out the investigation** and also whether the investigation will be **undercover**. Guidance produced by the accountancy firm KPMG has highlighted the importance of obtaining quickly a picture of the **activities** of the suspected fraudster by reviewing his personal paperwork (diaries, files, expense claims etc.) and also contacting the people who worked with him.

Ultimately the detection and prevention of fraud requires not only a **clear strategy** but also a **willingness to enforce controls**.

5 Responsibility for detecting and preventing fraud

It is the responsibility of the directors to take such steps as are reasonably open to them to **prevent and detect** fraud.

5.1 The responsibility of directors

In a **limited company**, or plc, it is the responsibility of the directors to prevent and detect fraud. They should:

(a)   Ensure that the **activities** of the entity are conducted honestly and that its **assets** are safeguarded

(b)   Establish arrangements to **deter** fraudulent or other dishonest conduct and to **detect** any that occurs

(c)   Ensure that, to the best of their knowledge and belief, **financial information**, whether used internally or for financial reporting, is reliable.

5.2 The role of the auditor

The responsibility of the external auditor is only to express an opinion upon whether the financial statements give a true and fair view of the company's financial situation and results.

The auditor should design audit procedures so as to have a **reasonable expectation** of detecting misstatements arising from fraud or error. It should be emphasised that, in the case of a sophisticated fraud, which has been designed to escape detection by the auditors, a **reasonable expectation** is all that they can have.

If the auditors become aware, during the audit, that fraud or error may exist, they should document their findings and report them to management.

In the case of fraud, the auditors should then consider whether the matter should be reported to an appropriate authority in the public interest. If they decide that this is the case, they request that **the directors** make the report. If the directors do not do so, or if the fraud casts doubt upon the integrity of the directors, the auditors should make the report themselves.

If the auditor takes the view that the financial statements are affected by fraud or error, he should qualify his report accordingly.

It is the responsibility of the **directors** to take reasonable steps to detect and prevent fraud and error.

Chapter Roundup

- In a corporate context fraud can fall into one of two main categories: **removal of funds or assets** from a business or the **intentional misrepresentation of the financial position of a business**.

- **Common frauds** include payroll frauds, conspiracy with other parties and stealing assets. More subtle measures including teeming and lading and manipulation of bank reconciliations and cashbooks to conceal theft.

- There are three broad **pre-requisites** or 'pre-conditions' that must exist in order to make fraud a possibility: dishonesty, motivation and opportunity.

- Signs of high fraud risk include indications of **lack of integrity**, **excessive pressures**, **poor control systems**, **unusual transactions** and **lack of audit evidence**.

- A number of factors tend to crop up frequently as **indicators** of potential fraud situations; these can be categorised under business and personnel risks.

- In order to prevent fraud, managers must be aware of the **risks** and **signs** of fraud.

- Prevention policies include emphasis on **ethics** and **personnel and training procedures**. Controls within particular business areas such as **segregation of duties** and **documentation requirements** are also significant.

- Controls must be developed in a structured manner, taking account of the whole spectrum of risk and focusing on the key risks identified in each area of the business.

- Managers and staff should be aware of their **responsibilities** to help in detecting fraud. Fraud detection is also helped by having **information readily available** and allowing **whistleblowing**.

- Organisations should establish a **fraud response plan**, setting out how the **method** and **extent** of the fraud and **possible suspects** should be investigated.

- It is the responsibility of the directors to take such steps as are reasonably open to them to **prevent and detect** fraud.

Quick Quiz

1   What is fraud?

2   What are the two main types of fraud from a corporate perspective?

3   Give two consequences of each type.

4   Give three examples of each type.

5   Why do computers increase the risk of fraud?

6   What is the key to devising successful internal controls?

7   What is the first step in assessing the risks faced by an organisation?

8   List five common indicators of fraud

9   In what manner should controls be developed?

10   List five examples of internal controls (not computer-related).

11   What factors might indicate fraudulent collusion with external parties?

12   Give three examples of problems in obtaining audit evidence that might indicate fraud.

13   What are the main factors that might prevent controls operating properly?

14   What are the main personnel controls that can be used to limit the risk of fraud?

Answers to Quick Quiz

1   Fraud may generally be defined as 'deprivation by deceit'.

2   The two types of corporate fraud are removal of funds or assets from a business and intentional misrepresentation of the financial position of the business.

3   Consequences of the former include lower profits and a reduction in working capital. Consequences of the latter include incorrect decision-making by management or by investors and fluctuations in share price.

4   Examples of the former include theft of cash or other assets, payroll fraud and teeming and lading. Examples of the latter include overvaluation of inventory, failure to adhere to bad debt or depreciation policy and manipulation of year-end events.

5   Computers tend to increase exposure to fraud because they are frequently the vehicles through which fraudulent activities are carried out.

6   The key to devising successful internal controls is to identify the risks clearly first.

7   The first step is to consider separately the extent to which external and internal factors may present a risk.

8   Common indicators of fraud include trends that start to deviate from the industry norms, complex changes to business structures, secretive behaviour, evidence of an expensive lifestyle not commensurate with earnings and an autocratic management style.

9   Controls must be developed in a structured manner, taking account of the whole spectrum of risk and focusing on the key risks identified in each area of business.

10   Examples include physical controls, segregation of duties, authorisation policies, using words rather than numbers and enforcing holiday policy.

11   Unusual discounts or commissions, or excessive eagerness to handle certain clients by oneself

12
- Inadequate records
- Inadequate documentation of transactions
- Differences between accounting records and third party confirmations
- Lack of response by management to enquiries
- Unreasonable time pressures from management

13
- Lack of emphasis on compliance
- Lack of understanding of why controls are required
- Staff problems
- Changes in senior personnel
- Excessive emphasis on the authority of line management

14
- Rigorous recruitment procedures including interviews and references
- Appraisals
- Procedures to deal with grievances

Part E
Leading and managing individuals and teams

11

Leading and managing people

Topic list	Syllabus reference
1 The purpose and process of management	E1 (c)
2 Writers on management	E1 (a)(b)
3 Management and supervision	E1 (a)
4 What is leadership?	E1 (a)
5 Leadership skills and styles	E1 (d)(e)

Introduction

In this chapter, we attempt to get an overview of the manager's task (**Section 1**). What is management? How should people be managed? What do managers actually do to manage resources, activities and projects?

Section 2 traces the **development of management theory** from its focus on efficiency and control (classical and scientific management), through a recognition of the importance of people factors (human relations and neo-human relations), to a more complex understanding that a variety of factors influence the managerial role.

In **Section 3**, we note the difference between a manager and a **supervisor**: the interface between managerial and non-managerial levels of the organisation.

The theories discussed in this chapter are noted specifically in the syllabus study guide, and some (such as Fayol's five functions of management and Mintzberg's managerial roles) are particularly useful as a framework for understanding management in general. The major challenge of this topic is learning the detail of the various theories.

In today's organisations, managers are also called upon to be 'leaders'. We explore leadership as a separate function (and skill-set) of management, in **Sections 4 and 5**.

Study guide

		Intellectual level
E1	**Leadership, management and supervision**	
(a)	Define leadership, management and supervision and the distinction between these terms.	1
(b)	Explain the nature of management:	1
(i)	Scientific/classical theories of management Fayol, Taylor	
(ii)	The human relations school – Mayo	
(iii)	The functions of a manager – Mintzberg, Drucker	
(c)	Explain the areas of managerial authority and responsibility.	2
(d)	Explain the qualities, situational, functional and contingency approaches to leadership with reference to the theories of Adair, Fiedler, Bennis, Kotter and Heifetz.	2
(e)	Explain leadership styles and contexts: using the models of Ashridge, and Blake and Mouton.	2

Exam guide

You need a thorough grasp of the work of the writers summarised in Sections 2 – 4 of this chapter. Even simple models could come up in the exam. Areas such as the difference between management and leadership, or specific **leadership style models**, could also be examined. Perhaps the key challenge of this topic is to grasp the difference between **trait theories** (leaders simply have certain characteristics), **style theories** (leaders have different approaches, some of which are more effective than others) and **contingency approaches** (leaders can adopt specific behaviours to suit the specific situation).

1 The purpose and process of management

Management is responsible for using the organisation's resources to meet its goals. It is accountable to the owners: shareholders in a business, or government in the public sector.

1.1 Managing organisations

Key term

Management may be defined, most simply, as 'getting things done through other people' (Stewart).

An organisation has been defined as 'a social arrangement for the controlled performance of collective goals.' This definition suggests the need for management.

    (a)   **Objectives** have to be set for the organisation.

    (b)   Somebody has to **monitor progress and results** to ensure that objectives are met.

    (c)   Somebody has to communicate and sustain **corporate values**, ethics and operating principles.

    (d)   Somebody has to look after the interests of the **organisation's owners** and other **stakeholders**.

John, Paul, George and Ringo set up in business together as repairers of musical instruments. Each has contributed $5,000 as capital for the business. They are a bit uncertain as to how they should run the business, and, when they discuss this in the pub, they decide that attention needs to be paid to planning what they do, reviewing what they do and controlling what they do.

Suggest two ways in which John, Paul, George and Ringo can manage the business assuming no other personnel are recruited.

Answer

The purpose of this exercise has been to get you to separate the issues of management functions from organisational structure and hierarchy. John, Paul, George and Ringo have a number of choices. Here are some extreme examples.

(a) All the management activities are the job of one person.

In this case, Paul, for example, could plan direct and control the work and the other three would do the work.

(b) Division of management tasks between individuals (eg: repairing drums *and* ensuring plans are adhered to would be Ringo's job, and so on).

(c) Management by committee. All of them could sit down and work out the plan together etc. In a small business with equal partners this is likely to be the most effective.

Different organisations have different structures for carrying out management functions. For example, some organisations have separate strategic planning departments. Others do not.

In a **private sector business**, managers act, ultimately, on behalf of shareholders. In practical terms, shareholders rarely interfere, as long as the business delivers profits year on year.

In a **public sector organisation**, management acts on behalf of the government. Politicians in a democracy are in turn accountable to the electorate. More of the objectives of a public sector organisation might be set by the 'owners' – ie the government – rather than by the management. The government might also tell senior management to carry out certain policies or plans, thereby restricting management's discretion.

1.2 Authority, accountability and responsibility

FAST FORWARD

It is the role of the manager to **take responsibility** and **organise people** to get things done. This involves the use of **authority** and **power** and implies a hierarchy in which power is delegated downwards while **accountability** is rendered upwards.

Authority is the decision making discretion given to a manager, while responsibility is the obligation to perform duties. Sufficient authority should be granted to permit the efficient discharge of the appointed responsibility. Delegation is essential wherever there is a hierarchy of management. Power is the *ability* to do something whereas authority is the *right* to do something; expert power is possessed by those acknowledged as experts.

It is easy to confuse **authority**, **accountability** and **responsibility** since they are all to do with the **allocation of power within an organisation**.

1.3 Authority

Key term

> **Organisational authority:** the scope and amount of discretion given to a person to make decisions, by virtue of the position he or she holds in the organisation.

The authority and power structure of an organisation defines two things.

- The part which each member of the organisation is expected to perform
- The relationship between the members

A person's (or office's) authority can come from a variety of sources, including from above (supervisors) or below (if the position is elected). Managerial authority thus has three aspects.

- Making decisions within the scope of one's own managerial authority
- Assigning tasks to subordinates
- Expecting and requiring satisfactory performance of these tasks by subordinates

1.4 Responsibility and accountability

Responsibility is the liability of a person to discharge duties. Responsibility is the obligation to do something; in an organisation, it is the duty of an official to carry out assigned tasks.

With responsibility, we must associate **accountability**. Managers are accountable *to* their superiors *for* their actions and are obliged to report to their superiors how well they have exercised the authority delegated to them.

1.5 Delegation

Delegation of authority occurs in an organisation where a superior gives to a subordinate the discretion to make decisions within a certain sphere of influence. This can only occur if the superior initially possesses the authority to delegate; a subordinate cannot be given organisational authority to make decisions unless it would otherwise be the superior's right to make those decisions. Delegation of authority is the process by which a superior gives a subordinate the authority to carry out an aspect of the superior's job. Without delegation, a formal organisation could not exist.

When a superior delegates authority to a subordinate, the subordinate is accountable to the superior. However, the superior **remains fully accountable** to **his** superiors; responsibility and accountability cannot be abdicated by delegation.

As well as being essential for running an organisation, delegation brings a number of other benefits.

(a) **Training**: subordinates gain experience of problems and responsibility, which helps to prepare them for promotion and contributes to the avoidance of crises of management succession.

(b) **Motivation**: *Herzberg* found that responsibility was an important factor in job satisfaction and motivation.

(c) **Assessment**: subordinates' performance in relation to delegated responsibility can be used as a measure of their need for further training and experience and their readiness for promotion.

(d) **Decisions**: delegation brings decisions closer to the situations that require them, potentially improving them by having them made by those with most knowledge of the problems and factors involved.

1.6 Authority and power

If an organisation is to function as a co-operative system of individuals, some people must have authority or power over others. Authority and power flow **downwards** through the formal organisation.

(a) **Authority** is the right to do something; in an organisation it is the right of a manager to require a subordinate to do something in order to achieve the goals of the organisation.

(b) **Power** is distinct from authority, but is often associated with it. **Whereas authority is the right to do something, power is the ability to do it.**

Weber put the kind of authority we see in organisations into a wider context, proposing that there were three ways in which people could acquire legitimate power (or authority).

(a) **Charismatic authority** arises from the personality of the leader and his or her ability to inspire devotion through, for example, sanctity, heroism or example.

(b) **Traditional authority** rests on established belief in the importance of immemorial tradition and the status it confers.

(c) **Rational-legal** authority raises from the working of accepted normative rules, such as are found in organisations and democratic governments.

1.7 Power and influence

Influence is the process by which one person in an organisation, A, modifies the behaviour or attitudes of another person, B. An individual may have the ability to make others act in a certain way, without having the organisational authority to do so: informal leaders are frequently in this position.

The following types of power from different sources have been identified in organisations (by Handy and others).

(a) **Physical power** is the power of superior force. Physical power is absent from most organisations (except the prison service and the armed forces), but it is sometimes evident in poor industrial relations (eg shop floor intimidation). Power based on fear of punishment is known as **coercive power**.

(b) **Resource power** is the control over resources which are valued by the individual or group to be influenced. Senior managers may have the resource power to grant promotion or pay increases to subordinates, in which case it is **reward power**. Trade unions possess the resource power to take their members out on strike. The amount of power a person has then depends on how far he controls the resource, how much the resource is valued by others, and how scarce it is. *French and Raven* identified **informational** power, which is a type of resource power. It derives from the ability to control access to information. Within formal organisation structures, such control is an aspect of management and therefore informational power is an aspect of **legitimate** power (see below).

(c) **Position power** or **legitimate power** is the power which is associated with a particular job in an organisation. **It is more or less the same as authority.** Handy noted that position power has certain 'hidden' benefits.

(i) Access to information

(ii) Access to people: for example, entitlement to membership of committees and contact with other powerful individuals in the organisation

(iii) The right to organise conditions of working and methods of decision-making

(d) **Expert power** is the power which is based on **expertise**, although it only works if others **acknowledge** that expertise. Many staff jobs in an organisation (eg computer systems analysts and personnel department managers) rely on expert power to influence line management. If the expert is seen to be incompetent or if his area of expertise is not widely acknowledged (which is often the case with personnel department staff) he will have little or no expert power.

(e)   **Referent power** lies in the personal qualities of the individual. Personal power is capable of influencing the behaviour of others, and helps to explain the strength of informal organisations.

(f)   **Negative power** is the use of disruptive attitudes and behaviour to stop things from happening. It is associated with low morale, latent conflict or frustration at work. Negative power is destructive and potentially very damaging to organisational efficiency.

Influence, the act of directing or modifying the behaviour of others, may be achieved in a variety of ways.

(a)   The application of force, such as physical or economic power

(b)   The establishment of rules and procedures that are enforced through position and/or resource power

(c)   Bargaining and negotiation, which depend on the relative strengths of each party's position

(d)   Persuasion

Question

Power

What kind of power is used by a manager who promises a pay increase if productivity rises?

A   Position power
B   Resource power
C   Reward power
D   Referent power

Answer

C   Reward power: reward power is an aspect of resource power so, while Option B is not incorrect, it is not as good an answer as Option C.

1.8 Power centres

The **degree** of power people exercise, and the **types** of power they are able to exploit, differ depending in part on their position in the organisation hierarchy. The effects of personal power vary: the chief executive's use of personal power will be more far-reaching in the organisation as a whole than that of a junior manager.

1.8.1 Senior management

Senior management enjoy position power. In theory, senior managers take the major decisions and set constraints over the decisions taken by other people. In practice, however, the senior manager's power is never absolute. Senior managers depend on decisions and information supplied by subordinates, and it is quite possible that the information is shaped at a lower level. Senior managers are likely to play a number of managerial roles.

Senior managers have coercive and reward powers, and most importantly take decisions relating to personnel.

Finally, it helps managers to be on a 'network'. This means that if a manager's allies are placed in certain positions, their loyalty might be useful.

1.8.2 Middle managers

Middle managers have a number of power sources. They have some reward power over their own subordinates. They may have expert power and negative power to delay or subvert decisions taken by senior managers. They need legitimate power, hence the need for formal job descriptions, authorisation limits and so on.

People at lower levels of the organisation derive power from several sources.

- Expert power (about organisational activities, or specific processes)
- Resource power over information
- Access to other important people
- Negative power

1.8.3 Interest groups

There are also formal interest groups, that is, groups which are perceived to represent the interests of their members. Such groups tend to wield greater power in conflict situations than their members as individuals.

(a) **Trade unions** are organisations whose purpose it is to promote their members' interests. The power of trade unions has been much reduced.

(b) **Occupational and professional groups** represent the interests of their members and of their clients. Professional bodies and other occupational associations are concerned to preserve standards of skill and knowledge, to ensure appropriate financial rewards (theoretically commensurate with their skills and knowledge) and to create a measure of independence, for example, in the right to control their own affairs.

1.8.4 Departmental power

The power exercised by individual departments will vary.

Some departments in the technostructure exercise power by the use of **functional authority,** for instance, by specifying procedures. Other departments are important as they deal with **key strategic contingencies**. These are 'events and activities both inside and outside an organisation that are essential for attaining organisational goals'. They can arise in several ways.

(a) **Dependency**. A department which depends on anther department may not be in a position to exercise power over that department, without support at a higher level. A department may use its **resource power** to make other departments dependent on it.

(b) **Financial resources.** This is another sort of dependency, but a department with a larger budget can spend it with more discretion.

(c) **Centrality.** How critical is the department in the **primary** activities of the organisation?

(d) **Non-substitutability**. Some departments cannot easily be broken up and their activities carried out elsewhere. This used to be the case with information systems departments, before the advent of cheap personal computers and software.

(e) **Uncertainty.** A department which reduces the levels of uncertainty faced by other departments (in dealing with key environmental variables) has a sort of expert power.

1.9 The manager's role in organising work

FAST FORWARD

Managers have **key roles** in work planning, resource allocation and project management.

1.9.1 Work planning

Work planning is the establishment of work methods and practices to ensure that predetermined objectives are efficiently met at all levels.

- (a)   **Task sequencing** or **prioritisation** ie considering tasks in order of importance for achieving objectives and meeting deadlines.

- (b)   **Scheduling** or **timetabling tasks**, and allocating them to different individuals within appropriate time scales.

- (c)   Establishing **checks and controls** to ensure that:

    - (i)   Priority deadlines are being met and work is not 'falling behind'
    - (ii)   Routine tasks are achieving their objectives

- (d)   **Contingency plans**: arrangements for what should be done if changes or problems occur, eg computer system failure or industrial action.

- (e)   **Co-ordinating** the efforts of individuals: integrating plans and schedules so that data and work flows smoothly from one stage of an operation to another.

Some jobs (eg assembly line work) are entirely routine, and can be performed one step at a time, but for most people, some kind of on-going planning and adjustment will be required.

1.9.2 Assessing where resources are most usefully allocated

In broad terms, managers and supervisors have access to the following resources, which can be allocated or deployed to further the unit's objectives.

- (a)   **Human resources:** staff time and skills

- (b)   **Material resources**, including raw materials, equipment, machine time, office space and so on

- (c)   **Financial resources**, within budget guidelines

- (d)   **Information**

The first three of these are sometimes called 'the 4Ms': Manpower, Machine capacity, Materials and Money.

A manager or supervisor may be responsible for allocating resources between:

- (a)   Different ways to achieve the same objective (eg to increase total profits, sell more – or cut costs)

- (b)   Competing areas, where total resources are limited

A piece of work will be **high priority** in the following cases.

- If it has to be completed by a certain time (ie a deadline)
- If other tasks depend on it
- If other people depend on it
- If it has important potential consequence or impact

Routine priorities or regular peak times (eg tax returns) can be planned ahead of time, and other tasks planned around them.

Non-routine priorities occur when unexpected demands are made. Thus planning of work should cover routine scheduled peaks and contingency plans for unscheduled peaks and emergencies.

1.9.3 Projects

Key term

A **project** is 'an undertaking that has a beginning and an end and is carried out to meet established goals within cost, schedule and quality objectives' (Haynes, *Project Management*).

The main difference between project planning and other types of planning is that a project is not generally a repetitive activity. Projects generally:

- Have specific start and end points
- Have well-defined objectives, cost and time schedules
- Cut across organisational and functional boundaries

The relocation of offices, the introduction of a new information system or the launch of a new product may be undertaken as a project. Other examples include building/capital projects, such as factory construction or bridge building.

1.9.4 Project management

The job of **project management** is to foresee as many contingencies as possible and to plan, organise, co-ordinate and control activities.

Management task	Comment
Outline project planning	• Developing project targets such as overall costs or timescale (eg project should take 20 weeks) • Dividing the project into activities (eg analysis, programming, testing), and placing these activities into the right sequence, often a complicated task if overlapping • Developing the procedures and structures, managing the project (eg plan weekly team meetings, performance reviews etc)
Detailed planning	Identifying the tasks and resource requirements; network analysis for scheduling
Teambuilding	The project manager has to meld the various people into an effective team
Communication	The project manager must let key project stakeholders know what is going on, and ensure that members of the project team are properly briefed
Co-ordinating project activities	Between the project team and clients/users, and other external parties (eg suppliers of hardware and software)
Monitoring and control	The project manager should determine causes of any departure from the plan, and take corrective measures
Problem-resolution	Unforeseen problems may arise, and it falls upon the project manager to sort them out, or to delegate the responsibility for so doing to a subordinate

2 Writers on management

The classical writers on management and organisation were largely concerned with **efficiency.**

2.1 Henri Fayol: five functions of management

Fayol was an administrator and proposed universal principles of organisation.

Fayol (1841-1925) was a French industrialist who put forward and popularised the concept of the '**universality of management principles**': in other words, the idea that all organisations could be structured and managed according to certain rational principles. Fayol himself recognised that applying such principles in practice was not simple: 'Seldom do we have to apply the same principles twice in identical conditions; allowance must be made for different and changing circumstances.'

Fayol classified five **functions of management** which apply to any organisation.

Function	Comment
Planning	This involves determining **objectives**, and strategies, policies, programmes and procedures for achieving those objectives, for the organisation and its sub-units.
Organising	Establishing a **structure of tasks** which need to be performed to achieve the goals of the organisation; grouping these tasks into jobs for individuals or teams; allocating jobs to sections and departments; **delegating** authority to carry out the jobs; and providing **systems of information** and communication, for the co-ordination of activities.
Commanding	Giving **instructions** to subordinates to carry out tasks, for which the manager has authority (to make decisions) and responsibility (for performance).
Co-ordinating	**Harmonising** the goals and activities of individuals and groups within the organisation. Management must reconcile differences in approach, effort, interest and timing, in favour of overall (or 'super-ordinate') shared goals.
Controlling	**Measuring** and **correcting** the activities of individuals and groups, to ensure that their performance is in accordance with plans. Deviations from plans are identified and corrected.

You may be struck by two key 'omissions' from Fayol's classification, from a more modern viewpoint.

(a) '**Motivating**' is not mentioned. It is assumed that subordinates will carry out tasks when 'commanded' or instructed to do so, regardless of whether or how far they may 'want' to.

(b) '**Communicating**' is not mentioned, although it is implied by the process of commanding (giving instructions), co-ordinating (sharing information) and controlling (giving feedback).

This reflects the classical view of the function of management as a matter of controlling resources and processes rather than people: an awareness of management as first of all an *interpersonal* process, involving communication and influence, only developed later, as we will see.

Exam focus point

Although Fayol's 'managerial functions' may seem like a minor topic – and rather old-fashioned – it is a foundational model. The five functions are a helpful framework or starting point for discussing the nature of management and supervision – even if you prefer more modern alternatives such as Mintzberg's more fluid managerial roles or more interpersonally-based interpretations (including 'leadership', discussed later in this chapter).

2.2 F W Taylor: scientific management

Taylor was an engineer and sought the most efficient methods.

Frederick W Taylor (1856-1915) pioneered the **scientific management** movement in the USA. He was among the first to argue that management should be based on 'well-recognised, clearly defined and fixed principles, instead of depending on more or less hazy ideas.' Taylor was a very skilled engineer and he took an engineering efficiency approach to management.

Principles of scientific management include the following.

(a) The development of a true **science of work**. 'All knowledge which had hitherto been kept in the heads of workmen should be gathered and recorded by management. Every single subject, large and small, becomes the question for scientific investigation, for reduction to law.'

(b) The **scientific selection** and **progressive development** of workers: workers should be carefully trained and given jobs to which they are best suited.

(c) The application of techniques to **plan**, **measure and control work** for maximum productivity.

(d) The constant and intimate **co-operation between management and workers**: 'the relations between employers and men form without question the most important part of this art'.

In practice, scientific management techniques included the following key elements.

(a) **Work study techniques** were used to analyse tasks and establish the most efficient methods to use. No variation was permitted in the way work was done, since the aim was to use the 'one best way'.

(b) **Planning and doing were separated**. It was assumed that the persons who were intellectually equipped to do a particular type of work were probably unlikely to be able to plan it to the best advantage: this was the manager's job.

(c) Jobs were **micro-designed**: divided into single, simple task components which formed a whole specialised 'job' for an individual, rather than permitting an individual to perform whole or part-task processes. (Task 'meaning' and 'significance', now considered essential to job satisfaction, had not yet emerged as important values.)

(d) Workers were **paid incentives** on the basis of acceptance of the new methods and output norms; the new methods greatly increased productivity and profits. Pay was assumed to be the only important motivating force.

Scientific management as practised by Taylor and contemporaries such as Gilbreth and Gantt was very much about **manual work**. However, elements of scientific management are still practised today, whenever there is a concern for productivity and efficiency.

Case Study

Persistent Taylorism?

It has been argued that elements of Taylorism – maximising managerial control through the micro-design of jobs, automation and close supervision – can be seen in the management of junior staff in businesses such as:

- Large fast-food franchises (such as McDonalds).

- Call-centres, where calls are scripted, timed and monitored – and (in some reported cases) staff must ask permission to leave the 'floor' to go to the toilet.

Exam focus point

The application of scientific management principles to modern working practices forms the subject of a question on the Pilot Paper.

2.3 Elton Mayo: human relations

FAST FORWARD

Mayo and his colleagues investigated individual and group behaviour at work, as a factor in productivity.

In the 1920s, research began to show that managers needed to consider the complexity of **human behaviour**. It was recognised that an exclusive focus on technical competence (under scientific management) had resulted in social incompetence: managers were not taught how to manage people. At the same time, it emerged that being a 'small cog in the machine' was experienced as alienating and demoralising by workers – whatever the financial incentives offered. A more complex picture of human motivation began to emerge.

Elton Mayo was Professor of Industrial Research at the Harvard Business School. He was involved in a series of large scale studies at the Western Electric Company's Hawthorne works in Chicago between 1924 and 1932. These studies were originally firmly set in the context of scientific management in that they began with an experiment into the effect of lighting on work output. However, it rapidly became apparent that **worker attitudes** and **group relationships** were of greater importance in determining the levels of production achieved than the lighting itself.

An important element in the Hawthorne studies was the investigation of the dynamics of work groups. The group was very effective in enforcing its behavioural norms in such matters as 'freezing out' unpopular supervisors and restricting output. It was concluded that people are motivated at work by a variety of psychological needs, including social or 'belonging' needs. This became the basis of the **human relations school** of management theory.

2.3.1 Neo-human relations

Later writers (such as Maslow and Herzberg) focused on a wider variety of workers' 'higher-order' needs, including the need for challenge, responsibility and personal development in the job. This became known as the **neo-human relations school**, which proposed important theories of motivation and job satisfaction.

The human relations approaches contributed an important awareness of the influence of the human factor at work (and particularly in the work group) on organisational performance. Most of its theorists attempted to offer guidelines to enable practising managers to satisfy and motivate employees and so (theoretically) to obtain the benefits of improved productivity.

However, the approach tends to emphasise the importance of work to the workers without really addressing the economic issues: there is still no proven link between job satisfaction and motivation, or either of these and productivity or the achievement of organisational goals, as we will see in Chapter 13.

2.4 Modern writers on management

Subsequent writers have taken a more **flexible** view of what managers do.

In the second half of the twentieth century, writing on management became more diverse.

(a) The early emphasis on the organisation of work has been continued in the field of **supervisory studies** and the development of specific management techniques such as **project management.** The search for efficiency continues in the field of **work study** and **industrial engineering.**

(b) Human relations theory has been enhanced by developments in the study of motivation, group and individual behaviour, leadership and other aspects of **industrial psychology**.

(c) There has been much new writing on the nature of the **manager's task**: what it is to be a manager and what managers do, in increasingly complex and chaotic business environments.

2.5 Peter Drucker: the management process

Drucker emphasised the economic objective of managers in businesses.

Peter Drucker worked in the 1940s and 1950s as a business adviser to a number of US corporations. He was also a prolific writer on management.

Drucker argued that the manager of a business has one basic function – **economic performance**. In this respect, the business manager is different from the manager of any other type of organisation. Management can only justify its existence and its authority by the economic results it produces, even though as a consequence of its actions, significant non-economic results occur as well.

2.5.1 Management tasks

Drucker described the jobs of management within this basic function of economic performance as follows.

(a) **Managing a business**. The purposes of the business are to create a customer and innovation.

(b) **Managing managers**. The requirements here are:
- Management by objectives (or performance management)
- Proper structure of managers' jobs
- Creating the right spirit (culture) in the organisation
- Making a provision for the managers of tomorrow (managerial succession)
- Arriving at sound principles of organisation structure

(c) **Managing workers and work**

A manager's performance in all areas of management, including management of the business, can be enhanced by a study of the principles of management, the acquisition of 'organised knowledge' (eg management techniques) and systematic self-assessment.

2.5.2 Management processes

Later, Drucker grouped the work of the manager into five categories.

(a) **Setting objectives for the organisation**. Managers decide what the objectives of the organisation should be and quantify the targets of achievement for each objective. They must then communicate these targets to other people in the organisation.

(b) **Organising the work**. The work to be done in the organisation must be divided into manageable activities and manageable jobs. The jobs must be integrated into a formal organisation structure, and people must be selected to do the jobs.

(c) **Motivating** employees and communicating information to them to enable them to do their work.

(d) **The job of measurement**. Management must:

  (i) Establish **objectives** or yardsticks of performance for all personnel

  (ii) Analyse **actual performance**, appraise it against the objectives or yardsticks which have been set, and analyse the comparison

  (iii) **Communicate** the findings and explain their significance both to subordinate employees and also to superiors

(e) **Developing people.** The manager 'brings out what is in them or he stifles them. He strengthens their integrity or he corrupts them'.

Every manager performs all five functions listed above, no matter how good or bad a manager (s)he is. However, a bad manager performs these functions badly, whereas a good manager performs them well. Unlike Fayol, Drucker emphasised the importance of **communication** in the functions of management.

2.6 Mintzberg: the manager's role

FAST FORWARD

> **Mintzberg** described managerial roles, arguing that management is a disjointed, non-systematic activity.

Henry Mintzberg (1989) did a study of a relatively small sample of US corporations to see how senior managers actually spend their time. He suggests that in their daily working lives, managers fulfil three **types** of managerial role.

Role category	Role	Comment
Interpersonal Based on manager's formal authority or position	**Figurehead** (or ceremonial)	A large part of a Chief Executive's time is spent representing the company at dinners, conferences and so on.
	Leader	Hiring, firing and training staff, motivating employees, and reconciling individual goals with the objectives of the organisation.
	Liaison	Making contacts outside the vertical chain of command. Some managers spend up to half their meeting time with their peers rather than with their subordinates.

Role category	Role	Comment
Informational Based on managers' access to: • Upward and downward channels • Many external contacts	**Monitor**	The manager monitors the environment, and receives information from subordinates, superiors and peers in other departments. Much of this information is of an informal nature, derived from the manager's network of contacts.
	Spokesperson	The manager provides information on behalf of the unit and/or organisation to interested parties.
	Disseminator	The manager disseminates relevant information to subordinates.
Decisional Based on the manager's formal authority and access to information, which allow him to take decisions relating to the work of the department as a whole.	**Entrepreneur**	A manager initiates projects to improve the department or to help it react to a changed environment.
	Disturbance handler	A manager has to respond to unexpected pressures, taking decisions when there is deviation from plan.
	Resource allocator	A manager takes decisions relating to the mobilisation and distribution of limited resources to achieve objectives.
	Negotiator	Both inside and outside the organisation, negotiation takes up a great deal of management time.

Mintzberg's research challenged the classical view of the manager as separate to, or above, the routine demands of day-to-day work.

(a) Managers are not always able to be reflective, systematic planners.

(b) Managerial work is disjointed and discontinuous.

(c) Managers do have routine duties to perform, especially of a ceremonial nature (receiving important guests) or related to authority (signing cheques as a signatory) – contrary to the myth that all routine work is done by juniors.

(d) Managers prefer verbal and informal information to the formal output of management information systems. Verbal information is 'hotter' and probably easier to grasp.

(e) Management cannot be reduced to a science or a profession. According to Mintzberg, managerial processes cannot be analysed scientifically or codified into an examinable body of theory.

Mintzberg states that general management is, in practice, a matter of **judgement and intuition**, gained from **experience** in **particular situations** rather than from abstract principles. 'Fragmentation and verbal communication' characterise the manager's work.

Question

Managerial roles

Who suggested that a primary managerial role is 'developing people'?

A   Handy
B   Taylor
C   Herzberg
D   Drucker

Answer

The correct answer is D. Drucker.

3 Management and supervision

There are different levels of management in most organisations. A finance department in an organisation might be headed by the finance director (A) supported by a chief financial accountant (B) and chief management accountant (C). Lower down in the hierarchy assistant accountants might report to (B) and (C).

FAST FORWARD

Supervision is the interface between the operational core (non-managerial workers) and management.

3.1 The supervisor's role

The supervisor is the lowest level of management, at the **interface** between managerial and non-managerial staff.

The key features of supervision are as follows.

(a)   A supervisor is usually a **front-line manager**, dealing with the levels of the organisation where the bread-and-butter work is done. (S)he will deal with matters such as staffing and health and safety at the day-to-day operational level, where a manager might deal with them at a policy-making level.

(b)   A supervisor does not spend all his or her time on the managerial aspects of his job. Much of the time will be spent doing **technical/operational work**.

(c)   A supervisor is a **gatekeeper** or filter for communication between managerial and non-managerial staff, both **upward** (conveying reports and suggestions) and **downward** (conveying policies, instructions and feedback).

(d)   The supervisor monitors and controls work by means of **day-to-day, frequent and detailed information:** higher levels of management plan and control using longer-term, less frequent and less detailed information, which must be 'edited' or selected and reported by the supervisor.

Above the supervisor there may be several levels of management. Authority, responsibility and the timescale for decision-making all increase as the scalar chain is ascended. However, all managerial work may be considered to have some elements of similarity: it may be argued that supervisors carry out Fayol's five functions of management at a lower level.

Question   **Supervising work**

Bert Close has decided to delegate the task of identifying the reasons for machine 'down' time (when machines are not working) over the past three months to Brenda Cartwright. This will involve her in talking to operators, foremen and supervisors and also liaising with other departments to establish the effects of this down time. What will Bert need to do to delegate this task effectively? List at least four items he will need to cover with Brenda.

LEARNING MEDIA

Answer

- Identify task objectives
- Explain limits within which Brenda will work
- Deadlines
- Formats of reporting results
- Progress monitoring

4 What is leadership?

Key term

Leadership has been defined as:

'The activity of influencing people to strive willingly for group objectives' (*Terry*)

'Interpersonal influence exercised in a situation and directed, through the communication process, toward the attainment of a specialised goal or goals' (*Tannenbaum et al*)

4.1 Management and leadership

FAST FORWARD

There are many different definitions of **leadership**. Key themes (which are also used to distinguish leadership from management) include: interpersonal influence; securing willing commitment to shared goals; creating direction and energy; and an orientation to change.

The terms 'management' and 'leadership' are often used interchangeably. In some cases, management skills and theories have simply been relabelled to reflect the more fashionable term. However, there have been many attempts to distinguish meaningfully between them. *Kotter* (2001) argues that leadership and management involve two distinct sets of action. Management is about coping with **complexity**: its functions are to do with logic, structure, analysis and control, and are aimed at producing order, consistency and predictability. Leadership, by contrast, is about coping with **change**: its activities include creating a sense of direction, communicating strategy, and energising, inspiring and motivating others to translate the vision into action.

Management can be exercised over resources, activities, projects and other essential non-personal things. Leadership can only be exercised over **people**.

4.2 Key leadership skills

FAST FORWARD

Key leadership skills may be identified in a range of interpersonal and business areas.

There is a range of business and managerial skills important to a good leader, including:

(a) **Entrepreneurship**: the ability to spot business opportunities and mobilise resources to capitalise on them

(b) **Interpersonal skills**, such as networking, rapport-building, influencing, negotiating, conflict resolution, listening, counselling, coaching and communicating assertively

(c) **Decision-making and problem-solving** skills, including seeing the big picture

(d) **Time-management and personal organisation**

(e) **Self-development** skills: the ability to learn continuously from experience, to grow in self-awareness and to exploit learning opportunities.

Exam focus point

Remember, when thinking about leadership skills that *skills* are learned abilities to do things effectively: they are *not* the same as personality traits or characteristics, such as 'integrity' or 'vision'.

4.3 Theories of leadership

FAST FORWARD

There are three basic **schools of leadership theory**: trait ('qualities') theories, style theories and contingency (including situational and functional) theories.

There are three basic 'schools' of leadership theory.

School	Comment
Trait theories	Based on analysing the personality characteristics or preferences of successful leaders.
Style theories	Based on the view that leadership is an interpersonal process whereby different leader behaviours influence people in different ways. More or less effective patterns of behaviour (or 'styles') can therefore be adopted.
Contingency theories	Based on the belief that there is no 'one best way' of leading, but that effective leaders adapt their behaviour to the specific and changing variables in the leadership context: the nature of the task, the personalities of team members, the organisation culture and so on.

We will look at each of these in turn.

Exam focus point

The study guide refers to 'qualities', 'situational', 'functional' and 'contingency' approaches to leadership.

5 Leadership skills and styles

5.1 Trait or 'qualities' theories

FAST FORWARD

Early theories suggested that there are certain personal **qualities** common to 'great men' or successful leaders. In other words, **'leaders are born, not made'**.

Various studies have attempted to determine exactly *which* qualities are essential in a leader. One American study cites the following.

- Judgement
- Drive
- Fairness
- Energy

- Initiative
- Human relations skill
- Ambition
- Emotional stability

- Integrity
- Decisiveness
- Dedication
- Co-operation

- Foresight
- Dependability
- Objectivity

Trait theory has been more or less discredited.

(a) The premise that certain traits (or qualities) are absolutely necessary for effective leadership has never been substantiated.

(b) The lists of traits proposed for leaders have been vast, varied and contradictory.

(c) Trait theories ignore the complexities of the leadership situation, and not everybody with leadership 'traits' turns out to be a good leader.

5.2 Style theories of leadership

FAST FORWARD

Leadership styles are clusters of leadership behaviour that are used in different ways in different situations. While there are many different classifications of style, they mainly relate to the extent to which the leader is focused primarily on task/performance (directive behaviour) or relationships/people (supportive behaviour). Key style models include:

- The **Ashridge Model**: tells, sells, consults, joins
- **Blake and Mouton**'s **Managerial Grid**: concern for task, concern for people

There are various classifications of leadership style. Although the labels and definitions of styles vary, style models are often talking (broadly) about the same thing: a continuum of behaviours from:

(a) Wholly task-focused, directive leadership behaviours (representing high leader control) at one extreme, and

(b) Wholly people-focused, supportive/relational leadership behaviours (representing high subordinate discretion) at the other.

Exam focus point

Leadership can be linked with theories of motivation and management style.

5.2.1 The Ashridge Management College model

The Research Unit at Ashridge Management College distinguished four different management styles. (These are outlined, with their strengths and weaknesses, in the following table.) The researchers labelled their styles:

- Tells
- Sells
- Consults
- Joins

The Ashridge studies found that:

(a) In an ideal world, subordinates preferred the 'consults' style of leadership.

(b) People led by a 'consults' manager had the most favourable attitude to their work.

(c) Most subordinates feel they are being led by a 'tells' or 'sells' manager.

(d) In practice, **consistency** was far more important to subordinates than any particular style. The least favourable attitudes were found amongst subordinates who were unable to perceive any consistent style of leadership in their superiors.

Style	Characteristics	Strengths	Weaknesses
Tells (autocratic)	The leader makes all the decisions, and issues instructions which must be obeyed without question.	(1) Quick decisions can be made when speed is required. (2) It is the most efficient type of leadership for highly–programmed routine work.	(1) It does not encourage subordinates to give their opinions when these might be useful. (2) Communication between leader and subordinates will be one-way and the leader will not know until afterwards whether the orders have been properly understood. (3) It does not encourage initiative and commitment from subordinates.
Sells (persuasive)	The leader still makes all the decisions, but believes that subordinates have to be motivated to accept them and carry them out properly.	(1) Employees are made aware of the reasons for decisions. (2) Selling decisions to staff might make them more committed. (3) Staff will have a better idea of what to do when unforeseen events arise in their work because the leader will have explained his intentions.	(1) Communications are still largely one-way. Subordinates might not accept the decisions. (2) It does not encourage initiative and commitment from subordinates.
Consults	The leader confers with subordinates and takes their views into account, but retains the final say.	(1) Employees are involved in decisions before they are made. This encourages motivation through greater interest and involvement. (2) An agreed consensus of opinion can be reached and, for some decisions, this can be an advantage (eg increasing ownership). (3) Employees can contribute their knowledge and experience to help solve more complex problems.	(1) It might take much longer to reach decisions. (2) Subordinates might be too inexperienced to formulate mature opinions and give practical advice. (3) Consultation can too easily turn into a façade, concealing a 'sells' style.
Joins (democratic)	Leader and followers make the decision on the basis of consensus.	(1) It can provide high motivation and commitment from employees. (2) It shares the other advantages of the consultative style (especially where subordinates have expert power).	(1) The authority of the leader might be undermined. (2) Decision making might become a very long process, and clear decisions might become difficult to reach. (3) Subordinates might lack experience.

Question

Suggest an appropriate style of leadership for each of the following situations. Think about your reasons for choosing each style in terms of the results you are trying to achieve, the need to secure commitment from others, and potential difficulties with both.

(a) Due to outside factors, the personnel budget has been reduced for your department and 25% of your staff must be made redundant. Records of each employee's performance are available.

(b) There is a recurring administrative problem which is minor, but irritating to every one in your department. Several solutions have been tried in the past, but without success. You think you have a remedy which will work, but unknown problems may arise, depending on the decisions made.

Answer

(a) You may have to 'tell' here: nobody is going to like the idea and, since each person will have his or her own interests at heart, you are unlikely to reach consensus. You could attempt to 'sell', if you can see a positive side to the change in particular cases: opportunities for retraining, say.

(b) You could 'consult' here: explain your remedy to staff and see whether they can suggest potential problems. They may be in a position to offer solutions – and since the problem effects them too, they should be committed to solving it.

5.2.2 Blake and Mouton's Managerial Grid

Robert Blake and Jane Mouton carried out research (The Ohio State Leadership Studies) into managerial behaviour and observed two basic dimensions of leadership: **concern for production** (or task performance) and **concern for people.**

Along each of these two dimensions, managers could be located at any point on a continuum from very low to very high concern. Blake and Mouton observed that the two concerns did not seem to correlate, positively or negatively: a high concern in one dimension, for example, did not seem to imply a high or low concern in the other dimension. Individual managers could therefore reflect various permutations of task/people concern.

Blake and Mouton modelled these permutations as a grid. One axis represented concern for people, and the other concern for production. Blake and Mouton allotted nine points to each axis, from 1 (low) to 9 (high).

A questionnaire was designed to enable users to analyse and plot the positions of individual respondents on the grid. This was to be used as a means of analysing individuals' **managerial styles** and areas of weakness or 'unbalance', for the purposes of management development.

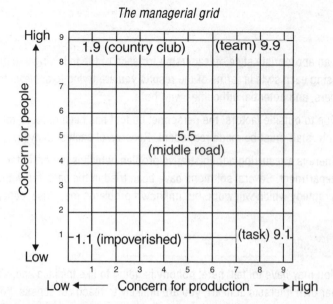

The managerial grid

The extreme cases shown on the grid are:

(a)   1.1 **impoverished:** the manager is lazy, showing little interest in either staff or work.

(b)   1.9 **country club:** the manager is attentive to staff needs and has developed satisfying relationships. However, there is little attention paid to achieving results.

(c)   9.1 **task management:** almost total concentration on achieving results. People's needs are virtually ignored.

(d)   5.5 **middle of the road** or the **dampened pendulum:** adequate performance through balancing (or switching between) the necessity to get out work with team morale.

(e)   9.9 **team:** high work accomplishment through 'leading' committed people who identify themselves with the organisational aims.

The managerial grid was intended as an appraisal and management development tool. It recognises that a balance is required between concern for task and concern for people, and that a high degree of both is possible (and highly effective) at the same time.

5.2.3 Evaluating the managerial grid

The grid thus offers a number of useful insights for the identification of management **training and development** needs. It shows in an easily assimilated form where the behaviour and assumptions of a manager may exhibit a lack of balance between the dimensions and/or a low degree of concern in either dimension or both. It may also be used in team member selection, so that a 1.9 team leader is balance by a 9.1 co-leader, for example.

However, the grid is a simplified model, and as such has practical limitations.

(a)   It assumes that 9.9 is the desirable model for effective leadership. In some managerial contexts, this may not be so. Concern for people, for example, would not be necessary in a context of comprehensive automation: compliance is all that would be required.

(b)   It is open to oversimplification. Scores can appear polarised, with judgements attached about individual managers' suitability or performance. The Grid is intended as a simplified 'snapshot' of a manager's preferred style, not a comprehensive description of his or her performance.

(c)   Organisational context and culture, technology and other 'givens' (*Handy*) influence the manager's style of leadership, not just the two dimensions described by the Grid.

(d)   Any managerial theory is only useful in so far as it is useable in practice by managers: if the grid is used only to inform managers that they 'must acquire greater concern for people', it may result in stress, uncertainty and inconsistent behaviour.

The features of Blake and Mouton's grid are examined on the Pilot Paper.

Question   **The managerial grid**

Here are some statements about a manager's approach to meetings. Which position on Blake's Grid do you think each might represent?

(a)   I attend because it is expected. I either go along with the majority position or avoid expressing my views.

(b)   I try to come up with good ideas and push for a decision as soon as I can get a majority behind me. I don't mind stepping on people if it helps a sound decision.

(c)   I like to be able to support what my boss wants and to recognise the merits of individual effort. When conflict rises, I do a good job of restoring harmony.

Answer

(a)   1.1: low task, low people
(b)   9.1: High task, low people
(c)   1.9: high people, low task

5.2.4 Limitations of style approaches

Perhaps the most important criticism of the style approach is that it does not consider all the variables that contribute to the practice of effective leadership.

(a)   The manager's personality (or 'acting' ability) may simply not be **flexible** enough to utilise different styles effectively.

(b)   The demands of the task, technology, organisation culture and other managers **constrain** the leader in the range of styles effectively open to him. (If his own boss practices an authoritarian style, and the team are incompetent and require close supervision, no amount of theorising on the desirability of participative management will make it possible...)

(c)   **Consistency** is important to subordinates. If a manager adapts his style to changing situations, they may simply perceive him to be fickle, or may suffer insecurity and stress.

Huczynski and Buchanan note that 'There is therefore no simple recipe which the individual manager can use to decide which style to adopt to be most effective.'

It is the consideration of this wide set of variables that has led to the development of the contingency approach to leadership.

5.3 Contingency approaches to leadership

In essence, contingency theory sees effective leadership as being dependent on a number of variable or contingent factors. There is no one right way to lead that will fit all situations. The ability of a manager to be a leader, and to influence his sub ordinate work group, depends on the particular situation and will vary from case to case. Gillen *(Leadership Skills)* suggests that: 'Using only one leadership style is a bit like a stopped clock: it will be right twice a day but, the rest of the time, it will be inaccurate to varying degrees. Leaders need to interact with their team in different ways in different situations. This is what we mean by "leadership style".'

FAST FORWARD

> Leaders need to adapt their style to the needs of the team and situation. This is the basis of **contingency approaches** such as:
>
> - **Fiedler**'s 'psychologically close' and 'psychologically distant' styles
> - **John Adair**'s 'action-centred' leadership model – based upon 'situations' or 'functions'

5.3.1 F E Fiedler

Perhaps the leading advocate of contingency theory is Fiedler. He carried out extensive research on the nature of leadership and found that people become leaders partly because of their own attributes and partly because of their situation. He studied the relationship between style of leadership and the effectiveness of the work group and identified two types of leader.

(a) **Psychologically distant managers** (PDMs) maintain distance from their subordinates.

  (i) They formalise the roles and relationships between themselves and their superiors and subordinates.

  (ii) They choose to be withdrawn and reserved in their inter-personal relationships within the organisation (despite having good inter-personal skills).

  (iii) They prefer formal consultation methods rather than seeking the opinions of their staff informally.

  PDMs judge subordinates on the basis of performance, and are primarily task-oriented: Fiedler found that leaders of the most effective work groups tend to be PDMs.

  Fiedler also argued that the leadership style adopted is relatively stable, and a feature of a leader's personality that could therefore be predicted.

(b) **Psychologically close managers** (PCMs) are closer to their subordinates.

  (i) They do not seek to formalise roles and relationships with superiors and subordinates.

  (ii) They are more concerned to maintain good human relationships at work than to ensure that tasks are carried out efficiently.

  (iii) They prefer informal contacts to regular formal staff meetings

Fiedler suggested that the effectiveness of a work group depended on the **situation**, made up of three key variables.

- The relationship **between the leader and the group** (trust, respect and so on)
- The extent to which the **task** is defined and structured
- The **power** of the leader in relation to the group (authority, and power to reward and punish)

A situation is **favourable** to the leader when:

- The leader is liked and trusted by the group
- The tasks of the group are clearly defined and unambiguous
- The position power of the leader (ie to reward and punish with organisation backing) is high

Fiedler suggested that:

(a) A structured (or psychologically distant) style works best when the situation is either very favourable, or very unfavourable to the leader

(b) A supportive (or psychologically close) style works best when the situation is moderately favourable to the leader.

(c) 'Group performance will be contingent upon the appropriate **matching of leadership styles** and the **degree of favourableness** of the group situation for the leader.' (*Fiedler*)

This is summed up in the diagram below.

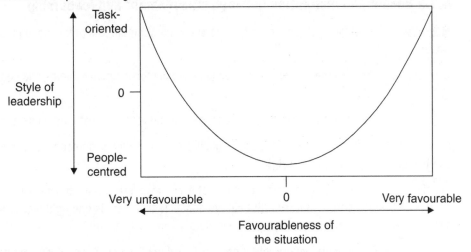

5.3.2 John Adair: action-centred leadership

John Adair's model (also called 'action-centred' or 'functional') is part of the contingency school of thought, because it sees the leadership process in a context made up of three interrelated variables: **task needs**, the individual needs of group members and the **needs of the group** as a whole. These needs must be examined in the light of the whole situation, which dictates the relative priority that must be given to each of the three sets of needs. Effective leadership is a process of identifying and acting on that priority, exercising a relevant cluster of roles to meet the various needs.

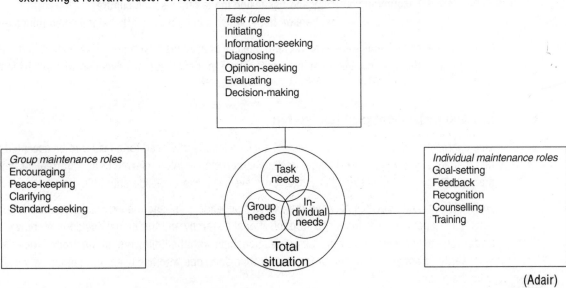

(Adair)

Adair argued that the common perception of leadership as 'decision making' was inadequate to describe the range of action required by this complex situation. He developed a scheme of leadership training based on precept and practice in each of eight leadership 'activities' which are applied to task, team and individual: hence, the **action-centred leadership** model.

- Defining the task
- Planning
- Briefing
- Controlling
- Evaluating
- Motivating
- Organising
- Setting an example

5.3.3 Bennis: the distinction between management and leadership

Warren Bennis puts forward some specific differences between the role of the manager and the role of the leader.

(a) **The manager** administers and maintains, by focusing on systems and controls and the short term.

(b) **The leader** innovates, focuses on people and inspires trust, and holds a long-term view.

As a further distinction, Bennis distinguishes between the manager as someone who **'does the right thing'** and the leader who **'does things right'**.

Bennis studied leadership by examining leaders of every description in the hope of finding some common characteristics. His book *Leaders* (1985) did not conclude that there is one right way to lead, but it does set out common competencies displayed by leaders. Bennis calls them:

(a) The **management of attention**: a compelling cause or vision, to give focus
(b) The **management of meaning**: the ability to communicate
(c) The **management of trust**: being consistent and honest
(d) The **management of self**: being aware of personal weaknesses and strengths.

Other tasks of the leader that Bennis sees as important are:

(a) Constantly reminding people why their work is important
(b) Creating an atmosphere of trust
(c) Encouraging curiosity and risk taking in the organisation culture
(d) Fostering an atmosphere of 'hope' which can be particularly helpful when things go wrong

Bennis believes that leadership in the modern age is a **shared task**, with power spread around rather than centralised. It could be that the most important role of modern leaders is deciding who will be in their teams.

5.3.4 Heifetz: dispersed leadership

This approach recognises the importance of social relations, the need for a leader to be accepted and the fact that nobody will be an ideal leader in every circumstance. Also referred to as 'informal' or 'emergent', it proposes that individuals at all organisational levels can exert a 'leadership influence'.

Heifetz (1994) distinguishes between the exercise of 'leadership' and the exercise of 'authority'. This separates leadership from the formal organisational hierarchy and traditional positions of 'power'. The leader can only be identified by examining relationships with the 'followers' in the group – he or she could quite easily be someone who 'emerges', rather than someone who has been pre-defined as the leader from the outset.

This approach is more sociological and political in its basis than traditional management thinking, drawing as it does open the prevailing organisational culture and context. A leader's individual qualities are less important than the leadership process, and the relationships created and sustained within it.

Case Study

Federal Express leadership qualities

FedEx has a system for rating aspiring leaders according to nine attributes:

- Charisma
- Individual consideration
- Intellectual stimulation
- Courage
- Dependability
- Flexibility
- Integrity
- Judgement
- Respect for others

Shell leadership framework

The leadership framework used by Shell includes nine key elements as indicated below:

- Builds shared vision
- Champions customer focus
- Maximises business opportunities
- Demonstrates professional mastery
- Displays personal effectiveness
- Demonstrates courage
- Motivates, coaches and develops
- Values differences

Vodafone Global leadership competencies

The Vodafone leadership competencies underlying their global leadership programme are divided into five categories:

- Values communication
- International team development
- Strategic vision
- Building organisational capability
- Commercial drive

5.3.5 An appraisal of contingency theory

Contingency theory usefully makes people aware of the factors affecting the choice of leadership style. However, *Schein* has pointed out that:

(a) Key variables such as task structure, power and relationships are difficult to measure in practice

(b) Contingency theories do not always take into account the need for the leader to have technical competence relevant to the task

Perhaps the major difficulty for any leader seeking to apply contingency theory, however, is actually to modify his or her behaviour as the situation changes.

Exam focus point

The syllabus Study Guide specifically mentions the work of:

- Adair
- Bennis
- Fiedler
- Heifetz
- Kotter

Keep in mind that most of the quoted theories are North American in origin, and do not necessarily take account of cultural differences in other countries.

Chapter Roundup

- **Management** is responsible for using the organisation's resources to meet its goals. It is accountable to the owners: shareholders in a business, or government in the public sector.

- It is the role of the manager to **take responsibility** and **organise people** to get things done. This involves the use of **authority** and **power** and implies a hierarchy in which power is delegated downwards while **accountability** is rendered upwards.

  Authority is the decision making discretion given to a manager, while responsibility is the obligation to perform duties. Sufficient authority should be granted to permit the efficient discharge of the appointed responsibility. Delegation is essential wherever there is a hierarchy of management. Power is the *ability* to do something whereas authority is the *right* to do something; expert power is possessed by those acknowledged as experts.

- Managers have **key roles** in work planning, resource allocation and project management.

- The classical writers on management and organisation were largely concerned with **efficiency**.

- **Fayol** was an administrator and proposed universal principles of organisation.

- **Taylor** was an engineer and sought the most efficient methods.

- **Mayo** and his colleagues investigated individual and group behaviour at work, as a factor in productivity.

- **Subsequent writers** have taken a more **flexible** view of what managers do.

- **Drucker** emphasised the economic objective of managers in businesses.

- **Mintzberg** described managerial roles, arguing that management is a disjointed, non-systematic activity.

- **Supervision** is the interface between the operational core (non-managerial workers) and management.

- There are many different definitions of **leadership**. Key themes (which are also used to distinguish leadership from management) include: interpersonal influence; securing willing commitment to shared goals; creating direction and energy; and an orientation to change.

- **Key leadership skills** may be identified in a range of interpersonal and business areas.

- There are three basic **schools of leadership theory**: trait ('qualities') theories, style theories and contingency (including situational and functional) theories.

- Early theories suggested that there are certain personal qualities common to 'great men' or successful leaders. In other words, **'leaders are born, not made'**.

- **Leadership styles** are clusters of leadership behaviour that are used in different ways in different situations. While there are many different classifications of style, they mainly relate to the extent to which the leader is focused primarily on task/performance (directive behaviour) or relationships/people (supportive behaviour). Key style models include:

  - The **Ashridge Model**: tells, sells, consults, joins
  - **Blake and Mouton**'s **Managerial Grid**: concern for task, concern for people

- Leaders need to adapt their style to the needs of the team and situation. This is the basis of **contingency approaches** such as:

  - **Fiedler**'s 'psychologically close' and 'psychologically distant' styles
  - **John Adair**'s 'action-centred' leadership model – based upon 'situations' or 'functions'

Quick Quiz

1   Which of the following is *not* one of Fayol's five functions of management?

A   Commanding
B   Controlling
C   Communicating
D   Co-ordinating

2   State Taylor's principles of scientific management.

3   What advance did the Hawthorne studies make in the management of people?

4   The overriding responsibility of the management of a business, according to Drucker, is employee development. *True or false?*

5   What managerial roles did Mintzberg describe and what categories did he group them into?

6   Is the statement below true or false?

'Frederick Taylor, despite his engineering background, was primarily concerned with the satisfaction workers obtained from their jobs.'

7   Which of the following is not one of the interpersonal roles of managers identified by Henry Mintzberg?

A   Handling disturbances
B   Reconciling individual needs with the requirements of the organisation
C   Training staff
D   Liaising outside the scalar chain

8   Complete the statement below using one of the words in the list given in brackets.

'.................................... authority cuts across departmental boundaries and enables managers to take decisions that affect staff in departments other than their own.'

(managerial, line, staff, functional, financial, formal)

9   A 'manager' might also be identified as a transformational leader. *True or false?*

10   If a manager confers with subordinates, takes their views and feelings into account, but retains the right to make a final decision, this is a:

A   Tells style
B   Sells style
C   Consults style
D   Joins style

11   What is the most effective style suggested by Blake and Mouton's Managerial Grid? Why is it so effective in theory, and why might it not be effective in practice?

12   John Adair formulated the:

A   Best fit model of leadership
B   Action-centred model of leadership
C   Follower-readiness model of leadership
D   Trait theory of leadership

BPP
LEARNING MEDIA

Answers to Quick Quiz

1   C: Communicating

2   The development of a true science of work; the scientific selection and progressive development of workers; the bringing together of the science and the workers; constant and intimate co-operation between management and workers.

3   An understanding that individual attitudes and group relationships help determine the level of output.

4   False: The overriding responsibility is economic performance.

5
Category	Roles
Interpersonal:	Figurehead; leader; liaison
Informational:	Monitor; spokesperson; disseminator
Decisional	Entrepreneur; disturbance handler; resource allocator; negotiator

6   False. Taylor was entirely concerned with engineering efficiency and believed that the increases in pay that ensued from the adoption of his method should be sufficiently motivating for any good worker.

7   A.   This is a decisional role. The 'disturbances' referred to are unpredictable situations that require managerial input to resolve.

8   Functional

9   False. Management is identified with 'transactional' leadership

10   C. Make sure you can define the other styles as well

11   9.9. It is effective if there is sufficient time and resources to attend fully to people's needs, if the manager is good at dealing with people and if the people respond. It is ineffective when a task has to be completed in a certain way or by a certain deadline, whether or not people like it

12   B. (You should be able to identify A as the work of Handy, and C as the work of Hersey and Blanchard.)

12

Individuals, groups and teams

Topic list	Syllabus reference
1 Individuals	E2 (a)–(c)
2 Groups	E2 (a)
3 Teams	E2 (b)(c) E3 (a)(b)
4 Team member roles	E3 (c)
5 Team development	E3 (c)
6 Building a team	E3 (c)(e)
7 Successful teams	E3 (d)(e)

Introduction

It is a useful reminder that managers do not just manage activities, processes and resources: they manage *people*. Organisations are made up of individuals and groups, with their own goals, needs and ways of seeing things.

In **Section 1**, we look at some useful concepts for understanding the behaviour of **individuals** at work, and how it can be managed.

In **Sections 2-7**, we look at how people behave in informal groups and in the more structured environment of **teams**. In particular, we consider how to create and maintain effective teams at work.

One of the key points to grasp is that an **effective team** is one which not only achieves its task objectives, but satisfies the needs of its members as well. As you will see in this chapter, **teamwork** involves both *task* functions (getting the job done) and *maintenance* functions (keeping the team together).

Teamwork is one of the hottest concepts in modern management. Fortunately, there are some useful models which can be learned: perhaps the major challenge of this topic is to get their details straight in your mind.

Study guide

		Intellectual level
E2	**Individual and group behaviour in business organisations**	
(a)	Describe the main characteristics of individual and group behaviour.	1
(b)	Outline the contributions of individuals and teams to organisational success.	1
(c)	Identify individual and team approaches to work.	1
E3	**Team formation, development and management**	
(a)	Explain the differences between a group and a team.	1
(b)	Define the purposes of a team.	1
(c)	Explain the role of the manager in building the team and developing individuals within the team:	1
(i)	Belbin's team roles theory	
(ii)	Tuckman's theory of team development	
(d)	List the characteristics of effective and ineffective teams.	1
(e)	Describe tools and techniques that can be used to build the team and improve team effectiveness.	1

Exam guide

Relationships within a team and the management of teams often figure in the examination, including named models such as Tuckman and Belbin. The Pilot Paper features a 2 mark question on Tuckman's stages, and another on Belbin's roles.

1 Individuals

1.1 Personality

FAST FORWARD

> **Personality** is the total pattern of an individual's thoughts, feelings and behaviours. It is shaped by a variety of factors, both inherited and environmental.

In order to identify, describe and explain the differences between people, psychologists use the concept of **personality**.

Key term

> **Personality** is the total pattern of characteristic ways of thinking, feeling and behaving that constitute the individual's distinctive method of relating to the environment.

1.1.1 Describing personality

Attempts to describe the 'components' of personality, or the ways people differ, focus on two broad concepts: traits and types.

(a) Personality **traits** are relatively stable, enduring qualities of an individual's personality which cause a tendency to behave in particular ways. If we say that someone is 'impulsive', for example, we are identifying one of his personality traits. This trait will make him tend to respond to situations in habitual ways: for example, by making rapid decisions and taking immediate liking to people.

Trait theories of personality account for individual differences by identifying the particular combination and strength of traits possessed by individuals.

(b) Personality **types** are distinct clusters of personality characteristics, which reflect the psychological preferences of the individual. If we say that someone is an 'extravert', for example, we may be suggesting that she is sociable, expressive, impulsive, practical and active. An 'introvert', by contrast, is unsociable, inhibited, controlled, reflective and inactive.

Type theories of personality account for individual differences by identifying the particular mix of preferences within personality types. Carl Jung suggested that 'People tend to develop behaviours, skills and attitudes associated with their type, and those with types different from yours will probably be opposite to you in many ways.'

The well-known **Myers Briggs Type Inventory**™ is based on detailed analysis of personality types. The aim of the inventory (and the value of personality theories to managers) is:

(a) To provide a shared language with which people can discuss and explore individual uniqueness (their own natural style) and ways of developing to their full potential

(b) To help people to understand areas of difference which might otherwise be the source of misunderstanding and mis-communication

(c) To encourage people to appreciate diversity by highlighting the value and complementary contributions of all personality types

Question

Personality

How is your personality 'cut out' to be an accountant? This is not a technical question: it merely invites you to think about your personality traits – and stereotypes about the 'type of person' who chooses to be an accountant or makes a good accountant. (This will be useful when we look at recruitment and selection in Chapter 15.)

1.1.2 Managing personality

An individual's personality should be compatible with his or her work requirements in three ways.

Compatibility	Comments
With the **task**	Different personality types suit different types of work. A person who appears unsociable and inhibited will find sales work, involving a lot of social interactions, intensely stressful – and will probably not be very good at it.
With the **systems** and **management culture** of the organisation	Some people hate to be controlled, for example, but others want to be controlled and dependent in a work situation, because they find responsibility threatening.
With other **personalities** in the team	Personality clashes are a prime source of conflict at work. An achievement-oriented personality, for example, tends to be a perfectionist, is impatient and unable to relax, and will be unsociable if people seem to be getting in the way of performance: such a person will clearly be frustrated and annoyed by laid-back sociable types working (or not working) around him.

Where incompatibilities occur, the manager or supervisor has three options.

(a)   **Restore compatibility**. This may be achieved by reassigning an individual to tasks more suited to his personality type, for example, or changing management style to suit the personalities of the team.

(b)   **Achieve a compromise**. Individuals should be encouraged to:

(i)   Understand the nature of their differences. Others have the right to be themselves (within the demands of the team): personal differences should not be taken personally, as if they were adopted deliberately to annoy

(ii)   Modify their behaviour if necessary.

(c)   **Remove the incompatible personality**. In the last resort, obstinately difficult or disruptive people may simply have to be weeded out of the team.

1.2 Perception

FAST FORWARD

Perception is the process by which the brain selects and organises information in order to make sense of it. People behave according to what they perceive – not according to what really is.

Different people see things differently and human beings behave in (and in response to) the world, not as it really is, but as they see it.

Key term

> **Perception** is the psychological process by which stimuli or in-coming sensory data are selected and organised into patterns which are meaningful to the individual.

1.2.1 Processes of perception

The process of **perceptual selection** deals with how we gather and filter out incoming data. Perception may be determined by any or all of the following.

(a)   **The context**. People see what they want to see: whatever is necessary or relevant in the situation in which they find themselves. You might notice articles on management in the newspapers while studying this module which normally you would not notice, for example.

(b)   **The nature of the stimuli**. Our attention tends to be drawn to large, bright, loud, contrasting, unfamiliar, moving and repeated (not repetitive) stimuli. Advertisers know it.

(c)   **Internal factors**. Our attention is drawn to stimuli that match our personality, needs, interests, expectations and so on. If you are hungry, for example, you will pick the smell of food out of a mix of aromas.

(d)   **Fear or trauma.** People are able to avoid seeing things that they *don't* want to see: things that are threatening to their security or self-image, or things that are too painful for them.

A complementary process of **perceptual organisation** deals with the interpretation of the data which has been gathered and filtered.

1.2.2 Managing perception

People do not respond to the world as it really is, but as they perceive it to be. If people act in ways that seem illogical or contrary to you, it is probably not because of stupidity or defiance, but because they simply do not see things in the same way you do. In order to manage differences in perception:

(a)   Consider whether you might be **misinterpreting** the situation

(b)   Consider whether others might be misinterpreting the situation or interpreting it **differently** from you

(c)   When tackling a task or a problem get the people involved to **define the situation** as they see it

(d)   Be aware of the most common clashes of perception at work

    (i)   **Managers and staff.** The experience of work can be very different for managerial and non-managerial personnel. Efforts to bridge the gap may be viewed with suspicion.

    (ii)   **Work cultures**. Different functions in organisations may have very different time-scales and cultures of work, and will therefore perceive the work, and each other, in different ways.

    (iii)   **Race, sex** and **religious beliefs.** A joke, comment or gesture that one person may see as amusing may be offensive – and construed as harassment under UK law – to another.

1.3 Attitudes

FAST FORWARD

People develop **attitudes** about things, based on what they think, what they feel and what they want to do about it. Attitudes are formed by perception, experience and personality which in turn are shaped by wider social influences.

Attitudes are our general standpoint on things: the positions we have adopted in regard to particular issues, things and people, as we perceive them.

Key term

An **attitude** is 'a mental state ... exerting a directive or dynamic influence upon the individual's response to all objects and situations with which it is related.'

Attitudes are thought to contain three basic components.

- Knowledge, beliefs or disbeliefs, perceptions
- Feelings and desires (positive or negative)
- Volition, will or the intention to perform an action

Behaviour in a work context will be influenced by:

(a)   **Attitudes to work:** the individual's standpoint on working, work conditions, colleagues, the task, the organisation and management

(b)   **Attitudes at work:** all sorts of attitudes which individuals may have about other people, politics, education or religion (among other things), and which they bring with them into the work place – to act on, agree, disagree or discuss

Positive, negative or neutral attitudes to other workers, or groups of workers, to the various systems and operations of the organisation, to learning – or particular training initiatives – to communication or to the task itself will obviously influence performance at work. In particular, they may result in varying degrees of:

- Co-operation or conflict between individuals and groups, or between departments
- Co-operation with or resistance to management
- Success in communication – interpersonal and organisation wide
- Commitment and contribution to the work

Question

Attitude

Suggest four elements which would make up a positive attitude to work. (An example might be the belief that you get a fair day's pay for a fair day's work.)

Answer

Elements of a positive attitude to work may include a willingness to:

(a) Commit oneself to the objectives of the organisation, or adopt personal objectives that are compatible with those of the organisation

(b) Accept the right of the organisation to set standards of acceptable behaviour for its members

(c) Contribute to the development and improvement of work practices and performance

(d) Take advantages of opportunities for personal development at work

1.4 Intelligence

Intelligence is a wider and more complex concept than the traditional view of 'IQ'. It includes useful attributes such as:

(a) **Analytic intelligence**: traditionally measured by IQ tests, including mental agility, logical reasoning and verbal fluency

(b) **Spatial intelligence**: the ability to see patterns and connections, most obvious in the creative artist or scientist

(c) **Practical intelligence**: practical aptitude, handiness

(d) **Intra-personal intelligence**: self awareness, self expression, self-control, handling stress

(e) **Inter-personal intelligence**: empathy, understanding of the emotional needs of others, influence, conflict resolution, assertiveness, co-operation

Intra-and inter-personal intelligence have recently attracted attention, through the work of Daniel **Goleman** (and others) as **emotional intelligence** (EQ). EQ is considered particularly important in managing people effectively, since it enables a person to manage the emotional components of situations, behaviour and communication.

1.5 Role theory

Role theory suggests that people behave in any situation according to other people's expectations of how they should behave in that situation.

A role may be seen as a part you play: people sometimes refer to wearing 'different hats' in different situations or groups of people.

(a) A **role set** is a group of people who respond to you in a given role. Staff in the accounts department will relate to the account manager in his role as professional and superior –

rather than as a father or husband (within the role set of the family) or friend (in the role set of non-work peers) and so on. Individuals need to be aware of which role set they are operating in, in order to behave appropriately for the role.

(b) **Role ambiguity** may occur if you do not know what role you are operating in at a given time. If a manager tries to be 'friends' with staff, this may create ambiguity and people will not know where they stand.

(c) **Role incompatibility** or **role conflict** occurs when you are expected to operate in two roles at once: for example, if you have to discipline a member of staff (in your role as superior) with whom you have become informally friendly (in your role as sociable person).

(d) **Role signs** indicate what role you are in at a given moment, so that others relate to you in that role without ambiguity or confusion. Role signs at work have traditionally included such things as style of dress (signalling professionalism) and styles of address (signalling respect and relative status).

(e) **Role models** are the individuals you aspire to be like: people you look up to and model your own behaviour on.

2 Groups

As an employee your relationship with the organisation is as an individual: the employment contract is with you as an individual, and you are recruited as an individual. In your working life, though, you will generally find yourself working as part of a **group** or **team**. If you are a supervisor or a manager, you may direct a team.

2.1 What are groups?

FAST FORWARD

> A **group** is a collection of individuals who perceive themselves as a group. It thus has a sense of **identity**.

Key term

A **group** is any collection of people who perceive themselves to be a group.

Groups have certain attributes that a random crowd does not possess.

(a) **A sense of identity**. There are acknowledged boundaries to the group which define who is in and who is out, who is us and who is them.

(b) **Loyalty to the group,** and acceptance within the group. This generally expresses itself as conformity or the acceptance of the norms of behaviour and attitudes that bind the group together and exclude others from it.

(c) **Purpose and leadership.** Most groups have an express purpose, whatever field they are in: most will, spontaneously or formally, choose individuals or sub-groups to lead them towards the fulfilment of those goals.

2.2 Why form groups?

Any organisation is composed of many groups, with attributes of their own. People in organisations will be **drawn together into groups** by a variety of forces.

- A preference for small groups, where closer relationships can develop
- The need to belong and to make a contribution that will be noticed and appreciated
- Familiarity: a shared office or canteen
- Common rank, specialisms, objectives and interests

- The attractiveness of a particular group activity (joining an interesting club, say)
- Resources offered to groups (for example sports facilities)
- Power greater than the individuals could muster alone (trade union, pressure group)
- Formal directives

2.3 Formal and informal groups

Informal groups will invariably be present in any organisation. Informal groups include workplace cliques, and networks of people who regularly get together to exchange information, groups of 'mates' who socialise outside work and so on. They have a constantly fluctuating membership and structure.

Formal groups will be intentionally organised by the organisation, for a task which they are held responsible – they are task oriented, and become **teams**. Although many people enjoy working in teams, their popularity in the work place arises because of their effectiveness in fulfilling the organisation's work.

Question   Small groups

What groups are you a member of in your study or work environment(s)? How big are these groups? How does the size of your class, study group, work team – or whatever:

(a) Affect your ability to come up with questions or ideas?

(b) Give you help and support to do something you couldn't do alone?

Answer

Your primary groups are probably your tutor group or class. If at work, it would be the section in which you work. If the groups are large, you may feel reluctant to put forward ideas or ask questions, but even within a large group you should feel there is support and that help is at hand if you need it.

Exam focus point

Aspects to look out for in exam questions include the distinction between teams and groups; factors in team success; Belbin's team roles and Tuckman's team development model. Revise teambuilding carefully: it is another key issue.

2.4 Individual and group contribution

FAST FORWARD

People **contribute differently in groups** (due to group dynamics and synergy) than they do individually. This may have a positive or negative effect.

People contribute different skills and attributes to the organisation as individuals than they do as group members, because:

(a) Human behaviour is different in groups than in solo or interpersonal situations: **group dynamics** have an effect on performance.

(b) Groups offer **synergy**: 2 + 2 = 5. The pooling and stimulation of ideas and energies in a group can allow greater contribution than individuals working on their own. ('None of us is as smart as all of us', *Blanchard*.)

(c) Group dynamics and synergy may also be **negative**: distracting the individual, stifling individual responsibility and flair and so on. Individuals may contribute more and better in some situations.

Individuals contribute:	Groups contribute:
• A set of skills	• A mix of skills
• Objectives set by manager	• Some teams can set their own objectives under the corporate framework
• A point of view	• A number of different points of view, enabling a swift overview of different ways of looking at a problem
• Creative ideas related to the individual's expertise	• Creative ideas arising from new combinations of expertise
• 'I can't be in two places at once'	• Flexibility as team members can be deployed in different ways
• Limited opportunity for self-criticism	• Opportunity for exercising control

3 Teams

FAST FORWARD

A **team** is more than a group. It has joint **objectives** and **accountability** and may be set up by the organisation under the supervision or coaching of a team leader, although **self-managed teams** are growing in popularity.

Exam focus point

The distinction between a group and a team is specifically noted in the Study Guide, and appears as a question on the Pilot Paper.

Key term

A **team** is a small number of people with complementary skills who are committed to a *common purpose*, performance *goals* and approach for which they hold themselves basically accountable.

(*Katzenbach and Smith*)

3.1 Strengths of team working

FAST FORWARD

Teamworking may be used for: **organising** work; **controlling** activities; **generating** ideas; **decision-making**; pooling **knowledge.**

Teams are particularly well-adapted to the following purposes.

Type of role	Comments
Work organisation	Teams combine the skills of different individuals. Teams are a co-ordinating mechanism: they avoid complex communication between different business functions.
Control	Fear of letting down the team can be a powerful motivator: team loyalty can be used to control the performance and behaviour of individuals.
Ideas generation	Teams can generate ideas, eg through brainstorming and information sharing.
Decision making	Decisions are evaluated from more than one viewpoint, with pooled information. Teams make fewer, but better-evaluated, decisions than individuals.

3.2 Limitations of team working

Problems with teams include **conflict** on the one hand, and **group think** (excessive cohesion) on the other.

Teams and teamworking are very much in fashion, but there are potential **drawbacks**.

(a) Teamworking is not suitable for all jobs – although some managers do not like to admit this.

(b) Teamwork should be introduced because it leads to better performance, not because people feel better or more secure.

(c) Team processes (especially seeking consensus) can delay decision-making. The team may also produce the compromise decision, not the right decision.

(d) Social relationships might be maintained at the expense of other aspects of performance.

(e) Group norms may restrict individual personality and flair.

(f) 'Group think' (*Janis*): team consensus and cohesion may prevent consideration of alternatives or constructive criticism, leading the team to make risky, ill-considered decisions.

(g) Personality clashes and political behaviour within a team can get in the way of effective performance.

3.3 Organising team work

Multi-disciplinary teams contain people from different departments, pooling the skills of specialists.

Multi-skilled teams contain people who themselves have more than one skill.

A team may be called together temporarily, to achieve specific task objectives (**project team**), or may be more or less permanent, with responsibilities for a particular product, product group or stage of the production process (a **product or process team**).

There are two basic approaches to the organisation of team work: multi-skilled teams and multi-disciplinary teams.

3.3.1 Multi-disciplinary teams

Multi-disciplinary teams bring together individuals with different skills and specialisms, so that their skills, experience and knowledge can be pooled or exchanged.

Multi-disciplinary teams can:

(a) Increase workers' awareness of their overall objectives and targets

(b) Aid co-ordination between different areas of the business

(c) Help to generate solutions to problems, and suggestions for improvements, since a multi-disciplinary team has access to more pieces of the jigsaw

3.3.2 Multi-skilled teams

A multi-skilled team brings together a number of individuals who can perform any of the group's tasks. These tasks can then be shared out in a more flexible way between group members, according to who is available and best placed to do a given job at the time it is required. Multi-skilling is the cornerstone of team empowerment, since it cuts across the barriers of job descriptions and demarcations to enable teams to respond flexibly to changing demands.

3.3.3 Virtual teams

Virtual teams bring together individuals working in remote locations, reproducing the social, collaborative and information-sharing aspects of team working using Information and Communications Technology (ICT).

4 Team member roles

4.1 Who should belong in the team?

Team members should be selected for their potential to contribute to getting things done (**task performance**) and establishing good working relationships (**group maintenance**). This may include:

(a) **Specialist skills**. A team might exist to combine expertise from different departments

(b) **Power** in the wider organisation. Team members may have influence

(c) **Access to resources**. Team members may contribute information, or be able to mobilise finance or staff for the task

(d) The **personalities and goals** of the individual members of the team. These will determine how the group functions

The blend of the individual skills and abilities of its members will (ideally) **balance** the team.

4.2 Belbin: team roles

FAST FORWARD

Ideally team members should perform a **balanced mix of roles**. **Belbin** suggests: co-ordinator, shaper, plant, monitor-evaluator, resource-investigator, implementer, team-worker, completer-finisher and specialist.

R Meredith *Belbin* (1981) researched business game teams at the Henley Management College and drew up a widely-used framework for understanding roles within work groups.

Belbin insisted that a distinction needs to be made between:

(a) **Team (process) role** ('a tendency to behave, contribute and interrelate with others at work in certain distinctive ways'), and

(b) **Functional role** ('the job demands that a person has been engaged to meet by supplying the requisite technical skills and operational knowledge')

Exam focus point

Belbin's model of nine roles addresses the mix of team/process roles required for a fully functioning team.

4.2.1 Nine team roles

Belbin identifies nine team roles.

Role and description	Team-role contribution	Allowable weaknesses
Plant Creative, imaginative, unorthodox	Solves difficult problems	Ignores details, too preoccupied to communicate effectively
Resource investigator Extrovert, enthusiastic, communicative	Explores opportunities, develops contacts	Over-optimistic, loses interest once initial enthusiasm has passed
Co-ordinator (chairman) Mature, confident, a good chairperson	Clarifies goals, promotes decision-making, delegates well	Can be seen as manipulative, delegates personal work
Shaper Challenging, dynamic, thrives on pressure	Has the drive and courage to overcome obstacles	Can provoke others, hurts people's feelings
Monitor-Evaluator Sober, strategic and discerning	Sees all options, judges accurately	Lacks drive and ability to inspire others, overly critical
Team worker Co-operative, mild, perceptive and diplomatic	Listens, builds, averts friction, calms the waters	Indecisive in crunch situations, can be easily influenced
Implementer (company worker) Disciplined, reliable, conservative and efficient	Turns ideas into practical actions	Somewhat inflexible, slow to respond to new possibilities
Completer-Finisher Painstaking, conscientious, anxious	Searches out errors and omissions, delivers on time	Inclined to worry unduly, reluctant to delegate, can be a nitpicker
Specialist Single-minded, self-starting, dedicated	Provides knowledge and skills in rare supply	Contributes only on a narrow front, dwells on technicalities, overlooks the 'big picture'

4.2.2 A balanced team

These team roles are not fixed within any given individual. Team members can occupy more than one role, or switch to 'backup' roles if required: hence, there is no requirement for every team to have nine members. However, since role preferences are based on personality, it should be recognised that:

- Individuals will be naturally inclined towards some roles more than others
- Individuals will tend to adopt one or two team roles more or less consistently
- Individuals are likely to be more successful in some roles than in others

The nine roles are complementary, and Belbin suggested that an 'ideal' team should represent a mix or balance of all of them. If managers know employees' team role preferences, they can strategically select, 'cast' and develop team members to fulfil the required roles.

Question

The following phrases and slogans project certain team roles: identify which. (Examples are drawn from Belbin, 1993.)

(a)   The small print is always worth reading.
(b)   Let's get down to the task in hand.
(c)   In this job you never stop learning.
(d)   Without continuous innovation, there is no survival.
(e)   Surely we can exploit that?
(f)   When the going gets tough, the tough get going.
(g)   I was very interested in your point of view.
(h)   Has anyone else got anything to add to this?
(i)   Decisions should not be based purely on enthusiasm.

Answer

(a)   Completer-finisher
(b)   Implementer/company worker
(c)   Specialist
(d)   Plant
(e)   Resource investigator
(f)   Shaper
(g)   Teamworker
(h)   Co-ordinator/Chairman
(i)   Monitor-evaluator

4.3 How do people contribute?

FAST FORWARD

Team members make different types of **contribution** (eg proposing, supporting, blocking) in the areas of **task performance** and **team maintenance.**

In order to evaluate and manage team dynamics, it may be helpful for the team leader to:

(a)   Assess who (if anybody) is performing each of Belbin's **team roles**. Who is the team's plant? monitor-evaluator? and so on. There should be a mix of people performing task and team maintenance roles.

(b)   Analyse the **frequency and type of individual members' contributions** to group discussions and interactions.

   (i)   Identify which members of the team habitually make the most contributions, and which the least. (You could do this by taking a count of contributions from each member, during a sample 10-15 minutes of group discussion.)

   (ii)   If the same people tend to dominate discussion *whatever* is discussed (ie regardless of relevant expertise), the team has a problem in its communication process.

Rackham and *Morgan* have developed a helpful categorisation of the types of contribution people can make to team discussion and decision-making, including the following.

Category	Behaviour	Example
Proposing	Putting forward suggestions, new concepts or courses of action.	'Why don't we look at a flexi-time system?'
Supporting	Supporting another person or his/her proposal.	'Yes, I agree, flexi-time would be worth looking at.'
Seeking information	Asking for more facts, opinions or clarification.	'What exactly do you mean by "flexi-time"?'
Giving information	Offering facts, opinions or clarification.	'There's a helpful outline of flexi-time in this article.'
Blocking/ difficulty stating	Putting obstacles in the way of a proposal, without offering any alternatives.	'What if the other teams get jealous? It would only cause conflict.'
Shutting-out behaviour	Interrupting or overriding others; taking over.	'Nonsense. Let's move onto something else – we've had enough of this discussion.
Bringing-in behaviour	Involving another member; encouraging contribution.	'Actually, I'd like to hear what Fred has to say. Go on, Fred.'
Testing understanding	Checking whether points have been understood.	'So flexi-time could work over a day or a week; have I got that right?'
Summarising	Drawing together or summing up previous discussion.	'We've now heard two sides to the flexi-time issue: on the one hand, flexibility; on the other side possible risk. Now … '

Each type of behaviour may be appropriate in the right situation at the right time. A team may be low on some types of contribution – and it may be up to the team leader to encourage, or deliberately adopt, desirable behaviours (such as bringing-in, supporting or seeking information) in order to provide balance.

5 Team development

You probably have had experience of being put into a group of people you do not know. Many teams are set up this way and it takes some time for the team to become effective.

FAST FORWARD

A team **develops in stages**: forming, storming, norming, performing (**Tuckman**) and dorming or mourning/adjourning.

5.1 Tuckman's stages of group development

Four stages in group development were identified by *Tuckman* (1965).

Step 1   **Forming**

The team is just coming together. Each member wishes to impress his or her personality on the group. The individuals will be trying to find out about each other, and about the aims and norms of the team. There will at this stage probably be a wariness about introducing new ideas. The objectives being pursued may as yet be unclear and a leader may not yet have emerged.

Step 2 **Storming**

This frequently involves more or less open conflict between team members. There may be changes agreed in the original objectives, procedures and norms established for the group. If the team is developing successfully this may be a fruitful phase, as more realistic targets are set and trust between the group members increases.

Step 3 **Norming**

A period of settling down: there will be agreements about work sharing, individual requirements and expectations of output. Norms and procedures may evolve which enable methodical working to be introduced and maintained.

Step 4 **Performing**

The team sets to work to execute its task. The difficulties of growth and development no longer hinder the group's objectives.

Later writers added two stages to Tuckman's model.

(a)   **Dorming**. Once a group has been performing well for some time, it may get complacent, and fall back into self-maintenance functions, at the expense of the task.

(b)   **Mourning/adjourning**. The group sees itself as having fulfilled its purpose – or, if it is a temporary group, is due to physically disband. This is a stage of confusion, sadness and anxiety as the group breaks up. There is evaluation of its achievements, and gradual withdrawal of group members. If the group is to continue, going on to a new task, there will be a re-negotiation of aims and roles: a return to the forming stage.

Question	Team formation stages

Read the following descriptions of team behaviour and decide to which category they belong (forming, storming, norming, performing, dorming).

(a)   Two of the group arguing as to whose idea is best
(b)   Progress becomes static
(c)   Desired outputs being achieved
(d)   Shy member of group not participating
(e)   Activities being allocated

Answer

Categorising the behaviour of group members in the situations described results in the following: (a) storming, (b) dorming, (c) performing, (d) forming, (e) norming.

6 Building a team

In Section 5, we suggested that teams have a natural evolutionary life cycle, and that four stages can be identified. Not all teams develop into mature teams and might be stuck, stagnating, in any one of the stages.

So, it often falls to the supervisor or manager to build the team. There are three main issues involved in team building.

Issues	Comments
Team identity	Get people to see themselves as part of this group.
Team solidarity	Encourage loyalty so that members put in extra effort for the sake of the team.
Shared objectives	Encourage the team to commit itself to shared work objectives and to co-operate willingly and effectively in achieving them.

FAST FORWARD

> Team development can be facilitated by active **team building** measures to support team identity, solidarity and commitment to shared objectives.

We can now discuss some of the techniques for building team identity, team solidarity and the commitment to shared-objectives. But first try the question below.

Question
Teambuilding exercises

Why might the following be effective as team-building exercises?

(a)   Sending a project team (involved in the design of electronic systems for racing cars) on a recreational day out karting.

(b)   Sending two sales teams on a day out playing 'War Games', each being an opposing combat team trying to capture the other's flag, armed with paint guns.

(c)   Sending a project team on a conference at a venue away from work, with a brief to review the past year and come up with a vision for the next year.

(These are actually commonly-used techniques. If you are interested, you might locate an activity centre or company near you which offers outdoor pursuits, war games or corporate entertainment and ask them about team-building exercises and the effect they have on people.)

Answer

(a)   Recreation helps the team to build informal relationships: in this case, the chosen activity also reminds them of their tasks, and may make them feel special, as part of the motor racing industry, by giving them a taste of what the end user of their product does.

(b)   A team challenge forces the group to consider its strengths and weaknesses, to find its natural leader. This exercise creates an 'us' and 'them' challenge: perceiving the rival team as the enemy heightens the solidarity of the group.

(c)   This exercise encourages the group to raise problems and conflicts freely, away from the normal environment of work and also encourages brainstorming and the expression of team members' dreams for what the team can achieve in the future.

6.1 Team identity

A manager might seek to reinforce the sense of identity of the group. Arguably this is in part the creation of boundaries, identifying who is in the team and who is not.

(a)   **Name**. Staff at McDonald's restaurants are known as the Crew. In other cases, the name would be more official, describing what the team actually does (eg Systems Implementation Task Force).

(b) **Badge or uniform**. This often applies to service industries, but it is unlikely that it would be applied within an organisation.

(c) Expressing the team's **self-image:** teams often develop their own jargon, especially for new projects.

(d) Building a team **mythology** – in other words, stories from the past ('classic mistakes' as well as successes).

(e) **A separate space**: it might help if team members work together in the same or adjacent offices, but this is not always possible. (A team intranet page may perform this function for a virtual team.)

6.2 Team solidarity

Team solidarity implies cohesion and loyalty inside the team. A team leader might be interested in:

(a) **Expressing** solidarity

(b) Encouraging **interpersonal relationships** – although the purpose of these is to ensure that work gets done

(c) **Dealing with conflict** by getting it out into the open; disagreements should be expressed and then resolved

(d) **Controlling competition**. The team leader needs to treat each member of the team fairly and to be seen to do so; favouritism undermines solidarity

(e) Encouraging some **competition with other groups**, if appropriate. For example, sales teams might be offered a prize for the highest monthly orders; London Underground runs best-kept station competitions

Question

Group cohesion

Can you see any dangers in creating a very close-knit group? Think of the effect of strong team cohesion on:

(a) What the group spends its energies and attention on
(b) How the group regards outsiders, and any information or feedback they supply
(c) How the group makes decisions

What could be done about these dangerous effects?

Answer

Problems may arise in an ultra close-knit group because:

(a) The group's energies may be focused on its own maintenance and relationships, instead of on the task.

(b) The group may be suspicious or dismissive of outsiders, and may reject any contradictory information or criticism they supply; the group will be blinkered and stick to its own views, no matter what; cohesive groups thus often get the impression that they are infallible: they can't be wrong – and therefore can't learn from their mistakes.

(c) The group may squash any dissent or opinions that might rock the boat. Close-knit groups tend to preserve a consensus – falsely, if required – and to take risky decisions, because they have suppressed alternative facts and viewpoints.

This phenomenon is called '**groupthink** ' (Janis). In order to limit its effect, the team must be encouraged:

(a)   Actively to seek outside ideas and feedback

(b)   To welcome self-criticism within the group, and

(c)   Consciously to evaluate conflicting evidence and opinions

6.3 Commitment to shared objectives

Getting commitment to the team's shared objectives may involve a range of leader activity.

- Clearly setting out the objectives of the team

- Allowing the team to participate in setting objectives

- Giving regular feedback on progress and results with constructive criticism

- Getting the team involved in providing performance feedback

- Offering positive reinforcement (praise etc) for co-operative working and task achievement by the team as a whole (rather than just 'star' individuals)

- Championing the success of the team within the organisation

7 Successful teams

FAST FORWARD

A team can be evaluated on the basis of quantifiable and qualitative factors, covering its **operations** and its **output**, and team member **satisfaction**.

7.1 Evaluating team effectiveness

The task of the team leader is to build a 'successful' or 'effective' team. The criteria for team effectiveness include:

(a)   **Task performance**: fulfilment of task and organisational goals

(b)   **Team functioning**: constructive maintenance of team working, managing the demands of team dynamics, roles and processes, and

(c)   **Team member satisfaction**: fulfilment of individual development and relationship needs.

There are a number of factors, both quantitative and qualitative, that may be assessed to decide whether or how far a team is operating effectively. Some factors cannot be taken as evidence on their own, but may suggest underlying problems: accident rates may be due to poor safety systems, for example – but may also suggest poor morale and lack of focus due to team problems. Some of the characteristics of **effective** and **ineffective** teams may be summarised as follows.

Factor	Effective team	Ineffective team
Quantifiable		
Labour turnover	Low	High
Accident rate	Low	High
Absenteeism	Low	High
Output and productivity	High	Low
Quality of output	High	Low
Individual targets	Achieved	Not achieved

Factor	Effective team	Ineffective team
Stoppages and interruptions to the work flow	Low	High (eg because of misunderstandings, disagreements)
Qualitative		
Commitment to targets and organisational goals	High	Low
Understanding of team's work and why it exists	High	Low
Understanding of individual roles within the team	High	Low
Communication between team members	Free and open	Mistrust
Ideas	Shared for the team's benefit	'Owned' (and hidden) by individuals for their own benefit
Feedback	Constructive criticism	Point scoring, undermining
Problem-solving	Addresses causes	Only looks at symptoms
Interest in work decisions	Active	Passive acceptance
Opinions	Consensus	Imposed solutions
Job satisfaction	High	Low
Motivation in leader's absence	High	'When the cat's away…'

7.2 Rewarding effective teams

Team-based rewards may be used to encourage co-operation and mutual accountability.

Organisations may try to encourage effective team performance by designing reward systems that recognise team, rather than individual success. Indeed, **individual performance rewards** may act *against* team co-operation and performance.

(a) They emphasise individual rather than team performance.

(b) They encourage team leaders to think of team members only as individuals, rather than relating to them as a team.

For **team rewards** to be effective, the team must have certain characteristics.

- Distinct roles, targets and performance measures (so the team knows what it has to do to earn the reward)

- Significant autonomy and thus influence over performance (so the team perceives that extra effort will be rewarded)

- Maturity and stability

- Co-operation

- Interdependence of team members (so that the team manages member contribution, everyone 'pulls their weight', no-one feels they could earn higher rewards on their own)

Reward schemes which focus on team (or organisation) performance include:

(a) **Profit sharing** schemes, based on the distribution of a pool of cash related to profit

(b) **Gainsharing** schemes, using a formula related to a suitable performance indicator, such as added value. Improvements in the performance indicator must be perceived to be within the employees' control, otherwise there will be no incentive to perform.

(c) **Employee share option** schemes, giving staff the right to acquire shares in the employing company at an attractive price.

Chapter Roundup

- **Personality** is the total pattern of an individual's thoughts, feelings and behaviours. It is shaped by a variety of factors, both inherited and environmental.

- **Perception** is the process by which the brain selects and organises information in order to make sense of it. People behave according to what they perceive – not according to what really is.

- People develop **attitudes** about things, based on what they think, what they feel and what they want to do about it. Attitudes are formed by perception, experience and personality which in turn are shaped by wider social influences.

- **Role theory** suggests that people behave in any situation according to other people's expectations of how they should behave in that situation.

- A **group** is a collection of individuals who perceive themselves as a group. It thus has a sense of **identity**.

- People **contribute differently in groups** (due to group dynamics and synergy) than they do individually. This may have a positive or negative effect.

- A **team** is more than a group. It has joint **objectives** and **accountability** and may be set up by the organisation under the supervision or coaching of a team leader, although **self-managed teams** are growing in popularity.

- Teamworking may be used for: **organising** work; **controlling** activities; **generating** ideas; **decision-making**; pooling **knowledge.**

- Problems with teams include **conflict** on the one hand, and **group think** (excessive cohesion) on the other.

- **Multi-disciplinary** teams contain people from different departments, pooling the skills of specialists.

  Multi-skilled teams contain people who themselves have more than one skill.

- Ideally team members should perform a **balanced mix of roles**. **Belbin** suggests: co-ordinator, shaper, plant, monitor-evaluator, resource-investigator, implementer, team-worker, completer-finisher and specialist.

- Team members make different types of **contribution** (eg proposing, supporting, blocking) in the areas of **task performance** and **team maintenance**.

- A team **develops in stages**: forming, storming, norming, performing (**Tuckman**) and dorming or mourning/adjourning.

- Team development can be facilitated by active **team building** measures to support team identity, solidarity and commitment to shared objectives.

- A team can be evaluated on the basis of quantifiable and qualitative factors, covering its **operations** and its **output**, and team member **satisfaction**.

- **Team-based rewards** may be used to encourage co-operation and mutual accountability.

Quick Quiz

1 List three factors for a manager to consider in managing 'personality' at work.

2 Give three examples of areas where people's perceptions commonly conflict.

3 What is a team?

4 List Belbin's nine roles for a well-rounded team.

5 Who described the stages of group development?

    A   Woodcock
    B   Belbin
    C   Tuckman
    D   Rackham and Morgan

6 Suggest five ways in which a manager can get a team 'behind' task objectives.

7 High labour turnover is a characteristic of effective teams. *True or false?*

Answers to Quick Quiz

1 The compatibility of an individual's personality with the task, with the systems and culture of the organisation and with other members of the team

2 Managers and staff, work culture, race and gender

3 A small number of people with complementary skills who are committed to a common purpose, performance goals and approach for which they hold themselves basically accountable

4 Co-ordinator (or chairman), shaper, plant, monitor-evaluator, resource-investigator, implementer (or company worker), team worker, completer-finisher, specialist

5 C: Tuckman. You should be able to identify the team-relevant theories of Woodcock and Belbin and Rackham and Morgan as well

6 Set clear objectives, get the team to set targets/standards, provide information and resources, give feedback, praise and reward, and champion the team in the organisation

7 False

Motivating individuals and groups

Topic list	Syllabus reference
1 Overview of motivation	E4 (a)
2 Content theories of motivation	E4 (b)
3 Process theories of motivation	E4 (b)
4 Choosing a motivational approach	E4 (a)
5 Rewards and incentives	E4 (c)(d)
6 Pay as a motivator	E4 (d)

Introduction

Human behaviour is a complex phenomenon. Managers need to understand something of what makes their team members 'tick' – particularly when it comes to the key question: how do you get them to perform well, or better?

That is what **motivation** is about.

Having explored motivation, and its impact on performance, in **Section 1**, we go on to look at a range of key **motivational theories** in **Sections 2-4.** There are some famous theoretical models here, and it is definitely worth learning them.

In **Sections 5-6**, we look at a range of **financial and non-financial rewards** that may be used to motivate people. Take note, as you proceed through the chapter, that money is by no means the only (or necessarily the most effective) incentive to higher levels of performance.

The ability to 'motivate' people is also a key skill of **leadership**, as we saw in Chapter 11.

Study guide

		Intellectual level
E4	**Motivating individuals and groups**	
(a)	Define motivation and explain its importance to the organisation, teams and individuals.	1
(b)	Explain content and process theories of motivation: Maslow, Herzberg, McGregor, and Vroom.	2
(c)	Explain and identify types of intrinsic and extrinsic reward.	1
(d)	Explain how reward systems can be designed and implemented to motivate teams and individuals.	1

Exam guide

Motivation is likely to appear regularly in the exam, since it is an essential aspect of managerial responsibility. Since there is a large body of academic work, you must understand the theories and authorities.

1 Overview of motivation

1.1 What is motivation?

FAST FORWARD

Motivation is 'a decision-making process through which the individual chooses desired outcomes and sets in motion the behaviour appropriate to acquiring them'. (*Huczynski and Buchanan*).

Key term

Motivation is 'a decision-making process through which the individual chooses desired outcomes and sets in motion the behaviour appropriate to acquiring them'. (*Huczynski and Buchanan*).

In practice, the words **motives** and **motivation** are commonly used in different contexts to mean the following.

    (a)   **Goals or outcomes** that have become desirable for a particular individual. We say that money, power or friendship are motives for doing something.

    (b)   The **mental process of choosing desired outcomes**, deciding how to go about them (and whether the likelihood of success warrants the amount of effort that will be necessary) and setting in motion the required behaviours.

    (c)   The **social process** by which other people motivate us to behave in the ways they wish. Motivation in this sense usually applies to the attempts of organisations to get workers to put in more effort.

1.2 Needs and goals

FAST FORWARD

People have certain **innate needs and goals**, through which they expect their needs to be satisfied Both these drive behaviour.

Individual behaviour is partly influenced by human biology, which requires certain basics for life. When the body is deprived of these essentials, biological forces called **needs** or **drives** are activated (eg hunger), and dictate the behaviour required to end the deprivation: eat, drink, flee and so on. However, we retain freedom of choice about *how* we satisfy our drives: they do not dictate specific or highly predictable behaviour. (Say you are hungry: how many specific ways of satisfying your hunger can you think of?)

Each individual also has a set of **goals**. The relative importance of those goals to the individual may vary with time, circumstances and other factors.

Influence	Comment
Childhood environment and education	Aspiration levels, family and career models and so on are formed at early stages of development.
Experience	This teaches us what to expect from life: we will either strive to repeat positive experiences, or to avoid or make up for negative ones.
Age and position	There is usually a gradual process of goal shift with age. Relationships and exploration may preoccupy young employees. Career and family goals tend to compete in the 20-40 age group: career launch and take-off may have to yield to the priorities associated with forming permanent relationships and having children.
Culture	Collectivist cultures (see Chapter 3) show a greater concern for relationships at work, while individualist cultures emphasise power and autonomy.
Self-concept	All the above factors are bound up with the individual's own self-image. The individual's assessments of his own abilities and place in society will affect the relative strength and nature of his needs and goals.

The **basic assumptions of motivation** are that:

(a) People behave in such a way as to **satisfy their needs** and fulfil their goals

(b) An organisation is in a position to **offer some of the satisfactions** people might seek: relationships and belonging, challenge and achievement, progress on the way to self-actualisation, security and structure and so on.

(c) The organisation can therefore **influence** people to behave in ways it desires (to secure work performance) by offering them the means to satisfy their needs and fulfil their goals in return for that behaviour. (This process of influence is called motivation).

(d) If people's needs are being met, and goals being fulfilled, at work, they are more likely to have a **positive attitude** to their work and to the organisation, and to experience **job satisfaction**.

1.3 How useful is 'motivation' as a concept?

FAST FORWARD

Motivation is a useful concept, despite the fact that the **impact** of motivation, job satisfaction and morale on performance are difficult to measure.

The impact of motivation and job satisfaction on **performance** is difficult to measure accurately.

(a) Motivation is about getting *extra* levels of commitment and performance from employees, over and above mere compliance with rules and procedures. If individuals can be motivated, by one means or another, they might work more efficiently (and productivity will rise) or they will produce a better quality of work.

(b) The case for job satisfaction as a factor in improved performance is not proven.

(c) The key is to work 'smarter' – not necessarily 'harder'.

Morale is a term drawn primarily from a military context, to denote the state of mind or spirit of a group (esprit de corps), particularly regarding **discipline** and **confidence**. It can be related to satisfaction, since low morale implies a state of dissatisfaction.

The signs by which **low morale or dissatisfaction** are gauged are also ambiguous.

(a)   **Low productivity** is not invariably a sign of low morale. There may be more concrete problems (eg with work organisation or technology).

(b)   **High labour turnover** is not a reliable indicator of low morale: the age structure of the workforce and other factors in natural wastage will need to be taken into account. Low turnover, likewise, is no evidence of high morale: people may be staying because of lack of other opportunities in the local job market, for example.

However, there is some evidence that satisfaction correlates with mental health, so symptoms of **stress** or psychological dysfunction may be a signal that all is not well. (Again, a range of non-work factors may be contributing.)

Attitude surveys may also be used to indicate workers' perception of their job satisfaction, by way of interview or questionnaire.

Question

Personal motivation

What factors in yourself or your organisation motivate you to:

(a)   Turn up to work at all?
(b)   Do an average day's work?
(c)   'Bust a gut' on a task or for a boss?

Go on – be honest!

1.4 Theories of motivation

FAST FORWARD

Many **theories** try to explain motivation and why and how people can be motivated.

One classification distinguishes between content and process theories.

(a)   **Content theories** ask the question: '**What** are the things that motivate people?'

They assume that human beings have a *set* of needs or desired outcomes. Maslow's hierarchy of needs and Herzberg's two-factor theory, both discussed shortly, are two of the most important approaches of this type.

(b)   **Process theories** ask the question: '**How** can people be motivated?'

They explore the process through which outcomes *become* desirable and are pursued by individuals. This approach assumes that people are able to select their goals and choose the paths towards them, by a conscious or unconscious process of calculation. Expectancy theory and Handy's 'motivation calculus', discussed later, are theories of this type.

Exam focus point

The distinction between process and content theories is a basic point – and a common pitfall for students: Note, as you read on, that despite the popularity of Maslow and Herzberg, they have their limitations – and they are not the *only* theories of motivation.

2 Content theories of motivation

Content theories of motivation suggest that the best way to motivate an employee is to find out what his/her needs are and offer him/her rewards that will satisfy those needs.

2.1 Maslow's hierarchy of needs

Maslow identified a hierarchy of needs which an individual will be motivated to satisfy, progressing towards higher order satisfactions, such as self-actualisation.

Abraham Maslow described five innate human needs, and put forward certain propositions about the motivating power of each need.

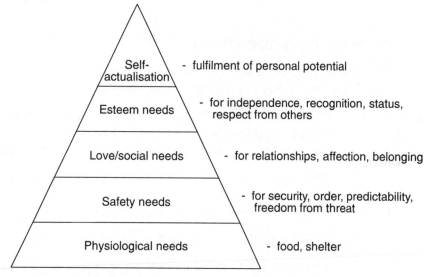

Self-actualisation - fulfilment of personal potential

Esteem needs - for independence, recognition, status, respect from others

Love/social needs - for relationships, affection, belonging

Safety needs - for security, order, predictability, freedom from threat

Physiological needs - food, shelter

(a)   An individual's needs can be arranged in a **'hierarchy** of relative pre-potency' (as shown). Each level of need is **dominant until satisfied**; only then does the next level of need become a motivating factor. A need which has been satisfied no longer motivates an individual's behaviour.

(b)   The need for self-actualisation can rarely be satisfied.

(c)   In addition, Maslow described:

   (i)   Freedom of enquiry and expression needs (for social conditions permitting free speech, and encouraging justice, fairness and honesty)

   (ii)   Knowledge and understanding needs (to gain knowledge of the environment, to explore, learn)

Question   Maslow's hierarchy of needs

Decide which of Maslow's categories the following fit into.

(a)   Receiving praise from your manager

(b)   A family party

(c)   An artist forgetting to eat

(d)   A man washed up on a desert island

(e)   A pay increase

(f)   Joining a local drama group

(g)   Being awarded the OBE

(h)   Buying a house

Answer

Maslow's categories for the listed circumstances are as follows.

(a) Esteem needs
(b) Social needs
(c) Self-actualisation needs overriding lower-level needs!
(d) Physiological needs
(e) Safety needs initially; esteem needs above in a certain income level
(f) Social needs or self-actualisation needs
(g) Esteem needs
(h) Safety needs or esteem needs

2.1.1 Evaluating Maslow's theory

Maslow's hierarchy is simple and intuitively attractive: you are unlikely to worry about respect if you are starving! However, it is only a theory and has been shown to have several major limitations.

(a) An individual's behaviour may be in response to **several needs**, and the same need may cause **different behaviour** in different individuals, so it is difficult to use the model to explain or predict an individual's behaviour in response to rewards.

(b) The hierarchy ignores the concept of **deferred gratification** (by which people are prepared to ignore current suffering for the promise of future benefits) and **altruistic behaviour** (by which people sacrifice their own needs for others).

(c) **Empirical verification** of the hierarchy is hard to come by.

(d) Research has revealed that the hierarchy reflects UK and US **cultural values**, which may not transfer to other contexts.

2.2 Herzberg's two-factor theory

FAST FORWARD

Herzberg identified two basic need systems: the need to avoid unpleasantness and the need for personal growth. He suggested factors which could be offered by organisations to satisfy both types of need: hygiene and motivator factors respectively.

Herzberg's two-factor theory is based on two needs: the need to avoid unpleasantness, and the need for personal growth.

(a) The need to avoid unpleasantness is satisfied through **hygiene factors**. Hygiene factors are to do with the environment and conditions of work, including:

- Company policy and administration
- Salary
- The quality of supervision
- Interpersonal relations
- Working conditions
- Job security

If inadequate, hygiene factors cause **dissatisfaction** with work (which is why they are also called 'dissatisfiers'). They work like sanitation, which minimises threats to health rather than actively promoting 'good health'.

(b)   The need for personal growth is satisfied by **motivator factors**.

These actively create job satisfaction (they are also called 'satisfiers') and are effective in motivating an individual to superior performance and effort. These factors are connected to the work itself, including:

- Status (although this may be a hygiene factor too)
- Advancement (or opportunities for it)
- Recognition by colleagues and management
- Responsibility

- Challenging work
- A sense of achievement
- Growth in the job

A lack of motivator factors will encourage employees to concentrate on the hygiene factors. These, although they can be regarded as motivators in the very short term, will eventually dissatisfy.

Herzberg suggested that where there is evidence of poor motivation, such as low productivity, poor quality and strikes, management should not pay too much attention to hygiene factors such as pay and conditions. Despite the fact that these are the traditional target for the aspirations of organised labour, their potential for bringing improvements to work attitudes is limited. Instead, Herzberg suggested three types of **job design** which would offer job satisfaction through enhanced motivator factors.

- Job enlargement
- Job rotation   } discussed in Section 3 below.
- Job enrichment

2.3 Evaluating Herzberg's theory

Herzberg's original study was concerned with 203 Pittsburgh engineers and accountants. His theory has therefore been criticised as being based on:

(a)   An inadequately small sample size

(b)   A limited cultural context (Western professionals)

The impact of job satisfaction (from motivator factors) on work performance has proved difficult to verify and measure.

Exam focus point

The Pilot Paper contains a question on monetary rewards and Herzberg's two-factor theory.

3 Process theories of motivation

FAST FORWARD

Process theories of motivation help managers to understand the dynamics of employees' decisions about what rewards are worth going for.

3.1 Vroom's expectancy theory

FAST FORWARD

Expectancy theory basically states that the strength of an individual's motivation to do something will depend on the extent to which he expects the results of his efforts to contribute to his personal needs or goals.

Victor Vroom stated a formula by which human motivation could be assessed and measured. He suggested that the strength of an individual's motivation is the product of two factors.

(a)   The strength of his **preference** for a certain outcome. Vroom called this **valence**: it can be represented as a positive or negative number, or zero – since outcomes may be desired, avoided or regarded with indifference.

(b)   His **expectation** that the outcome will in fact result from a certain behaviour. Vroom called this 'subjective probability' or **expectancy**. As a probability, it may be represented by any number between 0 (no chance) and 1 (certainty).

In its simplest form, the expectancy equation may be stated as:

$F = V \times E$

where: F = the force or strength of the individual's motivation to behave in a particular way
         V = valence: the strength of the individual preference for a given outcome or reward and
         E = expectancy: the individual's perception that the behaviour will result in the outcome/reward.

In this equation, the lower the values of valence or expectancy, the less the motivation. An employee may have a high expectation that increased productivity will result in promotion (because of managerial promises, say), but if he is indifferent or negative towards the idea of promotion (because he dislikes responsibility), he will not be motivated to increase his productivity. Likewise, if promotion is very important to him – but he does not believe higher productivity will get him promoted (because he has been passed over before, perhaps), his motivation will be low.

Exam focus point

> This equation is the subject of a 1 mark question on the Pilot Paper.

3.2 Managerial implications of process theories

Process theory suggests the following.

(a)   **Intended results should be made clear**, so that the individual can complete the motivation calculation by knowing what is expected, the reward, and how much effort it will take.

(b)   Individuals are more committed to **specific goals** which they **have helped to set themselves**, taking their needs and expectations into account.

(c)   Immediate and on-going **feedback** should be given. Without knowledge of actual results, there is no check that 'E' expenditure was justified (or will be justified in future).

(d)   If an individual is **rewarded** according to performance tied to standards (management by objectives), however, he or she may well set lower standards: the expectancy part of the calculation (likelihood of success and reward) is greater if the standard is lower, so less expense of 'E' is indicated.

4 Choosing a motivational approach

Two influential writers of the neo-human relations school argue that a manager's approach to motivating people depends on the **assumptions** (s)he makes about 'what makes them tick'.

4.1 McGregor: Theory X and Theory Y

FAST FORWARD

> **McGregor** suggested that a manager's approach is based on attitudes somewhere on a scale between two extreme sets of assumptions: Theory X (workers have to be coerced) and Theory Y (workers want to be empowered).

Douglas McGregor (*The Human Side of Enterprise*) suggested that managers (in the USA) tended to behave as though they subscribed to one of two sets of assumptions about people at work: Theory X and Theory Y.

(a) **Theory X** suggests that most people dislike work and responsibility and will avoid both if possible. Because of this, most people must be coerced, controlled, directed and/or threatened with punishment to get them to make an adequate effort. Managers who operate according to these assumptions will tend to supervise closely, apply detailed rules and controls, and use 'carrot and stick' motivators.

(b) **Theory Y** suggests that physical and mental effort in work is as natural as play or rest. The ordinary person does not inherently dislike work: according to the conditions it may be a source of satisfaction or dissatisfaction. The potentialities of the average person are rarely fully used at work. People can be motivated to seek challenge and responsibility in the job, if their goals can be integrated with those of the organisation. A manager with this sort of attitude to his staff is likely to be a consultative, facilitating leader, using positive feedback, challenge and responsibility as motivators.

Both are intended to be extreme sets of assumptions – not actual types of people. However, they also tend to be self-fulfilling prophecies. Employees treated as if 'Theory X' were true will begin to behave accordingly. Employees treated as if 'Theory Y' were true – being challenged to take on more responsibility – will rise to the challenge and behave accordingly.

Theory X and Theory Y can be used to heighten managers' awareness of the assumptions underlying their motivational style.

Exam focus point

McGregor's Theory X and Theory Y are relevant to the 'role of management' topic as well as motivation: you might like to bear it in mind as you study leadership styles.

5 Rewards and incentives

FAST FORWARD

Not all the **incentives** that an organisation can offer its employees are directly related to **monetary** rewards. The satisfaction of *any* of the employee's wants or needs may be seen as a reward for past performance, or an incentive for future performance.

Key terms

A **reward** is a token (monetary or otherwise) given to an individual or team in recognition of some contribution or success.

An **incentive** is the offer or promise of a reward for contribution or success, designed to motivate the individual or team to behave in such a way as to earn it. (In other words, the 'carrot' dangled in front of the donkey!)

Different individuals have different goals, and get different things out of their working life: in other words, they have different **orientations** to work. Why might a person work, or be motivated to work well?

(a) The **human relations** school of management theorists regarded **work relationships** as the main source of satisfaction and reward offered to the worker.

(b) Later writers suggested a range of 'higher-order' motivations, notably:

- **Job satisfaction**, interest and challenge in the job itself – rewarding work
- **Participation** in decision-making – responsibility and involvement

(c) **Pay** has always occupied a rather ambiguous position, but since people need money to live, it will certainly be part of the reward package.

5.1 Intrinsic and extrinsic factors

Rewards may be **extrinsic** (external to the work and individual) or **intrinsic** (arising from performance of the work itself).

Rewards offered to the individual at work may be of two basic types.

(a)   **Extrinsic rewards** are separate from (or external to) the job itself, and dependent on the decisions of others (that is, also external to the control of the workers themselves). Pay, benefits, non-cash incentives and working conditions (Herzberg's hygiene factors) are examples.

(b)   **Intrinsic rewards** are those which arise from the performance of the work itself (Herzberg's motivator factors). They are therefore psychological rather than material and relate to the concept of job satisfaction. Intrinsic rewards include the satisfaction that comes from completing a piece of work, the status that certain jobs convey, and the feeling of achievement that comes from doing a difficult job well.

5.2 A reward system

Child has outlined management criteria for a reward system. Such a system should do six things.

(a)   Encourage people to **fill job vacancies** and not leave

(b)   Increase the **predictability of employees' behaviour**, so that employees can be depended on to carry out their duties consistently and to a reasonable standard

(c)   Increase **willingness to accept change** and flexibility. (Changes in work practices are often 'bought' from trade unions with higher pay)

(d)   Foster and **encourage innovative behaviour**

(e)   **Reflect the nature of jobs** in the organisation and the skills or experience required. The reward system should therefore be consistent with seniority of position in the organisation structure, and should be thought fair by all employees

(f)   **Motivate**: that is, increase commitment and effort

5.3 Job design as a motivator

The **job** itself can be used as a motivator, or it can be a cause of dissatisfaction. **Job design** refers to how tasks are organised to create 'jobs' for individuals.

5.3.1 Micro-design

One of the consequences of mass production and scientific management was what might be called a **micro-division** of labour, or **job simplification**. Micro-designed jobs have the following **advantages**.

(a)   **Little training**. A job is divided up into the smallest number of sequential tasks possible. Each task is so simple and straightforward that it can be learned with very little training.

(b)   **Replacement**. If labour turnover is high, this does not matter because unskilled replacements can be found and trained to do the work in a very short time.

(c)   **Flexibility**. Since the skill required is low, workers can be shifted from one task to another very easily.

(d)   **Control**. If tasks are closely defined and standard times set for their completion, production is easier to predict and control.

(e)   **Quality**. Standardisation of work into simple tasks means that quality is easier to predict.

Disadvantages of micro-designed jobs, however, include the following.

(a) The work is **monotonous** and makes employees tired, bored and dissatisfied. The consequences will be high labour turnover, absenteeism, spoilage, unrest. People work better when their work is variable, unlike machines.

(b) An individual doing a simple task feels like a small cog in a large machine, and has no **sense of contributing** to the organisation's end product or service.

(c) Excessive specialisation **isolates** the individual in his or her work and inhibits not only social contacts with work mates, but knowledge generation.

(d) In practice, excessive job simplification leads to **lower quality,** through inattention and loss of morale.

5.3.2 Job enrichment

Frederick **Herzberg** suggested three ways of **improving job design**, to make jobs more interesting to the employee, and hopefully to improve performance: job enrichment, job enlargement and job rotation.

Key term

> **Job enrichment** is planned, deliberate action to build greater responsibility, breadth and challenge of work into a job. Job enrichment is similar to **empowerment**.

Job enrichment represents a 'vertical' extension of the job into greater levels of responsibility, challenge and autonomy. A job may be enriched by:

- Giving the job holder **decision-making tasks** of a higher order
- Giving the employee greater **freedom** to decide how the job should be done
- Encouraging employees to **participate** in the planning decisions of their superiors
- Giving the employee regular **feedback**

Job enrichment alone will not automatically make employees more productive. 'Even those who want their jobs enriched will expect to be rewarded with more than job satisfaction. Job enrichment is not a cheaper way to greater productivity. Its pay-off will come in the less visible costs of morale, climate and working relationships' *(Handy).*

5.3.3 Job enlargement

Key term

> **Job enlargement** is the attempt to widen jobs by increasing the number of operations in which a job holder is involved.

Job enlargement is a 'horizontal' extension of the job by increasing task variety and reducing task repetition.

(a) Tasks which span a larger part of the total production work should reduce boredom and add to task meaning, significance and variety.

(b) Enlarged jobs might be regarded as having higher status within the department, perhaps as stepping stones towards promotion.

Job enlargement is, however, limited in its intrinsic rewards, as asking workers to complete three separate tedious, unchallenging tasks is unlikely to be more motivating than asking them to perform just one tedious, unchallenging task!

5.3.4 Job rotation

Key term

Job rotation is the planned transfer of staff from one job to another to increase task variety.

Job rotation is a 'sequential' extension of the job. Herzberg cites a warehouse gang of four workers, where the worst job was seen as tying the necks of the sacks at the base of the hopper, and the best job as being the fork lift truck driving: job rotation would ensure that individuals spent equal time on all jobs. Job rotation is also sometimes seen as a form of training, where individuals gain wider experience by rotating as trainees in different positions.

It is generally admitted that the developmental value of job rotation is limited – but it can reduce the monotony of repetitive work.

5.3.5 Job optimisation

A well designed job should provide the individual with five **core dimensions** which contribute to job satisfaction.

(a) **Skill variety**: the opportunity to exercise different skills and perform different operations

(b) **Task identity**: the integration of operations into a 'whole' tasks (or meaningful segments of the task)

(c) **Task significance**: the task is perceived to have a role, purpose, meaning and value

(d) **Autonomy**: the opportunity to exercise discretion or self-management (eg in areas such as target-setting and work methods)

(e) **Feedback**: the availability of performance feedback enabling the individual to assess his progress and the opportunity to *give* feedback, be heard and influence results

5.4 Feedback as a motivator

FAST FORWARD Constructive performance **feedback** is important in job satisfaction and motivation.

There are two main types of feedback, both of which are valuable in enhancing performance and development.

(a) **Motivational feedback** is used to reward and reinforce positive behaviour and performance by praising and encouraging the individual. Its purpose is to increase **confidence**. By focusing on what is being done right (instead of on problems and shortcomings) the manager can energise employees to be more committed to overcoming their problems and shortcomings (*Blanchard and Bowles*).

(b) **Developmental feedback** is given when a particular area of performance needs to be improved, helping the individual to identify what needs to be changed and how this might be done. Its purpose is to increase **competence**. Note that this is still a 'positive' process: it should not be associated with 'negative' comments or criticism.

Constructive feedback is designed to widen options and encourage development. This does not mean giving only positive, motivational or 'encouraging' feedback about what a person has done: feedback about areas for improvement, given skilfully and sensitively, is in many ways more useful. It needs to be:

- Balanced with positives
- Specific
- Focused on behaviours/results – *not* personalities
- Objective (felt to be fair)

- Supportive/co-operative, emphasising the resources available to help the person improve
- Selective (not tackling all shortcomings at once)
- Encouraging

5.5 Participation as a motivator

FAST FORWARD

Participation in decision making (if genuine) can make people more committed to the task.

People generally want more interesting work and to have a say in decision-making. These expectations are a basic part of the movement towards greater **participation** at work.

The methods of achieving increased involvement have largely crystallised into two main streams.

(a)   **Immediate participation** is the term used to refer to the involvement of employees in the day-to-day decisions of their work group, eg through empowered or self-managed team working.

(b)   **Distant participation** refers to the process of including company employees in the decision-making machinery of the organisation at a senior level, dealing with long-term policy issues including investment and employment. (This is a contentious area of European industrial policy, also called 'industrial democracy'.)

Participation can involve employees and make them feel committed to their task, given the following conditions (5 Cs).

- **Certainty**: participation should be genuine.
- **Consistency**: efforts to establish participation should be made consistently over a long period.
- **Clarity**: the purpose of participation is made quite clear.
- **Capacity**: the individual has the ability and information to participate effectively.
- **Commitment**: the manager believes in and genuinely supports participation.

6 Pay as a motivator

FAST FORWARD

Pay is the most important of the hygiene factors, but it is ambiguous in its effect on motivation.

Pay is important because:

- It is a major cost for the organisation
- People feel strongly about it: it 'stands in' for a number of human needs and goals
- It is a legal issue (minimum wage, equal pay legislation)

6.1 How is pay determined?

There are a number of ways by which organisations determine pay.

(a)   **Job evaluation** is a systematic process for establishing the relative worth of jobs within an organisation. Its main purpose is to provide a rational basis for the design and maintenance of an equitable (and legally defensible) pay structure.

The salary structure is based on **job content**, and not on the personal merit of the job-holder. (The individual job-holder can be paid extra personal bonuses in reward for performance.)

(b)   **Fairness.** Pay must be **perceived** and felt to match the level of work, and the capacity of the individual to do it.

(c) **Negotiated pay scales** Pay scales, differentials and minimum rates may have been negotiated at plant, local or national level, according to factors such as legislation, government policy, the economy, the power of trade unions, the state of the labour market for relevant skills, productivity agreements and so on.

(d) **Market rates.** Market rates of pay will have most influence on pay structures where there is a standard pattern of supply and demand in the open labour market. If an organisation's rates fall below the benchmark rates in the local or national labour market from which it recruits, it will have trouble attracting and holding employees.

(e) **Individual performance in the job**, resulting in merit pay awards, or performance-related bonuses.

6.2 What do people want from pay?

Pay has a central – but ambiguous – role in motivation theory. It is not mentioned explicitly in any need list, but it offers the satisfaction of many of the various needs.

Individuals may also have needs unrelated to money, however, which money cannot satisfy, or which the pay system of the organisation actively denies (eg the need for leisure/family time – not overtime!) So to what extent is pay an inducement to better performance: a motivator or incentive?

Although the size of their income will affect their standard of living, most people tend not to be concerned to *maximise* their earnings. They may like to earn more but are probably more concerned to **earn enough** and to know that their pay is fair in comparison with the pay of others both inside and outside the organisation.

Pay is a 'hygiene' factor: it gets taken for granted, and so is more usually a source of dissatisfaction than satisfaction. However, pay is the most important of the hygiene factors, according to Herzberg. It is valuable not only in its power to be **converted** into a wide range of other satisfactions, but also as a consistent **measure of worth** or value, allowing employees to compare themselves and be compared with other individuals or occupational groups inside and outside the organisation.

Research has also illustrated that workers may have an **instrumental orientation** to work: the attitude that work is not an end in itself but a means to other ends, through earning money.

 Case Study

In what became known as the 'Affluent Worker' research, *Goldthorpe, Lockwood et al* found that highly-paid Luton car assembly workers experienced their work as routine and dead-end. The researchers concluded that they had made a rational decision to enter employment offering high monetary reward rather than intrinsic interest: they were getting out of their jobs what they most wanted from them.

The Luton researchers did not claim that all workers have an instrumental orientation to work, however, but suggested that a person will seek a suitable balance of:

- The rewards which are important to him
- The deprivations he feels able to put up with

Even those with an instrumental orientation to work have limits to their purely financial aspirations, and will cease to be motivated by money if the deprivations – in terms of long working hours, poor conditions, social isolation or whatever – become too great.

High taxation rates may also weigh the deprivation side of the calculation: workers may perceive that a great deal of extra effort will in fact earn them little extra reward.

Pay is only one of several intrinsic and extrinsic rewards offered by work. If pay is used to motivate, it can only do so in a wider context of the job and the other rewards. Thanks, praise and recognition, for example, are alternative forms of positive reinforcement.

Question

Pay as a motivator

Herzberg says that money is a **hygiene** factor in the motivation process. If this is true, it means that lack of money can demotivate, but the presence of money will not in itself be a motivator.

How far do you agree with this proposition? Can individuals be motivated by a pay rise?

6.3 Performance related pay (PRP)

FAST FORWARD

Performance related pay (PRP) is a form of incentive system, awarding extra pay for extra output or performance.

Key term

Performance related pay (PRP) is related to output (in terms of the number of items produced or time taken to produce a unit of work), or results achieved (performance to defined standards in key tasks, according to plan).

The most common individual PRP scheme for wage earners is straight **piecework**: payment of a fixed amount per unit produced, or operation completed.

For managerial and other salaried jobs, however, a form of **management by objectives** will probably be applied. PRP is often awarded at the discretion of the line manager, although guidelines may suggest, for example, that those rated exceptional get a bonus of 10% whereas those who have performed less well only get, say, 3%.

(a)   Key results can be identified and specified, for which merit awards will be paid.

(b)   There will be a clear model for evaluating performance and knowing when, or if, targets have been reached and payments earned.

(c)   The exact conditions and amounts of awards can be made clear to the employee, to avoid uncertainty and later resentment.

For service and other departments, a PRP scheme may involve **bonuses** for achievement of key results, or **points schemes**, where points are awarded for performance of various criteria (efficiency, cost savings, quality of service and so on). Certain points totals (or the highest points total in the unit, if a competitive system is used) then win cash or other awards.

6.3.1 Evaluating PRP

Benefits of PRP

- Improves commitment and capability
- Complements other HR initiatives
- Improves focus on the business's performance objectives
- Encourages two-way communication
- Greater supervisory responsibility
- It recognises achievement when other means are not available

Potential problems

- Subjectivity of awards for less measurable criteria (eg 'teamwork')
- Encouraging short-term focus and target-hitting (rather than improvements)
- Divisive/against team working (if awards are individual)
- Difficulties gaining union acceptance (if perceived to erode basic pay)

Question   PRP as a motivator

Why might PRP fail to motivate?

Answer

(a) The rewards from PRP are often too small to motivate effectively. Anyhow, some employees may not expect to receive the rewards and hence will not put in the extra effort.

(b) It is often unfair, especially in jobs where success is determined by uncontrollable factors.

(c) If people are rewarded individually, they may be less willing to work as a team.

(d) People may concentrate on short-term performance indicators rather than on longer-term goals such as innovation or quality. In other words, people put all their energy into hitting the target rather than doing their job better.

(e) PRP schemes have to be well designed to ensure performance is measured properly, people consider them to be fair and there is consent to the scheme.

6.4 Rewarding the team

> **FAST FORWARD**
>
> Various forms of **group rewards** can be used as an incentive to co-operative performance and mutual accountability.

6.4.1 Group bonus schemes

Group incentive schemes typically offer a bonus for a team which achieves or exceeds specified targets. Offering bonuses to a whole team may be appropriate for tasks where individual contributions cannot be isolated, workers have little control over their individual output because tasks depend on each other, or where team-building is particularly required. It may enhance team-spirit and co-operation as well as provide performance incentives, but it may also create pressures within the group if some individuals are seen not to be pulling their weight.

6.4.2 Profit-sharing schemes

Profit-sharing schemes offer employees (or selected groups) bonuses, directly related to profits or value added. Profit sharing is based on the belief that all employees can contribute to profitability, and that that contribution should be recognised. The effects may include profit-consciousness and motivation in employees, commitment to the future prosperity of the organisation and so on.

The actual incentive value and effect on productivity may be wasted, however, if the scheme is badly designed.

(a) The sum should be **significant**.

(b) There should be a **clear and timely link** between effort or performance and reward. Profit shares should be distributed as frequently as possible, consistent with the need for reliable information on profit forecasts, targets etc and the need to amass significant amounts for distribution.

(c)   The scheme should only be introduced if profit forecasts indicate a **reasonable chance of achieving** the above: profit sharing is welcome when profits are high, but the potential for disappointment is great.

(d)   The greatest effect on productivity arising from the scheme may in fact arise from its use as a focal point for **discussion** with employees, about the relationship between their performance and results, areas and targets for improvement etc. Management must be seen to be committed to the principle.

Chapter Roundup

- **Motivation** is 'a decision-making process through which the individual chooses desired outcomes and sets in motion the behaviour appropriate to acquiring them'. (*Huczynski and Buchanan*).

- People have certain **innate needs and goals**, through which they expect their needs to be satisfied. Both of these drive behaviour.

- **Motivation** is a **useful concept**, despite the fact that the impact of motivation, job satisfaction and morale on performance are difficult to measure.

- Many **theories** try to explain motivation and why and how people can be motivated.

- **Content theories** of motivation suggest that the best way to motivate an employee is to find out what his/her needs are and offer him/her rewards that will satisfy those needs.

- **Maslow** identified a hierarchy of needs which an individual will be motivated to satisfy, progressing towards higher order satisfactions, such as self-actualisation.

- **Herzberg** identified two basic need systems: the need to avoid unpleasantness and the need for personal growth. He suggested factors which could be offered by organisations to satisfy both types of need: hygiene and motivator factors respectively.

- **Process theories** of motivation help managers to understand the dynamics of employees' decisions about what rewards are worth going for.

- **Expectancy theory** basically states that the strength of an individual's motivation to do something will depend on the extent to which he expects the results of his efforts to contribute to his personal needs or goals.

- **McGregor** suggested that a manager's approach is based on attitudes somewhere on a scale between two extreme sets of assumptions: Theory X (workers have to be coerced) and Theory Y (workers want to be empowered).

- Not all the **incentives** that an organisation can offer its employees are directly related to **monetary** rewards. The satisfaction of *any* of the employee's wants or needs may be seen as a reward for past performance, or an incentive for future performance.

- **Rewards** may be **extrinsic** (external to the work and individual) or **intrinsic** (arising from performance of the work itself).

- The **job** itself can be used as a motivator, or it can be a cause of dissatisfaction. **Job design** refers to how tasks are organised to create 'jobs' for individuals.

- Frederick **Herzberg** suggested three ways of **improving job design**, to make jobs more interesting to the employee, and hopefully to improve performance: job enrichment, job enlargement and job rotation.

- Constructive performance **feedback** is important in job satisfaction and motivation.

- **Participation** in decision making (if genuine) can make people more committed to the task.

- **Pay** is the most important of the hygiene factors, but it is ambiguous in its effect on motivation.

- **Performance related pay (PRP)** is a form of incentive system, awarding extra pay for extra output or performance.

- Various forms of **group rewards** can be used as an incentive to co-operative performance and mutual accountability.

Quick Quiz

1   What is (a) positive reinforcement and (b) self actualisation?

2   List the five categories in Maslow's Hierarchy of Needs.

3   How might an individual's goals change with age?

4   List some ways in which an organisation can offer motivational satisfaction.

5   What is the difference between a reward and an incentive?

6   According to Herzberg, leadership style is a motivator factor. *True or false?*

7   Explain the formula 'F = V × E'.

8   'People will work harder and harder to earn more and more pay.' Do you agree? Why (or why not)?

9   A 'horizontal' extension of the job to increase task variety is called:

   A   Job evaluation
   B   Job enrichment
   C   Job enlargement
   D   Job rotation

Answer to Quick Quiz

1   (a)   Encouraging a certain type of behaviour by rewarding it
      (b)   Personal growth and fulfilment of potential

2   Physiological, safety, love/social, esteem, self-actualisation

3   Increasingly they include forming relationships, having children, power and autonomy

4   Relationships, belonging, challenge, achievement, progress, security, money

5   A reward is given for some contribution or success. An incentive is an offer of reward

6   False: it is a hygiene factor

7   Force of motivation = Valence × Expectation

8   This is true to an extent. There is however a physical limit to how much people can work, and in the end factors other than pay will become important once people believe they earn enough money for their needs.

9   C. Make sure you can define all the other terms as well

Part F

Recruiting and developing effective employees

Personal effectiveness and communication

14

Topic list	Syllabus reference
1 Personal development plans	F2 (a)(b)
2 Time management	F2 (c)(d)
3 The role of information technology	F2 (e)
4 Coaching, mentoring and counselling	F2 (f)
5 Communication in the workplace	F3 (a)
6 Formal communication processes	F3 (b)(c)(e)
7 Informal communication channels	F3 (c)
8 Barriers to communication	F3 (d)(f)
9 Communication methods	F3 (g)

Introduction

This chapter draws together a number of topics that relate to the way that people do their jobs. It is not always enough for them to deal with the routine work that comes to them. If the organisation is to prosper, they must be active and creative in their approach.

We start the chapter with a **Section 1** focuses on personal development plans, which are valuable for setting out the activities to ensure development and improved job performance.

Section 2 covers time management, a very necessary skill for all busy people. Good time management depends to some extent on ruthless prioritisation and this requires a good understanding by staff of just what their roles are. The role of information technology in improving personal effectiveness is discussed in **Section 3**.

Section 4 covers coaching, mentoring and counselling as tools in personal development.

The rest of this chapter (**Sections 5–9**) is principally concerned with **communication**. Communication is fundamental to the success of any organisation of any size, since it is only *via* communication that we know what is to be done, by whom and how. Communication is also fundamental to **motivation**, as you discovered in Chapter 13.

Study guide

		Intellectual level
F2	**Techniques for improving personal effectiveness at work and their benefits**	
(a)	Explain the purposes of personal development plans.	1
(b)	Describe how a personal development plan should be formulated, implemented, monitored and reviewed by the individual.	1
(c)	Explain the importance of effective time management.	1
(d)	Describe the barriers to effective time management and how they may be overcome.	1
(e)	Describe the role of information technology in improving personal effectiveness.	1
(f)	Explain the purposes and processes of coaching, mentoring and counselling and their benefits.	1
F3	**Features of effective communication**	
(a)	Define communications.	1
(b)	Explain a simple communication model: sender, message, receiver, feedback, noise.	1
(c)	Explain formal and informal communication and their importance in the workplace.	1
(d)	Identify the consequences of ineffective communication.	1
(e)	Describe the attributes of effective communication.	1
(f)	Describe the barriers to effective communication and identify practical steps that may be taken to overcome them.	1
(g)	Describe the main methods and patterns of communication.	1

Exam guide

Many of these topics – such as barriers to communication, qualities of effective communication, counselling – may be set as questions. An article in *student accountant* has pointed out that 'if there is one prerequisite that sets accountancy apart from other professions, it is the need to communicate clearly and concisely both internally and externally. Communication is the core of the accountancy profession, transmitting information from one person to another, from one organisation to another – or a combination of both – and to the shareholders and other stakeholders of the organisation.' The article goes on to discuss various barriers to communication and how they can be overcome. The nature and direction of organisational communication, the need for good communication, the qualities of good communication, barriers to communication and ways to improve it are all key examinable topics, because of their importance to the accountant's role.

1 Personal development plans

Key terms

> A **personal development plan** is a clear developmental action plan for an individual which incorporates a wide set of developmental opportunities, including formal training.
>
> **Self development** may be defined as: 'personal development, with the person taking primary responsibility for his or her own learning and for choosing the means to achieve this.' (Pedler, Burgoyne & Boydell)

1.1 Personal development objectives

Personal development implies a wide range of activities with the objectives of:

- Improving **performance** in an existing job
- Improving **skills and competences**, perhaps in readiness for career development or organisational change
- Planning experience and pathways for **career development** and/or advancement within the organisation
- Acquiring **transferable skills** and competences for general 'employability' or change of direction
- Pursuing **personal growth** towards the fulfilment of one's personal interests and potential

1.2 A systematic approach to personal development planning

A systematic approach to planning your own development will include the following steps.

Step 1   Select an **area for development**: a limitation to overcome or a strength to build on. Your goals might be based on your need to **improve performance** in your current job and/or on your **career goals**, taking into account possible changes in your current role and opportunities within and outside the organisation. You might carry out a personal SWOT (strengths, weaknesses, opportunities, threats) analysis. One helpful tool is an interest/ aptitude and performance matrix, on which you can identify skills which you require (don't do well) but for which you can build on your aptitudes and interests (like).

Performance

	High	Low
High (Aptitude/interest)	Like and do well	Like but don't do well
Low (Aptitude/interest)	Dislike but do well	Dislike and don't do well

Step 2   Set a SMARTER (specific, measurable, agreed, realistic, time-bounded, evaluated and reviewed) **learning objective**: what you want to be able to do or do better, and in what time scale.

Step 3   Determine how you will move towards your objective:

- **Research** relevant learning resources and opportunities
- **Evaluate** relevant learning resources and opportunities for suitability, attainability and cost-effectiveness

- Secure any **support or authorisation** required from your manager or training development

Step 4 Formulate a comprehensive and specific action plan, including:

- The SMARTER objective

- The learning approaches you will use, described as **specific actions** to take. (Ask a colleague to provide feedback; watch a training video; enrol in a course.) Each action should have a **realistic time scale** or schedule for completion.

- A **monitoring and review plan**. Precisely how and when (or how often) will you assess your progress and performance, against your objectives? (Seek feedback? review results? pass an end-of-course test?)

Step 5 Secure **agreement** to your action plan (if required to mobilise organisational support or resources)

Step 6 **Implement** your action plan.

Six marks were available in the Pilot Paper for this syllabus, for outlining the stages in preparing a PDP. A useful reminder not to neglect your study and revision in what may appear to be 'soft' syllabus topics!

2 Time management

FAST FORWARD

Time is a scarce resource and managers' time must be used to the best effect. **Urgency** and **importance** must be recognised and distinguished. Tasks must be prioritised and scheduled. In-trays can be managed using the ACIB method. Other important matters are correct use of the telephone, availability to callers and seeing tasks through to completion.

The scarcest resource any of us has is time. No amount of investment can add more hours to the day or weeks to the year. All we can do is take steps to make more effective use of the time which is available to us. Planning how we spend our time is as normal to us as planning how we will spend our income, and you should already have considerable experience of both.

To be worth his or her pay, every employee needs to add more value than he or she costs per hour. If you do the same exercise for the whole team, you can see how expensive the time of your section actually is, and why keeping colleagues waiting to start a meeting or training course is more serious than just a breach of manners. It is important, therefore, that managers work as efficiently as possible.

Key term

Time management is the process of allocating time to tasks in the most effective manner.

FAST FORWARD

Effective time management involves attention to:

- Goal or target setting
- Action planning
- Prioritising
- Focus
- Urgency
- Organisation

Time management tasks

(a) **Identifying objectives** and the key tasks which are most relevant to achieving them - sorting out what the supervisor **must** do, from what he **could** do, and from what he would **like** to do. *Urgent* is not always the same as *important*.

(b) **Prioritising and scheduling**: assessing key tasks for relative importance and amount of time required. Routine non-essential tasks should be delegated - or done away with if possible. Routine key tasks should be organised as standard procedures and systems. Non-routine key tasks will have to be carefully scheduled as they arise, according to their urgency and importance; an up-to-date diary with a **carry forward system** to follow-up action will be helpful.

(c) **Planning and control**: Schedules should be regularly checked for disruption by the unexpected: priorities will indicate which areas may have to be set aside for more urgent items. Information and control systems in the organisation should be utilised so that problems can be anticipated, and sudden decisions can be made on the basis of readily available information.

2.1 Principles of time management

The key principles of time management can be depicted as follows

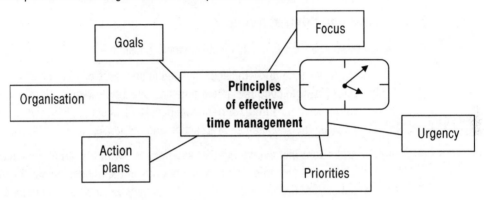

2.1.1 Goals

If you have no idea what it is you are supposed to accomplish all the time in the world will not be long enough to get it done. Nor is there any way of telling whether you have done it or not. To be useful, goals need to be SMART:

Specific

Measureable

Attainable

Realistic and

Time-bounded

In work terms you could probably set **specific goals** by reference to your job description: 'prepare and despatch invoices for all goods sold'; 'issue monthly statements'; 'monitor slow paying customers'.

However, **measurable** and **time-bounded goals** are very important for **effective time management**. If you say 'My goal is to see that invoices are issued and despatched for all goods sold on the day of sale' you have a very clear and specific idea of what it is that you have to achieve and whether you are achieving it or not.

2.1.2 Action plans

Now you must make **written action plans that set out how you intend to achieve your goals**: the timescale, the deadlines, the tasks involved, the people to see or write to, the resources required, how one plan fits in with (or conflicts with) another. These need not be lengthy or formal plans: start with **notes, lists** or **flowcharts** that will help you to capture and clarify your ideas and intentions.

2.1.3 Priorities

Now you can set priorities from your plan. You do this by deciding which tasks are the most important: what is the most valuable use of your time at that very moment?

Which task would you do if you only had time to do one task? That is your first priority. Then imagine that it will turn out that you have enough time to do one more thing before you have to leave. What would you do next? That is your second priority. Continue in this vein until you have identified three or four top priorities. Then get on with them, in order.

2.1.4 Focus: one thing at a time

Work on **one thing at a time** until it is finished, where possible.

(a) If a task cannot be completely finished in one 'session', complete everything that it is in your power to complete at that time and use a **follow-up system** to make sure that it is not forgotten in the future. Correspondence, in particular, will involve varying periods of delay between question and answer, action and response.

(b) **Make sure that everything that you need is available before you start work.** If it isn't, you may not be able to do the task yet, but one of the things on your 'to do' list will be to order supplies of the necessary forms or stationery, or to obtain the required information or do whatever it is that is holding you up.

(c) **Before you start a task clear away everything from your desk that you do not need for that particular task.** Put them where you will be able to retrieve them when you come to deal with the tasks that you need them for. It is quite hard to discipline yourself to do this because it might take some time and you might feel that that time could be spent doing other things. However, once tidy working becomes a habit, it will take no time at all, because your desk will always be either clear or have on it only the things you are using at that precise moment. One of the best ways of helping yourself to concentrate and handle things one at a time is to remove distractions.

2.1.5 Urgency: do it now!

Do not put off large, difficult or unpleasant tasks simply because they are large, difficult or unpleasant. If you put it off, today's routine will be tomorrow's emergency: worse, today's emergency will be even more of an emergency tomorrow. Do it now!

Think for a moment about how you behave when you know something is very urgent. If you oversleep, you leap out of bed the moment you wake up. If you suddenly find out that a report has to go out last post today rather than tomorrow afternoon, then you get on with it at once. We are saying that you should **develop the ability to treat everything that you have to do in this way.**

2.1.6 Organisation

Apart from working to plans, checklists and schedules, your work organisation might be improved by the following.

(a) **An ABCD method of in-tray management**. When a task or piece of paper comes into your in-tray or 'to do' list, you should never merely look at it and put it back for later. This would mean you would handle it more than once – usually over and over again, if it is a trivial or unpleasant item! Resolve to take one of the following approaches

Act on the item immediately

Bin it, if you are sure it is worthless, irrelevant and unnecessary

Create a definite plan for coming back to the item: get it on your schedule, timetable or 'to do list'

Delegate it to someone else to handle

(b) **Organise your work in batches** of jobs requiring the same activities, files, equipment and so on. Group your filing tasks or word processing tasks, for example, and do them in a session, rather than having to travel to and fro or compete for equipment time for each separate task.

(c) **Take advantage of your natural work patterns**. Self-discipline is aided by developing regular hours or days for certain tasks, like dealing with correspondence first thing, or filing at the end of the day. If you are able to plan your own schedules, you might also take into account your personal patterns of energy, concentration, alertness etc. Large or complex tasks might be undertaken in the mornings before you get tired.

2.2 Improving time management

Plan each day. A task list of things to be done each day will be a start, but a simple task list gives no idea of the priority of each task. The daily list should include the most important tasks as well as urgent but less important tasks.

Produce a longer-term plan. This can highlight the important tasks so that sufficient time is spent on them on a daily basis. A longer-term plan can also help cope with more complicated jobs, by breaking them down into a number of stages. In addition, long-term planning helps anticipate busy periods so that backlogs of routine work are cleared during quieter times.

Assess the opportunity costs. The opportunity cost of using time in a particular fashion is the benefit that would have been gained if it had been used in a different way. For example, travelling by car may be more convenient than travelling by train, but you may be able to work on the train.

The **half open door**. Although having an open door is a common policy, **do not be available to all comers at all times**. There are several ways of preventing interruptions.

(a) Be **unavailable**. Use call-diverting facilities on your telephone (and/or ask your secretary, if you have one). Alternatively you can try working somewhere other than your usual desk or office. Plan time for your own work.

(b) Set **'surgery hours'** during which your door is open to visitors.

(c) Determine which **people are 'urgent' or 'important'**. Your immediate boss might be asked to wait, whereas the Chief Executive must be attended to immediately.

(d) Arrange **regular meetings with people you have to deal with frequently** (immediate boss, subordinates). These meetings can be used to deal with routine business and also all but the most important problems.

(e) **Stay in control of meetings**, by asking people to come back later or saying that you can spare them X minutes (and no longer).

(f) **Do not allow people to by-pass the hierarchy**. Most people should deal with your staff first of all.

Stay in control of the telephone. The telephone can be a major barrier to good time management, by being a source of constant interruption and a means of communication which, through poor technique, is used inefficiently. The following are good ways of improving telephone time management.

(a) **Only take calls during certain times** and divert calls to your secretary during the rest of the day. Alternatively use your secretary as a screen so that only important calls are put through to you immediately.

(b) **Group calls** so that you make a number of calls together.

(c) If someone is unavailable when you call, say that you'll **ring back at a specified time,** rather than allowing the person to ring you back at an inconvenient time for you.

(d) You should **know what you aim to achieve by each telephone call**, also what information you will need to have handy and how long the call will take.

Make appointments with yourself. If you need to spend time alone, making plans, reviewing progress - or indeed making sure that you get personal time at work or at home for rest and relaxation - it is a good idea to treat this as if it were a meeting. Make a time for it in your diary, and stick to it: take it seriously, and do not let other activities encroach on it.

Work to schedules and checklists. Here is what you should do.

(a) Don't rely on memory for appointments, events and duties. Keep a monthly list of the tasks you want to achieve and a target date.

(b) Try to work on **one thing at a time**, and to **finish each task** you start. Split large tasks into smaller tasks.

(c) **Don't put off** large, difficult or unpleasant tasks simply because they are large, difficult or unpleasant. Today's routines will be tomorrow's emergencies, and today's emergencies will **still** be tomorrow's emergencies.

(d) **Learn to anticipate** and allow for work coming up; recognise and set reasonable deadlines.

Organise work in batches, with relevant files to hand, machines switched on and so on to save time spent in turning from one job to another.

Maintain a list of small jobs which can be completed whilst waiting for a meeting or telephone call.

Take advantage of work patterns. Self-discipline is aided by developing regular hours or days for certain tasks, like dealing with correspondence first thing or filing at the end of the day. If you are able to plan your own schedules, you might also take into account your personal patterns of energy, concentration and alertness. Large or complex tasks might be undertaken in the mornings before you get tired, or perhaps late at night with fewer distractions, while Friday afternoon is not usually a good time to start a demanding task in the office.

Follow up tasks and see them through. Uncompleted work, necessary future action, expected results or feedback should be scheduled for the appropriate time. Checklists are also useful for making sure an operation is completed, marking the stage reached in case it has to be handed over to someone else or temporarily laid aside.

Exam focus point	In the examination you are likely to be faced with questions involving helping others with their time management. The list of ideas above may be useful examples, or suggestions for such questions, but add more of your own.

2.3 Prioritisation

Prioritising tasks involves ordering tasks in order of preference or priority, based on:

- The relative consequences of timely or untimely performance
- Importance
- Dependency of other people of tasks
- Urgency
- Defined deadlines, timescales and commitments

Each of us has to identify a system for prioritising our work and this involves planning. If you treat work in a reactive and ad hoc way, then you will respond to tasks as they land on your desk with no consideration of their importance. Effective managers take the time to review what has to be done and consider each activity in terms of its importance, priority and urgency, as well as the potential for delegation.

Key term

> **Prioritisation** involves identifying key results (objectives which *must* be achieved if the section is to fulfil its aims) and key tasks (those things that *must* be done on time and to the required standard if the key results are to be achieved).

A job will be **important** compared to other tasks, if it satisfies at least one of three conditions.

- It adds value to the organisation's output.
- It comes from a source deserving high priority, such as a customer or senior manager.
- The potential consequences of failure are long-term, difficult to reverse, far reaching and costly.

One of the problems managers have in allocating their time, comes from determining what tasks are **important** as defined above and distinguishing these from **urgent** tasks, which may have a deadline but less importance.

- Tasks both urgent and important should be dealt with now, and given a fair amount of time.

- Tasks **not** urgent but still important will become urgent as the deadline looms closer. Some of these tasks can be delegated.

- Tasks urgent but not important should be delegated, or designed out of your job. The task might be urgent to someone else, but not to you.

- Tasks neither urgent nor important should be delegated or binned.

Question

Time management

According to Charles Handy, managers must live in two dimensions at once: the present and the future. This inevitably causes a conflict between focusing on the pressing demands of today and creating space in which to plan strategically for the opportunities of tomorrow. Assuming you agree with Charles Handy, how can we improve our personal time management so that both these activities can be achieved effectively?

Answer

Personal time management

Every manager faces a range of constraints and demands. Dealing with the two time dimensions of the **present** and the **future** requires the manager to have a clear view about how to manage personal time and how to organise the workload. *John Adair* in his book *How to Manage Your Time*, suggests that there are five problems common to almost all managers.

(a) **Procrastinating**

Particularly when a job seems boring, we can easily put it off only to add it to the next day's or next week's workload. Resolving to put aside an hour a day, for example, for those jobs that you would like to put off, will result in a better use of the time.

(b) **Delegating ineffectively**

Almost all managers have subordinates. However some managers seem to think that they have to carry out all the functions that have been delegated to them. Managers can save time by developing their subordinates by giving them tasks that are challenging and worthwhile to do. In many cases it is the manager's fear of 'letting go' which is the problem. To be effective, a manager needs to let go and develop the potential of the subordinate through delegation.

(c) **Mismanaging the paperwork**

Although we talk about the 'paperless office' managers are increasingly having to deal with large amounts of information and data. Being submerged in paper wastes time and does not allow the manager to spend time on matters that are more vital to the efficient running of the organisation. The old maxim 'never pick up a piece of paper and put it down without doing something with it' is good advice for managers. A short time organising papers can save time, particularly if these are vital documents that are needed for a meeting that day.

(d) **Holding unnecessary meetings**

All managers know just how valuable a meeting can be - whether it be a formal or informal meeting. However, managers need to ask themselves a number of questions such as 'What would happen if we didn't hold this meeting?' or 'Why are we meeting?' or 'What is the objective of the meeting?' Thus, meetings need to give value for the time they take and have the people with the skills and expertise that are essential for the objectives to be met.

(e) **Failing to set priorities**

Some managers can find it difficult to cope with changing pressures from above, in addition to running their departments or sections.

Setting priorities is therefore an essential part of the job.

2.4 Work planning

FAST FORWARD

Work planning includes the following basic steps:

- Establishing priorities
- Loading, allocation of tasks
- Sequencing of tasks
- Scheduling: estimating the time taken to complete a task and working forwards or backwards to determine start or finish times

Work planning, as the term implies, means planning how, when and by whom work should be done, in order that objectives can be efficiently met. At an individual level, this may involve the following.

Planning activity	Example
Scheduling **routine tasks** so that they will be completed at pre-determined times	You plan to complete bank reconciliations every month.
Handling **high-priority tasks and deadlines**: working into the routine any urgent tasks which interrupt the usual level of working	You adjust your plans so that you can prepare an urgent costing requested by the sales manager.
Adapting to **changes and unexpected demands**	A colleague may go off sick: there should be a contingency plan to enable to you to provide cover for him or her.
Setting **standards** against which performance will be measured	You set a target to complete a certain number of costings to a certain level of accuracy.
Co-ordinating your own plans and efforts with those of others	You plan to get your costings to the sales meeting in time for sales staff to prepare a quote for a client.

Work planning consists of a number of basic steps.

(a) **Allocating work** to people and machines (sometimes called **loading**)

(b) Determining the **order** in which activities are performed (prioritising: sometimes called **activity scheduling** or **task sequencing**)

(c) Determining exactly **when** each activity will be performed (timetabling: sometimes called **time scheduling**)

(d) Establishing **checks and controls** to ensure that deadlines are being met and that routine tasks are still achieving their objectives

2.4.1 Loading

The allocation of tasks to other people, or machines, will depend upon a number of factors.

- The skills and expertise required to do the task
- The other work already allocated to people with the appropriate skills
- The demand for commonly used facilities (such as computers and printers)

2.4.2 Sequencing

We have already discussed prioritising on the basis of commitments, urgency and importance. If these issues are not involved, here are some other possible criteria for sequencing tasks.

(a) **Arrival time**. This is the first come, first served basis that you encounter all the time, in the bank, or whenever you ring somebody, for example. The order in which things are done are determined by the things themselves.

(b) **Most nearly finished**. This is not very scientific, but it recognises that great frustration can be caused by interrupting a job just before it is completed.

(c) **Shortest queue at next operation**. For example, seeing that the typist is about to run out of work, you might draft some letters before making the lengthy series of phone calls that you are due to make.

(d) **Least changeover cost**. For example if you have too much to do and are about to go on holiday, you should finish off all the things that it will be difficult for someone else to take over while you are away.

(e)   **Shortest task first, then next shortest, and so on**. This is not very scientific, but it gets lots of things out of the way quickly.

(f)   **Longest job first, then next longest, and so on**. Again this is not very scientific, but it gets the most daunting task out of the way rather than letting it hang about becoming ever more daunting.

2.4.3 Scheduling

Activity scheduling provides a list of activities, in the order in which they must be completed: we have called this task sequencing. **Time scheduling** adds to this the timescale or start and end times/dates for each activity.

Determining the time that it will take to do a task – for the purpose of setting targets – is easy if it is a **routine task** that you have done a thousand times before. Simply keep a note of how long it takes you, on average.

With **non-routine tasks**, particularly substantial ones, it can be far more difficult to determine how long to allow. You can ask someone with more experience than you, or you might be able to break the new task down into smaller stages whose duration you can more easily estimate. The important thing is to be realistic.

Time schedules can be determined by different methods.

(a)   **Forward scheduling** can be used, starting with a given start time/date and working through estimated times for each stage of the task (allowing for some which may be undertaken simultaneously, by more than one person or machine) to the estimated **completion** time/date. This method can be used, for example, when completing routine accounting tasks.

(b)   **Reverse scheduling** is where you start with a **completion** time/date or deadline, and work **backwards** through estimated times for each stage of the task, determining **start times** for each stage – and for the task as a whole – which will enable you to meet the deadline. This method can be used to meet deadlines, for example, for a report to be prepared, for office relocation, and many other projects which have a set completion date.

Exam focus point

> This topic may seem like common sense, but do not be tempted to ignore it. The specifics of time management, and time management principles, lend themselves very nicely to exam questions.

3 The role of information technology

In this section we discuss some of the most significant developments in communication technology, and the impact these developments have had on the way people do their work.

Key terms

> **Digital** means 'of digits or numbers'. Digital information is information in a coded (binary) form.
>
> Information in **analogue** form uses continuously variable signals.

3.1 Modems and digital transmission

New technologies require **transmission systems** capable of delivering substantial quantities of data at great speed.

3.2 Mobile communications

Networks for portable telephone communications, also known as '**cellular**' or '**mobile phones**', have boomed in developed countries since the 1990s.

Digital networks have been developed which are better able to support data transmission than the older analogue networks, with **higher transmission speeds** and **less likelihood of data corruption**.

3.3 Voice messaging systems

Voice messaging systems answer and route telephone calls. Typically, when a call is answered a **recorded message** tells the caller to dial the extension required, or to hold if they want to speak to the operator.

3.4 Computer bulletin boards

A computer bulletin board consists of a central mailbox or area on a computer server where people can **deposit messages** for everyone to see, and, in turn, **read what other people have left** in the system.

Bulletin boards can be appropriate for a team of individuals at different locations to compare notes. It becomes a way of keeping track of progress on a **project** between routine team meetings.

3.5 Videoconferencing

Videoconferencing is the use of computer and communications technology to **conduct meetings**.

Videoconferencing has become increasingly common as the Internet and webcams have brought the service to desktop PCs at reasonable cost. More expensive systems feature a **separate room with several video screens**, which show the images of those participating in a meeting.

3.6 Electronic Data Interchange (EDI)

EDI is a form of computer-to-computer **data** interchange. Instead of sending each other reams of paper in the form of invoices, statements and so on, details of inter-company transactions are sent via telecoms links, **avoiding the need for output** and paper at the sending end, and **for re-keying of data** at the receiving end.

3.7 Deciding on a communication tool

FAST FORWARD

The **channel of communication** will impact on the effectiveness of the communication process. The characteristics of the message will determine what communication tool is best for a given situation.

Technological advances have increased the number of communication tools available. The features and limitations of ten common tools are outlined in the following table.

Tool	Features / Advantages	Limitations
Conversation	Usually unstructured so can discuss a wide range of topics Requires little or no planning Gives a real impression of feelings	Temptation to lose focus May be easily forgotten
Meeting	Allows multiple opinions to be expressed Can discuss and resolve a wide range of issues	Can highlight differences and become time-wasting confrontations 'Louder' personalities may dominate Costly in terms of personnel time A focused agenda and an effective Chair should minimise the impact of these limitations

Tool	Features / Advantages	Limitations
Presentation	Complex ideas can be communicated Visual aids such as slides can help the communication process The best presentations will leave a lasting impression	Requires planning and skill Poorly researched or presented material can lead to audience resentment
Telephone	Good for communications that do not require (or you would prefer not to have) a permanent written record Can provide some of the 'personal touch' to people in geographically remote locations Conference calls allow multiple participants	Receiver may not be available; 'phone-tag' is a frustrating pastime! (Voice-mail may help) Can be disruptive to receiver if in the middle of another task No written record gives greater opportunity for misunderstandings
Facsimile	Enables reports and messages to reach remote locations quickly	Easily seen by others Fax machine may not be checked for messages Complex images do not transmit well
Memorandum	Provides a permanent record Adds formality to internal communications	If used too often or the message is too general people may ignore it Can come across as impersonal
Letter	Provides a permanent record of an external message Adds formality to external communications Use a clear, simple structure, eg… • Letterhead • Reference or heading • Date • Recipient name and address • Greeting/salutation • Subject • Substance • Close • Signature • Author name and position • Enclosure/copy reference	If inaccurate or poorly presented provides a permanent record of incompetence May be slow to arrive depending on distance and the postal service

Tool	Features / Advantages	Limitations
Report	Provides a permanent, often comprehensive written record Use a clear, simple structure. There is no one correct format. An example that could be adapted to suit the report requirements is… • Meaningful Title • Author name and position • Purpose/Terms of Reference • Procedure followed • Findings • Conclusion/Recommendations Where necessary use a hierarchy of headings to aid clarity, eg… • 1 Section heading • 1.1 Related paragraph • 1.1(a) Related sub-paragraph	Complex messages may be misunderstood in the absence of immediate feedback Reports that reach (necessarily) negative conclusions can lead to negative impressions of the author
Electronic mail	Provides a written record Attachments (eg Reports or other documents) can be included Quick – regardless of location Automated 'Read receipts' or a simple request to acknowledge receipt by return message mean you know if the message has been received Can be sent to multiple recipients easily, can be forwarded on to others	Requires some computer literacy to use effectively People may not check their e-mail regularly Lack of privacy – can be forwarded on without your knowledge Long messages (more than one 'screen') may best be dealt with via other means, or as attached documents
Video-conference	This is in effect a meeting conducted using a computer and video system Provides more of a personal touch than the telephone, but less than a 'physical' meeting Some non-verbal messages (eg gestures) will be received	The hardware is expensive compared to telephone May be dominated by the most confident participant(s) Cross-border cultural differences may be unintentionally ignored as participants feel 'at home' Image quality is often poor – resulting in not much more than an expensive telephone conference call!

3.8 The effect of office automation on business

Office automation has an enormous effect on business. We discuss some of the most significant effects in this section.

3.8.1 Routine processing

The processing of routine data can be done in **bigger volumes**, at **greater speed** and with **greater accuracy** than with non-automated, manual systems.

3.8.2 The paperless office

There might be **less paper** in the office (but not necessarily so) with more data-processing done using computers. Many organisations print information held in computer files resulting in more paper in the office than with manual systems!

3.8.3 Management information

The nature and **quality of management information** has changed.

(a)   Managers are likely to have **access to more information** – for example from a database. Information is also likely to be **more accurate, reliable and up to date**. The range of **management reports** is likely to be wider and their content more comprehensive.

(b)   **Planning activities** should be more thorough, with the use of **models** (eg spreadsheets for budgeting) and **sensitivity analysis**.

(c)   Information for **control** should be more readily available. For example, a computerised sales ledger system should provide prompt reminder letters for late payers, and might incorporate other credit control routines. Stock systems, especially for companies with stocks distributed around several different warehouses, should provide better stock control.

(d)   **Decision making** by managers can be helped by **decision support systems**.

3.8.4 Organisation structure

The **organisation structure** might change. PC networks give local office managers a means of setting up a good **local management information system**, and **localised data processing** while retaining access to **centrally-held databases** and programs. Office automation can therefore encourage a tendency towards **decentralisation** of authority within an organisation.

On the other hand, such systems help **head office** to **keep in touch** with what is going on in local offices. Head office can therefore readily monitor and control the activities of individual departments, and retain a co-ordinating influence.

3.8.5 Customer service

Office automation, in some organisations, results in **better customer service**. When an organisation receives large numbers of telephone enquiries from customers, the staff who take the calls should be able to provide a prompt and helpful service if they have **on-line access** to the organisation's data files.

3.8.6 Homeworking or remote working

Advances in communications technology have, for some tasks, **reduced the need for the actual presence of an individual in the office**.

The **advantages to the organisation** of homeworking are as follows.

(a) **Cost savings on space**. Office rental costs and other charges can be very expensive. If firms can move some of their employees on to a homeworking basis, money can be saved.

(b) A **larger pool of labour**. The possibility of working at home might attract more applicants for clerical positions, especially from people who have other demands on their time (eg going to and from school) which cannot be fitted round standard office hours.

(c) If the homeworkers are **freelance**, then the organisation **avoids the need to pay them** when there is insufficient work, when they are sick, on holiday etc.

4 Coaching, mentoring and counselling

4.1 Coaching

Coaching is an approach whereby a trainee is put under the guidance of an experienced employee who shows the trainee how to perform tasks. It is also a fashionable aspect of leadership style and a feature of superior/subordinate relationships, where the aim is to *develop* people by providing challenging opportunities and guidance in tackling them.

Step 1 **Establish learning targets**. The areas to be learnt should be identified, and specific, realistic goals (eg completion dates, performance standards) stated by agreement with the trainee.

Step 2 **Plan a systematic learning and development programme.** This will ensure regular progress, appropriate stages for consolidation and practice.

Step 3 **Identify opportunities for broadening the trainee's knowledge and experience**, eg by involvement in new projects, placement on inter-departmental committees, suggesting new contacts, or simply extending the job, adding more tasks, greater responsibility etc.

Step 4 **Take into account the strengths and limitations of the trainee** in learning, and take advantage of learning opportunities that suit the trainee's ability, preferred style and goals.

Step 5 **Exchange feedback**. The coach will want to know how the trainee sees his or her progress and future. He or she will also need performance information in order to monitor the trainee's progress, adjust the learning programme if necessary, identify further needs which may emerge and plan future development for the trainee.

4.2 Mentoring

Key term

Mentoring is a long-term relationship in which a more experienced person as a teacher, counsellor, role model, supporter and encourager, to foster the individual's personal and career development.

Mentoring differs from coaching in two main ways.

(a) The mentor is not usually the protégé's immediate superior.
(b) Mentoring covers a wide range of functions, not always related to current job performance.

Career functions include:

- Sponsoring within the organisation and providing exposure at higher levels
- Coaching and influencing progress through appointments
- Protection
- Drawing up personal development plans
- Advice with administrative problems people face in their new jobs
- Help in tackling projects, by pointing people in the right direction

Psychosocial functions include:

- Creating a sense of acceptance and belonging
- Counselling and friendship
- Providing a role model

Organisational arrangements for coaching and mentoring will vary, but in general a coach needs to be an expert in the trainee's professional field. Mentors are often drawn from other areas of the organisation but can open up lines of communication to those with power and influence across it. For this reason, a mentor is usually in a senior position.

Exam focus point	A question on mentoring appears on the Pilot Paper.

4.3 Counselling

FAST FORWARD	**Counselling** is an interpersonal interview, the aim of which is to facilitate another person in identifying and working through a problem.

Key term	'**Counselling** can be defined as 'a purposeful relationship in which one person helps another to help himself. It is a way of relating and responding to another person so that that person is helped to explore his thoughts, feelings and behaviour with the aim of reaching a clearer understanding. The clearer understanding may be of himself or of a problem, or of the one in relation to the other.' (*Rees*)

The need for workplace counselling can arise in many different situations.

- During appraisal, to solve work or performance problems
- In grievance or disciplinary situations
- Following change, such as promotion or relocation
- On redundancy or dismissal
- As a result of domestic or personal difficulties
- In cases of sexual, racial or religious harassment or bullying at work (to support the victim and educate the perpetrator)

4.4 Benefits of counselling

Effective counselling is not merely a matter of pastoral care for individuals, but is very much in the organisation's interests. Counselling can:

(a) **Prevent underperformance**, reduce labour turnover and absenteeism and increase commitment from employees

(b) Demonstrate an organisation's **commitment** to and concern for its employees

(c) Give employees the **confidence and encouragement** necessary to take responsibility for self and career development

(d) Recognise that the organisation may be contributing to the **employees' problems** and provide an opportunity to reassess organisational policy and practice

(e) Support the organisation in **complying with its obligations** (eg in regard to managing harassment in the workplace).

4.5 The counselling process

Counselling is facilitating others through the process of **defining and exploring their own problems**: it is primarily a non-directive role.

Managers may be called on to use their expertise to help others make informed decisions or solve problems by:

(a) **Advising:** offering information and recommendations on the best course of action. This is a relatively *directive* role, and may be called for in areas where you can make a key contribution to the *quality* of the decision: advising an employee about the best available training methods, say, or about behaviours which are considered inappropriate in the workplace.

(b) **Counselling:** facilitating others through the process of defining and exploring their own problems and coming up with their own solutions. This is a relatively *non-directive* role, and may be called for in areas where you can make a key contribution to the *ownership* of the decision: helping employees to formulate learning goals, for example, or to cope with work (and sometimes non-work) problems.

The counselling process has three broad stages (*Egan*).

Step 1 **Reviewing the current scenario**: helping people to identify, explore and clarify their problem situations and unused opportunities. This is done mostly by listening, encouraging them to tell their 'story', and questioning/probing to help them to see things more clearly.

Step 2 **Developing a preferred scenario**: helping people to identify what they want, in terms of clear goals and objectives. This is done mostly by encouraging them to envisage their desired outcome, and what it will mean for them (in order to motivate them to make the necessary changes).

Step 3 **Determining how to get there:** helping people to develop action strategies for accomplishing goals, for getting what they want. This is done mostly by encouraging them to explore options and available resources, select the best option and plan their next steps.

Question   **Counselling skills**

Before you read on, which of the interpersonal skills covered in this chapter would you consider particularly helpful for a manager in the role of counsellor?

4.6 Counselling skills

Counselling skills include *orientations* (such as interest, sensitivity, empathy and non-judgement); *communication skills* (such as active listening, questioning and use of body language); and *problem-solving skills* (in order to explore goals and alternative options for pursuing them).

The aim of counselling is to help the other person to help himself. Counsellors need to have the **belief** that individuals have the resources to solve their own problems, albeit with facilitation and help.

Counsellors need to be **observant** and **knowledgeable** enough about people to notice and interpret behaviours which may indicate a problem: the other person may not have clearly identified or expressed what the problem is.

They need to be **sensitive** to beliefs and values which may be different from their own: for example, religious beliefs. They need to be **empathetic** (attempting to see the problem from the other person's point of view, and reflecting their understanding back to the other person so that they feel heard) – and yet also **impartial** (refraining from judging or giving advice unnecessarily).

They also need a range of first-order interpersonal skills:

(a) **Active listening:** to encourage the other person to talk (eg by **attentive** behaviour and giving supportive **feedback**); and to ensure (and demonstrate) that they are genuinely trying to understand the other person's viewpoint (eg by **reflecting back** what they think they are hearing).

(b) Using different **questioning styles:** to encourage the other person to speak; to think more deeply or clearly (probing and challenging); to check their own understanding.

(c) Using **body language** (to convey attentiveness, interest, support) and interpreting the other person's body language carefully (in order to explore the feelings underlying the other person's verbal messages).

4.7 Confidentiality

There will be situations when an employee cannot be completely open unless (s)he is sure that any comments will be treated confidentially. However, certain information, once obtained by the organisation (for example about fraud or sexual harassment) calls for action. In spite of the drawbacks, therefore, the CIPD *Statement on Counselling in the Workplace* is clear that employees must be made aware when their comments will be passed on to the relevant authority, and when they will be treated completely confidentially.

Case Study

'The findings of more than 80 studies on workplace counselling show that 90% of employees are highly satisfied with the process and outcome. Evidence suggests that counselling helps to relieve work-related stress and reduces sickness absence rates by up to half. That view is borne out by Mike Doig, medical director at Chevron Europe: "For every $1 spent on workplace counselling, $6–$10 was saved for our company, with the workforce receiving the direct benefit," he says. (*People Management*, May 2003)

5 Communication in the workplace

5.1 Communication in the organisation

FAST FORWARD

Communication is a two-way process involving the transmission or exchange of information and the provision of feedback. It is necessary to direct and co-ordinate activities.

Communication is required for planning, co-ordination and control.

(a) **Management decision-making requires data**. Managers are at the hub of a communications system.

(b) Interdepartmental co-ordination depends on information flows. All the interdependent systems for purchasing, production, marketing and administration can be synchronised to perform the right actions at the right times to co-operate in accomplishing the organisation's aims.

(c)   Individual motivation and effectiveness depends on communication, so that people know what they have to do and why.

Communication in the organisation may take the following forms.

- Giving **instructions**
- Giving or receiving **information**
- Exchanging **ideas**
- **Announcing** plans or strategies
- **Comparing** actual results against a plan
- **Rules or procedures**
- Communication about the **organisation structure** and job descriptions

5.2 Direction of communication

FAST FORWARD

Communication in an organisation **flows** downwards, upwards, sideways and diagonally.

Communication links different parts of the organisation.

(a)   **Vertical communication** flows up and down the scalar chain from superior to subordinate and back.

(b)   **Horizontal or lateral communication** flows between people of the same rank, in the same section or department, or in different sections or departments. Horizontal communication between peer groups is usually easier and more direct then vertical communication, being less inhibited by considerations of rank. It may be part of a **formal** work relationship, to co-ordinate the work of several people, and perhaps departments, who have to co-operate to carry out a certain operation. Alternatively, **informal** communication may furnish emotional and social support to an individual.

(c)   Interdepartmental communication by people of different ranks may be described as **diagonal communication**. Departments in the technostructure which serve the organisation in general, such as Human Resources or Information Systems, have no clear line authority linking them to managers in other departments who need their involvement.

Exam focus point

Lateral communication appears on the Pilot Paper.

5.3 Communication patterns (or networks)

A **communication pattern** channels communication between people. One of the purposes of a **formal organisation structure** is the design of a communications pattern for the organisation.

Leavitt, in a series of experiments, examined the effectiveness of four communication networks for **written** communication between members of a small group.

(a)   The **circle.** Each member of the group could communicate with only two others in the group, as shown.

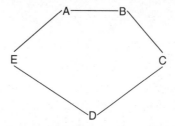

(b)   The **chain**

$$A—B—C—D—E$$

Similar to the circle, except that A and E cannot communicate with each other and are therefore at both ends of a communication chain.

(c)   The **'Y'**

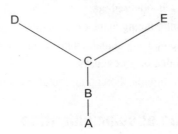

(d)   The **wheel**

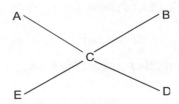

In both the 'Y' and the 'wheel' patterns, C occupies a more central position in the network.

In Leavitt's experiment, each member of a group of five people had to solve a problem and each had an essential piece of information. Only **written** communication, channelled according to one of the four patterns described above, was allowed. The findings of the experiment are tabulated below. A direct trade-off between speed and job-satisfaction is evident.

	Wheel	Y	Chain	Circle
Speed of problem solving	Fastest	2nd fastest	3rd fastest	Slowest
Leader	C	C	C (less so than wheel and Y)	None emerged
Job satisfaction	Lowest	3rd highest	2nd highest	Highest (?)

Exam focus point

This set of communication networks is the subject of a question on the Pilot Paper.

6 Formal communication processes

6.1 The communication process

FAST FORWARD

Communication can be depicted as the **radio signal** model. The sender encodes the message and transmits it through a medium to the receiver who decodes it into information.

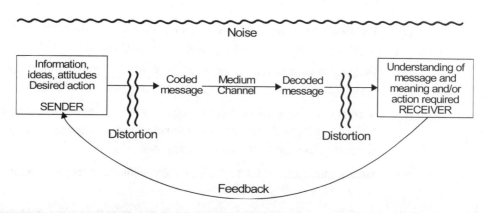

Process	Comment
Encoding of a message	The code or 'language' of a message may be verbal (spoken or written) or it may be non-verbal, in pictures, diagrams, numbers or body language.
Medium for the message	There are a number of channels for communication, such as a conversation, a letter, a notice board or via computer. The choice of medium used in communication depends on a number of factors such as urgency, permanency, complexity, sensitivity and cost.
Feedback	The sender of a message needs feedback on the receiver's reaction. This is partly to test the receiver's understanding of it and partly to gauge the receiver's reaction.
Distortion	The meaning of a message can be lost at the coding and decoding stages. Usually the problem is one of language and the medium used; it is very easy to give the wrong impression in a brief e-mail message.
Noise	Distractions and interference in the environment in which communication is taking place may be physical noise (passing traffic), technical noise (a bad telephone line), social noise (differences in the personalities of the parties) or psychological noise (anger, frustration, tiredness).

6.2 Desirable qualities of a communication system in an organisation

Clarity. The coder of a message must bear in mind the potential recipient. **Jargon can be used** - and will even be most appropriate - **where the recipient shares the same expertise**. It should be avoided for those who do not.

Recipient. The recipient should be clearly identified, and the right medium should be chosen, to minimise distortion and noise.

Medium. The channel or medium should be chosen to ensure it reaches the target audience. Messages of general application (eg Health and Safety signs) should be displayed prominently.

Timing. Information has to be timely to be useful.

6.3 Effective communication

FAST FORWARD

Effective communication: the right person receives the right information in the right way at the right time.

What does 'good communication' look like? It is perhaps easiest to identify *poor* or ineffective communication, where information is not given; is given too late to be used; is too much to take in; is inaccurate or incomplete; is hard to understand. **Effective communication** is:

(a)   **Directed to appropriate people**. This may be defined by the reporting structure of the organisation, but it may also be a matter of discretion, trust and so on.

(b)   **Relevant to their needs**: not excessive in volume (causing overload); focused on relevant topics; communicated in a format, style and language that they can understand.

(c)   **Accurate and complete** (within the recipient's needs). Information should be 'accurate' in the sense of 'factually correct', but need not be minutely detailed: in business contexts, summaries and approximations are often used.

(d)   **Timely:** information must be made available within the time period when it will be relevant (as input to a decision, say).

(e)   **Flexible**: suited in style and structure to the needs of the parties and situation. Assertive, persuasive, supportive and informative communication styles have different applications.

(f)   **Effective in conveying meaning**. Style, format, language and media all contribute to the other person's understanding or lack of understanding. If the other person doesn't understand the message, or misinterprets it, communication has not been effective.

(g)   **Cost-effective**. In business organisations, all the above must be achieved, as far as possible, at reasonable cost.

7 Informal communication channels

FAST FORWARD   Informal communication supplements the formal system.

The formal pattern of communication in an organisation is **always** supplemented by an informal one, which is sometimes referred to as the **grapevine**. People like to gossip about rumours and events.

7.1 The grapevine

A well known study into how the grapevine works was carried out by *K Davis* using his 'echo-analysis' technique: the recipient of some information, A, was asked to name the source of his information, B. B was then asked to name his source, C and so on until the information was traced back to its originator. Here are his findings.

(a)   The grapevine acts **quickly**.

(b)   The working of the grapevine is **selective**: information is not divulged randomly.

(c)   The grapevine usually operates **at the place of work** and not outside it.

(d)   Oddly, the grapevine is most active when the formal communication network is active: the **grapevine does not fill a gap** created by an ineffective formal communication system.

(e)   **Higher level executives were better communicators** and better informed than their subordinates. 'If a foreman at the sixth level had an accident, a larger proportion of executives at the third level knew of it than at the fourth level, or even at the sixth level where the accident happened.'

(f)   More technostructure executives were in the know about events than line managers (because the staff executives are more mobile and get involved with more different functions in their work).

7.2 The importance of informal communications

This can be seen by reassessing Mintzberg's roles of management. **Managers**, rather than staff, might rely on the grapevine, as opposed to formal communication channels, because of the qualities informal communication possesses.

(a) It is more current than the formal system.

(b) It is relevant to the **informal** organisation (where many decisions are actually determined).

(c) It relates to **internal politics**, which may not be reflected in formal communications anyway.

(d) It can **bypass excessively secretive management**.

7.3 Interpersonal skills

Interpersonal skills are needed in order to understand and manage roles, relationships, attitudes and perceptions. They enable us to communicate effectively and to achieve our aims when dealing with other people.

Interpersonal skills

(a) The ability to interpret **body language** and to use it to reinforce messages

(b) The ability to **listen attentively and actively**

(c) The ability to put others at their ease, to persuade and to smooth over difficult situations

(d) The ability to **identify when false or dishonest arguments** are being used, and to construct logical ones

(e) The ability to recognise how much information, and of what kind, another person will **need and be able to take in**

(f) The ability to **use communication media effectively**: to speak well, write legibly, use appropriate vocabulary and use visual aids where required

(g) The ability to **sum up** or conclude an argument clearly and persuasively

(h) The ability to communicate and show enthusiasm, ie **leadership** or inspiration

The above list is by no means exhaustive.

Here are some more important things to consider in interpersonal relations.

Factor	Comment
Goal	What does the other person want from the process? What do you want from the process? What will both parties need and be trying to do to achieve their aims? Can both parties emerge satisfied?
Perceptions	What, if any, are likely to be the factors causing distortion of the way both parties see the issues and each other? (Attitudes, personal feelings, expectations?)
Roles	What roles are the parties playing? (Superior/subordinate, customer/server, complainer/soother?) What expectations does this create of the way they will behave?
Resistances	What may the other person be afraid of? What may he or she be trying to protect? (His or her ego/self-image, attitudes?) Sensitivity will be needed in this area.
Attitudes	What sources of difference, conflict or lack of understanding might there be, arising from attitudes and other factors which shape them (sex, race, specialism, hierarchy)?

Factor	Comment
Relationships	What are the relative positions of the parties and the nature of the relationship between them? (Superior/subordinate? Formal/ informal? Work/non-work)? What style is appropriate to it?
Environment	What factors in the immediate and situational environment might affect the issues and the people? (eg competitive environment; customer care; pressures of disciplinary situation; nervousness; physical surroundings formality/ informality)

7.3.1 Listening

Listening in the communications model is about decoding and receiving information. Effective listening has three consequences.

- It encourages the sender to listen effectively in return to what you have to say
- It reduces the effect of noise
- It helps resolve problems by encouraging understanding from someone else's viewpoint

Advice for good listening

(a) **Be prepared to listen**. Put yourself in the right frame of mind and be prepared to grasp the main concepts.

(b) **Be interested**. Make an effort to analyse the message for its relevance.

(c) **Keep an open mind**. Your own beliefs and prejudices can get in the way of what the other person is actually saying.

(d) **Keep an ear open for the main ideas**. An awareness of how people generally structure their speech can help the process of understanding. Be able to distinguish between the thrust of the argument and the supporting evidence.

(e) **Listen critically**. This means trying to assess what the person is saying by identifying any **assumptions, omissions and biases**.

(f) **Avoid distraction**. People have a natural attention curve, high at the beginning and end of an oral message, but sloping off in the middle.

(g) **Take notes**, although note taking can be distracting.

7.3.2 Non-verbal communication: body language

The hidden messages in face-to-face communication can be a common cause for communication breakdown, as they cause decoding problems. Observe others, in meetings, presentations, interviews or just talking in the bar. Notice the signs of boredom or disagreement, support and interest. Picking up these signals will help you improve your own communication skills.

Whilst watching others, also become more aware of yourself. Be aware of the signals you are sending and transmit only those you intend to.

Non-verbal communication can be controlled and used for several purposes.

(a) It can **provide appropriate feedback** to the sender of a message (a yawn, applause, clenched fists, fidgeting)

(b) It can **create a desired impression** (smart dress, a smile, punctuality, a firm handshake)

(c) It can **establish a desired atmosphere** or conditions (a friendly smile, informal dress, attentive posture, a respectful distance)

(d) It can **reinforce spoken messages** with appropriate indications of how interest and feelings are engaged (an emphatic gesture, sparkling eyes, a disapproving frown)

If we can learn to **recognise** non-verbal messages, our ability to listen is improved.

(a)   When we are speaking, non-verbal **feedback** helps us to modify our message.

(b)   We may recognise people's **real feelings** when their words are constrained by formal courtesies (an excited look, a nervous tic, close affectionate proximity).

(c)   We can **recognise existing or potential personal problems** (the angry silence, the indifferent shrug, absenteeism or lateness at work, refusal to look someone in the eye).

Non-verbal cues

- Facial expression
- Gesture
- Posture and orientation
- Proximity and contact
- Movement and stillness
- Silence and sounds
- Appearance and grooming
- Response to norms and expectations

7.4 Observation

While not really a form of communication, **observation** as a management skill is linked to topics in communication such as interviewing, so it is convenient to deal with it here.

Observation is an important data-gathering technique. It can be used to measure the effectiveness of procedures, or, indeed, to establish just what procedures and processes are in use. It is perhaps most useful in establishing the nature of less formal aspects of the organisation, such as how the informal organisation works; how individuals perform their tasks; who interacts with whom; and how specified procedures are informally modified.

8 Barriers to communication

FAST FORWARD

Barriers to communication include 'noise' from the environment, poorly constructed or coded/decoded messages (distortion) and failures in understanding caused by the relative position of the senders and receivers.

8.1 General faults in the communication process

Distortion or omission of information by the sender

Misunderstanding due to lack of clarity or technical jargon

Non-verbal signs (gesture, posture, facial expression) contradicting the verbal message, so that its meaning is in doubt

'Overload' - a person being given too much information to digest in the time available

People hearing **only what they want** to hear in a message

Differences in social, racial or educational **background**, compounded by age and personality differences, creating barriers to understanding and co-operation

(Mnemonic using words in bold above: Distorted Messages Never Overcome Personal Differences.)

8.2 Communication difficulties at work

Status (of the sender and receiver of information)

- A senior manager's words are listened to closely and a colleague's perhaps discounted.
- A subordinate might mistrust his or her superior believing that he or she might look for hidden meanings in a message.

Jargon. People from different job or specialist backgrounds (eg accountants, personnel managers, IT experts) can have difficulty in talking on a non-specialist's wavelength.

Suspicion. People discount information from those not recognised as having expert power.

Priorities. People or departments have different priorities or perspectives so that one person places more or less emphasis on a situation than another.

Selective reporting. Subordinates giving superiors incorrect or incomplete information (eg to protect a colleague, to avoid bothering the superior); also a senior manager may only be able to handle edited information because he does not have time to sift through details.

Use. Managers may be prepared to make decisions on a hunch without proper regard to the communications they may or may not have received.

Timing. Information which has **no immediate** use may be forgotten.

Opportunity. Opportunity, formal or informal, for people to say what they think may be lacking.

Conflict. Where there is conflict between individuals or departments, communications will be withdrawn and information withheld.

Personal differences, such as age, educational/social background or personality mean that people have different views as to what is important or different ways of expressing those views. Sometimes individuals' views may be discounted because of who they are, not what they say.

8.2.1 Culture

Secrecy. Information might be given on a need-to-know basis, rather than be considered as a potential resource for everyone to use.

Can't handle bad news. The culture of some organisations may prevent the communication of certain messages. Organisations with a 'can-do' philosophy may not want to hear that certain tasks are impossible.

8.2.2 Categories of communication problems

(a) **System.** There may be a bad formal communication system.
(b) **Misunderstanding.** There may be misunderstanding about the actual content of a message.
(c) **Personality.** Inter-personal difficulties may hamper communication.

8.3 Improving the communications system

Establish better communication links.

- **Standing instructions** should be recorded in easily accessible manuals which are kept fully up-to-date.
- Management **decisions** should be sent to all people affected by them, preferably in writing.
- Regular **staff meetings**, or formal consultation with trade union representatives should be held.

- **A house journal** should be issued regularly.

- **Appraisal interviews** should be held between a manager and his subordinates, to discuss the job performance and career prospects of the subordinates.

- **New technology** such as e-mail should be used but not so as to overload everybody with messages of no importance.

Use the **informal organisation** to supplement this increased freedom of communication.

8.4 Clearing up misunderstandings

Confirmation: issuing a message in more than one form (eg by word of mouth at a meeting, confirmed later in minutes) can help.

Reporting by exception should operate to prevent **information overload** on managers.

Train managers who do not express themselves clearly and concisely. Necessary jargon should be taught in some degree to people new to the organisation or unfamiliar with the terminology of the specialists.

 Case Study

Procter and Gamble have a rule that no memo should be longer than one side of paper.

Communication between superiors and subordinates will be improved when **interpersonal trust** exists. Exactly how this is achieved will depend on the management style of the manager, the attitudes and personality of the individuals involved, and other environmental variables. Peters and Waterman advocate 'management by walking around' (MBWA), and informality in superior/subordinate relationships as a means of establishing closer links.

 Question   **Communication**

Is the statement below true or false?

'A clearly expressed verbal message will always be understood.'

Answer

False. 'Clear expression' is a matter of opinion and perception, or in terms of the communications model, of coding and decoding. We must also consider the effect of noise, such as cultural differences.

9 Communication methods

9.1 Oral communication

Face-to-face communications (eg meetings and interviews) and oral communication (eg phone calls) bring a range of listening and non-verbal skills into play.

Face-to-face communication plays an important part in the life of any organisation, whether it is required by government legislation or the Articles of Association of a company, or occurs informally for information exchange, problem-solving and decision-making.

Face-to-face communication is good for four purposes.

- **Generating new ideas**
- **'On the spot' feedback**, constructive criticism and exchange of views
- **Co-operation** and sensitivity to personal factors
- **Spreading information quickly** through a group of people

However, such communication can be counter productive.

- People must **know the reason** for the group discussion.
- Participants must be willing and effective communicators.
- There must be sufficient **guidance** or leadership to control proceedings.
- People must maintain standards of **courtesy.**

9.2 Meetings

Formal meetings, such as the Board meeting of a company, the Annual General Meeting of a society, or a Local Council meeting, are governed by strict **rules, conventions** and **procedures**.

- Attendance rights (for members of the public, shareholders and so on)
- Adequate notice of forthcoming meetings
- The minimum number of members required to hold the meeting (the quorum)
- The timing of meetings
- The type of business to be discussed
- The binding power of decisions upon the participants

Meetings in organisations are rarely formal, although Board meetings might require a minimum number of people to attend.

9.3 Team briefings

Team briefings are a form of face-to-face communication mechanism which are designed to increase the commitment and understanding of the workforce.

A team briefing is a means of communicating at team level, not in the more impersonal or abstract level of the house journal or noticeboard. It is given by a **team leader**, who should have been thoroughly trained and briefed or, occasionally, by a more senior member of management. They are specially relevant in modern-style manufacturing plants, where the workforce is organised into smallish teams, each with a team leader.

The **purpose of a team briefing** is to communicate and explain management decisions in the hope that this will reduce any disruption, dispel any rumours, and enhance employees' commitment. Subjects include:

- Policies (new or changed, and why)
- Plans
- Progress
- Personnel issues

A survey by the Manchester School of Management *(Financial Times* 27 July 1992*)* reported that most workers **welcomed** such schemes, but did **not** feel any more or less committed to the organisation. Neither did they **understand** management decisions any better!

Reasons for failure

- Lack of senior management commitment
- Interference
- A lack of enthusiasm shown by middle managers
- The reluctance of management to allow the discussion of matters of real importance.

Team briefings can be seen as a tool which tries to **motivate** by **communicating**. However, it is **not** clear whether, using Herzberg's model, information has a role in motivation.

(a) If lack of information (as a result of management secrecy) is a **hygiene** factor, you would expect little **long-term** change in the level of motivation from a more open management approach.

(b) If providing more information and being more open is a **motivator** factor, you would expect greater enthusiasm.

9.4 Conferences

A body which has a large membership spread over a wide area, such as a professional body or a trade union, may find conferences a useful means of improving contact between the organisation's central administration and the body of the membership. A conference is a means of bringing together a much larger number of members to discuss matters of current interest or concern. It can give members a better understanding of what their organisation is trying to do for them and lead to a greater commitment to it.

9.5 Interviews

The interview, informal or otherwise is an excellent internal system for handling the problems or queries of individuals, allowing **confidentiality** and flexible response to personal factors. Interviews are, however, costly in terms of managerial time. Some interviews are built into the **formal** communication system.

(a) Grievance interviews allow employees to voice their complaints.

(b) Disciplinary interviews help the organisation to maintain its standards.

(c) Appraisal interviews are used to discuss the employee's performance, progress and possible need for improvement.

9.6 Telephone calls and voice mail

The **telephone** provides all the interactive and feedback advantages of face to face communication, while saving the travel time. It is, however, more impersonal than an interview for the discussion of sensitive personal matters, and it does not **by itself** provide the concreteness of written media.

Voice mail is a means of leaving spoken memos, for someone to listen to later. It can be useful as an extension of **paging**, so that a person can leave detailed messages for someone who is absent without the inconvenience of having to write a memorandum or the hazard of leaving a message.

Video conferencing has grown in popularity since the Gulf War and with the decreasing cost of technology compared to the cost and inconvenience of flying. It is a meeting conducted over long distance. Each participant shares a room, and interacts with a video broadcast image of the other participants.

9.7 Forms

Routine information flow is largely achieved through the use of **forms**. A well designed form can be completed quickly and easily with brief, relevant and specifically identified details of a request or instruction. They are simple to file, and information is quickly retrieved and confirmed. Examples include: expense forms, timesheets, insurance forms and stock request forms.

9.8 Notice board

A notice board is a channel through which various written media can be cheaply transmitted to a large number of people. It allows the organisation to present a variety of information to any or all employees: items may have a limited time span of relevance but will at least be available for verification and recollection for a while. However, they have their drawbacks.

(a)   They can easily fall into **neglect**, and become untidy or irrelevant (or be sabotaged by graffiti).

(b)   They are wholly **dependent** on the intended recipient's **curiosity** or desire to receive information.

9.9 House journal

Larger companies frequently run an **internal magazine** or newspaper to give employees routine information.

- Staff appointments and retirements
- Meetings, sports and social events
- Results and successes; customer feedback
- New products or machinery

Propaganda? The journal usually **avoids controversy**: it may **not deal with sensitive issues** such as industrial relations or pollution of the environment, and may stop short of criticising policy, management, products and so on. It is, after all, designed to improve rather than threaten communication and morale, and it may be seen by outsiders (especially customers) who might get an unfavourable impression of the organisation.

9.10 Organisation manual or handbook

An organisation (or office) manual is useful for drawing together and **keeping up to date a** variety of information.

- The structure of the organisation (perhaps an organisation chart)
- Background: the organisation's history and geography
- The organisation's products, services and customers
- Rules and regulations
- Conditions of employment: pay structure, hours, holidays, notice and so on
- Standards and procedures for health and safety

- Procedures for grievance, discipline, salary review
- Policy on trade union membership
- Facilities for employees

9.11 Letters and faxes

The letter is flexible in a wide variety of situations, and useful in providing a written record and confirmation of the matters discussed.

(a) It is widely used for external communication, via the **external mailing system** or courier.

(b) A direct letter may be used internally in certain situations where a confidential written record is necessary or personal handling required.

Fax achieves the same object as a letter, but is more immediate. Faxes are sometimes followed up with a letter.

9.12 Memoranda

A memorandum is the equivalent of the letter in internal communication. It is sent via the **internal mail system** of an organisation. Memoranda are useful for exchanging many sorts of message and particularly for confirming telephone conversations: sometimes, however, they are used instead of telephone conversations, where the call would have been quicker, cheaper and just as effective. Many memoranda are unnecessarily typed where a short hand-written note would be adequate.

9.13 Electronic communications

The introduction of personal computer networks facilitates new sorts of communication, of which **email** is probably by far the most prevalent. It is particularly useful in organisations which are widely dispersed over several sites in one or more countries.

Email has many **advantages** above the telephone and over paper memos, which explains why it has been so widely adopted.

(a) Emails can be sent to **large numbers of people at the same time** without having to be physically distributed on paper.

(b) Email messages **need not interrupt the recipient's flow of work**, unlike a phone call.

Email has **drawbacks**.

(a) Some people use email when face to face contact is more appropriate.

(b) Although email can feel as informal as a spoken conversation, email records can be used in legal proceedings, eg for former employees suing the company for unfair dismissal. They may also be cited in defamation.

(c) They contribute to information overload: there is a temptation to copy email to people that do not really need to see it.

(d) If email is the main means of communication with external parties, the company's corporate identity may be compromised if people send emails in a variety of formats.

Asda were successfully sued by a disgruntled customer because untrue rumours that a customer was guilty of fraud had been circulated via the company's email system. Employees have also used email in 'unfair dismissal' cases.

These legal problems emphasise the need for **internal guidance** on how email should be used. If email is used to communicate with other customers or suppliers, it should be treated in the same way as other business correspondence, including obtaining appropriate authorisation. The guidance should prohibit defamatory or other abusive messages. Above all employees should be made aware that communication by email is permanent and not transitory in nature.

9.14 Report writing

A formal **report** enables a number of people to review the complex facts and arguments relating to an issue on which they have to base a plan or make a decision. This is primarily an **internal medium** used by management, but can be used externally for the information of such recipients as shareholders, the general public, government agencies and banks (eg the company's Annual Report).

The written report does not allow for effective discussion or immediate feedback, as does a meeting, and can be a time-consuming and expensive document to produce. However, as a medium for putting across a body of ideas to a group of people, it has several **advantages.**

(a)   People can **study the material in their own time**, rather than arranging to be present at one place and time

(b)   **No time need be wasted on irrelevancies** and the formulation of arguments, such as may occur in meetings

(c)   The report should be **presented objectively and impartially**, in a formal and impersonal style: emotional reactions or conflicts will be avoided.

Chapter Roundup

- **Time** is a scarce resource and managers' time must be used to the best effect. **Urgency** and **importance** must be recognised and distinguished. Tasks must be prioritised and scheduled. In-trays can be managed using the ACIB method. Other important matters are correct use of the telephone, availability to callers and seeing tasks through to completion.

- **Effective time management** involves attention to:

  - Goal or target setting
  - Action planning
  - Prioritising

  - Focus
  - Urgency
  - Organisation

- **Prioritising tasks** involves ordering tasks in order of preference or priority, based on

  - The relative consequences of timely or untimely performance
  - Importance
  - Dependency of other people of tasks
  - Urgency
  - Defined deadlines, timescales and commitments

- **Work planning** includes the following basic steps:

  - Establishing priorities

  - Loading, allocation of tasks

  - Sequencing of tasks

  - Scheduling estimating the time taken to complete a task and working forwards or backwards to determine start or finish times

- The **channel of communication** will impact on the effectiveness of the communication process. The characteristics of the message will determine what communication tool is best for a given situation.

- **Counselling** is an interpersonal interview, the aim of which is to facilitate another person in identifying and working through a problem.

- Counselling is facilitating others through the process of **defining and exploring their own problems**: it is primarily a non-directive role.

- **Counselling skills** include *orientations* (such as interest, sensitivity, empathy and non-judgement); *communication skills* (such as active listening, questioning and use of body language); and *problem-solving skills* (in order to explore goals and alternative options for pursuing them).

- **Communication** is a two-way process involving the transmission or exchange of information and the provision of feedback. It is necessary to direct and co-ordinate activities.

- Communication in an organisation **flows** downwards, upwards, sideways and diagonally.

- Communication can be depicted as the **radio signal** model. The sender codes the message and transmits it through a medium to the receiver who decodes it into information.

- **Effective communication**: the right person receives the right information in the right way at the right time.

- Informal communication supplements the formal system.

- Barriers to communication include 'noise' from the environments, poorly constructed or coded/decoded messages (distortion) and failures in understanding caused by the relative position of the senders and receivers.

- **Face-to-face** communications (eg meetings and interviews) and oral communication (eg phone calls) bring a range of listening and non-verbal skills into play.

Quick Quiz

1 List six elements of effective time management.

2 Which of the following necessarily makes a piece of work high priority?

    A   Importance

    B   Urgency

    C   Importance and urgency

    D   Other people want you to do the work by a given deadline

3 A list of activities in the order in which they must be completed is the product of task loading.
True or false?

4 When scheduling routine accounting tasks, are you most likely to use forward scheduling or reverse scheduling?

5 Draw a simple diagram of the communication process using dotted or broken lines where 'distortion' may be a problem.

6 Give five examples of non-verbal communication, and suggest what they might be used to indicate.

7 Communication between two members of a project team from different functions, but the same level of authority, is:

    A   Upward

    B   Downward

    C   Lateral

    D   Diagonal

8 What are the main purposes of upward communication in organisations?

9 What are the stages of the counselling process?

10 Is the statement below true or false?

'Informal communication does not fill a gap created by an ineffective formal communication system, but co-exists with it.'

11 Is the statement below true or false?

'Coaching encompasses a much wider range of functions than mentoring.'

Answers to Quick Quiz

1   Goals; action plans; priorities; focus; urgency; organisation

2   C. An important point: work may be urgent-but-not-important or important-but-not-urgent. You may have paused over D – but this is an assertiveness issue: if someone else 'wants' you to do something, you still have a right to consult your own priorities and commitments, assess their right to ask and so on.

3   False: it is a product of task sequencing. Task loading is allocating tasks to people or machines.

4   Forward scheduling. Reverse scheduling is more suitable for scheduling tasks for which you already have a completion date or deadline.

5   Refer to Section 6.1

6   A nod of agreement; a smile to encourage; a frown to disapprove; a yawn to show boredom; turning away to discourage

7   C

8   To give feedback, to inform and to make suggestions

9   Reviewing the current scenario; developing a preferred scenario; determining how to get there

10   True.

11   False.

Recruitment and selection

Topic list	Syllabus reference
1 Recruitment and selection	F1 (a)
2 Responsibility for recruitment and selection	F1 (c)
3 The recruitment process	F1 (b)
4 Advertising vacancies	F1 (d)
5 A systematic approach to selection	F1 (a)
6 Selection methods in outline	F1 (d)
7 Interviews	F1 (e)
8 Selection testing	F1 (e)
9 Other selection methods	F1 (e)
10 Evaluating recruitment and selection practices	F1 (e)

Introduction

Recruitment and selection (**Section 1**) are two core activities in the field of Human Resource Management (HRM). Together, they are broadly aimed at ensuring that the organisation has the human resources (labour and skills) it needs, when it needs them, in order to fulfil its objectives.

In this chapter, we look at the process of **recruitment (Sections 2 and 3)**, which is about **obtaining candidates** and advertising the vacancy in the labour market **(Section 4)**.

We then go on to cover the process of **selection**, which is about deciding which of the applicants is the **right candidate**.

Once candidates have been attracted to apply, there needs to be a systematic process to separate out those who are most suitable for the job **(Section 5)**.

In **Sections 6 to 9**, we examine a range of selection tools. **Interviews** are the most popular – but not necessarily the most effective in their ability to predict future job performance! Organisations are increasingly using 'back-up' methods such as tests and group assessments.

In **Section 10**, we complete the planning and control cycle by suggesting how a manager might **evaluate** the effectiveness of the recruitment and selection process – and what might be done to improve it where necessary.

Bear in mind what these procedures are designed to *do*: identify the best person for the job *and* ensure fair treatment for all potential applicants.

Study guide

		Intellectual level
F1	**Recruitment and selection, managing diversity and equal opportunity**	
(a)	Explain the importance of effective recruitment and selection to the organisation.	1
(b)	Describe the recruitment and selection processes and explain the stages in these processes.	1
(c)	Describe the roles of those involved in the recruitment and selection processes.	1
(d)	Describe the methods through which organisations seek to meet their recruitment needs.	1
(e)	Explain the advantages and disadvantages of different recruitment and selection methods.	1

Exam guide

A question requirement on recruitment may be combined with a requirement relating to selection. Some aspects of recruitment and/or selection will inevitably come up in the exam. Bear in mind that there are a number of procedures and techniques involved in selection. The pilot paper contains questions on the advertising of vacancies, selection tests, training and the learning process. This part of the syllabus is a rich source of questions.

1 Recruitment and selection

The process of recruitment should be part of the organisation's human resource plan. People are a major organisational resource and must be managed as such.

1.1 Overview of recruitment and selection

FAST FORWARD

Effective recruitment practices ensure that a firm has enough **people with the right skills**.

The **overall aim of the recruitment and selection process** in an organisation is to obtain the quantity and quality of employees required to fulfil the objectives of the organisation.

This process can be broken down into three main stages.

(a) **Defining requirements**, including the preparation of job descriptions, job specifications and person specifications (or personnel specifications).

(b) **Attracting applicants**, including the evaluation and use of various methods for reaching appropriate sources of labour (both within and outside the organisation).

(c) **Selecting** the appropriate candidates for the job, or the appropriate job for the candidate.

Key terms

Recruitment is the part of the process concerned with finding applicants: it is a positive action by management, going into the labour market (internal and external), communicating opportunities and information, generating interest.

Selection is the part of the employee resourcing process which involves choosing between applicants for jobs: it is largely a 'negative' process, eliminating unsuitable applicants.

In times of low unemployment, employers have to compete to *attract* desirable categories of labour. In times of high unemployment, and therefore plentiful supply, 'the problem is not so much of attracting candidates, but in deciding how best to *select* them' (Cole, *Personnel Management Theory and Practice*). In times of low demand for labour, however, socially responsible employers may have the additional policy of using *existing staff* (internal recruitment) rather than recruiting from outside, in order to downsize staff levels through natural wastage and redeployment.

1.2 The importance of recruitment and selection

The founding belief of the human resources management (HRM approach is that employees represent a scarce and crucial resource which must be obtained, retained, developed and mobilised for organisational success.

(a) Recruitment (and training) issues are central to the business strategy.

(b) Organisations need to deploy skills in order to succeed. Although the labour market might seem a 'buyer's market', in practice there are:

(i) Skill shortages in key sectors (eg computing services) and local areas

(ii) Mismatches between available skill supply and the demands of particular markets and organisations

Even in conditions of high overall employment, particular skill shortages still exist and may indeed be more acute because of recessionary pressures on education and training. Engineers and software designers, among other specialist and highly trained groups, are the target of fierce competition among employers, forcing a revaluation of recruitment and retention policies.

2 Responsibility for recruitment and selection

FAST FORWARD

> The recruitment process involves **personnel specialists** and **line managers**, sometimes with the help of recruitment **consultants**.

The people involved in recruitment and selection vary from organisation to organisation.

2.1 Senior managers

Senior managers/directors may be involved in recruiting people – from within or outside the organisation – for **senior positions**, or in authorising key appointments. For most other positions, they will not be directly involved. However, they are responsible for **human resources (HR) planning**: identifying the overall skill needs of the organisation, and the types of people it wishes to employ (perhaps as part of the corporate mission statement).

2.2 The human resources department

Some firms employ specialists to manage their recruitment and other (HR) activities, often under the authority of the **human resources manager**.

The role of the human resources (HR) function in recruitment and selection may include:

- Assessing needs for human resources (HR planning)
- Maintaining records of people employed
- Keeping in touch with trends in the labour market
- Advertising for new employees
- Ensuring the organisation complies with equal opportunities and other legislation
- Designing application forms
- Liaising with recruitment consultants
- Preliminary interviews and selection testing

2.3 Line managers

In many cases the recruit's prospective boss will be involved in the recruitment.

(a)   In a small business (s)he might have sole responsibility for recruitment.

(b)   In larger organisations, line managers may be responsible for:

- Asking for more human resources: notifying vacancies or issuing a job requisition
- Advising on skill requirements and attributes required
- Selection interviewing (perhaps collaborating with HR specialists)
- Having a final say in the selection decision

The current trend is towards devolving recruitment and selection (among other Human Resource Management activities) increasingly to line management.

2.4 Recruitment consultants

Specialist recruitment consultants or agencies may be contracted to perform some recruitment tasks on the organisation's behalf, including:

(a)   Analysing, or being informed of, the requirements

(b)   Helping to draw up, or offering advice on, job descriptions, person specifications and other recruitment and selection aids

(c)   Designing job advertisements (or using other, informal methods and contacts, eg by 'head hunting')

(d)   Screening applications, so that those most obviously unsuitable are weeded out immediately

(e)   Helping with short-listing for interview

(f)   Advising on, or conducting, first-round interviews

(g)   Offering a list of suitable candidates with notes and recommendations

2.4.1 Factors in the outsourcing decision

The decision of whether or not to use consultants will depend on a number of factors.

(a)   **Cost**.

(b)   The level of expertise, specialist **knowledge and contacts** which the consultant can bring to the process.

(c)   The level of recruitment expertise available **within the organisation**.

(d)   Whether there is a need for **impartiality** which can only be filled by an outsider trained in objective assessment. If fresh blood is desired in the organisation, it may be a mistake to have insiders selecting clones of the common organisational type.

(e)   Whether the use of an outside agent will be **supported** or resented/rejected by in-house staff.

(f)   Whether the organisation **culture** supports in-house staff in making HR decisions. (Consultants are not tied by status or rank and can discuss problems freely at all levels.)

(g)   **Time**. Consultants will need to learn about the vacancy, the organisation and its requirements.

(h) **Supply of labour**. If there is a large and reasonably accessible pool of labour from which to fill a post, consultants will be less valuable. If the vacancy is a standard one, and there are ready channels for reaching labour (such as professional journals), the use of specialists may not be cost-effective.

3 The recruitment process

FAST FORWARD

Recruitment is a systematic process of (a) identifying and defining skill needs and (b) attracting suitably skilled candidates.

3.1 A systematic approach

The recruitment process is part of a wider whole.

(a) Detailed **human resource planning** (as seen in Chapter 1) defines what resources the organisation needs to meet its objectives, and what sources of labour (internal and external) are available. The organisation's skill requirements may be met through recruitment – but there may also be plans for reducing staff numbers, redeployment, training and development, promotion, retention (to reduce loss of skills through staff turnover) and so on.

(b) **Job analysis** produces two outputs.

    (i) A **job description**: a statement of the component tasks, duties, objectives and standards involved in a job.

    (ii) A **person specification**: a reworking of the job description in terms of the kind of person needed to perform the job.

(c) Recruitment as such *begins with the identification of vacancies*, from the requirements of the human resource plan or by a **job requisition** from a department that has a vacancy.

(d) Preparation and publication of **recruitment advertising** will have three aims.

    (i) Attract the attention and interest of potentially suitable candidates.

    (ii) Give a favourable (but accurate) impression of the job and the organisation.

    (iii) Equip those interested to make an appropriate application (how and to whom to apply, desired skills, qualifications and so on).

(e) Recruitment merges into **selection** when processing applications and assessing candidates.

(f) **Notifying applicants** of the results of the selection process is the final stage of the combined recruitment and selection process.

3.2 Job analysis, competences and job design

3.2.1 Job analysis

Job analysis determines the requirement for a job. The job's tasks are set out in a job description. A **job specification** describes the skills or competences required for the job. A **person specification** describes the sort of person suitable for the job.

The management of the organisation needs to analyse the sort of work needed to be done in order to recruit effectively. The type of information needed is outlined below.

Type of information	Comments
Purpose of the job	This might seem obvious. As an accountant, you will be expected to analyse, prepare or provide financial information; but this has to be set in the context of the organisation as a whole.
Content of the job	The tasks you are expected to do. If the purpose of the job is to ensure, for example, that people get paid on time, the tasks involve include many activities related to payroll.
Accountabilities	These are the results for which you are responsible. In practice they might be phrased in the same way as a description of a task.
Performance criteria	These are the criteria which measure how good you are at the job. These are largely task related.
Responsibility	This denotes the importance of the job. For example, a person running a department and taking decisions involving large amounts of money is more responsible that someone who only does what he or she is told.
Organisational factors	Who does the jobholder report to directly (line manager)?
Developmental factors	Likely promotion paths, if any, and career prospects. Some jobs are 'dead-end' if they lead nowhere.
Environmental factors	Working conditions, security and safety issues and equipment.

 Case Study

Chase Manhattan Bank has clear procedures.

The competence definition and the scale are used to assess to what extent the individual has developed the competence, through seven points ranging from 'minimal knowledge' to 'recognisable ability' (representing a firm professional standard) and up to 'advisory level' (related to the best in the external market). This range is positioned as an external, absolute scale, not an internal relative measure. As such, it is used for individuals (always starting with self-analysis) to agree with their manager their individual competence profile, or for managers to specify the competence demands of given roles or specific job vacancies, or for the business to profile the differing requirements of customers.

It reaches the strategic needs of the organisation at its most macro level, but equally - and vitally, as a prerequisite for a successful corporate agenda - it supports a stream of products which get to the individual's agenda of professional development, career opportunity ad performance-related reward.

3.2.2 Competences

A current approach to job design is the development and outlining of **competences**.

> A person's **competence** is 'a capacity that leads to behaviour that meets the job demands within the parameters of the organisational environment and that, in turn, brings about desired results'. (*Boyzatis*)

Some take this further and suggest that a competence embodies the ability to **transfer** skills and knowledge to new situations within the occupational area.

Different sorts of competences

(a) **Behavioural/personal** competences are underlying personal characteristics and behaviour required for successful performance, for example, 'ability to relate well to others'. Most jobs require people to be good communicators.

(b) **Work-based/occupational competences** are 'expectations of workplace performance and the outputs and standards people in specific roles are expected to obtain'. This approach is used in NVQ systems. They cover what people have to do to achieve the results of the job. For example, a competence for a Chartered Certified Accountant might be to 'produce financial and other statements and report to management'.

(c) **Generic competences** can apply to all people in an occupation.

Some competences for managers are shown in the following table.

Competence area	Competence	
Intellectual	• Strategic perspective • Analytical judgement • Planning and organising	
Interpersonal	• Managing staff • Persuasiveness • Assertiveness and decisiveness	• Interpersonal sensitivity • Oral communication
Adaptability	• Flexibility • Coping with change	
Results	• Initiative • Motivation to achievement • Business sense	

These competences can be elaborated by identifying **positive** and **negative** indicators.

3.2.3 Job design

Parameters of job design (*Mintzberg*).

(a) **Job specialisation**

(i) **How many different tasks** are contained in the jobs and how broad and narrow are these tasks? **The task may be determined by operations management.** Until recently, there has been a trend towards narrow specialisation, reinforced, perhaps by demarcations laid down by trade unions. On the production line, a worker did the same task all the time. Modern techniques, however, require workers to be **multi-skilled**.

(ii) **To what extent does the worker have control over the work?** At one extreme ('scientific management') the worker has little control over the work. At the other extreme (eg an electrician) the worker controls the task.

(b) **Regulation of behaviour.** Co-ordination requires that organisations formalise behaviour so as to predict and control it.

(c) **Training** in **skills** and indoctrination in **organisational values**.

Belbin (1997) described a way of **tailoring job design** to delayered, team based structures and flexible working systems.

(a) Flattened delayered hierarchies lead to greater flexibility but also to uncertainty and sometimes to a **loss of control**.

(b) Old hierarchies tended to be **clearer** in establishing responsibilities.

3.2.4 Job description

Key term

> A **job description** sets out the purpose of the job, where it fits in the organisation structure, the context of the job, the accountabilities of the job and the main tasks the holder carries out.

Purposes of job descriptions

Purpose	Comment
Organisational	Defines the job's place in the organisational structure
Recruitment	Provides information for identifying the sort of person needed (person specification)
Legal	Provides the basis for a contract of employment
Performance	Performance objectives can be set around the job description

Contents of a job description

(a) **Job title** (eg Assistant Financial Controller). This indicates the function/department in which the job is performed, and the level of job within that function.

(b) **Reporting to** (eg the Assistant Financial controller reports to the Financial Controller), in other words the person's immediate boss. (No other relationships are suggested here.)

(c) **Subordinates** directly reporting to the job holder.

(d) **Overall purpose** of the job, distinguishing it from other jobs.

(e) **Principal accountabilities or main tasks**

(i) Group the main activities into a number of broad areas.

(ii) Define each activity as a statement of accountability: what the job holder is expected to achieve (eg **tests** new system to ensure they meet agreed systems specifications).

(f) The current fashion for multi-skilling means that **flexibility** is expected.

3.2.5 Role definitions

Whereas a **job** is a group of tasks, a role is more than this. A **role** is a part played by people in meeting their objectives by working competently and flexibly within the context of the organisation's objectives, structures and processes. A **role definition** is wider than a job description. It is less concerned with the details of the job content, but how people interpret the job.

Case Study

Guinness

Guinness Brewing Great Britain introduced a new pay system based on competences.

Restrictive job definitions, lengthy job descriptions and a 24-grade structure were replaced by broad role profiles and three pay bands. Roles are now specified in terms of 'need to do' (primary accountabilities), 'need to know' (experience and knowledge requirements) and 'need to be' (levels of competence).

Competences are defined as 'the skill, knowledge and behaviours that need to be applied for effective performance'. There are seven of them, including commitment to results and interpersonal effectiveness. Roles are profiled against each relevant competence and individuals' actual competences are compared with the requirements through the performance management process.

3.2.6 Person specification

Possible areas the specification may cover include:

- Personal skills
- Qualifications
- Innate ability

- Motivation
- Personality

3.2.7 Seven-point plan

Alec Rodgers devised a framework for the selection process that includes seven points.

Point	Examples
Physical make-up	Strength, appearance, health
Attainments	Qualifications, career achievements
General intelligence	Average, above average
Special aptitudes	Manual dexterity, metal sharpness
Interests	Mechanical, people-related
Disposition	Calm, independent
Circumstances	Location, car owner

The diagram on the next page shows recruitment activities in more detail.

3.3 Recruitment policy

FAST FORWARD

Detailed procedures for recruitment should only be devised and implemented within the context of a fair, consistent and coherent **policy**, or code of conduct.

A typical recruitment policy might deal with:

- Internal advertisement of vacancies, where possible
- Efficient and courteous processing of applications
- Fair and accurate provision of information to potential recruits
- Selection of candidates on the basis of suitability, without discrimination

The Recruitment Process

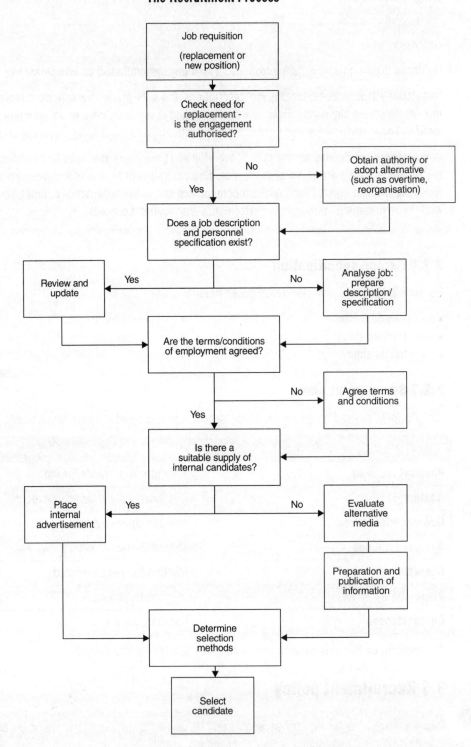

As an example the Chartered Institute of Personnel and Development has issued a Recruitment Code.

The CIPD Recruitment Code

1 Job advertisements should state clearly the form of reply desired, in particular whether this should be a formal application form or by curriculum vitae. Preferences should also be stated if handwritten replies are required.

2 An acknowledgement of reply should be made promptly to each applicant by the employing organisation or its agent. If it is likely to take some time before acknowledgements are made, this should be made clear in the advertisement.

3 Applicants should be informed of the progress of the selection procedures, what they will be (eg group selection, aptitude tests etc), the steps and time involved and the policy regarding expenses.

4 Detailed personal information (eg religion, medical history, place of birth, family background, etc) should not be called for unless it is relevant to the selection process.

5 Before applying for references, potential employers must secure permission of the applicant.

6 Applications must be treated as confidential.

The code also recommends certain courtesies and obligations on the part of the applicants.

Detailed procedures should be devised in order to make recruitment activity **systematic** and **consistent** throughout the organisation (especially where it is decentralised in the hands of line managers). Apart from the human resourcing requirements which need to be effectively and efficiently met, there is a **marketing** aspect to recruitment, as one 'interface' between the organisation and the outside world: applicants who feel they have been unfairly treated, or recruits who leave because they feel they have been misled, do not enhance the organisation's reputation in the labour market or the world at large.

3.4 Recruit or promote?

FAST FORWARD

A recruitment policy should cover areas such as the factors to be considered when deciding whether to **recruit** someone from **outside** or to **promote** or **transfer** someone from the existing workforce instead.

Some of the factors to be considered in this decision are as follows.

(a) **Availability in the current staff** of the skills and attributes required to fill the vacancy. If the lead time to develop current staff to 'fit' the vacancy is too long, there may be no immediate alternative to external recruitment.

(b) **Availability in the external labour pool** of the skills and attributes required. Where there are skill shortages, it may be necessary to develop them within the organisation.

(c) **Accuracy of selection decisions**. Management will be familiar with an internal promotee and his or her performance. An outside recruit will be a relatively unknown quantity and the organisation will be taking a greater risk attempting to predict job performance.

(d) **Time for induction**. An internal promotee has already worked within the organisation and will be familiar with its culture, structures, systems and procedures, objectives and other personnel. This gives a head start for performance in the new position. An external recruit may have to undergo a period of induction before performing effectively.

(e) **Staff development**. Internal promotion is evidence of the organisation's willingness to develop people's careers, which may build morale (and avoid resentments). It may also be part of a systematic **succession plan** which maintains managerial continuity and individual performance improvement over time.

(f)   **Fresh blood**. Insiders may be too socialised into the prevailing culture to see faults or be willing to change. Organisations in fast-changing and innovative fields may require new people with wider views, fresh ideas and competitor experience.

4 Advertising vacancies

Job advertising is aimed at attracting quality applicants and aiding self-selection.

The object of recruitment advertising is to attract suitable candidates and deter unsuitable candidates.

4.1 Qualities of a good job advertisement

Job advertisements should be

(a)   **Concise**, but comprehensive enough to be an accurate description of the job, its rewards and requirements

(b)   **Attractive** to the maximum number of the right people

(c)   **Positive and honest** about the organisation. Disappointed expectations will be a prime source of dissatisfaction when an applicant actually comes into contact with the organisation

(d)   **Relevant and appropriate to the job and the applicant**. Skills, qualifications and special aptitudes required should be prominently set out, along with special features of the job that might attract – on indeed deter – applicants, such as shiftwork or extensive travel.

4.2 Contents of a job advertisement

Typical contents of an advertisement targeted at external job seekers would include information about:

(a)   The **organisation**: its main business and location, at least

(b)   The **job**: title, main duties and responsibilities and special features

(c)   **Conditions**: special factors affecting the job

(d)   **Qualifications and experience** (required, and preferred); other attributes, aptitudes and/or knowledge required

(e)   **Rewards**: salary, benefits, opportunities for training, career development, and so on

(f)   **Application process**: how to apply, to whom, and by what date.

It should encourage a degree of **self-selection**, so that the target population begins to narrow itself down. The information contained in the advertisement should deter unsuitable applicants as well as encourage potentially suitable ones.

4.3 Advertising media

A number of print, electronic and interpersonal **media** are used for job **advertising**.

Media for recruitment advertising include the following

(a)   **In-house magazine, noticeboards**, e-mail or intranet. An organisation might invite applications from employees who would like a transfer or a promotion to the particular vacancy advertised, from within the internal labour pool.

(b)   **Professional and specialist newspapers or magazines,** such as *Accountancy Age, Marketing Week* or *Computing*.

(c)   **National newspapers:** often used for senior management jobs or vacancies for skilled workers, where potential applicants will not necessarily be found through local advertising.

(d)   **Local newspapers:** suitable for jobs where applicants are sought from the local area.

(e)   **Local radio, television and cinema**. These are becoming increasingly popular, especially for large-scale campaigns for large numbers of vacancies.

(f)   **Job centres**. Vacancies for unskilled work (rather than skilled work or management jobs) are advertised through local job centres, although in theory any type of job can be advertised here.

(g)   **School and university careers offices**. Ideally, the manager responsible for recruitment in an area should try to maintain a close liaison with careers officers. Some large organisations organise special meetings or **careers fairs** in universities and colleges, as a kind of showcase for the organisation and the careers it offers.

(h)   The **Internet**. Many businesses advertise vacancies on their websites, or register vacancies with on-line databases. The advantages of '*e-recruitment*' include:

        (i)   Large audience, reached at low cost

        (ii)   Interactivity with links to information, downloadable application forms, email contacts and so on

        (iii)   Pre-selection of people with Internet skills

4.4 Choosing

FAST FORWARD

The choice of advertising medium depends on criteria such as **reach, targeting** and **cost.**

There is a variety of advertising media available to recruiters. Factors influencing the choice of medium include the following.

(a)   **The type of organisation**. A factory is likely to advertise a vacancy for an unskilled worker in a different way to a company advertising for a member of the Chartered Institute of Personnel and Development for an HRM position.

(b)   **The type of job**. Managerial jobs may merit national advertisement, whereas semi-skilled jobs may only warrant local coverage, depending on the supply of suitable candidates in the local area. Specific skills may be most appropriately reached through trade, technical or professional journals, such as those for accountants or computer programmers.

(c)   **The cost of advertising**. It is more expensive to advertise in a national newspaper than on local radio, and more expensive to advertise on local radio than in a local newspaper etc.

(d)   The **readership and circulation** (type and number of readers/listeners) of the medium, and its suitability for the number and type of people the organisation wants to reach.

(e)   The **frequency** with which the organisation wants to advertise the job vacancy, and the duration of the recruitment process.

Exam focus point

A two-mark question on the Pilot Paper asks about a job advertisement that is discriminatory. This ties the material in this section with that in the following chapter on diversity and equal opportunities.

5 A systematic approach to selection

The process of **selection** begins when the recruiter receives details of candidates interested in the job. A systematic approach includes short-listing, interviewing (and other selection methods), decision-making and follow-up.

A systematic approach to selection may be outlined as follows.

Step 1   Deal with responses to job advertisements. This might involve sending **application forms** to candidates.

Step 2   Assess each application against **key criteria** in the job advertisement and specification. Critical factors may include qualifications and experience.

Step 3   **Sort applications** into 'possible', 'unsuitable' and 'marginal'. 'Possibles' will then be more closely scrutinised, and a shortlist for interview drawn up. Ideally, this should be done by both the personnel specialist and the prospective manager of the successful candidate.

Step 4   Invite candidates **for interview.**

Step 5   Reinforce interviews with **selection testing,** if suitable.

Step 6   **Review** un-interviewed 'possibles', and 'marginals', and put potential future candidates on hold, or in reserve.

Step 7   Send **standard letters** to unsuccessful applicants, and inform them simply that they have not been successful. Reserves will be sent a holding letter: 'We will keep your details on file, and should any suitable vacancy arise in future...'.

Step 8   Make a **provisional offer** to the successful candidate.

6 Selection methods in outline

All **selection methods** are **limited** in their ability to predict future job performance!

6.1 A range of methods

We will briefly list the main selection methods here. The more important are discussed in the following sections.

Methods	Examples
Interviewing	• Individual (one-to-one) • Interview panels • Selection boards
Selection tests	• Intelligence • Aptitude • Personality • Proficiency • Medical
Reference checking	• Job references • Character references

Methods	Examples
Work sampling	• Portfolios • Trial periods or exercises
Group selection methods	• Assessment centres

6.2 Which method is best?

Smith and Abrahamsen developed a scale that plots selection methods according to how accurately they predict a candidate's future performance in the job. This is known as a **predictive validity** scale. The scale ranges from 1 (meaning that a method is right every time) to 0 (meaning that a method is no better than chance).

Method	% use by firms	Predictive validity
Interviews	92	0.17
References	74	0.13
Work sampling	18	0.57
Assessment centres	14	0.40
Personality tests	13	0.40
Cognitive tests	11	0.54
Biodata (biography analysis)	4	0.40
Graphology (handwriting analysis)	3	0.00

The results surprisingly show a pattern of employers relying most heavily on the *least* accurate selection methods. Interviews in particular (for reasons which we will discuss below) seem not much better than tossing a coin.

7 Interviews

FAST FORWARD

Most firms use selection **interviews**, on a one-to-one or panel basis. Interviews have the advantage of flexibility, but have limitations as predictors of job performance.

Most firms use the interview as the main basis for selection decisions.

7.1 Purposes of selection interviews

Purposes of the selection interview include:

(a) Finding the **best person** for the job, by giving the organisation a chance to assess applicants (and particularly their interpersonal and communication skills) directly

(b) Making sure that applicants **understand** what the job involves, what career prospects there are, and other aspects of the employment relationship on offer

(c) Giving the best possible **impression** of the organisation as a prospective employer

(d) Offering **fair treatment** to all applicants, whether they get the job or not: in the UK, this is covered by anti-discrimination legislation, but it is also part of the organisation's 'employer brand' and reputation in the labour market

7.2 Preparation of the interview

Candidates should be given clear instructions about the date, time and location of the interview.

The layout of the interview room should be designed to create the desired impression of the organisation, and to create the atmosphere for the interview. In most cases, it will be designed to put the candidate at ease and facilitate communication (eg removing unnecessary formal barriers such as a desk between interviewers and interviewee) – but it may also be used to create pressures on the candidate, to test his or her response to stress.

The agenda and questions should be at least partly prepared in advance, based on *documentation* such as:

(a)   The job description (which sets out the requirements of the job)

(b)   The person specification (which describes the ideal candidate)

(c)   The application form and/or the applicant's CV (which outline the candidate's claim to suitability)

7.3 Conduct of the interview

Questions should be paced and put carefully. The interviewer should not be trying to confuse the candidate, plunging immediately into demanding questions or picking on isolated points; neither, however, should the interviewee be allowed to digress or gloss over important points. The interviewer must retain control over the information-gathering process.

Various questioning techniques may be used, and they are listed on the table on the next page.

Type of question	Comment
Open questions	('Who…? What…? Where…? When…? Why….?) These force candidates to put together their own responses in complete sentences. This encourages them to talk, keeps the interview flowing, and is most revealing ('Why do you want to be an accountant?')
Probing questions	These aim to discover the deeper significance of the candidate's answers, especially if they are initially dubious, uninformative, too short, or too vague. ('But what was it about accountancy that *particularly* appealed to you?')
Closed questions	Invite only 'yes' or 'no' answers: ('Did you…?, 'Have you…?'). This may be useful where there are points to be pinned down ('Did you pass your exam?') but there are several disadvantages to such questions. (a) They elicit an answer *only* to the question asked. (b) Candidates cannot express their personality, or interact with the interviewer on a deeper level. (c) They make it easier for candidates to conceal things ('You never *asked* me…'). (d) They make the interviewer work very hard.
Problem solving questions	Present the candidate with a situation and ask him/her to explain how s(he) would deal with it. ('How would you motivate your staff to do a task that they did not want to do?') Such questions are used to establish whether the candidate will be able to deal with the sort of problems that are likely to arise in the job.
Leading questions	Encourage the candidate to give a certain reply. ('We are looking for somebody who likes detailed figure work. How much do you enjoy dealing with numbers?' or 'Don't you agree that…?' or 'Surely…?'). The danger with this type of question is that the candidate will give the answer that (s)he thinks the interviewer wants to hear.

Question

Identify the type of question used in the following examples, and discuss the opportunities and constraints they offer the interviewee who must answer them.

(a)   'So, you're interested in a Business Studies degree, are you, Jo?'

(b)   'Surely you're interested in Business Studies, Jo?'

(c)   'How about a really useful qualification like a Business Studies degree, Jo? Would you consider that?'

(d)   'Why are you interested in a Business Studies degree, Jo?

(e)   'Why particularly Business Studies, Jo?'

Answer

(a)   Closed. (The only answer is 'yes' or 'no', unless Jo expands on it, at his or her own initiative.)

(b)   Leading. (Even if Jo was not interested, (s)he should get the message that 'yes' would be what the interviewer wanted, or expected, to hear.)

(c)   Leading closed multiple! ('Really useful' leads Jo to think that the 'correct' answer will be 'yes': there is not much opportunity for any other answer, without expanding on it unasked.)

(d)   Open. (Jo has to explain, in his or her own words.)

(e)   Probing. (If Jo's answer has been unconvincing, short or vague, this forces a specific answer.)

Evaluating the response to questions requires another set of interpersonal skills.

(a)   The interviewer must **listen carefully** to the responses and evaluate them so as to judge what the candidate is:

(i)   Wanting to say
(ii)   Trying not to say
(iii)   Saying, but does not mean, or is lying about
(iv)   Having difficulty saying

(b)   In addition, the interviewer will have to be aware when (s)he is hearing:

(i)   Something (s)he needs to know

(ii)   Something (s)he *doesn't* need to know

(iii)   Only what (s)he *expects* to hear

(iv)   Inadequately – when his or her own attitudes, perhaps prejudices, are getting in the way of an objective response to the candidate.

Candidates should also be given the opportunity to ask questions. The choice of questions might well have some influence on how the interviewers assess a candidate's interest in and understanding of the job. Moreover, there is information that the candidate will need to know about the organisation, the job, and indeed the interview process.

7.4 Types of interview

7.4.1 Individual interviews

Individual, one-to-one or face-to-face interviews are the most common selection method.

Advantages include:

(a)   Direct face-to-face communication, with opportunities for the interviewer to use both verbal and non-verbal cues to assess the candidate

(b)   Rapport between the candidate and the interviewer: each has to give attention solely to the other, and there is potentially a relaxed atmosphere, if the interviewer is willing to establish an informal style

(c)   Flexibility in the direction and follow-up of questions.

Disadvantages include the following.

(a)   The candidate may be able to disguise lack of knowledge in a specialist area of which the interviewer knows little.

(b)   The interviewer's perception may be selective or distorted, and this lack of objectivity may go unnoticed and unchecked.

(c)   The greater opportunity for personal rapport with the candidate may cause a weakening of the interviewer's objective judgement.

7.4.2 Panel interviews

Panel interviews are designed to overcome such disadvantages. A panel may consist of two or three people who together interview a single candidate: most commonly, an HR specialist and the departmental manager who will have responsibility for the successful candidate. This saves the firm time and enables better assessment.

7.4.3 Selection boards

Large formal panels, or **selection boards**, may also be convened where there are a number of individuals or groups with an interest in the selection.

Advantages include the following.

(a)   A number of people see candidates, and share information about them at a single meeting.

(b)   Similarly, they can compare their assessments on the spot, without a subsequent effort at liaison and communication.

Drawbacks include the following.

(a)   Questions tend to be more varied, and more random, since there is no single guiding force behind the interview strategy. The candidate may have trouble switching from one topic to another so quickly, especially if questions are not led up to, and not clearly put – as may happen if they are unplanned.

(b)   If there is a dominating member of the board, the interview may have greater continuity – but that individual may also influence the judgement of other members.

(c)   Some candidates may not perform well in a formal, artificial situation such as the board interview, and may find such a situation extremely stressful.

(d)   Research shows that board members rarely agree with each other in their judgements about candidates.

7.5 Advantages of interviews

Interviews in general are by far the most popular selection method used by organisations. They offer some significant advantages.

(a) They are highly interactive, allowing flexible question and answers. This allows candidates opportunities to ask questions, and allows questions and responses to be adapted to the direction and style of the interview.

(b) They offer opportunities to use non-verbal communication, which might confirm or undermine spoken answers (eg a candidate looking hesitant or embarrassed when making competence claims). This is particularly helpful to interviewers when challenging or probing in relation to inconsistencies or gaps in a candidate's application or answers.

(c) They offer opportunities to assess a candidate's personal appearance (relevant in areas such as grooming), interpersonal and communication skills.

(d) They offer initial opportunities to evaluate rapport between the candidate and his or her potential colleagues/bosses.

7.6 The limitations of interviews

Interviews are criticised, however, because **they fail to provide accurate predictions** of how a person will perform in the job, partly because of the nature of interviews, partly because of errors of judgement by interviewers.

Problem	Comment
Scope	An interview is too **brief** to 'get to know' candidates in the kind of depth required to make an accurate prediction of work performance.
Artificiality	An interview is an **artificial situation**: candidates may be on their best behaviour or, conversely, so nervous that they do not do themselves justice. Neither situation reflects what the person is really like.
The halo effect	A tendency for people to make an **initial general judgement** about a person based on a single obvious attribute, such as being neatly dressed or well-spoken. This single attribute will colour later perceptions, and make an interviewer mark the person up or down on every other factor in their assessment.
Contagious bias	The interviewer changes the behaviour of the applicant by **suggestion**. The applicant might be led by the wording of questions, or non-verbal cues from the interviewer, to change what (s)he is doing or saying in response.
Stereotyping	Stereotyping groups together people who are assumed to share certain characteristics (women, say, or vegetarians), then attributes certain traits to the group as a whole. It then assumes that each individual member of the supposed group will possess that trait.
Incorrect assessment	Qualitative factors such as motivation, honesty or integrity are very difficult to define and assess objectively.
Logical error	For example, an interviewer might decide that a young candidate who has held two or three jobs in the past for only a short time will be unlikely to last long in any job. (This isn't necessarily the case.)

Problem	Comment
Inexperienced interviewers	Inexperienced or unskilled interviewers may undermine the process through: • Inability to evaluate information about a candidate properly • Failure to compare a candidate against the job description or person specification • Failure to take control of the direction and length of the interview • Using inappropriate question types to elicit data or put candidates at ease • A reluctance to probe into facts or challenge statements where necessary.

Exam focus point

Interviews are relevant to many areas of personnel management. Many of the issues described above may also be relevant to appraisal interviews.

The limitations of interviews as a selection method is a particularly contentious issue which would lend itself to an exam question.

Selection tests are tested on the Pilot Paper.

8 Selection testing

FAST FORWARD

Selection tests can be used before or after interviews. Intelligence tests measures the candidate's general intellectual ability, and personality tests identify character traits and behavioural preferences. Other tests are more specific to the job (eg proficiency tests).

8.1 Types of selection test

In some job selection procedures, an interview is supplemented by some form of **selection test**. In order to be effective, tests must be:

(a)   **Sensitive** enough to discriminate between different candidates

(b)   **Standardised** on a representative sample of the population, so that a person's results can be interpreted meaningfully

(c)   **Reliable**: in that the test should measure the same thing whenever and to whomever it is applied

(d)   **Valid**: measuring what they are supposed to measure

There are two basic types of test.

(a)   **Proficiency and attainment** tests measure an individual's demonstrated competence in particular job-related tasks.

(b)   **Psychometric** tests measure such psychological factors as aptitude, intelligence and personality.

8.1.1 Proficiency, attainment or competence tests

Proficiency tests are designed to measure an individual's current ability to perform particular tasks or operations relevant to the job: for example, giving a secretarial candidate a typing test. **Attainment** (or competence) tests are a similar measurement of the standard an individual has reached at a particular skill. There is a wide range of proficiency testing material available, including 'in-tray' exercises (simulating work tasks). **Work sampling** requires the candidate to demonstrate work outputs: selectors may observe the candidate working, or the candidate may bring a portfolio of past work.

8.1.2 Intelligence tests

Tests of general intellectual ability typically test memory, ability to think quickly and logically, and problem solving skills. Most people have experience of IQ tests and the like, and few would dispute their validity as good measure of general intellectual capacity. However, there is no agreed definition of intelligence, and tests have now been devised to measure other forms of intelligence, notably emotional intelligence factors (such as self-awareness, interpersonal ability and self-control).

8.1.3 Aptitude tests

Aptitude tests are designed to measure and predict an individual's potential for performing a job or learning new skills. Aptitudes include:

- **Reasoning**: verbal, numerical and abstract
- **Spatio-visual ability**: practical intelligence, non-verbal ability and creative ability
- **Perceptual speed and accuracy**: clerical ability
- **Physical abilities**: mechanical, manual, musical and athletic

8.1.4 Personality tests

Personality tests may measure a variety of characteristics, such as an applicant's skill in dealing with other people, ambition and motivation, or emotional stability. Examples include the 16PF, the Myers-Briggs Type Indicator™ and the Minnesota Multiphasic Personality Inventory (MMPI).

The validity of such tests has been much debated, but is seems that some have been shown by research to be valid predictors of job performance, so long as they are used properly.

8.2 Limitations of testing

Despite current enthusiasm for selection testing, it has its limitations.

(a) There is not always a direct relationship between ability in the test and **ability in the job**: the job situation is very different from artificial test conditions.

(b) The **interpretation of test results** is a skilled task, for which training and experience is essential. It is also highly subjective (particularly in the case of personality tests), which belies the apparent scientific nature of the approach.

(c) Additional difficulties are experienced with **particular kinds of test**. For example:

(i) An aptitude test measuring arithmetical ability would need to be constantly revised or its content might become known to later applicants.

(ii) Personality tests can often give misleading results because applicants seem able to guess which answers will be looked at most favourably.

(iii)   It is difficult to design intelligence tests which give a fair chance to people from different cultures and social groups and which test the kind of intelligence that the organisation wants from its employees: the ability to score highly in IQ tests does not necessarily correlate with desirable traits such as mature judgement or creativity, merely mental ability.

(iv)   Most tests are subject to coaching and practice effects.

(d)   It is difficult to exclude **bias** from tests. Many tests (including personality tests) are tackled less successfully by women than by men, or by some candidates born overseas than by indigenous applicants, because of the particular aspect chosen for testing.

9 Other selection methods

9.1 Group selection methods (assessment centres)

Group selection methods might be used by an organisation as the final stage of a selection process, as a more 'natural' and in-depth appraisal of candidates.

Group assessments (sometimes called **assessment centres**) tend to be used for posts requiring leadership, communication or teamworking skills: advertising agencies often use the method for selecting account executives, for example.

9.1.1 Methods used in group selection

Assessment centres consist of a series of tests, interviews and group situations over a period of two days, involving a small number of candidates for a job. After an introductory session to make the candidates feel at ease, they will be given one or two tests, one or two individual interviews, and several group scenarios in which the candidates are invited to discuss problems together and arrive at solutions as a management team.

A variety of tools and techniques are used in group selection, including:

(a)   **Group role-play exercises**, in which candidates can explore (and hopefully display) interpersonal skills and/or work through simulated managerial tasks

(b)   **Case studies**, where candidates' analytical and problem-solving abilities are tested in working through described situations/problems, as well as their interpersonal skills, in taking part in (or leading) group discussion of the case study.

9.1.2 Advantages of group selection

These group sessions might be useful for the following reasons.

(a)   They give the organisation's selectors a longer opportunity to study the candidates.

(b)   They reveal more than application forms, interviews and tests alone about the ability of candidates to persuade others, negotiate with others, explain ideas to others, investigate problems efficiently and so on. These are typically management skills.

(c)   They reveal more about how the candidate's personality and skills will affect the work team and his or her own performance in the job.

9.2 Reference checking

References provide further information about the prospective employee.

This may be of varying value, as the subjectivity and reliability of all but the most factual information provided by chosen reference sources must be questioned. A reference should contain two types of information.

(a) Straightforward **factual information.** This confirms the nature of the applicant's previous job(s), period of employment, pay, and circumstances of leaving.

(b) **Opinions** about the applicant's personality and other attributes. These should obviously be treated with some caution. Allowances should be made for prejudice (favourable or unfavourable), charity (withholding detrimental remarks), and possibly fear of being actionable for libel (although references are privileged, as long as they are factually correct and devoid of malice).

At least two **employer** references are desirable, providing necessary factual information, and comparison of personal views. **Personal** references tell the prospective employer little more than that the applicant has a friend or two.

9.2.1 Written references

Written references save time, especially if a standardised letter or form has been pre-prepared. A simple letter inviting the previous employer to reply with the basic information and judgements required may suffice. A standard form may be more acceptable, and might pose a set of simple questions about:

- Job title
- Main duties and responsibilities
- Period of employment
- Pay/salary
- Attendance record

If a judgement of character and suitability is desired, it might be most tellingly formulated as the question: 'Would you re-employ this individual? (If not, why not?)'

9.2.2 Telephone references

Telephone references may be time-saving if standard reference letters or forms are not available. They may also elicit a more honest opinion than a carefully prepared written statement. For this reason, a telephone call may also be made to check or confirm a poor or grudging reference which the recruiter suspects may be prejudiced.

It should be noted that with the giving and taking-up of references there are **legal issues** to consider. Those who issue references need to be aware of the potential for claims of negligence from the prospective employer relying on the reference, or even defamation from the employee about whom the reference is being written. In addition, confidentiality must never be breached. Former employees have sued for slander and subsequent employers have brought an action where a person was recommended for an unsuitable post and their incompetence caused damage. Because of the legal implications, employers nowadays write a reference that is purely factual, confirming the dates, salary and role of the person in question. An alternative new method of assessment for new recruits comes in the form of a detailed questionnaire, which has been designed to ask skill-based, quality questions that should provide accurate answers.

10 Evaluating recruitment and selection practices

FAST FORWARD

The **effectiveness and cost-effectiveness** of recruitment and selection should be systematically **evaluated**, using a variety of measures.

10.1 How effective are recruitment and selection?

To get a clear idea of how efficient their recruitment and selection practices are, firms can ask themselves these questions.

- Can we identify human resources requirements from the business plans?
- How fast do we respond to demands from line managers for human resources?
- Do we give/receive good advice on labour market trends?
- Do we select the right advertising media to reach the market?
- How effective (and cost effective) is our recruitment advertising?
- How do our recruits actually perform – do we end up employing the right people?
- Do we retain our new recruits?

Recruitment and selection practices can be reviewed in various ways.

Review	Comment
Performance indicators	Each stage of the process can be assessed by performance indicators, for example the time it takes to process an application. Data can be collected to check any deviation from standard.
Cost-effectiveness	For example, number of relevant responses per recruitment ad, or cost of various advertising media per application elicited (or person employed).
Monitoring the workforce	High staff turnover, absenteeism and other problems (particularly among new recruits) may reflect poor recruitment and selection. Lack of workforce diversity may highlight discriminatory practices.
Attitude surveys	The firm can ask its recruits what they thought of the process.
Actual individual job performance	A person's actual performance can be compared with what was expected when (s)he was recruited.

10.2 Improving recruitment and selection procedures

A systematic model has been proposed in this chapter. If it is considered that recruitment and selection procedures need to be improved, attention may be given to matter such as:

(a) Improvement of **policies and guidelines** for selectors: eg in equal opportunities and recruit/promote decisions

(b) Establishment of **systematic procedures** for all stages of the process

(c) Improved **education and training** of selectors: eg in interviewing skills and testing techniques

(d) **Auditing of job advertising** content and media, in order to improve the attractiveness and realism of the organisation's offerings and the cost-effectiveness of advertising

(e) Widening the organisation's **repertoire of selection techniques**, to aim for the highest possible accuracy in predicting job performance and confirming candidate claims

(f) The possible use of external recruitment and selection **agencies and consultants**

Chapter Roundup

- Effective recruitment practices ensure that a firm has enough **people with the right skills**.

- The recruitment process involves **personnel specialists** and **line managers**, sometimes with the help of recruitment **consultants**.

- **Recruitment** is a systematic process of (a) identifying and defining skill needs and (b) attracting suitably skilled candidates.

- **Job analysis** determines the requirement for a job. The job's tasks are set out in a job description. A **job specification** describes the skills or competences required for the job. A **person specification** describes the sort of person suitable for the job.

- Detailed procedures for recruitment should only be devised and implemented within the context of a fair, consistent and coherent **policy**, or code of conduct.

- A recruitment policy should cover areas such as the factors to be considered when deciding whether to **recruit** someone from **outside** or to **promote** or **transfer** someone from the existing workforce instead.

- **Job advertising** is aimed at attracting quality applicants and aiding self-selection.

- A number of print, electronic and interpersonal **media** are used for job **advertising.**

- The choice of advertising medium depends on criteria such as **reach, targeting** and **cost**.

- The process of **selection** begins when the recruiter receives details of candidates interested in the job. A systematic approach includes short-listing, interviewing (and other selection methods), decision-making and follow-up.

- All **selection methods** are **limited** in their ability to predict future job performance!

- Most firms use selection **interviews**, on a one-to-one or panel basis. Interviews have the advantage of flexibility, but have limitations as predictors of job performance.

- **Selection tests** can be used before or after interviews. Intelligence tests measures the candidate's general intellectual ability, and personality tests identify character traits and behavioural preferences. Other tests are more specific to the job (eg proficiency tests).

- **Group selection methods** might be used by an organisation as the final stage of a selection process, as a more 'natural' and in-depth appraisal of candidates.

- **References** provide further information about the prospective employee.

- The effectiveness and cost-effectiveness of **recruitment and selection** should be systematically **evaluated**, using a variety of measures.

Quick Quiz

1   What is the underlying principle of human resources management?

2   What, in brief, are the stages of the recruitment and selection process?

3   What is the role of line managers in the recruitment process?

4   List the factors determining whether a firm should use recruitment consultants.

5   What are the characteristics of a good job advertisement?

6   What factors should be taken into account in an organisation's interview strategy?

7   The question 'Did you complete your accountancy qualification?' is:

   A   An open question
   B   A closed question
   C   A leading question
   D   A probing question

8   Why do interviews fail to predict performance accurately?

9   List the desirable features of selection tests.

10   Give examples of group selection methods.

11   'Personality and cognitive tests are more reliable predictors of job performance than interviews.' True or false?

12   How can firms improve their recruitment and selection practices?

Answers to Quick Quiz

1   People are a scarce resource and need to be managed effectively

2   Identifying/defining requirements; attracting potential employees; selecting candidates

3   It depends – making a requisition, identifying departmental needs, interviewing, reviewing the job analysis, job description etc

4   Cost; expertise; impartiality; organisation structure and politics; time; supply of labour

5   Concise; reaches the right people; gives a good impression; relevant to the job; identifies skills required etc

6   In brief, giving the right impression of the organisation and obtaining a rounded, relevant assessment of the candidate

7   B. (You might try to rephrase this question as the other types, for extra practice)

8   Brevity and artificiality of interview situation combined with the bias and inexperience of interviewers.

9   Sensitive; standardised; reliable; valid

10   Role play exercises; case studies

11   True

12   Clearly identifying what they want from the candidate; not relying on interviews alone.

BPP
LEARNING MEDIA

16

Diversity and equal opportunities

Topic list	Syllabus reference
1 Discrimination at work	F1 (f)
2 Equal pay	F1 (g)
3 Equal opportunity	F1 (g)
4 The practical implications	F1 (h)
5 Diversity	F1 (f)

Introduction

This chapter addresses a key issue in recruitment and selection (following on from Chapter 15), but it also has wider implications for HR policy and practice.

Employers are slowly starting to realise that equal opportunity policies have social and business benefits (as discussed in **Section 1**) and are seeking not just to comply with the legal framework **(Sections 2 and 3)**, but to develop positive action initiatives **(Section 4)**.

It is also being recognised that the workforce is increasingly **diverse** – and not just in the rather 'obvious' ways referred to by equal opportunities. Managing diversity is discussed in **Section 5**.

This chapter refers to the UK framework. Non-UK students may choose to use this material or may prefer to make use of their knowledge of similar matters in their own countries. Arguably, the UK legal framework raises important issues and sets certain minimum standards which should be regarded as good practice in any employment market.

Study guide

		Intellectual level
F1	**Recruitment and selection, managing diversity and equal opportunity**	
(f)	Explain the purposes of a diversity policy within the human resources plan.	2
(g)	Explain the purpose and benefits of an equal opportunities policy within human resource planning.	2
(h)	Explain the practical steps that an organisation may take to ensure the effectiveness of its diversity and equal opportunities policy.	1

Exam guide

Discrimination and equal opportunities are topics of great importance for managers in real life, relevant to all aspects of people management. The topic features on the Pilot Paper in the context of recruitment advertising.

1 Discrimination at work

1.1 Equal opportunities

> **FAST FORWARD**
>
> **Equal opportunities** is an approach to the management of people at work based on equal access to benefits and fair treatment.

Key term

> **Equal opportunities** is an approach to the management of people at work based on equal access and fair treatment, irrespective of gender, race, ethnicity, age, disability, sexual orientation or religious belief.

Equal opportunities employers will seek to redress inequalities (eg of access to jobs, training, promotion, pay or benefits) which are based around differences, where they have no relevance to work performance.

Certain aspects of equal opportunities (such as discrimination on the basis of sex, race or disability) are enshrined in law; others (such as, up to now, discrimination on the basis of age) rely upon models of good practice.

1.1.1 Why is equal opportunities an issue?

Despite the fact that women have contributed directly to the national product since medieval times, the acceptance of women in paid employment, on equal terms to men, has been a slow process. Many assumptions about women's attitudes to work, and capabilities for various types of work, have only recently been re-examined. Meanwhile, earnings surveys report that across all occupations, women are still earning 60-70% of male earnings in the same occupational group.

The TUC reports that the level of unemployment for black and Asian communities in the UK is significantly higher than for the white population. There is also ethnic segregation in the labour market, with a concentration of minority (male) employees in comparatively low-paying sectors. Meanwhile, the proportion of ethnic minority employees falls sharply at higher levels of the organisation (only 1% of senior managers in FTSE 100 companies).

The choice of jobs for the disabled is often restricted, resulting in higher and longer unemployment rates than the general population. Jobs are concentrated in plant/machine operative jobs, which tend to be low-paid.

Despite demographic and educational changes (and associated skill shortages among the younger population) a certain amount of discrimination is still directed at mature-age workers.

1.1.2 Why is equal opportunity an issue for employers?

FAST FORWARD

Sound **business arguments** can be made for having an equal opportunities policy.

Reasons argued for adopting non- or anti-discrimination measures include the following.

(a)   Common decency and fairness, in line with business ethics.

(b)   Good HR practice, to attract and retain the best people for the job, regardless of race or gender.

(c)   Compliance with relevant legislation and Codes of Practice, which are used by employment tribunals.

(d)   Widening the recruitment pool in times of skill shortages.

(e)   Other potential benefits to the business through its image as a good employer, and through the loyalty of customers who benefit from (or support) equality principles.

2 Equal pay

FAST FORWARD

Specific legislation (Equal Pay Act 1970) covers the offer of **equal pay** to a woman for work that is:
- Similarly evaluated in a job evaluation scheme
- 'The same or broadly similar' to the man's
- 'Of equal value' (Equal Pay (Amendment) Regulations)

2.1 Equal Pay Act 1970

The Equal Pay Act was the first major attempt to tackle sexual discrimination. It was intended 'to prevent discrimination as regards terms and conditions of employment between men and women'.

(a)   Where there is an element of sex discrimination in a collective agreement, this must be removed to offer a unisex pay rate.

(b)   Where a job evaluation scheme is operated to determine pay rates, a woman can claim equal pay for a job which has been rated as equivalent under the scheme.

(c)   Where job evaluation is not used, a women can claim equal pay for work that is 'the same or broadly similar' as the work of a man in the same establishment, ('broadly similar' having to be interpreted in the courts, in many cases. The defending employer must show differences of 'practical importance' in the two jobs).

2.2 Equal pay for work of equal value

The Equal Pay (Amendment) Regulations 1984 established the right to equal pay for 'work of equal value', so that a woman would no longer have to compare her work with that of a man in the same or broadly similar work, but could establish that her work has equal value to that of a man in the same establishment, as measured by a *job evaluation* scheme.

The Equal Opportunities Commission issued a 1997 Code of Practice on Equal Pay, covering definitions, pay systems, methods of identifying discrimination, job evaluation methods and a model policy.

3 Equal opportunity

FAST FORWARD

Discrimination of certain types is illegal in the UK on grounds of:

- Sex and marital status (Sex Discrimination Act 1986)
- Colour, race, nationality and ethnic or national origin (Race Relations Act 1996)
- Disability (Disability Discrimination Acts 1995 and 2005)
- Sexual orientation and religious beliefs (Employment Equality Regulations 2003)
- Age (Employment Equality (Age) Regulations 2006)

3.1 The legal framework on sex and race

In Britain, several main Acts have been passed to deal with inequality of opportunity.

(a) The **Sex Discrimination Act 1986,** and the **Sex Discrimination and Equal Pay (Miscellaneous Amendments) Regulations 1996**, outlawing certain types of discrimination on the grounds of sex, marital status and sex change.

(b) The **Race Relations Act 1996**, outlawing certain types of discrimination on grounds of colour, race, nationality, or ethnic or national origin. The **Race Relations (Amendment) Act 2000** added the requirement that larger public organisations (more than 150 employees) must draw up detailed plans for achieving racial equality in all employment practices.

3.1.1 Types of discrimination

FAST FORWARD

Employers should note the implications of the Acts for both:

- **Direct discrimination** – less favourable treatment of a protected group

- **Indirect discrimination** – when requirements or conditions cannot be justified on non-discriminatory grounds and work to the detriment of a protected group.

There are three types of discrimination under the Acts.

Key terms

> **Direct discrimination** occurs when one interested group is treated less favourably than another (except for exempted cases). It is unlikely that a prospective employer will practise direct discrimination unawares.
>
> **Indirect discrimination** occurs when a policy or practice is fair in form, but discriminatory in operation: for example, if requirements or conditions are imposed, with which a substantial proportion of the interested group cannot comply, to their detriment.
>
> **Victimisation** occurs when a person is penalised for giving information or taking action in pursuit of a claim of discrimination.

In addition, **harassment** is the use of threatening, intimidatory, offensive or abusive language or behaviour. This is covered by UK law in relation to race, religious belief and sexual orientation: sexual harassment will also be covered in forthcoming legislation.

An employer must, if challenged, justify apparently discriminatory conditions on non-discriminatory grounds. It is often the case that employers are not aware that they are discriminating indirectly, and this concept was a major breakthrough when introduced by the Acts.

Question | Indirect discrimination

Suggest four examples of practices that would constitute indirect discrimination on the grounds of sex.

Answer

(a)   Advertising a vacancy in a primarily male environment, where women would be less likely to see it.

(b)   Offering less favourable terms to part-time workers (given that most of them are women).

(c)   Specifying age limits which would tend to exclude women who had taken time out of work for child-rearing.

(d)   Asking in selection interviews about plans to have a family (since this might be to the detriment of a woman, but not a man).

3.1.2 Applying the law

In both Acts, the obligation of non-discrimination applies to all aspects of employment, including advertisements, recruitment and selection programmes, access to training, promotion, disciplinary procedures, redundancy and dismissal.

In both Acts, too, there are certain exceptions ('genuine occupational qualifications'), in which discrimination of a sort may be permitted. For example, a firm may prefer a man over a woman if there are reasons of physiology (not strength), privacy/decency (closely defined) or legal restrictions, eg work outside the UK, where 'laws or customs are such that the duties could not, or could not effectively, be performed by a woman'.

The legislation does not (except with regard to training) permit **positive discrimination**: actions which give preference to a protected person, regardless of genuine suitability and qualification for the job.

Exam focus point

> Bear in mind that the above provisions apply in the UK. Other countries, for reasons of social policy, may have different legislative measures in place. The *principles* of UK law may represent good practice anywhere.

Training may be given to particular groups exclusively, if the group has in the preceding year been substantially under-represented. It is also permissible to encourage such groups to apply for jobs where such exclusive training is offered, and to apply for jobs in which they are under-represented.

The Equal Opportunities Commission and Commission for Racial Equality have powers, subject to certain safeguards, to investigate alleged breach of the Acts, to serve a 'non-discrimination notice', and to follow-up the investigation until satisfied that undertakings given (with regard to compliance and information of persons concerned) are carried out.

3.1.3 Watch this space

The Equality Act 2006 amends some of the provisions on religious belief, sexual orientation and sexual discrimination in public bodies. It also sets out a framework for disbanding the Equal Opportunities Commission, Commission for Racial Equality and Disability Rights Commission – and creating a new umbrella body: The Commission for Equality and Human Rights (CEHR). These amendments will not take effect until 2007 – but it is worth being aware that they are on their way ... Watch out for updates in the quality press and professional journals.

3.2 The legal framework on disability

The **Disability Discrimination Act 1995** contains the following key points.

(a) A disabled person is defined as a person who has a physical or mental impairment that has a substantial and long-term (more than 12 months) adverse effect on his ability to carry out normal day to day activities. Severe disfigurement is included, as are progressive conditions such as HIV even though the current effect may not be substantial.

(b) The effect includes mobility, manual dexterity, physical co-ordination, and lack of ability to lift or speak, hear, see, remember, concentrate, learn or understand or to perceive the risk of physical danger.

(c) The Act makes it unlawful for an employer (of more than 20 employees) to discriminate against a disabled person/employee in three respects.

    (i) In deciding who to interview or who to employ, or in the terms of an employment offer

    (ii) In the terms of employment and the opportunities for promotion, transfer, training or other benefits, or by refusing the same

    (iii) By dismissal or any other disadvantage

(d) The employer has a duty to make reasonable adjustments to working arrangements or to the physical features of premises where these constitute a disadvantage to disabled people.

The Disability Discrimination Act 2005 extends protection to people with HIV, cancer and multiple sclerosis – and imposes additional duties on public bodies to protect and promote equality for disabled people.

3.3 Sexual orientation and religious beliefs

The **Employment Equality Regulations 2003** outlawed discrimination and harassment on grounds of sexual orientation and religious belief. Employers can be held responsible for conduct deemed offensive or harassing (including inappropriate jokes) in regard to either issue. In addition, firms may need to review policies on staff benefits (for gay partners as well as married couples), dress codes (to allow religious expressions) and staff absence (to allow for religious holidays).

3.4 Age discrimination

The 1999 **Voluntary Code of Practice on Age Diversity in Employment** (currently used as guidance for employment tribunals) states that employers should:

(a) Recruit on the basis of skills and abilities; refrain from using age limits or phrases that imply restrictions (such as 'newly-qualified' or 'recent graduate') in job advertisements; refrain from asking for medical references only from older applicants

(b) Select on merit and use, where possible, a mixed-age panel of interviewers, trained to avoid decisions based on prejudices and stereotypes

(c) Promote on the basis of ability, having openly advertised opportunities

(d) Train and develop all employees and regularly review training to avoid age being a barrier

(e) Base redundancy decisions on job-related criteria and ensure that retirement schemes are applied fairly.

Employment Equality (Age) Regulations 2006 implement EU directives. They will prohibit unjustified age discrimination in employment and vocational training; support later retirement and retirement planning; and remove upper age limits for unfair dismissal and redundancy rights.

Exam focus point

> Although the legal framework is clearly important, because of the organisation's compliance obligations, you should be aware of the wider implications of equal opportunity. Think about the ethical and business arguments for eliminating discrimination. Think about the components of a proactive and positive sexual, racial and age diversity policy.

4 The practical implications

The practical implications of the legislation for employers are set out in **Codes of Practice**, currently issued by the Commission for Racial Equality and the Equal Opportunities Commission. These do not have the force of law, but may be taken into account by employment tribunals.

4.1 Formulating an effective equal opportunities policy

FAST FORWARD

> Many organisations now establish their own **policy statements** or **codes of practice on equal opportunities**: apart from anything else, a statement of the organisation's position may provide some protection in the event of complaints.

Some organisations make minimal efforts to avoid discrimination, paying lip-service to the idea only to the extent of claiming 'We are an Equal Opportunities Employer' on advertising literature. To turn such a claim into reality, the following are needed.

(a) **Support** from the top of the organisation for the formulation of a practical policy.

(b) A **working party** drawn from – for example – management, unions, minority groups, the HR function and staff representatives. This group's brief will be to produce a draft Policy and Code of Practice, which will be approved at senior level.

(c) **Action plans and resources** (including staff) to implement and monitor the policy, publicise it to staff, arrange training and so on.

(d) **Monitoring**. The numbers of women and ethnic minority staff can easily be monitored

- On entering (and applying to enter) the organisation
- On leaving the organisation
- On applying for transfers, promotions or training schemes

(It is less easy to determine the ethnic origins of the workforce through such methods as questionnaires: there is bound to be suspicion about the question's motives, and it may be offensive to some workers.)

(e) **Positive action**: the process of taking active steps to encourage people from disadvantaged groups to apply for jobs and training, and to compete for vacancies. (Note that this is not positive discrimination.) Examples might be: using ethnic languages in job advertisements, or implementing training for women in management skills. In addition, there may be awareness training, counselling and disciplinary measures to manage sexual, racial and religious harassment.

4.2 Recruitment and selection

Recruitment and selection are areas of particular sensitivity to claims of discrimination – as well as genuine (though often unintended) inequality.

There is always a risk that disappointed job applicants, for example, will attribute their lack of success to discrimination, especially if the recruiting organisation's workforce is conspicuously lacking in representatives of the same ethnic minority, sex or group. The following guidelines should be borne in mind.

(a)   **Advertising**

   (i)   Any wording that suggests preference for a particular group should be avoided (except for genuine occupational qualifications).

   (ii)   Employers must not indicate or imply any 'intention to discriminate'.

   (iii) Recruitment literature should state that the organisation is an Equal Opportunities employer (where this can be justified).

   (iv)   The placing of advertisements only where the readership is predominantly of one race or sex is construed as indirect discrimination. This includes word-of-mouth recruiting from the existing workforce, if it is not broadly representative.

(b)   **Recruitment agencies**. Instructions to an agency should not suggest any preference.

(c)   **Application forms**. These should include no questions which are not work-related (such as domestic details) and which only one group is asked to complete.

(d)   **Interviews**

   (i)   Any non-work-related question must be asked of all subjects, if at all, and even then, some types of question may be construed as discriminatory. (You cannot, for example, ask only women about plans to have a family or care of dependants, or ask – in the most offensive case – about the Pill or PMT.)

   (ii)   It may be advisable to have a witness at interviews, or at least to take detailed notes, in the event that a claim of discrimination is made.

(e)   **Selection tests**. These must be wholly relevant, and should not favour any particular group. Even personality tests have been shown to favour white male applicants.

(f)   **Records**. Reasons for rejection, and interview notes, should be carefully recorded, so that in the event of investigation the details will be available.

4.3 Other initiatives

In addition to responding to legislative provisions, some employers have begun to address the **underlying problems** of discrimination.

Measures such as the following may be used as positive action initiatives.

(a)   Putting equal opportunities **higher on the agenda** by appointing Equal Opportunities Managers (and even Directors) who report directly to the HR Director.

(b)   **Flexible hours** or part-time work, term-time or annual hours contracts (to allow for school holidays) to help women to combine careers with family responsibilities. Terms and conditions, however, must not be less favourable.

(c)   **Career-break or return-to-work** schemes for women.

(d) **Fast-tracking school-leavers**, as well as graduates, and posting managerial vacancies internally, giving more opportunities for movement up the ladder for groups (typically women and minorities) currently at lower levels of the organisation.

(e) **Training for women-returners** or women in management to help women to manage their career potential. Assertiveness training may also be offered as part of such an initiative.

(f) **Awareness training** for managers, to encourage them to think about equal opportunity policy.

(g) **Counselling and disciplinary policies** to raise awareness and eradicate sexual, racial and religious harassment.

(h) **Positive action** to encourage job and training applications from minority groups.

5 Diversity

FAST FORWARD

The concept of **'managing diversity'** is based on the belief that the dimensions of individual difference on which organisations currently focus are crude and performance-irrelevant classifications of the most obvious differences between people.

Diversity in employment, as a concept, goes further than equal opportunities.

The ways in which people meaningfully differ in the work place include not only race and ethnicity, age and gender, but personality, preferred working style, individual needs and goals and so on.

5.1 Managing diversity

A 'managing diversity' orientation implies the need to be proactive in managing the needs of a diverse workforce in areas (beyond the requirements of equal opportunity and discrimination regulations) such as:

(a) Tolerance of individual differences

(b) Communicating effectively with (and motivating) ethnically diverse work forces

(c) Managing workers with increasingly diverse family structures and responsibilities

(d) Managing the adjustments to be made by an increasingly aged work force

(e) Managing increasingly diverse career aspirations/patterns, flexible working etc

(f) Dealing with differences in literacy, numeracy and qualifications in an international work force

(g) Managing co-operative working in ethnically diverse teams.

5.2 Diversity policy

Ingham (2003) suggests the following key steps in implementing a **diversity policy** taking into account all the equal opportunity requirements.

Step 1　**Analyse your business environment**

(a) Internally – does the diversity of the organisation reflect the population in its labour market?

(b) Externally – does the diversity of the workforce mirror that of the customer base?

Step 2   **Define diversity and its business benefits**

(a)   Legal, moral and social benefits

(b)   Business benefits: better understanding of market segments; positive employer brand; attraction and retention of talent

(c)   Employee benefits: more representative workforce; value and respect for people; opportunity to contribute fully; enhanced creativity

Step 3   **Introduce diversity policy into corporate strategy**

Weave diversity into corporate values and mission.

Step 4   **Embed diversity into core HR processes and system**

Review and refocus recruitment and selection, induction, reward and recognition, career management and training and development.

Step 5   **Ensure leaders implement policy**

(a)   Leaders and top management need to provide long-term commitment and resources

(b)   Use diversity as a key factor in coaching, awareness training and development of managers

Step 6   **Involve staff at all levels**

- Educate the workforce through awareness training
- Create a 'diversity handbook'
- Set up diversity working parties and councils
- Establish mentoring schemes

Step 7   **Communicate, communicate, communicate**

- Communicate diversity policy and initiatives clearly
- Internally: updates, briefings, training, intranet pages
- Externally: to boost employer brand and recruitment

Step 8   **Understand your company's needs**

(a)   Match resources to the size of the organisation and the scale of change required

(b)   Consider using diversity consultants or best practice representatives to provide advice, support and training

Step 9   **Evaluate**

- Benchmark progress at regular intervals
- Internally: diversity score cards, employee climate surveys
- Externally: focus groups, customer/supplier surveys

Exam focus point

The examiner has stated that while the details of Ingham's framework will not be examined, it is useful in aiding an understanding of how diversity may be implemented.

Chapter Roundup

- **Equal opportunities** is an approach to the management of people at work based on equal access to benefits and fair treatment.

- Sound **business arguments** can be made for having an equal opportunities policy.

- Specific legislation (Equal Pay Act 1970) covers the offer of **equal pay** to a woman for work that is:
    - Similarly evaluated in a job evaluation scheme
    - 'The same or broadly similar' to the man's
    - 'Of equal value' (Equal Pay (Amendment) Regulations)

- **Discrimination** of certain types is illegal in the UK on grounds of:
    - Sex and marital status (Sex Discrimination Act 1986)
    - Colour, race, nationality and ethnic or national origin (Race Relations Act 1996)
    - Disability (Disability Discrimination Acts 1995 and 2005)
    - Sexual orientation and religious beliefs (Employment Equality Regulations 2003)
    - Age (forthcoming Employment Equality (Age) Regulations 2006)

- Employers should note the implications of the Acts for both:
    - **Direct discrimination** – less favourable treatment of a protected group
    - **Indirect discrimination** – when requirements or conditions cannot be justified on non-racial grounds and work to the detriment of a protected group.

- Many organisations now establish their own **policy statements** or **codes of practice on equal opportunities**: apart from anything else, a statement of the organisation's position may provide some protection in the event of complaints.

- **Recruitment and selection** are areas of particular sensitivity to claims of discrimination – as well as genuine (though often unintended) inequality.

- In addition to responding to legislative provisions, some employers have begun to address **the underlying problems** of discrimination.

- The concept of **'managing diversity'** is based on the belief that the dimensions of individual difference on which organisations currently focus are crude and performance-irrelevant classifications of the most obvious differences between people.

Quick Quiz

1   Matt Black and Di Gloss run a small DIY shop. They're recruiting an assistant. Matt puts up an ad on the notice board of his Men's Club. It says: 'Person required to assist in DIY shop. Fulltime. Aged under 28. Contact...' Two candidates turn up for interview the following day: a man and a woman (who's heard about the job by word of mouth, through Di). Matt interviews them both, asking work-related questions. He also asks the woman whether she has children and how much time she expects to spend dealing with family matters.

Under the Sex Discrimination Act, Matt has laid himself open to allegations of:

A   One count of discrimination
B   Two counts of discrimination
C   Three counts of discrimination
D   No discrimination at all

2   List four causes of high minority unemployment in the UK.

3   List five possible measures that might support an equal opportunities policy in an organisation.

4   What is sexual harassment?

5   Under Equal Pay legislation, women are entitled to equal pay for 'similar' jobs. *True or false*?

Answers to Quick Quiz

1   C. Advertising in a place where the readership is predominately male. Asking the women about (1) children and (2) time spent on family matters

2   Low average age of minority populations; lack of UK recognised skills and qualifications; racial discrimination; concentrations of minority populations in places and industries with falling or static economic activity

3   Support from top management; a policy and code of practice on equal opportunities; resources to implement the policy; monitoring of implementation; positive action to encourage minority applications

4   Any unwanted conduct of a sexual nature, or based on sex, affecting the dignity of men and women at work

5   False. This was the previous position: the benchmark is now 'jobs of equal value' as determined by job evaluation

Training and development

Topic list	Syllabus reference
1 The learning process	F4 (a)–(c)
2 Development and training	F4 (d)–(f)
3 Training needs and objectives	F4 (d)
4 Training methods	F4 (d)
5 Responsibility for training and development	F4 (c) (d)
6 Evaluating training programmes	F4 (d)
7 Development	F4 (e)

Introduction

The development of people to meet current – and changing – job demands is a key leadership task.

In **Section 1**, we describe how people learn, and in **Sections 2-6**, we look at key aspects of a systematic approach to training: identifying training needs, selecting training **methods** and designing training that suits how people learn. **Evaluating** the effectiveness of training is also very important.

There are detailed procedures and models to learn, but at the core of this topic is the need to ensure that trainee learning is **applied** in the work context. Bear this in mind as you explore training methods, in particular.

In **Section 7**, we look at the wider topic of **development**, which is about more than just improving job performance.

This topic looks forward to performance appraisal (Chapter 18) because that's one of the formal ways of identifying training needs and development potential.

Study guide

		Intellectual level
F4	**Training, development and learning in the maintenance and improvement of business performance**	
(a)	Explain the importance of learning in the workplace.	2
(b)	Describe the learning process: Honey and Mumford, Kolb.	1
(c)	Describe the role of the human resources department and individual managers in the learning process.	1
(d)	Describe the training and development process: identifying needs, setting objectives, programme design, delivery and validation.	1
(e)	Explain the terms 'training', 'development' and 'education' and the characteristics of each.	1
(f)	List the benefits of effective training and development in the workplace.	1

Exam guide

'Training and development' contains a wide range of examinable topics. It could be linked with appraisal and performance management, where training needs are identified.

1 The learning process

FAST FORWARD

There are different schools of thought as to **how people learn**.

1.1 Approaches to learning theory

There are different schools of learning theory which explain and describe how people learn.

(a)   **Behaviourist psychology** concentrates on the relationship between stimuli (input through the senses) and responses to those stimuli. 'Learning' is the formation of new connections between stimulus and response, on the basis of conditioning. We modify our responses in future according to whether the results of our behaviour in the past have been good or bad.

(b)   The **cognitive approach** argues that the human mind takes sensory information and imposes organisation and meaning on it: we interpret and rationalise. We use feedback information on the results of past behaviour to make rational decisions about whether to maintain successful behaviours or modify unsuccessful behaviours in future, according to our goals and our plans for reaching them.

1.2 Lessons from learning theory

Whichever approach it is based on, learning theory offers certain useful propositions for the design of **effective training programmes** and the role of the human resources department in developing such program.

Proposition	Comment
The individual should be **motivated** to learn.	The advantages of training should be made clear, according to the individual's motives – money, opportunity, valued skills or whatever.
There should be clear **objectives and standards** set, so that each task has some meaning.	Each stage of learning should present a challenge, without overloading trainees or making them lose confidence. Specific objectives and performance standards will help trainees in the planning and control process that leads to learning, and provide targets against which performance will constantly be measured.
There should be timely, relevant **feedback** on performance and progress.	This will usually be provided by the trainer, and should be concurrent – or certainly not long delayed. If progress reports or performance appraisals are given only at the year end, for example, there will be no opportunity for behaviour adjustment or learning in the meantime.
Positive and negative **reinforcement** should be judiciously used.	Recognition and encouragement enhance individuals' confidence in their competence and progress: punishment for poor performance – especially without explanation and correction – discourages the learner and creates feelings of guilt, failure and hostility.
Active **participation** is more telling than passive reception (because of its effect on the motivation to learn, concentration and recollection).	If a high degree of participation is impossible, practice and repetition can be used to reinforce receptivity. However, participation has the effect of encouraging 'ownership' of the process of learning and changing – committing individuals to it as their own goal, not just an imposed process.

1.3 Learning styles: Honey and Mumford

FAST FORWARD

> Different people have different **learning styles** or preferences.

The way in which people learn best will differ according to their psychological preferences. That is, there are **learning styles** which suit different individuals. Peter **Honey** and Alan **Mumford** have drawn up a popular classification of four learning styles.

(a) **Theorists** seek to understand basic principles and to take an intellectual, 'hands-off' approach based on logical argument. They prefer training to be:

- Programmed and structured
- Designed to allow time for analysis
- Provided by teachers who share their preference for concepts and analysis

(b)   **Reflectors**

- Observe phenomena, think about them and then choose how to act
- Need to work at their own pace
- Find learning difficult if forced into a hurried programme
- Produce carefully thought-out conclusions after research and reflection
- Tend to be fairly slow, non-participative (unless to ask questions) and cautious

(c)   **Activists**

- Deal with practical, active problems and do not have patience with theory
- Require training based on hands-on experience
- Are excited by participation and pressure, such as new projects
- Are flexible and optimistic, but tend to rush at something without due preparation

(d)   **Pragmatists**

- Only like to study if they can see a direct link to real, practical problems
- Are good at learning new techniques through on-the-job training
- Aim to implement action plans and/or do the task better
- May discard good ideas which only require some development

Training programmes should ideally be designed to accommodate the preferences of all four styles, or to suit individual trainees (where feasible).

Question   Learning styles

With reference to the four learning styles drawn up by Honey and Mumford, which of these styles do you think most closely resembles your own? What implications has this got for the way you learn?

Answer

Depending on your answer you will learn most effectively in particular given situations. For example, the theorist will learn best from lectures and books, whereas the activist will get most from practical activities.

Exam focus point

Learning styles are the basic theories underpinning training. Bear in mind, though, that more practical aspects (such as training needs analysis and programme planning or the benefits of training), would be equally well suited to exam questions.

1.4 The Learning cycle: Kolb

FAST FORWARD

People can learn from everyday work experience, using the **learning cycle** of reflection, generalisation and application.

Another useful model is the **experiential learning cycle** devised by David **Kolb** and popularised by Honey and Mumford. Experiential learning involves doing and puts the learner in an active problem-solving role: a form of self-learning which encourages learners to formulate and commit themselves to their own learning objectives.

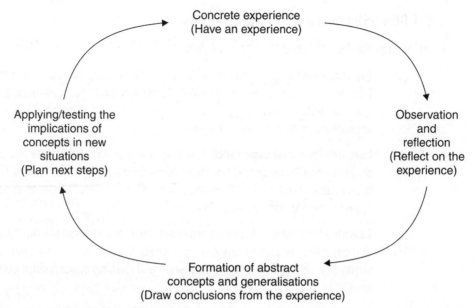

Concrete experience
(Have an experience)

Observation
and
reflection
(Reflect on the
experience)

Formation of abstract
concepts and generalisations
(Draw conclusions from the experience)

Applying/testing the
implications of
concepts in new
situations
(Plan next steps)

Suppose that an employee interviews a customer for the first time (concrete experience). He observes his own performance and the dynamics of the situation (observation) and afterwards, having failed to convince the customer to buy the product, the employee thinks about what he did right and wrong (reflection). He comes to the conclusion that he failed to listen to what the customer really wanted and feared, underneath his general reluctance: he realises that the key to communication is active listening (abstraction/ generalisation). He decides to apply active listening techniques in his next interview (application/testing). This provides him with a new experience with which to start the cycle over again.

Simplified, this **learning by doing** approach involves:

Act ⟶ Analyse action ⟶ Suggest principles ⟶ Apply principles ⟶ Act … (etc)

Exam focus point

Honey and Mumford and Kolb are specifically mentioned in the Study Guide for this syllabus.

1.5 Organisational learning

FAST FORWARD

The **learning organisation** is an organisation that facilitates the learning of all its members (*Pedler, Burgoyne, Boydell*), by gathering and sharing knowledge, tolerating experience and solving problems analytically.

Key term

The **learning organisation** is an organisation that facilitates the acquisition and sharing of knowledge, and the learning of all its members, in order continuously and strategically to transform itself in response to a rapidly changing and uncertain environment.

The key dimensions of a learning organisation are:

- The generation and transfer of knowledge
- A tolerance for risk and failure as learning opportunities
- A systematic, on-going, collective and scientific approach to problem-solving

1.5.1 Strengths of learning organisations

Learning organisations are good at certain key processes.

(a) **Experimentation**. Learning organisations systematically search for and test new knowledge. Decision-making is based on 'hypothesis-generating, hypothesis-testing' techniques: the plan-do-check-act cycle. Application of information and learning is key. Innovation is encouraged, with a tolerance for risk.

(b) **Learning from past experience**. Learning organisations freely seek and provide feedback on performance and processes: they review their successes and failures, assess them systematically and communicate lessons to all employees. Mistakes and failures are regarded as learning opportunities.

(c) **Learning from others**. Learning organisations recognise that the most powerful insights and opportunities come from looking 'outside the box' of the immediate environment. They encourage employees to seek information and learning opportunities outside the organisation as well as inside.

(d) **Transferring knowledge quickly and efficiently throughout the organisation.** Information is made available at all levels and across functional boundaries. Education, training and networking opportunities are constantly available.

2 Development and training

FAST FORWARD

> In order to achieve its goals, an organisation requires a **skilled workforce**. This is partly achieved by training.

2.1 Factors affecting job performance

There are many factors affecting a person's performance at work. Training and development are one method by which an organisation may seek to improve the performance of its staff.

2.2 What are training and development?

FAST FORWARD

> The main **purpose** of training and development is to raise competence and therefore performance standards. It is also concerned with personal development, helping and motivating employees to fulfil their potential.

Key terms

Development is 'the growth or realisation of a person's ability and potential through the provision of learning and educational experiences'.

Training is 'the planned and systematic modification of behaviour through learning events, programmes and instruction which enable individuals to achieve the level of knowledge, skills and competence to carry out their work effectively'.
(Armstrong)

Education is defined as that knowledge acquired gradually, by learning and instruction. Someone who is 'educated' is regarded as being in possession of particular knowledge or skills, and having gone through a particular process in order to acquire them. Education is crucial for a person's professional development, but it is only one part of the development process.

The overall purpose of employee development is:

- To ensure the firm meets current and future performance objectives by...
- Continuous improvement of the performance of individuals and teams, and...
- Maximising people's potential for growth (and promotion)

We will discuss development separately in Section 7 of this chapter.

Question

Note down key experiences which have developed your capacity and confidence at work, and the skills you are able to bring to your employer (or indeed a new employer!).

Answer

Few employers throw you in at the deep end – it is far too risky for them! Instead, you might have been given induction training to get acclimatised to the organisation, and you might have been introduced slowly to the job. Ideally, your employer would have planned a programme of tasks of steadily greater complexity and responsibility to allow you to grow into your role(s).

2.3 Training and development strategy

Organisations often have a **training and development strategy**, based on the overall strategy for the business. Development planning includes the following broad steps.

Step 1 Identify the **skills and competences** needed by the business plan or HR plan.

Step 2 Draw up the **development strategy** to show how training and development activities will assist in meeting the targets of the corporate plan.

Step 3 **Implement** the training and development strategy.

The advantage of such an approach is that the training is:

- Relevant
- Problem-based (ie corrects a real lack of skills)
- Action-oriented
- Performance-related
- Forward-looking

2.4 Benefits of training

FAST FORWARD

Training offers significant **benefits** for both employers and employees – although it is *not* the solution to every work problem!

2.4.1 Benefits for the organisation

Training offers some significant benefits for the organisation.

Benefit	Comment
Minimised the costs of obtaining the skills the organisation needs	Training supports the business strategy.
Increased productivity, improving performance	Some people suggest that higher levels of training explain the higher productivity of German as opposed to many British manufacturers.

Benefit	Comment
Fewer accidents, and better health and safety	EU health and safety directives require a certain level of training.
Less need for detailed supervision; reduced supervisory costs	If people are trained they can get on with the job, and managers can concentrate on other things. Training is an aspect of empowerment.
Flexibility	Training ensures that people have the variety of skills needed: multi-skilling is only possible if people are properly trained.
Recruitment and succession planning	Opportunities for training and development attract new recruits and ensure that the organisation has a supply of suitable managerial and technical staff for the future.
Retention	Training and development supports an internal job market (through transfer and promotion). It also helps to satisfy employees' self-development needs internally, without the need to change employers for task variety and challenge.
Change management	Training helps organisations manage change by letting people know why the change is happening and giving them the skills to cope with it.
Corporate culture	(1) Training programmes can be used to build the corporate culture or to direct it in certain ways. (2) Training programmes can build relationships between staff and managers in different areas of the business.
Motivation	Training programmes can increase commitment to the organisation's goals, by satisfying employees' self-actualisation needs (discussed in Chapter 13).

Note, however, that training cannot do everything! (Look at the wheel in Section 2.1 again.) Training cannot by itself improve performance problems arising out of:

- Bad management
- Poor job design
- Poor equipment, workplace layout or work organisation
- Lack of aptitude or intelligence
- Poor motivation (training gives a person the ability, but not necessarily willingness)

Question

Limitations of training

Despite all the benefits to the organisation, many are still reluctant to train. Suggest reasons for this.

Answer

Cost: training can be costly. Ideally, it should be seen as an investment in the future or as something the firm has to do to maintain its position. In practice, many firms are reluctant to train because of poaching by other employers – trained staff are more marketable elsewhere. While some organisations encourage this 'employability' training, recognising their inability to offer employees long-term job security, others may experience it as a resource drain. In addition, it must be recognised that training by itself is not the solution to performance problems: it must be effectively planned and managed, as we will see later in this chapter.

2.4.2 Benefits for the employee

For the **individual employee**, the benefits of training and development are more clear-cut, and few refuse it if it is offered.

Benefit	Comment
Enhances portfolio of **skills**	Even if not specifically related to the current job, training can be useful in other contexts. The employee becomes more attractive in the labour market ('employability') and more profitable within the firm.
Psychological benefits	The trainee might feel reassured that (s)he is of continuing value to the organisation. A perception of competence also enhances self-esteem and confidence.
Social benefit	People's social needs can be met by training courses, which can also develop networks of contacts.
The job	Training can help people do their job better, thereby increasing job satisfaction, and possibly promotion and earning prospects.

2.5 A systematic approach to training

FAST FORWARD

A **systematic approach** to training includes: need definition; objective setting; planning training programmes; delivering training; and evaluating results.

In order to ensure that training meets the real needs of the organisation, larger firms adopt a systematic approach.

Step 1 **Identify and define** the **organisation's training needs** (from the human resource plan). (It may be that recruitment is a better solution to skill shortfalls.)

Step 2 **Define the learning required** – in other words, specify the knowledge, skills or competences that have to be acquired. (For technical training, this is not difficult: for example, all finance department staff will have to become conversant with a new accounting system.)

Step 3 **Define training objectives** – what must be learnt and what trainees must be able to do after the training exercise.

Step 4 **Plan training programmes.** Training and development can be structured and implemented in a number of ways, as we shall discuss in Section 3. This covers:

- Who provides the training
- Where the training takes place

- Division of responsibilities between trainers, managers and the individual
- What training approaches, techniques, styles and technologies are used

Step 5   **Implement the training programme**

Step 6   **Monitor, review and evaluate** training. Has it been successful in achieving the learning objectives?

Step 7   **Go back to Step 2** if more training is needed.

We will now look at the stages of this process in more detail.

3 Training needs and objectives

FAST FORWARD

> A thorough analysis of **training needs** should be carried out to ensure that training programmes meet organisational and individual requirements.

3.1 Indicators of the need for training

Some training requirements will be obvious and 'automatic'.

(a)   If a piece of legislation is enacted which affects the organisation's operations, training in its provisions will automatically be indicated. Thus, for example, HR staff have needed training as various EU Directives have been enacted in UK law.

(b)   The introduction of new technology similarly implies a training need: for relevant employees to learn how to use it.

Other training requirements may emerge in response to **critical incidents**: problems or events which affect a key area of the organisation's activity and effectiveness. A service organisation may, for example, receive bad press coverage because of a number of complaints about the rudeness of its customer service staff on the telephone. This might highlight the need for training in telephone skills, customer care, scheduling (for the team manager, if the rudeness was a result of unmanageable workloads) and so on.

Some **qualitative indicators** might be taken as symptoms of a need for training: absenteeism, high labour turnover, grievance and disciplinary actions, crises, conflict, poor motivation and performance. Such factors will need to be investigated to see what the root causes are, and whether training will solve the problem.

3.2 Assessment for training

Another alternative is **self-assessment** by the employee. This may be highly informal (a list of in-house or sponsored courses is posted on the notice board or intranet and interested employees are invited to apply) or more systematic (employees complete surveys on training needs). The advantage of self-assessment, or self-nomination for training, is that it pre-supposes motivation on the part of the trainee and harnesses employees' knowledge of their own job requirements and skill weaknesses. The drawback, however, is that employees may be reluctant to admit to performance deficiencies.

A further alternative, therefore, is the use of **attitude surveys** and **360º feedback appraisal reports**, since the employee's superiors, subordinates, colleagues and customer contacts will be in a good position to identify performance deficiencies in areas that affect them: this will be particularly important in the case of customers.

3.3 Formal training need analysis

Other training requirements may only emerge from a formal **learning gap (or training need) analysis**.

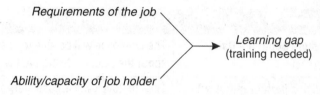

Training needs may be defined as the gap between what people should be achieving and what they actually are achieving. In other words:

Required level of competence *minus* present level of competence = training need.

The **required level of competence for the job** can be determined by:

(a) **Job analysis**, identifying the elements of the task

(b) **Skills analysis**, identifying the skill elements of the task, such as:

    (i)   What senses (vision, touch, hearing etc) are involved?
    (ii)   What left-hand/right-hand/foot operations are required?
    (iii) What interactions with other operatives are required?

(c) **Role analysis,** for managerial and administrative jobs requiring a high degree of co-ordination and interaction with others

(d) **Existing records**, such as job specifications and descriptions, person specifications, the organisation chart (depicting roles and relationships) and so on

(e) **Competence analysis** or existing competence frameworks, such as NVQs relevant to the job.

The **present level of employees' competence** (which includes not only skill and knowledge, but the employee's inclination or willingness to work competently as well) can be measured by an appropriate **pre-training test** of skills, knowledge, performance, attitude and so on.

The ongoing system of **performance appraisal** (discussed in Chapter 18) will furnish some of this information. A **human resources audit** or **skills audit** may also be conducted for a more comprehensive account of the current level of competence, skill, knowledge (and so on) in the workforce.

3.4 Setting training objectives

Once training needs have been identified, they should be translated into **training objectives**.

If it is considered that training would improve work performance, training **objectives** can be defined. They should be clear, specific and related to observable, measurable targets, ideally detailing:

- **Behaviour** – What the trainee should be able to do?
- **Standard** – To what level of performance?
- **Environment** – Under what conditions (so that the performance level is realistic)?

For example:

'At the end of the course the trainee should be able to describe … or identify … or distinguish x from y … or calculate … or assemble …' and so on. It is insufficient to define the objectives of training as 'to give trainees a grounding in …' or 'to encourage trainees in a better appreciation of …': this offers no target achievement which can be measured.

Training objectives link the identification of training needs with the content, methods and technology of training. Some examples of translating training needs into learning objectives are given in *Personnel Management, A New Approach* by Torrington and Hall.

Training needs	Learning objectives
To know more about the Data Protection Act	The employee will be able to answer four out of every five queries about the Data Protection Act without having to search for details.
To establish a better rapport with customers	The employee will immediately attend to a customer unless already engaged with another customers. The employee will greet each customer using the customer's name where known. The employee will apologise to every customer who has had to wait to be attended to.
To assemble clocks more quickly	The employee will be able to assemble each clock correctly within thirty minutes.

Having identified training needs and objectives, the manager will have to decide on the best way to approach training: there are a number of approaches and techniques, which we will discuss below.

3.5 Incorporating training needs into an individual development programme

FAST FORWARD

> Individuals can incorporate training and development objectives into a **personal development plan**.

Key term

> A **personal development plan** is a clear developmental action plan for an individual which incorporates a wide set of developmental opportunities, including formal training.

The purposes of a personal development plan include:

- Improving performance in the existing job
- Developing skills for future career moves within and outside the organisation

3.5.1 Steps in personal development planning

Personal development planning includes the following basic steps.

Step 1 **Analyse the current position**. You could do a personal SWOT (strengths, weaknesses, opportunities, threats) analysis, or a **skills analysis** (as depicted in the following diagram).

Performance

	High	Low
High *Liking of skills*	Like and do well	Like but don't do well
Low	Dislike but do well	Dislike and don't do well

The aim is to try to incorporate more of the employees' interests into their actual roles.

Step 2 **Set goals** to cover performance in the existing job, future changes in the current role, moving elsewhere in the organisation, developing specialist expertise. Such goals should have the characteristic of SMART objectives (specific, measurable, achievable, relevant and time-bounded).

Step 3 **Draw up an action plan** to achieve the goals, including:

- The objective

- Methods you will use to develop the identified skills (including learning experiences, opportunities to try and practise new behaviours and so on)

- Timescales for review of progress

- Methods of monitoring and reviewing progress and achievement of the objective

4 Training methods

FAST FORWARD

There are a variety of **training methods**. These include:
- Off-the-job education and training
- On-the-job training

4.1 Off the job training

FAST FORWARD

Off the job training minimises risk but does not always support transfer of learning to the job.

Off the job training is formal training conducted outside the context of the job itself in special training rooms or off-site facilities.

(a) **Courses** may be run by the organisation's training department or may be provided by external suppliers. These may be:

  (i) **Day release**: the employee works in the organisation and on one day per week attends a local college or training centre for theoretical learning.

  (ii) **Distance learning, evening classes and correspondence courses**, which make demands on the individual's time outside work.

  (iii) **Revision courses** for examinations of professional bodies.

  (iv) **Block release** courses which may involve four weeks at a college or training centre followed by a period back at work.

  (v) **Sandwich courses**, which usually involve six months at college then six months at work, in rotation, for two or three years.

  (vi) A **sponsored full-time course** at a university for one or two years.

(b) **Computer-based training** involves interactive training via PC. The typing program *Mavis Beacon* is a good example.

(c) **E-learning**

  E-learning is computer-based learning through a network of computers or the Internet (rather than stand-alone CD-Rom or software). Learning support is available from online tutors, moderators and discussion groups. This is a major element of the UK government's Lifelong Learning initiative, through the University for Industry (UfI) and 'learndirect'.

(d)   **Techniques** used on the course might include lectures and seminars (theory and information) or role plays, case studies and in-tray exercises (to simulate work activities).

4.1.1 Evaluation of off-the-job training

The advantages and disadvantages of off-the-job training may be summarised as follows.

Advantages	Disadvantages
Allows exploration/experimentation without the risk of consequences for actual performance	May not be directly relevant or transferable to the job and/or job content
Allows focus on learning, away from distractions and pressures of work	May be perceived as a waste of working time
Allows standardisation of training Suits a variety of learning styles (depending on the method used)	Immediate and relevant feedback may not be available (eg if performance is assessed by exam)
May confer status, implying promotability	Tends to be more theoretical: does not suit 'hands on' learning styles
	May represent a threat, implying inadequacy

4.2 On the job training

> **On the job training** maximises transfer of learning by incorporating it into 'real' work.

On the job training utilises real work tasks as learning experiences. Methods of on the job training include the following.

(a)   **Demonstration/instruction:** show the trainee how to do the job and let them get on with it. It should combine telling a person what to do and showing them how, using appropriate media. The trainee imitates the instructor, and asks questions.

(b)   **Job rotation:** the trainee is given several jobs in succession, to gain experience of a wide range of activities. (Even experienced managers may rotate their jobs, to gain wider experience; this philosophy of job education is commonly applied in the Civil Service, where an employee may expect to move on to another job after a few years.)

(c)   **Temporary promotion:** an individual is promoted into his/her superior's position whilst the superior is absent. This gives the individual a chance to experience the demands of a more senior position.

(d)   **'Assistant to' positions (or work shadowing):** an employee may be appointed as assistant to a more senior or experienced person, to gain experience of a new or more demanding role.

(e)   **Action learning:** managers are brought together as a problem-solving group to discuss a real work issue. An 'advisor' facilitates, and helps members of the group to identify how their interpersonal and problem-solving skills are effecting the process.

(f)   **Committees:** trainees might be included in the membership of committees, in order to obtain an understanding of inter-departmental relationships.

(g)   **Project work:** work on a project with other people can expose the trainee to other parts of the organisation.

4.2.1 Evaluation of on-the-job training

The advantages and disadvantages of on-the-job training may be summarised as follows.

Advantages	Disadvantages
Takes account of job context: high relevance and transfer of learning	Undesirable aspects of job context (group norms, corner-cutting) also learned
Suits 'hands on' learning styles: offers 'learning by doing'	Doesn't suit 'hands off' learning styles
No adjustment barriers (eg anti-climax after training) to application of learning on the job	Trial and error may be threatening (if the organisation has low tolerance of error!)
Develops working relationships as well as skills	Risks of throwing people in at the deep end with real consequences of mistakes
	Distractions and pressures of the workplace may hamper learning focus

Question

Training methods

Suggest a suitable training method for each of the following situations.

(a)   A worker is transferred onto a new machine and needs to learn its operation.

(b)   An accounts clerk wishes to work towards becoming qualified with the relevant professional body.

(c)   An organisation decides that its supervisors would benefit from ideas on participative management and democratic leadership.

(d)   A new member of staff is about to join the organisation.

Answer

Training methods for the various workers indicated are as follows.

(a)   Worker on a new machine: on-the-job training, coaching

(b)   Accounts clerk working for professional qualification: external course – evening class or day-release

(c)   Supervisors wishing to benefit from participative management and democratic leadership: internal or external course. However, it is important that monitoring and evaluation takes place to ensure that the results of the course are subsequently applied in practice

(d)   New staff: induction training

4.3 Induction training

FAST FORWARD

Induction is the process whereby a person is formally introduced and integrated into an organisation or system.

4.3.1 The purposes of induction

The purposes of induction are:

(a)   To help new recruits to find their bearings

(b)   To begin to socialise new recruits into the culture and norms of the team/organisation

(c)   To support recruits in beginning performance

(d)   To identify on-going training and development needs

(e)   To avoid initial problems at the 'induction crisis' stage of the employment lifecycle, when frustration, disorientation and disappointment may otherwise cause new recruits to leave the organisation prematurely

4.3.2 The process of induction

The immediate superior should commence the **on-going process of induction**.

Step 1   Pinpoint the areas that the recruit will have to learn about in order to start the job. Some things (such as detailed technical knowledge) may be identified as areas for later study or training.

Step 2   Introduce the recruit to the work premises and facilities, so (s)he can get his or her bearings.

Step 3   Briefing by the HR Manager on relevant policies and procedures: conditions of employment, sickness and holiday absences, health and safety and so on.

Step 4   Introduce the recruit to key people in the office: co-workers, health and safety officers, etc. One particular colleague may be assigned to recruits as a **mentor**, to keep an eye on them, answer routine queries, 'show them the ropes'.

Step 5   Introduce work procedures.

(a)   Explain the nature of the job, and the goals of each task

(b)   Explain hours of work

(c)   Explain the structure of the department: to whom the recruit will report, to whom (s)he can go with complaints or queries and so on.

Step 6   Plan and implement an appropriate training programme for whatever technical or practical knowledge is required. Again, the programme should have a clear schedule and set of goals so that the recruit has a sense of purpose, and so that the programme can be efficiently organised to fit in with the activities of the department.

Step 7   Monitor initial progress, as demonstrated by performance, as reported by the recruit's mentor, and as perceived by the recruit him or herself. This is the beginning of an on-going cycle of feedback, review, problem-solving and development planning.

Note that induction is an **on-going process**, embracing mentoring, coaching, training, monitoring and so on. It is not just a first day affair! After three months, six months or one year the performance of a new recruit should be formally appraised and discussed. Indeed, when the process of induction has been finished, a recruit should continue to receive periodic appraisals, just like every other employee in the organisation.

5 Responsibility for training and development

FAST FORWARD

> Increasingly, **responsibility for training and development** is being devolved to the individual learner, in collaboration with line managers and training providers.

5.1 The trainee

Many people now believe that the ultimate responsibility for training and development lies, not with the employer, but with the **individual**. People should seek to develop their own skills and improve their own careers, rather than wait for the organisation to impose training upon them. Why?

(a) Delayering means there are fewer automatic promotion pathways: individuals need to seek non-'vertical' paths to greater interest and challenge in the job.

(b) Technological change means that new skills are always needed, and people who can learn new skills will be more employable.

5.2 The human resources (HR) department or training department

The human resources department is centrally concerned with developing people. Larger organisations often have extensive learning and career planning programmes, managing the progression of individuals through the organisation, in accordance with the performance and potential of the individual and the needs of the organisation.

5.3 Line managers

Line managers bear some of the responsibility for training and development within the organisation by:

- Identifying the training needs of the department or section
- Assessing the current competences of the individuals within the department
- Identifying opportunities for learning and development on the job
- Coaching staff
- Offering performance feedback for on-the-job learning
- Organising training programmes where required

5.4 The training manager

The training manager is a member of staff appointed to arrange and sometimes run training. The training manager generally reports to the **human resources** or **personnel director**, but also needs a good relationship with line managers in the departments where the training takes place.

Responsibilities of the training manager include:

Responsibility	Comment
Liaison	With HR department and operating departments
Scheduling	Arranging training programmes at convenient times
Needs identification	Discerning existing and future skills shortages
Programme design	Developing tailored training programmes
Feedback	To the trainee, the department and the HR department
Evaluation	Measuring the effectiveness of training programmes

6 Evaluating training programmes

Key terms

Validation of training means observing the results of the course and measuring whether the training objectives have been achieved.

Evaluation of training means comparing the costs of the scheme against the assessed benefits which are being obtained.

6.1 The five-level evaluation model

The effectiveness of a training scheme may be measured at different levels (*Hamblin*).

Level 1   **Trainees' reactions to the experience**. These are usually measured by post-training feedback forms.

Level 2   **Trainee learning** (new skills and knowledge): measuring what the trainees have learned on the course usually by means of a test at the end of it.

Level 3   **Changes in job behaviour following training**: observing work practices and outputs (products, services, documents) to identify post-training differences.

Level 4   **Impact of training on organisational goals/results:** seeing whether the training scheme has contributed to the overall objectives of the organisation, in terms of quality, productivity, profitability, employee retention and so on.

Level 5   **Ultimate value**: the impact of training on the wider 'good' of the organisation in terms of stakeholder benefits, greater social responsibility, corporate growth/survival.

Question   **Evaluating and validating training**

Outline why it is important to evaluate and validate a training programme.

Answer

Validation of a new course is important to ensure that objectives have been achieved. Evaluation of it is more difficult, but at least as important because it identifies the value of the training programme to the organisation. Both are required to improve effectiveness or cost-effectiveness next time.

7 Development

FAST FORWARD

Development includes a range of learning activities and experiences (not just training) to enhance employees' or managers' portfolio of competence, experience and capability, with a view to personal, professional or career progression.

7.1 What is development?

As we noted at the beginning of this chapter, development is a 'wider' approach to fulfilling an individual's potential than training and education. Development may include training, but may also include a range of learning experiences whereby employees are:

(a)   Given **work experience** of increasing challenge and responsibility, which will enable them to other more senior jobs in due course of time

(b)   Given **guidance, support and counselling** to help them to formulate personal and career development goals

(c)   Given suitable **education and training** to develop their skills and knowledge

(d)   Helped to **plan their future** and identify opportunities open to them in the organisation

7.2 Approaches to development

Approaches to development include the following.

Approach	Comment
Management development	'An attempt to improve managerial effectiveness through a planned and deliberate learning process' (*Mumford*). This may include the development of management/leadership skills (or competences), management education (such as MBA programmes) and planned experience of different functions, positions and work settings, in preparation for increasing managerial responsibility.
Career development	Individuals plan career paths. The trend for delayered organisations has reduced opportunities for upward progression: opportunities may be planned for sideways/lateral transfers, secondments to project groups, short external secondments and so on, to offer new opportunities.
Professional development	Professional bodies offer structured programmes of continuing professional development (CPD). The aim is to ensure that professional standards are maintained and enhanced through education, development and training self-managed by the individual. A CPD approach is based on the belief that a professional qualification should be the basis for a career lifetime of development *and* adherence to a professional code of ethics and standards.
Personal development	Businesses are increasingly offering employees wider-ranging development opportunities, rather than focusing on skills required in the current job. Personal development creates more rounded, competent employees who may contribute more innovatively and flexibly to the organisation's future needs. It may also help to foster employee job satisfaction, commitment and loyalty.

Chapter Roundup

- There are different schools of thought as to **how people learn**.

- Different people have different **learning styles** or preferences.

- People can learn from everyday work experience, using the **learning cycle** of reflection, generalisation and application.

- The **learning organisation** is an organisation that facilitates the learning of all its members (*Pedler, Burgoyne, Boydell*), by gathering and sharing knowledge, tolerating experience and solving problems analytically.

- In order to achieve its goals, an organisation requires a **skilled workforce**. This is partly achieved by training.

- The main **purpose** of training and development is to raise competence and therefore performance standards. It is also concerned with personal development, helping and motivating employees to fulfil their potential.

- **Training** offers significant **benefits** for both employers and employees – although it is *not* the solution to every work problem!

- A **systematic approach** to training includes: need definition; objective setting; planning training programmes; delivering training; and evaluating results.

- A thorough analysis of **training needs** should be carried out to ensure that training programmes meet organisational and individual requirements.

- Once training needs have been identified, they should be translated into **training objectives**.

- Individuals can incorporate training and development objectives into a **personal development plan**.

- There are a variety of **training methods**. These include:

    - Off-the-job education and training
    - On-the-job training

- **Off the job training** minimises risk but does not always support transfer of learning to the job.

- **On the job training** maximises transfer of learning by incorporating it into 'real' work.

- **Induction** is the process whereby a person is formally introduced and integrated into an organisation or system.

- Increasingly, **responsibility for training and development** is being devolved to the individual learner, in collaboration with line managers and training providers.

- **Development** includes a range of learning activities and experiences (not just training) to enhance employees' or managers' portfolio of competence, experience and capability, with a view to personal, professional or career progression.

Quick Quiz

1   What does learning theory tell us about the design of training programmes?

2   Which of the following is not one of the learning styles defined by Honey and Mumford?

    A   Pragmatist
    B   Theorist
    C   Abstractor
    D   Reflector

3   List the four stages in Kolb's experiential learning cycle.

4   List examples of development opportunities within organisations.

5   List how training can contribute to:

    (a)   Organisational effectiveness
    (b)   Individual effectiveness and motivation

6   The formula 'required level of competence *minus* present level of competence describes
    .... '.

7   How should training objectives be expressed?

8   List the available methods of on-the-job training.

9   What are the levels of training validation/evaluation?

10   What is the supervisor's role in training?

Answers to Quick Quiz

1   The trainee should be motivated to learn. There should be clear objectives and timely feedback. Positive and negative reinforcement should be used carefully, to encourage active participation where possible

2   C: the correct 'A' word (you may like to use the acronym PART or TRAP to remember the model) is 'Activist'

3   Concrete experience, observation/reflection, abstraction/generalisation, application/testing

4   Career planning, job rotation, deputising, on-the-job training, counselling, guidance, education and training

5   (a)   Increased efficiency and productivity; reduced costs, supervisory problems and accidents; improved quality, motivation and morale

    (b)   Demonstrates individual value, enhances security, enhances skills portfolio, motivates, helps develop networks and contacts

6   Training needs

7   Actively – 'after completing this chapter you should be able to describe how to design and evaluate training programmes'

8   Induction, job rotation, temporary promotion, 'assistant to' positions, project or committee work

9   Reactions, learning, job behaviour, organisational change, ultimate impact

10   Identifying training needs of the department or section. Identifying the skills of the individual employee, and deficiencies in performance. Providing or supervising on-the-job training (eg coaching). Providing feedback on an individual's performance

Performance appraisal

18

Topic list	Syllabus reference
1 Performance management and assessment	F5 (a) (b)
2 The purpose of performance appraisal	F5 (c) (e)
3 The process of performance appraisal	F5 (d)
4 Barriers to effective appraisal	F5 (f)
5 How effective is the appraisal scheme?	F5 (g)

Introduction

The **Accountant in Business** syllabus contains key management and people
issues within its overall framework of 'business structure and purpose'. The
general purpose of performance appraisal is to improve the efficiency of the
organisation by ensuring that individuals within it are performing to the best of
their ability, by developing their own potential (**Sections 1** and **2**). This links to
training and development in Chapter 17.

This chapter also discusses the process of **appraisal** or **competence
assessment** (**Section 3**): the measurement and evaluation of the individual's
performance in relation to given plans and criteria. Barriers to effective
appraisal often need to be overcome (**Section 4**).

You should be aware that this is part of a broader process of:

* Goal setting
* Performance monitoring
* Feedback giving
* Performance adjustment

This process occurs firmly within an organisational context, so that the
performance of human resources supports the objectives of the organisation. It
is therefore important that the effectiveness of the appraisal scheme is
evaluated (**Section 5**).

Study guide

		Intellectual level
F5	**Review and appraisal of individual performance**	
(a)	Explain the importance of performance assessment.	1
(b)	Explain how organisations assess the performance of human resources.	1
(c)	Define performance appraisal and describe its purposes.	1
(d)	Describe the performance appraisal process.	1
(e)	Explain the benefits of effective appraisal.	2
(f)	Identify the barriers to effective appraisal and how these may be overcome.	1
(g)	Explain how the effectiveness of performance appraisal may be evaluated.	2

Exam guide

The process of appraisal and the detailed procedures associated with it could be a rich source of exam questions. The approaches taken with performance appraisal feature in a question on the Pilot Paper.

1 Performance management and assessment

FAST FORWARD

Performance management aims to get better results for the organisation via the measurement and evaluation of individual performance.

Appraisal is part of the system of performance management, including goal setting, performance monitoring, feedback and improvement planning.

Key term

Performance management is: a means of getting better results by managing performance within an agreed framework of goals, standards and competence requirements. It is a process to establish a shared understanding about what is to be achieved, and an approach to managing and developing people in order to achieve it.

This definition highlights key features of performance management.

Aspect	Comment
Agreed framework of goals, standards and competence requirements	The manager and the employee agree about a standard of performance, goals and the skills needed.
Performance management is a **process**	Managing people's performance is an on-going activity, involving continual monitoring and assessment, discussion and adjustment.
Shared understanding	The goals of the individual, unit and organisation as a whole need to be integrated: everyone needs to be 'on the same page' of the business plan.
Approach to **managing and developing people**	Managing performance is not just about plans, systems or resources: it is an **interpersonal** process of influencing, empowering, giving feedback and problem-solving.
Achievement	The aim is to enable people to realise their potential and maximise their contribution to the organisation's success.

1.1 The process of performance management

A systematic approach to performance management might include the following steps.

Step 1   From the **business plan**, identify the requirements and competences required to carry it out.

Step 2   Draw up a **performance agreement**, defining the expectations of the individual or team, covering standards of performance, performance indicators and the skills and competences people need.

Step 3   Draw up a **performance and development plan** with the individual. These record the actions needed to improve performance, normally covering development in the current job. They are discussed with job holders and will cover, typically:

- The areas of performance the individual feels in need of development
- What the individual and manager agree is needed to enhance performance
- Development and training initiatives

Step 4   **Manage performance continually throughout the year,** not just at appraisal interviews done to satisfy the personnel department. Managers can review actual performance, with more informal interim reviews at various times of the year.

(a)   High performance is reinforced by praise, recognition and increasing responsibility. Low performance results in coaching or counselling

(b)   Work plans are updated as necessary.

(c)   Deal with performance problems, by identifying what they are, establish the reasons for the shortfall, take control action (with adequate resources) and provide feedback

Step 5   **Performance review**. At a defined period each year, success against the plan is reviewed, but the whole point is to assess what is going to happen in future.

In order for learning and motivation to be effective, it is essential that **people know exactly what their objectives are**. This enables them to do the following.

(a)   Plan and direct their effort towards the objectives

(b)   Monitor their performance against objectives and adjust (or learn) if required

(c)   Experience the reward of achievement once the objectives have been reached

(d)   Feel that their tasks have meaning and purpose, which is an important element in job satisfaction

(e)   Experience the motivation of a challenge: the need to expend energy and effort in a particular direction in order to achieve something

(f)   Avoid the de-motivation of impossible or inadequately rewarded tasks. As we have discussed in the chapter on motivation, there is a calculation involved in motivated performance. If objectives are vague, unrealistic or unattainable, there may be little incentive to pursue them: hence the importance of SMART objectives.

Some principles for devising performance measures are as follows.

Principle	Comment
Job-related	They should be related to the actual job, and the key tasks outlined in the job description
Controllable	People should not be assessed according to factors which they cannot control

Principle	Comment
Objective and observable	This is contentious. Certain aspects of performance can be measured, such as volume sales, but matters such as courtesy or friendliness which are important to some businesses are harder to measure
Data must be available	There is no use identifying performance measures if the data cannot actually be collected

2 The purpose of performance appraisal

2.1 Main components of appraisal

FAST FORWARD

Appraisal can be used to **reward** but also to identify **potential**. It is part of performance management and can be used to establish areas for improvement and **training and development** needs.

The general purpose of any appraisal system is to improve the efficiency of the organisation by ensuring that the individuals within it are performing to the best of their ability and developing their potential for improvement. This has three main components.

(a)   **Reward review**. Measuring the extent to which an employee is deserving of performance-related bonuses or pay increases

(b)   **Performance review**, for planning and following-up training and development programmes: identifying training needs, validating training methods and so on

(c)   **Potential review**, as an aid to planning career development and succession, by attempting to predict the level and type of work the individual will be capable of in the future

2.2 Specific objectives of appraisal

More specific objectives of appraisal may be summarised as follows.

(a)   Establishing **what the individual has to do** in a job in order that the objectives for the section or department are realised

(b)   Establishing the **key or main results** which the individual will be expected to achieve in the course of his or her work over a period of time

(c)   Comparing the individual's level of performance against a standard, to provide a basis for **remuneration** above the basic pay rate

(d)   Identifying the individual's **training and development needs** in the light of actual performance

(e)   Identifying potential candidates **for promotion**

(f)   Identifying **areas for improvement**

(g)   Establishing an **inventory** of actual and potential performance within the undertaking, as a basis for human resource planning

(h)   Monitoring the undertaking's **selection procedures** against the subsequent performance of recruits

(i)   **Improving communication** about work tasks between different levels in the hierarchy

2.3 Why have formal appraisal?

Formal appraisal systems support objective, positive, relevant, consistent feedback by managers.

You may argue that managers gather performance evaluations, and give feedback, on an on-going basis, in the course of supervision. Why is a formal appraisal system required? What are the benefits?

(a) Managers and supervisors may obtain random impressions of subordinates' performance (perhaps from their more noticeable successes and failures), but rarely form a **coherent, complete and objective** picture.

(b) They may have a fair idea of their subordinates' shortcomings – but may not have devoted time and attention to the matter of **improvement and development**.

(c) Judgements are easy to make, but less easy to **justify** in detail, in writing, or to the subject's face.

(d) Different assessors may be applying a **different set of criteria**, and varying standards of **objectivity** and judgement. This undermines the value of appraisal for comparison, as well as its credibility in the eyes of the appraisees.

(e) Unless stimulated to do so, managers rarely give their subordinates adequate **feedback** on their performance.

An article in *student accountant* (April 2004) sets out the advantages and benefits for the individual and the organisation:

	Benefits
Individual	• Objectives are established in relation to the whole organisation • Key results and timescales are established • Compares past performance and future activities against standards • Basis for performance related pay schemes
Organisation	• Suitable promotion candidates are identified • Areas of improvement can be seen • Communication is improved • Basis for medium to long term HR planning

Question   Formal appraisal

List four disadvantages to the individual of not having a formal appraisal system.

Answer

Disadvantages to the individual of not having an appraisal system include: the individual is not aware of progress or shortcomings, is unable to judge whether s/he would be considered for promotion, is unable to identify or correct weaknesses by training and there is a lack of communication with the manager.

3 The process of performance appraisal

3.1 Overview of the appraisal process

Three basic requirements of a **formal appraisal system** are: defining what is to be appraised, recording assessments, and getting the appraiser and appraisee together for feedback and planning.

There are three basic requirements for a formal appraisal system.

(a) The **formulation of desired traits and standards** against which individuals can be consistently and objectively assessed.

(b) **Recording assessments**. Managers should be encouraged to utilise a standard framework, but still be allowed to express what they consider important, and without too much form-filling.

(c) **Getting the appraiser and appraisee together**, so that both contribute to the assessment and plans for improvement and/or development.

A systematic appraisal system would include the following stages.

Step 1 **Identification of criteria** for assessment, perhaps based on job analysis, performance standards, person specifications and so on.

Step 2 The preparation by the subordinate's manager of an **appraisal report**. In some systems both the appraisee and appraiser prepare a report. These reports are then compared.

Step 3 An **appraisal interview**, for an exchange of views about the appraisal report, targets for improvement, solutions to problems and so on.

Step 4 **Review of the assessment** by the assessor's own superior, so that the appraisee does not feel subject to one person's prejudices. Formal appeals may be allowed, if necessary to establish the fairness of the procedure.

Step 5 The preparation and implementation of **action plans** to achieve improvements and changes agreed.

Step 6 **Follow-up:** monitoring the progress of the action plan.

This can be depicted as a control system, as follows.

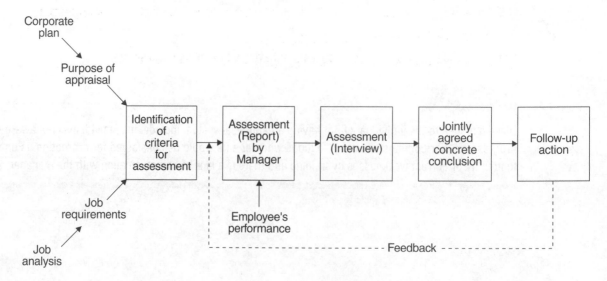

BPP
LEARNING MEDIA

3.2 What is appraisal?

Assessments must be related to a common standard, in order for comparisons to be made between individuals: on the other hand, they should be related to meaningful **performance criteria**, which take account of the critical variables in each job.

Some basic criteria might appear in a simple appraisal report form as follows.

APPRAISAL REPORT						
Name: Time in position:						
Position: Period of review:						
Company:						
Overall assessment	A	B	C	D	E	Comment
Job knowledge						
Effective output						
Co-operation						
Initiative						
Time-keeping						
Other relevant facts (specify)						

A = Outstanding   B = Above standard   C = To required standard

D = Short of standard in some respects   E = Not up to required standard

Potential	A	B	C	D	E	Comment

A = Overdue for promotion   B = Ready for promotion   C = Potential for promotion

D = No evidence of promotion potential at present

E = Has not worked long enough with me for judgement

Training, if any, required:

Assessment discussed with employee?	Yes	No
Signed	Date	
Confirmed	Date	

BPP LEARNING MEDIA

3.3 Appraisal techniques

A variety of appraisal **techniques** can be used to measure different criteria in a different ways.

A variety of appraisal techniques may be used, measuring different criteria in different ways.

(a) **Overall assessment** The manager writes in narrative form his judgements about the appraisee. There will be no guaranteed consistency of the criteria and areas of assessment, however, and managers may not be able to convey clear, effective judgements in writing.

(b) **Guided assessment**. Assessors are required to comment on a number of specified characteristics and performance elements, with guidelines as to how terms such as 'application', 'integrity' and 'adaptability' are to be interpreted in the work context. This is more precise, but still rather vague.

(c) **Grading**. Grading adds a comparative frame of reference to the general guidelines, whereby managers are asked to select one of a number of levels or degrees to which the individual in question displays the given characteristic. These are also known as **rating scales**.

Numerical values may be added to ratings to give rating scores. Alternatively a less precise **graphic scale** may be used to indicate general position on a plus/minus scale.

Factor: job knowledge

High _____ ⇥ _____   Average _____   Low _____

(d) **Behavioural incident methods**. These concentrate on employee behaviour, which is measured against typical behaviour in each job, as defined by common critical incidents of successful and unsuccessful job behaviour reported by managers.

(e) **Results-orientated schemes**. This reviews performance against specific targets and standards of performance agreed in advance by manager and subordinate together. There are significant advantages to such an approach.

(i) The subordinate is more involved in appraisal because (s)he is able to evaluate his/her progress in achieving jointly-agreed targets.

(ii) The manager is relieved of a critic's role, and becomes a coach.

(iii) Clear and known targets help modify behaviour.

The effectiveness of the scheme will depend on the **targets set** (are they clearly defined? realistic?) and the **commitment** of both parties to make it work.

Question   Appraisal techniques

What sort of appraisal systems are suggested by the following examples?

(a) The Head Teacher of Dotheboys Hall sends a brief report at the end of each term to the parents of the school's pupils. Typical phrases include 'a satisfactory term's work', and 'could do better'.

(b) A firm of auditors assess the performance of their staff in four categories: technical ability, relationships with clients, relationships with other members of the audit team, and professional attitude. On each of these criteria staff are marked from A (= excellent) to E (= poor).

(c) A firm of insurance brokers assesses the performance of its staff by the number of clients they have visited and the number of policies sold.

Answer

(a) Overall assessment of the blandest kind
(b) A grading system, based on a guided assessment
(c) Results-orientated scheme

3.4 Self-appraisals

Self-appraisals occur when individuals carry out their own self-evaluation as a major input into the appraisal process.

Advantages include the following.

(a) It **saves the manager time**, as the employee identifies the areas of competence which are relevant to the job and his/her relative strengths.

(b) It offers **increased responsibility** to the individual, which may improve motivation.

(c) This **reconciles the goals** of the individual and the organisation.

(d) In giving the responsibility to an individual, the scheme may offer more **flexibility** in terms of the timing and relevance of the appraisal.

Disadvantages the following.

(a) People are often not the best judges of their own performance.

(b) People may deliberately over- (or under-) estimate their performance, in order to gain approval or reward – or to conform to group norms.

Many schemes combine managerial and self appraisal.

3.5 The appraisal interview

The appraisal **interview** is an important stage in the process, as it can be used to encourage collaborative problem solving and improvement planning. A 'problem-solving' style is preferable to a 'tell and sell' or 'tell and listen' style (*Maier*).

The process of an appraisal interview may be as follows.

Step 1 **Prepare**

- Plan interview time and environment: the aim is to facilitate collaborative problem-solving and communication. Privacy is essential

- Prepare relevant documentation: job description, employee records, and statement of performance (or appraisal form)

- Review employee's history and self-appraisals/peer appraisals (if used)

- Prepare for the interview

- Prepare report. Review employee's self-appraisal

Step 2 **Interview**

- Select an appropriate style (see below): directional, persuasive or collaborative
- Encourage employee to talk, identify problems and solutions
- Be fair

Step 3 **Agree**

- Summarise to check understanding
- Gain employee commitment
- Agree plan of action

Step 4 **Report**

- Complete appraisal report, if not already prepared

Step 5 **Follow up**

- Take action as agreed
- Monitor progress
- Keep employee informed

3.5.1 Three approaches: Maier

Maier (The Appraisal Interview) identifies three types of approach to appraisal interviews. Most appraisees prefer the third of the alternatives suggested.

(a) The **tell and sell style**. The manager tells the subordinate how (s)he has been assessed, and then tries to 'sell' (gain acceptance of) the evaluation and the improvement plan. This requires unusual human relations skills in order to convey constructive criticism in an acceptable manner, and to motivate the appraisee to alter his/her behaviour.

(b) The **tell and listen style**. The manager tells the subordinate how (s)he has been assessed, and then invites the appraisee to respond. The manager therefore no longer dominates the interview throughout, and there is greater opportunity for coaching or counselling as opposed to pure direction.

  (i) The employee is encouraged to participate in the assessment and the working out of improvement targets and methods: it is an accepted tenet of behavioural theory that participation in problem definition and goal setting increases the individual's commitment to behaviour and attitude modification.

  (ii) This method does not assume that a change in the employee will be the sole key to improvement: the manager may receive helpful feedback about how job design, methods, environment or supervision might be improved.

(c) The **problem-solving style**. The manager abandons the role of critic altogether, and becomes a coach and helper. The discussion is centred not on the assessment, but on the employee's work problems. The employee is encouraged to think solutions through, and to commit to the recognised need for personal improvement. This approach encourages intrinsic motivation through the element of self-direction, and the perception of the job itself as a problem-solving activity. It may also stimulate creative thinking on the part of employee and manager alike, to the benefit of the organisation's adaptability and methods.

Exam focus point

> This is the accepted framework for discussing appraisal interviews and so is worth learning, especially as it appears on the Pilot Paper.

3.6 Follow-up

After the appraisal interview, the manager may complete the report, with an overall assessment, assessment of potential and/or the jointly-reached conclusion of the interview, with **recommendations for follow-up action**. The manager should then discuss the report with the counter-signing manager (usually his or her own superior), resolving any problems that have arisen in making the appraisal or report, and agreeing on action to be taken. The report form may then go to the development adviser, training officer or other relevant people as appropriate for follow-up.

Follow-up procedures may include the following.

(a) **Informing appraisees of the results** of the appraisal, if this has not been central to the review interview

(b) **Carrying out agreed actions** on training, promotion and so on

(c) **Monitoring the appraisee's progress** and checking that (s)he has carried out agreed actions or improvements

(d) Taking necessary steps to **help the appraisee to attain improvement objectives**, by guidance, providing feedback, upgrading equipment, altering work methods and so on.

Question	Follow-up

What would happen without follow-up?

Answer

The appraisal would merely be seen as a pleasant chat with little effect on future performance, as circumstances change. Moreover the individual might feel cheated.

The appraisal can also be used as an input to the employee's **personal development plan** (see Chapter 14).

4 Barriers to effective appraisal

FAST FORWARD

Problems with appraisal are its implementation in practice and a range of misperceptions about it (*Lockett*). New techniques of appraisal aim to monitor effectiveness from a number of perspectives.

4.1 Problems in practice

Lockett *(Effective Performance Management)* suggests that barriers to effective appraisal can be identified as follows.

Appraisal barriers	Comment
Appraisal as confrontation	Many people dread appraisals, or use them 'as a sort of show down, a good sorting out or a clearing of the air.' In this kind of climate: • There is likely to be a lack of agreement on performance levels and improvement needs. • The feedback may be subjective or exaggerated. • The feedback may be negatively delivered. • The appraisal may focus on negative aspects, rather than looking forward to potential for improvement and development.
Appraisal as judgement	The appraisal 'is seen as a one-sided process in which the manager acts as judge, jury and counsel for the prosecution'. This puts the subordinate on the defensive. Instead, the process of performance management 'needs to be jointly operated in order to retain the commitment and develop the self-awareness of the individual.'

Appraisal barriers	Comment
Appraisal as chat	The appraisal is conducted as if it were a friendly chat 'without … purpose or outcome … Many managers, embarrassed by the need to give feedback and set stretching targets, reduce the appraisal to a few mumbled "well dones!" and leave the interview with a briefcase of unresolved issues.'
Appraisal as bureaucracy	Appraisal is a form-filling exercise, to satisfy the personnel department. Its underlying purpose, improving individual and organisational performance, is forgotten.
Appraisal as unfinished business	Appraisal should be part of a continuing future-focused process of performance management, not a way of 'wrapping up' the past year's performance issues.
Appraisal as annual event	Many targets set at annual appraisal meetings become irrelevant or out-of-date. Feedback, goal adjustment and improvement planning should be a continuous process.

A *student accountant* article (April 2004) suggests that: 'Perhaps the greatest problem with appraisals is that they are often regarded as a nuisance' by employees and managers alike.

4.2 Appraisal and pay

Another problem is the extent to which the appraisal system is related to the **pay and reward system**. Many employees consider that positive appraisals should be rewarded, but there are major drawbacks to this approach.

(a) **Funds available** for pay rises rarely depend on one individual's performance alone – the whole company has to do well.

(b) **Continuous improvement** should perhaps be expected of employees as part of their work and development, not rewarded as extra.

(c) Performance management is about a lot more than pay for *past* performance – it is often **forward looking** with regard to future performance.

4.3 Upward appraisal

FAST FORWARD

New techniques of appraisal aim to monitor the appraisee's effectiveness from a number of perspectives. These techniques include upward, customer and 360 degree feedback.

A notable modern trend, adopted in the UK by companies such as BP and British Airways and others, is **upward appraisal**, whereby employees are not rated by their superiors but by their subordinates. The followers appraise the leader.

Advantages of upward appraisal include the following.

(a) Subordinates tend to know their superior better than superiors know their subordinates.

(b) As all subordinates rate their managers statistically, these ratings tend to be more reliable – the more subordinates the better. Instead of the biases of individual managers' ratings, the various ratings of the employees can be converted into a representative view.

(c) Subordinates' ratings have more impact because it is more unusual to receive ratings from subordinates. It is also surprising to bosses because, despite protestations to the contrary, information often flows down organisations more smoothly and comfortably than it flows up. When it flows up it is qualitatively and quantitatively different. It is this difference that makes it valuable.

Problems with the method include fear of reprisals, vindictiveness, and extra form processing. Some bosses in strong positions might refuse to act, even if a consensus of staff suggested that they should change their ways.

4.4 Customer appraisal

In some companies part of the employee's appraisal process must take the form of **feedback from 'customers' (whether internal or external).** This may be taken further into an influence on remuneration (at *Rank-Xerox*, 30% of a manager's annual bonus is conditional upon satisfactory levels of 'customer' feedback). This is a valuable development in that customers are the best judges of customer service, which the appraisee's boss may not see.

4.5 360 degree appraisal

Taking downwards, upwards and customer appraisals together, some firms have instituted **360 degree appraisal** (or multi-source appraisal) by collecting feedback on an individual's performance from the following sources.

(a)   The person's immediate manager.

(b)   People who report to the appraisee, perhaps divided into groups.

(c)   Peers and co-workers: most people interact with others within an organisation, either as members of a team or as the receivers or providers of services. They can offer useful feedback.

(d)   Customers: if sales people know what customers thought of them, they might be able to improve their technique.

(e)   The manager personally: all forms of 360 degree appraisal require people to rate themselves. Those 'who see themselves as others see them will get fewer surprises'.

Sometimes the appraisal results in a counselling session, especially when the result of the appraisals are conflicting. For example, an appraisee's manager may have a quite different view of the appraisee's skills than subordinates.

5 How effective is the appraisal scheme?

FAST FORWARD

Like any organisational programme, the effectiveness and cost-effectiveness of appraisal should be systematically **evaluated**.

5.1 Criteria for evaluating appraisal

The appraisal scheme should itself be evaluated (and regularly re-assessed) according to the following general criteria.

Criteria	Comment
Relevance	• Does the system have a useful purpose, relevant to the needs of the organisation and the individual? • Is the purpose clearly expressed and widely understood by all concerned, both appraisers and appraisees? • Are the appraisal criteria relevant to the purposes of the system?

Criteria	Comment
Fairness	• Is there reasonable standardisation of criteria and objectivity throughout the organisation? • Is it reasonably objective?
Serious intent	• Are the managers concerned committed to the system – or is it just something the personnel department thrusts upon them? • Who does the interviewing, and are they properly trained in interviewing and assessment techniques? • Is reasonable time and attention given to the interviews – or is it a question of 'getting them over with'? • Is there a genuine demonstrable link between performance and reward or opportunity for development?
Co-operation	• Is the appraisal a participative, problem-solving activity – or a tool of management control? • Is the appraisee given time and encouragement to prepare for the appraisal, so that he can make a constructive contribution? • Does a jointly-agreed, concrete conclusion emerge from the process? • Are appraisals held regularly?
Efficiency	• Does the system seem overly time-consuming compared to the value of its outcome? • Is it difficult and costly to administer?

5.2 Methods of evaluation

Evaluating the appraisal scheme may involve:

(a)   Asking appraisers and appraisees how they **felt** about the system (addressing issues of perceived usefulness, fairness and so on)

(b)   Checking to see if there have been enhancements in **performance** by the individual and the organisation (as a result of problem solving and improvement planning)

(c)   Reviewing other **indicative** factors, such as staff turnover or disciplinary problems, lack of management succession and so on.

However, firms should not expect too much of the appraisal scheme. Appraisal systems, because they target the individual's performance, concentrate on the lowest level of performance feedback: they ignore the organisational and systems context of performance.

Chapter Roundup

- Performance management aims to get better results for the organisation and evaluation of individual performance.

  Appraisal is part of the system of performance management, including goal setting, performance monitoring, feedback and improvement planning.

- Appraisal can be used to **reward** but also to identify **potential**. It is part of performance management and can be used to establish areas for improvement and **training and development** needs.

- **Formal appraisal systems** support objective, positive, relevant, consistent feedback by managers.

- Three basic requirements of a **formal appraisal system** are: defining what is to be appraised, recording assessments, and getting the appraiser and appraisee together for feedback and planning.

- A variety of appraisal **techniques** can be used to measure different criteria in a different ways.

- The appraisal **interview** is an important stage in the process, as it can be used to encourage collaborative problem solving and improvement planning. A 'problem-solving' style is preferable to a 'tell and sell' or 'tell and listen' style (*Maier*).

- **Problems** with appraisal are its implementation in practice and a range of misperceptions about it (*Lockett*). New techniques of appraisal aim to monitor effectiveness from a number of perspectives.

- New techniques of appraisal aim to monitor the appraisee's effectiveness from a number of perspectives. These techniques include upward, customer and 360 degree feedback.

- Like any organisational programme, the effectiveness and cost-effectiveness of appraisal should be systematically **evaluated**.

Quick Quiz

1   What are the purposes of appraisal?

2   What bases or criteria of assessment might an appraisal system use?

3   Outline a results-oriented approach to appraisal.

4   What is a 360-degree feedback, and who might be involved?

5   When a subordinate rates his or her manager's leadership skills, this is an example of:

    A   Job evaluation
    B   Job analysis
    C   Performance management
    D   Upward appraisal

6   What follow-up should there be after an appraisal?

7   How can appraisals be made more positive and empowering to employees?

8   What kinds of criticism might be levelled at appraisal schemes by a manager who thought they were a waste of time?

9   What is the difference between performance appraisal and performance management?

10 The most empowering style of appraisal interview, according to Maier, is the 'tell and listen' approach. *True or false?*

Answers to Quick Quiz

1   Identifying performance levels, improvements needed and promotion prospects; deciding on rewards; assessing team work and encouraging communication between manager and employee

2   Job analysis, job description, plans, targets and standards

3   Performance against specific mutually agreed targets and standards

4   A 360 degree appraisal involves doing a downwards, upwards and customer appraisal together. Feedback on an individual's performance is collected from the following sources.

  (a)   The person's immediate manager
  (b)   People who report to the appraisee
  (c)   Peers and co-workers
  (d)   Customers
  (e)   The individual personally

5   D. Make sure you can define all these terms clearly

6   Appraisees should be informed of the results, agreed activity should be taken, progress should be monitored and whatever resources or changes are needed should be provided or implemented

7   Ensure the scheme is relevant, fair, taken seriously, and co-operative

8   The manager may say that he has better things to do with his time, that appraisals have no relevance to the job and there is no reliable follow-up action, and that they involve too much paperwork

9   Appraisal *on its own* is a backward-looking performance review. But it is a vital input into performance management, which is forward-looking

10   False. The most empowering style is 'problem solving'

Pilot paper questions and answers

Pilot paper

Paper F1

Accountant in Business

Time allowed: 2 hours

Do NOT open this paper until instructed by the supervisor.

During reading and planning time only the question paper may be annotated. You must NOT write in your answer booklet until instructed by the supervisor.

This question paper must not be removed from the examination hall.

Warning

The pilot paper cannot cover all of the syllabus nor can it include examples of every type of question that will be included in the actual exam. You may see questions in the exam that you think are more difficult than any you see in the pilot paper.

ALL FIFTY questions are compulsory and MUST be attempted

1   Span of control is concerned with the number of levels of management in an organisation.

    A   True
    B   False   **(1 mark)**

2   Which of the following is the main function of marketing?

    A   To maximise sales volume
    B   To identify and anticipate customer needs
    C   To persuade potential consumers to convert latent demand into expenditure
    D   To identify suitable outlets for goods and services supplied   **(2 marks)**

3   Which one of the following has become an established best practice in corporate governance in recent years?

    A   An increasingly prominent role for non-executive directors
    B   An increase in the powers of external auditors
    C   Greater accountability for directors who are in breach of their fiduciary duties
    D   A requirement for all companies to establish an internal audit function   **(2 marks)**

4   According to Charles Handy's four cultural stereotypes, which of the following organisations would adopt a task culture?

    A   The cost accounting department of a large steel producing company
    B   The consulting division of a 'big four' accountancy firm
    C   A civil service department
    D   A small clothes and design fashion house   **(2 marks)**

5   At what stage of the planning process should a company carry out a situation analysis?

    A   When converting strategic objectives into tactical plans
    B   When formulating a mission statement
    C   When validating the effectiveness of plans against outcomes
    D   When formulating strategic objectives   **(2 marks)**

6   Which one of the following is a potential advantage of decentralisation?

    A   Greater control by senior management
    B   Risk reduction in relation to operational decision-making
    C   More accountability at lower levels
    D   Consistency of decision-making across the organisation   **(2 marks)**

7   Which one of the following is an example of an internal stakeholder?

    A   A shareholder
    B   An non-executive director
    C   A manager
    D   A supplier   **(2 marks)**

8   According to Mendelow, companies must pay most attention to the needs of which group of stakeholders?

    A   Those with little power and little interest in the company

    B   Those with a high level of power but little interest in the company

    C   Those with little power but a high level of interest in the company

    D   Those with a high level of power and a high level of interest in the company   **(2 marks)**

9   What is the responsibility of a Public Oversight Board?

    A   The establishment of detailed rules on internal audit procedures

    B   The commissioning of financial reporting standards

    C   The creation of legislation relating to accounting standards

    D   The monitoring and enforcement of legal and compliance standards   **(2 marks)**

10   The ageing population trend in many European countries is caused by a increasing birth rate and an increasing mortality rate.

    A   True

    B   False   **(1 mark)**

11   Which one of the following is consistent with a government's policy objective to expand the level of economic activity?

    A   An increase in taxation

    B   An increase in interest rates

    C   An increase in personal savings

    D   An increase in public expenditure   **(2 marks)**

12   Which of the following is the name given to unemployment arising from labour in the market place being of the wrong type or available in the wrong place?

    A   Structural unemployment

    B   Cyclical unemployment

    C   Frictional unemployment

    D   Marginal unemployment   **(2 marks)**

13   When an organisation carries out an environmental scan, it analyses which of the following?

    A   Strengths, weaknesses, opportunities and threats

    B   Political, economic, social and technological factors

    C   Strategic options and choice

    D   Inbound and outbound logistics   **(2 marks)**

14   Which of the following is data protection legislation primarily designed to protect?

    A   All private individuals and corporate entities on whom only regulated data is held

    B   All private individuals on whom only regulated data is held

    C   All private individuals on whom any data is held

    D   All private individuals and corporate entities on whom any data is held   **(2 marks)**

15 Which of the following types of new legislation would provide greater employment opportunities in large companies?

    A   New laws on health and safety

    B   New laws to prevent discrimination in the workplace

    C   New laws making it more difficult to dismiss employees unfairly

    D   New laws on higher compensation for employer breaches of employment contracts

(2 marks)

16 The total level of demand in the economy is made up of consumption, ... , government expenditure and net gains from international trade.

Which of the following correctly completes the sentence above.

    A   Savings

    B   Taxation

    C   Investment   **(1 mark)**

17 Which set of environmental factors does a lobby group intend to directly influence?

    A   Political

    B   Technological

    C   Demographic

    D   Economic   **(2 marks)**

18 The use of advanced technology solutions in order to maximise the productivity and effectiveness of call centre operations is an application of the principles established by which school of management thought?

    A   Human relations

    B   Empirical

    C   Scientific

    D   Administrative   **(2 marks)**

19 The original role of the accounting function was which one of the following?

    A   Providing management information

    B   Recording financial information

    C   Maintaining financial control

    D   Managing funds efficiently   **(2 marks)**

20 Tax avoidance is a legal activity whilst tax evasion is an illegal activity.

Is this statement true or false?

    A   True

    B   False   **(1 mark)**

21 The system used by a company to record sales and purchases is an example of which of the following?

    A   A transaction processing system

    B   A management information system

    C   An office automation system

    D   A decision support system   **(2 marks)**

22 The implementation of a budgetary control system in a large organisation would be the responsibility of the internal auditor.

Is this statement true or false?

A   True
B   False   (1 mark)

23 Which type of organisation would have the retail prices it charges to personal consumers subject to close scrutiny by a regulator?

A   A multinational corporation
B   A multi-divisional conglomerate
C   A national utilities company
D   A financial services provider   (2 marks)

24 The central bank has announced a 2% increase in interest rates.

This decision has the most impact on which department of a large company?

A   Marketing
B   Treasury
C   Financial accounting
D   Production   (2 marks)

25 The major purpose of the International Accounting Standards Board (IASB) is to ensure consistency in ....

Which two words complete this sentence?

A   Financial control
B   Corporate reporting
C   External auditing   (1 mark)

26 X Co has a financial accountant and a management accountant.

Which group of activities would fall within the responsibility of the financial accountant?

A   Payroll, purchase ledger, sales invoicing
B   Inventory valuation, budgetary control and variance analysis
C   Fraud avoidance, segregation of duties, internal review and control
D   Funds management, risk assessment, project and investment appraisal   (2 marks)

27 In an economic environment of high price inflation, those who owe money will gain and those who are owed money will lose.

Is this statement true or false?

A   True
B   False   (1 mark)

28 To whom is the internal auditor primarily accountable?

A   The directors of the company
B   The company as a separate entity
C   The shareholders of the company
D   The employees of the company   (2 marks)

29   Which one of the following is a DISADVANTAGE of a computerised accounting system over a manual accounting system?

A   A computerised system is more time consuming to operate
B   The operating costs of a computerised system are higher
C   The computerised system is more costly to implement
D   A computerised system is more error prone   (2 marks)

30   The identification, evaluation, testing and reporting on internal controls is a feature of which of the following?

A   Operational audit
B   Transactions audit
C   Social responsibility audit
D   Systems audit   (2 marks)

31   What is the primary responsibility of the external auditor?

A   To verify all the financial transactions and supporting documentation of the client

B   To ensure that the client's financial statements are reasonably accurate and free from bias

C   To report all financial irregularities to the shareholders of the client

D   To ensure that all the client's financial statements are prepared and submitted to the relevant authorities on time   (2 marks)

32   Which of the following are substantive tests used for in the context of external audit of financial accounts?

A   To establish whether a figure is correct
B   To investigate why a figure is incorrect
C   To investigate whether a figure should be included
D   To establish why a figure is excluded   (2 marks)

33   In the context of fraud, 'teeming and lading' is most likely to occur in which area of operation?

A   Sales
B   Quality control
C   Advertising and promotion
D   Despatch   (2 marks)

34   In order to establish an effective internal control system that will minimise the prospect of fraud, which one of the following should be considered first?

A   Recruitment policy and checks on new personnel
B   Identification of areas of potential risk
C   Devising of appropriate sanctions for inappropriate behaviour
D   Segregation of duties in critical areas   (2 marks)

35   The leadership style that least acknowledges the contribution that subordinates have to make is

....

Which word correctly completes this sentence?

A   Authoritarian
B   Autocratic
C   Assertive   (1 mark)

36 The Blake and Mouton managerial grid examines the relationship between 'concern for production' and which of the following?

    A   Concern for people
    B   Concern for sales
    C   Concern for quality
    D   Concern for service   **(2 marks)**

37 Jackie leads an established team of six workers. In the last month, two have left to pursue alternative jobs and one has commenced maternity leave. Three new staff members have joined Jackie's team.

    Which one of Tuckman's group stages will now occur?

    A   Norming
    B   Forming
    C   Performing
    D   Storming   **(2 marks)**

38 Richard is a valuable member of his team. He is enthusiastic and curious, highly communicative and has a capacity for contacting people and exploring anything new.

    Which of Belbin's team roles does Richard fulfil?

    A   Monitor-evaluator
    B   Plant
    C   Resource-investigator
    D   Company worker   **(2 marks)**

39 Which one of the following statements is correct in relation to monetary rewards in accordance with Herzberg's Two-Factor theory?

    A   Pay increases are a powerful long-term motivator
    B   Inadequate monetary rewards are a powerful dissatisfier
    C   Monetary rewards are more important than non-monetary rewards
    D   Pay can never be used as a motivator   **(2 marks)**

40 Which one of the following is a characteristic of a team as opposed to a group?

    A   Members agree with other members
    B   Members negotiate personal roles and positions
    C   Members arrive at decisions by consensus
    D   Members work in cooperation   **(2 marks)**

41 According to Victor Vroom:

    Force (or motivation) = ... × expectancy

    Which of the following words completes Vroom's equation.

    A   Needs
    B   Valence
    C   Opportunity   **(1 mark)**

42 According to Handy's 'shamrock' organisation model, which one of the following is becoming progressively less important in contemporary organisations?

A The permanent, full-time work force
B The part-time temporary work force
C The role of independent sub-contractors
D The role of technical support functions (2 marks)

43 Which pattern of communication is the quickest way to send a message?

A The circle
B The chain
C The Y
D The wheel (2 marks)

44 Poor quality lateral communication will result in which of the following?

A Lack of direction
B Lack of coordination
C Lack of delegation
D Lack of control (2 marks)

45 Role playing exercises using video recording and playback would be most effective for which type of training?

A Development of selling skills
B Regulation and compliance
C Dissemination of technical knowledge
D Introduction of new processes or procedures (2 marks)

46 In the context of marketing, the 'four P's' are price, place, promotion and ....

Which word correctly completes this sentence?

A Processes
B Production
C Product (1 mark)

47 In relation to employee selection, which type of testing is most appropriate for assessing the depth of knowledge of a candidate and the candidate's ability to apply that knowledge?

A Intelligence testing
B Personality testing
C Competence testing
D Psychometric testing (2 marks)

48 A company has advertised for staff who must be at least 1.88 metres tall and have been in continuous full-time employment for at least five years.

Which of the following is the legal term for this unlawful practice?

A Direct discrimination
B Indirect discrimination
C Victimisation
D Implied discrimination (2 marks)

49   Which one of the following is most appropriate for the purpose of supporting the individual
      through the learning process with a view to promoting career development?

      A   Buddy
      B   Counsellor
      C   Mentor
      D   Instructor   **(2 marks)**

50   Gils is conducting an appraisal interview with his assistant Jill. He initially invites Jill to talk about
      the job, her aspirations, expectations and problems. He adopts a non-judgmental approach and
      offers suggestions and guidance.

      This is an example of which approach to performance appraisal?

      A   Tell and sell approach
      B   Tell and listen approach
      C   Problem solving approach
      D   360 degree approach   **(2 marks)**

1	B	The span of control refers to the number of subordinates immediately reporting to a superior official. The scalar chain is concerned with the chain of command and the number of levels of management.
2	B	According to the Chartered Institute of Marketing, marketing is 'the management process which identifies, anticipates and satisfies customer needs profitably'. The other answer options relate to specific activities carried out by a marketing department.
3	A	Non-executive directors should provide a balancing influence and play a key role in reducing conflicts of interest between management and shareholders.
4	B	The principal concern in a task culture is to get the job done. Large consultancy firms usually have the flexibility required to implement this.
5	D	A situation analysis is carried out when formulating strategic objectives.
6	C	In decentralisation, the motivation and accountability of local managers is increased.
7	C	The others are known as connected stakeholders.
8	D	The answer A group need minimal effort. The answer B group need to be treated with care and the C answer group need to be kept informed.
9	D	Their aim is to minimise breaches of legislative requirements and ensure compliance of the relevant standards.
10	B	The aging population trend is caused by a decreasing birth rate and a decreasing mortality rate.
11	D	Answers A and B would have the reverse effect. Increasing public expenditure should increase the level of consumer demand and therefore the level of economic activity.
12	C	Friction in the labour market means that there are difficulties in matching workers with the jobs available.
13	B	These are the external factors which impact the business.
14	B	The (UK) Data Protection Act 1998 protects individuals about whom data is held.
15	B	Discrimination can arise on the basis of gender, race, lifestyle and age.
16	C	Consumption is consumer spending. Investment means investment by enterprises.
17	A	Lobbyists put their case to individual ministers or civil servants.
18	C	The scientific management aim is for increased efficiency in production, that is, increased productivity.
19	B	The original role was that of recording financial information. The role today is much wider.
20	A	Tax avoidance involves making decisions which will minimise the tax liability. Tax evasion is deliberating not paying tax which is lawfully due.
21	A	A system used to record sales and purchases is a transaction processing system.
22	B	The internal auditor's role is to monitor the effectiveness of the controls in place. It is not their responsibility to implement systems.
23	C	Some privatised firms are monopolies, in that they have no competitors. To ensure that they do not abuse their position, there are regulatory bodies (eg OFWAT for water) which control their policies.
24	B	The interest rate is the price of money. A rise in interest rates will raise the price of borrowing, and increase the interest that can be made on surplus funds.

25	B	The IASB forms financial reporting standards which businesses must implement. This ensures consistency in corporate reporting.
26	A	The payroll, purchase ledger and sales invoicing would normally be the responsibility of the financial accountant. B might be covered by the management accountant. C might be covered by the internal audit department. D might be covered by the treasury department or the management accountant.
27	A	Where price inflation is high the value of money reduces steadily over time.
28	A	The internal auditor is accountable to the highest executive level in the organisation.
29	C	The computerised system is more costly to implement in the beginning. This is only a short-term disadvantage and the advantages outweigh the disadvantage.
30	D	A systems audit is based on a testing and evaluation of the internal controls.
31	B	The external auditor expresses an opinion on the financial statements.
32	A	Substantive tests are used to discover errors and omissions.
33	A	Teeming and lading is the theft of cash or cheque receipts. It is done by setting subsequent receipts against the outstanding debt to conceal the theft.
34	B	One of the prerequisites for fraud is opportunity. Identifying areas of potential risk should reduce the opportunities to commit fraud.
35	B	The Ashridge model states that authorisation acknowledges the least contribution from subordinates.
36	A	Blake and Mouton designed the management grid. It is based on two fundamental ingredients of behaviour, namely concern for production (or the task) and concern for people.
37	B	Forming the stage where the team is just coming together and may still be seen as a collection of individuals.
38	C	A resource-investigator is popular, sociable, extrovert, relaxed; source of new contacts, but not an originator, needs to be made use of.
39	B	Pay is a hygiene factor. According to Herzberg, hygiene factors, no matter how advanced and favourable could never motivate; however dissatisfaction with them could demotivate.
40	C	A consensus is the majority of opinion so the input of all team members is considered.
41	B	Valence is the strength of the individual preference for a given outcome or reward.
42	A	Pressure to reduce personnel costs and to adapt to new market imperatives has increased the use of part-time and temporary contracts of employments.
43	D	The wheel is the fastest followed by the Y, then the chain, and finally the circle.
44	B	Lateral communication may be used to co-ordinate the work of several people and perhaps departments who have to co-operate to carry out a certain operation.
45	A	Role playing exercises are most useful for developing and practising skills.
46	C	'Product' can also be replaced with the word 'service'.
47	C	A tests memory and problem solving skills. B tests a variety of characteristics such as ambition and motivation. D tests psychological factors such as aptitude, intelligence and personality.
48	B	On average men are taller than women so this is an indirect discrimination on the grounds of gender.

49 C Answers A, B and D are shorter term roles than a mentor.

50 B The tell and listen approach is where the manager tells the subordinate how (s)he has been assessed and then invites the appraisee to respond.

Exam question bank

1   A .... company has a separate legal personality from its owners (shareholders).

Which word correctly completes this sentence?

A   Private
B   Public
C   Limited   **(1 mark)**

2   Henry Mintzberg model analysed organisation structure into five basic components.

Which of the following components includes analysts and designers of control systems?

A   Strategic apex
B   Technostructure
C   Middle line
D   Support staff   **(2 marks)**

3   Which of the following is NOT one of the main objectives of Human Resource Management?

A   To obtain the right number and type of skilled employees for the organisation's current and future requirements.

B   To develop and deploy the organisation's employees in such a ways as to maximise flexibility and productivity

C   To ensure compliance with the organisation's social and legal responsibilities in relation to employees

D   To minimise labour turnover and maximise employee retention within the organisation

                                                                                               (2 marks)

4   Committees are particularly effective for carrying out research work.

Is this statement true or false?

A   True
B   False   **(1 mark)**

5   Which of the following would be identified as an operational-level information system?

A   Executive Support System (ESS)
B   Knowledge Work System (KWS)
C   Decision Support System (DSS)
D   Transaction Processing System (TPS)   **(1 mark)**

6   What is the name given to a collection of structured data which can be accessed and manipulated by multiple users?

A   A database management system (DBMS)
B   A database
C   Data independence
D   Data integration   **(2 marks)**

7   Which of the following is most likely to be an example of an 'existential culture' in Harrison's model of cultural types?

A   An entrepreneurial start-up business
B   A partnership of graphic designers
C   A construction project
D   A large telecommunications company   **(2 marks)**

8   Which of the following statements is true?

A   The grapevine springs up where there is inadequate formal communication in an organisation.

B   Cliques and other informal groups can be either helpful or dysfunctional in an organisation

C   Not all organisations have in informal organisation
D   The informal organisation promotes employee health and safety   **(2 marks)**

9   .... comprise all those individuals or groups who have a legitimate interest in an organisation's activities.

Which word or phrase correctly completes this sentence?

A   Key players
B   Shareholders
C   Stakeholders   **(1 mark)**

10   Which approach to ethics considers which actions are likely to result in 'the greatest good for the greatest number of people'?

A   Legalism
B   Deontology
C   Categorical imperatives
D   Utilitarianism   **(2 marks)**

11   What is the meaning of the ethical principal of 'independence in appearance'?

A   Accountants must complete their work free from bias or prejudice

B   Accountants must complete their work without excessive supervision

C   Accountants must complete their work in such a way as to give a reasonable person no cause to question their objectivity

D   Accountants must complete their work in such a way as to give a reasonable person confidence that they can work without supervision   **(2 marks)**

12   Which of the following is NOT a major theme of corporate governance?

A   Ensuring the confidentiality of information
B   Accountability
C   Ethical treatment of stakeholders
D   The management and reduction of risk   **(2 marks)**

13   According to the Greenbury committee in the UK, who should set directors' remuneration?

    A   An audit committee
    B   Independent non-executive directors
    C   The board of directors
    D   The London Stock Exchange   **(2 marks)**

14   Corporate social responsibility (CSR) is incompatible with the interests of shareholders in a business organisation.

    According to the stakeholder view, is this statement true or false?

    A   True
    B   False   **(1 mark)**

15   Which type of government policy focuses on taxation, public borrowing and public spending?

    A   Fiscal
    B   Monetary
    C   Social policy
    D   Industry policy   **(2 marks)**

16   Which of the following is NOT likely to result from a fall in the exchange rate?

    A   A stimulus to exports
    B   An increase in the costs of imports
    C   Reducing demand for imports
    D   A reduction in the rate of domestic inflation   **(2 marks)**

17   …………… inflation arises from an excess of aggregate demand over the productive capacity of the economy.

    Which word or words correctly complete this sentence?

    A   Demand pull
    B   Cost push
    C   Frictional   **(1 mark)**

18   For which of the following reasons is dismissal automatically considered unfair under UK law?

    A   Redundancy
    B   Non-capability
    C   Pregnancy
    D   Misconduct   **(2 marks)**

19   Under which component of PEST analysis would an organisation analyse the media through which segments of the youth market access new digital music products?

    A   Political
    B   Economic
    C   Social
    D   Technological   **(2 marks)**

20   The bargaining power of customers in an industry will be greater in which of the following circumstances?

A   There are one or two dominant suppliers in the industry
B   The product is highly important to the customer's business
C   There are many customers in the industry
D   Switching costs are low   **(2 marks)**

21   An organisation has to decide whether to buy or lease machinery for its new factory.

Which of the following members of the finance function would be responsible for this decision?

A   The financial manager
B   The management accountant
C   The financial accountant   **(1 mark)**

22   Goods inwards checks are an example of a control in which business financial system?

A   Payroll
B   Purchasing
C   Sales
D   Cash management   **(2 marks)**

23   An organisation has a policy of checking all invoices from suppliers against goods received notes before paying the invoices.

This is an example of what type of control procedure?

A   Accounting controls
B   Detect controls
C   Correct controls
D   Prevent controls   **(2 marks)**

24   Which of the following is NOT a feature of external audit?

A   Its ultimate objective is to add value and improve operations
B   The auditors report to the shareholders or members of the organisation
C   It focuses on the financial statements and records of the organisation
D   The auditors are independent of the organisation and its management   **(2 marks)**

25   The purpose of .... data is to ensure that the most recent usable copy of the data can be recovered and restored in the event of loss or corruption on the primary storage medium.

Which word correctly completes this sentence?

A   Password-protecting
B   Backing-up
C   Validating
D   Verifying   **(2 marks)**

26   A warehouse manager instructs staff not to record returns of goods to suppliers, if the goods have already been entered into inventory records, as this will be 'sorted out by the accounts department'.

Is this action potentially fraudulent?

A   No
B   Yes, as an example of removal of assets from a business
C   Yes, as an example of intentional misrepresentation of the financial position of a business

(1 mark)

27   Which of the following would be regarded as fraud prevention measures?

A   Requiring all quantities to be written in words rather than numbers
B   Requiring all staff to take full holiday entitlements
C   Defining standard procedures for normal business operations
D   All of the above   (2 marks)

28   Which type of power is associated with line authority?

A   Physical power
B   Resource power
C   Legitimate power
D   Expert power   (2 marks)

29   Which school of management thinking focused on a range of higher-order needs of workers for job satisfaction?

A   Scientific management
B   Human relations
C   Neo-human relations
D   Contingency   (2 marks)

30   What two factors in leadership style are plotted on Blake & Mouton's managerial grid?

A   Managerial discretion and subordinate discretion
B   Concern for production and concern for people
C   Psychological distance and favourability of the situation
D   Exercise of leadership and exercise of authority   (2 marks)

31   Cohesive groups generally take more risky decisions than the same individuals working separately.

Is this statement true or false?

A   True
B   False   (1 mark)

32   In a project team, Jane is the person everyone turns to with their problems and inter-personal conflicts, knowing that she will listen and mediate.

Which of Belbin's team roles does Jane fulfil?

A   Plant
B   Shaper
C   Co-ordinator
D   Team worker   (2 marks)

565

33   In which order does a team ordinarily progress through Tuckman's stages of development?

      A   Norming, storming, forming, performing
      B   Storming, forming, norming, performing
      C   Forming, storming, norming, performing
      D   Norming, forming, storming, performing   **(2 marks)**

34   What type of motivation theory is expectancy theory?

      A   Process theory
      B   Content theory   **(1 marks)**

35   Bill believes that his team are innately lazy and will shirk work and responsibility unless he directs
      and supervises them closely, and applies strict discipline.

      Which writer's motivational theory accounts for Bill's motivational approach?

      A   Herzberg
      B   Maslow
      C   Vroom
      D   McGregor   **(2 marks)**

36   Which of the following is NOT identified as a core dimension in job design for job satisfaction?

      A   Skill variety
      B   Task identity
      C   Performance-related pay
      D   Feedback   **(2 marks)**

37   Fred is a team leader who keeps a detailed checklist of his daily tasks, and ranks them in order of
      importance and urgency. He only takes phone calls during particular times of day, to avoid
      interruptions. Even so, at the end of the day, he has to work late to complete a large number of
      urgent but low-level tasks for the following day.

      Which of the following is Fred's weakness in the area of time management?

      A   Planning
      B   Delegation
      C   Focus
      D   Prioritisation   **(2 marks)**

38   Jihander, the payroll supervisor, has been asked to meet with Tom once a week for eight weeks, in
      order to help Tom to plan, implement and review a learning programme to improve his knowledge
      of the company's payroll system.

      What term would be given to this type of relationship?

      A   Coaching
      B   Mentoring
      C   Counselling   **(1 mark)**

39   Which of the following is NOT usually a barrier to effective communication?

      A   Distortion
      B   Noise
      C   Rapport
      D   Jargon   **(2 marks)**

40 What does a person specification describe?

A The main tasks, responsibilities and conditions involved in a job
B The attributes of the ideal person for a given job
C The performance rating of a given job-holder
D The number of people required to fill job vacancies **(2 marks)**

41 An organisation urgently needs to recruit an experienced cost accountant, but does not have a large budget for recruitment advertising.

Which of the following would be its most appropriate recruitment medium?

A Recruitment consultancy
B Advertisement in a national newspaper
C Advertisement on local radio
D Register with an on-line accountancy recruitment database **(2 marks)**

42 According to research, what selection method is the most reliable predictor of job performance?

A Interviews
B References
C Work sampling
D Personality tests **(2 marks)**

43 Justine has offered to give evidence at an Employment Tribunal on behalf of a colleague who is claiming that he has been passed over for promotion because he is not married. Over the following weeks, her department head repeatedly denies her requests for work breaks, because she is already having 'time off in court'.

Under UK legislation, Justine herself may have a claim for what form of discrimination?

A Direct discrimination
B Indirect discrimination
C Victimisation
D Harassment **(2 marks)**

44 It is illegal in the UK to use age limits or phrases that imply restrictions (such as 'recent graduate') in job advertisements.

Is this statement true or false?

A True
B False **(1 mark)**

45 What learning style would have a natural preference for (and learn best from) on-the-job training using methods such as project work or job instruction?

A Theorist
B Reflector
C Activist
D Pragmatist **(2 marks)**

46 Which of the following is an advantage of on-the-job training?

A Allows focus on learning
B Supports transfer of learning
C Allows standardisation of training
D Minimises risk **(2 marks)**

47   What is the lowest level at which the effectiveness of training can be evaluated?

A   Trainee learning
B   Changes in trainees' job behaviour
C   Trainee reaction
D   Changes in results   (2 marks)

48   What is the key objective of a performance appraisal system?

A   To ensure that employees are performing to the best of their ability and developing their
     potential for improvement

B   To underpin the reward system of the organisation

C   To support promotion planning

D   To give employees feedback on the previous year's performance   (2 marks)

49   An organisation uses an appraisal form which enables managers to measure employees' behaviour
      in key situations against descriptions of key successful and unsuccessful job behaviour reported by
      managers.

      What appraisal technique is being used by this organisation?

A   Overall assessment
B   Guided assessment
C   A behavioural incident method
D   A results-oriented scheme   (2 marks)

50   Which approach to appraisal interviewing gives the interviewer the least critical and dominant role
      in the process?

A   Tell and sell
B   Tell and listen
C   Problem-solving   (1 mark)

Exam answer bank

1   C   A limited company is incorporated specifically to create a separate legal entity, allowing for the concept of limited liability. A limited company may be either public or private – but this is a separate distinction, based mainly on different sources of share capital. *(Chapter 1)*

2   B   The technostructure is concerned with standardisation of work processes and outputs. The strategic apex and middle line are layers of management (controlling the operating core). Support staff fulfil ancillary functions. *(Chapter 1)*

3   D   An organisation may not wish to minimise labour turnover and maximise retention, if the HR plan requires downsizing by natural wastage. The other three options are key objectives of HRM. *(Chapter 1)*

4   B   Committees are useful for generating new ideas, but inefficient for on-going work. *(Chapter 1)*

5   D   A TPS performs and records routine transactions, at an operational level. An ESS is a strategic-level system, a DSS a management-level system and a KWS a knowledge-level system. *(Chapter 2)*

6   B   A database is a collection of structured data. A DBMS is the software that builds, manages and provides access to a computerised database. Data independence and integration are two features of a well-designed database system. *(Chapter 2)*

7   B   An existential culture is shaped by the interests of contributing members, such as a professional partnership. An entrepreneurial start-up is likely to be a power culture; a construction project a task culture; and a large telecom firm a bureaucracy or role culture. *(Chapter 3)*

8   B   Cliques can be helpful in encouraging cross-functional communication, but they can also 'freeze out' individuals and focus on their own agendas. The other statements are untrue: a grapevine flourishes even where formal communication is good; all organisations also have informal social systems; and informal organisation can undermine health and safety (eg by creating informal 'short-cuts' or a culture of recklessness). *(Chapter 3)*

9   C   Stakeholders are all individuals or groups with a 'stake' in the organisation's activities or results. Shareholders are merely one (connected) stakeholder group, while key players are one 'category' of stakeholders in Mendelow's power-interest matrix. *(Chapter 3)*

10   D   Utilitarianism is based on the outcomes or consequences of actions. Deontology is based on duty: categorical imperatives are the 'rules' by which duty (or moral responsibility) can be judged. Legalism is based on the agreed rules or laws laid down by a group or society. *(Chapter 4)*

11   C   Independence in appearance is being *seen* to be independent or objective: it is an additional requirement to being objective in fact (independence of mind) – and nothing to do with freedom from supervision (or autonomy). *(Chapter 4)*

12   A   Confidentiality may legitimately be breached in the public interest: corporate governance depends on the free flow of information to stakeholders. The other options are key themes in corporate governance. *(Chapter 5)*

13   B   Non-executive directors (sitting on a remuneration committee) have the independence required for this task – while the board of directors (including executive directors) does not. An audit committee has responsibilities for review of financial statements, internal controls and internal audits, and liaison with external auditors. The London Stock Exchange regulates corporate governance through the Combined Code for members. *(Chapter 5)*

14   B   According to the stakeholder view, CSR is in the long-term interests of shareholders because it helps to secure stakeholder support, access to resources, sustainable business relationships and so on. *(Chapter 5)*

15   A   Monetary policy focuses on money supply, the monetary system, interest rates, exchange rates and the availability of credit. Social policy focuses on workplace regulation, labour supply, education and skills. Industry policy focuses on matters such as freedom of trade, entry barriers and capacity, and industry regulation. *(Chapter 6)*

16   D   A fall in the exchange rate makes a country's exports cheaper to overseas buyers, and imports more expensive: it therefore has the first three effects. The increase in the cost of imports, however, is likely to add to the rate of domestic inflation. *(Chapter 6)*

17   A   Demand pull inflation occurs when the economy is buoyant and there is a high aggregate demand, in excess of the economy's ability to supply. Cost push inflation occurs where the costs of factors of production rise. 'Frictional' is not a term applied to inflation, but to unemployment (referring to the lead time required to match workers with jobs). *(Chapter 6)*

18   C   Redundancy, non-capability and misconduct are potentially fair grounds for dismissal, provided that the employee was fairly handled. Dismissal on the grounds of pregnancy is automatically unfair, partly as a form of sexual discrimination. *(Chapter 7)*

19   C   The developments in digital music products may be analysed under technological factors, but media consumption and buying patterns are socio-cultural factors. *(Chapter 7)*

20   D   If the costs of switching to alternative suppliers is low, customers can demand more from their suppliers. The other circumstances tend to increase the power of suppliers, by reducing the customers' ability to take their business elsewhere (options A and B) or by decreasing the importance of individual customers' business (option C). *(Chapter 7)*

21   A   The financial manager is responsible for raising finance and controlling financial resources. The management accountant presents accounting information to support the management of the business. The financial accountant reports the results and financial position of a business. *(Chapter 8)*

22   B   Purchasing system tests are based around buying and goods inwards. The equivalent for sales would be selling and goods outwards. Payroll concerns the payment of wages and salaries. Cash management focuses on the authorisation, verification and recording of payments and receipts. *(Chapter 8)*

23   D   Prevent controls are designed to prevent errors (in this case, wrong payments) from happening. Detect controls are designed to detect errors once they have happened; correct controls to minimise or negate the effect of errors; and accounting controls to provide accurate accounting records. *(Chapter 9)*

24   A   This is the objective of internal audit. The (narrower) objective of external audit is to enable auditors to express an opinion on the financial statements of the organisation. *(Chapter 9)*

25   B   Backing-up is making separately-stored duplicate copies of data for this purpose. The other three options are other forms of integrity control: verification involves ensuring data entered matches source documents, while validation involves ensuring that it is not incomplete or unreasonable. *(Chapter 9)*

26   C   There is potential for inventory to be fraudulently over-valued for accounts purposes. *(Chapter 10)*

27   D   Trivial and unrelated as some of the options may seem, they are all fraud prevention controls: making it difficult to alter quantities; creating time for frauds to come to light; and highlighting deviations from norms. *(Chapter 10)*

28   C   Also known as 'position' power, as it derives from a given role in the chain of command. Physical power is based on superior force; resource power on control over valued resources or rewards; and expert power on possession of valued knowledge or expertise. *(Chapter 11)*

29   C   The neo-human relations school argued that a wide range of employee motivations impacts on performance: the human relations school pioneered this insight, but focused on social or belonging needs. Scientific management focused instead on technical efficiency. The contingency school argued that a wide range of factors – human and non-human – impacts on performance. *(Chapter 11)*

30   B   The grid plots concern for production and concern for people. A balance between managerial and subordinate discretion can be seen in other style theories such as 'Tells-sells-consults-joins'. Psychological distance and situation are factors in Fiedler's contingency theory. The distinction between leadership and authority is used by Heifetz to distinguish between leaders (potentially informal or emergent) and managers (in positions of formal authority). *(Chapter 11)*

31   A   This is known as the 'risky-shift' phenomena: it is also a symptom of 'group think'. It is one of the ways in which people contribute differently in groups than they do individually – and not always in positive ways. *(Chapter 12)*

32   D   The Plant solves more conceptual, strategic problems for the team. The Shaper is a leader, but uses dynamism and challenge. The Co-ordinator pulls the team together, but more as organiser or chairperson. It is the team worker who fulfils the relationship-maintenance function. *(Chapter 12)*

33   C   Forming is the 'coming together' stage, followed by conflict (storming) as roles and goals are tested, settling down (norming) as ways of working together are developed, and finally focus on the task (performing). *(Chapter 12)*

34   A   Expectancy theory is a process theory, because it explores the process or 'calculation' by which outcomes become desirable and are pursued by individuals. Content theory focuses on the 'package' of needs or desired outcomes that motivate people (eg Herzberg's and Maslow's models). *(Chapter 13)*

35   D   McGregor's Theory X/Y accounts for the motivational approach of managers, based on their assumptions about their subordinates. You should be able to identify the other theories as two-factor theory, hierarchy of needs and expectancy theory respectively. *(Chapter 13)*

36   C   PRP is not an element of job design: nor is it directly related to job satisfaction. The five core dimensions are skill variety, task identity, task significance, autonomy and feedback: any or all of these can be increased in a job to increase employee satisfaction and commitment. *(Chapter 13)*

37   B   Fred is not delegating tasks to his team: this is an important aspect of time management. The mini-scenario indicates that Fred plans, focuses and prioritises well. *(Chapter 14)*

38   A   This can be identified as coaching because it is short-term, job-specific and carried out by the immediate supervisor: unlike mentoring, which is long-term, broad in focus and often carried out by an off-line mentor. Counselling is a specific intervention in the case of personal or disciplinary problems, rather than directly addressing skill improvement. *(Chapter 14)*

39   C   Rapport is the term for establishing a 'connection' between yourself and another person, which generally facilitates communication: it involves a range of verbal and non-verbal communication techniques. Distortion refers to a fault in the 'coding' or 'decoding' of a

message; noise to interference in the transmission or receipt of a message; and jargon to the use of technical vocabulary which non-users cannot understand. *(Chapter 14)*

40 B Option A is a job description: often confused with a person specification. One describes the job, while the other describes the ideal candidate for the job. A performance rating would be contained in a performance appraisal, and the number of people required in a job requisition or recruitment plan. *(Chapter 15)*

41 D This e-recruitment option is suitably targeted (compared to a national newspaper or local radio), and low-cost and low-lead-time (compared to retaining a consultancy). *(Chapter 15)*

42 C Work sampling allows candidates to demonstrate actual capability in job-relevant tasks. Various forms of testing are less accurate. Interviews are very low on predictive validity, due to their limited scope, artificiality and subjectivity. References are even less accurate, due to bias and caution. *(Chapter 15)*

43 C Victimisation occurs when a person is penalised for giving information or taking action in pursuit of a claim of discrimination. Direct discrimination occurs when one interested group is treated less favourably than another, and indirect discrimination when a policy or practice appears fair but is discriminatory in practice. Harassment is the use of threatening, intimidatory, offensive or abusive language or behaviour. *(Chapter 16)*

44 A As of October 2006, the Employment Equality (Age) Regulations make this practice unlawful in the UK: previously, age discrimination was subject only to a voluntary code of practice. *(Chapter 16)*

45 D Methods of learning-by-doing suit both Activists and Pragmatists, but Pragmatists have the additional preference for practical, job-related problem-solving. Theorists and Reflectors prefer to conceptualise or observe before applying learning. *(Chapter 17)*

46 B On-the-job learning supports application of learning to the job (transfer of learning) far better than off-the-job learning. However, it is subject to the distractions and pressures of work, is not easy to standardise for large numbers of trainees, and creates the risk of poor initial performance and experimentation in real-work situations. *(Chapter 17)*

47 C Trainee reaction or satisfaction is level 1; trainee learning is level 2; changes in job behaviour (ie application of learning) is level 3; and impact on goals/results is level 4. *(Chapter 17)*

48 A The key objective of performance appraisal is performance improvement, through feedback, problem-solving and development planning. This is often not directly related to reward and/or promotion planning. While retrospective feedback is one tool of appraisal, it is not regarded as an end in itself. *(Chapter 18)*

49 C Overall assessment is an unguided narrative evaluation; guided assessment a comment on specified characteristics and performance elements; and a results-oriented scheme a review of performance against specific targets and standards agreed in advance by the assessor and assessee. *(Chapter 18)*

50 C The three options are listed in decreasing order of interviewer dominance and critical role, using Maier's popular classification. *(Chapter 18)*

Index

Note: **Key Terms** and their page references are given in **bold.**

BPP
LEARNING MEDIA

Review Form & Free Prize Draw – Paper F1 Accountant in Business (2/07)

All original review forms from the entire BPP range, completed with genuine comments, will be entered into one of two draws on 31 January 2008 and 31 July 2008. The names on the first four forms picked out on each occasion will be sent a cheque for £50.

Name: _____   **Address:** _____

_____

_____

How have you used this Text?
(Tick one box only)

☐ Home study (book only)

☐ On a course: college _____

☐ With 'correspondence' package

☐ Other _____

Why did you decide to purchase this Text? *(Tick one box only)*

☐ Have used BPP Texts in the past

☐ Recommendation by friend/colleague

☐ Recommendation by a lecturer at college

☐ Saw advertising

☐ Saw information on BPP website

☐ Other _____

During the past six months do you recall seeing/receiving any of the following?
(Tick as many boxes as are relevant)

☐ Our advertisement in *ACCA Student Accountant*

☐ Our advertisement in *Pass*

☐ Our advertisement in *PQ*

☐ Our brochure with a letter through the post

☐ Our website www.bpp.com

Which (if any) aspects of our advertising do you find useful?
(Tick as many boxes as are relevant)

☐ Prices and publication dates of new editions

☐ Information on Text content

☐ Facility to order books off-the-page

☐ None of the above

Which BPP products have you used?

Text	☑	*Success CD*	☐	*Learn Online*	☐
Kit	☐	*i-Learn*	☐	*Home Study Package*	☐
Passcard	☐	*i-Pass*	☐	*Home Study PLUS*	☐

Your ratings, comments and suggestions would be appreciated on the following areas.

	Very useful	Useful	Not useful
Introductory section (Key study steps, personal study)	☐	☐	☐
Chapter introductions	☐	☐	☐
Key terms	☐	☐	☐
Quality of explanations	☐	☐	☐
Case studies and other examples	☐	☐	☐
Exam focus points	☐	☐	☐
Questions and answers in each chapter	☐	☐	☐
Fast forwards and chapter roundups	☐	☐	☐
Quick quizzes	☐	☐	☐
Question Bank	☐	☐	☐
Answer Bank	☐	☐	☐
Index	☐	☐	☐

Overall opinion of this Study Text	Excellent ☐	Good ☐	Adequate ☐	Poor ☐

Do you intend to continue using BPP products?   Yes ☐   No ☐

On the reverse of this page are noted particular areas of the text about which we would welcome your feedback. The BPP author of this edition can be e-mailed at: heatherfreer@bpp.com

Please return this form to: Nick Weller, ACCA Publishing Manager, BPP Learning Media Ltd, FREEPOST, London, W12 8BR

Review Form & Free Prize Draw (continued)

TELL US WHAT YOU THINK

Because the following specific areas of the Text contain new material and cover highly examinable topics etc, your comments on their usefulness are particularly welcome.

Please note any further comments and suggestions/errors below

Free Prize Draw Rules

1   Closing date for 31 January 2008 draw is 31 December 2007. Closing date for 31 July 2008 draw is 30 June 2008.

2   Restricted to entries with UK and Eire addresses only. BPP employees, their families and business associates are excluded.

3   No purchase necessary. Entry forms are available upon request from BPP Learning Media. No more than one entry per title, per person. Draw restricted to persons aged 16 and over.

4   Winners will be notified by post and receive their cheques not later than 6 weeks after the relevant draw date.

5   The decision of the promoter in all matters is final and binding. No correspondence will be entered into.